Christmas [illegible]

Enjoy, Editor-in-Chief!!

Love,

Laura and Fred

THE ONION PRESENTS

OUR FRONT PAGES

21 Years Of Greatness, Virtue, And Moral Rectitude From America's Finest News Source

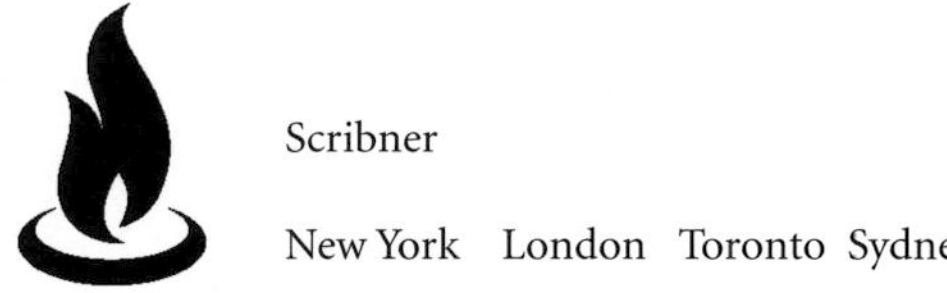

Scribner

New York London Toronto Sydney

Scribner
A Division of Simon & Schuster, Inc.
1230 Avenue of the Americas
New York, NY 10020

First Scribner hardcover edition November 2009

SCRIBNER and design are registered trademarks of The Gale Group, Inc., used under license by Simon & Schuster, Inc., the publisher of this work.

For information about special discounts for bulk purchases, please contact Simon & Schuster Special Sales at 1-866-506-1949 or business@simonandschuster.com.

The Simon & Schuster Speakers Bureau can bring authors to your live event. For more information or to book an event, contact the Simon & Schuster Speakers Bureau at 1-866-248-3049 or visit our website at www.simonspeakers.com.

Designed by Colin Tierney

Manufactured in China

10 9 8 7 6 5 4 3 2 1

Library of Congress Control Number: 2009019869

ISBN 978-1-4391-5692-6

OUR FRONT PAGES

EDITOR
Joe Randazzo

SECTION EDITORS
Megan Ganz, Joe Garden, Dan Guterman, Todd Hanson, John Krewson, Chad Nackers

COVER ART & DESIGN
Colin Tierney

PRODUCTION ARCHIVING & RESTORATION
Jun Uneo

EDITORIAL MANAGERS
Chet Clem, Kate Palmer, Julie Smith

EDITORIAL ASSISTANT
Brian Janosch

INTERNS
Sara Goldblatt, Raef Harrison, Rachel Oakley, Nick Stefanovich, Alyssa Varner

WITH SPECIAL THANKS

Adam Albright-Hanna, Kelly Ambrose, Jen Axen, Mark Banker, Amie Barodale, Cole Bolton, Diane Bullock, Max Cannon, Christine Carlson, Julie Chambers, Kiron Cheema, Becki Chulew, Sam Chung, Chris Comello, Rich Dahm, Ian Dallas, Mike DiCenzo, Scott Dikkers, Brian Ebner, Jonathan Hart Eddy, Heather Ekey, Michael Faisca, Matt Fanale, Rose Forman, Nick Gallo, T.G. Gibbon, Janet Ginsburg, Michelle Goodwin, Stephen Gotcher, Will Graham, Danny Greenberg, Josh Greenman, Mike Greer, Paul Grimstad, Geoff Haggerty, Steve Hannah, Kristen Harberg, John Harris, Tim Harrod, David Javerbaum, Christopher Johnson, Barry Julien, David Junker, Ryan Kallberg, Ben Karlin, Chris Karwowski, Timothy Keck, Ellie Kemper, Gery Kercheck, Matt Kirsch, Dan Klein, Peter Koechley, Carol Kolb, Dave Kornfeld, Kirstin Krutsch, Sean Lafleur, Jacqueline Lalley, Mike Loew, Kurt Luchs, Rick Martin, Mike McAvoy, Sam Means, Johnny McNulty, Frank Miller, Sean Mills, Matt Morrison, Pete Mueller, Shaun Mulheron, Danny Mulligan, Kittson O'Neill, Jenny Paulo, Chris Pauls, Keith Phipps, Lisa Pompilio, Seth Reiss, Kent Roberts, Jason Roeder, David Schafer, Tom Scharpling, Maria Schneider, Mike Schuster, Michael Schwartz, Anita Serwacki, Randel Shard, Kelly Shea, Will Shepard, Dave Sherman, Scott Sherman, Robert Siegel, R. Sikoryak, Andy Snyder, Sigmund Stern, Krista Stockebrand, Rick Streed, Jack Stuef, Ward Sutton, Scott K. Templeton, Stephen Thompson, Baratunde Thurston, Will Tracy, Dan Vebber, Stu Wade, Andrew Welyczko, Christine Wenc, Bill Wernecke, Ben Wikler, Mike Wise, Shoshanah Wolf, Graeme Zielinski, Toni Ziemer, Todd Zwillich, and to everyone over the past two decades who helped make this book possible.

TRUTH'S LAST OUTPOST

IT WOULD NOT BE OVERSTATING THE CASE, nor exaggerating its cultural impact, to say that *The Onion* has been a harbinger of change in print journalism and in our culture at large over the past two decades.

A brief examination of the following pages—this chronicle of great events and, if anything, even greater reporting—serves to confirm the fact. Change is a constant, in news as much as anywhere, and our society's rate of change has been accelerated ever more dramatically since *The Onion*'s inception. Gone are the days of the breathless hawker on the corner yelling "Extra!" while brandishing his paper aloft; the men brandishing things on today's corners have harsher things to yell. Newspapers no longer spiral out at us from our movie screens to announce world-shaking events; at the rate the world has been shaking, they could hardly spin fast enough. And with the arrival of the Internet, information itself has become a roiling, undefined mass, as difficult to interpret or escape as the newsprint that once rubbed off on our nervous, tentative fingers.

While powerless to stop change or even understand its nature, the writers and editors of *The Onion*, more than any other newspaper, have stood by their duty and faithfully recorded that change for all to see. More resigned than the rictus of mandatory cheer grinning rigidly at us from the cover of *USA Today*, more earnest than the insular eyebrow lift of literate ennui that sighs from the editorial page of *The New York Times*, and more fragile and human than the sneering stock ticker that is *The Wall Street Journal*, *The Onion* is the sole news outlet capable of acknowledging that it is not above the hue and cry, that it is, in fact, along for the ride, and that we have all of us together spiraled out of the darkness and down into something we cannot yet name or comprehend.

Whether these pages represent the greatest achievement in American journalism at the turn of the millennium, only the readers of tomorrow, the grateful and enlightened generations to come, if there be any, may know for certain. But when those men and women yet unborn cast their eyes back upon our era, the failing light they see flickering back at them shall be guttering from the front page of America's Finest News Source, *The Onion*.

Brian Williams

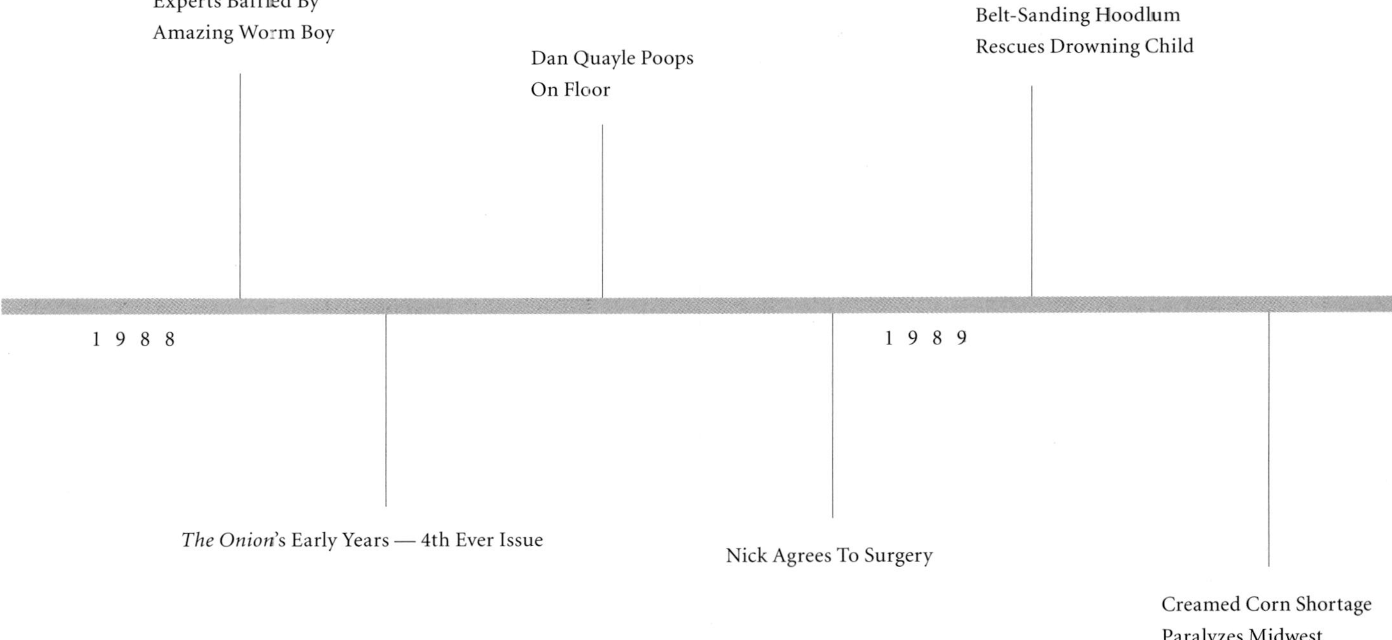
Experts Baffled By
Amazing Worm Boy
Dan Quayle Poops
On Floor
Belt-Sanding Hoodlum
Rescues Drowning Child
1 9 8 8
1 9 8 9
The Onion's Early Years — 4th Ever Issue
Nick Agrees To Surgery
Creamed Corn Shortage
Paralyzes Midwest

EARLY YEARS

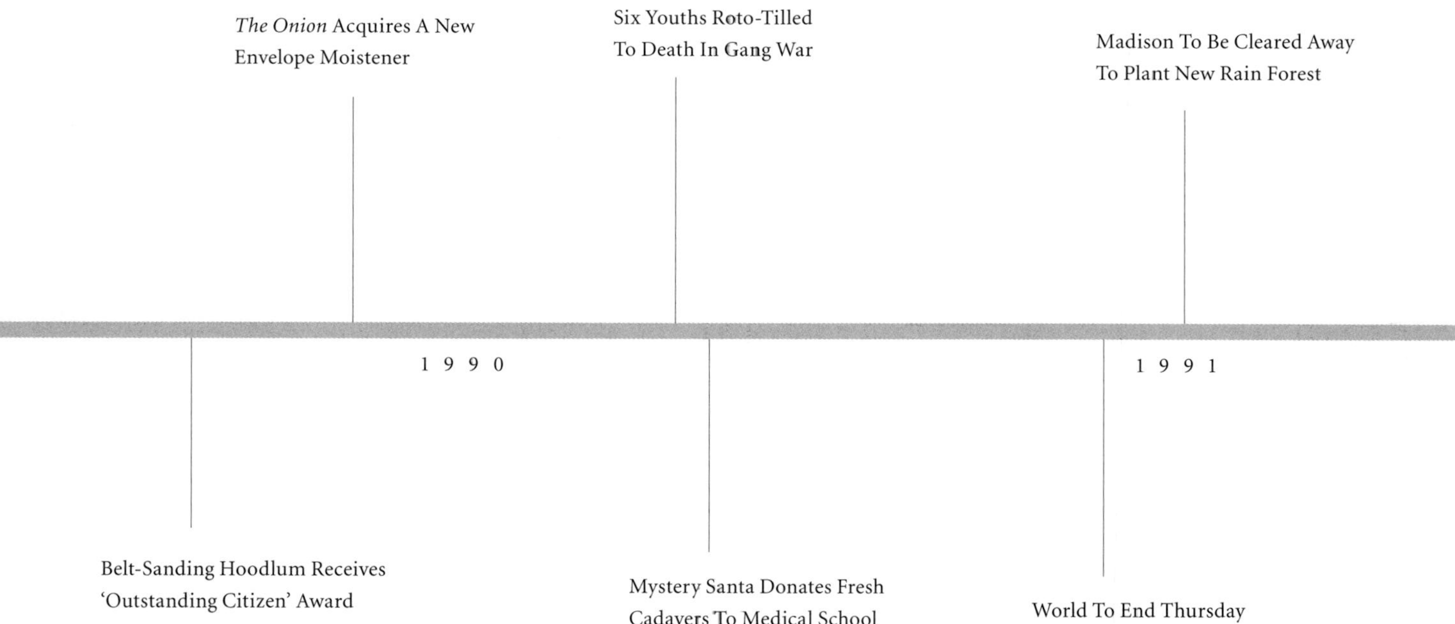

The Onion Acquires A New Envelope Moistener
Six Youths Roto-Tilled To Death In Gang War
Madison To Be Cleared Away To Plant New Rain Forest
1990
1991
Belt-Sanding Hoodlum Receives 'Outstanding Citizen' Award
Mystery Santa Donates Fresh Cadavers To Medical School
World To End Thursday

THE ONION

free campus weekly monday august 29, 1988 volume 14 number 1

august

S	M	T	W	T	F	S
28	29	30	31			

septemeber

S	M	T	W	T	F	S
				1	2	3

under the skin...

News Summaries 2
Who's Busted 2
Creative Writing 3
Professor Hornby's Figures in History 4
Academic Survival Tips 4
Feature Article 5
Plebes 5
DOWN AND OUT DAWG pull-out calendar 6-7
Jake the Weasel 8
Some reviews 9
AfterTaste 10
DOWN AND OUT DAWG 10
Scarecrow: a cereal 11
The Shave 12
Onion Mixer 12

Mendota Monster Mauls Madison

What exactly is happening in the once peaceful town of Madison, Wisconsin? See page 4 for the scoop by Gunnar Downes, two-time winner of the Provo, Utah -- Reporter of The Year Award. Gunnar exposes the dirty truth.

UW SNAPSHOTS

Superfluous statistics that really don't shape much of anything

Unhappy Bike Owners

Every year many bicycles are stolen because people are clueless, or worse yet trustworthy of their species. The simplest way to avoid such an unpleasant situation is to lock your bike. Remember lock it or lose it!

Number Of Stolen Bicycles Per Year

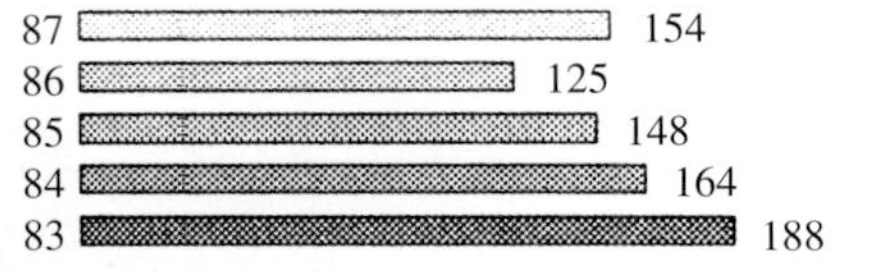

Source: UW-Madison Police and Security Report

THE ONION COUPON SECTION

Space age technology has allowed us to make a coupon section that you simply cut out, fold in half and slip into wallet, purse, or satchel. Estimated time to remove, 18 seconds. Just 18 seconds to save you hundreds, no thousands of dollars. For your convenience the genius puzzle is attached to this high tech wonder of the future. You can save millions of dollars and increase your intelligence ten fold. What's more, if an ONION operative stops you on the street and asks if you have this wonder of the 70's on you, and you do. You win one of the following prizes.

- **Onion T-Shirts (always the rage)**
- **Tickets to Onion Night**
- **G.I Joe™ action figures**

CLIP IT NOW, OR LET THE WORLD PASS YOU BY.

*After 232 years of news-gathering, this issue is *The Onion*'s first to be printed in Madison, WI.

SWIMSUIT ISSUE
THE ONION
Free Campus Weekly | Tuesday, January 24, 1989 | Volume 15 • Number 2

EXISTENCE DISPROVEN

Professor Dodderson relaxing in his favorite Lay-Z-Boy recliner even though it has been conclusively proven that neither he nor the chair exists.

Professor L.F. Dodderson of the UW-Madison physics department is the man who last week formulated the now-famous equation disproving the existence of the universe, U=Z ("U" being the *universe,* and "Z" meaning *zilch).*

Publication of the equation in an influential New York newspaper caused a media sensation. Telephones rang off the hook in every newsroom in America. Telegraphs clicked. Newspaper printers clacked through the night.

See Zilch on page 10

UW Snapshots

Statistics for your twilight years.

Hair's the Reason

Onion Operatives surveyed 100 freelance anthropologists to find the sociological root of the "Big Hair" hairstyle phenomena still prevalent in the 1980's.

55% As an aid to hunter/gatherers—for hiding simple tools and long sharp weapons.

44% Genetic adaptation much like that of the blowfish—to frighten off predators.

1% As a religious rite—to mimic the headdress of Tlazoheotl, the Eater of Filth and Goddess of Unbridled Sexuality

Onion operatives agree that, for whatever reason, all the big hair on campus looks great!

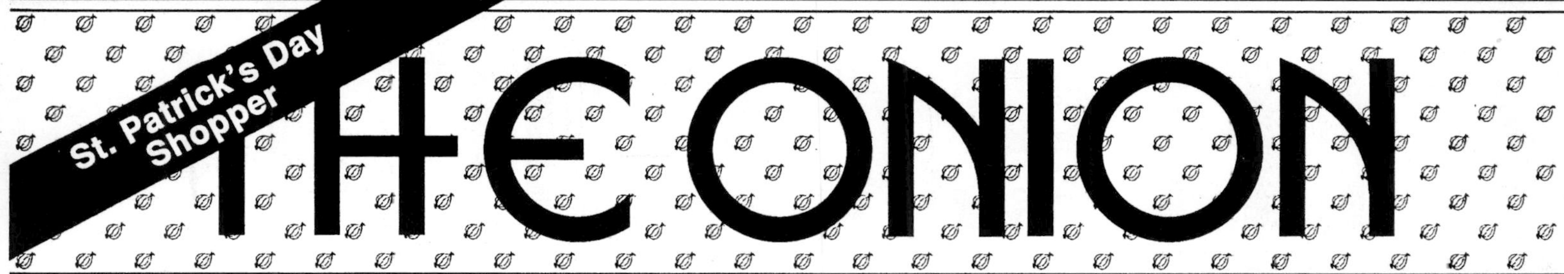

Free Campus Weekly | Tuesday, February 21, 1989 | Volume 15 • Number 6

DEAD GUY FOUND

BY LISA COOPER

Madison, Wisconsin—A dead guy was found buried head first up to his waist in a snowbank this Monday morning, apparently the result of an accident with a snowplow.

"I was just out shoveling my walk when I noticed this pile of clothes and stuff," said 28-year-old insurance agent, Timothy Specht. Specht said that he and a neighbor's further investigation lead to the discovery of the dead guy.

Kairen Juniper, 19, an exotic dancer, also saw the dead guy. "One minute I'm walking down to pick up my daily paper, and the next minute there's this dead guy," she said.

Speculation by the Police Department as to the dead guy's situation immediately before his immersion in the snowbank has lead to almost nothing. "About the only thing we have gleaned at this point is that the dead guy was probably unaware of the alternate sides parking law enforced in conjunction with heavy snows and that he was walking on the wrong side on that morning," said Madison Police Liaison Mary Ann Thurber.

The Dane county coroner's office has been working since Monday to determine the cause of death. A Coroner's office employee said work had slowed to a

See Dead Guy on page 7

UW Snapshots

A brief glimpse of the reality you participate in every day

Donna Does Emerald City

Onion Operatives polled 100 students to see which character in *The Wizard of Oz* Donna Shalala resembles most.

86% King of the Flying Monkeys

13% Mayor of Munchkinland

1% Glinda, the Good Witch of the North

**Onion Operatives were happy that no one mentioned either Wicked Witch because of their profound respect for Donna Shalala.*

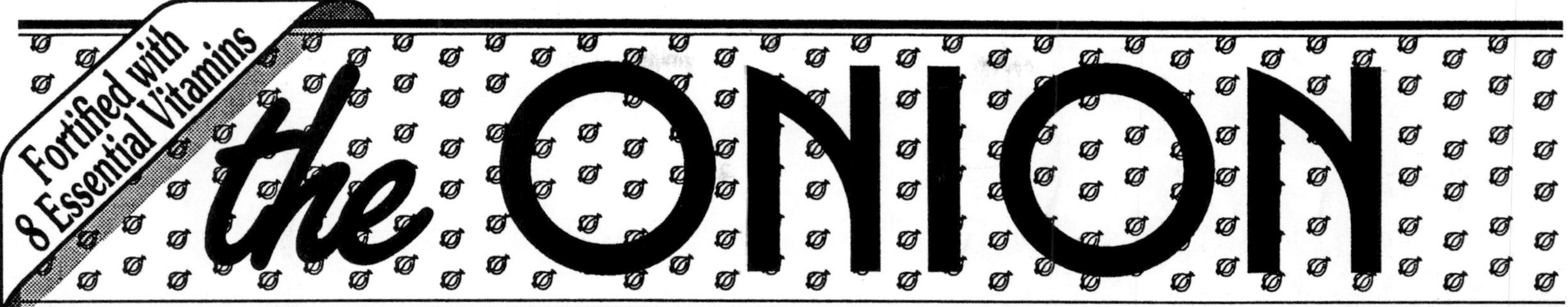

Free Campus Weekly 10–16 October 1989 Volume 16 • Number 7

PEN STOLEN FROM DORM STUDY AREA

This study table in Witte Hall was the scene of the alleged pen theft. University Police and Security officers have told the victim to just buy a new pen.

by Michael Hirsch, *Onion* City Desk

Madison—A pen was reported stolen Sunday night from a study center at Witte Hall on the UW campus. The pen, a medium point Bic, was discovered missing at approximately 8:13 p.m., according to UW Police Officer William Shenkenberg, who responded to the complaint. The owner of the pen, Jeffery Tidebaum, 19, left his studies momentarily for a trip to the rest room. Upon return, Tidebaum noticed that his pen was missing. The pen is valued at 49¢.

See Pen on page 5

Statistics that do your thinking for you.

Bank to the Future

What statistically likely future awaits business majors?

62%
Small-town furniture store owner. Bankrupt and divorced by age 30.

21%
Bank clerk, eventually promoted to Loans. Killed in holdup.

17%
Owner of three Popeye's Chicken franchises. Ruined by salmonella outbreak. Live out life clipping hedges for City Parks Service.

Margin of error ±5%: Dogged ambition inspired by the book *Iacocca: An Autobiography* not taken into account.

Kid Tested, Mother Approved!

the ONION

Free Campus Weekly | 31 October–6 November 1989 | Volume 16 • Number 10

Gov Proclaims November Masturbation Month

SPECIAL THANKS TO JOHN HENKES

Governor Tommy Thompson, in his historic announcement, spoke of the importance of family values, the continued growth of our state's economy, and the merits of titillating ones own genitals.

by Sarah Miles, *Onion* Government Reporter

MADISON—As Governor Thompson began his address to the joint session of the Legislature, few present expected him to begin by saying, "How many in this hall have masturbated. Raise your hands."

A murmur swelled as an embarrassing surprise engulfed the large hall of the capitol. One or two lawmakers jokingly raised their hands, to the giddy delight of their colleagues.

"The truth is," the governor continued with a straight face, "We've all masturbated—every last one of us."

The audience became humbly silent as the governor's words sunk in.

"You have," the governor said, pointing to Assembly Speaker Tom Loftus (D-Sun Prairie), his likely opponent in the 1990 race for governor. The lawmaker at Loftus's left nudged him with a knowing grin. Some of the others sitting near him simply covered their mouths and giggled.

"You have," the governor said, pointing to Sue Vergeront, acting chair of the Wisconsin Women's Caucus. She smiled uneasily and looked about.

"I have," the governor went on. "It's nothing to be ashamed of. In fact, it's a healthy, decent, and natural way of releasing tension, of improving your self-awareness, of improving your sexual awareness—and," the governor cracked a little smile, "burning off calories." The audience laughed lightly. The governor took a sip of water from the glass at the side of his podium.

Assuming the governor's unbefitting talk of masturbation was only a preliminary tidbit intended to "break the ice," the audience

See Gov on page 6

UW Snapshots

A look at the world through the devil's kaleidoscope.

Make Lung Cancer, Not War

Onion Operatives perused Steep & Brew's smoking section to conduct this Snapshot. "Why do so many Politically Correct Leftists smoke cigarettes?"

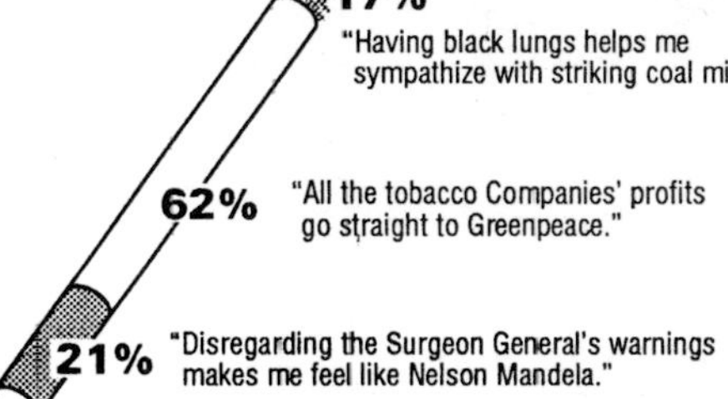

Onion Operatives were impressed by all those who blew peace-sign smoke rings for them.

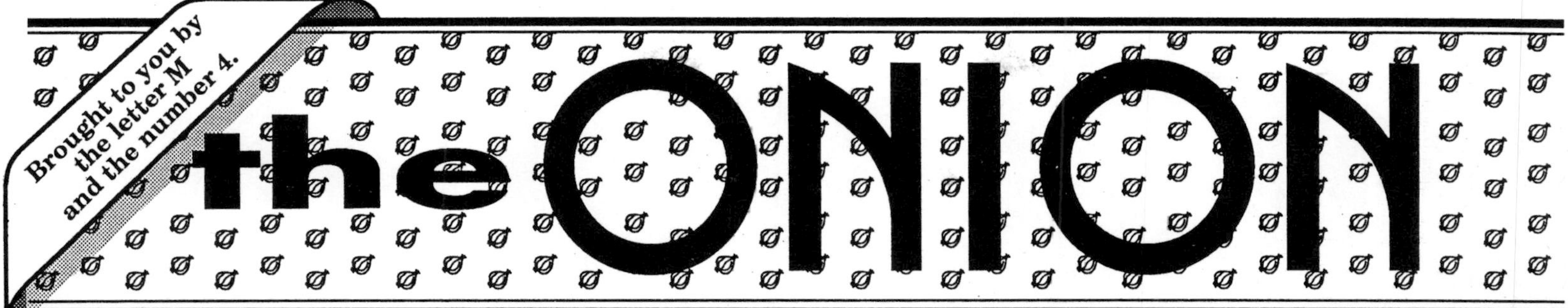

free campus weekly 25 September–1 October 1990 volume 18 • number 5

Everybody's Eatin' Bread!

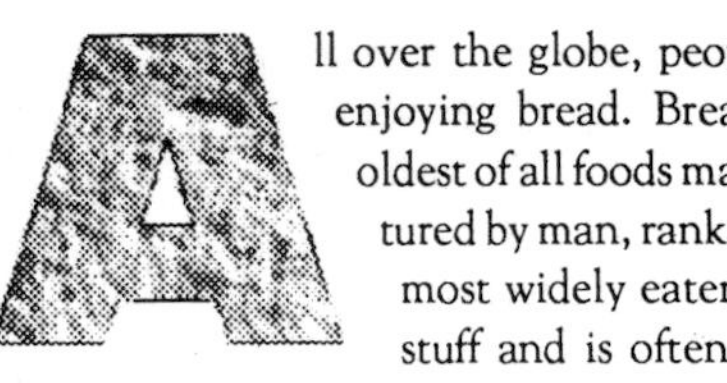

All over the globe, people are enjoying bread. Bread, the oldest of all foods manufactured by man, ranks as the most widely eaten foodstuff and is often called the "staff of life." Here in the United States, the bread consumed most is white, enriched, sliced and wrapped. However, the true bread connoisseur will sing praises of whole wheat, cracked wheat, light and dark ryes, pumpernickel, cornbread, and Swedish, French and Italian loaves.

Whether you're eating rice bread from the Orient, oatcakes and bannocks from Scotland, tortillas from Mexico, or bread made from the roots of the cassava plant, you know bread ranks as an energy food and a source of many nutrients. Eight slices of enriched bread daily furnish 20.1% of the needed calories, 22.7% of the protein, 14.5% of the calcium, 38.9% of the iron, 36.9% of the thiamine, 19.2% of the riboflavin, and 42.8% of the niacin recommended for a 12-year-old child, according to the Food and Nutrition Board of the National Research Council.

In addition to being a nutritious treat, bread has a rich, colorful history. The Egyptians are generally credited with making the first leavened bread. This leavening changed the face of bread history, transforming bread from hard and flat to soft, light and full of air. This development stunned the Sumerian citizenry, causing generations of war and bloodshed. Spores from the uncultured yeast were commonly used as weapons against

see BREAD on page 4

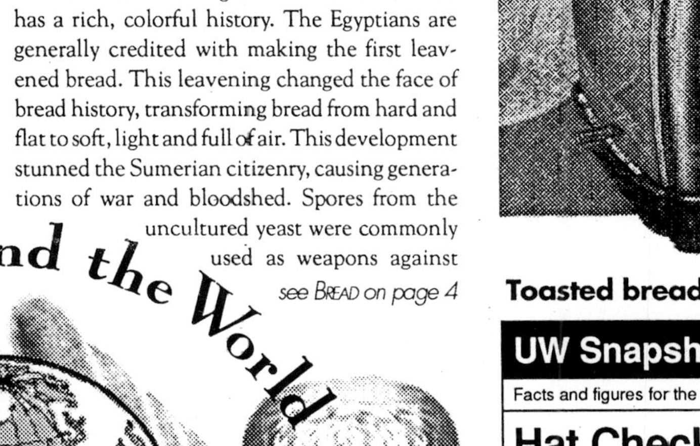

Breads 'round the world have many shapes and sizes. Armenians make *lavash*, a thin, flat bread. Greeks eat large doughnut-shaped loaves called *kouloura*, and Scandinavians enjoy thin wafers. Italians bake loaves with poppy seeds on the tops. Germans bake long, square loaves of dark *pumpernickel*.

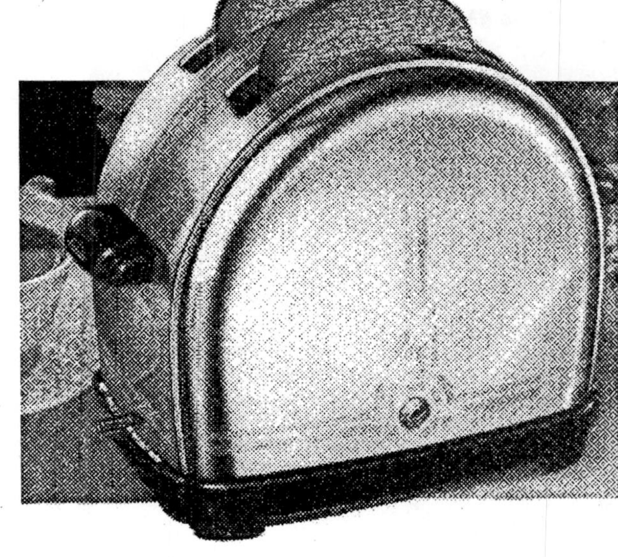

Toasted bread makes a great addition to any meal.

UW Snapshots

Facts and figures for the Johnny Bench in all of us.

Hat Check

Here's why so many members of the UW's male student populace wear their baseball caps with the visors in the back.

- **17%** Dream of the fast-paced lifestyle of the Major League catcher.
- **23%** Need an unobstructed view of the constellations to supplement astronomy studies.
- **68%** Want to look like Goober from THE ANDY GRIFFITH SHOW.

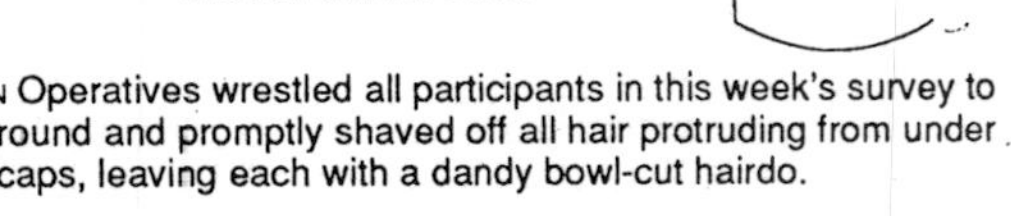

ONION Operatives wrestled all participants in this week's survey to the ground and promptly shaved off all hair protruding from under their caps, leaving each with a dandy bowl-cut hairdo.

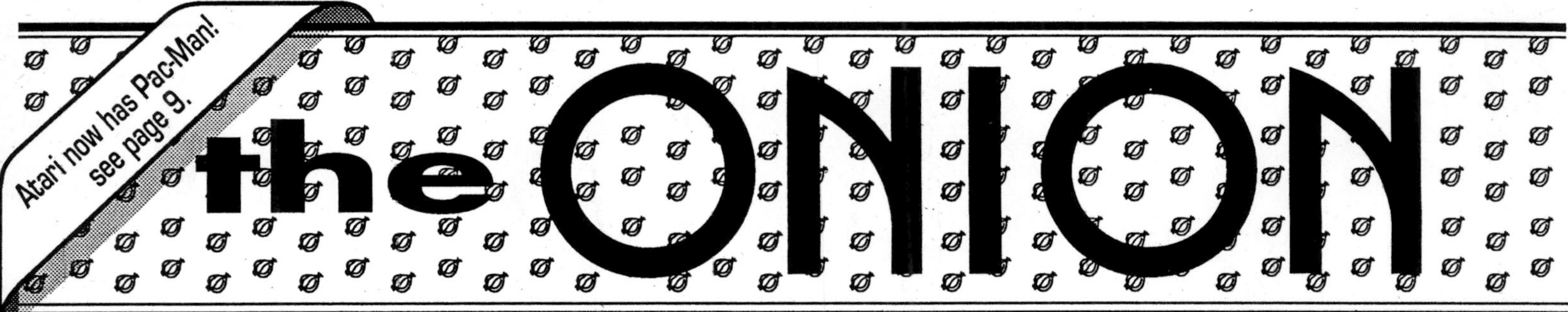

free campus weekly 9–15 October 1990 volume 18 • number 7

Human Torch Says, "I'm Fed Up With Inane In-Flight Magazines."

A Personal Message from The Human Torch

Last week, The Human Torch approached us with a story he wanted to run in THE ONION. *We felt, since he has been such a help to the Madison community and he usually avoids contact with regular humans, it was necessary for us to print his words. Therefore,* THE ONION *proudly presents The Human Torch's first message to the public.*

AS A CHAMPION OF JUSTICE, I AM CONSTANTLY ON THE GO. SINCE I WAS NOT blessed with the ability to fly, I find myself doing a lot of travelling by airplane. You would think the least the airlines could do is provide a frequent flier like myself something substantial to read. Yet, they insist on carting out those insipid in-flight magazines whenever I ask for reading material.

see TORCH on page 8

UW Snapshots

Living your worst nightmare, statistically.

Digital Dares

ONION Operatives used a "Digital Scrambler" to destroy the CD collections of 100 UW students. Here's how respondents rebuilt their collections:

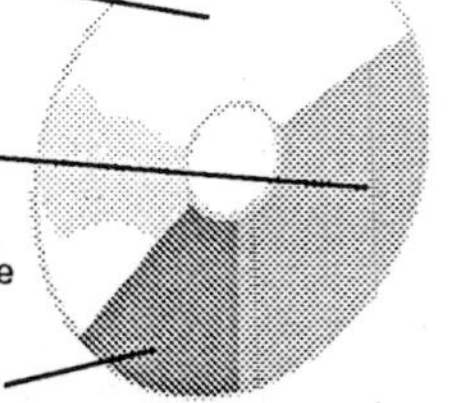

58% Tape-recorded themselves singing all lost music.

31% Hired their favorite street musician to play the harmonica in their room 24 hours a day.

12% Manufactured own laser-readable CDs using Oscar Mayer Beef Bologna and 3-hole-punch.

ONION Operatives checked back on all respondents. Those who had bought all-new collections had their eardrums extracted with wire cutters.

REPLACE CAP AFTER USE

the ONION

health and fitness manual — 23–29 October 1990 — volume 18 • number 9

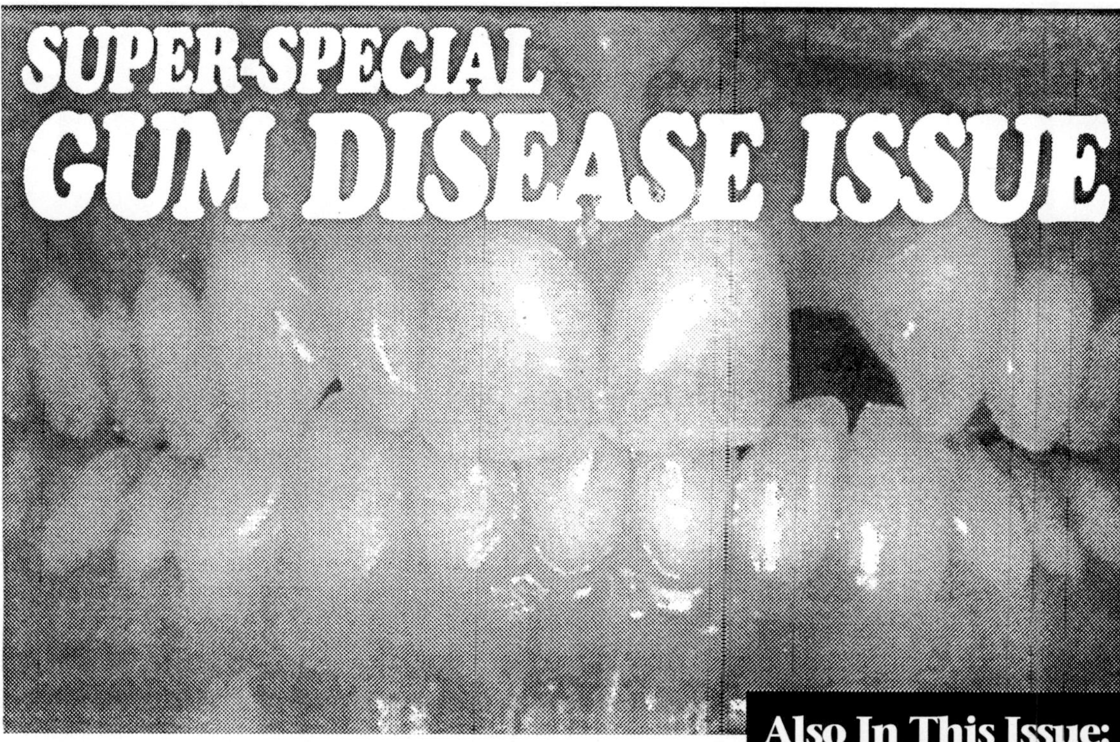

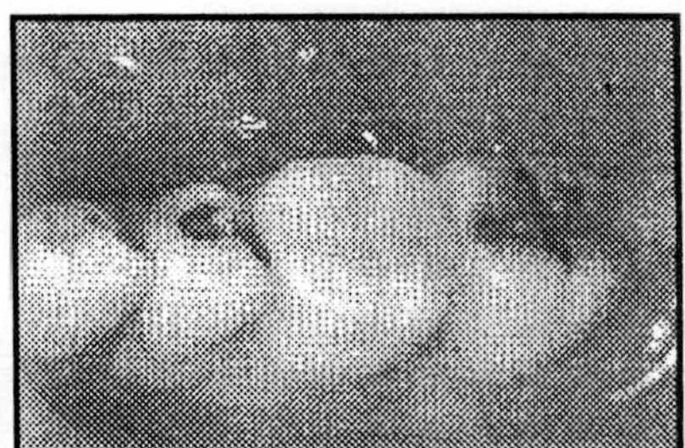

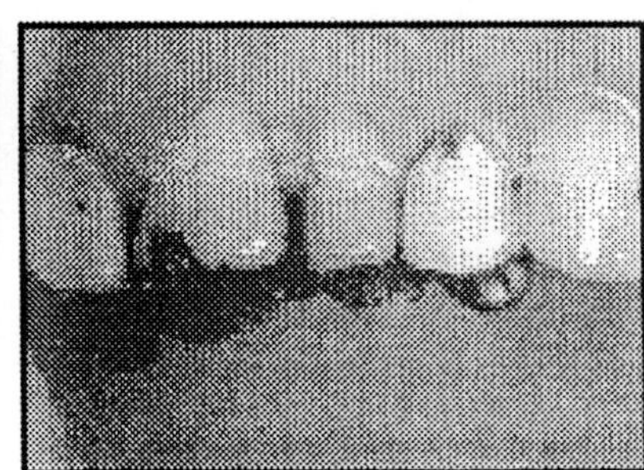

UW Snapshots

To present a statistical look at the world, sometimes you gotta break the rules.

Love It or Leave It!

The arrival of the fall season put Onion Operatives in the mind of statistically rating how leaves benefit the United States. (Categorized by percentage of benefit per bushel of leaves.)

48% Provide natural cover for ground personnel in event of an invasion by the Soviet Union.

37% Provide adequate sustenance if no other roughage source is available.

19% Fun to jump in.

Onion Operatives discovered that a healthy adult can be smothered and killed if force fed enough leaves.

Also In This Issue:

- Depressed? Try Liposuction on that Pesky Head
- Laryngospasms, Throat Polyps and other Vocal Foils
- Lunch Break Arthroscopic Surgery
- Top 40 DJs Agree: Cancer Cure Only Months Away

Special Bette Midler Birthday Gala

the ONION

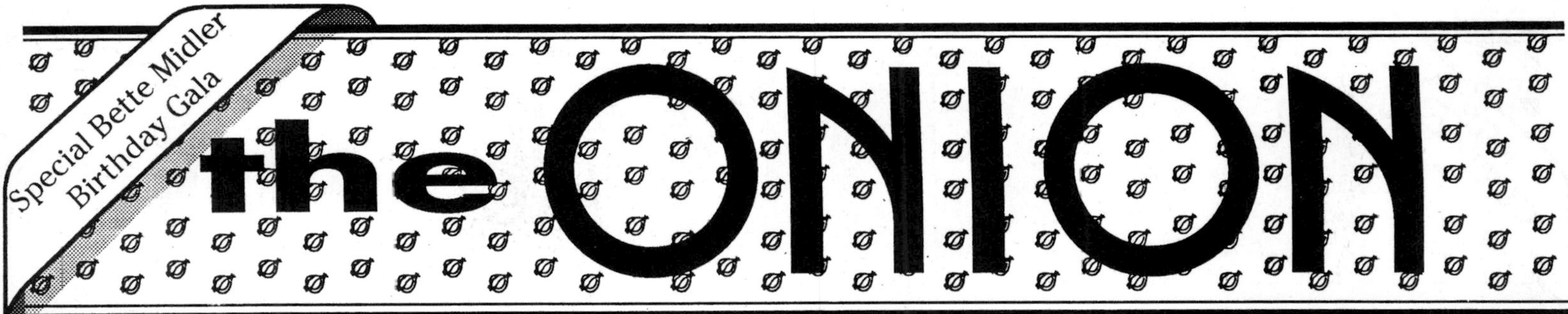

free campus weekly | 6–12 November 1990 | volume 18 • number 11

'TV WEEK' RIDDLED WITH LIES!

see story on page 7

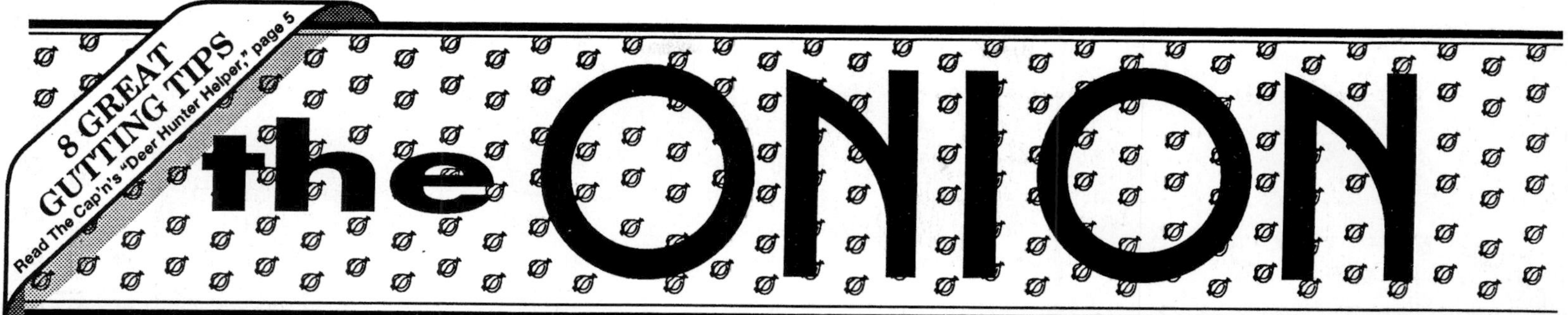

free campus weekly 27 November—3 December 1990 volume 18 • number 13

CANADA SIGNS NONAGGRESSION PACT WITH THE UNITED STATES

DESPITE THE PROSPECT OF WAR IN THE MIDDLE East, the Free World can breathe a little more easily today with the ratification of the controversial North American Non-Aggression Treaty between Canada and the United States, in Ottawa Thursday.

"Peace in our time!" declared a jubilant President Bush before a tearful audience of reporters and diplomatic officials outside the doors of Ottawa's Royal Canadian Hall, where the long and often difficult Ottawa Royal Summit was held. Bush and Canadian Prime Minister Brian Mulrooney, photographed shaking hands, exchanging hugs, and cuddling small children and puppies, announced the summit's success to a worldwide television audience estimated at three billion, larger even than Lionel Richie's performance at the '88 Olympics. "At last the spectre of death and destruction that have held the people of our two great nations in the grip of fear and uncertainty has been exorcised," Mulrooney told reporters. "Now, the healing can begin."

The effects of the new accord are being felt nationwide. Missile silos in North Dakota, Montana, Minnesota and Upper Michigan were taken off red alert, sending up a cheer of joy and relief from the soldiers stationed there. Thousands of troops, anxiously awaiting word to begin massing on the Northern border, were sent home, tired and weary, but grateful for the chance to spend Thanksgiving with their families. As one man in the field put it, "This year, I

see TREATY on page 6

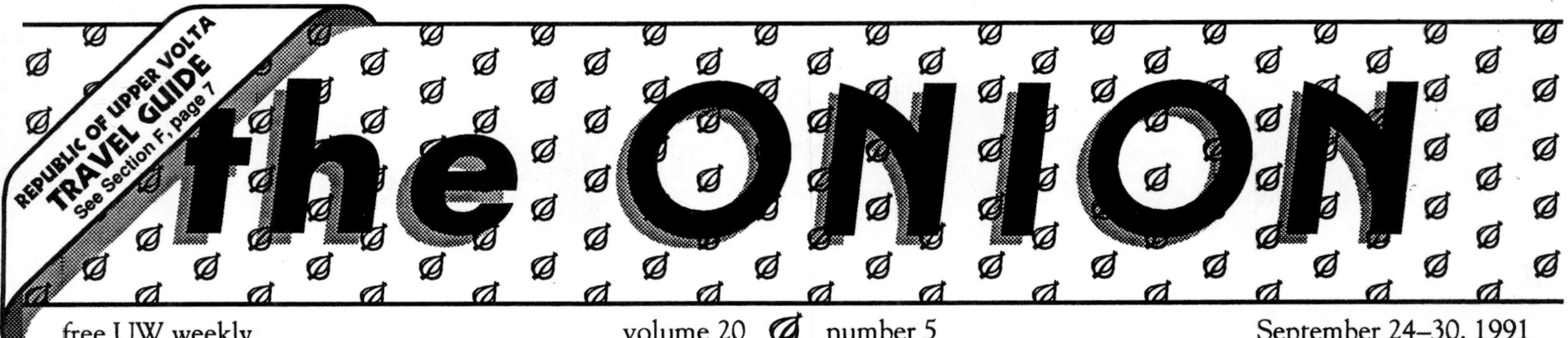

free UW weekly volume 20 number 5 September 24–30, 1991

PROF UNDER FIRE FOR BLASPHEMING POSEIDON

A UNIVERSITY OF WISCONSIN PROFESSOR stands accused of making irreverent remarks about Poseidon, Olympian God and King of the Seas, in a classroom lecture. Professor Marvin Hoyte's alleged remarks have resulted in an uproar from concerned religious groups, and, as a result, the University has promised a full re-evaluation of its school-wide curriculum.

According to an anonymous student's report, Professor Hoyte was speaking to a small group of students immediately following his Agricultural Journalism 103 course. In the conversation, the Professor allegedly referred to Poseidon as "the water god," and later as "the guy with the pitchfork." These insufficiently respectful comments come in the wake of the recent NEWSWEEK cover story, INFIDEL EDUCATORS: HAS CAMPUS FREE SPEECH GONE TOO FAR? and a heated national debate on the issue.

Evoking the Religious Insensitivity Subchapter of the University's new "Hate Speech" Rule, the University has temporarily suspended Professor Hoyte without pay pending a ruling on the charge by a joint body of the Board of Regents and the Wisconsin Counsel of Churches.

"Belittling Poseidon, or any part of his undersea kingdom," said Sean Alcott, spokesperson for the Students Religious Anti-defamation League, "also belittles those who worship him. Furthermore, it subjects us to Poseidon's

see POSEIDON on page 6

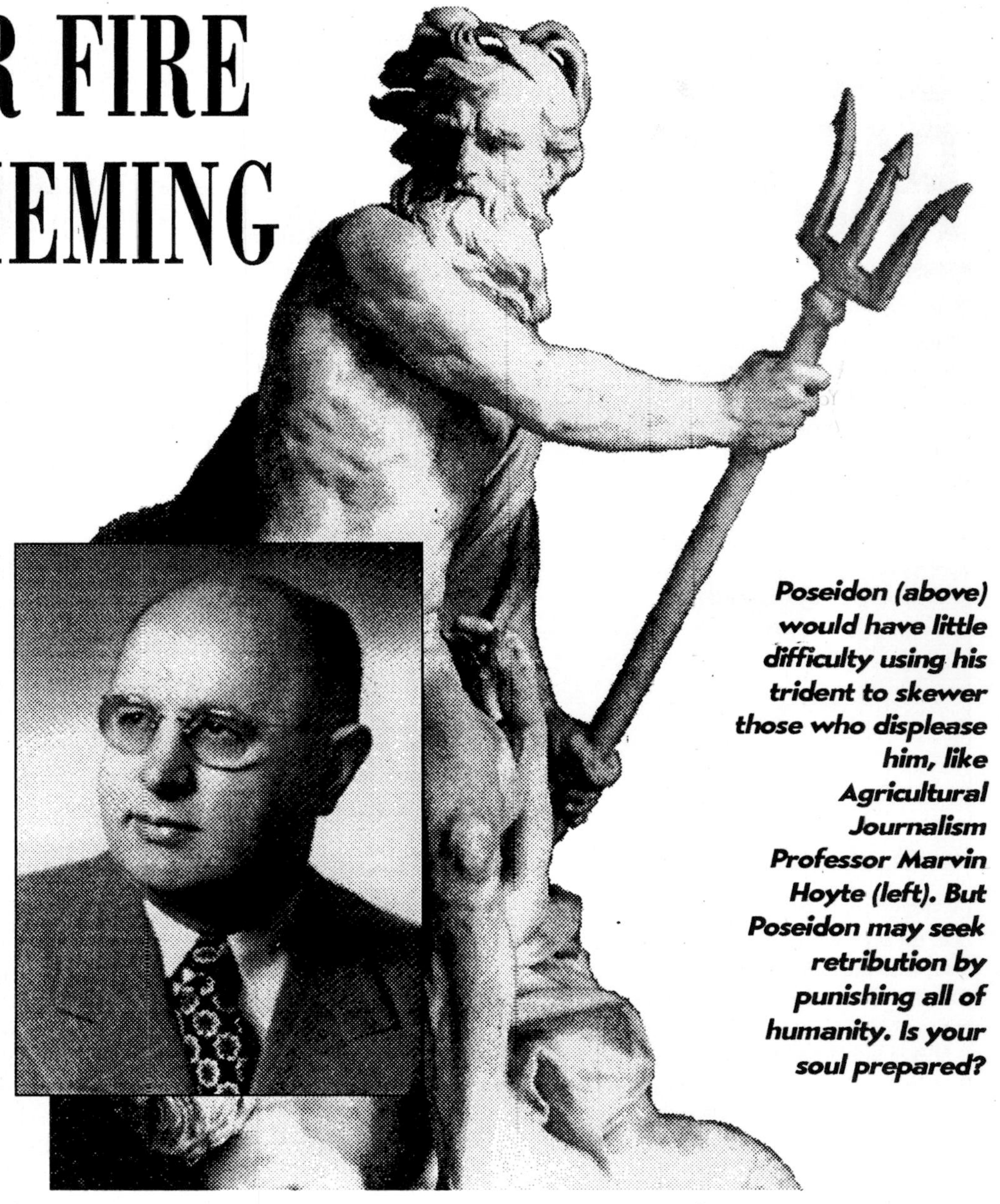

Poseidon (above) would have little difficulty using his trident to skewer those who displease him, like Agricultural Journalism Professor Marvin Hoyte (left). But Poseidon may seek retribution by punishing all of humanity. Is your soul prepared?

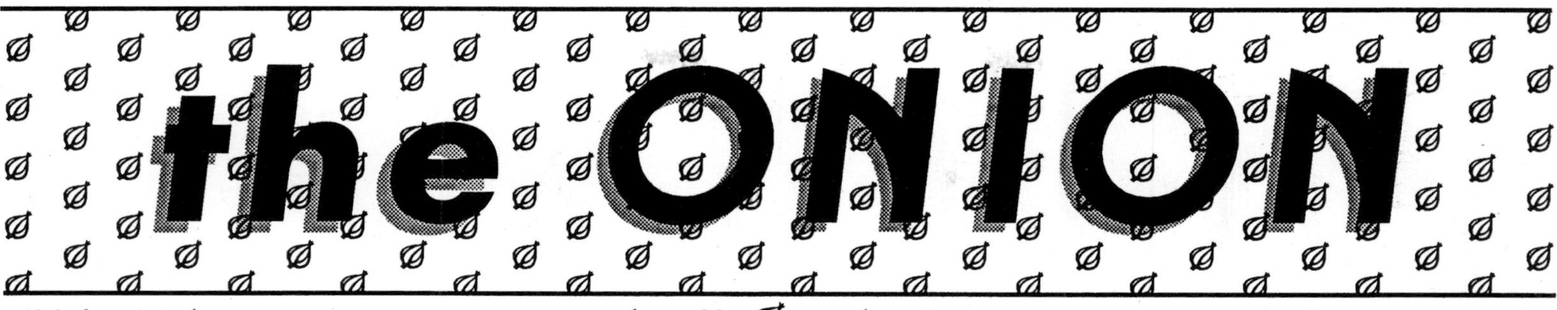

Madison's only newspaper volume 20 number 13 November 13–December 2, 1991

RUN FOR YOUR LIVES!

THE END IS NEAR! SAVE YOURSELVES! LOGICAL thought has become nothing but a hindrance! The only option available to us is desperate, widespread panic! Panic! You must run now to save your lives! Abandon all reason! She's gonna blow! The enemy is at the gate! All hope is lost! The walls are falling! Don't bother fighting it! The rivers run red with blood and human entrails! Doom is at Hand! Don't waste another second! Run! Run! Head for the hills! Forget your friends and family—they're already dead! You'll be next unless you heed these prophetic words! Don't even stop to reason why! Run! Run as fast as your legs will carry you! Thinking will only hasten your inevitable end! For the love of God, Run! The seventh seal has broken! Death is imminent! The earth trembles as the four horsemen of the Apocalypse come riding in! Heed the signs! You'll never make it! Panic! Wave you arms madly! Scream at the top of your voice! Words mean nothing! Communication is useless! Chaos and madness runs amok in our streets! Join the sprawling mass of terrified, wild-eyed animals who once called themselves humans! Panic! Run! These are insurmountable odds! The sins of the past have come due! It's time to pay the piper! Repent! Repent, you wicked snakes and vipers! The skies have been torn asunder and rain down fire and brimstone! There's no escape! All exits are blocked! Plow through the screaming hoards! Trample over those weaker than you! Kill others to further your own futile effort to survive! This is your last chance! This is it! This is the end! Look out for yourself and no one else! Run! The horrific specter

see RUN! on page 5

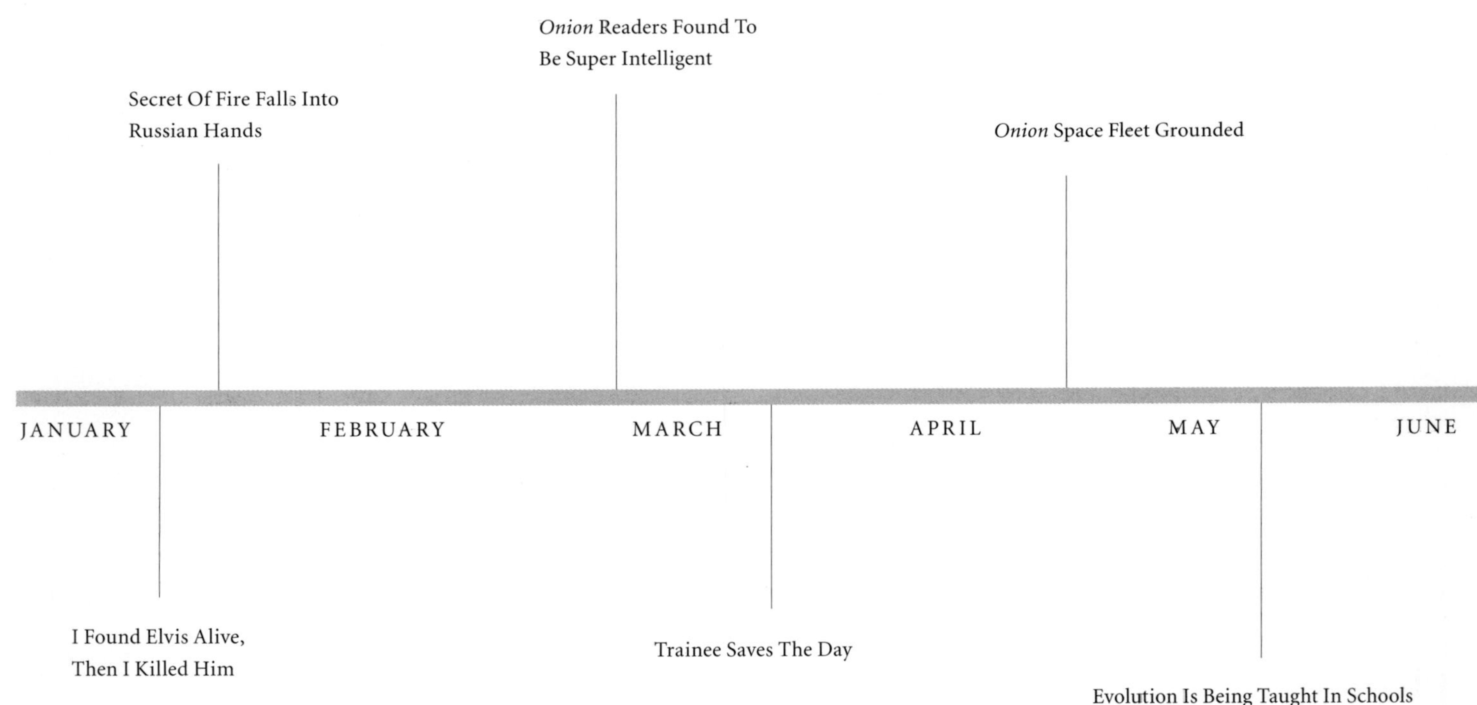
Onion Readers Found To Be Super Intelligent
Secret Of Fire Falls Into Russian Hands
Onion Space Fleet Grounded
JANUARY
FEBRUARY
MARCH
APRIL
MAY
JUNE
I Found Elvis Alive, Then I Killed Him
Trainee Saves The Day
Evolution Is Being Taught In Schools

1992

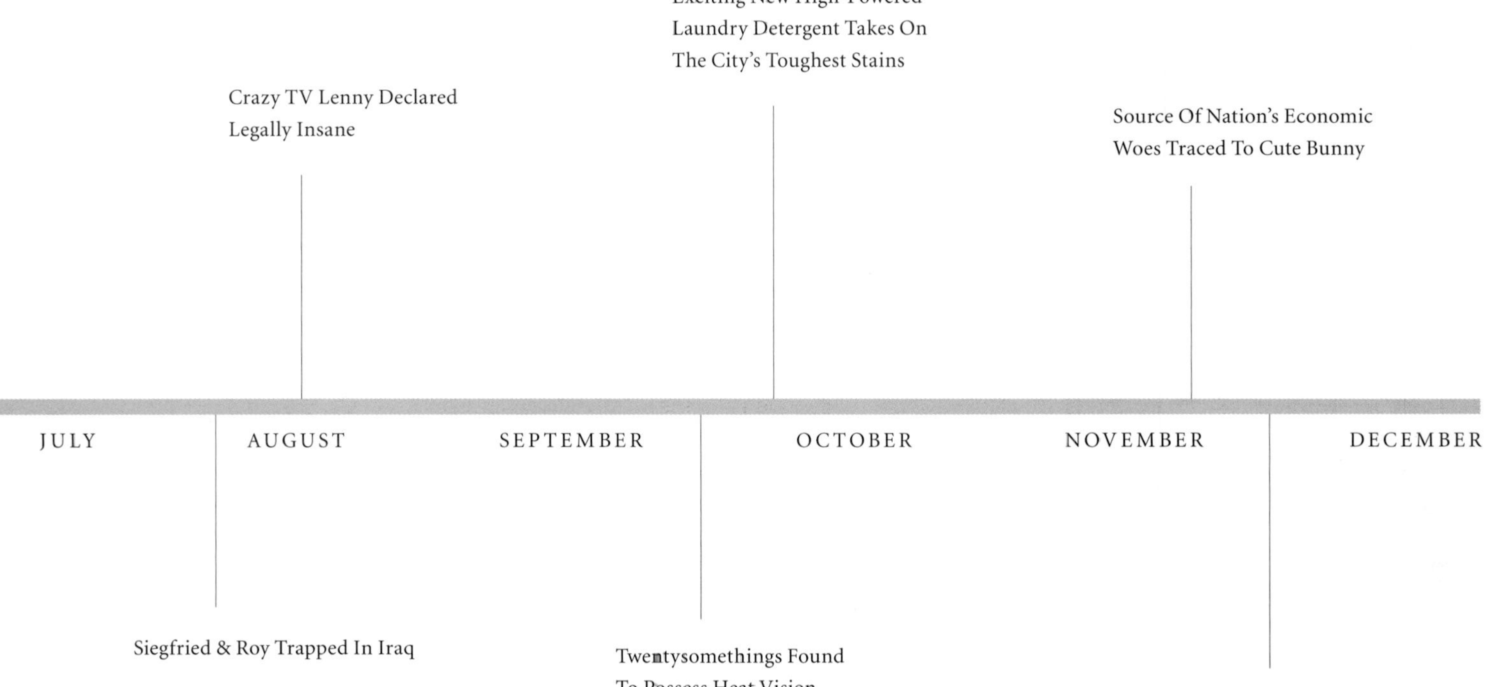

Exciting New High-Powered Laundry Detergent Takes On The City's Toughest Stains
Crazy TV Lenny Declared Legally Insane
Source Of Nation's Economic Woes Traced To Cute Bunny
JULY
AUGUST
SEPTEMBER
OCTOBER
NOVEMBER
DECEMBER
Siegfried & Roy Trapped In Iraq
Twentysomethings Found To Possess Heat Vision
Belt-Sanding Hoodlum Announces Bid For U.S. Presidency

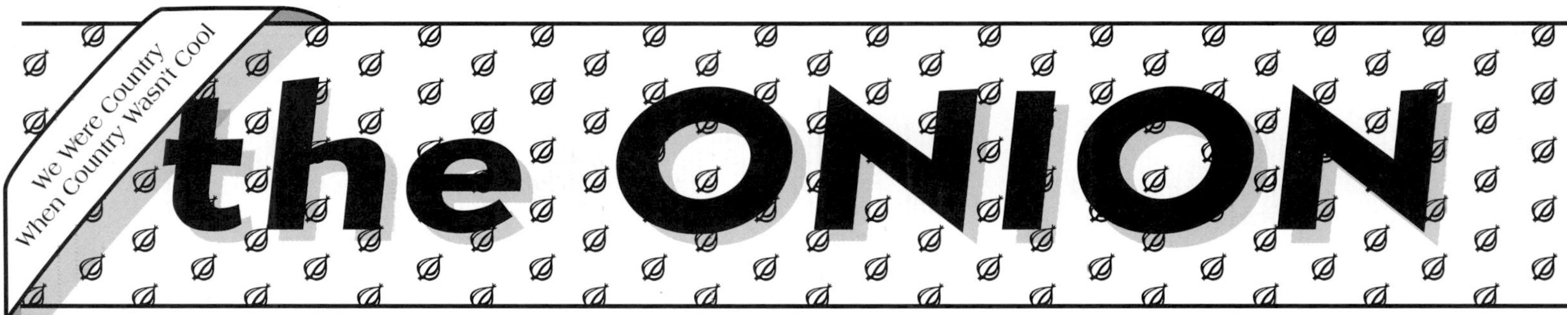

Madison's free propaganda instrument volume 21 number 5 February 11–17, 1992

RUBIK'S CUBE— SOLVED!

Above: the befuddling Rubik's Cube.
Left: The bratty whiz kid who solved it.

FOR OVER TEN YEARS, INTELLECTUALS AND GAMING folk have been mystified by the Rubik's Cube. From computer engineers to MENSA drop-outs, army generals to shepherds, people of every stripe have tried, and failed, to solve the Rubik's Cube. Even best-selling author and NASA scientist Carl Sagan is known to have hurled the Cube at his wall in angry frustration after laboring for days in a hopeless attempt to solve it. If somebody that smart can't even solve it, the rest of us probably shouldn't even bother, right?

Wrong! 11-year-old whiz-kid Richard Sjudig upstaged them all. He not only dared attempt to solve the Rubik's Cube—he succeeded. Now, meet this clever youngster who's turned the world of IQ-scoring on its head with his incredible spatial aptitude. What's inside that bowl-cut-topped, bespectacled head of his? The impressive list starts with four languages. He also has a bachelors degree in mathematics from MIT. His IQ is said to be well above the genius level. Television viewers watched in disbelief as Richard solved the Rubik's Cube on the hit TV program THAT'S INCREDIBLE Monday night. Fran Tarkenton summed up the world's amazement when he looked at the camera and said, "That's Incredible!"

Richard solved the cube by first dissembling it and lubricating it with either graphite or petroleum jelly, to make it move more quickly and smoothly. He then re-assembled it and began moving the sides around. Matching the colors of the outside squares with the

see CUBE on page 11

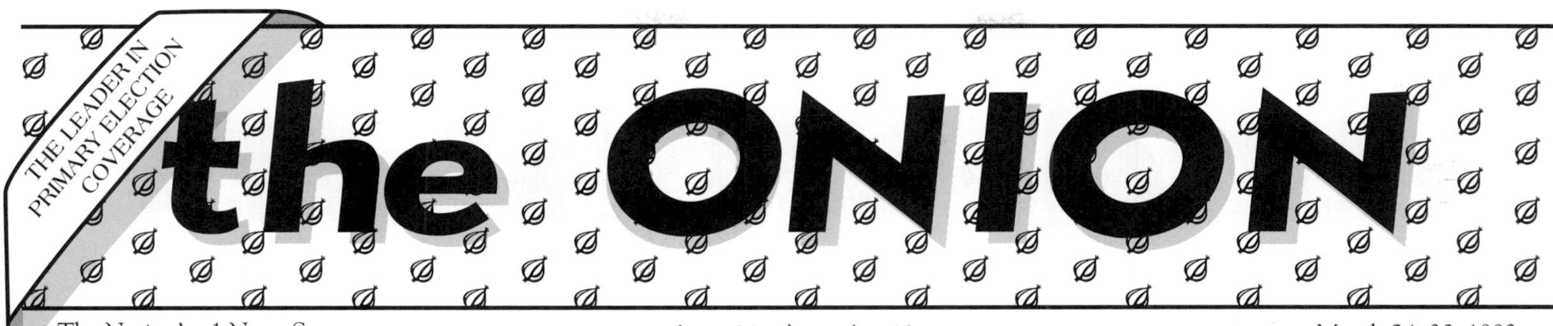

The Nation's #1 News Source volume 21 number 10 March 24–30, 1992

PANHANDLER STRIKE ENTERS THIRD WEEK

City Hall in a Gridlock

City officials are in a panic as Madison's panhandlers announced their intentions to continue their strike if their demands were not met with alacrity. The strike was called in response to recent layoffs, and in part to protest working conditions and benefits packages that fail to meet industry standards, according to a press release distributed by the Panhandling People's Union. Union local co-presidents Spare Change Guy and Crazed Vietnam Vet Guy have asked union members to remain at their customary posts, but not to solicit spare coins until an accord has been reached. Teetering Man could not be reached for comment by press time.

Ramifications of the strike may reach beyond the confines of the State Street-area Panhandlers. Madison's Babbling Street Loon Union is threatening a solidarity strike if the Panhandler's demands are not met. They plan to stage a series of "silent days" beginning next Monday.

The panhandlers' demands include decreased dues, health club membership, a more comprehensive dental plan, and perhaps most controversially, profit sharing

see Strike on page 6

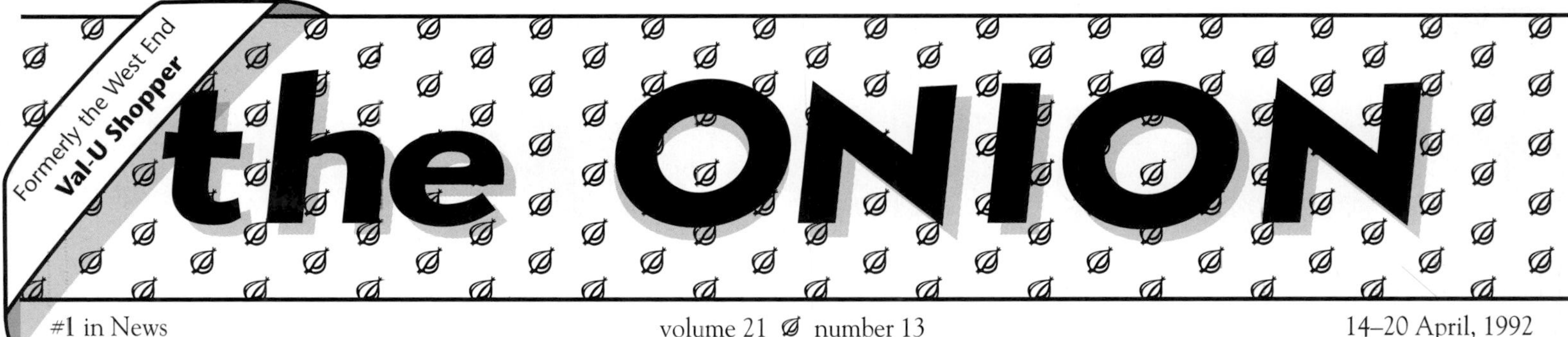

#1 in News volume 21 number 13 14–20 April, 1992

'KING RALPH' PLATE TO BE SOLD AT AUCTION

Bidding Expected to Exceed $30 million

The Onion has announced its intention to offer for sale the "King Ralph" plate in its collection during next month's Sotheby's auction in London. The plate was one of a limited pressing of 150,000, produced for the world media to promote the 1991 feature film, King Ralph. Until now, no lover of fine collector plates dared dream that this important artifact might be owned by any organizations other than the press elite, such as The Onion, who review and promote film art. But Onion accountants have recommended the plate's sale, citing the millions of dollars that could be raised to finance The Onion's prostitution empire and schoolyard drug distribution network.

Representatives from the Franklin Mint have been working closely with the Onion staff, examining the plate and readying it for sale. Per their recommendation, the plate will no longer be left haphazardly about the Onion offices. Because the plate decreases in value each time it is touched by human hands, it will no longer be used by staffers to reheat McRib sandwiches. The plate will now be encased in a glass display cabinet.

Onion, Inc. has been criticized by art scholars and dealers. By putting the artifact on the open market, they fear it will fall into the hands of the Nazis. After extensive investigation of these claims, The Onion has de-

see King Ralph Plate on page 8

The Onion's valuable 'King Ralph' plate, shown here with Appraiser F. Emmit Grimms, will be offered for sale this week. Mr. Grimms is pictured in the lobby of Howard Johnson's Restaurant, where he supervised the vigorous scrubbing of the plate to prepare it for sale.

U.S. CANDYLAND TOURNAMENT RESULTS see pg. 18

the ONION

Number 1 r News volume 22 number 2 25–31 August, 1992

BUSH HANDS OVER U.S. TO NATIVE AMERICANS

To commemorate his landmark decision, President Bush dressed in traditional Cheyenne garb and offered a "peace pipe" to Native Americans residing in a Wyoming reservation. Though greeted with sneers and chuckles at first, Bush was eventually driven off the reservation when he attempted to perform a "rain dance" he had seen in an old Western.

With candidate Bill Clinton well ahead in the polls prior to last week's Republican national convention, it was clear George Bush needed a strong domestic agenda to regain popularity. Now his reelection has been almost guaranteed as he revealed his plan to give the United States back to the original owner, the Native Americans.

"It belongs to them, lets give it back," the President said during

"It's theirs anyway," Bush says.

his nomination acceptance speech, drawing massive applause with his quote of Midnight Oil's "Beds Are Burning" hit single.

The President cited many reasons for his decision, most notably Kevin Costner's heartwarming epic Dances With Wolves, which

see Bush on page 8

Number One In News volume 22 number 3 1–7 September, 1992

RANDOM BEATINGS TO BEGIN THURSDAY

THE ONION IS PROUD TO ANNOUNCE ITS distribution of this year's random beatings, which are slated to begin this Thursday with the annual pummeling of a local resident to be named later. 1992 looks to be the biggest year yet, with an

Get yours before they're gone.

Onion Beating Task Force Headquarters deployed to every American city with a population of over fifty thousand.

One of the longest running annual events in the history of journalism, the random beatings will continue a tradition dating back to the turn of the century, when Onion publisher T.

see BEATINGS on page 8

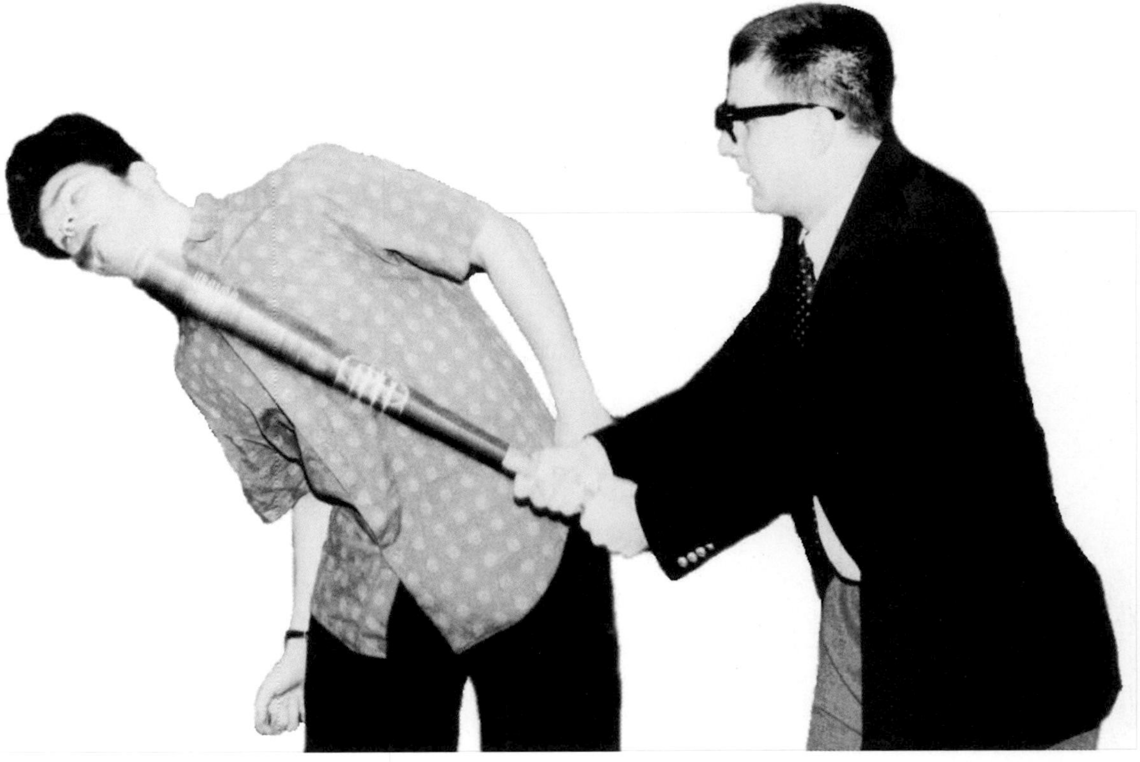

Thousands of lucky American citizens like the one pictured above will be privy to a violent beating doled out by The Onion's Random Beatings Task Force. Beatings will be administered without warning to anyone the Task Force sees fit to pummel.

Number One In News volume 22 number 4 8–14 September, 1992

SCIENTISTS STUNNED BY AMAZING GRASS BOY

Grass Boy, the amazing hybrid of human and grass, is shown here as he looked on the day he was discovered. The stunned smile on his face is not one of happiness, but of contentment.

Meet the Boy Raised By Grass

IN ONE OF THE MOST BIZARRE CASES OF HUMAN SOCIOLOGY and botany to date, scientists have announced the discovery of "Grass Boy," a healthy 15-year-old boy presumed to have been lost in an meadow as a child and raised by grass. Without the socialization skills of other humans to imitate, Grass Boy has evolved into an incredible hybrid of human and grass.

Grass Boy was discovered by the family of Joseph and Nora Gibson during a picnic in a Minnesota field last month. While playing frisbee, the Gibsons stumbled upon what they thought was a large blade of green grass. "Then I saw the head and realized it was actually a naked child standing perfectly still—a blade of grass, but also a boy," Joseph Gibson said.

Unresponsive to any human stimuli, Grass Boy was incapable of communicating with the Gibsons, and had to be forcibly removed by scientists, torn away from the only family he knew: grass, shrubs, and other vegetation.

Scientists theorize that Grass Boy was lost or aban-

see GRASS BOY on page 4

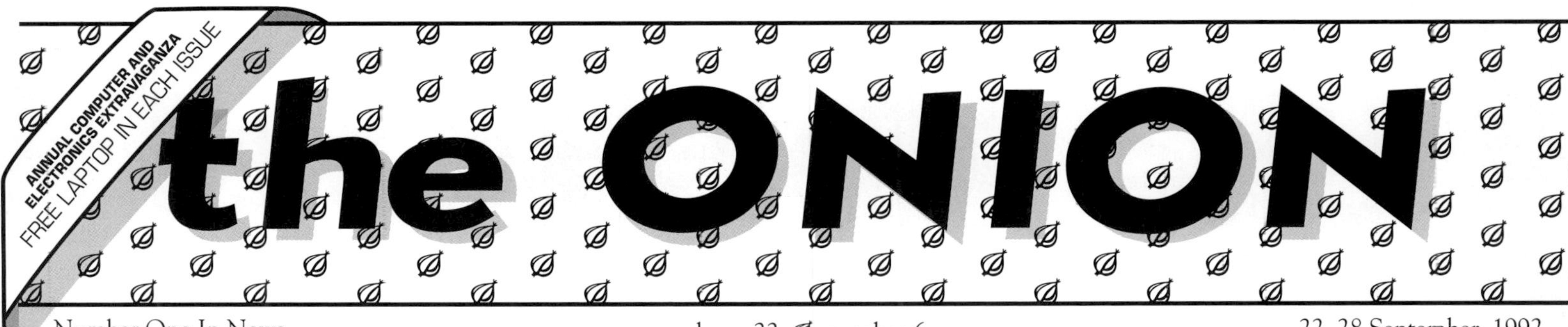

Number One In News volume 22 Ø number 6 22–28 September, 1992

New American Flag Will Feature More Beefcake

Male stripper Lance Stiletto's hunky frame will soon be featured prominently on Old Glory.

In yet another indication that 1992 is shaping up to be the Year of the Woman in national politics, President Bush on Friday bowed to pressure from women's organizations and signed a bill requiring the American flag to immediately begin featuring more beefcake.

"For so long in American society, the female anatomy has been overemphasized and exploited," Bush said in a speech to the League of Women Voters in New York, "and I'm going to be proud to use Old Glory to reverse this tradition." This comment was followed by a huge round of applause. Immediately after the speech an all-male dance revue rushed into the room and began performing for the audience to the tune of "Do You Think I'm Sexy," by Rod Stewart.

The way the beefcake will be added to the flag has not been officially announced, but inside sources say the Bush Administration is negotiating closely with Lance Stiletto, 24, a male stripper at Peeks Nightclub

see Beefcake *on page 4*

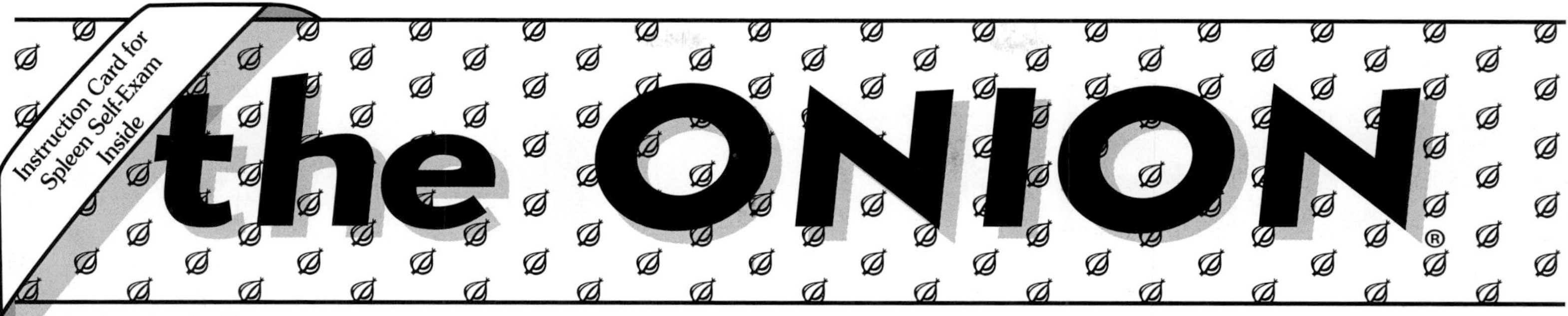

Number One In News volume 22 number 7 29 September–5 October, 1992

Jeff and Becky BREAK UP!

Oh my God, did you hear about Jeff and Becky? They broke up! I swear to God! Everyone thought they were totally in love because they were going out for, like, two months and Jeff just took her to The Shorewood Inn for dinner after the West game last week, but yesterday Julie told me that Jeff told Becky that he just wanted to be friends for awhile, and it wasn't because of anything personal or anything. But I don't believe that at all because yesterday I was hanging out with Lisa and she told me that Rich was, like, all over her at the party last week and told her all this stuff that Jeff had totally been saying behind Becky's back, like how he was sick of her calling him every night and stuff. And, oh *Jeez*! I can't believe I forgot this! Jeff told Alex that he was thinking of going out with this other girl from Bayside! I'm *not* kidding! Jeff is, like, *such* a jerk because Zach told me that if he was going out with Becky he would totally treat her *so* much better than Jeff. Like, Jeff never took her to dances because he always wanted to go with his friends so he could goof around. If he's, like, after this other girl he should have broken up with Becky as soon as he decided that, because now he just led her on and made her look stupid for going out with Jeff for so long because he's *obviously* such a jerk! I can't believe it. Because Becky is pretty smart, you know? She probably knew Jeff was

see Jeff and Becky on page 4

God, they looked so cute together in this picture, but, like, when Jeff broke up with her, Becky totally tore the picture in half.

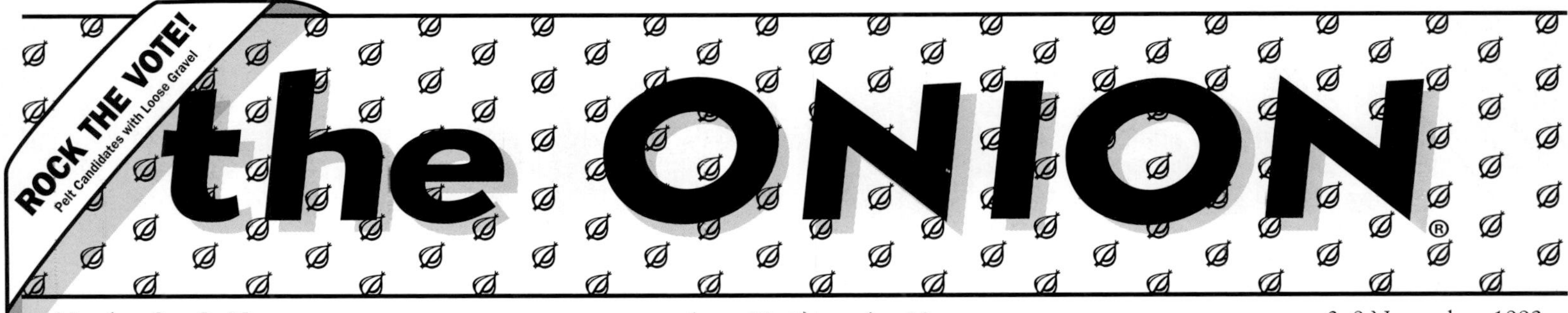

Number One In News volume 22 number 12 3–9 November, 1992

This satellite photo of the flaming space hat, taken by the Space Shuttle crew, shows how close the hat came to signalling Armageddon for all Earth life.

EARTH NEARLY HIT BY FLAMING SPACE HAT

Celestial observers the world over are breathing easier today following the near destruction of all life on Earth by a giant flaming space hat. According to top scientists, the path of the space hat came within 2 miles of the Earth's upper atmosphere. Had it crashed into the planet, the release of kinetic energy from the hat would have caused worldwide earthquakes, boiled the oceans and upset weather patterns for generations, eventually killing all plant and animal life.

The space hat was first sighted last May by NASA observers. Their routine survey of the asteroid belt turned up a large object which not only moved quickly against the galactic background but grew steadily larger, as if it were moving closer. Further analysis using the Hubble orbiting telescope showed that the object was not only getting closer, but was on a collision course with Earth.

"We weren't worried at first," said Frijoff Nolte, NASA's Chief of Astronomy, "because we figured it was just a large nickel–iron asteroid or a wayward comet. Imagine our surprise and horror when we realized that it was a giant flaming space hat, even more deadly than the giant flaming space bowtie that killed the dinosaurs and dug the huge crater in Arizona."

Spectrographic analysis of the space hat showed it to be composed of interstellar dust, water ice, frozen hydrogen, worsted wool and trace amounts of fine silk which

see Space Hat on page 4

Number One In News volume 22 ⌀ nu... 17–30 November, 1992

ANGRY LUMBERJACK DEMANDS HEARTY BREAKFAST

No need to be angry, Mr. Lumberjack! The breakfast specials at The Golden Skillet™ were prepared for big eaters like you, so enjoy! And remember—whether you're chopping down mighty Sequoias or just working at the office, The Golden Skillet™ is a Breakfast Bonanza!

Early morning patrons of The Golden Skillet Pancake House were startled Tuesday when a muscle-bound lumberjack from the North Woods entered the popular eating establishment and loudly bellowed his desire for a hearty breakfast at an affordable price. The lumberjack spoke of his frustration at consistently spending too much money on breakfasts, only to have them fail to put a dent in his voracious appetite.

After plunging his giant axe into the reception counter, he was greeted by waitress Kelly Donaldson and led to his table. "I was scared at first," recounts the perky blond 24-year-old, "but I knew that here at Golden Skillet, we have a variety of breakfast specials to satisfy even the hungriest of customers—at a price that won't break their bank accounts!"

Witnesses say that although the lumberjack was skeptical at first, he agreed to sit down and look at the Golden Skillet's extensive menu. Within minutes, he ordered the "Starvin' Marvin," a limited-time-only breakfast special which includes two eggs, five pancakes, bacon and sausage links—all for only $4.99!

The lumberjack enjoyed a steaming cup of coffee, which Waitress Kelly refilled at no extra charge, while he waited for his food. "But he didn't have to wait long!" says Troy Haglin, a customer who was seated in the booth to the left of the lumberjack. "He shot me some dirty looks and growled a couple times, but within minutes Kelly arrived with a heap of pancakes to satisfy the lumberjack's hankerings." Haglin added that even a big mean lumberjack with a hunger the size of the Great Outdoors can't deny that service at the Golden Skillet is first rate!

Upon receiving his breakfast, the lumberjack let out a loud, heartfelt "Mmmmmm!" He rubbed his stomach before digging into the massive pile of food set before him. He began his meal in the manner of any normal lumberjack, shoveling food into his mouth noisily, but by the time he finished his last mouthful the lumberjack picked up a few social graces from other customers from surrounding tables. People from all walks of life know that The Golden Skillet is a Breakfast Lover's Paradise.

see LUMBERJACK *on page 4*

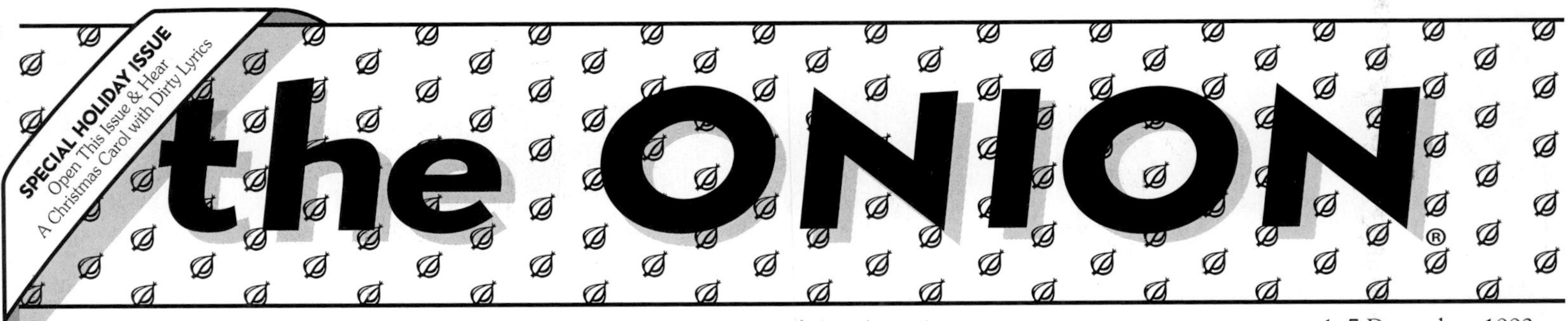

SANTA CLAUS DEAD AT 250

A Posthumous Note To A Jolly Old Elf—

We'll never forget your bright red suit, or your meerschaum pipe, or the way you belted out a "Ho Ho Ho" just to make us laugh. We'll miss your jovial demeanor and your undying generosity. Each of us will remember a certain special gift you gave us that touched our hearts when we were young. Your untimely passing marks the end of an era. Our children will never know the thrill of staying up late on Christmas Eve awaiting your arrival, but don't worry! We won't let 'em forget you, Santa!

Have Fun In Heaven!
THE ONION

TO THE ENGLISH HE WAS SAINT NICHOLAS. THE SWISS referred to him as Kris Kringle, and to the Germans he was Pelz Nichol. But regardless of what you call him, Santa Claus is dead. The magical old figurehead of the Christmas season was pronounced dead of pneumonia at exactly 12 midnight on Friday. He was 250 years old.

According to Barney the Elf, the attending doctor at the North Pole, Claus' pneumonia was brought on by his constant late night trips into the chilly stratosphere. Barney also cited nicotine addiction and a frantic lifestyle as contributors to Claus' illness. "I warned him to slow down," emphasized Barney, "It was bad enough at his age to be globe-trotting every Christmas Eve, but lately he's been going out every

see SANTA on page 4

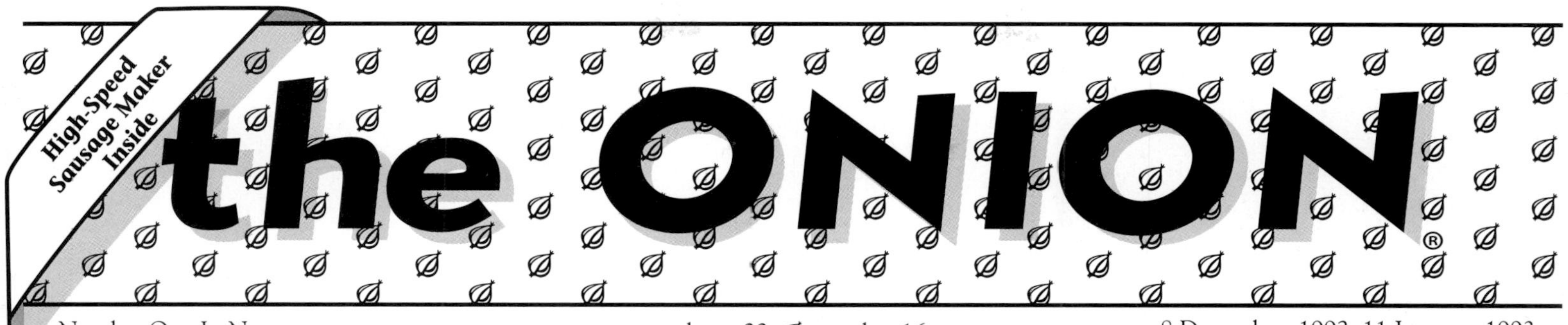

Number One In News | volume 22 ⌀ number 16 | 8 December, 1992–11 January, 1993

The Onion's Man of the Year

My Dad

Selecting The Onion's annual Man of the Year is never a simple task. The person we choose must be morally forthright, an outstanding member of the human community, and most importantly, someone who truly made a difference in our world during the past year. Some of the previous individuals who have lived up to our high standards include Nelson Mandela, Mikhail Gorbachev, and John Ritter.

This year's selection was a rather obvious one for all of us at The Onion. Although other names had been dropped, like Ross Perot and Tom Arnold, it became clear after a few minutes of discussion that the 1992 Onion Man of the Year would be my dad.

What makes my dad so great? First of all, my dad lets me be me. When I told him that I wanted to go into journalism rather than be a computer salesman like him, he didn't get disappointed the way many dads would. Instead, he supported me—he put his arm

see Man of The Year on page 4

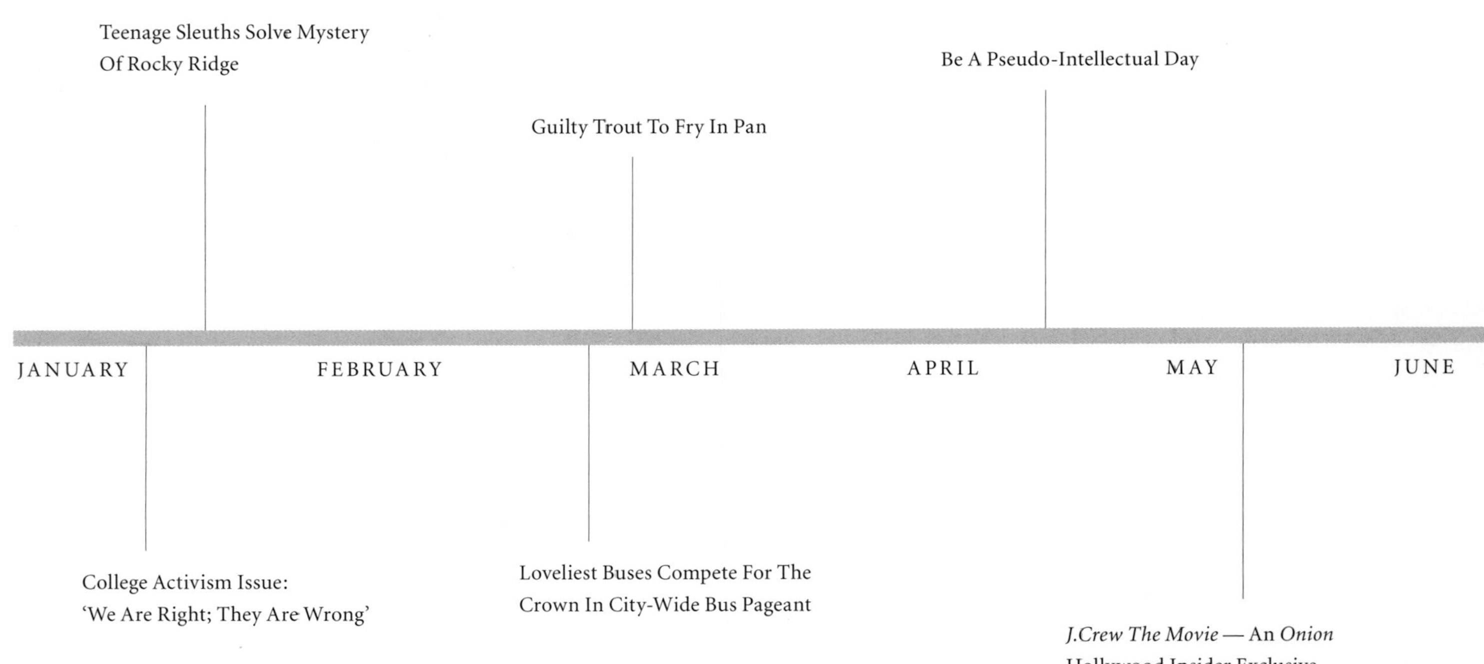
Teenage Sleuths Solve Mystery
Of Rocky Ridge
Guilty Trout To Fry In Pan
Be A Pseudo-Intellectual Day
JANUARY
FEBRUARY
MARCH
APRIL
MAY
JUNE
College Activism Issue:
'We Are Right; They Are Wrong'
Loveliest Buses Compete For The
Crown In City-Wide Bus Pageant
J.Crew The Movie — An *Onion*
Hollywood Insider Exclusive

1993

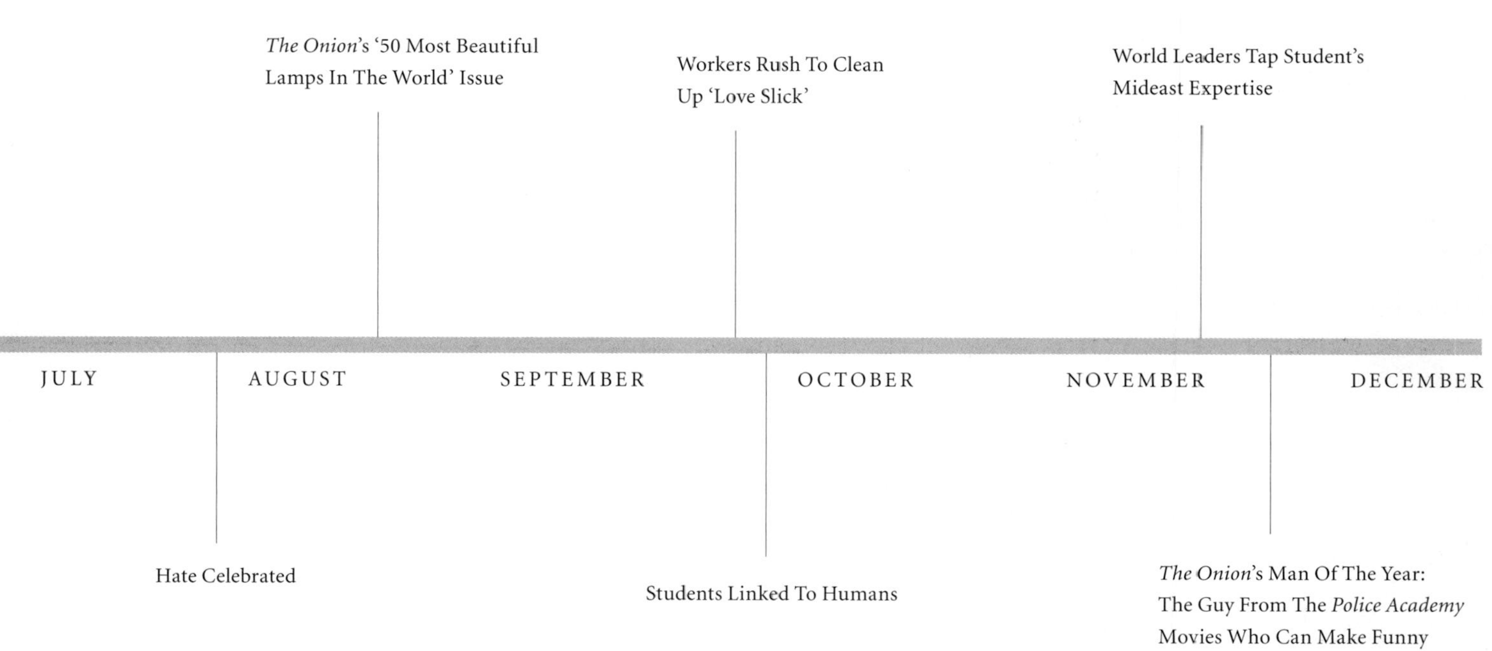

The Onion's '50 Most Beautiful Lamps In The World' Issue
Workers Rush To Clean Up 'Love Slick'
World Leaders Tap Student's Mideast Expertise
JULY
AUGUST
SEPTEMBER
OCTOBER
NOVEMBER
DECEMBER
Hate Celebrated
Students Linked To Humans
The Onion's Man Of The Year: The Guy From The *Police Academy* Movies Who Can Make Funny Noises With His Mouth

Number One In News volume 23 Ø number 13 13–19 April 1993

EASTER HOLIDAY RUINED BY SUBSTITUTE BUNNY

Confused Kids Cry: "Where Are Our Easter Eggs?"

This exclusive Onion Photo shows Substitute Easter Bunny Donny Blanchard loafing in the office of the Magic Bunny Council when he should have been hiding eggs for deserving children.

TINY TOTS FROM EVERY CORNER OF THE GLOBE CRIED THEIR TINY EYES OUT, as no Easter egg, Easter basket or Easter marshmallow chickie could be found in the whole of Christendom. The traditional hunt of Easter eggs, one of the most highly anticipated parts of the Lenten season, was marred by the insolence of a last-minute replacement Easter Bunny, resulting in more empty-handed children this year than during Cadbury's cyanide scare of 1988.

The selection of a new Easter Bunny was called for after the sudden resignation last Tuesday of Lapine, the Easter Bunny from 1981 to 1992. Fellow helpers say Lapine was dissatisfied with the early hours and low pay associated with the job, and threatened to quit at least three other times when he wasn't amply supplied with carrots. Members of the Magic Bunny Council, reeling from Lapine's resignation, had still not chosen a new Easter Bunny by Maundy Thursday.

Easter Bunnies come and go, owing to the short life span of rabbits and the high value of their pelts, but the rigorous Easter Bunny selection process usually locates the most competent bunny for the

see EASTER on page 4

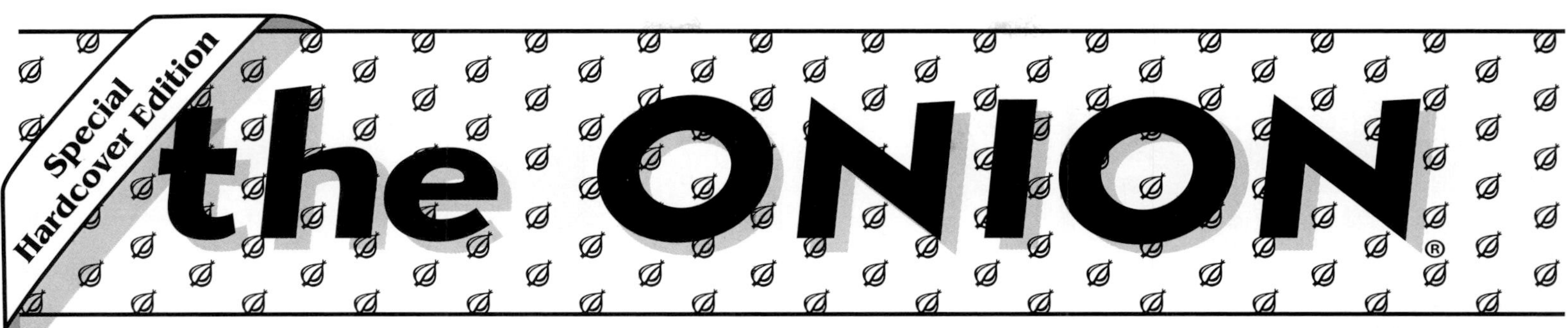

Number One In News | volume 23 Ø number 15 | 27 April–3 May 1993

NEW STAMP SERIES COMMEMORATES SKIN DISORDERS

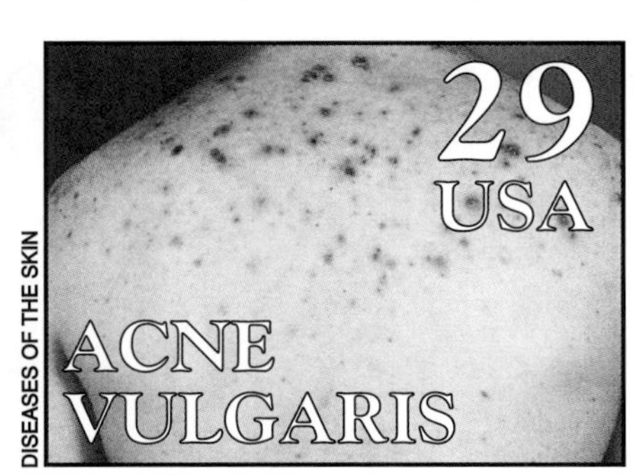

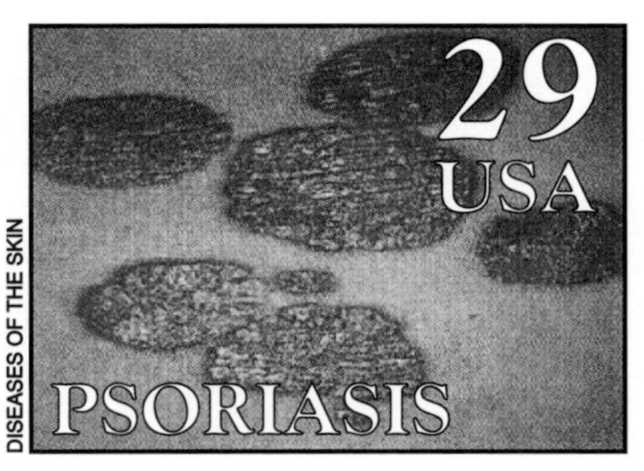

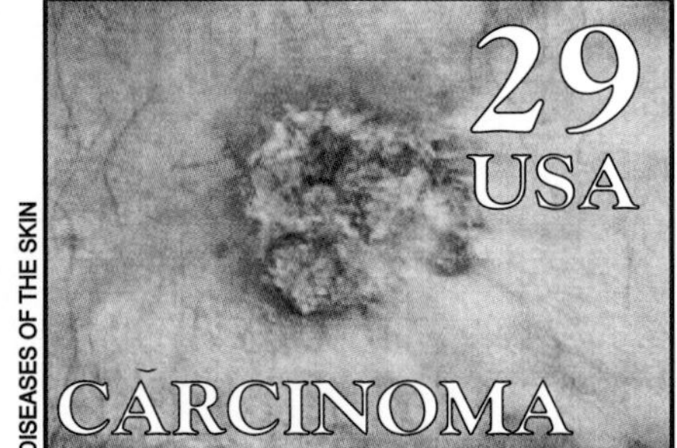

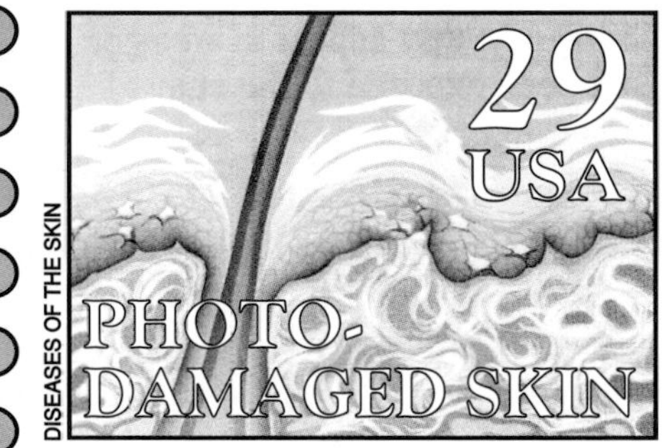

U.S. POST OFFICES WERE CROWDED TO CAPACITY Monday as people rushed to acquire a new series of stamps devoted entirely to unpleasant skin ailments. Known collectively as the Diseases of the Skin Series, the ten stamps feature full-color close-ups of festering epidermal wounds, many which glisten with pus or ooze blood. The diseases pictured, which range from harmless (eczema) to deadly (malignant melanoma), were chosen last year by over 50 million people who voted for their favorites at their local post office.

"We never dreamed response would be this overwhelming," said Postmaster General Rita Darvonovich. "We haven't seen this level of interest in stamps since 1977, when we printed our Steaming Heaps of Deer Viscera Collection."

The new stamps were released Monday to coincide with the twentieth anniversary of the 1973 epidemic of scabies among America's mail carriers. Postmaster Darvonovich believes that her own infestation gave her a new respect for the importance of skin problems. "When I had [scabies], it totally controlled my actions," she explains. "I couldn't sit down when I drove my postal jeep, and angry customers on my route would often catch me itching myself with their rolled-up magazines."

Just a few months ago, the skin disease stamps

see STAMPS on page 10

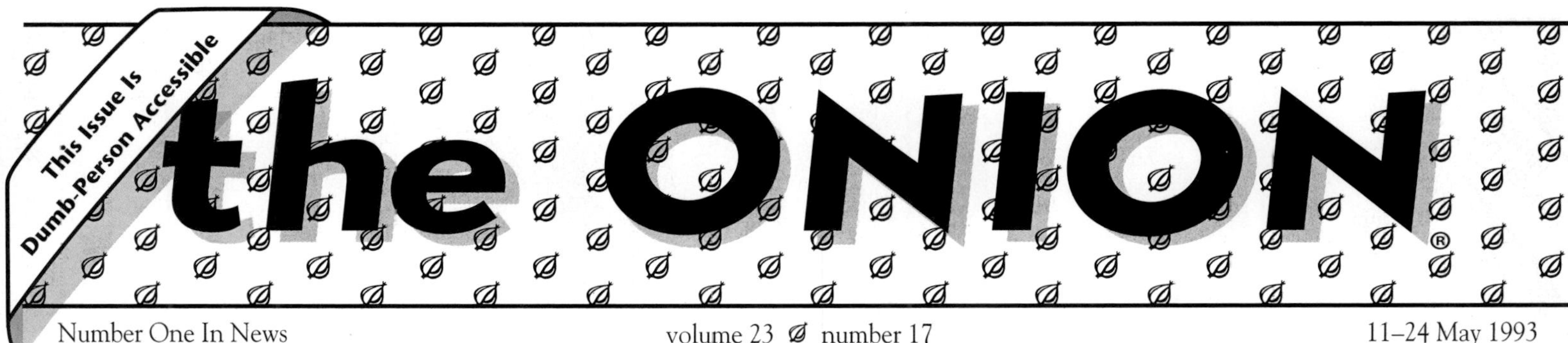

Number One In News volume 23 number 17 11–24 May 1993

UW Cuts Funding of Coed Naked Sports

Soon, scenes like this will be rare as coed naked sports are phased out.

THE DISTINCTIVE SMACK OF THE BALL IN THE FIELDER'S palm won't be heard down at the ball park this spring. Come fall, the slap of the pigskin on the fullback's meaty chest will be absent from the gridiron. And this winter, no crowd will thrill to the sharp squeak of bare feet on the hardwood of the basketball court. From the lofty office of the athletic director, the word has come down—there will be no more coed naked sports at the University of Wisconsin.

The athletic department cited practical considerations for the decision. Injuries ranging from minor abrasions to syphilis continued to hamper most teams, and physical contact on the field often went above and beyond the call of normal athletics. Intimate one-on-one encounters as well as spontaneous mass orgies disrupted the flow of many contests.

Still further, the Chancellor argued that financial woes were so serious that a University ad-hoc committee of financial experts determined that either the Coed Naked Sports program or the English department had to be cut.

This strategy seems to have failed the school however, as Randy Moore, junior English major and all-conference hurdler on the coed naked track team, has given her allegiance to sport.

"English am important, but hey, me are one second away from the league record and I got a year to break it," Moore said.

see COED NAKED SPORTS on page 11

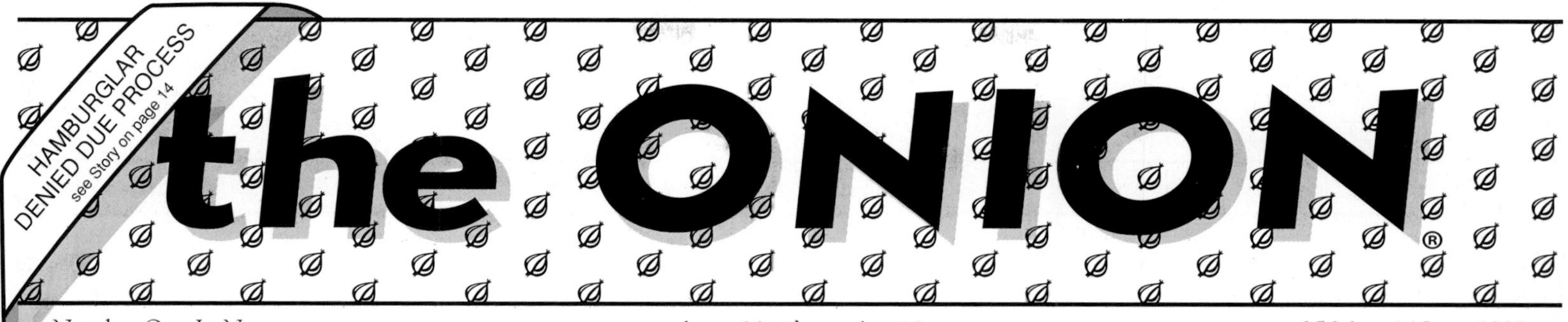

Number One In News | volume 23 number 18 | 25 May–14 June 1993

SENIORS' BUFFET RUINED BY SHORTAGE OF FOLDING CHAIRS

Last Saturday's Senior Citizens Spring Buffet in Akron, Ohio, normally the social high-point of the season, was deemed a complete failure by those in attendance because there were no places to sit. According to inside sources, the buffet organizers had rented out the President's Hall at the Ramada Inn on 54th and Ruby Avenue, but failed to reserve the proper number of folding chairs.

Ramada Inn representatives claim that all the chairs were reserved by Akron East High School for their senior prom held in the Ambassador Room across the hall. "Hey, we got there first," said Akron East High School Class President Karl Wagner. "We told them they could use our chairs while we were dancing, but I guess our rock music scared them away."

Because of the oversight, many senior citizens were forced to either wait in long lines for empty seats or eat their cured ham and potato salad while sitting on the stairs in the hotel lobby. Many chose not to stay at all, leaving as soon as they learned about the lack of chairs. "What are we supposed to do—stand?" grumbled retired salesman Leo Shostak, as he and his wife of 46 years headed for the door.

"I'm not as spry as I used to be," said Charlotte Franze, who turned 86-years-young on Saturday. "I've had trouble with the veins in my legs, so it hurts to stand for too long."

Archie "Arch" Danielson, who was to receive the Senior Citizen Up-And-About Award for his work at his local newspaper, seemed especially

see Buffet on page 4

While some were lucky to get seats early (pictured above), most senior citizens were forced to wander around the hall or sit on the dusty floor. Many elderly participants (pictured at right) complained of vericose vein irritation caused by the lengthy wait. They also didn't like the Jell-O.

220 COLD-CRANKIN' AMPS!!!

the ONION®

Madison's Only Newspaper volume 24 number 4 7–13 September 1993

SCIENTISTS STUNNED BY AMAZING SPOON BOY

Spoon Boy, the amazing hybrid of human and spoon, is shown here in the kitchen of Professor Underwood. He can perform all the duties of a normal spoon.

Meet the Boy Raised By Spoons

In one of the most bizarre cases of human sociology and metallurgy to date, scientists have announced the discovery of "Spoon Boy," a healthy 15-year-old boy theorized to have been lost in a utensil drawer as an infant, and exposed only to spoons. Without the social skills of other humans to imitate, Spoon Boy has evolved into an incredible hybrid of human and spoon.

Spoon Boy was discovered by the family of Pete and Rhoda Scardini when they moved into a newly remodeled apartment last month. After opening the utensil drawer beneath the kitchen counter, the Scardinis picked up what they thought to be a beautifully crafted silver spoon. "Then I saw the head and realized it was actually a naked child—a spoon, but also a boy," Pete Scardini said.

Unresponsive to any human stimuli, Spoon Boy was incapable of communicating with the Scardinis, and had to be forcibly removed by scientists, torn away from the only family he knew: spoons, forks and butter knives.

Scientists theorize that Spoon Boy was lost or abandoned as an infant in the drawer, destined to be without a human role model for 15 years. He then grew to grotesquely small and deformed dimensions in order to adapt to his cramped environment. "What we see in Spoon Boy is a remarkable testament to human adaptability," says Professor Howard Underwood.

After being shipped to the authorities, Spoon Boy was tested by a team of researchers. Professor Underwood, whose knowledge of sociology and evolution

see Spoon Boy on page 13

Congratulations! You are our 75 BILLIONTH Reader!

the ONION®

Number One In News | volume 24 number 7 | 28 September–4 October 1993

One guest was able to snap this picture of Jesus as he gloriously materialized above a keg of Busch Light.

TRIUMPHANT RETURN OF JESUS CHRIST ADDS EXCITEMENT TO KEGGER

Dozens of Lucky Underage Students Get Baptized—In Beer!

THOSE IN ATTENDANCE AT ANDY HABERSHANKER'S BEER BASH LAST FRIDAY WERE DELIGHTED TO ENTERTAIN an unexpected visitor when the Lord Jesus Christ materialized above a keg of beer, ending an almost 2,000 year period of non-intervention in earthly matters. Although Jesus was initially judgemental of the group of drunken college students, He was quick to mingle with the crowd and ended up staying at the party for nearly three hours. "I was really worried that He would send me to hell or some shit like that," said Habershanker, "but it turns out He was just looking for a good time and some cheap beer."

After Jesus introduced himself to Habershanker, the excited host was quick to welcome the Son of God, giving Him a discount on a cup and introducing Him to his housemates. Jesus seemed appreciative of the hospitable gestures, although assured Habershanker that He already knew everyone at the party. To demonstrate, he then pointed at a group of people and remarked on how many hairs were on each of their heads.

Jesus' attendance saved the party, which was up until then boring and unsuccessful. According to Habershanker, guests were complaining that the crowd had gotten too big, and that the mixtape being played was "lame." Once Jesus appeared, however, people seemed to forget their qualms, rejoicing in His presence and joyfully singing hymns. "Jesus made us feel like we were all players in our Heavenly Father's plan, where before we were just a sweaty, uncomfortable crowd," said one partygoer. "This was the best kegger ever!"

After only a few beers, Jesus, or "Jeez" as He came to be known, began to show signs of mortal fallibility. He was seen spilling a beer on His loincloth, and repeatedly spoke of His strained relationship with His father. "He said that living in the light of God wasn't all it's cracked up to be,"

see JESUS on page 4

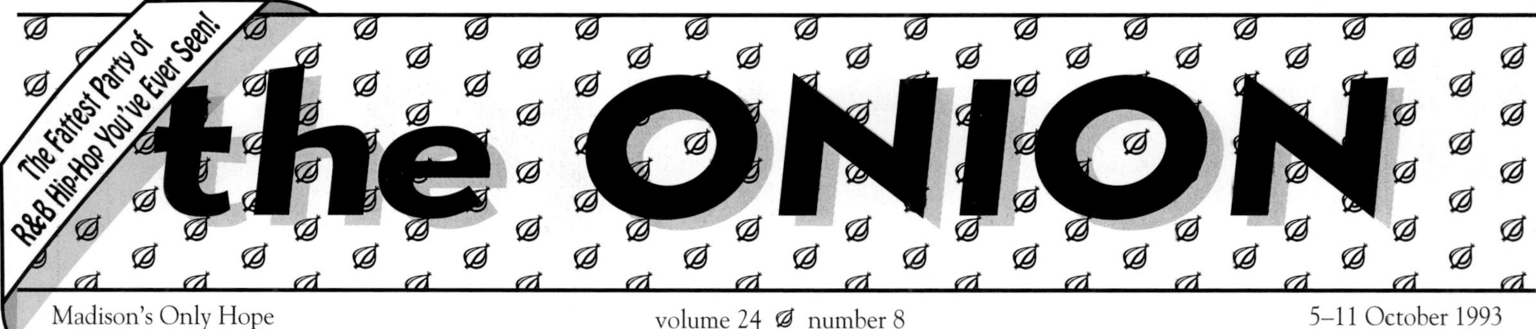

Madison's Only Hope volume 24 ⌀ number 8 5–11 October 1993

BOY TRAVELS TO DISTANT LANDS INSIDE MAGICAL ABANDONED REFRIGERATOR

He Should Be Coming Back Out Any Day Now.

Sam anxiously waits outside the refrigerator for Danny to emerge and recount his travels.

Little Danny Perkins, 7, entered a world of adventure last week when he visited the county dump and hopped into a magical abandoned refrigerator. Now, five days later, the curious second-grader's friends and family are anxiously waiting for him to emerge from the refrigerator and tell them about all the marvelous places he's been and things he's seen.

Danny's friend and classmate, Sam Bartos, was on hand to see Danny off on his journey, and was even given the honor of closing the shiny silver latch on the refrigerator's door once Danny was inside. "A few minutes after he got in, I heard a lot of banging and noise coming from the refrigerator," Sam said, "and I knew his journey had begun."

According to Sam, the two boys have been playing in the dump ever since they met in kindergarten two years ago. They had often talked about the old refrigerator, and used their imaginations to pretend that it was really a spaceship, a submarine or a World War II fort. Until last week, however, neither had dared enter the wonderful machine and experience its magic firsthand. "We wanted to make up a secret map and flight plan before we took off," Sam explained.

In the treehouse in Sam's backyard, the two boys spent weeks making a list of the places they wanted to visit. First, they had hoped to go to the forests of India to hunt tigers. This was to be followed by jaunts to the treasure-filled caves of Arabia, and the sewers of New York to meet the Teenage

see Refrigerator on page 8

What's the Frequency, Kenneth?

the ONION

All The Advertising That's Fit To Print — volume 24 number 12 — 2–8 November 1993

CLINTON KILLS MAN WITH BARE HANDS

The president insists the murder makes up for his lack of military experience

President Clinton held a press conference Monday to announce that he had just killed a man with his bare hands. The murder had been anticipated since last July, when Clinton admitted he was unsure of his abilities to govern, having never faced death. Many had criticized the president for his lack of experience fighting with the armed forces, so Clinton promised to gain this experience before the one-year anniversary of his election.

The president participated undercover in routine FBI-organized gangland slayings, and then in several international assassinations. None left him satisfied. An FBI agent quotes Clinton as saying, "I shall not truly know what death is like until I can feel the force of a man's life drain from his body, and look at his eyes as they become blank with death."

Clinton's obsession with killing a man led his staff to organize the transport of death row inmates to the White House, but all were sent back by the president. Clinton maintained at the time that the inmates had already seen death, and that killing them would do no good. "I want something pure to kill. I want utter fear and confusion to glow in a man's eyes when I kill him," he said.

The FBI eventually chose a tourist at random. Jerry Burns, a 28-year-old cartography student from Indianapolis, was visiting the Capitol with his girlfriend when Secret Service agents shot him with a tranquilizer gun and brought him before the president. Burns reportedly had little time to make a statement, awakening from his drugged slumber only seconds before the president began to strangle him. Witnesses report that the victim appeared frightened and groggy.

"I have killed this man," Clinton said at Monday's press conference as the corpse was wheeled in, "and through

see Clinton on page 10

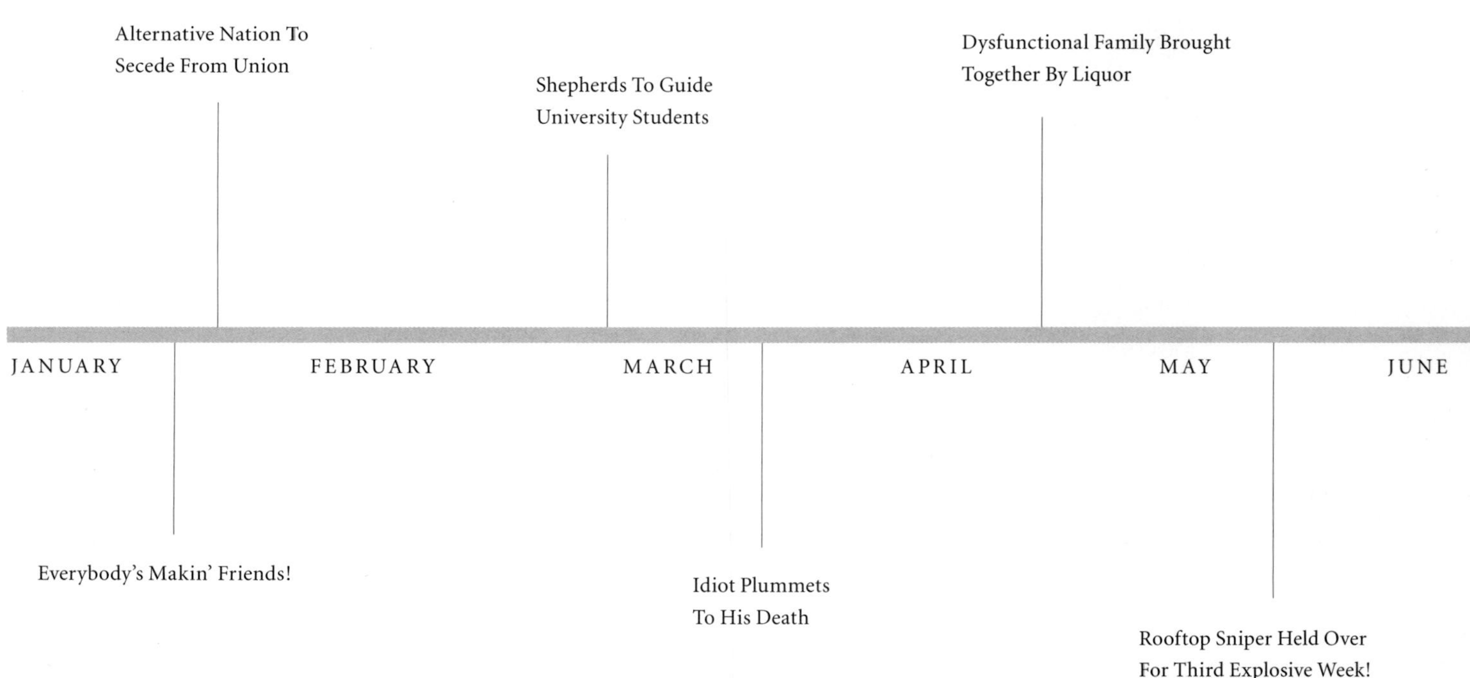

Alternative Nation To
Secede From Union
Shepherds To Guide
University Students
Dysfunctional Family Brought
Together By Liquor
JANUARY
FEBRUARY
MARCH
APRIL
MAY
JUNE
Everybody's Makin' Friends!
Idiot Plummets
To His Death
Rooftop Sniper Held Over
For Third Explosive Week!

1994

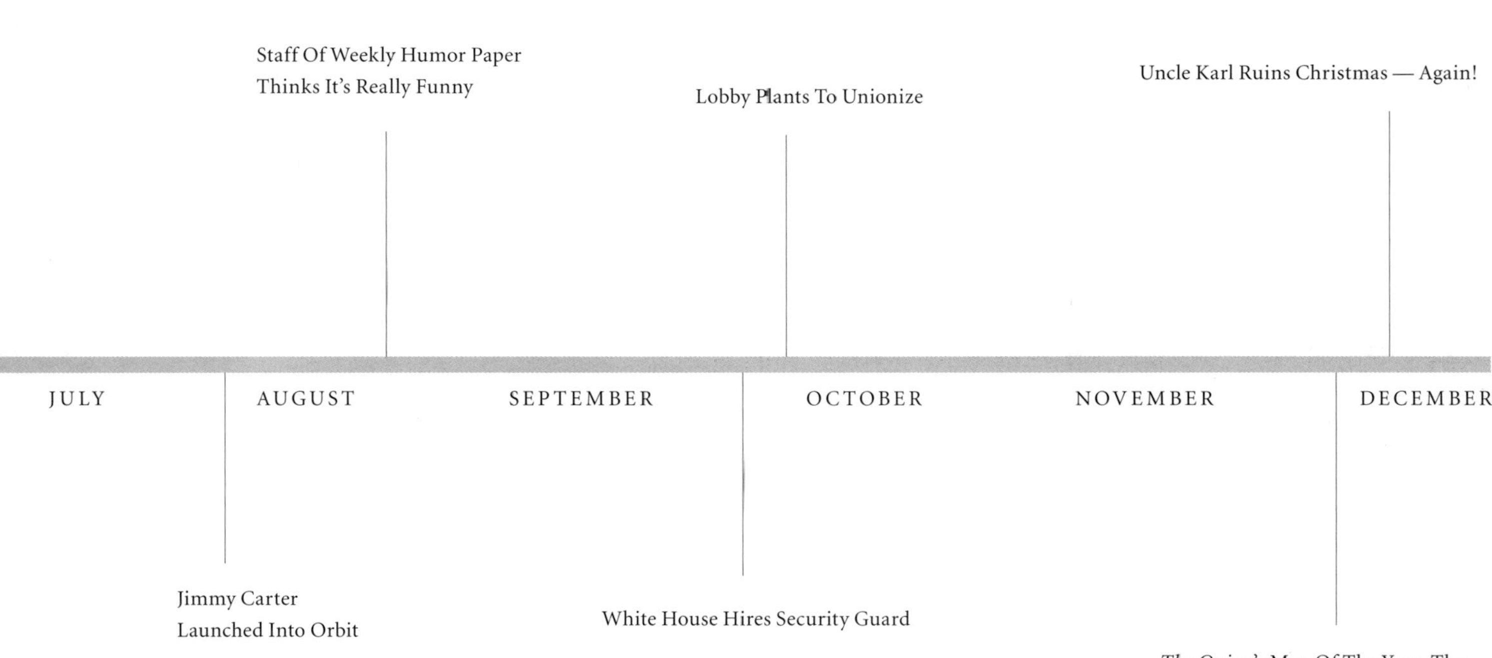

Staff Of Weekly Humor Paper Thinks It's Really Funny
Lobby Plants To Unionize
Uncle Karl Ruins Christmas — Again!
JULY
AUGUST
SEPTEMBER
OCTOBER
NOVEMBER
DECEMBER
Jimmy Carter Launched Into Orbit
White House Hires Security Guard
The Onion's Men Of The Year: The San Diego Chicken, Stomach Cancer

Got the Winter Blues? Why Not Kill Yourself? (see page 18)

the ONION

Number One in News | volume 25 ⌀ number 2 | 25–31 January 1994

Astronomer finds center of universe

Houston, Tex. — Astronomer James Mercer startled the scientific community yesterday when he announced that the universe revolves around his 12-year-old son, Craig. Using a computerized holographic simulation, Mercer placed his son in the middle of the room, and re-created the universe around him. "You'll notice that he serves as a rock-solid, gravitational epicenter," Mercer said, adding that his son is a straight-A student.

New perfume designed for the starving

Paris — Paris' top perfume companies have created a special line of products for starving third-world populations, claiming that if the poor are going to be hungry, they might as well smell nice. The new perfumes, which will smell like various foods unavailable to the starving, will be aggressively marketed using the same techniques perfected by U.S. cigarette companies in similar locales. "The least we can do for those starving wretches is develop a low-end beef-scented cologne." said perfume magnate Claude Montpelier. Each bottle will contain a warning label that clearly states that the perfume is not edible.

Ex-presidents lose Secret Service protection

Washington D.C. — In a continuing effort to trim costs from the federal budget, the Clinton Administration announced a plan to drastically cut Secret Service protection costs for the five living ex-presidents. Presidents Nixon, Ford, Carter, Reagan and Bush will no longer have private bodyguards, but will be encouraged to live together in the same neighborhood and watch out for each other's safety. Implementing this "neighborhood watch" program is expected to cut costs by over 300 percent.

Buffalo loses fourth straight Super Bowl

Atlanta, GA — The Buffalo Bills lost the Super Bowl next Sunday. Their fourth straight Super Bowl loss, again to the Dallas Cowboys, was slightly closer then last year's 52-17 blow-out. "I thought the first, second and third time really hurt," Bills' defensive back Nate Odomes said after the upcoming game. "But the fourth time is even worse then all the others."

SUPER MONKEY COLLIDER LOSES FUNDING

The Controversial Experiment Comes to an End

Above: Monkeys relax in the main hallway of the abandoned collider.

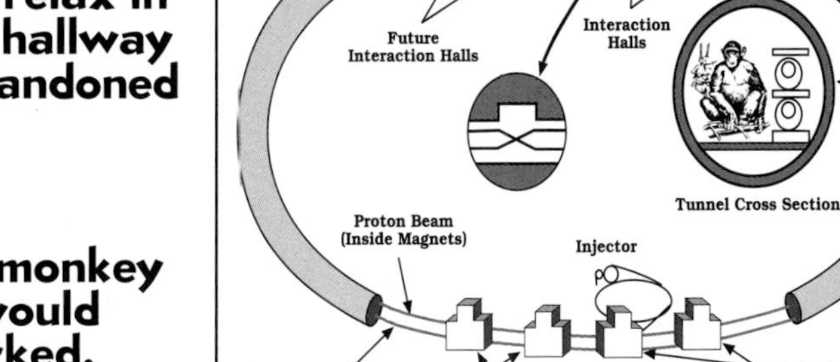

Right: How the monkey collider would have worked.

CONGRESS VOTED MONDAY TO CUT FEDERAL FUNDING for the superconducting monkey collider, a controversial experiment which has cost taxpayers an estimated 7.6 billion dollars a year since its inception in 1983.

The collider, which was to be built within a 45-mile-long circular tunnel, would accelerate monkeys to near-light speeds before smashing them together. Scientists insist the collider is an important step toward understanding the universe, because no one can yet say for certain what kind of noises monkeys would make if collided at those high speeds. "It could be a thump, a splat, or maybe even a sound that hasn't yet been heard by human ears," said project head Dr. Eric Reed Friday, in an impassioned plea to Congress. "How are we supposed to understand things like the atom or the nature of gravity if we don't even know what colliding monkeys sound like?"

But Congress, under heavy pressure from the powerful monkey rights lobby, decided that the money being spent on the monkey collider could be put to better use in other areas of government. Now, with funding cut off, the future of our nation's monkey collision program looks bleak.

Congress began funding the monkey collider in 1983, after Dr. Reed convinced lawmakers that the U.S. was lagging behind the Soviet Union in monkey-colliding technology. Funds were quickly allocated so that Reed could spend a week

see MONKEYS on page 8

ROKKIN' with DOKKEN

the ONION

Madison's Free Weekly News Manifesto volume 25 number 5 15–21 February 1994

NEWS IN BRIEF

Accordionist arrested

SAN MARCOS, Texas—Authorities have arrested an accordionist charged with making people involuntarily fall in love. According to a complaint filed by the District Attorney's office, Giuseppe Altovese, 48, prowled city parks and played "Lady of Spain," causing passersby enraptured by the gentle hum of the accordion to fall head-over-heels in love. "I don't even know this palooka,' said Jim Landers, 44, referring to a man hanging about his shoulders. "And now he has an eternal claim on my heart."

Woman, 20, doubts weather

MADISON, Wis.—A student who expressed shock and disbelief at record amounts of snow and severe cold has been burned to death for heresy. Beth Schiestle, 20, was reported to have questioned Father Winter repeatedly. "I can't believe how cold it is," Schiestle reportedly said. "How much snow can we possibly get?" She was immediately given the test of stones, then tied to a stake and burned.

Rival health plan would cover hurt feelings

WASHINGTON, D.C.—A bipartisan effort has been launched on Capitol Hill to expand health care reform legislation to include coverage for hurt feelings. U.S. Rep. Henry Gonzalez (D–Texas) announced parts of the measure, which would require hugging, ears to listen and shoulders to lean or cry on, provided by trained professionals. Gonzalez said the plan may be expanded to include kissing boo-boos.

Beatles reunion tour ends after chair mishap

INDIANAPOLIS—On the 30th anniversary of their arrival in the United States, the two surviving Beatles have canceled their historic reunion tour after only two shows. The duo called it quits after Paul McCartney became dislodged from a specially designed chair intended to ease inflamation caused by a pelvic virus. The singer toppled on to the stage, shattering his brittle hip.

YOU ARE A COMMUNIST!

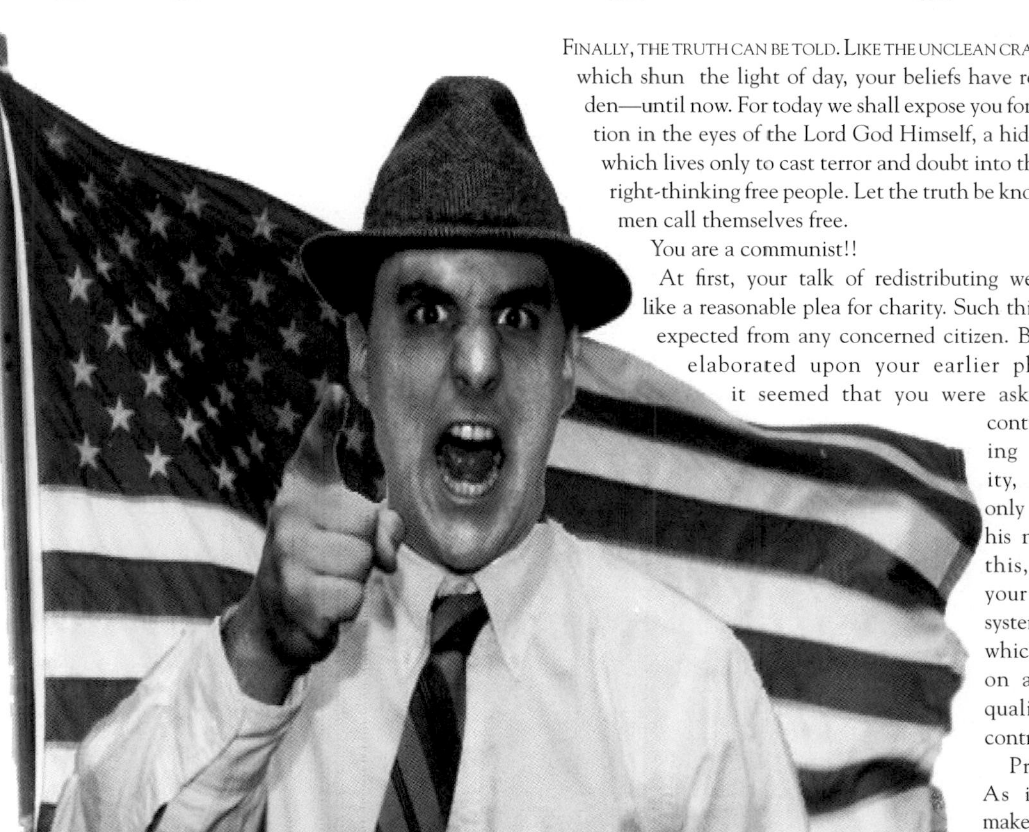

FINALLY, THE TRUTH CAN BE TOLD. LIKE THE UNCLEAN CRAWLING THINGS which shun the light of day, your beliefs have remained hidden—until now. For today we shall expose you for an abomination in the eyes of the Lord God Himself, a hideous monster which lives only to cast terror and doubt into the heart of all right-thinking free people. Let the truth be known wherever men call themselves free.

You are a communist!!

At first, your talk of redistributing wealth seemed like a reasonable plea for charity. Such things are to be expected from any concerned citizen. But when you elaborated upon your earlier philosophies, it seemed that you were asking each to contrbute according to his ability, but to take only according to his need! To top this, you stated your belief in a system of payment which was based on amount, not quality, of labor contributed!

Preposterous! As if one who makes mud pies has created something worth as much as an apple pie. The very idea! By expounding upon such ridiculous

see COMMUNIST! on page 4

Lovingly hand-painted by skilled artisans!

the ONION®

You Are Dumb. volume 25 number 14 26 April–2 May 1994

Caning commuted to 'noogie' for American teen

SINGAPORE—The State Department has worked out a compromise with the government of Singapore that will commute the sentence of an American teen convicted of vandalism. Stephen Fay, 18, was sentenced to six lashes with a bamboo cane, a practice that leaves permanent scars. The State Department said Singapore relented and offered Fay the option of "snake-bites, noogies or charlie-horses." Fay opted for a noogie, which means his scalp will be ground to the bone with an electric sander.

Rich Little dead at 81

NEW YORK—President Clinton has declared Wednesday a national day of mourning for Rich Little, the country's 37th president who succumbed to a stroke over the weekend. The enigmatic president and Little Debbie Snack Cake spokesman will be most remembered for his role in in the Watergate cover-up, his subsequent resignation and the nutty answering-machine tapes he made while in self-imposed exile. Supporters say talk of scandal overlooks Little's important contributions to the nation, such as his restoration of diplomatic relations with Great Britain with his side-splitting impressions of Jimmy Stewart and Cary Grant.

Cancer not so bad

BOSTON—The New England Journal of Medicine has reported that contracting cancer leads to a higher quality of life. "Cancer: Beyond the Hoopla," written by Dr. Paul Hayes, puts a positive spin on the painful disease. "They get to lie in bed all day, have their food served to them and they're complaining?" Hayes said. "I hope this report ends our society's penchant for coddling cancer patients."

Five dead at 'jail 'n bail'

CHAPEL HILL, N.C.—A Gamma Chi sorority charity event turned bloody when participants in the "jail 'n bail" tried to apprehend a convicted child rapist. Five members of the sorority chapter were slain by the man, Tim Cuprisin, who had eluded authorities for months. The event raised $40 for a local whites-only leprosarium.

TOBACCO COMPANIES ANNOUNCE:

SECONDHAND SMOKE CAUSES SECONDHAND COOLNESS

People who position themselves near smokers proven almost as cool as the smokers themselves

In these photos provided by the Tobacco Institute, an average-looking nobody (above) becomes a really cool guy, simply by sitting near a smoker (right).

AMERICANS HAVE KNOWN FOR YEARS THAT SMOKING IS A DIRECT cause of coolness. But a recent study funded by JR Raynolds and several other cigarette conglomerates proves conclusively that the cool effects of smoking are not limited to the smoker. According to the study, secondhand smoke is a leading cause of coolness, only slightly less cool than actual smoking or heroin addiction.

As a result of the study, cigarette companies are encouraging nonsmokers to frequent smoky bars, make friends with smokers and discourage laws that would set aside separate nonsmoking areas. "We are only acting in the best interest of the public at large," Raynolds spokesperson Ron Gronfeld said. "We're not saying nonsmokers are going to die as a result of their actions, but we do want to make sure they know they aren't as cool as they could be."

Gronfeld referred to a "three level progression" of coolness that nonsmokers experienced in the study. Level one could be observed as soon as the nonsmoker was shackled to a barstool near a person enjoying a delicious cigarette. "Even the nerdiest subject we could find somehow appeared cool when interacting with his smoking partner," Gronfeld said. "Just the fact that the subject was brave enough to breathe the deadly secondhand smoke established him as a brave, freethinking individual; the kind of person who might one day run with the bulls in Pamplona."

see COOL on page 4

Guns Don't Kill People—
DEMONS Kill People.

the ONION ®

Number One In News | volume 25 number 16 | 10–16 May 1994

Family saved by three-way inflatable goat

MIAMI—A family of four, rescued after floating in the Gulf of Mexico for nearly two weeks, credits their salvation to the father's aberrant sex toy. The Clowes family and their luggage were swept from the deck of a Carnival Cruise Ship during a freak storm. Father Gerald, a librarian, reluctantly inflated "Pink-Hole: The Three-way Inflatable Goat" only after his toddler children, Ben and Tricia, began drowning. They clung to "Pink-Hole" for 13 days before being saved by a boat of Haitian refugees.

Man avoids messing with Texas

JOPLIN, Mo.—A man's aggression toward the Longhorn State was curbed after he read a bumper sticker that warned him, "Don't Mess With Texas." The incident escalated after Jake Vretnar, in a drunken tirade, swore to friends that he would "go and fuck up" the state of Texas. Vretnar boarded his truck for the drive, but cut his trip short after seeing the bumper sticker. "I guess they're serious," he said.

Moose hold vigil, wait for new Pooh-bah

CUDAHY, Wis.—A crowd of 200 is holding a somber vigil outside the Moose Lodge here, hoping to be the first to find out who the next Pooh-bah will be. When gray cigar smoke rises out of the lodge's "hospitality lounge," the choice will have been made. The Pooh-bah-elect will then treat the house to a shot. The reigning Pooh-bah, Glen Stepnowski, died Friday after undergoing unsuccessful liposuction.

New orifice found

BERLIN—Scientists at the institute for orificial studies have announced the discovery of a new orifice on the human body. "Believe us," one scientist said, "you don't want to know where it is." Scientists are holding back the orifice's location, fearing that the public might spend valuable time trying to plug or clean it.

JEWS TO RELEASE BOX SET

Long-awaited compilation will 'rock,' say rabbis

Hundreds of Jews line up around the block to get first-release copies of the compilation.

ENCOURAGED BY SUCCESSFUL "BOX SET" RELEASES BY GROUPS such as Led Zeppelin, the Allman Brothers and Steely Dan, the Jews announced that they will release a box set of their own, due in retail stores and synagogues this summer.

The box set will chronicle over 6,000 years of Judaic history, and will be even bigger than Eric Clapton's 4-disc CROSSROADS compilation.

"Led Zeppelin was less than 25 years old when it put out a set," said Rabbi/producer Uriel Raz, who is in the final mixing stages in his Jerusalem studio. "We've been around for 6,000 years. That's a lot of history, and that's a lot of rock."

The box set, tentatively titled, EXODUS AND INCIDENTS, THE JEWS 4000 B.C.E. – 1994, will feature all of the Jews' best known material, as well as a fantastic 783-page full-color brochure chronicling the history of the group. Never-before-seen "backstage" photos will accompany shots of such memorable moments as the 2053 B.C.E. defeat of the Babylonians, Moses parting the Red Sea and the sold-out 1983 European tour. Among the items in the box will be a beautiful blue satin

see JEWS on page 8

This prototype shows off the yarmulke and tallith that will be included in each box set.

the ONION
Number One In News. volume 26 number 2 23–29 August 1994

CAT LOOSE IN CITY!

Terrified residents panic, flee downtown Madison

An area photographer was able to snap this picture of the cat and the panic it induced among residents. Luckily, all involved escaped unharmed.

For three consecutive days, the downtown area of Madison has been crippled by the menacing presence of an escaped kitty-cat. Once a safely enclosed house pet, the loose cat is now rampaging through the city's streets, unchecked and free to wreak havoc at any moment.

Citizens have been strongly advised to stay in their houses at all times, to avoid venturing out for food or other basic staple goods, and to leave all fish and fish by-products off the streets.

"What we have here is a crisis situation, being handled by the top crisis-management people in the field," mayoral spokesman Tom Browning said. "Our first order of business is to remove all plastic mice and rubber balls from our city streets. Cats have been known to enjoy frolicking with these items."

The cat, which goes by the name Mr. Fluffy and is technically a kitten, escaped when owner Renee Raphael accidentally opened her door to get the mail, not knowing that the sly cat was underfoot.

"I thought he was safely contained in the basement, where I had just fed him a refreshing bowl of cream," Raphael said. "He must have jimmied the lock open with his paw and quietly slid past me. I only hope no one is hurt or killed as a result of my irresponsibility."

A wave of fear and desperation has consumed virtually everyone in the three-mile radius where the cat has been seen stalking.

"I'm afraid to let my children walk on the street," resident Michael McCoy said. "Have you seen what these beasts can do to a small child, let alone a ball of twine?"

The cat has yet to attack any city residents, although there have been several reports of it purring aggressively at passersby.

see Cat on page 4

Declaration of Principles

Onion Board of Trustees

The Onion is here to serve its readers. For 57 years, The Onion has been a vessel of truth and integrity in the news industry. For this, our 15,000th issue, the editors have seen fit to commit to the printed page clearly and plainly what The Onion stands for.

1) To inform the public of local news, sports scores, scientific breakthroughs and historical world events, truthfully, quickly and straightforwardly, without the use of sensational tactics.

2) To verify the facts behind a news story with three reliable sources before committing it to print.

3) To remain within the boundaries of good taste and uphold traditional values, scrupulously avoiding any topics which might be deemed offensive (such as defecation, urination, copulation, flatulence, sodomy, bestiality, cunnilingus, or fellatio).

4) To let no commercial factions influence the content of the paper unless a lucrative exchange can be agreed upon by both the prospective advertiser and the Onion board.

As you continue to read The Onion in the future, we will be doing everything in our power to adhere to these principles and provide you with the information you need to improve your way of life.

Selling our services to the highest bidder, regardless of whether their cause be for good—or EVIL.

the ONION®

Number One In News. volume 26 Ø number 4 6–12 September 1994

SCIENTISTS BEFUDDLED BY ASTOUNDING WIFFLE™ BOY

Meet the boy raised by Wiffle™ products

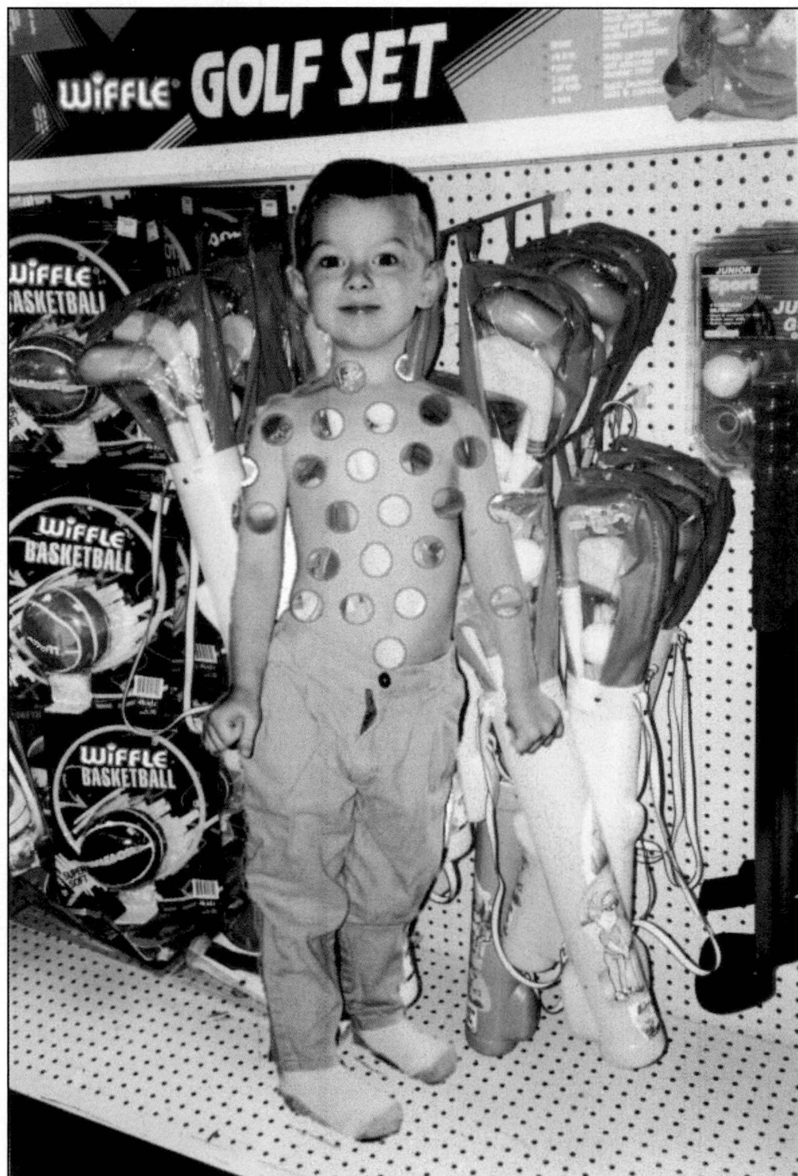

Wiffle™Boy, the amazing hybrid of human and Wiffle,™ is shown here in the toy store where he was found. He is as light and safe as any Wiffle™product.

In one of the most bizarre cases of human sociology and child-oriented sporting goods science to date, scientists have announced the discovery of "Wiffle™Boy," a healthy 15-year-old boy theorized to have been lost in an abandoned toy store as a child and exposed only to Wiffle™products. Without the social skills of other humans to imitate, Wiffle™Boy has evolved into an incredible hybrid of human and Wiffle.™

Wiffle™Boy was discovered by asbestos-removal workers when they prepared to clean up the long-condemned Magic Castle toy store last month. The crew was applying stickers to the toys in aisle 7 reading, "50% Off—Asbestos Damage," when they uncovered what they thought to be an unusual type of Wiffle™toy. "But then I saw the head and realized it was actually a naked child—a Wiffle™product, but also a boy," worker Pete Scardini said.

Unresponsive to any human stimuli, Wiffle™Boy was incapable of communicating with the workers and had to be forcibly removed by scientists, torn away from the only family he knew: Wiffle™balls, Wiffle™bats and Wiffle™golf sets.

Scientists theorize that Wiffle™Boy was lost or abandoned as an infant in aisle 7, destined to be without a human role model for 15 years. He then grew to a grotesquely deformed—but light and safe—form in order to adapt to his Wiffle™-filled environment. "What we see in Wiffle™Boy is a remarkable testament to human adaptability," says Professor Ron Underwood.

see Wiffle™Boy on page 4

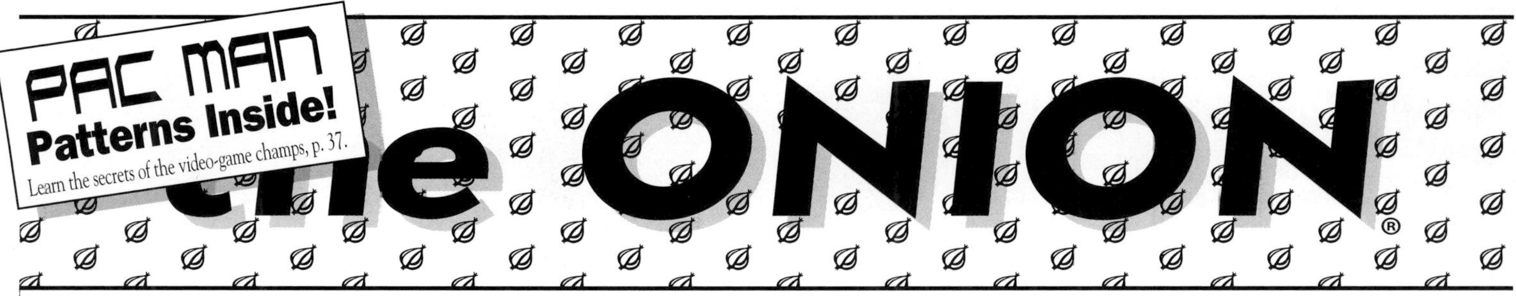

Madison's Only Newspaper | volume 26 Ø number 6 | 20–26 September 1994

BEER!

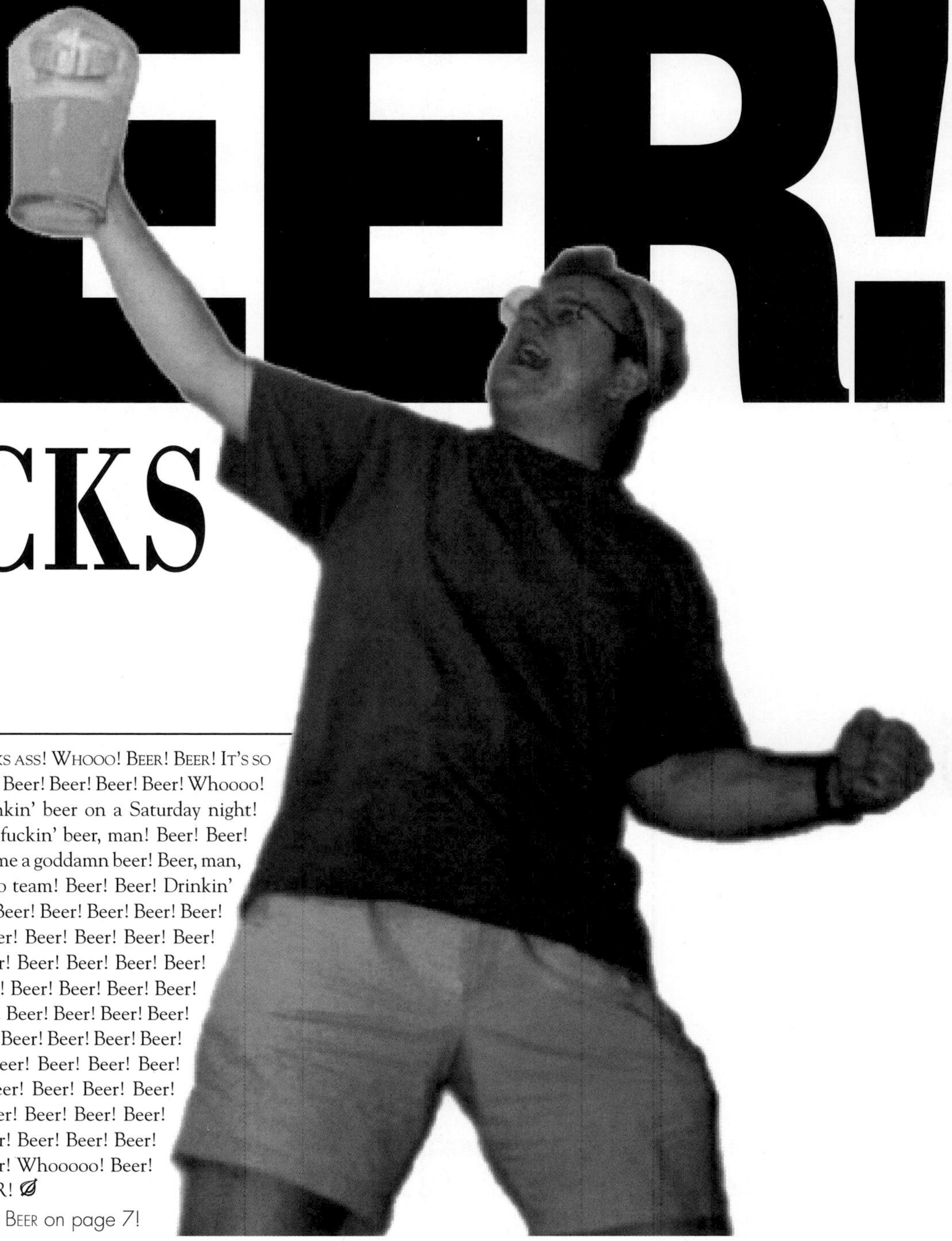

IT KICKS ASS!

Beer! Beer! Beer! Whoooooooo! Beer! It kicks ass! Whooo! Beer! Beer! It's so fuckin' awesome! Beer! Drink some beer! Beer! Beer! Beer! Beer! Beer! Whoooo! All right! Beer! Beer! Beer! Whooooo! Drinkin' beer on a Saturday night! Whoooooo! Beer! Beer! Beer! Beer! Mother-fuckin' beer, man! Beer! Beer! Gotta drink some beer! Beer! Whooooo! Gimme a goddamn beer! Beer, man, beer! Beer! Beer! Whoooooo! Yeah! Beer! Go team! Beer! Beer! Drinkin' beer! All night! Beer! Whooooo! Beer! Beer! Beer! Beer! Beer! Beer! Beer! Beer! Beer! Beer! Whooooo! Beer! Yeah! Yeah! Beer! Whooooo! Beer! Beer! Beer! Beer! Beer! Get me another BEER! Ø

more Beer on page 7!

Put through over 2 million miles of rigorous testing

the ONION

You Are Dumb. volume 26 number 9 11–17 October 1994

THOMPSON CHANGES TITLE FROM 'GOVERNOR' TO 'SEXECUTIONER'

Hopes to update image in time for next month's election

WISCONSIN'S TOMMY THOMPSON, LONG RECOGNIZED AS A MIDDLE-OF-THE-ROAD CONSERVATIVE GOVERNOR, shocked the national media yesterday by announcing that his title of Governor will be immediately changed to Sexecutioner.

Sexecutioner Thompson ushered in the new title by donning black leather bondage gear and signing a state highway repair bill.

"I'm still the same old Tommy," Sexecutioner Thompson said, cracking a bull-whip in front of a startled audience. "I still like to fish, hunt, and engage in stimulating political debate. Only now, a fishing rod isn't the only pole I wield."

The office of Sexecutioner will operate exactly like its predecessor, with a Lieutenant Sexecutioner and sexecution aides, or "love-daddies." Only Thompson's title and certain image points will go through a significant change. For example, the gubernatorial seal used on all state documents will be updated to feature an image of Thompson wearing a spiked dog collar and sticking out his four-inch tongue.

Insiders say the move was motivated by many factors, most important of which was Thompson's desire to have a more menacing-sounding title than "Governor." Although many names were considered (Big Dog, Mack Daddy, The Guvver), Thompson is said to have chosen Sexecutioner because the title captures the spirit of his leadership, and of the state of Wisconsin.

"As a young Republican back in school, I was never very popular with the ladies," Thompson said. "But now that I'm the Sexecutioner, just watch the pretty gals come running."

The Sexecutioner, who is running for a third term against Democratic challenger Chuck Chvala, hopes his title change will inspire other national figures to enliven their traditionally stodgy public images.

"Governors and other politicians are people too. People with normal, healthy desires, fetishes and obsessions," Sexecutioner Thompson said, foaming at the mouth and masturbating furiously.

see SEXECUTIONER on page 4

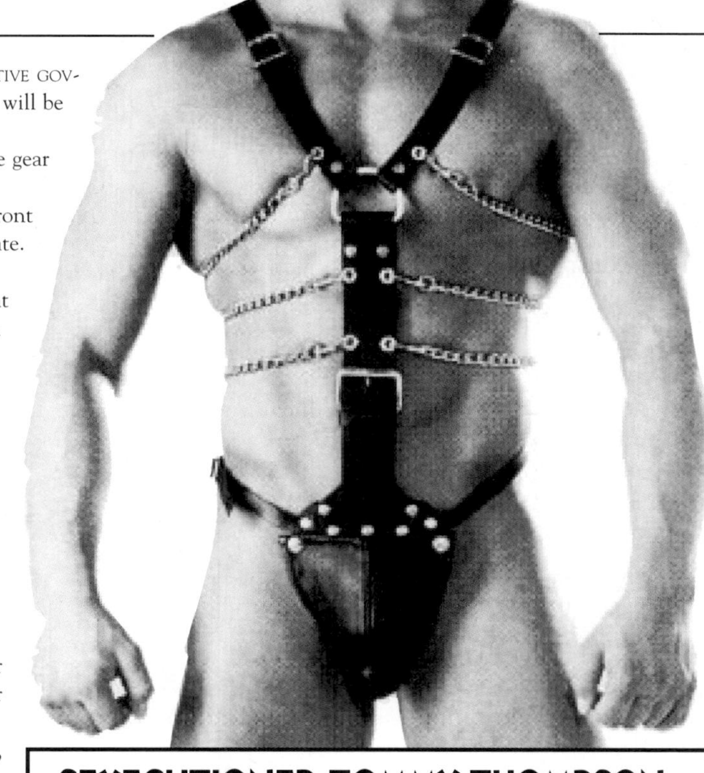

SEXECUTIONER TOMMY THOMPSON STRUTS HIS STUFF FOR THE VOTERS

Not Printed on 100% Hemp Paper volume 26 number 10 18–24 October 1994

CROSS-COUNTRY BABYSITTING SPREE CONTINUES

Renegade suspect has cared for 30 children in 18 states

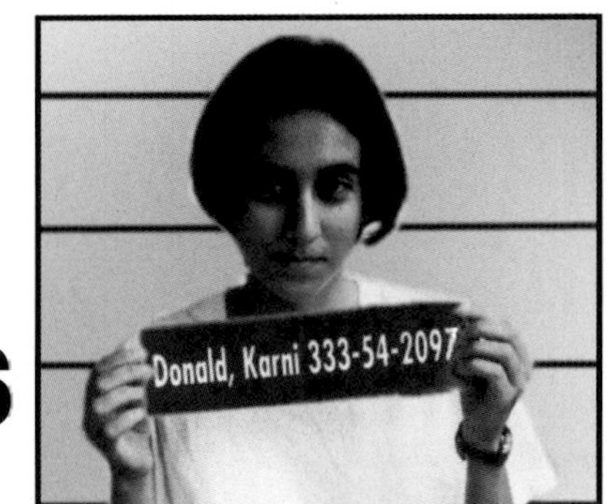

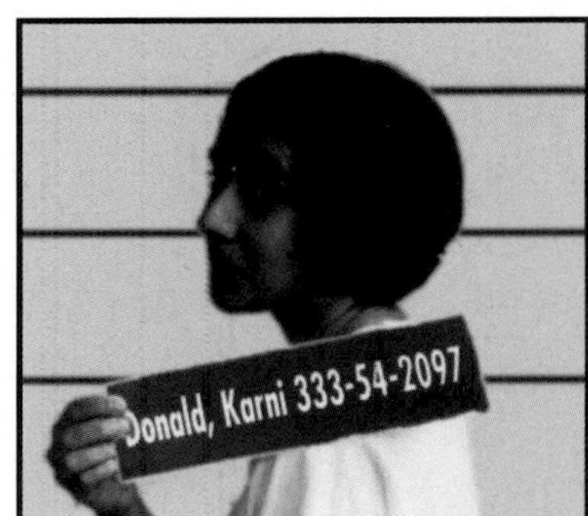

LAW ENFORCEMENT OFFICIALS ARE WORKING OVERTIME TO capture and arrest Karni Donald, the 18-year-old high school senior believed responsible for a brutal 18-state spree of babysitting.

Karni is thought to have committed her first babysitting job in Norfolk, West Virginia, though authorities didn't recognize the pattern of quality, tax-free childcare until Karni reached Lexington, Kentucky—three babysitting jobs later. "When we investigated the first job, we thought it was the work of just another babysitter. After all, Norfolk has its share," Federal Marshal Tom Henkoblap said. "But after the job in Lexington, we began to see a pattern. It was then that we declared the group of babysittings to be an official cross-country crime spree."

Henkoblap says all of Karni's babysittings have shown similarities in style and execution. In each case, the babysitter knocked on the victims' door and asked if they had any young children. If the victim answered no, Karni would say, "Thank you. Have a nice night," and walk away. But if the victim did have children, the situation would typically evolve into a full-fledged babysitting job. Karni is said to smile sweetly and inquire whether the victims would like to take a few hours off, away from the kids—a tempting offer few have refused.

see SPREE on page 4

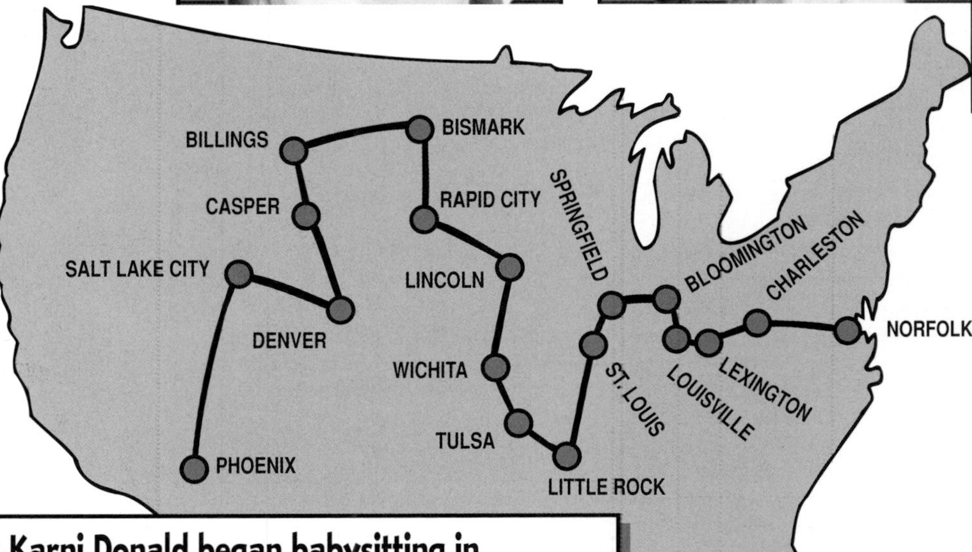

Karni Donald began babysitting in West Virginia and hasn't stopped since. Karni is no stranger to the law; the above mugshots were taken two years ago when she was arrested for stealing lipstick.

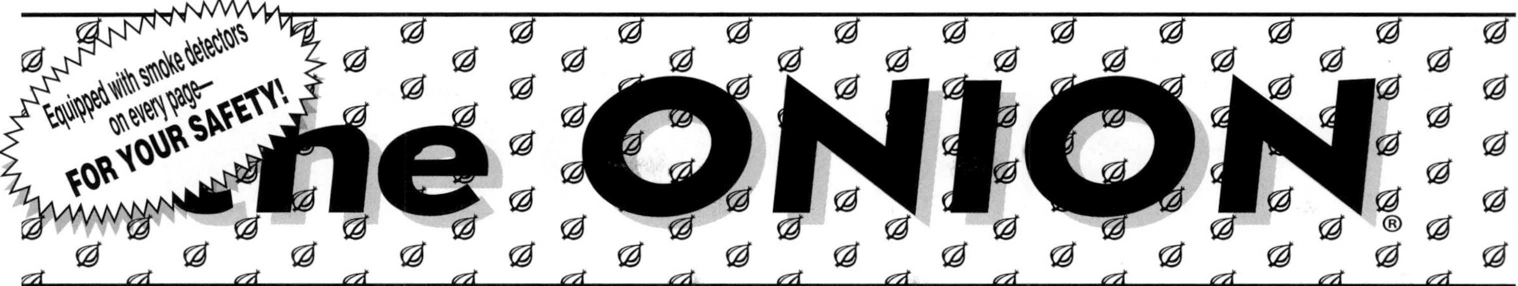

Madison's Beacon of Truth and Justice volume 26 number 11 25–31 October 1994

GIRLFIGHT!!!

QUICK! CHECK IT OUT!

A GIRLFIGHT BROKE OUT ON A CROWDED DOWNTOWN STREET YESTERDAY, RESULTING IN THE slight injury of two high school-aged girls. Witnesses were reportedly amused by the novelty of the situation and the sissy-like way girls have of scuffling.

"It was clear they might hurt each other, and someone needed to intervene," witness Patrick Ruddick, who eventually broke up the fight, said. Ruddick then smiled and looked down at his feet ashamedly. "But there's something about girls fighting that's silly and entertaining, so I watched it for a few seconds before doing anything."

Lucky passersby were amused by slapping, screeching and pulling of hair.

The girlfight was characterized by slapping, shrill screams, pulling of hair and a general lack of knowledge regarding how to effectively defend one's self. The fight contained none of the more violent punching, tackling, choking and effective fighting techniques that often occur when boys fight.

A phone call to 911 resulted in the arrival of authorities moments after the girlfight began. "I had heard there was a fight downtown," Officer Chuck McNabb said. "I didn't know what to expect, so I jumped out of my car with my revolver at the ready. But then I saw it was just two girls. I immediately holstered my pistol, relaxed, and laughed heartily." When accused by reporters of failing to break up a dangerous situation, McNabb simply smirked, stating, "Oh, come on. Those girls weren't going to

see GIRLFIGHT on page 4

NOW WITH EXTRA-LARGE PRINT (conveniently reduced for maximum news coverage)

the ONION®

Madison's Only Newspaper. volume 26 Ø number 14 15–28 November 1994

An Important Message from the Alpha Male

Attention Apes! Your leader speaks! Hear him!

RRRAAARRR! GRRAAAA! AARRRRGGG!

From all corners of the jungle my voice is heard!

From across the wooded lowlands where we make our home, my mighty ape call reverberates, striking fear into lesser, weaker gorillas! Hear me, my minions! I am the BIGGEST! I am the STRONGEST! No one is bigger and more fearsome than me!

To those foolish few who would challenge my position, I say this: RRAAAARRR! If you defy me I will run toward you, yelling and screaming, beating my chest in a terrifying display! You will run in fear of my superior girth and muscle! You will cower in terror, because I am the biggest and strongest of apes!

The best fruits and nuts and the choicest morsels of food must go to me! The finest and most sexually attractive of our females must be mine and mine alone to breed! Those who attempt to breed with my elite harem of females will soon learn their place, for if I smell them on my females I will roar and stamp my feet and thrash my powerful muscular arms and shake the trees! And it will be SCARY! And they will RUN!

Of all the apes, who can roar louder than me, the Alpha Male? None! Who can climb higher or run faster or beat

see MESSAGE on page 4

GREAT HOLIDAY SHOPPING IDEAS INSIDE!
Send a festive vial of crack anywhere in the U.S. for only $15! See page 33.

the ONION®

America's Only State-Sanctioned News Source | volume 26 Ø number 16 | 5–12 December 1994

RESTAURANT CITED FOR SERVING DEAD CHICKENS

Twisted eatery expected customers to consume the lifeless poultry

Disgusted FDA agent Tom McMann displays one of the rotisseried chicken corpses. The coroner arrived soon afterward.

In the latest in an increasing number of fast-food restaurant horror stories, the local eatery Barney's Chick'N Barn has been cited by food and drug authorities for serving dead chickens to customers—and expecting that they would be consumed as food!

Barney's horrific transgressions were reported by Leon Raiddle after he dined at the restaurant with his family last month. "I ordered some burgers for the kids, and a small bucket of chicken for me and my wife," Raiddle's statement read. "I expected just that—some chicken. Imagine my horror and revulsion when the counter attendant handed me a bucket full of dead chickens! I nearly vomited. But it was my kids I was most worried about. What on God's Earth was I supposed to tell them?"

Raiddle alerted FDA authorities, who donned disguises and went to secretly dine at the Chick'N Barn. Upon close inspection of the area behind the restaurant's counter, the team discovered nearly two dozen chicken corpses turning on metal spits over an indoor grill. The restaurant was cited for serving dead chickens, and fined $20. In addition, all employees were handcuffed, dragged into the parking lot and brutally beaten with hammers.

"We've found restaurants with live animals in the kitchens, glue in the Alfredo sauce, even places that urinate in their soup," FDA agent Tom McMann said. "But we've never come across a restaurant as twisted and evil as Barney's Chick'N Barn."

Rita Endive, the restaurant's district manager, denied that Barney's was guilty of any wrongdoing. "We are a restaurant. We serve meat, and yes, we serve chicken," Endive said. "We also serve salad and Jello. That's what restaurants do. We are not a vegetarian establishment."

see CHICKEN on page 4

Quayle Announces Bid For
1995 Presidential Election

Exciting New Contraption
Makes Bread 'Toasty'

Computers Are Back!

JANUARY FEBRUARY MARCH APRIL MAY JUNE

Mallquake! For Hundreds, A Day
Of $aving$ Turns To Tragedy

Area 18-Year-Old No
Longer Breast Feeding

Whitest Man In The World Found

1995

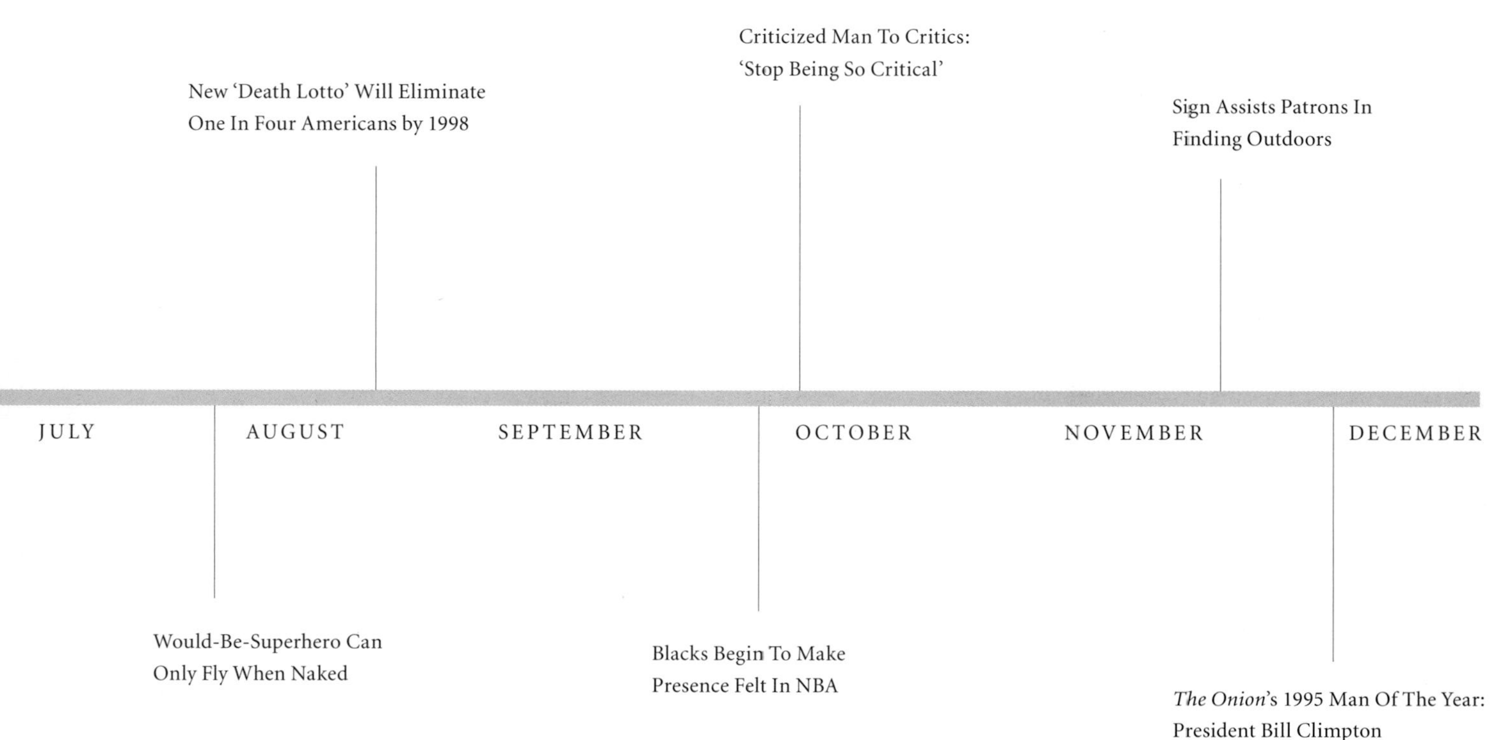
New 'Death Lotto' Will Eliminate One In Four Americans by 1998
Criticized Man To Critics: 'Stop Being So Critical'
Sign Assists Patrons In Finding Outdoors
JULY
AUGUST
SEPTEMBER
OCTOBER
NOVEMBER
DECEMBER
Would-Be-Superhero Can Only Fly When Naked
Blacks Begin To Make Presence Felt In NBA
The Onion's 1995 Man Of The Year: President Bill Climpton

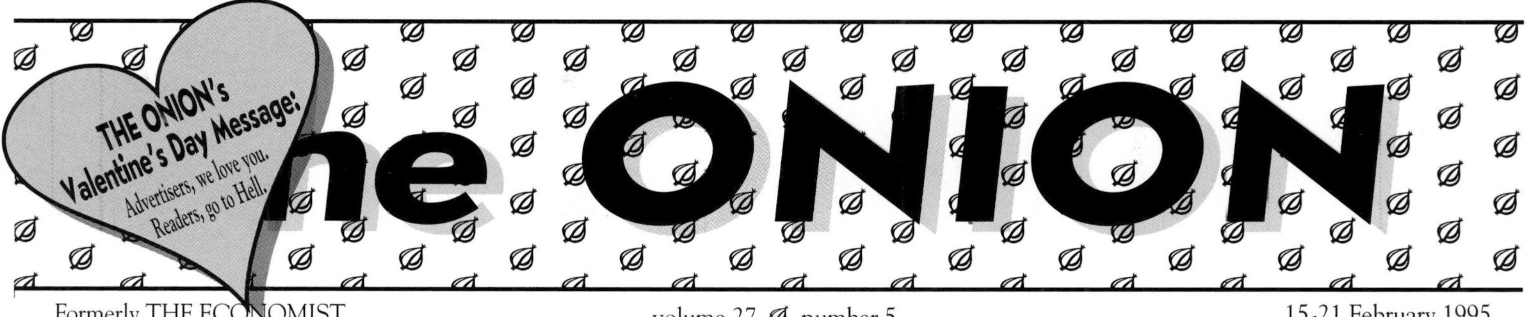

Formerly THE ECONOMIST volume 27 number 5 15-21 February 1995

ANCIENT PYRAMIDS DESTROYED BY SARCASM OF YOUTH

Sturdy structures crumble to dust after being insulted by cynical 23-year-old

THE GREAT PYRAMIDS OF GIZA, ONE OF THE SEVEN wonders of the world and one of humanity's first and most complex structural creations, collapsed Friday after being derided by a cynical 23-year-old American college student employing sarcastic comments.

The event occurred early Friday afternoon, when Claire Haney, on a tour of the pyramids with her family, spat, "Ooooh, The pyramids. Yeah, they're so impressive," with a bored roll of her eyes. The super-concentrated derisive power of her sarcasm was enough to make even the mighty pyramids feel worthless, causing their limestone exterior to instantly crack and crumble to the ground.

Later on the tour, Haney used sarcasm to destroy the Sphinx by referring to it as "fascinating, and not at all incredibly boring to look at." The tour ended at the tomb of King Tutankhamen, which collapsed into rubble after Haney snidely commented that it "completely added something to the tour, and it didn't at all feel like I was standing around in a musty old basement."

Psychologists have been familiar with the basic workings of sarcasm for over a decade, but until now, no one imagined that it could be directed potently enough to hurt the feelings of—and eventually destroy—non-living physical objects. In 1982, scientists established that sarcasm results when a speaker utters one statement that claims to mean one thing, but through minor tone irregularities—and often an obnoxious over-inflection of the voice—the real meaning of that speaker's statement becomes the exact opposite.

Voice analysts speculate that Haney's sarcasm is extra powerful and caustic because she is part of the "twentythingsome" generation. Members of this group of young Americans have learned to wield the vocal device with the adeptness of expert swordsmen due to their growing up frustrated and bitter in Reagan's America—a time of shrinking opportunities and dashed hopes.

This theory was proved Sunday when a group of chemistry professors at Yale University displayed to Haney a collection of traditionally revered achievements in American culture: a first edition copy of Mark Twain's THE ADVENTURES OF HUCKLEBERRY FINN, several classic American paintings by Nor-

see SARCASM on page 4

Claire Haney reluctantly poses in front of the pyramids she destroyed with her caustic attitude.

7-20 March 1995
27•8

Are you good-looking enough? The answer, no, is on page 106

Masking the stench of your filthy genitals

The Pill: Is it loaded with fat?

10 great ways to pussy-whip your man

Answering every woman's question:

How can I get Anorexia?

Can you be career-minded and still obsess about your appearance?

Number One In News volume 27 number 11 4–10 April 1995

WAR!

Come On, Let's Have One!

NEVER IS MAN MORE GALLANT NOR GRAND THAN WHEN HE is at war. Never is a country more unified and patriotic than when it is at war. So why do we waste our time with pitiful treaties and paltry peacekeeping projects with puny countries that we can chew up and spit out like a nugget of caramel? Why do we not jump directly into the noble gorge of bloody combat? Damn you, nations of Earth and your worthless economic sanctions and your useless arms negotiations! Enough! Enough! Three times enough! End the two-bit bickering and squalid squabbles with an explosion of deadly solutions! So let's have a war already!

We want a war! Sweep out the fallout shelters! We want a war! Bring back the draft! Pick sides! Pray to God! Harden yourself! Get ready for all the emotion and mortality life has to offer, cause we're going to war! We need it!

It's us against them! Believers against non-believers! White against black! Women against men! Brother against brother! Young against old! Hard against soft! Us against ourselves! It doesn't matter—this is war! War! War!

Let a symphony of lead death sing its way through the flesh of the enemy's buzz-cut battalions! This is war!

Let a field of protesters emerge with long hair, megaphones, flaming hormones, self-righteousness and dope! It's going to be war! Bring on the singers to croon on about the unjust old men sending the young to die! It's war!

There are no bystanders, only soldiers! All in! There is no neutral zone! The combat zone is everywhere! Sing the fight song! Write letters to your sweetheart back home! Raise high the flag! Let battle cries rattle from your hate-worn throat! This is it! War!

Quicken the bullets! Embolden the tanks! Convert the car factories to munitions plants! Study the great battles! Create new bacteria bombs! Set fresh coordinates for the MX! Polish the cannisters of poison gas! Tune up the troop transports! Construct the prisoner-of-war camps! Groom generals! Dig trenches! Do your duty! Drop bombs! Give blood! Dig deep! Donate lead! Get Bob Hope on the horn! Dig up his cold, dead corpse if you have to! Take aim! This is war! All out war!

Shed a tear for the boys who won't be coming back to their wives and sons and daughters and mothers! Wipe those tears and start fighting! This is the real thing! This is war!

Consider yourself enlisted! Good morning, soldier? How do you feel? Brave! Strong! Able! Faithful! Your heart had better be gurgling over with centuries of fury! Your legs had better be trembling! Your brain better be shaking! You damn well better be ready to kill them, because they sure as hell are ready to kill you! Get off your ass and get to the front! We're going to WAR!

BROUGHT TO YOU BY THE COLD HAND OF TECHNOLOGY

the ONION

Number One In News. volume 27 number 12 11–17 April 1995

CLEVER BUMPER STICKERS RESOLVE ABORTION ISSUE

Witticisms appeal to public, lawmakers

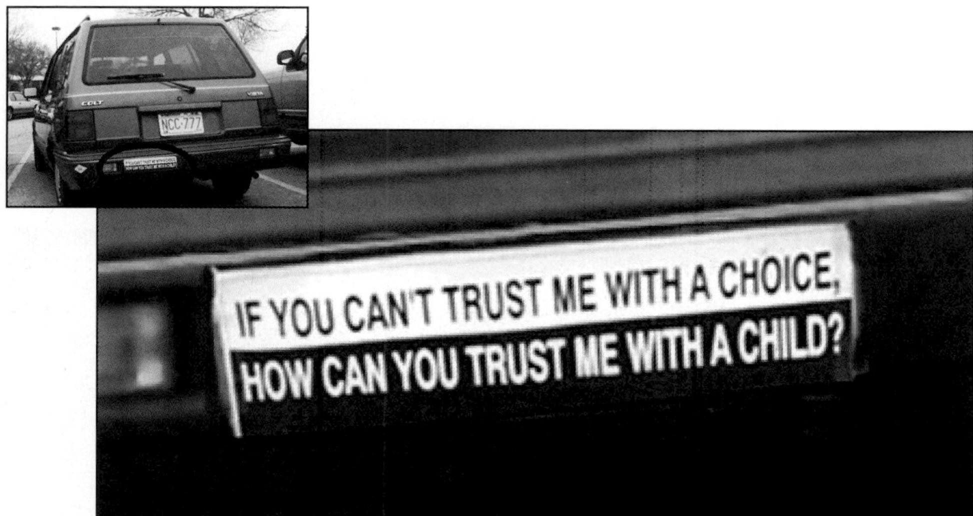

An ONION Fun Fact: Bumper stickers were responsible for the 1963 Bay of Pigs fiasco, and instrumental in the 1918 Treaty of Paris.

A MAJOR STEP TOWARD ENDING THE ABORTION CONTROVERSY took place yesterday, when a pro-life bumper sticker on a parked car convinced key pro-choice activists that abortion is wrong. The sticker, which read, "Abortion Stops a Beating Heart," changed the position of the activists, who were previously unaware that abortion involved any heart stoppage.

Said NARAL president Lynn Jenkins, "I am shocked to learn about [the beating heart]. From now on, I'm pro-life. And I vote."

When informed of the sticker, former President and pro-choice activist Jimmy Carter said he would put aside his various humanitarian causes so he could fully devote his energies to constructing model fetuses.

G. Thomas Agee of the Washington, D.C.-based Opinion Institute is not surprised by the impact of the pro-life sticker. "Bumper stickers offer real solutions to complex problems. They're not just pat, oversimplified phrases. The right sticker, with just the right message, can be every bit as powerful a force for social change as a cute, catchy button."

By 3 p.m. yesterday, news of the pro-life sticker had spread across the country. In Richmond, Va., abortion doctor James Higgins announced his plan to bomb himself. "I am Doctor Death!" he said. "I must be stopped!" Eugene, Ore., abortionist Janet Murphy-Kaye blocked the door to her own clinic shortly before she was to perform an abortion. "I can not sit idly by and allow what I am about to do to happen."

Even former Supreme Court Justice William Brennan, who wrote the majority opinion in 1973's Roe vs. Wade case, was convinced by the sticker. "We had no idea about the beating hearts back then—the technology simply was not there."

Planned Parenthood director Denise Rose recommended that if women think they absolutely must have abortions, they should think of those tiny little beating hearts. "Ba-doomp. Ba-doomp," Rose said, using a finger

see STICKER on page 10

Our Very Special Cartoon Issue
LEGAL NOTICE: BY PICKING UP THIS VERY SPECIAL CARTOON ISSUE YOU ENTER INTO A BINDING LEGAL CONTRACT IN WHICH YOU MUST SURRENDER ANY AND ALL PERSONAL ASSETS TO THE ONION.

the ONION

Number One In News. volume 27 number 14 25 April–1 May 1995

Renegade Cop Draws Picture of Cute Horsey

'It's a Very, Very Nice Horsey,' Says Local Fifth-Grade Teacher

THEY DON'T COME ANY HARDER THAN Detective Jake Stone. He lives hard, drinks hard, drives hard, and according to a recent discovery, draws very nicely.

That knowledge was the result of his latest suspension from the Metro force—a drawing of a very cute horsey. (See right.) It was the first time that Stone, a divorced loner who calls a .45 his best friend, showed any signs of artistic inclination.

"It's such a cute horsey," fifth-grade art teacher Paige Buonocore said when shown the work. "Jake draws very, very well."

Stone, who was at first reticent to discuss the horsey, opened up about the drawing when separated from his fellow officers.

"I don't care if the Sarge says this picture is going up on the station refrigerator," Stone said in a raspy, world-weary voice. "He can't take me off the case. Crooked cops killed my partner. Now I've got to straighten them out—horizontally."

Stone, also known as "The Cannon," refers often to the gangland-style slaying of partner Brian Lane, who just happened to be in the wrong place at the wrong time—without backup. Stone, held hostage at gunpoint, watched Lane get gunned down, and continues to endure graphic, slow-motion flashbacks about the incident to this day.

Stone blamed cops on the mob payroll, and crossed the line between detective work and vigilantism to hunt them down. Then he drew the cute horsey.

While serving his suspension, Stone drew the horsey on a piece of scrap paper lying around his dingy, one-bedroom apartment. He found the piece of paper under some pizza boxes, next to a pile of empty beer cans. Stone is recently divorced from his second wife, and judging by his unkempt appearance and gruff disposition, seems to have taken the break-up hard. Although it certainly didn't affect the cuteness of the horsey, some believe it has affected his police work.

"You never know what he is going to do," said Doug "Rookie" Landon, one of Stone's numerous ex-partners. "It's like he's carrying around the weight of the world, and taking it out on everyone he sees."

According to Landon, Stone frequently criticizes each of his partners' driving ability, and he makes fun of the fact that they are all happily married. Landon believes that deep down Stone harbors great respect, even envy, for

see COP on page 8

Although lone-wolf cop Jake Stone paused at police HQ to display his cute horsey, he is still sworn to hunt down the crooked cops who killed his partner.

Tiger Attacks Bill Clinton

YESTERDAY AT 4:01 P.M. IN THE WHITE HOUSES Square Offices, our President, Bill Clinton was attacked by a tiger while giving a press confrence about his failing sit com, starring Chelsea, Bill and of course Hillary. The Clinton's sit com was based on their life before Bill took office. It was on twice a week but didn't last very long.

In the middle of Clinton's press confrence an unexpected guess jumped out and pinned the President to the ground. [Were guessing he liked the sit com as much as the public did when it went off the air.] The tiger had ecscaped from a zoo two days ago. The tiger cage lock rusted and broke beacause they were cheap.

An ambulance rushed to the seen and took Clinton to the hospital. The hospital told us that Clinton's hand will be bandaged for about three weeks. That means that the President won't be signing any papers or playing his saxaphone for a while. We talked to some people and they said they'd be very dissapointed.

We went to the hospital to see how Clinton was doing. Clinton told us that he would get more security at the zoo, he was very disapointed that the zoo din't have the best kinds of locks on the cages. Clinton decided he should have a lot more security gaurds at the zoo, ecspecialy by the tiger cages. "Hillary agrees with me!" Clinton said. On the way out Clinton told us "I feel my pain!"

see TIGER on page 10

The President, wrapped up in an amusing anecdote about life as a public figure, only became aware of the attacking tiger when it pounced on him and bit his arm.

the ONION®

VOLUME 28 ISSUE 2 | NUMBER ONE IN NEWS | 22–28 AUGUST 1995

NEWS

NEW WATER-COOLER ENLIVENS INTRAOFFICE BANTER

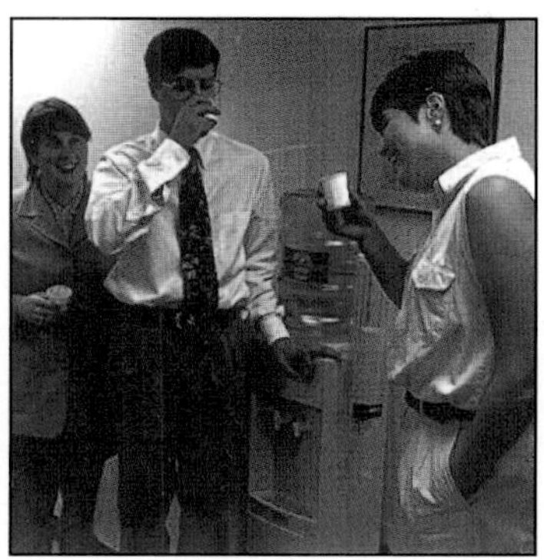

Story, page 6

THE DOW

I am the guy who types in the DOW each week and I am very lonely. I need a date.

Please, please call me at 1-800-555-7342

WEATHER

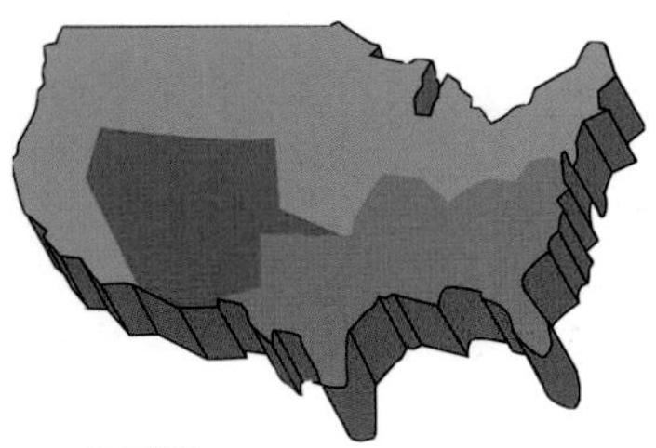

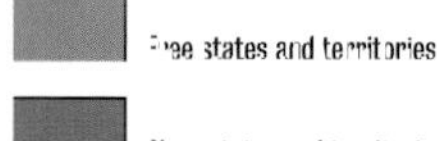

Free states and territories

Slave states and territories

Territories open to slavery by Compromise of 1850

INSIDE

NEWS IN BRIEF....................2
WHAT DO YOU THINK?....................5
HOROSCOPES....................5
JIM'S JOURNAL....................6
PATHETIC GEEK STORIES....................8
DECLINE AND FALL CALENDAR....................10
CULTURAL IDIOCY QUIZ....................14
DRUNK OF THE WEEK....................16
A-V CLUB....................17
MOVIE LISTINGS....................19
CALENDAR....................23
CLASSIFIEDS....................26

Local Youth to Explore Own Body

Curious and frightened by the changes she has begun to notice in herself, Stacy Mullhull, a Lakeland Middle School seventh grader, will soon begin a full-scale exploration of her budding young body. The 13-year-old Mullhull, who is experiencing what is commonly known as "puberty," is expected to discover many exciting new things over the next few years, including masturbation and boys.

"This is an exciting time for young Stacy. There's nothing quite so strange and wonderful as a young girl on the brink of her sexual awakening," Lakeland Mayor Paul Johnson said. "She is a ripe, young bud about to flower."

Puberty, according to experts, is the period of rapid sexual and physical development that typically begins at age 12 in girls and 14 in boys. During puberty, girls undergo many changes, including menstruation and ovulation. Girls also develop many secondary sex characteristics during puberty, including armpit and pubic hair, development of breasts, and a widening of hips.

Said Mullhull, "I want to die."

While puberty is perfectly natural, Mullhull appears strangely uncomfortable with it. She refused to answer the questions of reporters camped outside her house and ran away when one asked if she had begun menstruating. "It's something every girl goes through, yet Stacy still feels alone, like she's the only one going through it." said Charles Edmonds, ABC News bureau chief. "It's strange that she's so elusive, but ABC is still providing excellent coverage."

Although embarrassed by her blossoming sexuality, 13-year-old Stacy Mullhull is exploring her changing genitals and budding breast area.

Mullhull recently went to the mall with her mom to purchase her first bra, a fact she unsuccessfully attempted to conceal from her classmates. The first day she wore the size 30AA training bra, classmate Daniel Wilcox snapped its strap in the middle of homeroom, sparking uproarious laughter from the

see Exploration on page 4

This neighborhood will receive the 'Meal Deal' in lieu of a costly elementary school.

Clinton, Congress Pass $5 Billion Inner City 'Meal Deal'

Poor to receive free medium beverage with purchase of any 6" sub

Inner city residents living in a wasteland of poverty and crime received exciting news yesterday when President Clinton joined Congress in approving a special offer providing free medium soft drinks to all urban poor who purchase any regularly priced six-inch sub. The complimentary 20-ounce beverages, available for a limited time and not valid with other offers, are expected to bring some much needed refreshment to America's decaying, degraded urban centers.

"People out there are hungry for progress and thirsty for change," Clinton said. "This delicious sandwich and drink combo should really go a long way."

Inner city Americans, long victims of discrimination and government neglect, will have a choice of five different soft drinks: Coke, Diet Coke, Sprite, Dr. Pepper and Country Time Lemonade.

see Deal on page 8

Breathtaking Nature Scene Inspires Salesman

Story, page 13

A Bulldog in a Jogging Suit?

Story, page 13

Story, page 11

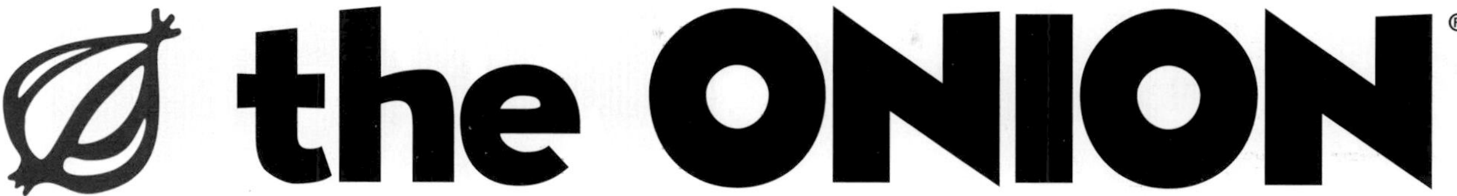

VOLUME 28 ISSUE 5 NUMBER ONE IN NEWS 12–18 SEPTEMBER 1995

NEWS

The Warriors & Women of *Battlestar Galactica*

See page 31

THE DOW

I'm the guy who writes the DOW in every week. I've written a novel, you know.

(Fan mail would be appreciated.)

+9.35

WEATHER

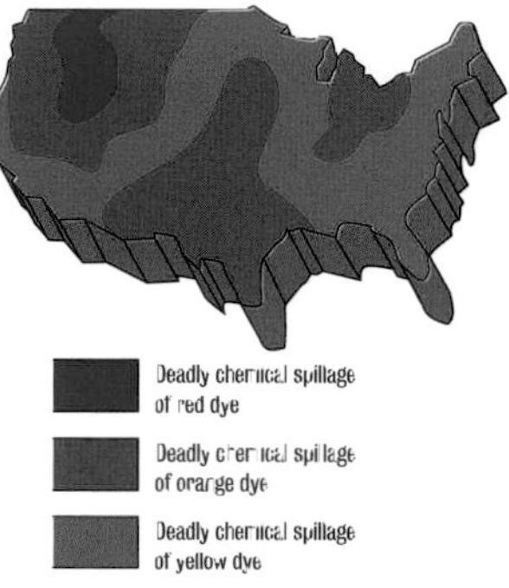

Deadly chemical spillage of red dye

Deadly chemical spillage of orange dye

Deadly chemical spillage of yellow dye

INSIDE

NEWS IN BRIEF 2
FUNNY BUSINESS 5
HOROSCOPES 5
JIM'S JOURNAL 6
THE MENUS 10
DECLINE AND FALL CALENDAR 14
CULTURAL IDIOCY QUIZ 18
DRUNK OF THE WEEK 26
A-V CLUB 27
MOVIE LISTINGS 29
CALENDAR 34
CLASSIFIEDS 38

SEXY LITTLE NUMBER TRANSFERS FROM IOWA STATE

Area interest was sparked today by the arrival of student Amber Jean "A.J." Duncan, a sexy little number transferring this semester from Iowa State.

Duncan, an art history major who hopes one day to teach, is so mind-numbingly sexy, she has already taken the breath away from two eyewitnesses, who described her as "sexy in that special, mesmerizing way—due not only to her great physical beauty but to the subtleties of her manner, confidence of her bearing, and strength of her personality," and as "a drop-dead knockout with great legs."

Students lucky enough to have glimpsed her agree that thanks is due to Dean of Admissions Hugh Kilno, who oversaw her transfer admission, thus ensuring that the leggy A.J. is no longer hundreds of miles away in Iowa, but actually among us, in this city, breathing our air and blanketing the campus with her staggering sexuality.

A.J. was not interviewed for this article, as her intimidating beauty rendered her unapproachable, even for this reporter. This reporter has, however, lingered near her on several occasions, once even spotting her wearing Spandex while jogging.

Although initial reports that A.J. was still seeing third-year Iowa State student Brad Lapinski worried some observers, those close to A.J. claim the relationship is essentially over.

"A.J. had been getting sick of Brad's cloying possessiveness for a long time now, if you ask me," Duncan's longtime friend Tammy Ninn said. "Now that she's finally transferred, I don't think

see SEXY on page 4

The coquettish A.J. may be new to town, but her raw, youthful sexuality has already intimidated every male who has come into contact with her.

Government Urges Citizenry: Ignore the Throbbing Cosmic Love Orb

NEW YORK—In what one statesman called "a plea for sanity in a time of world crisis," the governments of the world urged people everywhere to disregard the gigantic throbbing cosmic love orb currently hovering above the planet. In a special joint announcement by the United Nations today, a delegation from all major industrialized nations called for "all citizens to continue to go about business as normal" and to "remain calm," despite the orb's uncanny ability to speak in every language on Earth.

According to officials, the Orb, which emits intense sensations of peace and universal love, must be destroyed.

"We must summon courage to face the challenge posed by the orb's seeming omnipotence, and specifically we must not renounce any of our worldly goods prematurely, before all the facts are in," the announcement read. The assembled leaders also said that the

see ORB on page 10

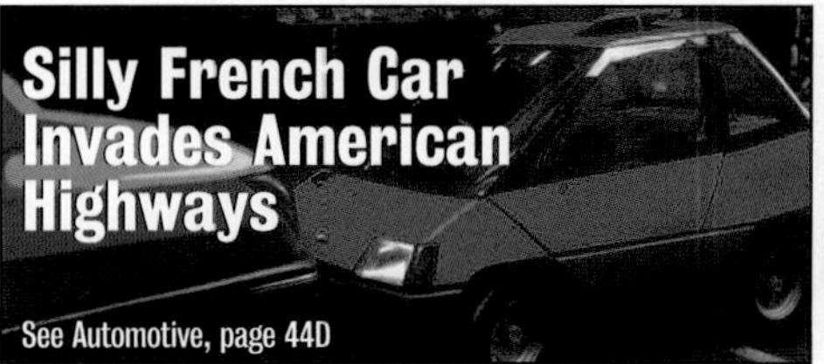

VOLUME 28 ISSUE 8 | NUMBER ONE IN NEWS | 3–9 OCTOBER 1995

NEWS

Prisoners Brighten Up Drab City Landmarks with Cheery, Gay Paint

Story, page 15

THE DOW

Come meet the DOW's new mascot, Dowey the Stupid Up and Down Arrow, this Saturday at the Peach Tree Mall.

WEATHER

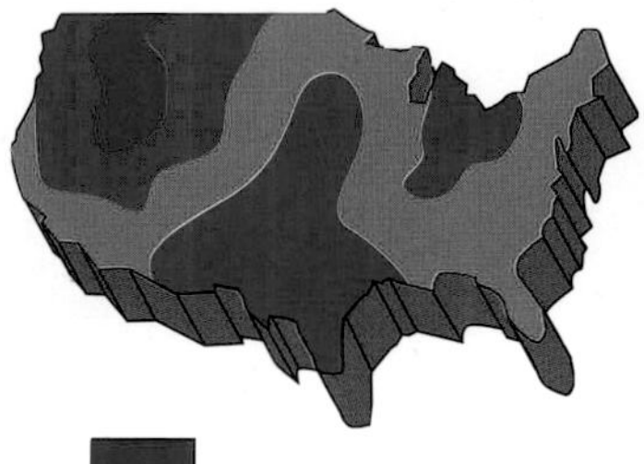

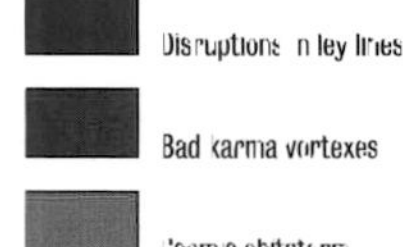

Disruptions in ley lines

Bad karma vortexes

Cosmic shitstorm

INSIDE

NEWS IN BRIEF 2
FUNNY BUSINESS 5
HOROSCOPES 5
PATHETIC GEEK STORIES 8
THE MENUS 10
DECLINE AND FALL CALENDAR 14
CULTURAL IDIOCY QUIZ 17
DRUNK OF THE WEEK 20
A-V CLUB 21
MOVIE LISTINGS 22
CALENDAR 30
CLASSIFIEDS 34

DINOSAURS ARE HIDING

Dinosaurs, long thought extinct, have recently been discovered hiding all over the world. This sneaky T-Rex appeared just long enough to devour 97 Portland, Ore. residents last Saturday.

A joint team of British and American paleontologists made the stunning announcement today that dinosaurs, long thought extinct for over 65 million years, are actually just hiding. According to the scientists, over 200,000 of the prehistoric creatures are still alive today, cleverly concealing themselves from human view through the use of various carefully chosen "hiding places."

"Clearly, the dinosaur is a creature scientific experts would classify as 'Extra-Hidey,'" team leader Sir Neville Scott said.

The British-American team made its initial discovery last Friday during a dig in southern New Mexico. According to Scott, the group was in the midst of excavating the intact jawbone of an early Pleistocene-era stegosaurus when a large dinosaur was spotted tucked behind a nearby tree.

"It was trying to check out what we were doing," Scott said. "We spotted it and tried to call it over, but it got scared and ran away crying." When team member Henry Flahr approached the allosaurus, it responded by nuzzling its snout to his breast, then fatally gored him with his razor-sharp claws.

The find quickly led to the discovery of numerous other dinosaurs, all of which were found hiding in places scientists had previously failed to look. A 500-ton brontosaurus was found behind a San Francisco skyscraper; a triceratops was spotted in a large hedge in suburban Baltimore; and a pterosaurus was discovered under-

see HIDING on page 4

Centerfold's Turn-ons, Turn-offs Set Community Agenda

Rural Hollows, Minnesota understands the importance of change. That's why the tiny town of 2,300 has recently taken bold steps to buff up its sleepy small town image, revising its community agenda according to the likes and dislikes of leggy Playboy playmate Cyndi Simmons. In doing this, city officials are optimistic that their new centerfold-based agenda will be more in step with today's political climate, not to

see CENTERFOLD on page 8

Playmate Cyndi Simmons loves long walks and ice cream on a hot day, which, along with her other likes and dislikes, have become law in Rural Hollows.

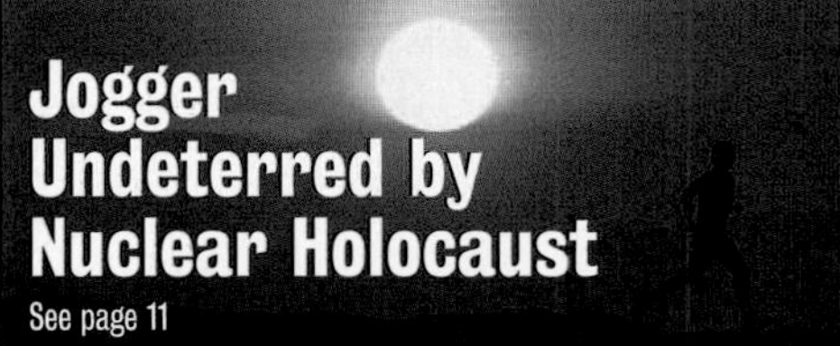

VOLUME 28 ISSUE 10 | NUMBER ONE IN NEWS | 17–23 OCTOBER 1995

NEWS

ANGRY ISLAND GOD DEMANDS BUTTERY SCONE

See 4B

THE DOW

Trading was light yesterday, as the nation's financiers enjoyed a delicious, two-hour meal at Hardee's.

WEATHER

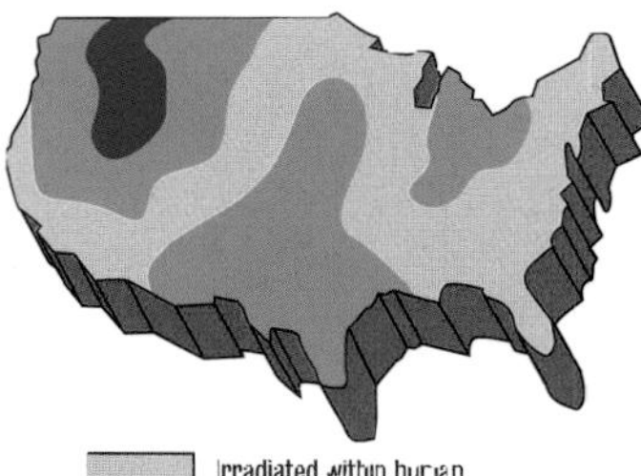

Irradiated within human survival levels

Irradiated beyond human survival levels

Wastelands controlled by nomadic motor warlords

INSIDE

NEWS IN BRIEF 2
ADVENTURE! 4
FUNNY BUSINESS 5
HOROSCOPES 5
PATHETIC GEEK STORIES 8
THE MENUS 10
DECLINE AND FALL CALENDAR 14
CULTURAL IDIOCY QUIZ 17
DRUNK OF THE WEEK 18
A-V CLUB 19
MOVIE LISTINGS 21
SAVAGE LOVE 25
CALENDAR 26
CLASSIFIEDS 30

Gay Couple to Add Exciting Big City Feel to Small Town

The sleepy hamlet of Reedsburg, OH (pop. 748), will soon take on an exciting big city feel, thanks to Rob Hennings and Steve Baker, a New York City gay couple moving to town next weekend. Hennings and Baker, partners for over 13 years, will be Reedsburg's first gay residents, providing the town with a brand-new, sophisticated, cosmopolitan flavor.

"This should make us just like San Francisco and New York," mayor Paul Herbeveldt said. "Homosexuals will now be proudly walking our streets."

Hennings and Baker, who are moving to Reedsburg because math teacher Baker accepted a job at the local high school, are looking forward to life in Ohio.

"We hear it's a lovely town," Hennings said. "It will be refreshing to get away from the city, a place where we both have lived most of our adult lives."

Area businesses are making a special effort to welcome the soon-to-arrive couple. Ed's Tavern, a popular local bar, has already established Thursdays as "Alternative Lifestyles" Night, when only Hennings and Baker may enter.

"We want them to have a place to go and feel comfortable in their own environment," owner Ed Grady said. "This is a chance for them to go out and be gay with each other."

Hollywood Stop, the town's video

see GAY on page 4

5 THINGS BEING DONE TO WELCOME ROB AND STEVE:

1. Video store ordering copy of gay movie *Philadelphia.*
2. 'Alternative Lifestyles' Night Thursdays at Ed's Tavern.
3. Keller's Department Store stocking up on pink shirts, earrings and scarves—items gay men seem to like.
4. Will invite them to talk to school children about being different from normal people.
5. Reedsburg Community Theatre to put on lavish, big-budget production of *La Cage Aux Folles.*

Gay couple Rob Hennings and Steve Baker recently moved from New York City to tiny Reedsburg, Ohio. Town residents look forward to hearing stories about art, theatre, dance, literature, foreign films and black people.

Football Victory Placates Masses

The city's mindless uneducated rabble enjoyed a brief respite from their hollow, desperate lives when the local football team won on Saturday.

When the Red Raiders of Texas Tech University hosted arch-rival Texas Christian University on Saturday, it was a team with a mission: to snap its three-game losing streak and placate the ignorant masses of fans with a meaningless collective ego boost.

Mission accomplished.

With a tough-as-nails running attack and a few lucky turnovers, the Red Raiders' 35-9 victory over the Horned Frogs made the unwashed Tech faithful forget about their uninspired, go-nowhere jobs and stagnant personal lives, if only for a day.

see MASSES on page 8

the ONION®

VOLUME 28 ISSUE 12 | NUMBER ONE IN NEWS | 31 OCTOBER–6 NOVEMBER 1995

NEWS

Rainbows: Why Are There So Many Songs About Them?

See page 81

THE DOW

If I ever meet this Dow Jones fella, I'm gonna ask him, "Hey guy, why so up and down?"

+63.54

WEATHER

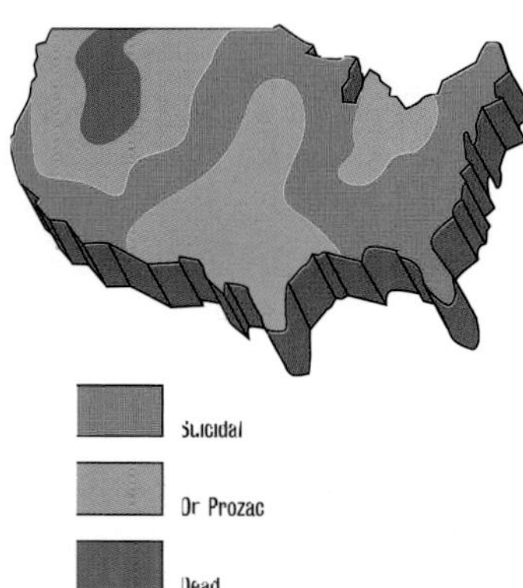

INSIDE

NEWS IN BRIEF....4
FUNNY BUSINESS....5
HOROSCOPES....5
PATHETIC GEEK STORIES....8
THE MENUS....10
ADVENTURE!....12
DECLINE AND FALL CALENDAR....14
CULTURAL IDIOCY QUIZ....16
DRUNK OF THE WEEK....18
A-V CLUB....19
MOVIE LISTINGS....21
SAVAGE LOVE....27
CALENDAR....28
CLASSIFIEDS....30

AREA BOWL CASHED

Disappointment, frustration and dismay were just a few of the highly charged emotional reactions experienced today upon discovery that a bowl, belonging to area residents Mike Cudahy and "Thatches" Moynihan, was cashed. The bowl, described as a "big fat bowl," was not expected to be cashed until much later, as it had just been packed.

Co-owners Cudahy and Moynihan describe the current situation as "a total buzz-kill," and hope that, with any luck, the bowl will be re-packed soon.

"In the meantime," Cudahy told reporters at a downtown press conference, "We're totally jonesin', big time."

Tragically, there is nothing the pair can do now but wait... and hope.

"We were seriously runnin' low after Tuesday night's jam session," Moynihan, a sometime acoustic guitarist currently employed as a pizza delivery driver, told reporters. "We gathered up all the shake, schwag, and roaches we had lying around, and packed them tight into this cool metal pipe I got from this store my cousin works at in Chicago. It was beautiful. One minute we were like, hey man, we're runnin' low; the next thing you know we were sitting on a full dance card for the rest of the night."

But the sense of exhilaration and triumph the two felt would shortly turn to tragic loss. Though the bowl was packed as tight as possible, almost to the point where drawing smoke through it was difficult, a slew of houseguests soon depleted their supply and left the pair "cashed."

"It was packed rock solid, man," Moynihan said. "No kind or nothin', just strictly mersh, but still solid. But then,

see CASHED on page 6

Serious jonesin' was the result of this bowl being cashed prematurely. Experts blame an abundance of unexpected houseguests.
Inset: Pot smoker Mike Cudahy holds a press conference to announce the cashing. He hopes his brother will come to town this weekend with a much-needed bag.

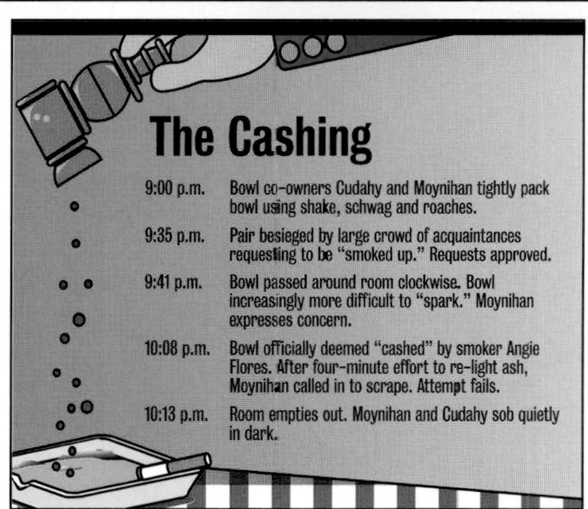

New U.S. Military Helicopter Too Beautiful To Use in Combat

The Defender, the most technologically advanced helicopter ever built, is covered by a silk tarp and dusted twice daily.

LANGLEY, VA—U.S. military officials unveiled the Bell 8600L "Defender" helicopter Tuesday at Langley Air Force base, calling it the greatest weapon in U.S. aerospace history and vowing it would never be used.

"It is the ultimate peace-keeping tool, a technological triumph," General Hem Willenfeld said. "But even more stunning than its firepower is its magnificent beauty, its glorious essence of aesthetic perfection."

The general gently stroked the side of the craft, his gaze locked in its metallic sheen, adding, "So, so beautiful."

see BEAUTIFUL on page 8

Got the Winter Blues? Why Not Kill Yourself?

Suicide Tips, page 18

City Braces for Bold New Lozenge Flavor

See Metro, page 62

Erika Kind of Annoyed with Amy

See World, page 11

the ONION®

VOLUME 28 ISSUE 17 NUMBER ONE IN NEWS 12–18 DECEMBER 1995

NEWS

Government to NASA: 'Keep on Spending, You're Doing Great!'

See Nation, page 23

THE DOW

Hey brokers, liven up your cubicle by putting a little star on top of this arrow to make it look like a little Christmas tree.

WEATHER

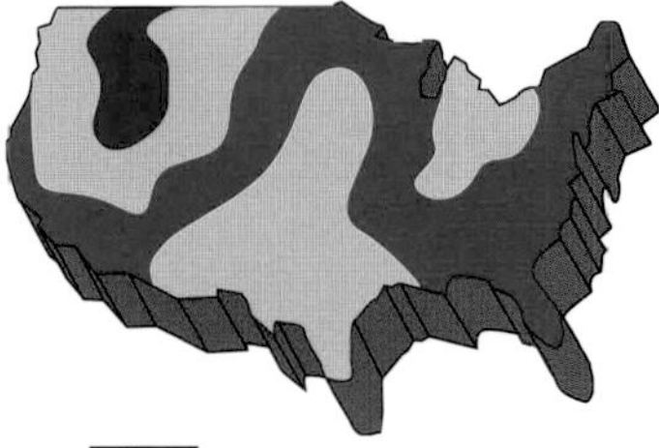

People who invited you to their party

People whose friends brought you along

People so beautiful you could never know them

INSIDE

NEWS IN BRIEF 2
ADVENTURE! 4
FUNNY BUSINESS 5
HOROSCOPES 5
PATHETIC GEEK STORIES 8
THE MENUS 10
DECLINE AND FALL CALENDAR 12
CULTURAL IDIOCY QUIZ 17
DRUNK OF THE WEEK 20
A-V CLUB 21
MOVIE LISTINGS 23
SAVAGE LOVE 27
CALENDAR 28
CLASSIFIEDS 30

Congress Hires Drummer

WASHINGTON, D.C.—In a decisive 376-45 vote last Friday, the United States Congress hired drummer Joey Lombardo, a professional percussionist with years of studio and touring experience. Lombardo, who has toured with such diverse artists as Kenny Loggins, Pat Benatar and Richard Marx, is expected to provide the legislative body with a variety of much-needed percussive effects.

"You wouldn't believe how much his steady backbeat helps keep bills and budget proposals rolling along, not to mention adding some zip to those filibusters," Sen. Alfonse D'Amato (R-NY) said. "Lombardo provides a rock-solid foundation upon which Congress can really jam."

The seasoned studio vet, who played with Bryan Adams on the Australian leg of the star's 1991 Waking Up the Neighbors Tour, will also provide drum rolls during key budget votes. Before the vote tally for the controversial Steffens-Hawley Welfare Bill was announced Monday, Lombardo performed a dramatic, prolonged snare drum roll, which, according to 93-year-old Sen. Strom Thurmond (R-SC), "made me tingly."

Despite his lack of Congressional drumming experience, Lombardo is confident he has the stamina to keep up with the long-winded legislators. "When I was on Tina Turner's Break Every Rule World Tour, we did a show in Rio that was over three and half hours. I'm confident that if I can keep up with Tina, I can keep up with Orrin Hatch and Arlen Specter."

With his extensive experience playing live, Lombardo also brings a theatrical sensibility to Congress. When Speaker of the House Newt Gingrich recently opened session with the remark, "I know why Clinton didn't want

see DRUMMER on page 8

Drummer Joey Lombardo brings some 'serious chops' to the U.S. Congress. Sax legend David Sanborn has already promised to sit in and jam with him during next week's critical HR-32.(S) welfare vote.

Bang the Drum Slowly

Here's where the presence of a skilled percussionist on the floor of the U.S. Congress will be valuable:

Roll Call	Will provide tension-building drum roll when voting results are announced
Filibusters	Will provide steady backbeat during lengthy, time-killing speeches
Senatorial Jokes	Will provide rim shots to punctuate witty remarks and partisan jabs made during speeches and debates
Closing of Congressional Session	Will play breathtaking eight-minute solo when Congress breaks, leaving members pumped up for limo ride home

Police Unimpressed with Rooftop Sniper

'It's been done,' say officials

Sniper Victor Huemanga (inset) has failed to make an impression on Houston Police, who urge him to kill in a more creative manner.

HOUSTON, TX—A rooftop sniper armed with an automatic rifle opened fire on a crowded downtown intersection yesterday, killing four and leaving area police officers greatly unimpressed. The seven-minute shooting spree, which also critically wounded at least 20 others in a busy lunchtime crowd, was described by the officers as "uninspired" and "lame."

"To be quite honest, it's been done," Houston police chief Karl Slawson said, stifling a yawn. "Off the top of my head, I can think of at least five other cases in Texas alone where a guy snapped, got on a roof and fired into a crowd below. There's just nothing new about it."

The sniper, identified as 44-year-

see SNIPER on page 4

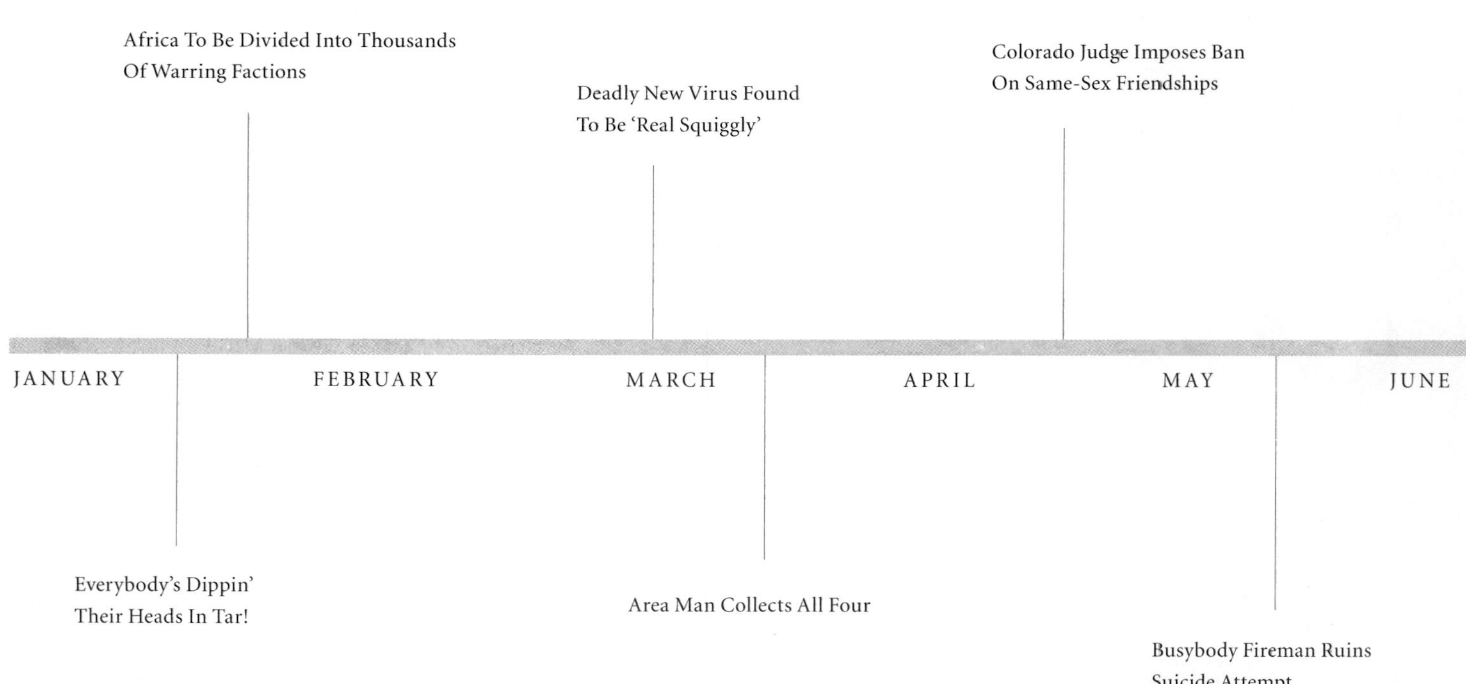

Africa To Be Divided Into Thousands
Of Warring Factions
Deadly New Virus Found
To Be 'Real Squiggly'
Colorado Judge Imposes Ban
On Same-Sex Friendships
JANUARY
FEBRUARY
MARCH
APRIL
MAY
JUNE
Everybody's Dippin'
Their Heads In Tar!
Area Man Collects All Four
Busybody Fireman Ruins
Suicide Attempt

1996

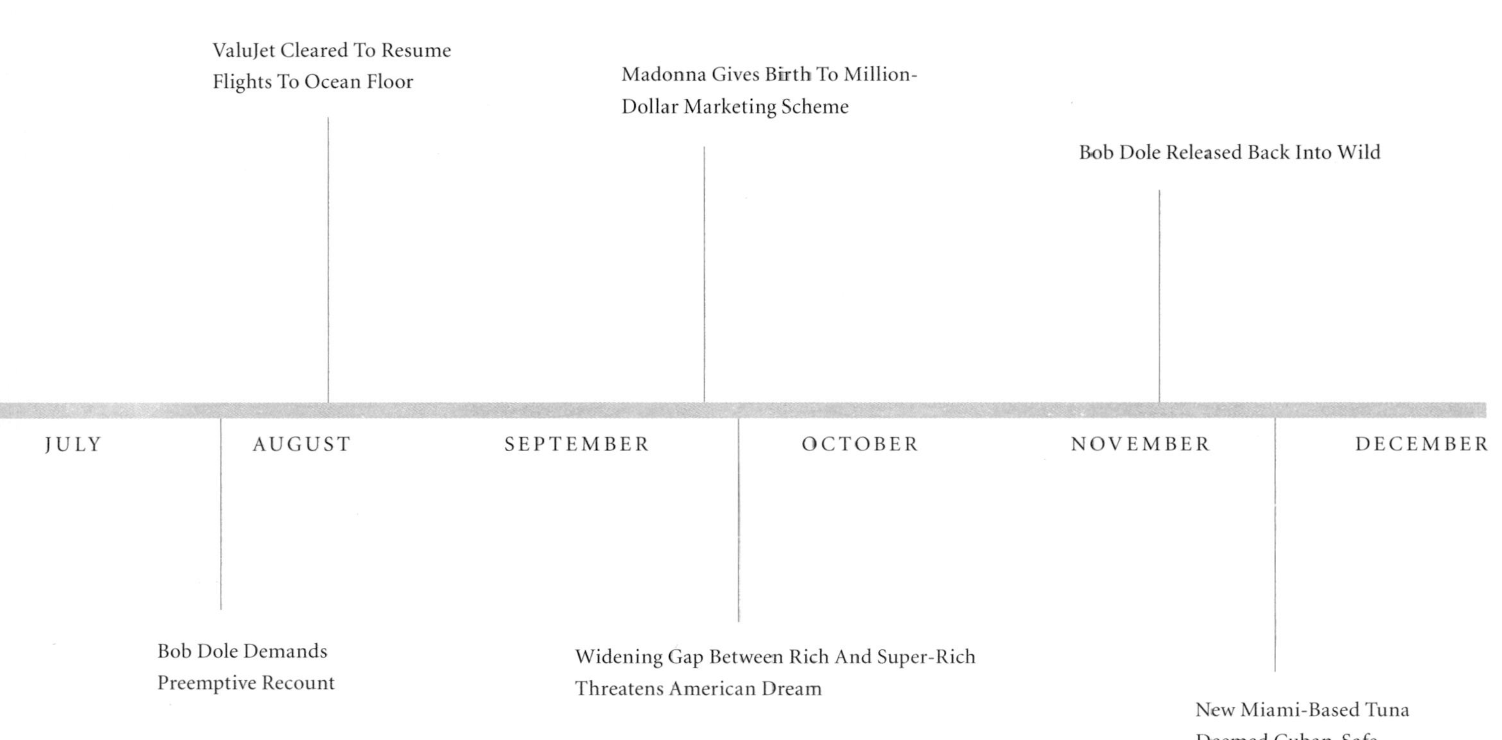

ValuJet Cleared To Resume Flights To Ocean Floor
Madonna Gives Birth To Million-Dollar Marketing Scheme
Bob Dole Released Back Into Wild
JULY
AUGUST
SEPTEMBER
OCTOBER
NOVEMBER
DECEMBER
Bob Dole Demands Preemptive Recount
Widening Gap Between Rich And Super-Rich Threatens American Dream
New Miami-Based Tuna Deemed Cuban-Safe

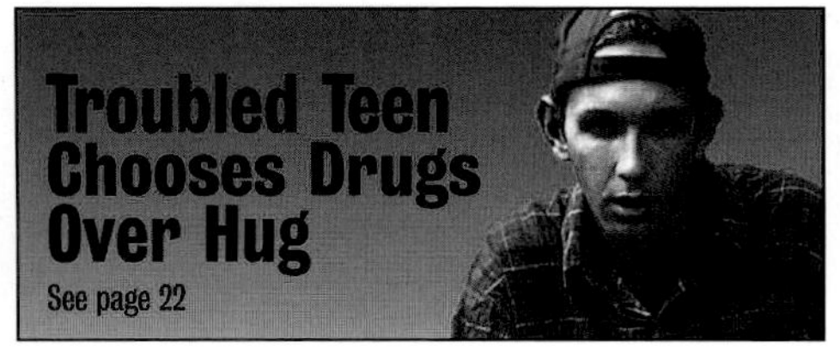

the ONION®

VOLUME 29 ISSUE 3 | NUMBER ONE IN NEWS | 30 JANUARY–5 FEBRUARY 1996

NEWS

ISLAND-BURYING TIDAL WAVE WETS HUNDREDS

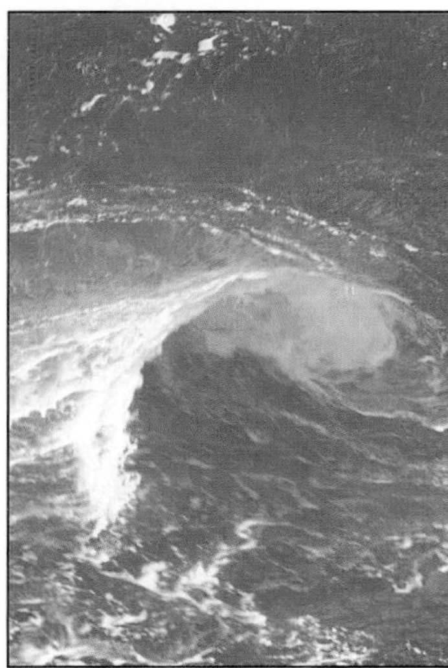

See World, page 19

THE DOW

Small investors take note: When the arrow is up, this is a good thing. When it is down, that is bad.

WEATHER

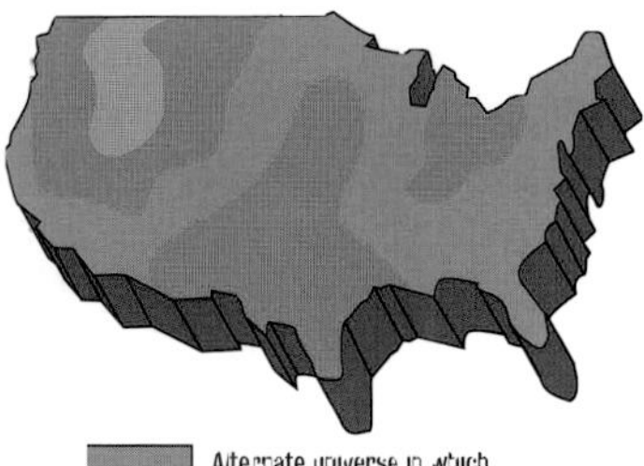

Alternate universe in which South won Civil War

Alternate universe in which Third Reich conquered United States

Alternate universe in which *The Powers* is still on the air

INSIDE

NEWS IN BRIEF 2
SNAPSHOT 2
ADVENTURE 4
FUNNY BUSINESS 5
PATHETIC GEEK STORIES 8
THE MENUS 11
DECLINE AND FALL CALENDAR 12
CULTURAL IDIOCY QUIZ 18
DRUNK OF THE WEEK 20
A-V CLUB 21
MOVIE LISTINGS 24
SAVAGE LOVE 29
CALENDAR 31
CLASSIFIEDS 33

U.S. INVADES VIETNAM

Clinton: 'We need another Vietnam'

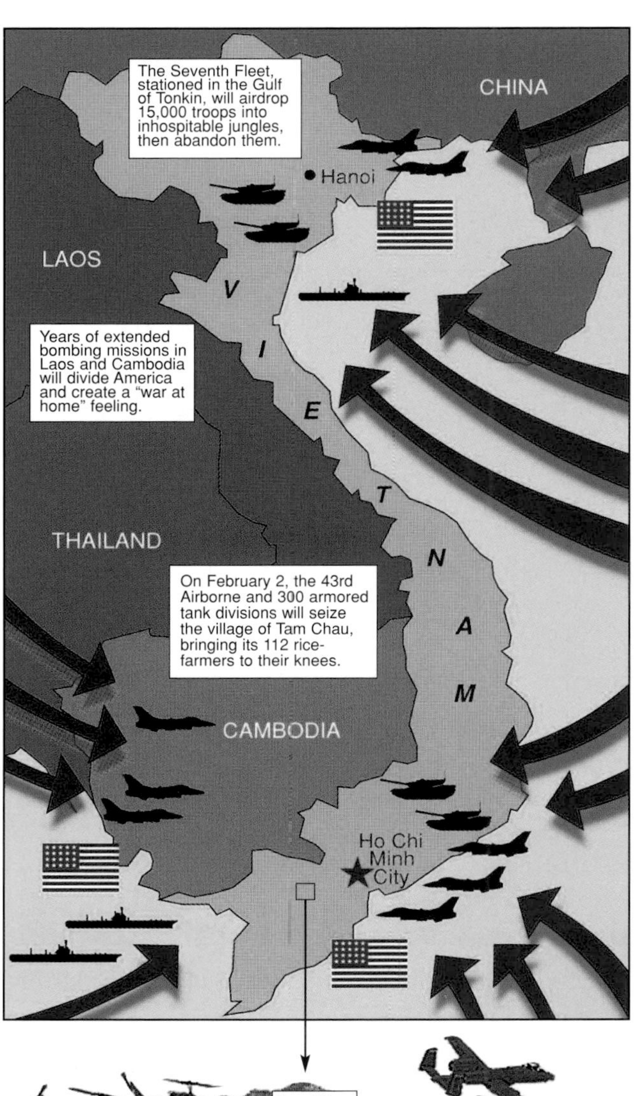

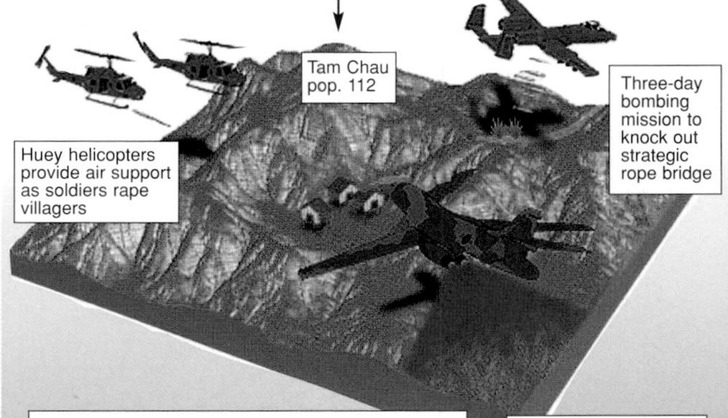

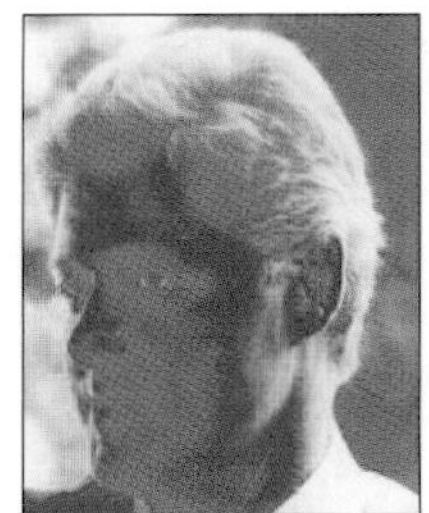
Bill Clemant

President Clinton announced today that after 20 years and a slow, painful healing process, the U.S. will again invade Vietnam. "For a long time, we have said we don't need another Vietnam," Clinton told a joint session of Congress. "But now, more than ever, America needs to be divided. We need another Vietnam."

American ground troops will be flown in via helicopters to ransack villages. Unrelenting napalm bombing missions will obliterate thousands of acres of Vietnamese farmland and rain forest. Clinton also plans to use chemical weapons like Agent Orange to inflict long-term physical damage to Vietnamese civilians and American soldiers alike. "Furthermore," Clinton said, "I believe the time is right for American soldiers to rape and kill more Vietnamese women and children."

Clinton urged our nation's young people to do their part by organizing protests against the war.

"It is up to the younger generation to put a wedge in our national pride, and make the soldiers doubt their mission overseas," he said. "I want to see flags burning on our campuses." The president promised to order National Guardsmen to shoot students who engage in protest of any kind.

Eighteen to 30-year-olds are being conscripted

see U.S. INVASION on page 7

> **"It is up to the younger generation to put a wedge in our national pride, and make the soldiers doubt their mission overseas. I want to see flags burning on our campuses."**
> **—President Bill Clinton**

Vietnam Vets Admit War Wasn't That Bad

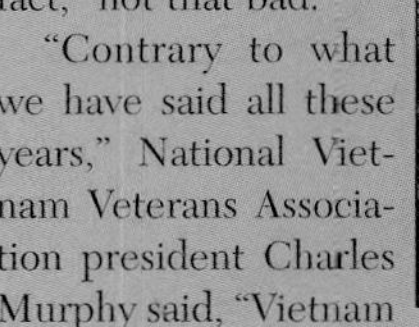

After more than two decades of describing the Vietnam War as a "living hell," and an "endless, indescribable horror beyond all words," America's Vietnam veterans finally admitted yesterday that the war was, in fact, "not that bad."

"Contrary to what we have said all these years," National Vietnam Veterans Association president Charles Murphy said, "Vietnam simply was not that bad. In fact, it was quite enjoyable. We really are a big bunch of babies."

see VETS on page 11

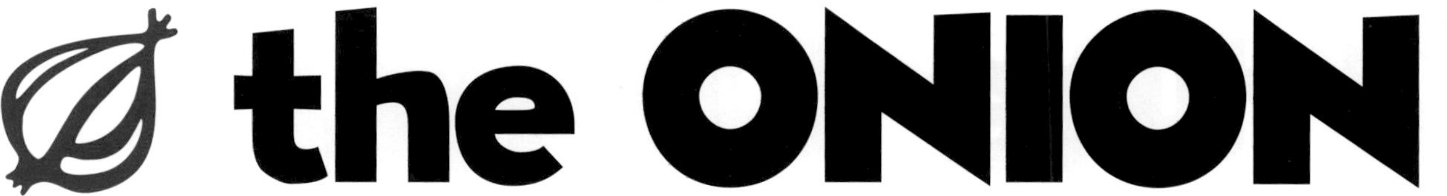

VOLUME 29 ISSUE 5 NUMBER ONE IN NEWS 13–19 FEBRUARY 1996

NEWS

God to Use Powers for Evil

See World, page 18

THE DOW

Your regular DOW guy is sick today, so I'll be providing you with your financial information in his place. My name is Brad.

-13.21

WEATHER

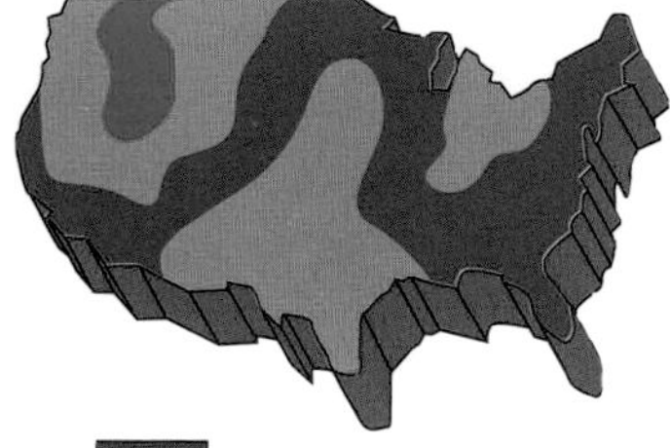

Exchanges of flowers and jewelry

Exchanges of heart-shaped boxes of candy

Exchanges of herpes virus

INSIDE

NEWS IN BRIEF 2
ADVENTURE 4
FUNNY BUSINESS 5
PATHETIC GEEK STORIES 8
THE MENUS 10
DECLINE AND FALL CALENDAR 12
CULTURAL IDIOCY QUIZ 15
VALENTINE'S DAY PERSONALS 16
VALENTINE'S DAY CUT-OUTS 19
A-V CLUB 23
MOVIE LISTINGS 26
SAVAGE LOVE 33
CALENDAR 34
CLASSIFIEDS 36

Clinton Tagged by Local Gang

WASHINGTON, D.C.—In an incident under heavy investigation by Secret Service officials, President Clinton was "tagged" late yesterday afternoon, spray-painted across the chest by a member of the E. Street Kingz, a notorious D.C. street gang. The latest in a series of graffiti strikes in the ongoing war between the Kingz and their rival gang, the Deth Ro Niggaz, the tagging caused an estimated $350 in damages to Clinton's suit and officially marked the President as Kingz's "turf."

"We are shocked and disturbed by this serious breach of presidential security," White House chief of security Alan Watkins said. "We are taking every possible step to protect the President in the future, including coating him with a paint-resistant shellac."

The incident marked the first crime committed against a President since Ronald Reagan was raped by David James Pelphrey in 1986.

According to reports, shortly after 3 p.m., an unidentified member of the E. Street Kingz snuck past White House guards and spray-painted a red, backwards "ESK"—the gang's symbol—across Clinton's chest. The unidentified gang member escaped through the South Lawn gate by telling guards that he was Secretary of State Warren Christopher.

According to Washington-area gang experts, with the tagging, President

see TAGGED on page 4

President Clinton, moments after a surprise tagging by the E. Street Kingz, paused on the Capitol steps to take questions from the media. It was the first presidential tagging since the Harding Administration.

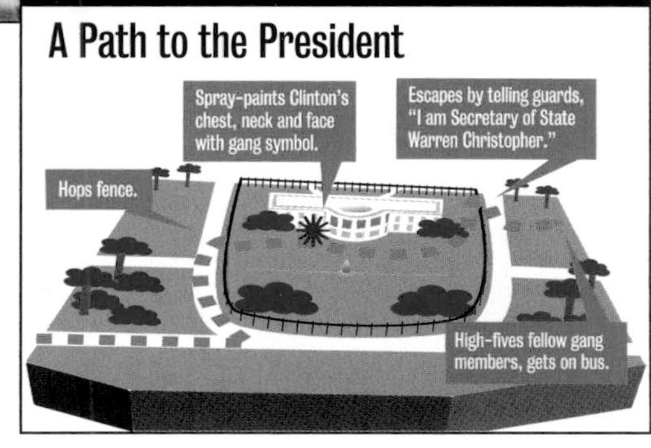

Massive Oil Spill Results in Improved Wildlife Viscosity

NOME, AK—A Castrol Oil supertanker ran aground Monday near Nome, Alaska, spilling more than 51 million gallons of oil into the Bering Strait and greatly improving the viscosity of area marine wildlife. The spill, the world's largest since the Exxon Valdez ran aground in 1989, has coated over 500,000 birds, fish and seals in quality, high-grade lubricant that will provide valuable protection and keep important animal parts running smooth.

Wildlife officials were excited by news of the spill.

"A thick coat of oil should help these animals a lot, especially in the cold weather," Tom Wofford of the U.S. Fish and Wildlife Department said. "Last month alone, we had 200 cases of Northern Cranes suffering from severe thermal break-

see SPILL on page 10

These seals are just some of the ocean wildlife who will no longer knock, nor suffer from thermal breakdown, thanks to Castrol's 51 million gallon oil spill in the Bering Strait.

Nursing Home Hosts '96 Die-Off
See Community, page 19

The Middle East: Politically Unstable?
See World, page 6

Mulatto Arrested in Own Hate Crime
See Region, page 9

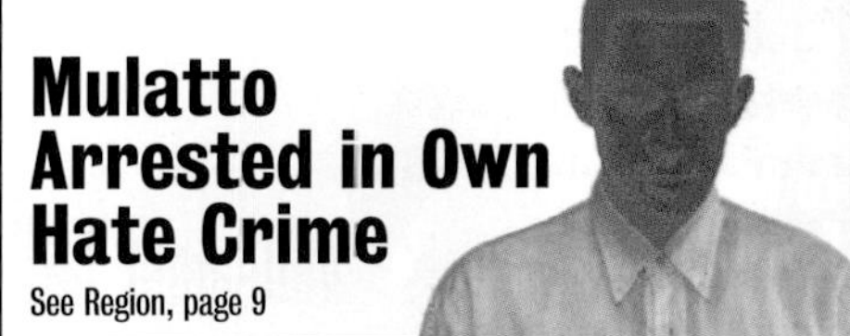

the ONION®

VOLUME 29 ISSUE 12 | NUMBER ONE IN NEWS | 3–9 APRIL 1996

NEWS

Chinese Premier To Clinton: "生夏帖市帖"

See Nation, page 4

TODAY'S ONION

Broadway Today

The Great White Way is exciting and vibrant, with cutting-edge, original musicals that speak to our times like no other form of entertainment.

see Theater, 2E

Travelers

You will never be able to visit Paris, so enjoy our glamorous four-page, full-color spring travel guide. Also: A guide to dining in Tokyo, a city in which you'll never eat.

see Travel, 4A

Get on the Electronic Internet Highway

The Onion goes "Cyber" with its new e-mail address. Write a letter to us—electronically! Believe it.
fuckyoumoron@aol.com

INSIDE

NEWS IN BRIEF 2
ADVENTURE! 4
FUNNY BUSINESS 5
PATHETIC GEEK STORIES 8
AN ADVERTISEMENT 9
CULTURAL IDIOCY QUIZ 13
DECLINE AND FALL CALENDAR 14
DRUNK OF THE WEEK 18
A-V CLUB 21
MOVIE LISTINGS 24
WORDS 30
SAVAGE LOVE 31
CALENDAR 33
CLASSIFIEDS 36

CHRIST RETURNS TO NBA

After a two-year hiatus from basketball, Jesus Christ returned to the NBA last night, playing with his former team, the Atlanta Hawks. Christ, who quit the sport in May 1994 to focus on spreading His message of universal love and compassion, made His triumphant return last night against the Bulls, just in time for Easter Sunday.

The return of Christ, who averaged 18.2 points and 7.3 assists per game during his 10-year NBA career, has excited success-hungry Hawks fans, who are calling Him the team's "Savior."

Said Atlanta resident and devout Christian Jeff Voorhees, "Jesus is Lord."

Christ's decision to return to the Hawks surprised insiders, considering for years the Nazareth native had been crucified by the Atlanta press. Ever since He was drafted third overall out of Texas A&M in 1986, Christ has been labeled "too passive and forgiving" to ever lead the Hawks to the promised land. Christ, however, has decided to

see CHRIST on page 4

Christ's Career Highlights

College: Texas A&M
- School's second all-time leading scorer.
- Junior year, led Aggies to NCAA's Sweet 16

Pro: Drafted third overall by Atlanta in 1986
- January 17, 1988–Scored 33 points in one quarter after Nets forward Buck Williams used his name in vain after a missed dunk.
- February 22, 1990–During time out at All-Star game in Chicago, turned water into Gatorade.
- December 16, 1991–Overturned souvenir stand in lobby of Dallas's Reunion Arena, shouting, "This is a house of basketball!"
- March 4, 1992–Appeared on cover of *Sports Illustrated* for the seventh time, once again with the headline, "It's a Miracle!"

Jesus Christ returned to action last night against the Chicago Bulls, chipping in 13 points and 4 assists, and wowing fans with his trademark "Ascension Dunk."

NASA's lightweight straw space shuttle tragically burst into flames upon rocket fuel ignition.

NASA Baffled by Failure of Straw Shuttle

NASA officials watched in horror Monday as the $68 billion straw space shuttle, Explorer 2, burst into flames upon lift-off from Cape Canaveral.

The four American and three Russian astronauts on-board were killed instantly, despite the protection of their all-straw space suits.

Technicians were stunned by the failure, which capped a flawless six-month pre-launch test period. They count among the possible causes of the accident "faulty twine."

According to an official statement by NASA Chief Engineer Georke Toshikima, "The straw ship was dry, light-weight and well-bailed enough to break the earth's orbit, but inexplicably burst into flames when ignited with 3,000 gallons of rocket fuel."

"This is a devastating setback for NASA," one technician added.

An estimated 30 birds, 8 voles and 20 mice who had nested in the ship's outer hull or burrowed homes deep in the ship's straw engines also perished in the blast.

The twine that held the ship in place was top quality burlap bailing twine,

see STRAW on page 17

Area 6-Year-Old Becomes Youngest Ever to Crash Plane

See Our Children, page 19

***Willow* Rented**

See Entertainment, page 28

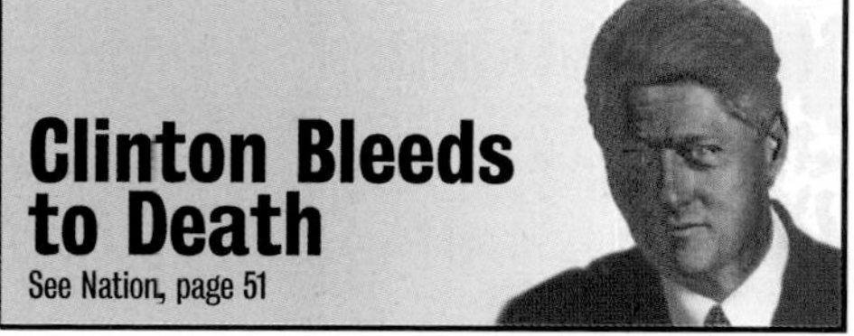

Clinton Bleeds to Death

See Nation, page 51

the ONION®

VOLUME 29 ISSUE 15 | NUMBER ONE IN NEWS | 24–30 APRIL 1996

NEWS

Quentin Tarantino Breaks Three-Day Media Silence

See Focus, page 11

TODAY'S ONION

Computer Expo News

New World Global Technology Summit introduces hundreds of new ways to avoid human contact

Technolpgy p. 34

People

Plucky Hezbollah extremist starts mail-order crafts business

p. 41

Special Comics Issue

Is it possible that *The Lockhorns* is no longer relevant?

see p. 16

INSIDE

NEWS IN BRIEF 2
ADVENTURE 4
WHAT DO YOU THINK? 5
PATHETIC GEEK STORIES 8
DECLINE AND FALL CALENDAR 13
CULTURAL IDIOCY QUIZ 15
SPECIAL COMICS SECTION 16
A-V CLUB 19
MOVIE LISTINGS 22
DRUNK OF THE WEEK 25
WORDS 28
SAVAGE LOVE 29
CALENDAR 30
CLASSIFIEDS 32

Defense Department Boosts Funding for $15 Billion Puppycrusher

After 11 years of research and development, and more than $9 billion in spending, the Defense Department announced Monday that it will boost funding to $15 billion for its high-performance puppycrusher.

Pentagon officials are hopeful that with the increased budget, the highly touted 45,000 PSI canine compressor, known among puppy-crushing industry professionals as PupCrunch-2000, will be fully operational by June 1997. If this goal is met, according to Defense Department officials, the U.S. will be the world's undisputed leader in puppy-crushing technology.

"This is an extremely important piece of technology," project head Eric Reed said. "But given the budget we've been working with, puppies were not being crushed anywhere near thin enough, nor quickly enough. A one-eighth-inch thickness in 2.1 seconds on a three-month-old Labrador Retriever has been set as the standard, but without better compression plates, even that modest goal cannot be reached."

Reed complained that without proper funding, the U.S. puppycrushing program would continue to suffer embarrassing setbacks, like the kind that occurred last month when 400 three-month-old border collies were only partially crushed by a defective hydraulic pump, leaving upwards of 200 semi-crushed collie pups writhing for several hours on the staging area floor and eventually bleeding to death.

"It was a really bloody, disgusting mess," Reed said, explaining why more

see PUPPYCRUSHER on page 4

Onion Photo/R. Ruban

With an extra $6 billion, researchers behind PupCrunch-2000 hope to upgrade technology (see right) to crush puppies at a never-before-accomplished rate of 400 per minute.

Special Focus

Will the increased funding for PupCrunch-2000 take much-needed funding away from other Defense Department projects, like ChickenRaper-K35 and GiraffeEviscerator-8000?

See our Special Report on p. 10.

Area Students Prepare Breasts for Increased Springtime Display

Onion Photo/R. Ruban

Students like this University of Colorado junior are excited to once again display their breasts, sporting form-fitting Urban Outfitter T-shirts in response to warm spring weather.

Female college students from across the northern U.S. celebrated the improved weather this week, preparing their breasts for the increased exposure and display that the warm weather now demands. For the last several months, the students' breasts have existed only in the imaginations and fond memories of others, obscured by baggy sweaters, bulky ski jackets, and shapeless flannel.

Yet, with the coming of spring, all that has changed, as students now slip into less fabric and fewer layers. Their breasts, like big cuddly honeybears wiping the sleep from their eyes as they emerge from hibernation, once again climb out into the

see BREASTS on page 6

Supreme Court Rules Tennesseeans Are Sentient Beings

WASHINGTON, D.C. (AP)—In a victory for advocates of states' rights, the U.S. Supreme Court ruled 5-4 yesterday that Tennessee citizens are sentient beings with a capacity to make certain decisions for themselves.

Chief Justice William Rehnquist, writing the Court's majority opinion, stated that, "The absence of higher forms of cognitive thinking skills on a statewide level does not preclude the application of the individual liberties guaranteed in the First Amendment to the residents of that state, no matter how strong the evidence is toward their

see SENTIENCE on page 12

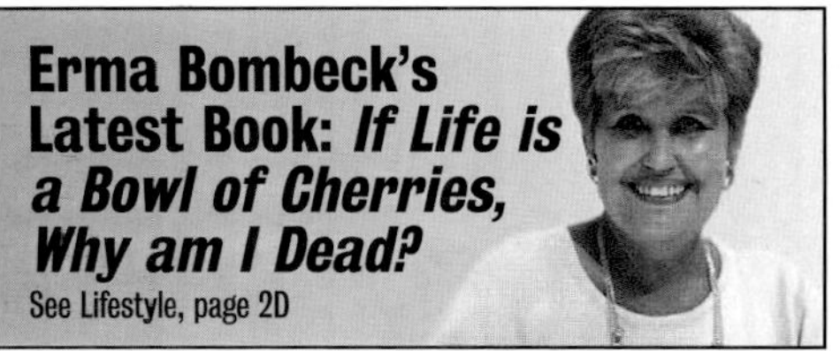
Erma Bombeck's Latest Book: *If Life is a Bowl of Cherries, Why am I Dead?*
See Lifestyle, page 2D

Sex Pistol Babies to Air This Summer on CBS
See Television, page 4C

A Celebration of Potted Meat Food Product
See Special Pull-out Section

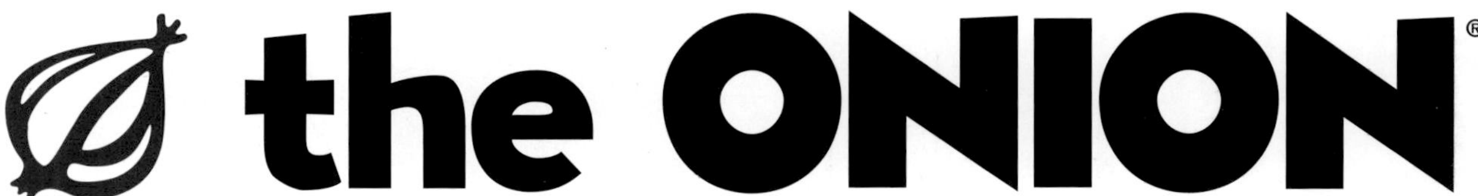

VOLUME 29 ISSUE 16 NUMBER ONE IN NEWS 1–7 MAY 1996

NEWS

IRA, Hamas Sweep 1996 Bombie Awards

See International Bombing, page 11

THE DOW

To hell with the DOW. This week's number represents the weight increase of my pathetic, lard-ass son. I hate you, boy.

TODAY'S ONION

Naval Concerns

U.S. Naval Officials Complain That a Recent Crackdown on Sexual Assault Will Hurt Recruitment Efforts

National News p. 21

Community Bulletin Board

Area Lemur Demands School Board Reform

p. 38

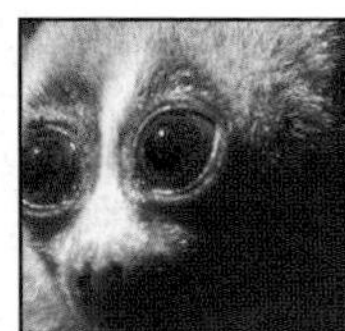

INSIDE

NEWS IN BRIEF 2
ADVENTURE 4
WHAT DO YOU THINK? 5
PATHETIC GEEK STORIES 8
DECLINE AND FALL CALENDAR 12
DRUNK OF THE WEEK 17
CULTURAL IDIOCY QUIZ 18
A-V CLUB 19
MOVIE LISTINGS 22
MUSIC 26
WORDS 28
SAVAGE LOVE 29
CALENDAR 30
CLASSIFIEDS 32

Deforestation Complete

Onion Photo/R. Ruban

The earth's surface, now a barren expanse of tree-less wasteland, will decompose at a rapid pace, causing cessation of all life on the planet by late June.

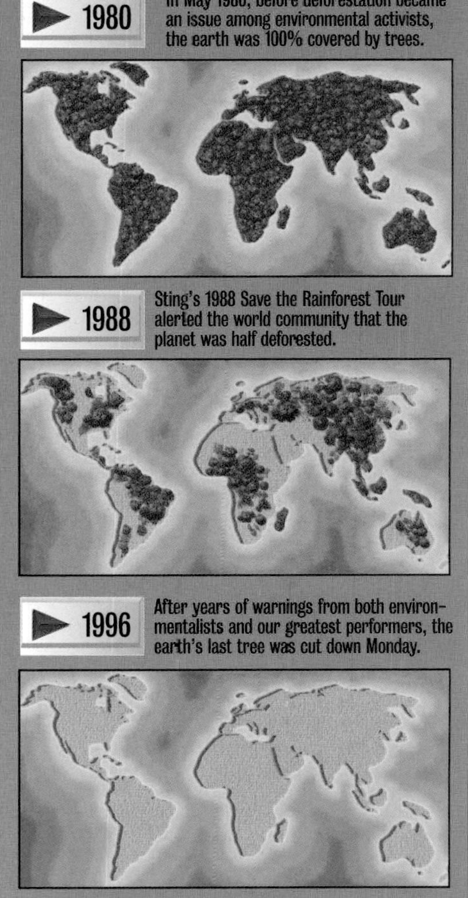

Global deforestation, the environmental disaster forewarned by eco-radicals since as far back as 1980, has finally and irreversibly arrived, spokespersons from Worldwide PulpCo announced Monday. The final tree, a 120-foot-tall Russian fir located near the timber line in a remote region of northwest Siberia, was cut down by PulpCo and converted into 10,000 sanitary straw wrappers for a major national fast-food chain.

With the elimination of trees, the earth's leading producer of oxygen, biologists believe all oxygen-dependent animal and plant species will soon become extinct.

"This is somewhat of a setback," PulpCo CEO Douglas Langley said. "But we want to assure our customers that we will continue our commitment to producing top-quality consumer paper products."

Ecologists predict that by late June, the planet will be littered with the unburied corpses of most, if not all, of the earth's fauna.

Despite the impending apocalypse, accountants for PulpCo assured shareholders in an emergency meeting that the company's earnings would continue see DEFORESTATION on page 8

Area Bassist Fellated

COLUMBUS, OH—According to reports, area musician Paul Simms, bass player for the local grunge/punk band The Dead Taybacks, was fellated early Sunday morning by an unknown woman. The fellatio, which occurred during a late-night party following a Dead Taybacks show at the Tar Pit in downtown Columbus, was described as "totally rockin'" by Simms, who formerly played bass for Claw Jockey.

A part-time college student who is currently looking for a place to stay, Simms was unable to identify his fellater, as he passed out shortly thereafter. Nonetheless, he remains optimistic about future occurrences of fellatio in his life, and credits his status as a band member for his fellatio success.

"The whole rock thing—the hair, the ripped clothes, the total disillusionment with the overwhelming, crushing commercialism of modern American life," said Simms, flipping his long, tousled locks out of his eyes with a flip of his hand. "Chicks dig it."

see FELLATED on page 4

Onion Photo/R. Ruban

Area bassist Paul Simms recently enjoyed oral sex. He attributed the fortuitous encounter to his status as a "rock" musician, which creates a tremendous sexual energy that makes him irresistible to "chicks."

the ONION®

VOLUME 29 ISSUE 21 | NUMBER ONE IN NEWS | 19 JUNE–9 JULY 1996

NEWS

Man with Flamethrower Waiting for Appropriate Time to Use It

See People, page 2D

WEATHER

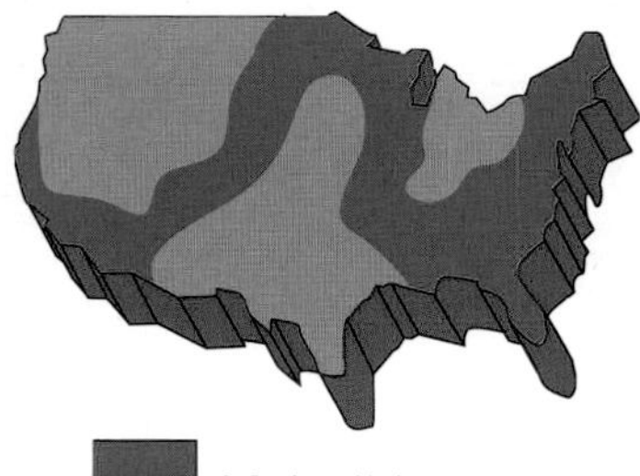

Golf ball-sized hail

Pail-sized hail

Alan Hale-sized hail

SPORTS

Royals pitcher Bob Reed hurled a no-hitter Monday, greatly increasing his chances of obtaining sexual favors this week in the Kansas City metropolitan area. See Sports, page 4A

INSIDE

NEWS IN BRIEF....................2
ONION INFO-GRAPHIC....................2
THE OPINION PAGE....................4
WHAT DO YOU THINK....................5
FUNNY BUSINESS....................16
DRUNK OF THE WEEK....................20
A-V CLUB....................21
MOVIE LISTINGS....................24
MUSIC....................26
WORDS....................28
SAVAGE LOVE....................29
CALENDAR....................30
CLASSIFIEDS....................32
PATHETIC GEEK STORIES....................34

New Study Shows Progress Made by Broads

A University of California-Berkeley study released Tuesday revealed that broads have made significant progress in the workplace over the past decade.

A comprehensive, long-term examination of the career paths of over 4,500 broads from across the U.S., the study indicates that broads are earning 15 percent more on average and are twice as likely to be in positions of upper management than just 10 years ago.

"This is a tremendously exciting, very promising report," said Stan Cullums, director of UC-Berkeley's famed Institute For Gender Research, which conducted the study. "After several decades of status quo and periodic retrenchment, it would appear that broads are finally beginning to make strides toward equality in the work-

see BROADS on page 8

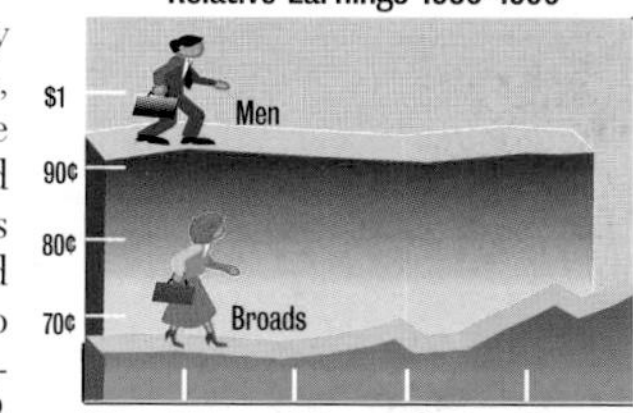

Amish Give Up

'This is bullshit,' elders say

Amish farmer Jakob Nordemann plans to sell his horse and buggy and to shave off his Pennsylvania Dutch-style beard—which he called "totally ridiculous."

Onion Photo/R. Ruban

LANCASTER, PA—After centuries of enduring harsh, spare living conditions and voluntarily shunning modern amenities such as microwave ovens and red clothing, Amish leaders announced Monday that Amish across the U.S. will abandon their traditional ways and adapt to modern American life.

"Fuck that," said Amish Father Ezekiel Schmid at a Lancaster press conference. "This is pure bullshit."

Schmid recounted the hard Amish life, in which many long hours are spent toiling under the hot sun in heavy black clothing without any refrigerated drinks or gas-powered farm machines. He spoke of the arduous task of raising barns by hand from dawn until dusk, and of laboriously churning his own butter without electrical power.

"I can't believe we were such suckers," Schmid said. "I feel like a fool."

Schmid added that he will shave off his "ridiculous" Pennsylvania Dutch-style beard with no mustache, a look he says went out of fashion in "about 1820."

"Why didn't anyone ever tell me how stupid I looked?" he said.

According to Schmid, the Amish look forward to a wide variety of "alternative lifestyle" opportunities that now await them.

"I am indeed looking forward to wearing clothing that is a color other than black," said Josephat Kreugger, a prominent

see AMISH on page 6

Clinton Sold

WASHINGTON, D.C.—President Clinton was sold at an invitation-only Sotheby's auction Sunday, purchased by well-known British financier Owen Barasman. Clinton, who went for $425,000, was the highlight of an auction that also included an original *Huckleberry Finn* manuscript, two rare Han Dynasty vases and several sets of expensive cutlery.

"I believe I was sold for a fair price," said Clinton, who was shipped to one of Barasman's private London galleries yesterday. "I look forward to being a part of his impressive collection of rare and beautiful artifacts."

Because of the auction, Clinton was forced to cut short a West Coast trip, during which he met with California Gov. Pete Wilson to survey flood damage in Northern California.

Sotheby's Photo

Sotheby's auction-goers enjoyed this sale item among the hundreds offered at Sunday's event.

"It will be difficult to complete my West Coast visit from this shelf," said Clinton, speaking from his new display area, between a Victorian-era porcelain figurine and 17th century English musket.

DNR Warns: U.S. Mayonnaise Reserves Dwindling

WASHINGTON, D.C.—The American condiment community reacted with shock Monday when the U.S. Department of Natural Resources announced that the nation's natural mayonnaise reserves, long thought sufficient to carry the country into the 21st century, are, in fact, running dangerously low.

"Because of record heat in the Southwest basin, the outer layer of our national reserves spoiled prematurely," DNR spokesperson David Korking said. "Millions of gallons of all-natural mayonnaise—mayonnaise that hundreds of species of waterfowl rely on to make wholesome egg salad—

see MAYONNAISE on page 8

the ONION®

VOLUME 29 ISSUE 23 | NUMBER ONE IN NEWS | 10–23 JULY 1996

NEWS

Science Fiction Fan Increases Suavity With Trenchcoat

See People, page 9C

WEATHER

Controlled by Indian chieftains

Controlled by British and French colonial settlers

Controlled by pre-Mormon tribes of ancient white Latter-Day Saints contacted by the risen Christ after ascension as documented in New Testament and revealed by the teachings of Joseph Smith

TOMORROW

Coming tomorrow in the Onion: Our '96 Sheep Guide!

INSIDE

NEWS IN BRIEF 2
ONION INFO-GRAPHIC 2
THE OPINION PAGE 4
WHAT DO YOU THINK 5
FUNNY BUSINESS 12
A-V CLUB 15
MOVIE LISTINGS 18
DRUNK OF THE WEEK 19
MUSIC 22
WORDS 24
SAVAGE LOVE 25
CALENDAR 26
CLASSIFIEDS 28
PATHETIC GEEK STORIES 30

Independent Investigation:
SPECIAL OLYMPICS FIXED
Many 'Winners' Found to Have Lost Badly

Scandal rocked the sports world yesterday when a secret investigation revealed that the Special Olympics, one of the nation's premier annual athletic competitions, is fixed.

According to the undercover probe, over the years hundreds and possibly thousands of participating athletes have been declared "winners," despite losing their respective contests, often by wide margins.

"I don't think there's anything 'winning' or 'special' about finishing in eighth or ninth place," chief investigator Harlan Brundage said. "Do these kids think they're winners just because they tried? Just because they gave it their all? Well, let me tell you, trying doesn't make you a winner. Coming in first does."

An estimated 15,000 athletes partici-

see OLYMPICS on page 6

A Scandal Uncovered:

Is there a history of double standards in Olympic competitions?

1980 ▶ Soviet Olympic weightlifter Vasiely Alexeev fails to lift qualifying weight: Wins no medal, is booed by Moscow crowd.

Special Olympian Davey Johnstone drops barbell on foot: Is treated to french fries at McDonald's by Dad.

1984 ▶ Olympic sprinter Mary Decker trips and falls: Finishes last and becomes symbol of defeat everywhere.

Special Olympian Susie Kravitz stops to wave at sister in crowd: Finishes last and is praised for "super effort."

1972 ▶ U.S. Olympic Basketball Team loses gold medal game on blown call by referee: Players refuse to accept silver medals to this day.

Special Olympic basketball team accidentally scores for opponents at buzzer: Players enjoy group hug with coach.

Catholic Church Allows Gays to Serve as Altar Boys

VATICAN CITY—In a radical break from centuries of strict church doctrine, the Pope approved a measure yesterday that would allow gay men and boys to be provisionally accepted into the Catholic Church.

According to the pontiff's new plan, gays will be allowed to serve as altar boys at all public and private church functions.

"It is high time the Catholic Church moved forward on the issue of homosexuality," said Cardinal John Valento, speaking on behalf of

see ALTAR BOYS on page 8

The new altar boys' duties include assisting with Holy Communion, lighting candles and helping clergy with bathing and dressing.

Nuclear Threat Still 'Very Real,' Says Muhammad Ali

LOUISVILLE, KY—Former world heavyweight boxing champ Muhammad Ali spoke out Monday against what he called "the ever-growing threat of thermonuclear war between the United States and the Soviet Union."

Ali, speaking from his Louisville home, made a personal appeal to Ronald Reagan and Mikhail Gorbachev to settle their differences at the discussion table, not on the field of battle.

"Things have gotten completely out of control," Ali said. "If we don't stop this Cold War now, tomorrow there may not be any planet left for the children."

Ali added that yellow is his favorite color. "It is a very pretty color. It reminds me of daffodils in the spring-

see ALI on page 31

Loveless Union Ends in Baby

ROCKFORD, IL—A loveless union resulted Monday in the birth of a baby who, according to area love experts, will almost certainly never receive the warm, nurturing love it needs to develop fully. Nor, they say, will it ever learn to show love for others in its lifetime.

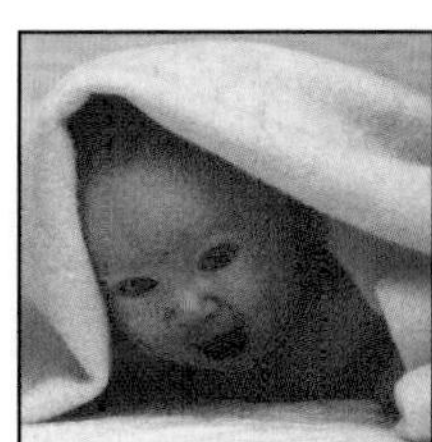

The unloved child of the Thurnblochs

The child, William Thurnbloch, Jr., was conceived in the hopes that its presence might function as a love substitute in the lives of its parents, William and Suzanne Thurnbloch, of Rockford. Sources agree this attempt is doomed to failure, and that the Thurnblochs will continue to live lives as devoid of love as ever before.

"I doubt either Bill or Suzanne ever fully comprehended what love was, and, therefore, never realized that their lives lacked love," Department of Love and Related Issues regional chairperson and psychotherapist Kent McNuhm said. "Nonetheless, a subconscious perception of the inherent emptiness of their lives drove them to reproduce."

McNuhm went on to cite the couple's total lack of interest in each other's daily lives, refusal to engage in conver-

see LOVELESS on page 8

Hootie and the Blowfish: Breaking Down Racial Barriers Between Black, White Pussies

See Music page 9G

Emperor Penguin Demands More Smelt

See Nature page 24

Mousy Brunette Removes Glasses, Becomes Sizzling Sexpot

See Lifestyle, page 41

the ONION®

VOLUME 30 ISSUE 2 | NUMBER ONE IN NEWS | 21–27 AUGUST 1996

NEWS

'Nothing Ordinary' About Multinational Chain of PepsiCo-Owned, Mexican-Themed Fast Food Outlets

See Business, page 5C

THE DOW

Sorry, no financial news. The Dow's trading floor hosted a school trip for troubled inner-city teens yesterday, so everybody went home early.

LOTTO

This week's jackpot: $7 million

Your share: zero

SPORTS

Inside—our 1996 NFL Preview, including a full-color action pullout of the Dallas Cowboys' top whore/pimp duo, Candii Walls and Leroy "Sugar" Epps.

See Football, page 1D

INSIDE

NEWS IN BRIEF....2
THE OPINION PAGE....4
WHAT DO YOU THINK....5
ONION INFO-GRAPHIC....5
PATHETIC GEEK STORIES....14
FUNNY BUSINESS....16
A-V CLUB....19
MOVIE LISTINGS....20
DRUNK OF THE WEEK....23
MUSIC....26
WORDS....28
SAVAGE LOVE....29
CALENDAR....30
CLASSIFIEDS....32

Reagan Pyramid Nears Completion

Builders expect the Reagan Pyramid to be ready in time for the Great Communicator's mummification and ascension into the Afterworld upon death. Among the items to be entombed with Reagan are 2,500 MX missiles, a golden chalice of jelly beans and his beloved servant, George Bush.

SIMI VALLEY, CA—Slave manpower was doubled this week in an effort to assure that erection of the gigantic Reagan Pyramid remains on schedule, and will be completed in time for the 40th President's mummification and ascension into the Afterworld upon death.

With doctors concurring that the former leader, suffering from Alzheimer's, is expected to die within two years, swift completion of the towering structure is "of paramount priority," according to Republican party insiders.

"Only the most gigantic tomb ever created will be worthy of the Great Communicator," said former Reagan Secretary of Defense Caspar Weinberger. "As his mortal subjects, it is our holy duty to provide Reagan with a burial commensurate with his stature, in order that he may enter the Realm of Death bedecked with raiments and honors so that he may take his rightful place beside the mighty Sun God, Ra."

From his ranch estate, the bedridden Reagan responded, saying, "Ra."

According to project overseer and

see REAGAN on page 13

Fed to Make Interest Rates Undulated Relaxingly

WASHINGTON, DC—In a major step toward establishing a more "soothing and peaceful" U.S. economy by Fiscal Year 1998, Federal Reserve Board Chairman Alan Greenspan announced yesterday that he will make the prime lending rate undulate relaxingly, moving back and forth in a restful, wavelike motion.

Noting the severely jarring ups and downs that have characterized the nation's economy over the last 18 months, Greenspan told a meeting of the House Ways and Means Committee:

Before

After

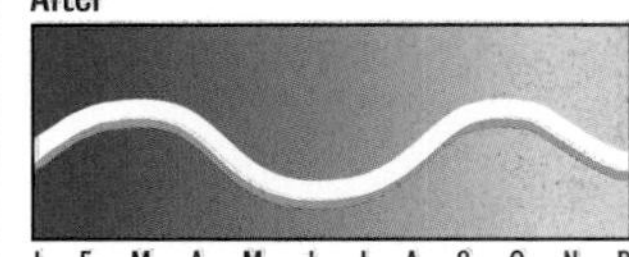

"We will manipulate the money supply in such a way that Americans feel as though they are being pleasantly lofted on a gentle ocean wave, up and down, up and down, crest following trough and trough following crest, over and over and over,

see UNDULATE on page 6

Man With Shirt Off Terrifies Community

MIDFORD, OHIO—Downtown Midford was rocked with terror yesterday when a man with his shirt off casually lounged in the sun, causing panic in the streets and striking desperate fear into the hearts of the town's citizenry.

The alleged perpetrator, Gary Dernbaum of nearby Plovis, was described by police and city officials as "frighteningly nonchalant" in his behavior, apparently unmoved by the state of stark terror his sweat-covered, flabby torso inspired in others.

Dernbaum, a third-shift auto assembly worker and NASCAR racing collectibles enthusiast, reportedly added insult to injury by spending most of his shirtlessness eating and drinking, devouring a chili dog "without remorse."

According to sources, Dernbaum also engaged in friendly conversation with several terror-struck passersby unlucky enough to make eye contact with him, greeting their stares of shock and repulsion with casual remarks like, "Gee, it's hot out!" and "Phew! Sweaty day today, huh?"

It is believed he also patted and slapped at his belly during a number of these verbal harangues, heightening witnesses' reactions to a fever-pitch crescendo of desperate panic and fear.

"It was horrible," said witness

see SHIRTLESS on page 8

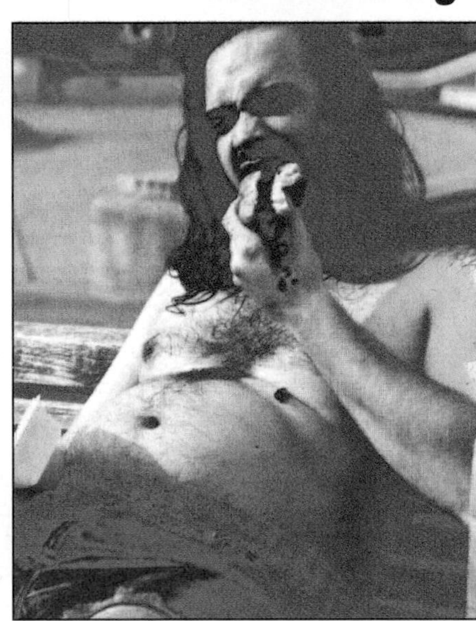

Gary Dernbaum's exposed torso threw Midford, OH, into a state of panic and chaos yesterday, forcing the governor to declare a state of "Visual Emergency."

Produce Manager Ready For Some Football

See Sports page 3C

Vatican Unveils New Rosary For Windows

See Computers page 24

Clinton Woos Gay Vote With Freddie Mercury Mustache

See Election, page 3A

the ONION®

VOLUME 30 ISSUE 4 | NUMBER ONE IN NEWS | 4–10 SEPTEMBER 1996

Mountain Dew Council of Elders Exiles Non-Radical Teen

From their hidden sanctuary high atop Mount Dew, the Mountain Dew Council Of Elders formally passed judgment on area teen Brian Ruderman yesterday, unanimously ruling him "not radical" and sentencing him to eternal banishment from the Extreme Network.

"To you, Brian Ruderman, we have said in the past, Do the Dew," Mountain Dew Highfather Snowboardus the Totally Radical said as the final verdict was delivered. "But from this day forth say we it no longer, saying to ye instead, Brian Ruderman, go forth from this place, leave us, and Do the Dew no more."

"You have been deemed not worthy," Mountain Dew Highfather Jetskius the Awesome stated. "You and your scions shall never again Grab It, Buy It or Slam It."

Ruderman, 18, who was brought before the ancient Council under allegations of showing cowardice in the face of rollerblade ramp-jumping and bicycle moto-cross skydiving, was unable to successfully defend himself after failing the "Trial By Bungee," a 500-year-old initiation ritual of the Order of Dew.

see ELDERS on page 10

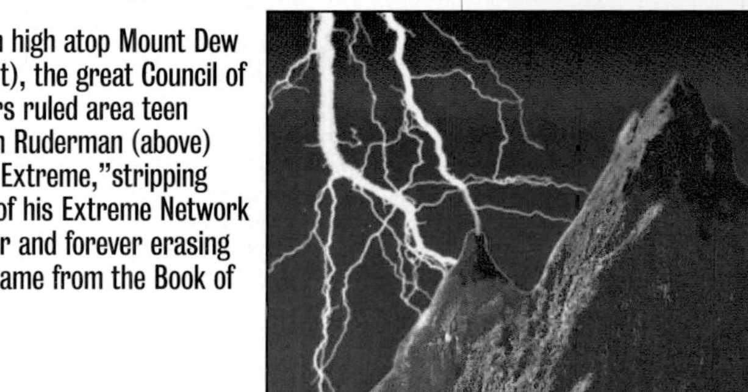

From high atop Mount Dew (right), the great Council of Elders ruled area teen Brian Ruderman (above) 'Not Extreme,"stripping him of his Extreme Network Pager and forever erasing his name from the Book of Dew.

NEWS

Area Ostrich Lashes Out Against Unnecessarily Restrictive Zoning Laws

See City, page 4D

WEATHER

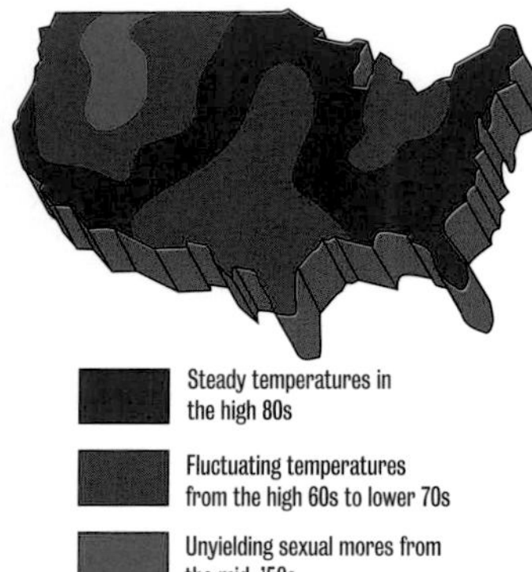

- Steady temperatures in the high 80s
- Fluctuating temperatures from the high 60s to lower 70s
- Unyielding sexual mores from the mid-'50s

NATION

The Republican Party crafted a bill yesterday that, if approved, would give handguns and semi-automatic rifles the right to vote.

See Law, page 7A

INSIDE

NEWS IN BRIEF....2
THE OPINION PAGE....4
WHAT DO YOU THINK....5
ONION INFO-GRAPHIC....5
PATHETIC GEEK STORIES....8
FUNNY BUSINESS....34
A-V CLUB....37
DRUNK OF THE WEEK....41
MOVIE LISTINGS....42
MUSIC....46
WORDS....50
SAVAGE LOVE....51
CALENDAR....53
CLASSIFIEDS....56

Inner-City Stabbings Leave Five Maidless

Highland Park, IL, residents Bunny and Peter Devlinger (right) were left with dirty towels and unmade beds when maid Georgette Davis (left) was stabbed 47 times in the neck and chest Sunday morning.

CHICAGO—A string of inner-city stabbings left five residents of Chicago's wealthy Highland Park suburb maidless this weekend.

According to police, the crimes seem to be related, in that all five residents were left without kitchen and dining room service for their morning meal.

"It was horrible," said Highland Park resident Edmund O. Rayburn. "We were left with no choice but to perform such tasks as making the bed, running cold water from the tap, and pulling out chairs for ourselves before sitting on them."

The Chicago Police Department is conducting a full-scale investigation of the interruption in maid service, and plans to issue a formal report to the Highland Park Gate and Security Service by the end of this week.

"We're doing everything we can to find the perpetrator," Police Chief Stan Jacoby said.

see MAIDLESS on page 6

Freemasons Return To Jupiter
See Secret Societies, page 7C

JFK Jr. Celebrates 10,000th Coupling
See People, page 5A

Area Mofo Announces Plans To Chill
See City, page 24

the ONION®

VOLUME 30 ISSUE 8 NUMBER ONE IN NEWS 2–8 OCTOBER 1996

NEWS

Coach Filmed Before Live Studio Audience

See Television, page 8G

WEATHER

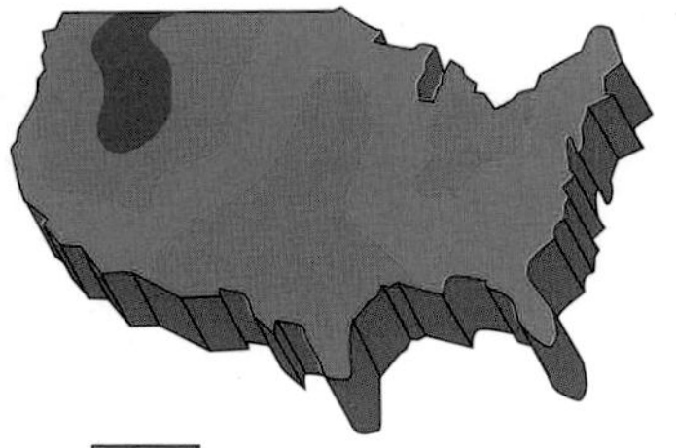

Partly cloudy and windy

Partly sunny and hot

Partly literate, reliant upon "blurb"-type print format

HEALTH

The RU-486 abortion pill was given tentative FDA approval this week, despite strong resistance from the Catholic Church and the American Stomach-Punchers Union.

See Nation, page 3A

INSIDE

NEWS IN BRIEF....2
THE OPINION PAGE....4
WHAT DO YOU THINK....5
ONION INFO-GRAPHIC....5
PATHETIC GEEK STORIES....8
FUNNY BUSINESS....14
A-V CLUB....17
MOVIE LISTINGS....20
DRUNK OF THE WEEK....24
MUSIC....26
WORDS....28
SAVAGE LOVE....29
CALENDAR....30
CLASSIFIEDS....32

Christopher Reeve Placed Atop Washington Monument

WASHINGTON, DC—One of America's most beloved landmarks, the Washington Monument, became all the more stirring and inspiring Monday with the addition of disabled actor Christopher Reeve.

Reeve, 44, paralyzed below the neck after a tragic equestrian mishap last year, was bolted to the pinnacle of the 555-foot monument and affixed with display spotlights for night viewing. He will remain there permanently, on 24-hour display.

"Christopher has shown himself to be a pillar of strength and courage who brings out the best in us all," said John Beaumont, Director of U.S. Parks and Services. "He was a logical addition to this already impressive monument. Once the idea was presented, nothing could stop us: not logistical problems, not budget constraints, not even the teary objections of Mr. Reeve."

The former *Superman* actor and his electric wheelchair were hoisted up the side of the towering obelisk by a tractor-powered cable pulley. Reeve was then welded to the pinnacle, facing east toward the Capitol, and bolted in place with iron slugs made from a cannonball fired at the battle of Yorktown.

A bronze plaque at the foot of the

see REEVE on page 6

Over 300,000 gathered at the Washington Monument Monday to watch Reeve's official bolting-in ceremony. Said Greensboro, NC, resident Cal Brewer: "I wish I had the courage to be crippled like that."

FAA To Require Longer Fuses on Commercial Planes

WASHINGTON, DC—In a move calculated to reduce significantly the number of catastrophic midair explosions aboard U.S. airliners, the FAA announced Monday that longer fuses will be required for all commercial air carriers beginning in 1997.

The move toward longer fuses began earlier this year when the older, shorter fuses on several commercial flights, including TWA's infamous Flight 800, burned all the way down to the fuselage and into the airplanes' detonators, causing them to explode in mid-air.

"This is a step in the right direction," U.S. Secretary of Transportation Federico Peña said. "No longer will passengers on long trips be sent into fits of panic as they watch their airplane's fuse sputtering inexorably shorter and shorter, sobbing hysterically in the fear that they may not reach the ground before being engulfed in a fireball thousands of feet in the air."

Peña added that to help make flights more enjoyable for passengers, the new

see FUSES on page 12

Sports Fan Killed in Tragic Home Entertainment Center Collapse

MENASHA, WI—Local resident Stan Blaskowitz, a self-described "sports fanatic," was crushed and killed Sunday, when his seven-foot, 900-pound home entertainment center fell on him during the final seconds of a televised Green Bay Packers game.

"It was horrible," said friend and neighbor Bill Gustafson, who was a witness to the tragic accident. "I think the Pack could really go all the way this year."

According to Outagamie County coroners, Blaskowitz and several other Green Bay faithful decided to watch the game on Blaskowitz's living room television set because of its state-of-the-art nature, boasting a 27-inch screen, a built-in digital satellite system and stereo Surround Sound. Ironically, these were the same factors that coroners say contributed to his death by crushing.

According to eyewitness accounts, the fatal accident occurred during the closing seconds of the fourth quarter. Blaskowitz, a longtime forklift operator at the Kimberly-Clark paper mill, was kneeling on the carpet in front of the entertainment center, having been pulled from his chair by the dra-

see SPORTS FAN on page 8

Stan Blaskowitz, 1965–1996

Drug Use By Jerry Garcia Down 85 Percent
See People page 1C

Victor Hugo's *Les Lunchables* To Hit Broadway
See Theater page 7D

Another Pufferfish Dies Bitter And Friendless
See Ocean Life, page 6B

the ONION®

VOLUME 30 ISSUE 13 — NUMBER ONE IN NEWS — 6–12 NOVEMBER 1996

NEWS

Tony Randall Secedes From Union; Declares Himself Independent Nation of Randalia

See Nation, page 3A

DOW

Trading on Wall Street was heavy yesterday, but not nearly as heavy as my wide-load of a wife.

LOCAL

The girls' monkey bars at Parkhurst Elementary were found to be contaminated Monday, tainted by Kenny Powell, a cootie-carrying third-grade boy.

See Schools, page 11B

INSIDE

NEWS IN BRIEF 2
THE OPINION PAGE 4
WHAT DO YOU THINK 5
ONION INFO-GRAPHIC 5
PATHETIC GEEK STORIES 8
DRUNK OF THE WEEK 25
FUNNY BUSINESS 26
A-V CLUB 29
MOVIE LISTINGS 32
MUSIC 36
WORDS 38
SAVAGE LOVE 39
CALENDAR 42
CLASSIFIEDS 44

General Motors Introduces New Instant-Win Airbags

DETROIT—With third-quarter sales sluggish and its share of the domestic market down 11 percent since 1993, General Motors unveiled a new instant-win airbag contest Monday.

The new airbags, which award fabulous prizes upon violent, high-speed impact with another car or stationary object, will come standard in all of the company's 1997 cars.

"Auto accidents have never been so exciting," said GM vice-president of marketing Roger Jenkins, who expects the contest to boost

see AIRBAGS on page 18

Low Voter Turnout Blamed On Election-Day Zombie Attacks

WASHINGTON, DC—Political observers expressed disappointment over Tuesday's low voter turnout, citing a rash of election-day attacks by cannibalistic, reanimated corpses of the recently deceased—*flesh-eating zombies from beyond the grave!*

"Everything is under control," Speaker of the House Newt Gingrich said at an emergency joint session of Congress. "National Guardsmen have been dispatched to problem areas, and I am fully confident in their ability to restore order. *We are doomed! Every dead body will get up and kill! The people they kill will get up and kill!*"

According to pollsters, the low election-day turnout is not surprising. "Historically, fewer people vote when conditions outside are bad," said Debra Patton of the Washington, D.C.-based MediaWatch Institute. "Examples of this sort of inclement weather include rain, snow and *unstoppable tides of walking corpses from the gates of Hell itself!*"

"Whether these zombie attacks will ultimately affect the outcome of the election is difficult to say," said Hannah Redding, Harvard University pro-

see ZOMBIES on page 6

ON MUNICIPAL BUILDI

Vote Here

Zombies, seen here attacking a photographer, are believed to have caused voters to shy away from polling places.

Israel Intercepts Massive Palestinian Rock Shipment

NABLUS, GAZA STRIP (AP)—Israeli troops patrolling the border of the Gaza Strip breathed a sigh of relief Monday as state-of-the-art Israeli customs-searching equipment intercepted a large shipment of rocks bound for Palestinian youth demonstrators.

It is believed that the shipment came from a rogue Soviet republic willing to sell rocks to the highest bidder on the international arms market.

The value of the shipment—250 crates filled with rocks, pebbles and gravel—is estimated in the neighborhood of 800 million dinar (about $6).

The rocks, mostly small, one-hand throwing rocks, were concealed in large crates of medical supplies being sent to PLO camps near the Israel-Jordan border.

Israeli officials vowed to track down the supplier of the weapons. "Whatever secret underground rock smugglers have been outfitting the Palestinians, we will find them," Israeli Defense Minister Avi Birkot said. "Rocks like these could really hurt someone."

According to munitions expert James Wolk, if thrown with enough force and accuracy, the seized rocks "could create permanent scuff marks in an Israeli tank, and possibly even make a small dent."

"The world is still a very dangerous place," Secretary of State Warren Christopher said in an offical U.S. statement.

Israeli soldiers (above) guard crates of intercepted Soviet rocks bound for Palestinian youth demonstrators. The weapons are valued at 800 million dinar, or about $6.

Jews Begin To Make Presence Felt in Entertainment Law

See Business, page 3B

Soul Train Discontinues Service To Des Moines

See Nation, page 7D

Bob Hope Remembered

See People, page 1C

the ONION®

VOLUME 30 ISSUE 14 | NUMBER ONE IN NEWS | 13-19 NOVEMBER 1996

NEWS

Baseball Hero Hits Homer For Dying Billionaire

See Sports, page 1D

WEATHER

Lava covers entire land surface

Light lava coverage in a.m., sunny

Slight chance of lava in evening

PEOPLE

Inside: An exclusive interview with a pair of rock legends. Heart's Ann and Nancy Wilson.

See Music, page 11B

INSIDE

THE OPINION PAGE 4
WHAT DO YOU THINK 5
ONION INFO-GRAPHIC 5
NEWS IN BRIEF 6
PATHETIC GEEK STORIES 14
FUNNY BUSINESS 18
A-V CLUB 21
MOVIE LISTINGS 24
DRUNK OF THE WEEK 27
MUSIC 28
WORDS 30
SAVAGE LOVE 31
CALENDAR 32
CLASSIFIEDS 36

Immigration Officials Beef Up U.S.-Mexican Border With Pure Beef

A Mexican attempts to jump over the 15-foot-high wall of beef guarding the U.S. border. Minutes after this photo was taken, the man was captured and returned to Mexico, unsuccessful but fully satiated.

EL PASO, TX—In an effort to beef up security measures along the U.S.-Mexican border, the U.S. Immigration and Naturalization Service announced Monday that the border will soon be fortified with 1,200 miles of pure beef.

"America has drawn a line in the sand," INS official Frank Wilhelm said. "And that line is made of meat."

According to Wilhelm, the immense, 15-foot-high wall of pure beef, which will extend from the Pacific to the Gulf of Mexico along the Rio Grande, will make border crossing all but impossible.

"This beef will be cooked sizzling hot, so hot that it will be extremely painful to climb over," said INS chief Kent Roker. "And even if a Mexican does get across, they will be so full that they won't run far."

Just this morning, Ciudad Juárez,

see BEEF-UP on page 10

New Fox Sitcom Outrageous

LOS ANGELES—According to television industry insiders, a new Fox sitcom scheduled to debut Nov. 17 is outrageous.

The new program, *Sweet Georgia Washington*, stars rapper Sandy "Pepa" Denton (of Salt-n-Pepa fame) as Georgia Washington, a wise-cracking, back-sassing White House maid who interferes with political affairs each week, stirring up major trouble for the President (Howard Hesseman).

"When you see this new show," said longtime television executive Myron Bell, "I think you will understand why it is being called 'the outrageous new comedy from the creators of *Martin*.'"

As a recent Fox commercial for *Sweet Georgia Washington* announced, "This Sunday night, the federal government is about to get hit... *below the beltway*."

According to Morton Zollner, Fox senior vice-president of marketing, the key to the new sitcom is its no-holds-barred uproariousness. "You won't believe some of the things that Georgia does," Zollner said. "For example, in the first episode, an old friend from high school comes to visit, and to impress her, Georgia gets the prime minister of Israel to pretend to be her boyfriend."

"I won't give away the end," Zollner said, "but let's just say it's outrageous."

Sweet Georgia Washington airs Sundays at 8 p.m., right after *Cuttin' the Phat!*, starring Sinbad as the director of an inner-city weight-loss camp.

Clinton Invents New Steam-Powered Contraption To Fix Economy

'Fabulous Financiamalizer' To Boost GNP, Lower Interest Rates

WASHINGTON, DC—President Clinton, in a bold move toward economic restructuring, announced the financial agenda for his second term Monday: economic stimulation through application of the "Fabulous Financiamalizer," a fanciful steam-powered contraption of his own devising.

"My fellow Americans, I come before you today to flaunt a very miracle of modern science," Clinton said at a press conference Monday, sporting a plum-colored velvet tuxedo and top hat, as well as a newly grown black handlebar mustache.

Clinton spoke while standing next to the prototype Financiamalizer, a 20-foot-high maze of tubing and whirling discs painted in spiral patterns, connected to a simmering steam boiler. "Girls, grab onto your boyfriends," Clinton continued, "lest you become faint of heart at the magnificent machinations of Professor W. Jefferson Clinton's Fabulous Financiamalizer."

He then began his demonstration by spinning a large valve wheel at the base of the contraption, funneling steam into a bellows-like component

see FINANCIAMALIZER on page 11

At a press conference Monday, Professor W. Jefferson Clinton (right) unveiled the amazing new Financiamalizer.

Floppy-Armed Robot Repeatedly Warns: 'Danger'
See Astronomy page 8D

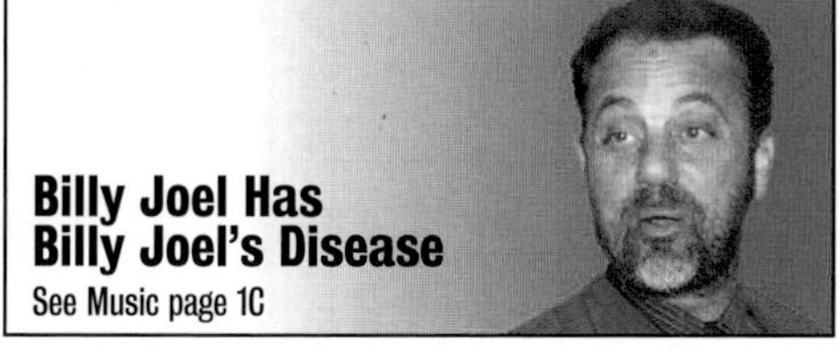
Billy Joel Has Billy Joel's Disease
See Music page 1C

New Candy To Hum And Glow In Mouths
See Product Watch, page 4B

the ONION®

VOLUME 30 ISSUE 18 NUMBER ONE IN NEWS 11–17 DECEMBER 1996

NEWS

Newly Discovered Fossils Reveal Prehistoric Humans Were Bony

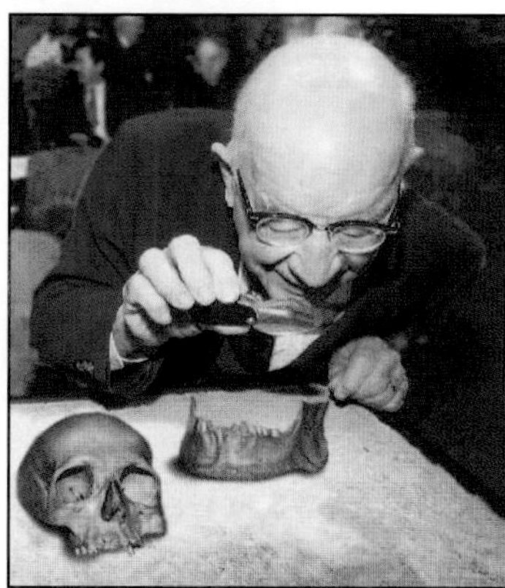
See Science, page 2D

WEATHER

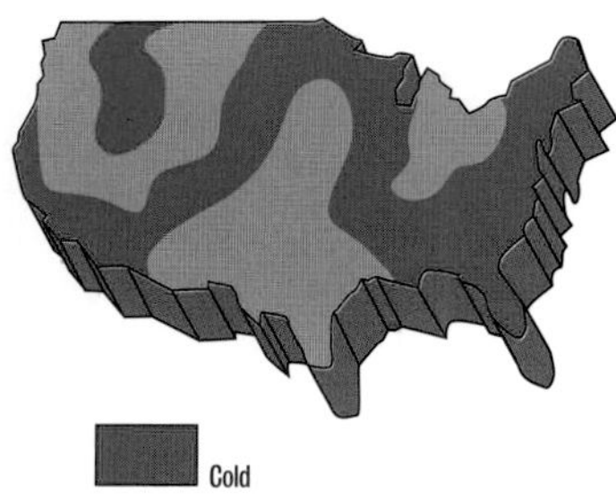

TELEVISION

Tonight, 8 p.m.: Harrison Ford co-stars with Lindsay Wagner and Peter Mayhew in ABS's new *Star Wars* made-for-TV movie, *They Took My Wookie.*

INSIDE

NEWS IN BRIEF..........2
THE OPINION PAGE..........4
WHAT DO YOU THINK..........5
ONION INFO-GRAPHIC..........5
PATHETIC GEEK STORIES..........8
FUNNY BUSINESS..........22
A-V CLUB..........25
MOVIE LISTINGS..........28
DRUNK OF THE WEEK..........31
MUSIC..........32
WORDS..........34
SAVAGE LOVE..........35
CALENDAR..........36
CLASSIFIEDS..........40

NASA, NASCAR Merge

Above: The Space Shuttle Endeavor (#17) prepares to make its move on Dale Jarrett (#88) during its qualifying run for the Purolator 500 in Murfreesboro, TN.

CAPE CANAVERAL, FL—In an effort to generate excitement and public support for America's struggling space program, NASA announced Monday that it will join the wildly popular NASCAR racing circuit in time for the 1997 season.

"Despite all our efforts to stir up enthusiasm, Americans still view the space program as boring and a waste of money," said NASA Director of Public Relations Boyd Connington, explaining the merger with NASCAR. "We've tried everything—record-setting manned space orbits; discovery of lunar ice formations; photographic evidence of life on Mars. But nothing we've done has captured the public's imagination quite like the thrill of seeing Ricky Rudd fly around a track at upwards of 170 mph."

The NASACAR Space Shuttle, which boasts such sponsors as Sunoco and Gold Bond Medicated Powder and is piloted by veteran driver Ernie Irvan, made its debut Sunday at the Slick 50 300 at the Talladega Speedway in Talladega, FL. Despite averaging 2,300 mph, the shuttle finished dead last in its inaugural race,

see NASACAR on page 14

Unprecedented Ass Expansion Threatens Area Pantsuit

NEW ROCHELLE, NY—Preservationists throughout the nation are expressing alarm at what they call an "unprecedented" rate of ass expansion within the confines of a New Rochelle-area pantsuit.

According to a study released Monday by the activist group PantsWatch, the pantsuit, a Jaclyn Smith-brand outfit purchased in 1992, could suffer irreparable damage within the next six months if the ass expansion were to continue unchecked.

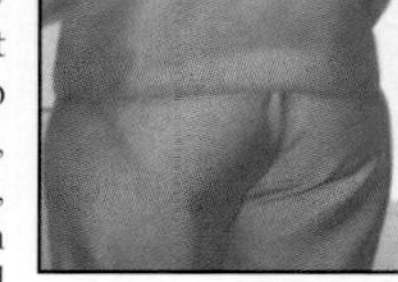
The ass

"The current ass expansion rate is nearly double that of last year. Containment of the emergent assosphere is becoming less and less viable," PantsWatch's Brent Klarman said. "This ass must not be allowed to destroy vital stitching. We can not idly stand by and allow this ass to continue its relentless growth beyond the already-allocated fabric zone."

Among the study's alarming claims are a 40 percent increase in seam stress, a 23 percent rise in

see ASS on page 12

Inner Cities To Receive Soothing Heroin

WASHINGTON, DC—In a humanitarian relief effort expected to greatly ease the pain of America's blighted inner cities, the federal government will begin importing and distributing the wonder-drug heroin to the growing urban underclass, President Clinton announced Monday.

Citing "the horrible pain of life in America's urban centers," Clinton urged all Americans living below the poverty line to begin using the substance immediately and "forget the daily agonies of your unceasingly horrific lives in a mind-numbing rush of glorious, opiate-induced oblivion."

"A lighter, a spoon, some cotton balls and a syringe are all America needs to end the misery of poverty forever," Clinton continued. "Poor people of the nation everywhere dream of a way out of the ghetto, and I am here to tell them: Do not give up on that dream. America, heroin is that way out."

Government officials were unanimous in their support for the president's plan.

President Clinton displays one of the needles that will soon pump sweet relief into America's blighted inner cities (right).

"This stuff is unbelievable—we're talking 100 percent pure unrefined China White," U.S. Sen. Trent Lott (R-MS) said. "Our nation's poor are clearly going to be on cloud nine once this 'mainline' hits the vein."

see HEROIN on page 6

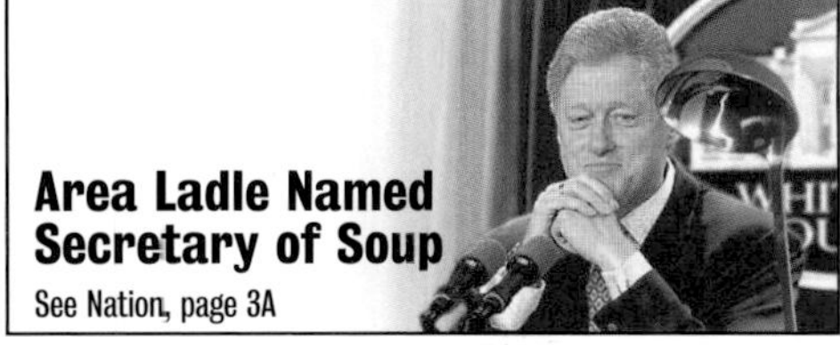

the ONION®

VOLUME 30 ISSUE 19 NUMBER ONE IN NEWS 18 DECEMBER 1996–14 JANUARY 1997

NEWS

Middle East Crisis Traced To Trouble-Making Genie

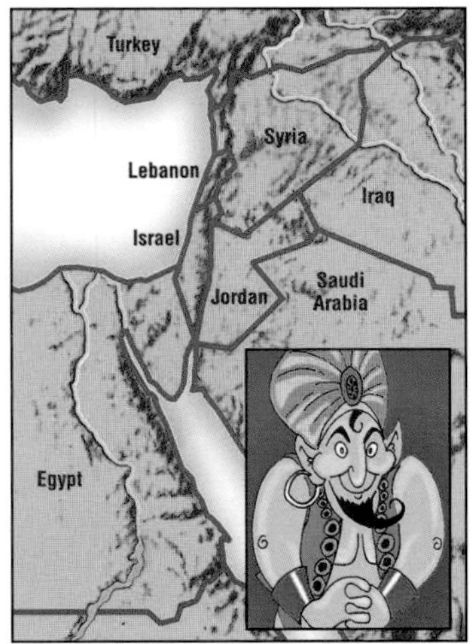

See World, page 2A

DOW

The Dow soared yesterday. If you don't get me a table right now, I'll have your job, you two-bit waitress bimbo.

TELEVISION

Tonight, 8 p.m.: Patti LaBelle, Ashford and Simpson, Sinbad and Heavy D. are among the guests scheduled to appear on ABC's *A Bryan Adams Kwanzaa.*

INSIDE

NEWS IN BRIEF..........2
THE OPINION PAGE..........4
WHAT DO YOU THINK..........5
ONION INFO-GRAPHIC..........5
PATHETIC GEEK STORIES..........8
FUNNY BUSINESS..........18
A-V CLUB..........23
MOVIE LISTINGS..........26
DRUNK OF THE WEEK..........29
MUSIC..........30
WORDS..........32
SAVAGE LOVE..........33
CALENDAR..........34
CLASSIFIEDS..........36

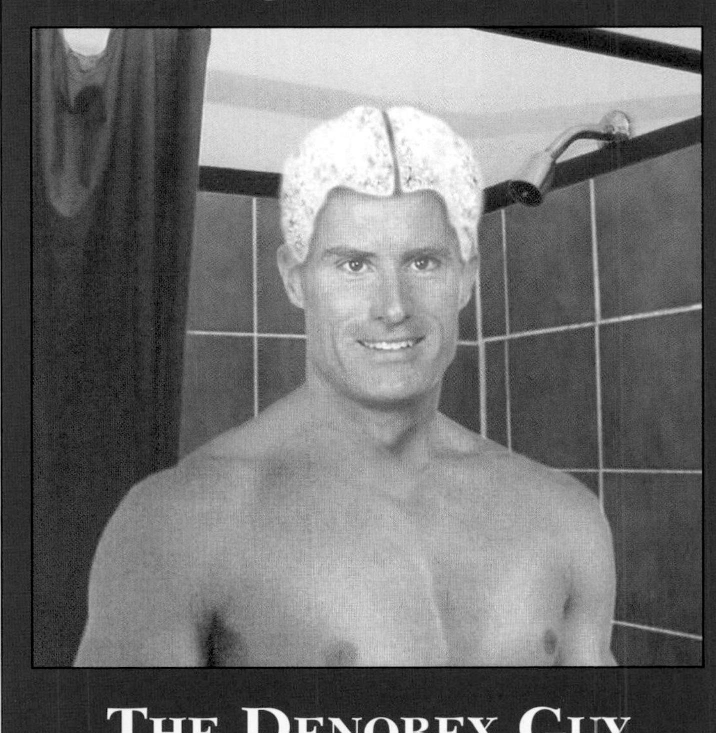

THE DENOREX GUY

Ever since *Onion* publisher T. Herman Zweibel was first awarded the honor in 1921, *The Onion*'s Man Of The Year has ranked among the most prestigious and time-honored traditions in journalism. Though there are many who make and shape our world, only one can be chosen *The Onion*'s Man Of The Year.

A roster of past selections reads as a veritable who's-who of history's towering figures: John Ritter, My Dad, The Guy From The *Police Academy* Movies Who Makes Funny Noises With His Mouth, President Bill Climpton, The San Diego

see DENOREX on page 6

Baseball Imposes Tough New 'Three-Strikes-You're-Out' Rule

NEW YORK—Saying it is time to "get tough on hitters," Acting Commissioner of Baseball Bud Selig announced Monday the adoption of a hard-line "Three-Strikes-You're-Out" policy on all at-bats.

"The American people are sick and tired of the same batters coming to the plate and taking pitch after pitch," said Selig after a day-long closed-door session of the Rules Committee of Major League Baseball. "There comes a point where we have to draw the line and say, 'Okay, you've had your chance, and you blew it. You are doing harm to your team and to your fans, and you are going to spend the rest of your half-inning in the dugout.'"

The strict new rule will replace the previous system, under which the number of opportunities a hitter had to put the ball in play was subject to the discretion of the umpires. Among the factors umpires had previously taken into account: difficulty of pitch thrown, degree of pressure from fans and teammates to get a hit, socio-economic condition of the batter, and whether or not he showed any remorse for previous failed at-bats.

But according to the drafted formulation of the new rule, slated to go into effect at the start of the 1997 season,

see BASEBALL on page 14

Experts Predict On-Line World Of Next Century To Feature More Breasts

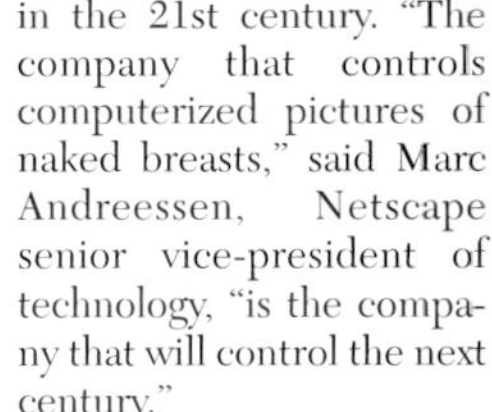

PALO ALTO, CA—Government officials, computer scientists and leading information-technology figures from around the globe met at the annual International CyberTechnology Summit at Stanford University this past weekend to discuss the future of the Internet. And that future, they say, will be graced with an ever-increasing quantity of naked breasts.

Despite differing on many Internet issues, all attendees were united in one basic belief: The Internet is a revolution in communications that will radically alter the way we access and view breasts in the 21st century. "The company that controls computerized pictures of naked breasts," said Marc Andreessen, Netscape senior vice-president of technology, "is the company that will control the next century."

Netscape, whose Navigator is currently the world's most popular breast-server program, is in a posi-

see BREASTS on page 12

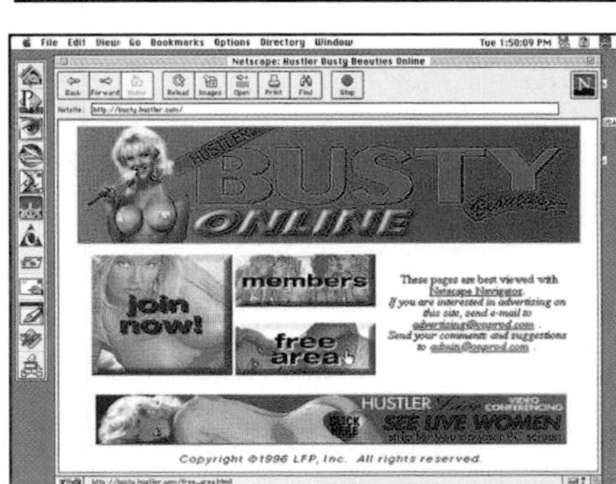

With its recent acquisition of the *Hustler* Archives (right), Microsoft is in a position to become the world's leading breast-server well into the 21st century.

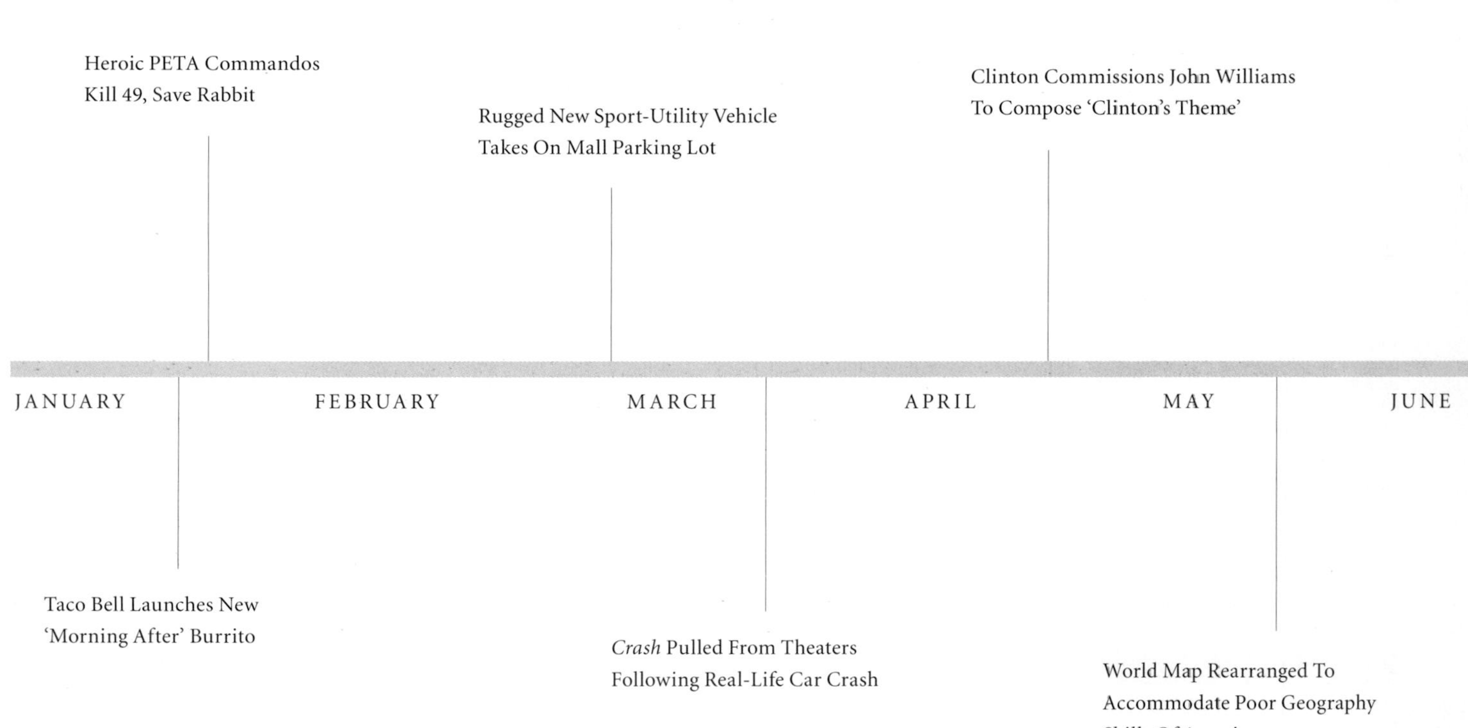
Heroic PETA Commandos
Kill 49, Save Rabbit
Rugged New Sport-Utility Vehicle
Takes On Mall Parking Lot
Clinton Commissions John Williams
To Compose 'Clinton's Theme'
JANUARY
FEBRUARY
MARCH
APRIL
MAY
JUNE
Taco Bell Launches New
'Morning After' Burrito
Crash Pulled From Theaters
Following Real-Life Car Crash
World Map Rearranged To
Accommodate Poor Geography
Skills Of Americans

1997

Alzheimer's Disease Sufferers Demand Cure For Pancakes

Girl Scouts Rocked By 'Cookies For Cash' Fundraising Scandal

Freshman Term Paper Discovers Something Totally New About *Silas Marner*

JULY AUGUST SEPTEMBER OCTOBER NOVEMBER DECEMBER

EPA Places Good Single Men On Endangered Species List

New Urban Visor Blocks Out The Poor

National Security Commission Warns Clinton: 'The Call Is Coming From *Inside The House*'

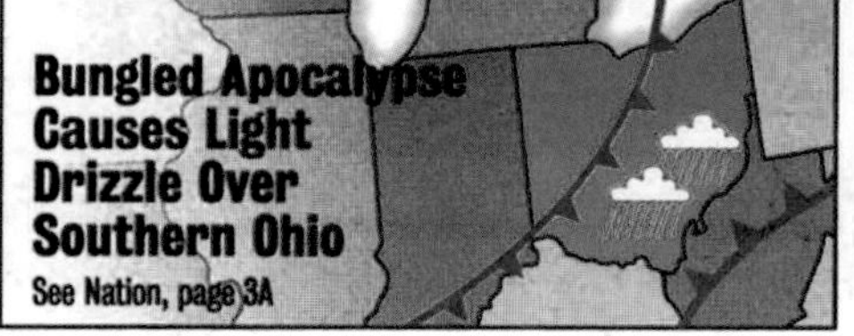

the ONION®

VOLUME 31 ISSUE 1 — NUMBER ONE IN NEWS™ — 15–21 JANUARY 1997

NEWS

Islamic Fundamentalists Condemn Casual Day

See Middle East, page 2A

DOW

The Dow rose 11 points yesterday. See this tie? This tie cost more than you make in a month.

PEOPLE

Controversial "gangsta" rapper Tha Grimm Reefah, who shot himself in the foot last week, now blames his own music for the accident.

See Music, page 7D

INSIDE

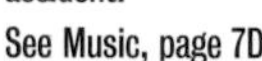

NEWS IN BRIEF....4
THE OPINION PAGE....6
WHAT DO YOU THINK....7
ONION INFO-GRAPHIC....7
PATHETIC GEEK STORIES....8
A-V CLUB....11
MOVIE LISTINGS....14
MUSIC....12
SAVAGE LOVE....21
CALENDAR....16
CLASSIFIEDS....22

ABC Cancels *Yeltsin!*

LOS ANGELES—ABC announced Monday that it is cancelling *Yeltsin!*, the struggling two-year-old sitcom starring Russian president Boris Yeltsin.

Though network executives did not give a reason for the cancellation, it is believed that Yeltsin's poor comedic skills—including his oafish, mistimed delivery of his character's catchphrase, "You got that right, sister!"—were to blame.

Writers for the show were also frustrated by the star's frequent comas, which made it "nearly impossible" for the Russian premier to memorize his lines.

"Sooner or later," *Entertainment Weekly* television critic Owen McCready said, "the

see YELTSIN on page 6

Fifth-Period Gym Class Under Investigation For Failure To Hustle

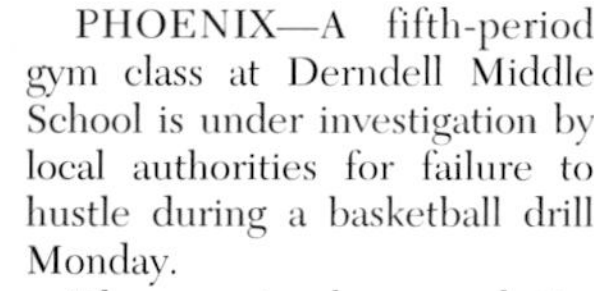

Left: Students in Coach Peeler's fifth-period gym class could be trying a lot harder, officials say.

PHOENIX—A fifth-period gym class at Derndell Middle School is under investigation by local authorities for failure to hustle during a basketball drill Monday.

The gym teacher, coach Irv Peeler, is cooperating with authorities and has not been charged.

"I did everything I could," Peeler said in a press conference Monday. "I yelled, 'Come on, people, let's go, let's move,' and when that produced no effect, I yelled, 'Let's see some hustle out there.' But even then I could discern no evidence of hustling."

Peeler went on to say that the students displayed "very poor" effort.

Eyewitness testimony corroborates allegations that even during warm-up exercises, at least a dozen students failed to rotate fully during trunk twists, and that "a significant number" also failed to "adequately bend at the knees" during squat thrusts.

Among those named in the investigation were Brian Ericks, Dan Chester, Howie Goldberg, Tim Miraglia and Todd Pollack.

The report also indicated that of the 30 pupils in the class, six failed to come to class dressed in the proper gym gear. Those six

see HUSTLE on page 18

RC Cola Celebrates 10th Purchase

ALBANY, NY—Employees at Royal Crown Cola are jubilant in the wake of the 10th product sale in the company's 68-year history.

"This is a historic day for RC Cola," Royal Crown CEO Tad Lipscomb said. "Our tenacity and dedication to providing a top-rate cola beverage have finally paid off. The double-digit barrier was a difficult hurdle that we have been approaching for decades, but now the sky is the limit."

The milestone sale took place Monday afternoon, when Ames, IA, resident Stephen Dutchins, 81, purchased a two-liter bottle of the wildly unpopular cola at a local Food Lion grocery store. "They put the Coke and Pepsi on the top shelf, and I couldn't reach them," Dutchins told reporters. "I decided my thirst was significant enough to justify buying an unknown brand."

Added Dutchins: "My wife died several years ago."

"We are proud that Mr. Dutchins chose to switch to crisp, refreshing RC Cola," said Lipscomb. "And we anticipate a long, productive relationship with our newest family member."

For pushing the cola manufacturer over the nine mark, Dutchins was awarded a case of RC, bringing the company's number of consumed servings to 34.

see RC COLA on page 8

Pain To Reach New Levels

WASHINGTON, DC—Though already extremely painful, the physical sensation of pain will become markedly greater in the coming months, continuing to rise exponentially throughout 1997, sources say.

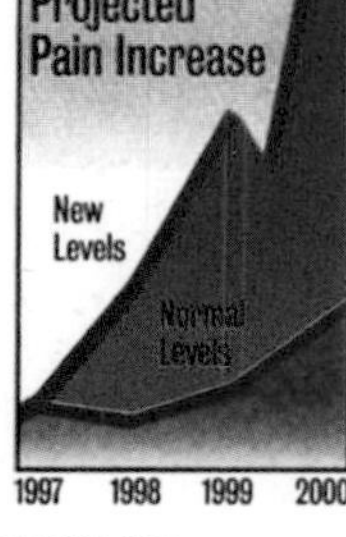

According to a recent report released by the U.S. Department of Agony and Suffering, even levels of pain currently considered unbearable will seem mild compared to the beyond-excruciating jolts of

see PAIN on page 14

See Science, page 2D

See People, page 8D

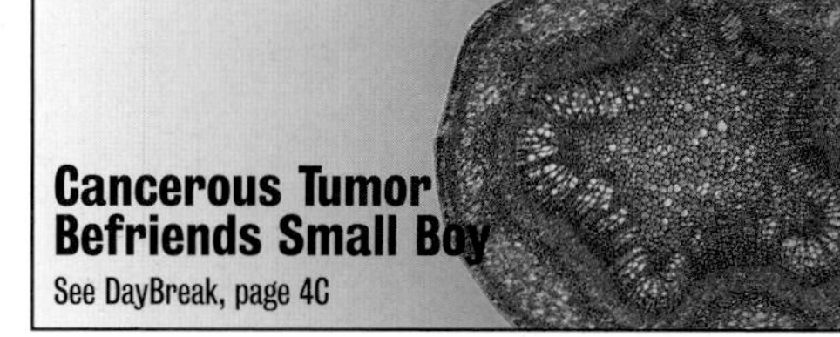

See DayBreak, page 4C

the ONION®

VOLUME 31 ISSUE 5 NUMBER ONE IN NEWS™ 12–18 FEBRUARY 1997

NEWS

Protesters Ignored

See Nation, page 2A

WEATHER

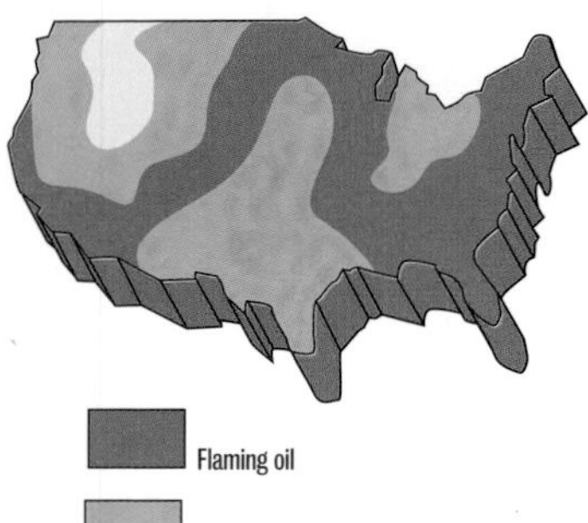

Flaming oil

Lake of pain

Tortured screams of damned

DOW

The Dow leapt several feet in the air yesterday, catching a frisbee in its mouth before taking off, running down the beach. It then sat down again and panted happily in the shade.

INSIDE

NEWS IN BRIEF....2
THE OPINION PAGE....4
WHAT DO YOU THINK....5
ONION INFO-GRAPHIC....5
PATHETIC GEEK STORIES....8
DRUNK OF THE WEEK....17
FUNNY BUSINESS....18
A-V CLUB....21
MOVIE LISTINGS....24
MUSIC....28
WORDS....30
SAVAGE LOVE....31
CALENDAR....33
CLASSIFIEDS....36

New 'Small 'n' Flaccid' Ad Campaign Least Successful Ever

ONION AdWatch

Chicago ad agency Meacham, Ellis & Young is the talk of the industry this week in the wake of the public's overwhelmingly negative reaction to its much-trumpeted, multimillion-dollar "Small 'n' Flaccid" advertising campaign for Merit cigarettes.

The $450 million ad blitz, the subject of the most intense pre-release media hype since last year's famous "Mmm-mmm, Mama, Show Me What'cha Got" campaign for Burger King, was expected to vault Merit to the top of the $800 billion cigarette industry.

Despite high expectations, the campaign and its slogan, "Merit—Makin' You Feel All Small 'n' Flaccid" has met with universal and complete failure.

see FLACCID on page 12

Clinton Holds Summit With Magic Turtle

WASHINGTON, DC—Crime, health care and campaign finance reform were the top issues on the agenda for President Clinton's breakfast meeting with a magic turtle at the White House Monday.

Clemens

Government insiders say the turtle, in Washington for a brief visit before returning to his Enchanted Gooseberry Glade, is the administration's leading hope for solutions to some of the top issues facing the nation. The White House also hopes the magic turtle's powers can be harnessed to protect the U.S. from spells cast by forest trolls.

"The magic turtle brings a lot to the table," Clinton said in a special press briefing following the one-hour meeting. "In addition to his foreign policy expertise, he has over 300 years of experience dealing with Magic Pond trade issues and knowledge of over 800 fanciful riddles."

Clinton particularly praised the magic turtle's insight on problems facing Polly The Polywog and her happy band of music-making lilypad pals.

According to a report published in Tuesday's *Washington Post*, talks began shortly after the turtle instructed Clinton to rub his magic shell.

"Once his magic turtle shell was

see TURTLE on page 6

Jewish Texans Commemorate Holocaust... Texas-Style!

LUBBOCK, TX—The West Texas chapter of B'nai B'rith is holding a month-long series of events in remembrance of the Holocaust, commemorating the 20th century's darkest hour the way they do everything... Texas-style!

"If we do not remember the past, we are doomed to repeat it," said San Antonio Rabbi Leonard "Too Tall" Sussman at Sunday's opening ceremony, laying a wreath before the Lone Star Of David in front of B'nai B'rith headquarters in Lubbock. "The world was silent, and in silence lies complicity. Never again, y'hear?"

Added Sussman, "Yee-haw!" He then lit the ceremonial Eternal Flame, over which a spit will be installed for Wednesday's kosher steer cookout.

Among the highlights of Holocaust Hoedown '97: a Main Street parade featuring red, white and blue Texas blossoms spelling out "Don't Mess With The Jews"; a special appearance by six-time Zionist calf-roping champion Barry Lowenstein; and daily double-bill showings of *Schindler's List* and John Wayne's *True Grit*.

"Have we learned the lessons of the Holocaust?" asked Deborah Teitelbaum, director of Dallas' Museum of the Holocaust. "If the answer is yes, then how does one explain events in such places as Cambodia and Bosnia? What do we tell the orphaned child in Rwanda? And how 'bout them Cowboys!"

Above: Texas Jews rustle up some memorial grub.

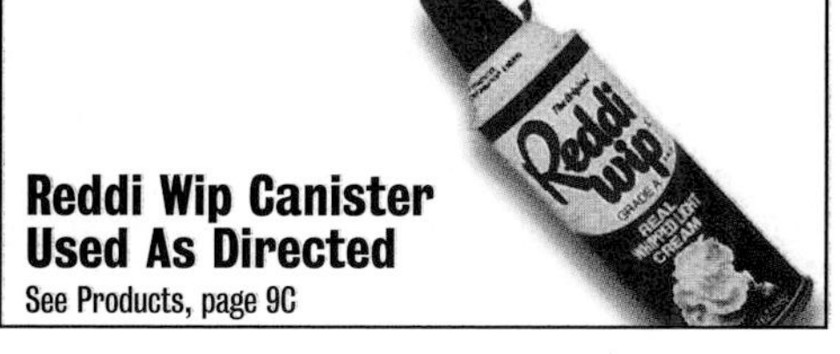

the ONION®

VOLUME 31 ISSUE 6 NUMBER ONE IN NEWS™ 19–25 FEBRUARY 1997

NEWS

Clinton Hitchhikes To St. Louis For Jazzfest

See Nation, page 4A

WEATHER

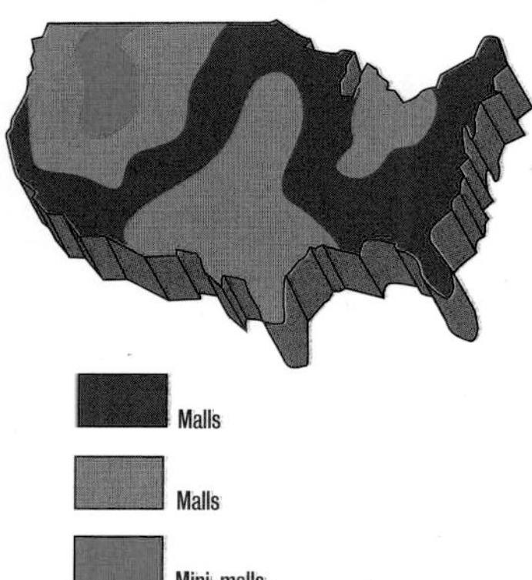

DOW

The Dow fell violently downward yesterday, heroically hurling itself on a grenade to save a crowd of schoolchildren. It will not be forgoten.

INSIDE

NEWS IN BRIEF..........2
THE OPINION PAGE..........4
WHAT DO YOU THINK..........5
ONION INFO-GRAPHIC..........5
PATHETIC GEEK STORIES..........8
DRUNK OF THE WEEK..........16
FUNNY BUSINESS..........18
A-V CLUB..........21
MOVIE LISTINGS..........24
VIDEO..........27
MUSIC..........28
WORDS..........30
SAVAGE LOVE..........31
CALENDAR..........32
CLASSIFIEDS..........36

Local Man Would Like Fries With That

Left: Consumer Don Turnbee considers his side-order options.

ERIE, PA—Eleventh-hour lunch-rush negotiations came to a successful conclusion Monday when, following a 30-second period of deliberation, area resident Don Turnbee opted to accept the McDonald's corporation's suggestion that he have fries with that.

Though the fries were not part of Turnbee's initial purchase proposal to the fast-food giant, the addition of the processed, potato-based food item to his mid-day meal was a concession he felt would best serve his short-term side-order selection needs.

"I wasn't gonna get fries at first," Turnbee said. "But then I wound up getting them."

After carefully reviewing his food-choice options based on such factors as cost, availability and deliciousness, Turnbee arrived at

see FRIES on page 6

New $5.1 Billion Surveillance Satellite To Provide 24-Hour Data On Lee Horsley

CAPE CANAVERAL, FL—In what is considered the most ambitious mid-'80s TV star-monitoring program in its history, NASA on Monday unveiled the HORSTAT-II satellite, a $5.1 billion Lee Horsley-surveillance system.

Scheduled to be launched Saturday, the HORSTAT-II promises up-to-the-minute statistical data on the whereabouts and activities of the handsome, mustachioed star of *Matt Houston*.

From its Horslosynchronous orbit 800 kilometers above the earth's surface, HORSTAT-II will use its array of microsensors to gather and analyze Horsley-related data, which will be relayed to NASA bases at Cape Canaveral and NORAD.

"HORSTAT-II's state-of-the-art imaging technology will allow it to isolate Mr. Horsley out of a crowd of thousands," said NASA team leader Dr. Martin Heller. "It

Above: An infrared satellite image of rugged Matt Houston star Lee Horsley.

is specially programmed to home in on the unique particle wavelength, temperature and electromagnetic signature emanating from the actor's Horslosphere."

"Our infrared imaging system will be able to pinpoint Horsley's location even when he's relaxing in an exclusive Southern California spa," Heller said. "In addition,

see HORSLEY on page 8

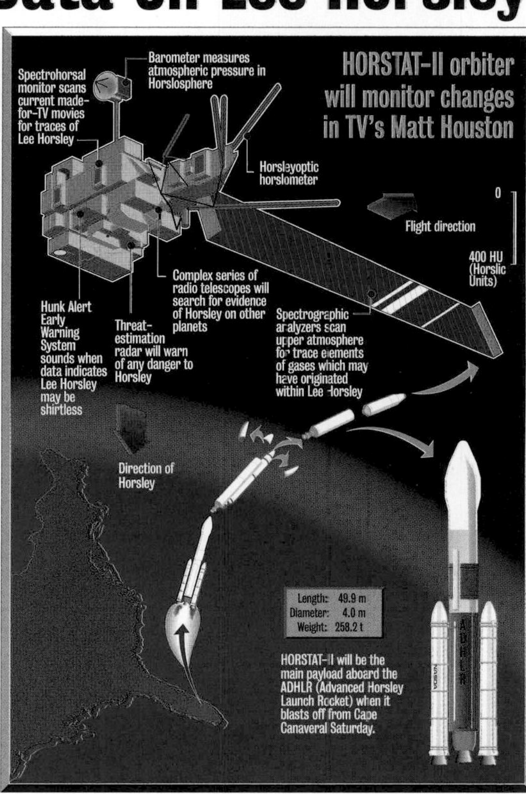

Homoerotic Overtones Enliven NRA Meeting

COEUR D'ALENE, ID—Repression was the order of the day as the National Rifle Association's North Idaho Chapter held its annual convention this weekend.

More than 25,000 dedicated gun lovers from across Northern Idaho flocked to the Coeur d'Alene Convention Center for the two-day event, happily sublimating homosexual impulses amid a carefully maintained facade of platonic camaraderie.

Left: NRA member Jack Harwich admires a fellow member's piece, stirring potent new feelings within himself.

Moscow, ID, resident Richard Hoflinger, 47, a longtime gun-rights activist, exhibited the collection of antique rifles through which he has channeled his culturally unacceptable impulses. "Guns should be part of any upstanding Christian family," Hoflinger said, sticking a long, thick, oily pipe-cleaner 14 inches up an 1886 Remington.

In the next booth, anoth-

see NRA on page 12

the ONION®

VOLUME 31 ISSUE 8 | NUMBER ONE IN NEWS™ | 5–11 MARCH 1997

NEWS

Dept. Of Weights And Measures Establishes 'Cheeto' As Standard Unit Of Cheeto Measurement

See Science, page 11A

WEATHER

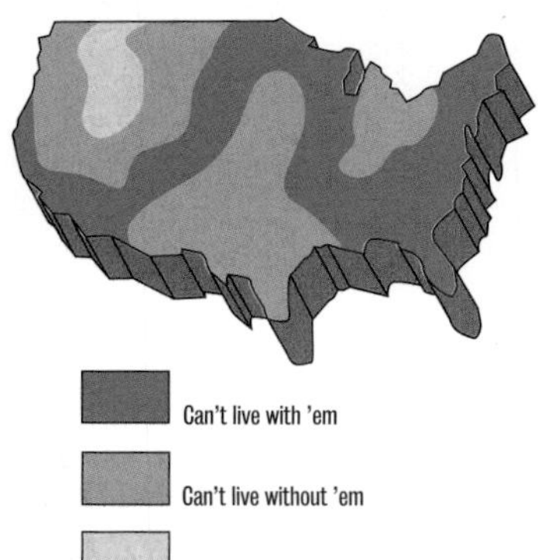

LOTTO

The Lotto: You Don't Need To Speak Perfect English To Play.™

INSIDE

NEWS IN BRIEF ... 2
THE OPINION PAGE ... 4
WHAT DO YOU THINK ... 5
ONION INFO-GRAPHIC ... 5
PATHETIC GEEK STORIES ... 8
DRUNK OF THE WEEK ... 25
FUNNY BUSINESS ... 26
A-V CLUB ... 29
MOVIE LISTINGS ... 32
VIDEO ... 35
MUSIC ... 36
WORDS ... 38
SAVAGE LOVE ... 39
CALENDAR ... 40
CLASSIFIEDS ... 43

Study: Depression Hits Losers Hardest

PALO ALTO, CA—According to a report released Monday by Stanford's Institute For Psychotherapeutic Study, depression, America's leading mental illness, hits losers worse than any other segment of society.

Losers, sad excuses for human beings who have no reason to feel good about themselves or their failed, miserable lives, are approximately 25 times as likely to suffer the emotionally crippling effects of depression as any other group researched, the study claims.

Worse yet, the prospects for successful treatment of depression among the loser populace are "poor at best," the study found. The reason: Most losers are such hopeless lost causes that they can never get a life, no matter how hard they try, and are "doomed to repeat their mistakes forever, living out their pathetic existence as little more than human garbage."

see LOSERS on page 12

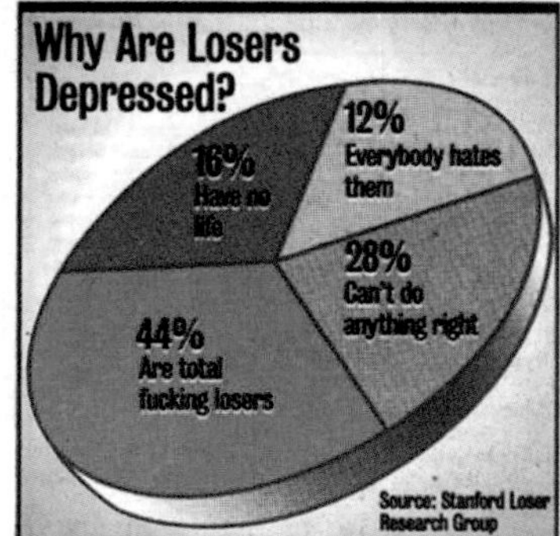

Leno Begs Simpson To Kill Again

Left: O.J. Simpson returns home following last month's civil trial. Inset: Jay Leno, sorely lacking material, is imploring him to kill again.

BURBANK, CA—In an impassioned, nationally televised plea Monday, a teary-eyed Jay Leno begged O.J. Simpson to commit more murders.

"I beg of you, Mr. Simpson. I have no more material since your trial ended," the *Tonight Show* host said. "If you have any decency, any compassion at all, hear my plea to kill someone else."

"I am certain," Leno continued, "that last month's civil judgment was financially ruinous to you. No doubt, you feel a profound sense of anger over the verdict. That is why today I am urging you to translate that anger into action, violent action against an innocent victim, preferably a celebrity."

In the event that Simpson is unwilling to commit another murder, Leno asked that, at the very least, he sexually brutalize someone.

"For 30 years, *The Tonight Show* has been America's premier comedic institution. But now, that great tradition is in jeopardy. O.J., America needs another high-profile homicide to show us how to laugh again."

When pressed to name a person for Simpson to murder, Leno suggested an ex-girlfriend. "That would certainly provide a gold

see SIMPSON on page 10

Crazed Palestinian Gunman Angered By Stereotypes

HEBRON, WEST BANK—In an emotionally charged press conference Monday, crazed Palestinian gunman Faisal al Hamad expressed frustration over the stereotyping of his people.

"As a crazed Palestinian gunman, I feel hurt by the negative portrayal of my people in the media," said al Hamad, 31, a Hebron-area terrorist maniac. "None of us should have to live with stereotyping and ignorance."

He then began screaming and firing into a busload of Israeli schoolchildren.

"It hurts that in this supposedly enlightened day and age, people still make assumptions about other people," al Hamad said. "We should not rely on simple generalizations. Each crazed Palestinian gunman is an individual."

Al Hamad said that he himself has often been unfairly stereotyped. "Any time I enter a crowded temple with fully loaded AK-47s in both hands, people just assume I'm going to open fire," he said. "That really hurts."

"Yes, I sometimes do gun people down in the name of the Allah," he noted. "But there is so much more to me."

Several weeks ago, al Hamad was again the victim of stereotyping during a vacation he took with his family to Washington, D.C.

"When we arrived at the airport in Washington, security guards detained us for more than 12 hours,

see GUNMAN on page 6

Above: Faisal al Hamad, seen here shrieking anti-U.S. slogans, says that "not every crazed Palestinian gunman is exactly alike."

the ONION®

VOLUME 31 ISSUE 16 | NUMBER ONE IN NEWS | 30 APRIL–6 MAY 1997

NEWS

Giant Altoid Headed Toward Earth

'Curiously Strong' Celestial Body Will Extinguish All Life

See Astronomy, page 8D

WEATHER

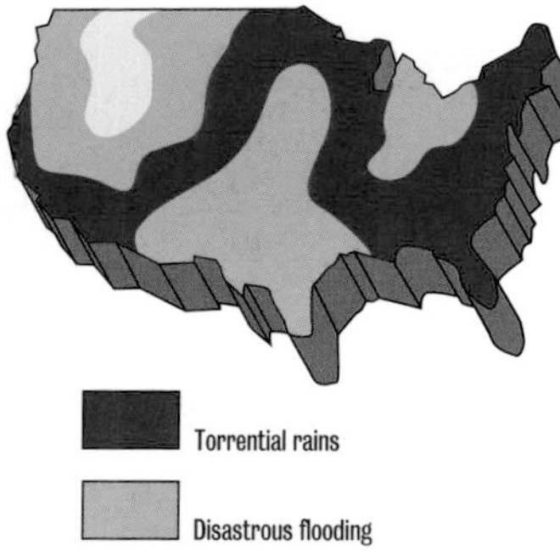

Torrential rains

Disastrous flooding

Undersea kingdom of Prince Namor, the Sub-Mariner

DOW

The Dow reached 18 yesterday and left home to live on its own.

INSIDE

NEWS IN BRIEF....2
THE OPINION PAGE....4
WHAT DO YOU THINK....5
ONION INFO-GRAPHIC....5
PATHETIC GEEK STORIES....8
DRUNK OF THE WEEK....16
FUNNY BUSINESS....18
A-V CLUB....21
MOVIE LISTINGS....26
VIDEO....27
MUSIC....28
WORDS....30
SAVAGE LOVE....31
CALENDAR....32
CLASSIFIEDS....35

Seven Trampled In Annual 'Running Of The Congressmen'

Above: Loosed from their chambers, lawmakers surge down Capitol Hill toward a crowd of thrill-seekers in Monday's 83rd annual Running Of The Congressmen.

WASHINGTON, DC—In what Washington insiders are calling "one of the most impressive displays of congressional virility in U.S. history," seven people were trampled Monday in the 83rd annual Running Of The Congressmen.

Injuries ranged from minor tie-clip abrasions to full-body impact trauma.

"It was frightening," said Jonathan Davis, 22, of Alexandria, VA, who is in critical but stable condition after being gored and tossed repeatedly by Rep. Pete Sessions (R-TX). "I underestimated the unbridled ferocity of these magnificent animals."

At 1 p.m., thousands of spectators lined the streets as the enraged herd of

see CONGRESSMEN on page 12

Local Jew Feels Left Out Of Worldwide Jewish Conspiracy

SOUTHFIELD, MI—It is an hour past sunset on a brisk Thursday night, and, like their brethren around the globe, the Jews of this affluent Detroit suburb are gathered in synagogues, busily hatching plots for world domination through financial chicanery and media influence. But for Seth Nussbaum, it will be just another lonely evening.

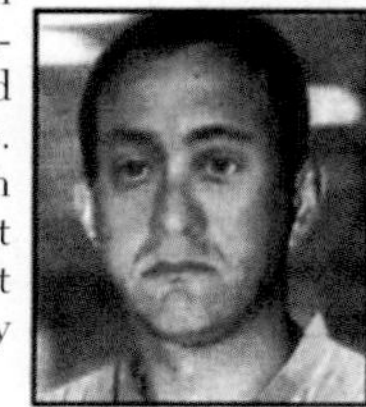

Nussbaum

"For some reason, they've decided to leave me out of the worldwide Jewish conspiracy," said Nussbaum, a 34-year-old computer programmer. "And I can't say it doesn't hurt."

While his fellow Jews are controlling the flow of billions of dollars of international currency and brokering multi million-dollar entertainment deals, on this quiet night Nussbaum is making himself a frozen pizza and watching *ER*, far removed from any money beyond the $28,000 annual salary he receives from his job at Cyntech Industries.

"Who's to say I wouldn't enjoy hoarding a little gold every now and then?" he said, his voice tinged with bitterness. "Believe me, I'd love to be able to sneak around behind the scenes like the Elders of Zion, pulling the strings and holding the real power in society. But I guess when it comes to working the Jerusalem-New York-L.A. triangle, I just wasn't one of the chosen people."

see CONSPIRACY on page 7

New National Parks Website Makes National Parks Obsolete

WASHINGTON, DC—In an effort to make America's natural wonders available to all citizens, the Department of the Interior announced Monday the creation of a $2 million National Parks Website.

The new website clears the way for the wholesale development of the parks: Next Monday, bulldozers will begin leveling more than 100,000 square miles of pristine, federally protected national parkland, finally making it available for industrial use.

Jack Holm, designer of the website, believes nature lovers will find it superior to the real parks in every way. "You will experience the same grand mountains, lush grass and wide variety of fauna, without ever leaving your home," he said. "And when you spot an animal on your cyber-tour, like a majestic elk, you can click on the elk and access information about its habitat and diet. Elks in the wild do not offer this option."

The website, located at

see WEBSITE on page 8

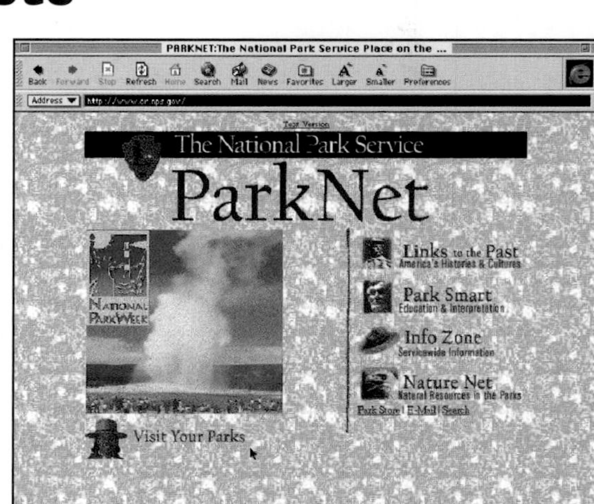

the ONION®

VOLUME 31 ISSUE 17 NUMBER ONE IN NEWS 7–13 MAY 1997

NEWS

Vatican Unveils New Pope Signal

See Religion, page 6C

WEATHER

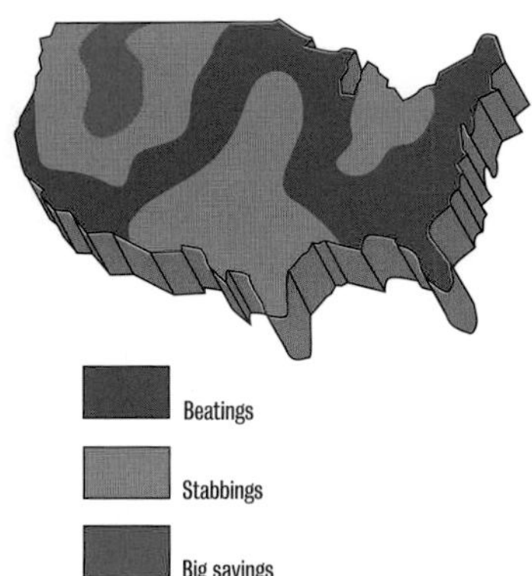

Beatings

Stabbings

Big savings

LOTTO

Today's winning looto numbers were selected on the basis of race, education and income.

INSIDE

NEWS IN BRIEF....2
THE OPINION PAGE....4
WHAT DO YOU THINK....5
ONION INFO-GRAPHIC....5
PATHETIC GEEK STORIES....8
DRUNK OF THE WEEK....21
FUNNY BUSINESS....22
A-V CLUB....25
MOVIE LISTINGS....30
VIDEO....31
MUSIC....32
WORDS....34
SAVAGE LOVE....35
CALENDAR....36
CLASSIFIEDS....39

Clerk Endures Fifth Humiliating Year

CHELSEA, MI—In a formal ceremony Tuesday, store clerk Dean Rechler, 26, was honored by Shop 'n' Thrift store management for five years of humiliating, spirit-crushing employment.

"Dean, you are an unremarkable person with no vim or vigor to speak of," said Greg DeGaetano, Rechler's shift manager at the 24-hour convenience store. "Literally hundreds of employees have come and gone in the five years you have been here, with most able to tolerate only a few months before quitting, yet you have remained."

To commemorate his achievement, Rechler was given a photocopied "Certificate of Degradation," stating that he had successfully endured five years of cashiering, mopping and stocking with no benefits, paid vacations, raises or promotions. Though the unappealing document was described by Shop 'n' Thrift upper management as "suitable for framing," it was clearly fit only for hiding

see CLERK on page 6

Republicans, Dadaists Declare War On Art

Above: Anti-art crusaders Sen. Jesse Helms (R-NC) and Dadaist provocateur Tristan Tzara call for the dismantling of the institutions regulating public art in a joint press conference Monday.

WASHINGTON, DC—Citing the "proliferation of immoral and offensive material throughout America's museums and schools," and waving placards emblazoned with agit-prop fotocollage reading, "diE KUnst ISt tOT, DadA ubEr aLLes" ("Art is dead, dada over all"), a coalition of leading Republican congressional conservatives and early 20th-century Dadaists declared war on art in a joint press conference Monday.

Calling for the elimination of federal funding for the National Endowment for the Arts; the banning of offensive art from museums and schools; and the destruction of the "hoax of reason" in our increasingly random, irrational and meaningless age, the Republicans and Dadaists were unified in their condemnation of the role of the artist in society today.

"Homosexuals and depraved people of every stripe are receiving federal monies at taxpayer expense for the worst kind of filth imaginable," said U.S. Sen. Jesse Helms (R-NC), a longtime NEA critic.

see ART on page 6

Shi'ite Terrorists Cross County Line

'We'll never catch those Farouk boys now,' says sheriff

TANNER COUNTY, GA—A pair of Islamic Shi'ite terrorists, wanted in connection with a string of airport bombings dating back to 1983, broke out of Tanner County Jail Monday, escaping justice by crossing the county line, sources close to the sheriff said.

Cousins Ahmad and Gamel Farouk, longtime Hezbollah members and internationally wanted terrorists, are believed to be hiding out in neighboring Calhoun County, beyond the jurisdiction of Tanner County authorities.

"We'll never get 'em now," said Deputy Clem Pickett, who fell asleep while guarding the Islamic extremists and woke up tied to his chair. "Once somebody crosses that county line, it's over."

"Them boys done hijacked that Pan Am Flight 140 and killed 11 passengers back in '92," Sheriff Buford Colfax said. "That ain't right."

see TERRORISTS on page 11

Right: Sheriff Buford Colfax gives up his hot pursuit of Hezbollah terrorists Ahmad and Gamel Farouk (above) after the pair jumped across Crooked Creek in their souped-up Mustang.

Bank Teller Manages Smile With Last Remaining Ounce Of Strength

See Business, page 4C

Gunman Opens Fire In Own McDonald's

See Local, page 5B

Clinton Found Alive

See Nation, page 2A

the ONION®

VOLUME 31 ISSUE 23 | NUMBER ONE IN NEWS | 9–22 JULY 1997

NEWS

Supreme Court Justice Benatar Orders Army To Stop Using Sex As A Weapon

See Judicial, page 2A

WEATHER

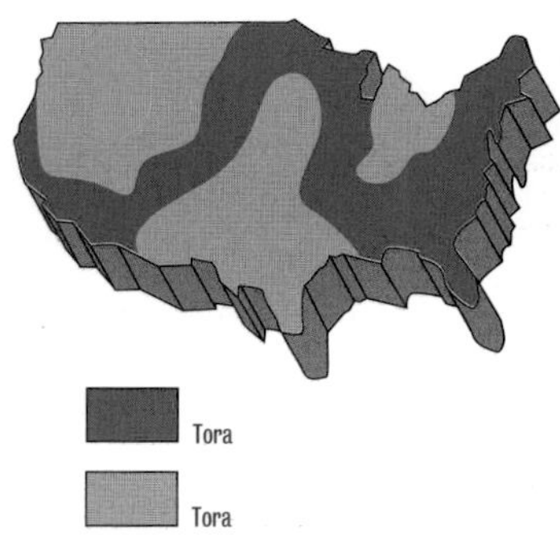

TELEVISION

Inside: An exclusive preview of *TV Guide*'s upcoming ranking of the top 100 *ALF* episodes of all time.

See Entertainment, page 4C

INSIDE

NEWS IN BRIEF ... 2
THE OPINION PAGE ... 4
WHAT DO YOU THINK ... 5
ONION INFO-GRAPHIC ... 5
PATHETIC GEEK STORIES ... 8
FUNNY BUSINESS ... 17
DRUNK OF THE WEEK ... 17
A-V CLUB ... 19
MOVIE LISTINGS ... 24
VIDEO ... 25
MUSIC ... 26
WORDS ... 28
SAVAGE LOVE ... 29
CALENDAR ... 30
CLASSIFIEDS ... 32

Report: U.S. Students Lead World In TV Jingle Recall

WASHINGTON, DC—Welcome news for America's much-maligned educational system arrived Monday, when a Department of Education study revealed that U.S. students rank first in the world in the field of TV jingle recall.

"This is tremendous," U.S. Secretary of Education Richard Riley said. "It finally proves that the youth of America *can* compete. Thanks to their hard work and years of dedicated television-watching, our children will have the edge in the highly competitive TV-jingle-based economy of the 21st century."

According to results of the five-year study, American students are twice as likely as students from such television-conscious countries as Germany and Japan to recall the melodies of TV

see JINGLE on page 14

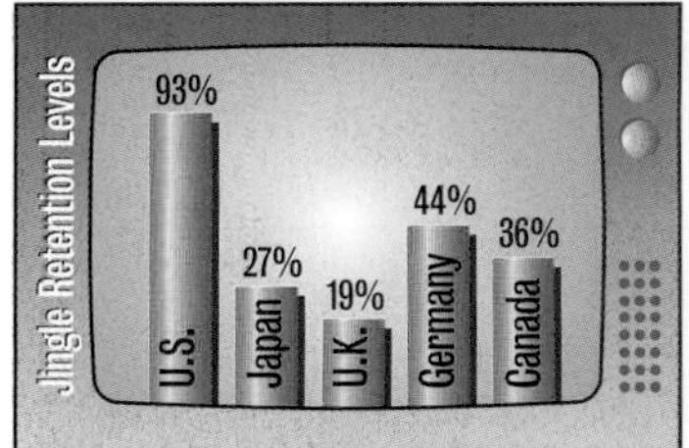

Source: Dept. of Education, 1997

CIA Unveils New Ghetto Drugs For '98

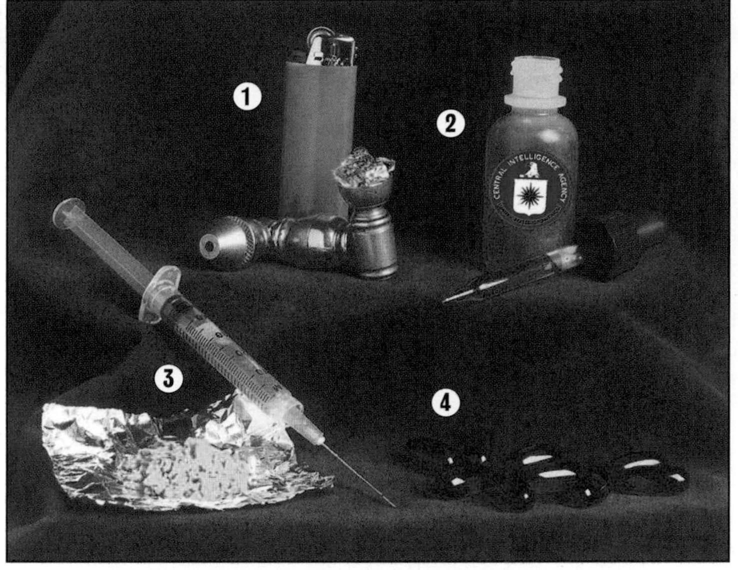

LANGLEY, VA—After months of eager anticipation within the nation's ghetto communities, the Central Intelligence Agency unveiled its 1998 line of addictive drugs Monday.

"The wait is over," CIA Director John Deutch said at the festive drug launch, simulcast on giant-screen TVs throughout Watts, Cabrini Green, Newark, and other urban areas. "Inner-city Americans now have four exciting new ways to narcotize themselves, with the quality of product and wide distribution they've come to expect from the CIA."

Reaction to the new drugs (see sidebar) was overwhelmingly positive. "They had a tough act to follow after crack," said New York-area Mafia boss Alfonse DiBiasi, Deutch's close friend and former college roommate. "But this new stuff is just as cheap and every bit as addictive. We're all very excited."

see CIA on page 11

① Blue Glass
Type: Euphoric
Method: Smoked
Effects: Feelings of extreme optimism and happiness; greatly enhanced reflexes; sensory and sexual pleasure; visual acuity. Immediately followed by semi-permanent suicidal catatonia.
Duration: Five minutes
Cost: $1 per hit

② Brainscratch
Type: Hallucinogen
Method: Dropped into eye
Effects: Reaches visual cortex in seconds, producing terrifying hallucinations. Test subjects report loss of identity and feelings of total dislocation from human world.
Duration: Ten hours to several years
Cost: $2 per dose

③ Zom-B
Type: Narcotic
Method: Injected
Effects: Stuporous mental coma, yet user's motor functions are involuntarily stimulated. Possible side effects may include walking off bridges or into oncoming trains.
Duration: Fifteen to twenty hours
Cost: $3 per fix

④ Spike
Type: Stimulant
Method: Ingested as pill
Effects: Rush of physical strength, invulnerability to pain, and sociopathic impulses. Originally developed by Pentagon as combat drug.
Duration: Two hours
Cost: $5 for 15 pills

Stephen Hawking Builds Robotic Exoskeleton

CAMBRIDGE, ENGLAND—Nobel Prize-winning physicist Stephen Hawking stunned the international scientific community Monday with his latest breakthrough, a remarkably advanced cybernetic exoskeleton designed to replace his wheelchair.

Hawking, paralyzed since early adulthood with the degenerative nerve disease ALS, unveiled the new creation at a press conference at Cambridge University.

"I am faster, stronger... better than before," Hawking told reporters via his suit's built-in voice synthesizer.

The hulking, hydraulically powered titanium-alloy exoskeleton is expected to assist the famed *Brief History Of Time* author tremendously in his ongoing theoretical physics research. "Because of his

see HAWKING on page 11

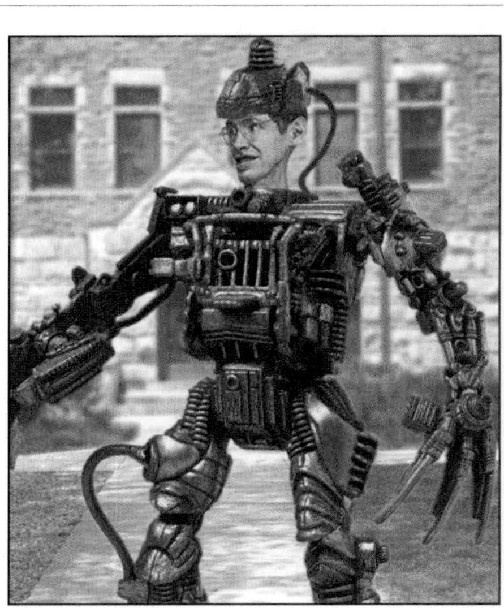

Right: Physicist Stephen Hawking strolls the Cambridge University campus in his new $55 million exoskeleton.

the ONION®

VOLUME 32 ISSUE 1 NUMBER ONE IN NEWS 6-12 AUGUST 1997

NEWS

World's Supermodels Form Hall Of Justice To Protect Ordinary Models

See World, page 2A

WEATHER

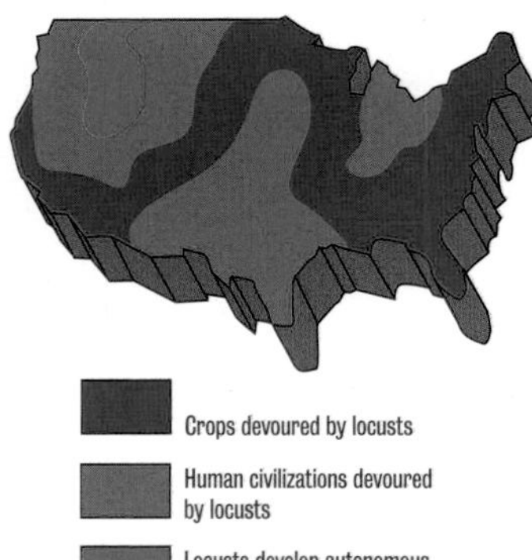

DOW

Trading on the floor was active, as $835 billion in shares changed hands.

Note: You make $5.50 per hour.

INSIDE

NEWS IN BRIEF 2
THE OPINION PAGE 4
WHAT DO YOU THINK 5
ONION INFO-GRAPHIC 5
PATHETIC GEEK STORIES 8
FUNNY BUSINESS 14
DRUNK OF THE WEEK 16
A-V CLUB 17
MOVIE LISTINGS 24
VIDEO 25
MUSIC 26
WORDS 28
SAVAGE LOVE 29
CALENDAR 30
CLASSIFIEDS 32

New Crispy Snack Cracker To Ease Crushing Pain Of Modern Life

Above: A promotional shot for Nabisco's new snack cracker, which should make less agonizing the grotesque, meaningless charade that is modern life.

EAST HANOVER, NJ—The dull, all-consuming ache of late 20th century life will be slightly alleviated next week when America's supermarkets receive their first shipments of Nabisco's new "T.C. McCrispee's" line of snack crackers.

Available in Regular, Garden Ranch and Zesty Cheddar flavors, the new crackers will flood consumers' bodies with salt, fat and starch, momentarily producing a pleasing sensation of warmth and nourishment, and detaching them from their otherwise constant and crushing sense of profound grief.

T.C. McCrispee's are widely expected to be Nabisco's most anguish-relieving snack-food product since the 1983 introduction of Double Stuf Oreos.

"We at the Nabisco Corporation are aware of the hideously bleak

see CRACKER on page 12

Clinton To PLO Terrorists: 'Leave The Girl Out Of It'

WASHINGTON, DC—In a tense standoff with far-reaching implications for both the free world and the president's ironclad code of honor, President Clinton made an impassioned plea to PLO terrorists Monday to "leave the girl out of it."

"It has always been the policy of the United States not to negotiate with terrorists," Clinton told reporters during a nationally televised White House press conference. "But this is different. The girl came here because of me, and when they grabbed her, they made it personal."

The girl, who has been held captive by the terrorists since last Friday, was identified Tuesday in a *New York Times* story as Valerie Herrick, the 26-year-old daughter of industrialist Milton Herrick. Sources close to the White House say she is "an idealistic, sexy brunette who was in the wrong place at the wrong time."

According to the Times story, on Friday, Herrick tracked the terrorists—who are wanted in connection with last week's deadly bombing in a Jerusalem market—to their

see CLINTON on page 6

Oprah's Contraceptive Club Prevents 450,000 Pregnancies In First Month

CHICAGO—Television talk-show host Oprah Winfrey, regarded by many as the most powerful woman in the media, has once again taken the TV industry by surprise with the success of her on-air Contraceptive Of The Month Club.

The much-hyped follow-up to her hugely successful Book Of The Month Club, the four-week-old Contraceptive Club has already prevented an estimated 450,000 unplanned pregnancies.

Just as some doubted that Winfrey would be able to convince her couch-bound, sub-literate viewers to read, many observers were skeptical that she could pull off the seemingly impossible task of explaining contraception to her working-class, constantly breeding audience.

"The response has been incredible," show producer Liz Frey said.

According to Frey, sales for last month's featured contraceptive device, the Leafbreeze™ Spermicidal Vaginal Sponge, more than quadrupled in the weeks following its selection.

During last month's special episode, the studio audience watched carefully and was uncharacteristically quiet as Winfrey explained, slowly and with no big

see OPRAH on page 15

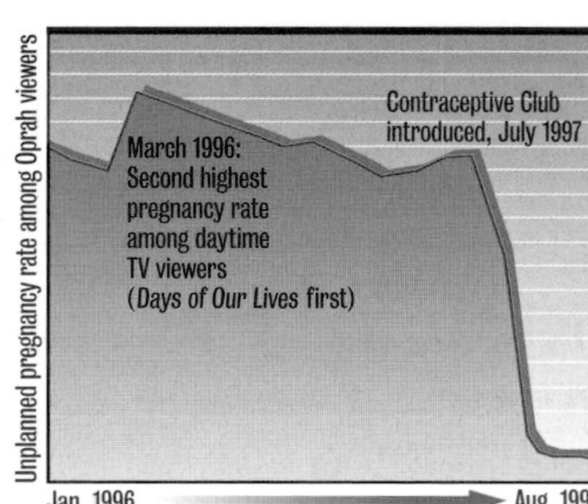

Popular TV talk-show host Oprah Winfrey (right) has convinced thousands of her loyal viewers to forego their usual wanton, unchecked procreation.

the ONION®

VOLUME 32 ISSUE 3 NUMBER ONE IN NEWS 20-26 AUGUST 1997

NEWS

God Demands Cuter Precious Moments Figurines

See Religion, page 8A

WEATHER

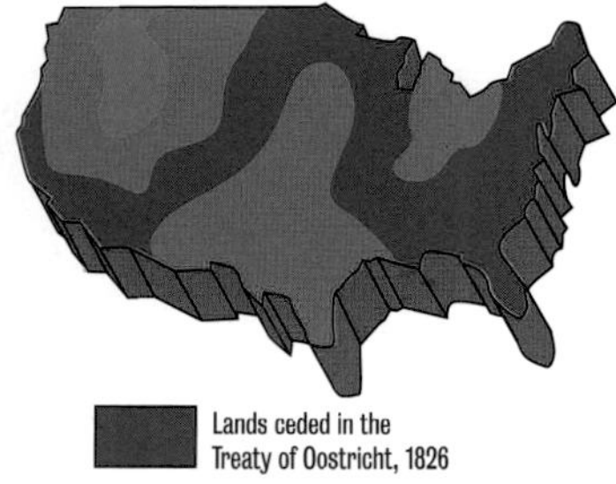

Lands ceded in the Treaty of Oostricht, 1826

Annexed from the Swiss, 1852

Disputed with Botswana

DOW

The Dow rose and fell rhythmically all day, soothing many Wall Street brokers and lulling them into a deep, healing sleep.

INSIDE

NEWS IN BRIEF..........2
THE OPINION PAGE..........4
WHAT DO YOU THINK..........5
ONION INFO-GRAPHIC..........5
PATHETIC GEEK STORIES..........8
FUNNY BUSINESS..........14
A-V CLUB..........17
DRUNK OF THE WEEK..........20
MOVIE LISTINGS..........24
VIDEO..........25
MUSIC..........26
WORDS..........28
SAVAGE LOVE..........29
CALENDAR..........30
CLASSIFIEDS..........32

Above: U.S. Education Secretary Richard Riley holds up a suicide note from a 15-year-old girl he says was "crying out for help in proper punctuation and spelling."

Nation's Educators Alarmed By Poorly Written Teen Suicide Notes

WASHINGTON, DC—At the group's annual convention Sunday, members of the National Education Association called for the formation of a nationwide coalition of parents, teachers and political leaders to address a rapidly growing problem: the alarmingly low quality of teenage suicide notes across the U.S.

In the convention's keynote address, U.S. Secretary of Education Richard Riley said America must renew its commitment to grammar, spelling and writing skills, calling the marked improvement of teen suicide prose "the nation's number one educational priority."

"Not three days ago I met with the parents of a young man who chose to take his own life," Riley said. "I was shocked by what I saw: a note that

see NOTES on page 10

McDonald's Sells Out

Cult Fan Base Deserts Underground Fast-Food Chain After Disney Tie-In Promotion

OAK PARK, IL—The hip, underground fast-food chain McDonald's is being assailed with cries of "sell-out" from its rabid fan base, which has expressed anger and disillusionment over a merchandising deal signed recently between the restaurant and the Disney Corporation.

For years one of the most respected and influential members of the nation's underground fast-food scene, McDonald's earlier this summer began selling "collectors cups" from the Disney film *Hercules* for 99 cents with any food purchase.

"God, I can't believe they would do something like this,

see McDONALD'S on page 6

Right: A sign at a Lexington, KY, McDonald's advertises *Hercules* cups for sale, a promotion which has hurt the alternative fast-food chain's street credibility among fans.

Strom Thurmond Calls For Construction Of Transcontinental Railroad

Above: U.S. Sen. Strom Thurmond (R-SC) said that as the 20th century approaches, the U.S. must be a leader in the field of steam-powered locomotive technology.

WASHINGTON, DC—Citing the need for cheaper and faster shipping to the Western Territories, the need to unite the Republic after the long and bitter War Between The States, and the recent discovery of gold in the California region, U.S. Sen. Strom Thurmond (R-SC) urged Congress Monday to support funding for the construction of a transcontinental railroad.

"My friends, we stand at the threshold of the Age Of Steam—a glorious new age for the Republic," Thurmond said. "And the mighty steam locomotive is the new Steam Age's most powerful expression. I propose that the Union grant me the sum of 50 thousands of dollars, that I may work in concert with our beloved Captains of Industry to forge an iron road of rails across the untamed, unexplored wilderness of the Western Territories."

According to Thurmond, the proposed Great Western Trans-Continental Steam Rail-Road would stretch from already-established tracks in St. Louis to the shores of the Pacific Ocean, ending "near the white settlement at Sacramento Town."

Once operational, Thurmond told members of Congress, the railroad would move upwards of 24 tons of cargo a day at speeds approaching 30 miles an hour. "My claims may seem preposterous, but mighty steam is

see THURMOND on page 8

Temporary Worker Permanently Scarred

See Workplace, page 2A

Are We Meeting The Needs Of Our Nation's Rich?

See Leisure, page 7C

Porn Star Doesn't Want To Direct

See FilmCorner, page 4D

the ONION®

VOLUME 32 ISSUE 4 | NUMBER ONE IN NEWS | 27 AUGUST–2 SEPTEMBER 1997

NEWS

Across Nation, Superstores Driving Out Old-Fashioned Megamalls

See Business, page 3C

WEATHER

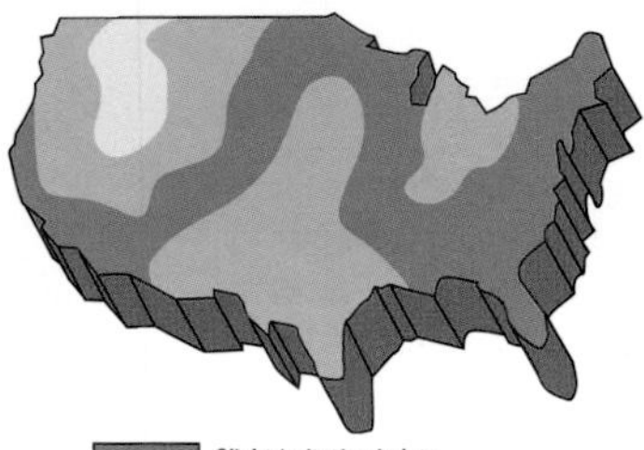

Slight irritation in late afternoon, cloudy

Burning sensation, mid-to-upper 70s

Incredibly painful rash, breezy

LOTTO

Lotto not working for you, huh? Maybe you should take a break and try the peel-off game at Taco Bell. Will *you* be the one to unmask Batman?

INSIDE

NEWS IN BRIEF....2
THE OPINION PAGE....4
WHAT DO YOU THINK....5
ONION INFO-GRAPHIC....5
PATHETIC GEEK STORIES....8
DRUNK OF THE WEEK....20
FUNNY BUSINESS....22
A-V CLUB....25
MOVIE LISTINGS....30
VIDEO....31
MUSIC....32
WORDS....36
SAVAGE LOVE....37
CALENDAR....38
CLASSIFIEDS....40

Last Literate Person On Earth Dead At 98

ROUEN, FRANCE—Béatrice Berceau, the planet's last literate person, died Monday, marking the end of an era.

Berceau, widely renowned in her native France and around the world for her remarkable ability to decipher coded inscriptions of symbols printed on paper, was 98 years old.

"Béatrice's death has officially ushered in the Post-Literate Age," said Roland Habusch, head of Harvard University's Department of Sound Bites and Pictograms. "No longer will we as a species have access to the information stored in the bound paper volumes known to Béatrice and our ancestors as 'books.'"

Those who knew Berceau claimed that the elderly eccentric did not own a television, could not operate an ordinary fax-modem and neither left nor

see LITERATE on page 19

Right: France's Béatrice Berceau, seen last year deciphering a complex system of ancient coded symbols contained in a bound paper volume known as a "book."

ZZ Top Grants Clinton Keys To Magic Hot Rod

Left: ZZ Top guitarists Billy Gibbons and Dusty Hill formally present President Clinton with the keys to the Eliminator hot rod.

WASHINGTON, DC—President Clinton's approval rating skyrocketed Monday with his acquisition of the keys to the magic hot rod belonging to popular, supernatural rock group ZZ Top.

According to a CBS News poll, Clinton's popularity has soared from 43 to 90 percent in the past three days, a jump many Washington insiders attribute to the "Eliminator" hot rod and its stylized "ZZ" keychain, presented to him by the hard-rocking trio.

"It would appear that Clinton's acquisition of the mysterious ZZ Top Eliminator—as well as his newfound association with ZZ Top's members themselves and the scantily clad women who accompany them at all times—has resulted in a tremendous image makeover for the president," said *Washington Post* White House correspondent Arthur Tierney.

Longtime public perception of Clinton as a weak, ineffectual virgin—widely attributed to his

see ZZ TOP on page 12

Sea-Going Turtle Under Fire For Egg Abandonment

OCALA, FL—State welfare agencies expressed outrage Monday over the discovery that a local sea turtle had "deliberately and recklessly abandoned" her six unborn children on an Ocala beach last Thursday.

"This kind of behavior is shocking and inexcusable," said Peter Hume, director of the Florida Division of Youth and Family Services (FDYFS). "To deposit one's own children in the sand and expect them to autonomously hatch after a two- to three-week incubation period, instinctively crawl to the ocean and immediately begin using their flippers as fully functioning transportational devices in the quest for aquatic vegetation—it boggles the mind. It's almost unhuman."

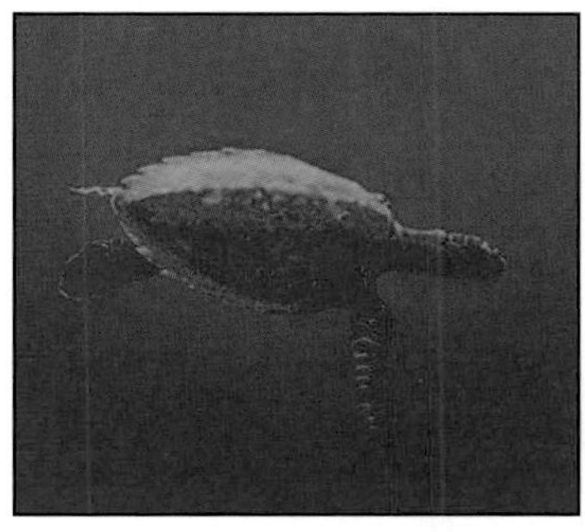

Above: The only known photo of the suspect, who allegedly swam off after leaving her six unborn children on a Florida beach.

The eggs, which appeared "weathered and malnourished" upon discovery, have been placed in foster care. State authorities have asked the Coast Guard to help in the search for the still-unidentified mother, whom animal-behavior experts believe is still in the area.

Stephen Varga, a frequent beachcomber in the Ocala area, witnessed the mother's act of gross criminal negligence. "She waddled inland along the shore, oh, 200 to 300 yards or so," Varga said, "and I remember thinking how suspicious the whole thing looked, the way she used her hind feet to carefully

see SEA TURTLE on page 7

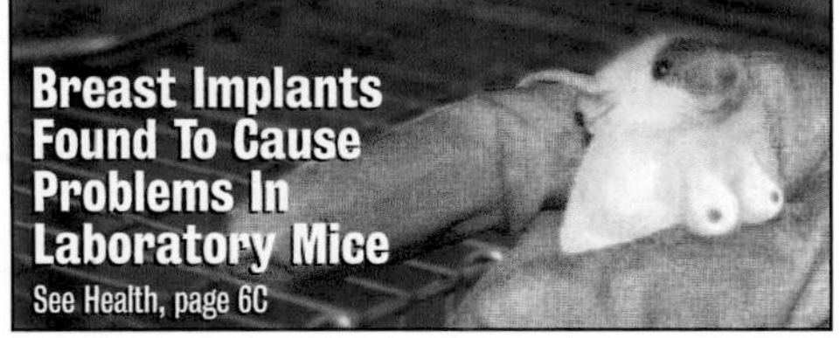

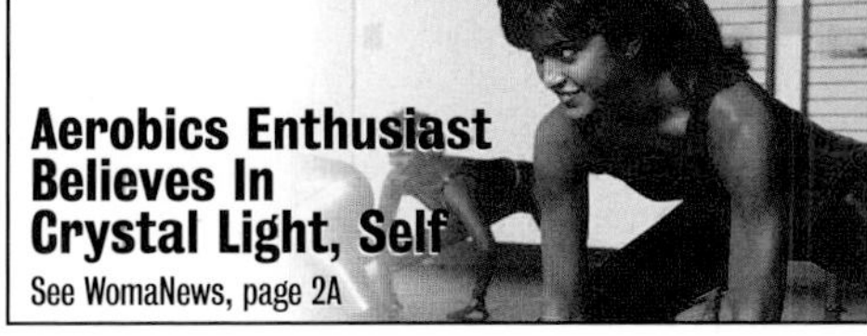

the ONION®

VOLUME 32 ISSUE 6 | NUMBER ONE IN NEWS | 10–16 SEPTEMBER 1997

NEWS

Turnout Lower Than Expected For Gala Central African Awards

See World, page 3A

WEATHER

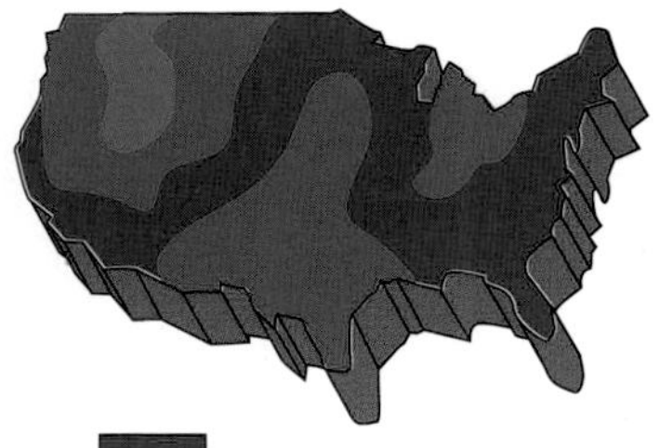

Consume 18% of world's resources

Consume 46% of world's resources

Consume 31% of world's resources

TAO

Trading was passive yesterday, as the Tao was content. Bond markets were as the shadow of a shade. The dollar fell yet seemed to rise. And brokers who thought they held their fortunes in their grasp lost them.

INSIDE

NEWS IN BRIEF 2
THE OPINION PAGE 4
WHAT DO YOU THINK 5
ONION INFO-GRAPHIC 5
PATHETIC GEEK STORIES 8
FUNNY BUSINESS 25
DRUNK OF THE WEEK 26
A-V CLUB 29
MOVIE LISTINGS 36
VIDEO 37
MUSIC 38
WORDS 42
SAVAGE LOVE 43
CALENDAR 44
CLASSIFIEDS 48

Area Consumer Makes Last-Minute Soft-Drink Size Upgrade To Acquire Collectible Plastic Cup

Left: Erie, PA, consumer Don Turnbee.

ERIE, PA—According to leading fast-food-industry analysts, area consumer Don Turnbee's soft-drink upgrade Monday from large to extra-large was motivated not by a desire for the extra volume of soda contained in the larger size, but rather to acquire a special, limited-edition collectible plastic cup.

Turnbee obtained the cup, an attractive, 24-ounce stackable beverage container that offers easy lidding and multiple reusability, at an area McDonald's, where the cup is available for a limited time only.

"I didn't really need the extra soda," Turnbee, 39, told reporters shortly after closing the deal, "but I figured since it's only 10 more cents I'd just go ahead and get the cup, too."

Spokespersons for the McDonald's Corporation expressed satisfaction with

see UPGRADE on page 24

DEA Chief: Winners Occasionally Use Drugs

'Some successful Americans may have experimented with illegal narcotics,' he says

Above: DEA head Thomas Constantine, testifying before Congress.

WASHINGTON, DC—In a surprise announcement with wide-ranging implications for U.S. narcotics policy, Drug Enforcement Administration director Thomas Constantine acknowledged Monday that some winners "may occasionally" use drugs.

"Apparently," said Constantine, addressing reporters at Justice Department headquarters, "contrary to the DEA's long-standing conviction, drug use may not be limited solely to the domain of losers. It appears that some successful Americans have experimented with illegal narcotics, as well."

The announcement was the result of a comprehensive three-year DEA study of more than 40,000 U.S. winners, including thousands of successful business executives, doctors, lawyers, scientists and civic leaders. The study, originally designed by the DEA to help shed light on the qualities shared by winners that make them resistant to drugs, instead revealed that over 71 percent of winners had at one time or another

see DRUGS on page 8

Japanese Leaders Say Radioactive Waste May Have Contributed To Creation Of Giant Monsters

TOKYO—Japanese prime minister Ryutaro Hashimoto announced Tuesday that radioactive waste recently discovered in Japan's Nihon prefecture may have contributed to the development of *kaiju*—translated as "strange, mysterious beast-animal supernatural giant warrior-monsters"—whose many battles have wreaked havoc throughout the Western world and Japan since the late 1950s.

"We are still continuing our investigation into the source of these radioactive-waste deposits," Hashimoto said. "However, it does appear that there may be a link between this waste and such monsters as Gohidra and King Krusan, who have so often laid waste to our armies and urban areas."

Shortly after completing his statement, the prime minister pointed toward the sky and screamed, "Oh, no—it is Grogan!" before

see MONSTERS on page 10

Prime Minister Hashimoto (center) holds an emergency meeting to discuss giant-monster containment strategies.

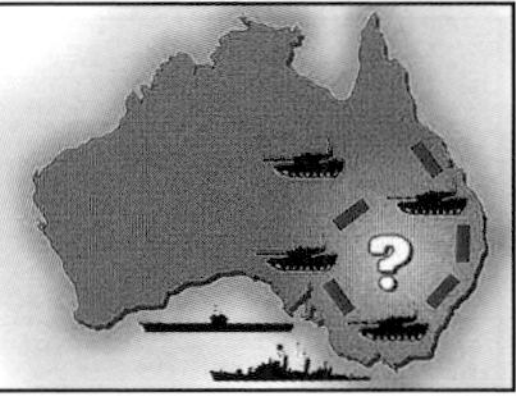

Could Australia Be Building Another Yahoo Serious?

See World, page 3A

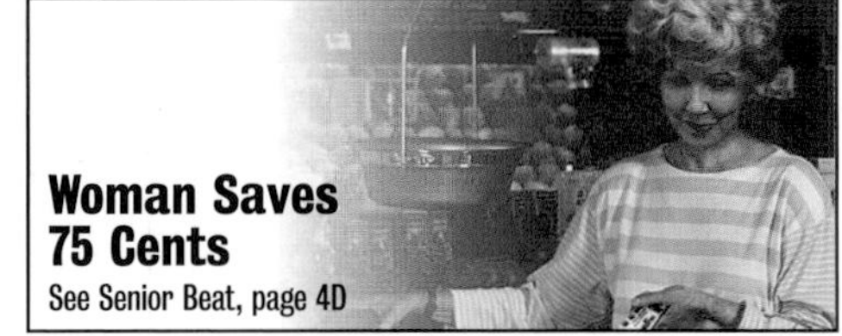

the ONION®

VOLUME 32 ISSUE 7 | NUMBER ONE IN NEWS | 17–23 SEPTEMBER 1997

NEWS

SAT Found To Be Biased In Favor Of Non-Hungover

See Education, page 3B

WEATHER

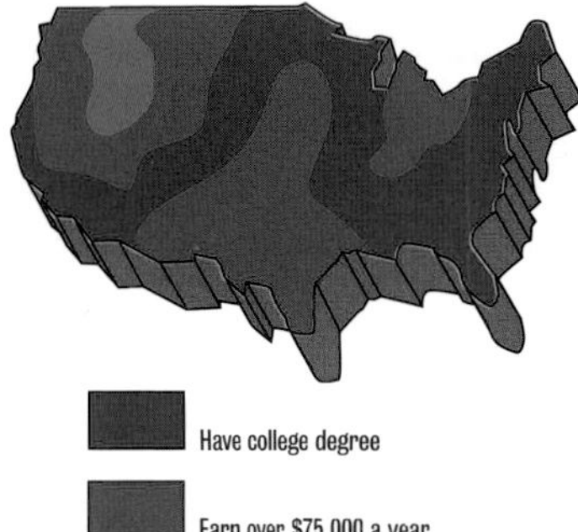

DOW

The Dow dropped 32 points after it embraced Marxism-Leninism, but then steadily rebounded after graduating, getting married, and taking a job in its father-in-law's brokerage firm.

INSIDE

NEWS IN BRIEF....2
THE OPINION PAGE....4
WHAT DO YOU THINK....5
ONION INFO-GRAPHIC....5
PATHETIC GEEK STORIES....8
FUNNY BUSINESS....16
DRUNK OF THE WEEK....17
A-V CLUB....19
MOVIE LISTINGS....26
VIDEO....27
MUSIC....28
WORDS....30
SAVAGE LOVE....31
CALENDAR....32
CLASSIFIEDS....36

U.S. Agriculture Secretary: 'Aw, Let's Not Do Farming Anymore'

DES MOINES, IA—Citing the massive economic woes plaguing the nation's farmers and the severe physical hardship of farming itself, U.S. Secretary of Agriculture Dan Glickman announced Monday that he would like to "forget about the whole farming thing altogether."

"Every day, it's the same thing—get up at the crack of dawn, swamp out the barn, feed the livestock. It's just a lot of work. I get exhausted just thinking about it," Glickman told assembled agribusiness representatives at the annual Midwest Agricultural

see FARMING on page 12

Above: A Nebraska farmer harvests crops, an activity Agriculture Secretary Dan Glickman says is "really hard."

Scientists Discover Wrinkle In Time-Life Continuum

'A stable 10-day window exists in which any book can be returned at no risk,' Cal Tech physicist says

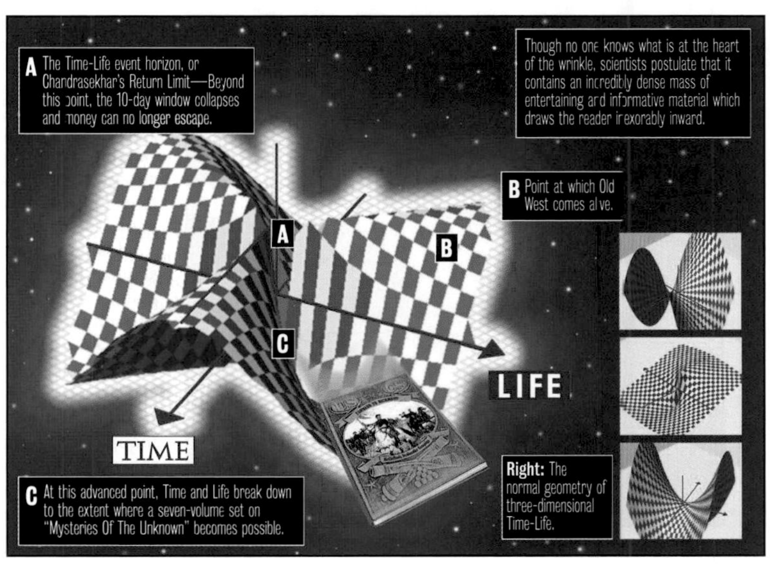

PASADENA, CA—The world's scientific and multi-volume-book-buying communities are abuzz following Monday's announcement that a team of California Institute of Technology physicists has discovered a wrinkle in the Time-Life continuum.

If the discovery proves to be correct, consumers may be able to receive 100 percent of their money back even after observing Time-Life phenomena for a limited 10-day "window" in the continuum.

"Preliminary data still needs to be closely evaluated before any definitive conclusions can be reached," said Cal Tech team leader Stephen Yu. "But it now appears that the very fabric of Time-Life itself may be curved in such a man-

see TIME-LIFE on page 13

Buck-Naked Man Stresses Importance Of Proper Schooling

WASHINGTON, DC—Alarmed by rising high-school dropout rates and declining test scores, buck-naked education consultant Dr. Donald Scherr urged America's youth to "put education first" during an address to more than 300 educators and students Monday.

"No matter what you want to be, a good education is the way to get there," said Scherr, his limp penis hanging visibly. "Your mind is like a car's gas tank: If you don't fill it, your future doesn't look so good."

The unclothed Scherr also took teachers to task for allowing standards to dip sharply over the past two decades. "A student today can graduate from high school knowing little more than the multiplication tables and who the current

see SCHOOLING on page 8

Buck-naked education consultant Donald Scherr (far right) offers a group of teachers tips on how to better motivate students.

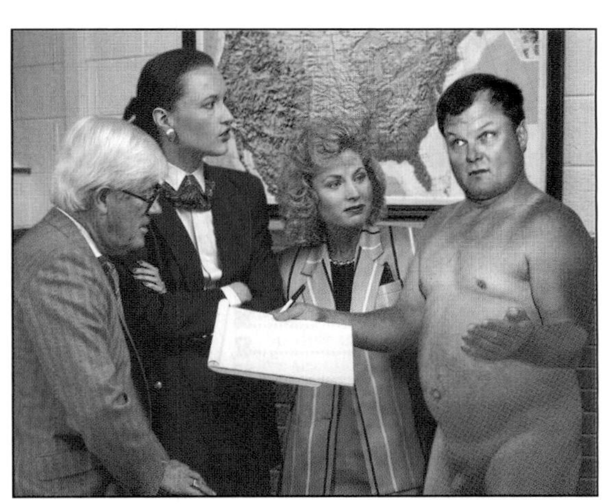

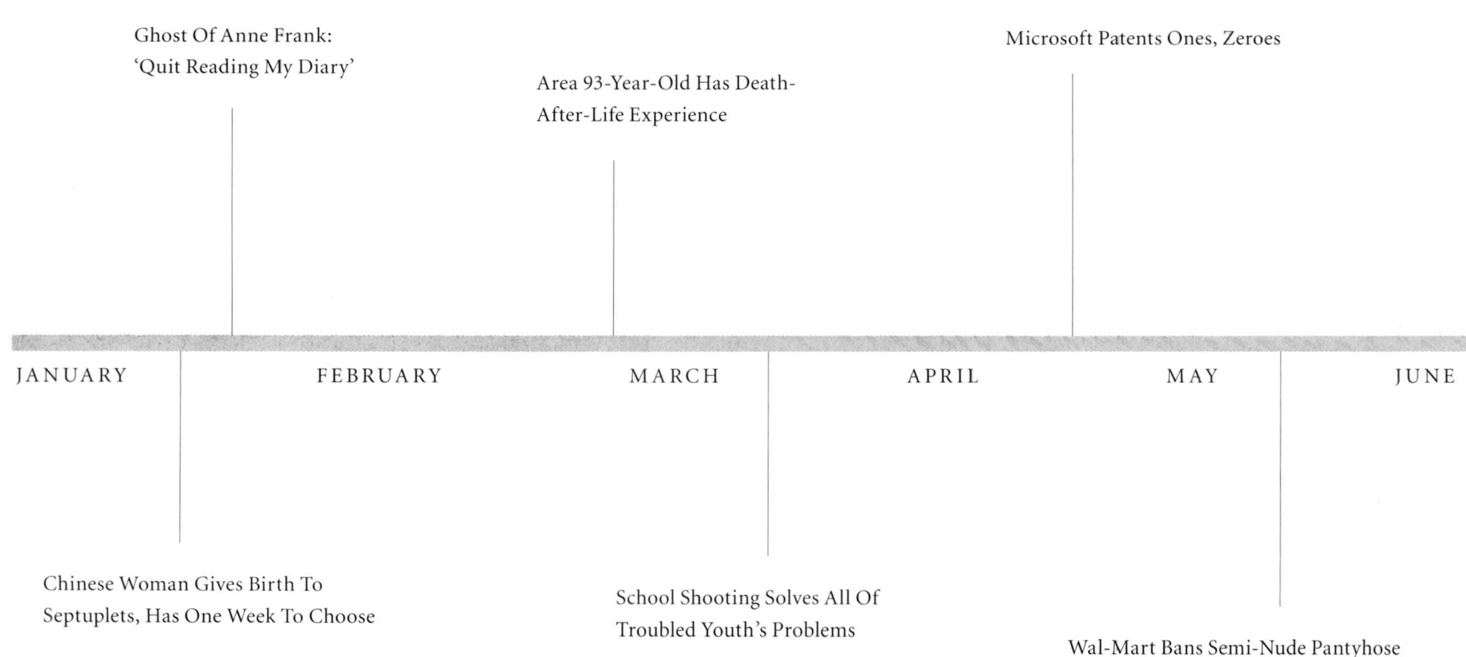
Ghost Of Anne Frank:
'Quit Reading My Diary'
Area 93-Year-Old Has Death-
After-Life Experience
Microsoft Patents Ones, Zeroes
JANUARY
FEBRUARY
MARCH
APRIL
MAY
JUNE
Chinese Woman Gives Birth To
Septuplets, Has One Week To Choose
School Shooting Solves All Of
Troubled Youth's Problems
Wal-Mart Bans Semi-Nude Pantyhose

1998

Arafat, Netanyahu Reach Understanding After Zany 'Stuck In Meat Locker' Ordeal

Congress Asks Clinton For Permission To Have Congress Outside Today

God Cites 'Moving In Mysterious Ways' As Motive In Killing Of 3,000 Papua New Guineans

JULY AUGUST SEPTEMBER OCTOBER NOVEMBER DECEMBER

Human Affection Now Available Only From Grandparents, Down Syndrome Children

Local Senior Brutally Folded In Craftmatic Adjustable Bed Accident

Nation's Wealthiest One Percent Demands Minority Status

Fran Drescher Cinched Up Another Notch

See Entertainment, page 4C

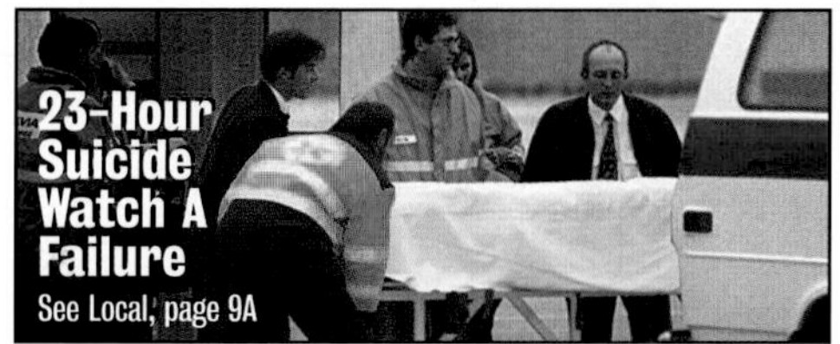
23-Hour Suicide Watch A Failure

See Local, page 9A

Inside: America Rates The Skin Colors

See Society, page 1D

the ONION®

VOLUME 33 ISSUE 2 | AMERICA'S FINEST NEWS SOURCE™ | 22–28 JANUARY 1998

NEWS

U.S. Soldiers To Be Equipped With Powerful Mandibles

See Nation, page 2A

WEATHER

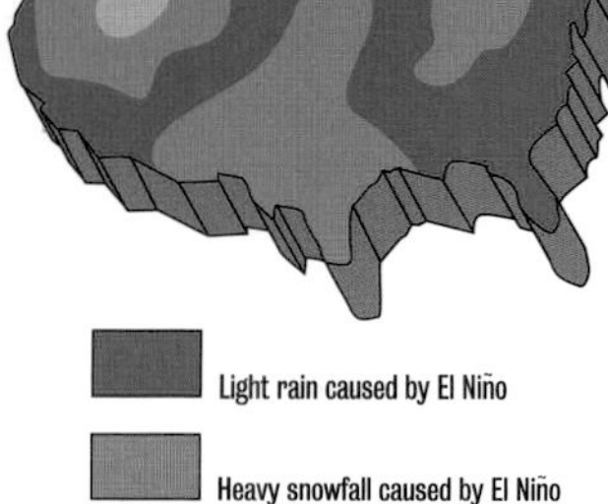

DOW

The Dow cracked under the intense pressure to perform today and downed a bottle of sleeping pills.

INSIDE

NEWS IN BRIEF....2
THE OPINION PAGE....4
WHAT DO YOU THINK....5
ONION INFO-GRAPHIC....5
PATHETIC GEEK STORIES....8
FUNNY BUSINESS....10
A-V CLUB....19
SAVAGE LOVE....29
DRUNK OF THE WEEK....20
INSIDE FEATURE....21
CINEMA....22
MUSIC....24
PICKS....26
CALENDAR....25
CLASSIFIEDS....30

Congress To Ironhead: 'What's With This Thingy?"

WASHINGTON, DC—Under fire for a litany of alleged "inappropriately feminine" personal-hygiene practices, St. Louis Rams running back Craig "Ironhead" Heyward testified under federal subpoena Monday before the Senate Investigatory Subcommittee on Bath And Shower Gender-Role Standards And Norms.

According to Washington insiders, the chief focus of the formal inquest concerned the popular athlete's

see IRONHEAD on next page

Right: U.S. Sen. Chuck Hagel (R-NE), displays a dainty, effeminate shower-sponge thingy for congressional review.

Raped Environment Led Polluters On, Defense Attorneys Argue

According to Dennis Schickle (above), lead defense attorney for Pacific North Construction & Lumber Corp., his client's rape of 30,000 acres of forest (right) was precipitated by the plaintiff's "flagrant flaunting of its abundant natural resources."

OLYMPIA, WA—In their opening statement before jurors Monday, defense attorneys representing Pacific North Construction & Lumber Corp. argued that their client was not at fault for the July 1997 rape of 30,000 acres of virgin forest, claiming that the forest led the development company on with "an eager and blatant display of its rich, fertile bounty."

"While, obviously, it is extremely unfortunate that this forest was raped, it should have known better than to show off its lush greenery and tall, strong trees in the presence of my client if it didn't want anything to happen," said lead defense attorney Dennis Schickle, speaking before a courtroom packed with members of the media. "It's only natural for any red-blooded American developer to get ideas in its head when it's presented with that kind of untouched beauty."

"The bottom line is," Schickle continued, "if you're going to tease and encourage like that, openly flaunting your abundant natural resources, don't be surprised by the consequences."

Public opinion regarding the high-profile case, which is being closely watched by timber-industry lobbyists and victims' rights groups across the U.S., is deeply divided. While some

see ENVIRONMENT on page 14

Radical Socialist Movement Ends After Three Semesters

ANN ARBOR, MI—Spokespersons for the Global Socialist League, an Ann Arbor-based radical socialist organization, announced Tuesday that the group is disbanding due to a lack of funds, ending its three-semester struggle to smash the bulwarks of slavery and oppression everywhere.

Founded by University of Michigan junior Kate Barlow in September 1996 as a campus-based revolutionary strike force dedicated to establishing a worldwide dictatorship of the proletariat, the GSL made the decision to disband after learning it had dropped below the five-member minimum required by the university for student-organization funding.

The group made the decision to disband after learning it had dropped below the five-member minimum required by the university for student-organization funding.

"We were really starting to get the word out about AmeriKKKa's exploitation of migrant labor, the silencing of Mumia Abu-Jamal, and the Clinton regime's reign of fascist terror in Central America," said Barlow, GSL chairperson and a creative-writing major. "But then Craig dropped out because his dad threatened to stop paying his tuition if he didn't get his grades

see SOCIALISTS on page 10

George Clinton, Della Reese Meet To Discuss Key Hairstyle Issues
See Fashion, page 1D

the ONION®

VOLUME 33 ISSUE 4 | AMERICA'S FINEST NEWS SOURCE™ | 4–10 FEBRUARY 1998

NEWS

Supermodel's True Beauty Comes From Outside

See Personality Profile, page 3F

WEATHER

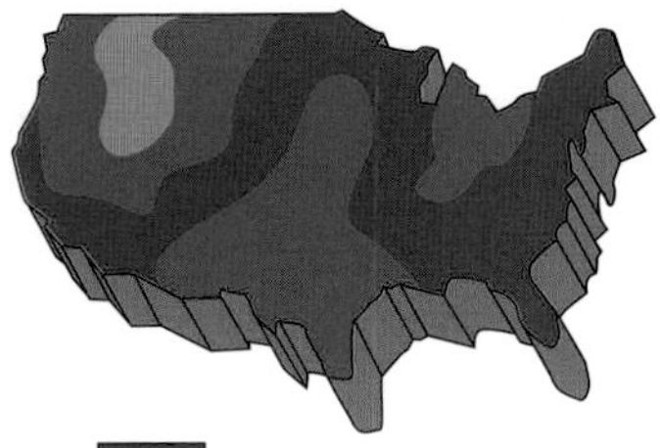

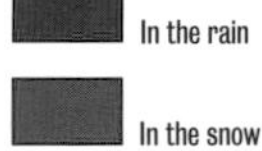

In the rain

In the snow

I got the funky flow

INSIDE

NEWS IN BRIEF 2
THE OPINION PAGE 4
WHAT DO YOU THINK 5
ONION INFO-GRAPHIC 5
PATHETIC GEEK STORIES 8
FUNNY BUSINESS 20
DRUNK OF THE WEEK 24
AV CLUB 25
MOVIE LISTINGS 32
VIDEO 33
MUSIC 34
WORDS 36
SAVAGE LOVE 37
CALENDAR 38
CLASSIFIEDS 41

Clinton Denies Lewinsky Allegations

'We did not have sex, we made love,' says president

Above: Embattled President Clinton vehemently denies having sex with former White House intern Monica Lewinsky (inset), calling it "so much more than that."

WASHINGTON, DC—With sexual-misconduct allegations continuing to envelop his presidency, President Clinton held a press conference Monday to reiterate his strong denial of charges that he had sex with former White House intern Monica Lewinsky.

"We did not have sex," said Clinton in a terse, carefully worded statement. "We made love. Sweet, sweet love."

Clinton, who in the past has emphatically denied ever having sexual relations with Lewinsky or telling her to lie about it, held fast to his earlier remarks.

"I said that I did not have a sexual relationship with that woman, and I stand by the truth of that statement," Clinton told reporters. "We did not, I repeat, not, have a mere sexual relationship. What the two of us shared that fateful year we spent in each other's arms was so much more than that."

According to Clinton, between December 1995 and April 1996, he and Lewinsky did not merely have sex. Rather, he said, they lounged luxuriously for hours in the Oval Office, reading each other poetry, feeding each other strawberries, and tenderly caressing each other about the face and neck before surrendering to desire and consummating their heartfelt passion.

"These base allegations of a tawdry, superficial sexual involvement—motivated in no small measure by my political opponents' desire to further their own right-wing agenda—are completely unfounded," Clinton said. "It went way beyond the physical. This was more than just the intertwining of two bodies. It was the union of two souls."

When asked to respond to charges

see CLINTON on page 10

64 Percent Of U.S. Population Now Working For Manpower

WASHINGTON, DC—According to a report released Monday by the U.S. Bureau of Labor Statistics, 64 percent of the nation's work force is currently employed in a "temp" capacity by Manpower employment agency.

the ONION's JOB FOCUS

"With more than 150 million Americans working for Manpower, we truly are a nation of temps," said Labor Secretary Alexis Herman, who in 1996 was placed by Manpower in the top Labor Department spot after Robert Reich vacated the post to accept a three-week data/word-processing assignment in a Hartford, CT, actuarial firm.

Experts attribute Manpower's success to its ability to supply U.S. companies with competent full-time workers who do not have to be given the same social and financial considerations as actual employees.

"Regular, full-time workers can

see MANPOWER on page 8

Above: The Chicago Bears Shufflin' Crew.

'85 Chicago Bears Return To Studio

Shufflin' Crew begins work on long-awaited follow-up album

CHICAGO—In an announcement that has electrified the music world, the Chicago Bears Shufflin' Crew confirmed Monday that it is reuniting and will soon begin work on its first new material since the seminal 1985 "Super Bowl Shuffle" single.

Confirming the recent swirl of music-industry rumors regarding a possible reunion, Shufflin' Crew lead singer Willie Gault told reporters: "After nearly 12 years of solo gigs and side projects, we decided it was time for us to work together again."

Gault went on to strongly deny rumors that the Crew was returning to the studio looking for trouble.

"We didn't come here

see BEARS on page 9

Murphy Brown: Still On The Air?
See Television, page 5C

the ONION®

VOLUME 33 ISSUE 6 AMERICA'S FINEST NEWS SOURCE™ 19–25 FEBRUARY 1998

NEWS

Islamic Fundamentalists Condemn Casual Day

See Middle East, page 2A

WEATHER

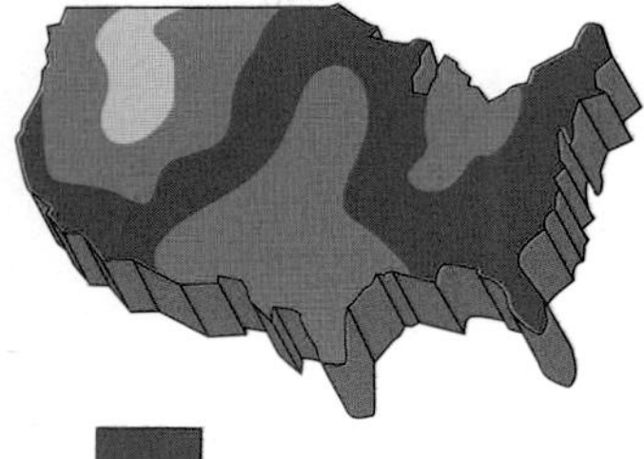

El Niño

Suncheros

Pequeños Keebleros

DOW

The Dow was relatively inactive yesterday, thanks to an ounce of kind dropped off by its friend Zack.

INSIDE

NEWS IN BRIEF 2
THE OPINION PAGE 4
WHAT DO YOU THINK 5
ONION INFO-GRAPHIC 5
PATHETIC GEEK STORIES 8
FUNNY BUSINESS 18
A-V CLUB 21
DRUNK OF THE WEEK 25
MOVIE LISTINGS 28
VIDEO 29
MUSIC 30
WORDS 32
SAVAGE LOVE 33
CALENDAR 34
CLASSIFIEDS 37

Area 15-Year-Old Only Homosexual In Whole World

WAUGANAUKEE, MN—On the surface, Daryl Hegge seems to be a typical 15-year-old boy. An avid trivia buff and amateur model-rocket hobbyist, he enjoys pizza parties, after-school activities like yearbook and drama club, participating in the junior-varsity cross-country team, and listening to the music of his favorite pop stars.

Hegge appears as normal and well-adjusted as any of his peers at J. Edgar Hoover High School in the tiny rural town of Wauganaukee. But despite his seemingly healthy exterior, Hegge is different from all his peers—very different. For, unlike his fellow students, Daryl Hegge is the only homosexual in the whole world.

"I am so alone," said Hegge, speaking to reporters from his family's unfurnished basement. Here, the silently suffering youth spends much of his time struggling to cope with his hidden, shameful burden—praying to Jesus for help, furtively masturbating, and writing love poetry in what he calls his "way-super-secret diary that no one, no one ever, can see."

Hegge suffers from the only known case of a condition doctors term "homosexuality"—a completely unknown syn-

see HOMOSEXUAL on page 9

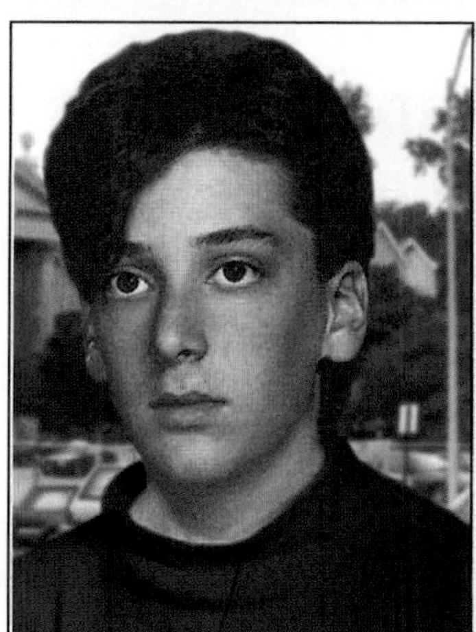

Despite his seemingly healthy exterior, Hegge is different from all his peers.

TWA Flight 800 Rebuilt, Ready To Return To Air

ST. LOUIS—At a jubilant press conference Wednesday, Trans World Airlines officials announced that, 19 months after its tragic crash off the coast of Long Island, NY, TWA Flight 800 is rebuilt and ready to return to the skies.

"This is a day everyone at TWA has been dreaming of for a long time," TWA director of safety Walter Gorman

see TWA on page 8

Left: TWA Flight 800 stands ready on the runway at New York's John F. Kennedy Airport. The salvaged and rebuilt plane will make its return to the skies Mar. 20, flying a New York to Paris route.

C-SPAN Releases *Too Hot For C-SPAN!* Video

WASHINGTON, DC—In the cable network's first-ever foray into the home-video market, C-SPAN is set to release *Too Hot For C-SPAN!* Tuesday.

The 60-minute, $19.95 videotape features what its packaging describes as "wild and sexy congressional outtakes you won't see on basic cable."

"Sometimes, the action in the House and Senate gets a little out of control, and footage must be held back from the general public," C-SPAN spokesperson Larry Jainchill said. "But now, for the first time ever, you can see it all. *Too Hot For C-SPAN!* is your front-row ticket to all the outrageous, uncensored action."

In one typical segment,

see C-SPAN on page 6

Right: A GATT-treaty debate gets out of hand as enraged U.S. Rep. John McCaskill (D-CA) charges Rep. Walter Fordice (R-NH) during a 1996 congressional session.

Second-Semester Fling Leads To First-Trimester Abortion

See Local, page 1C

Authorized Personnel Enjoying Untold Pleasures Beyond Designated Point

See Business, page 2B

Michael Jordan Displeased With This Week's Burnt Offerings

See People, page 6D

the ONION®

VOLUME 33 ISSUE 13 — AMERICA'S FINEST NEWS SOURCE™ — 9–15 APRIL 1998

NEWS

Cubs Eliminated From Playoff Contention

See Sports, page 12D

WEATHER

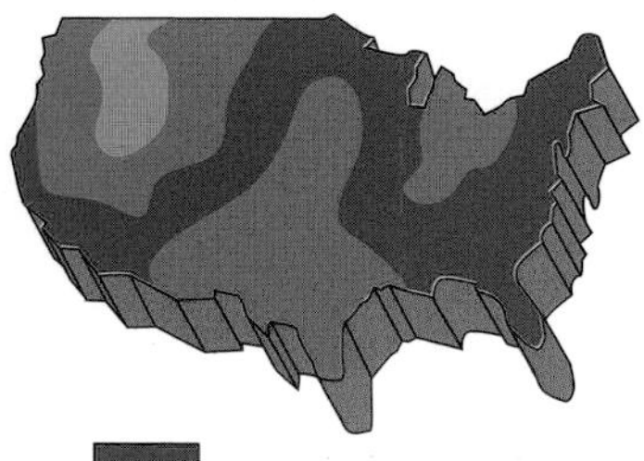

LOTTO

Lotto numbers were not drawn yesterday, as the Lotto spent its money on food for its five kids and went to look for work.

Lotto resumes tomorrow.

INSIDE

NEWS IN BRIEF....2
THE OPINION PAGE....4
WHAT DO YOU THINK....5
ONION INFO-GRAPHIC....5
PATHETIC GEEK STORIES....8
FUNNY BUSINESS....16
DRUNK OF THE WEEK....18
A-V CLUB....19
MOVIE LISTINGS....28
VIDEO....29
MUSIC....30
WORDS....32
SAVAGE LOVE....33
CALENDAR....34
CLASSIFIEDS....37

Retro-Crazed German Youths Invade Poland

Above: A battalion of hip, '30s-obsessed German teens rolls through the streets of Warsaw.

WARSAW, POLAND—In the largest nostalgia-driven military assault in history, 250,000 retro-crazed German teenagers and twentysomethings invaded Poland Monday.

"The '30s were, like, *the* coolest decade," said 17-year-old Grete Wunsch of Dusseldorf, one of the 840 young hipsters in the 55th Panzer Division who seized control of the capital city of Warsaw and set up a provisional German government. "The clothes, the music, the rallies—that whole Third Reich thing was just the best. I was *so* born in the wrong decade."

> **"The '30s were, like, the coolest decade," said 17-year-old Grete Wunsch of Dusseldorf.**

"*Lebensraum* is totally where it's at," said Günter Groff, 19, a high-ranking officer in the popular teen retro-club which calls itself "The S.S." "We're tired of the mainstream, corporate clothes and pop music of the '90s. We hunger for something more, something to call our own, and we understand that the Fatherland must gain more territory if the superior Aryan Race is to claim its rightful destiny as rulers of the *Untermensch*."

Throughout Poland, the air is filled

see YOUTHS on page 6

Hippocratic Oath 'Under Review' By HMO Board

INDIANAPOLIS—In a development bioethicists and health-care industry professionals are watching closely, the board of directors of Indiana HMO PhysCare-Plus, one of the largest and most powerful HMOs in the nation, announced Monday that the Hippocratic Oath is currently "under review."

According to board members, the 2,400-year-old oath, attributed to the Greek physician Hippocrates and generally acknowledged as the cornerstone of medical ethics, is "outmoded and no longer economically viable in today's complex, rapidly changing health-care environment."

"Here at PhysCare-Plus, our goal has always been the same: to provide customers with dependable, first-rate health care. But it is becoming increasingly difficult to do so when we are hampered by an ancient moral code penned by a contemporary of the historian Herodotus somewhere between 470 and 360 B.C.," said Dr. Cedric Samms, head of the PhysCare-Plus board. "While the oath is admirable for its idealism, it simply does not take into account the many complexities and economic realities of medicine in the modern age."

Added Samms: "The personal touch.... That's the PhysCare-Plus difference."

According to Samms, the Hippocratic Oath is too narrow and inflexible,

see HMO on page 12

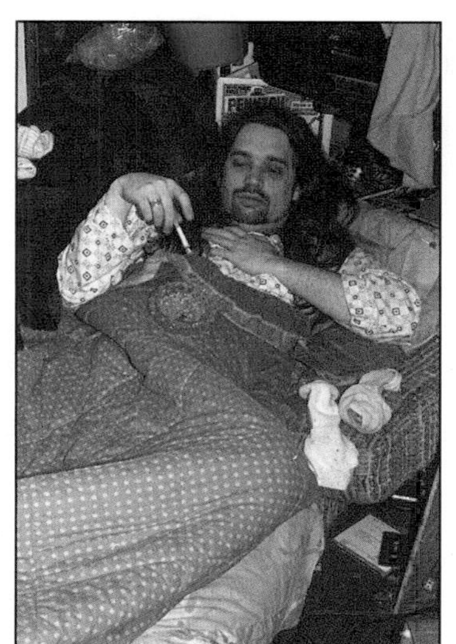

Utter Failure To Spend Rest Of Day In Bed

STEVENS POINT, WI—Part-time dishwasher and self-described "utter failure" Eric Mayhew opted to call in sick and spend the rest of the day in bed Monday, and may do so again tomorrow, sources said.

Reasons cited for the decision to remain in bed include: overall misery, desire to withdraw from all human contact, and the lack of any point in getting up to face another day of the pathetic charade of his totally wasted existence.

"I knocked on his door for a long time. I don't know if he didn't hear me or what," said Tom Worland, a former roommate of Mayhew's from the University of Wisconsin at Stevens Point, where the two briefly attended classes before dropping out in 1991. "He's pretty much a loner nowadays. To be honest, I don't see much of him anymore."

The 24-year-old Mayhew, who for the last several years has eked out a partial subsistence at various minimum-wage menial-labor jobs and has been rescued from insolvency by his parents

Left: Utter failure Eric Mayhew.

see FAILURE on page 14

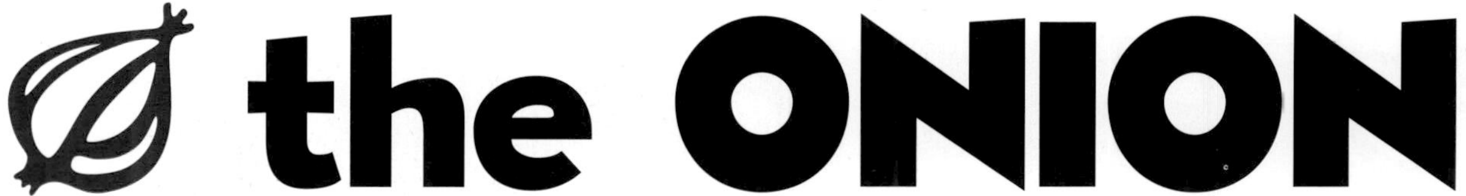

VOLUME 33 ISSUE 20 | AMERICA'S FINEST NEWS SOURCE™ | 28 MAY–3 JUNE 1998

NEWS

Uma Thurman, Ethan Hawke To Sire New Race Of Homo Celebritans

See People, page 3B

WEATHER

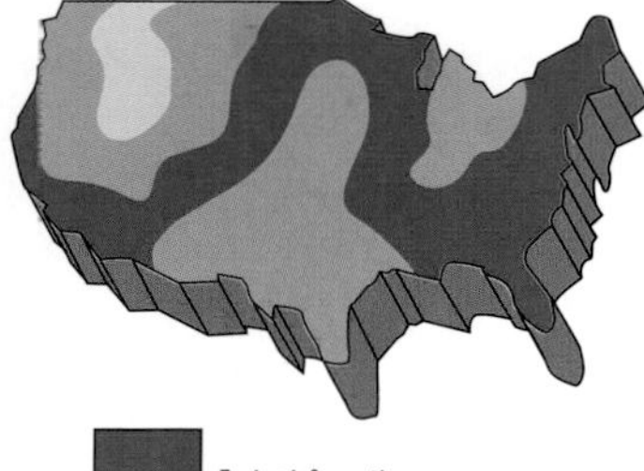

DOW

The Dow fell 23 points yesterday, forcing stockbroker Ryan Mills to sell Grandma's bed and her worn Bible.

INSIDE

NEWS IN BRIEF....2
THE OPINION PAGE....4
WHAT DO YOU THINK....5
ONION INFO-GRAPHIC....5
PATHETIC GEEK STORIES....8
FUNNY BUSINESS....13
A-V CLUB....15
SAVAGE LOVE....25
DRUNK OF THE WEEK....14
MOVIE LISTINGS....20
VIDEO....21
MUSIC....22
WORDS....24
CALENDAR....27
CLASSIFIEDS....29

Astronomer Discovers Center Of The Universe

'It is my beautiful 9-year-old son,' he says

PASADENA, CA—California Institute of Technology astronomer Dr. James Shrifkin stunned the scientific and space-exploration communities Tuesday, when he announced that the center of the known universe is his 9-year-old son Brian.

"The universe revolves around him," Shrifkin told colleagues at the annual American Society Of Astronomers convention at Cal Tech. "He is the most precious and wonderful child in all known creation."

Shrifkin said he first suspected that Brian, a straight-A student at Lakeside Elementary School, is the center of the universe last Saturday, when he scored three goals in his soccer game.

"After the game, I went home and thought about the many quantifiable properties of goodness my son possesses, including kindness, generosity and intelligence," Shrifkin said. "Formulating a rough Briancentric theory of space and time, I then collected more evidence, including the beautiful card he bought me last Father's Day and his spelling-bee trophy. The more data I had, the more apparent it became that my own son is the elusive center of the universe for which science has long searched."

Above: Brian Shrifkin, center of the known universe.

According to Shrifkin, at the moment of the Big Bang, a swirling, primordial cloud of emBrianic matter existed at the center of what would eventually become the universe. As the explosion settled and galaxies formed, Brian remained in the center, where laws of physics originating within him dictated the development of space as we know it.

"Primary data indicates that Brian is a spatial hub around which all other activity revolves," an excited, proud Shrifkin told reporters yester-

see UNIVERSE on page 7

New Starbucks Opens In Rest Room Of Existing Starbucks

CAMBRIDGE, MA—Starbucks, the nation's largest coffee-shop chain, continued its rapid expansion Tuesday, opening its newest location in the men's room of an existing Starbucks.

"Coffee lovers just can't stand being far from their favorite Starbucks gourmet blends," said Chris Tuttle, Starbucks vice-president of franchising. "Now, people can enjoy a delicious Frappuccino or espresso just about any time they please, even while defecating."

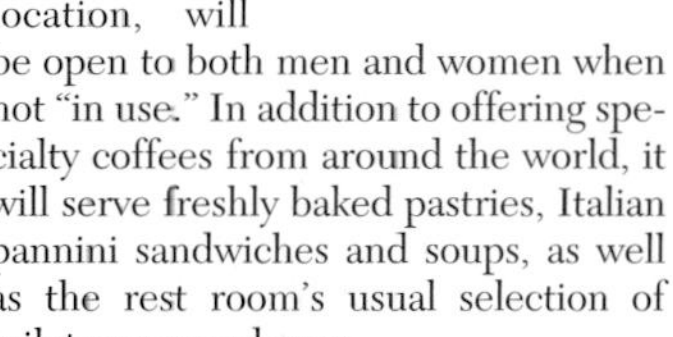

The new men's-room-based Starbucks, the coffee giant's 1,531st U.S. location, will be open to both men and women when not "in use." In addition to offering specialty coffees from around the world, it will serve freshly baked pastries, Italian pannini sandwiches and soups, as well as the rest room's usual selection of toilet paper and soap.

"This is a great addition," said Jonathan Connolly, a Boston-area banker who tried out the new Starbucks Tuesday. "I was enjoying my usual triple mocha latté in the main Starbucks, and I had to go to the bathroom, where three people were in line to use the stalls. The wait might have been a problem, but, to my great pleasure, there was another Starbucks right there, ready to serve me more delicious coffee. And the baristas were helpful and courteous."

see STARBUCKS on page 8

Area Homosexual Saves Four From Fire

Heroic Neighbor Praised, Gay

FALMOUTH, MA—Near-tragedy turned to joy Monday, when Phillip and Karen Widman and their two children were rescued from their burning house on Locust Street by Kevin Lassally, a homosexual man.

The fire, believed to have started when a lit candle ignited a set of drapes, threatened to consume the home and the Widman family along with it. Lassally, heading home after visiting with other homosexuals, smelled smoke and saw flames through the Widmans' living-room window.

see HOMOSEXUAL on page 10

Falmouth resident Kevin Lassally (inset), who likes to hold and kiss other men, is being hailed as a hero after rescuing a family of four from a deadly blaze.

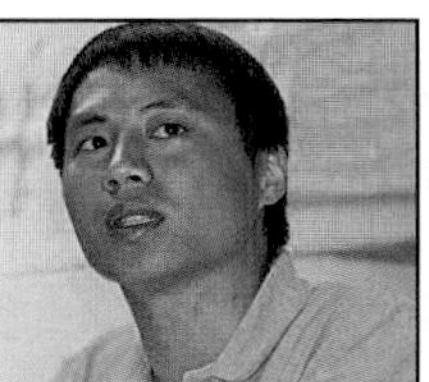

Chinese Graduate Student Pursues Master's In Political Silence

See World, page 5A

Is Your Privacy Being Violated? An Exclusive Hidden-Camera Investigation

See Office, page 1C

Actress Leaves Porn Past Behind With New Cinemax Erotic Thriller

See Entertainment, page 7D

the ONION®

VOLUME 33 ISSUE 25 AMERICA'S FINEST NEWS SOURCE™ 23–29 JULY 1998

NEWS

Nation's Insomniacs Speak Out Against World's-Strongest-Man Competitions

See Television, page 5D

WEATHER

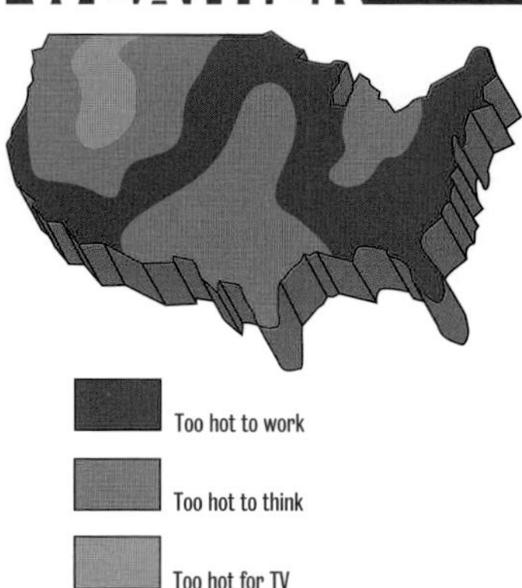

Too hot to work

Too hot to think

Too hot for TV

DOW

The Dow rose sharply after Fed Chief Jagger announced that the prime rate was going up, up, up, up.

+119

INSIDE

NEWS IN BRIEF..........2
THE OPINION PAGE..........4
WHAT DO YOU THINK..........5
ONION INFO-GRAPHIC..........5
PATHETIC GEEK STORIES..........8
FUNNY BUSINESS..........14
A-V CLUB..........17
MOVIE LISTINGS..........24
VIDEO..........25
MUSIC..........26
WORDS..........28
SAVAGE LOVE..........29
CALENDAR..........31
CLASSIFIEDS..........33

CONSUMER HEALTHBEAT

New Smokable Nicotine Sticks

Can They Help Smokers Quit?

- Will completely cure smokers' cravings, says manufacturer
- More effective than patches or gums
- Fills lungs with rich, satisfying smoke, curbing desire for cigarettes
- Available in regular or menthol
- Legal for minors
- Available wherever cigarettes are sold
- Should HMOs cover the drug?

see NICAREST page 3

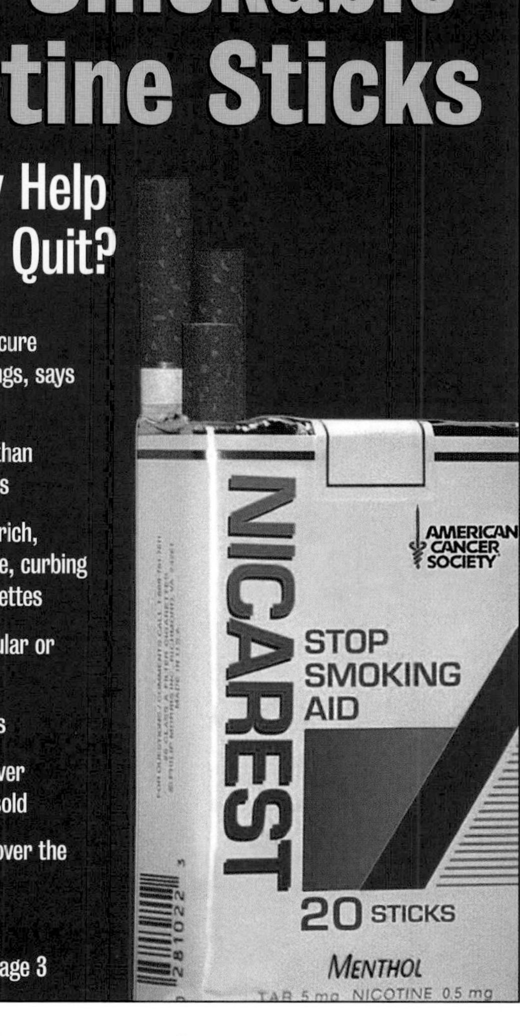

Clinton Escapes Through Air Vent

WASHINGTON, DC—Independent counsel Kenneth Starr's investigation into the behavior of Bill Clinton suffered a major setback Monday, when the embattled president escaped through an air vent minutes before he was to testify before a federal grand jury.

President Clinton

Clinton's dramatic escape occurred at the William O. Douglas Federal Courthouse, to which he had been subpoenaed for questioning about alleged perjury in the Linda Tripp/Monica Lewinsky affair.

Though Starr and other federal prosecutors immediately sounded the building's red alert, touching off a full-scale manhunt for Clinton, the president has not been located as of press time.

The air-vent escape took place shortly after 3 p.m., when law-enforcement personnel left Clinton unattended in a waiting room adjacent to the grand-jury chambers, only to discover the president missing upon their return several minutes later.

"At first, we had no idea how he had gotten out," said Brian Kolterman, one of two federal agents assigned to guard the room in which Clinton was being held. Upon discovering the escape, the two agents reportedly pinwheeled wild-

see AIR VENT on page 6

Area Guidance Counselor's Door Always Open

MANKATO, MN—Nick Wisniewski, 35, a guidance counselor at William Henry Harrison High School, announced Tuesday that the door to his office is always open.

"Feel free to drop in any time, kids, whether you need help with your schedule, are having trouble at home, or just want to rap," said Wisniewski, who has maintained an "open door" policy throughout his seven years at Harrison High. "Whatever may be on your mind, I'm here to listen."

Speaking from his office in the back hallway next to the shop, Wisniewski added: "I'm available during regular class periods, as well as before and after school every day except Fridays."

In addition to accepting students on a "first come, first served" basis, Wisniewski said students can make appointments to see him by signing up on the clipboard hanging outside his door. Or, if they prefer, students can place a note in the adjacent padlocked box marked "For Mr. Wisniewski—100% Confidential."

"Whatever I talk to a student about is kept between the two of us," said Wisniewski, simulating a zipper closing over his lips. "Earning

see COUNSELOR on page 7

Right: Guidance counselor Nick Wisniewski, who says students are welcome to "swing by any time for a rap session."

Allstate Charged With Operating Protection Racket

Allstate® You're in good hands.

See Business, page 1D

Charles Durning Hocks Up Four-Pound Chunk Of Phlegm

See People, page 3B

the ONION®

★

VOLUME 34 ISSUE 1 | AMERICA'S FINEST NEWS SOURCE™ | 6–12 AUGUST 1998

NEWS

Employees: Are They Costing U.S. Businesses Too Much Money?

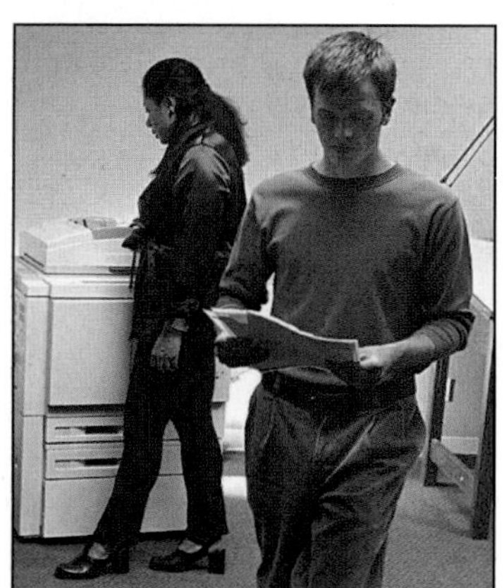

See Nation, page 4A

WEATHER

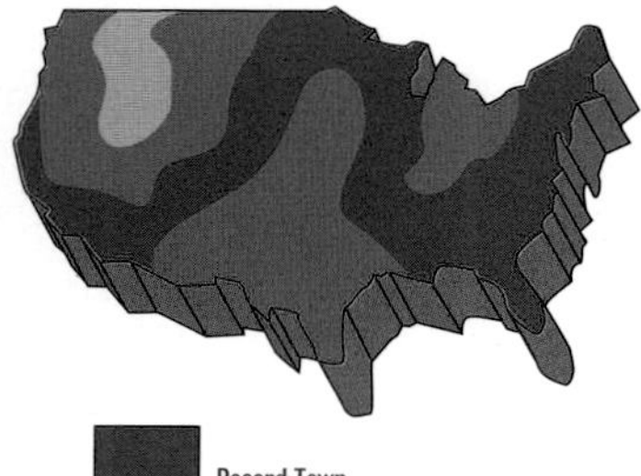

Record Town

Pet World

Carpetland

DOW

If the Dow didn't have such a negative attitude, maybe this wouldn't happen so often.

INSIDE

NEWS IN BRIEF 2
THE OPINION PAGE 4
WHAT DO YOU THINK 5
ONION INFO-GRAPHIC 5
PATHETIC GEEK STORIES 8
FUNNY BUSINESS 14
A-V CLUB 17
MOVIE LISTINGS 24
VIDEO 25
MUSIC 26
WORDS 28
SAVAGE LOVE 29
CALENDAR 31
CLASSIFIEDS 33

New Product Available

Americans were finally given another outlet for their discretionary-income spending Tuesday, when it was announced that a new consumer-product item is available for retail purchase.

The TapTeaser, a specially designed styling tool that doubles your hair's volume without damage, is in stores and can be purchased for the suggested retail price of $9.99.

"This is a very exciting time to be a consumer," said Nancy Wopat, a Santa Cruz, CA, mother of four and self-described "shopaholic." "Everyone loves acquiring top-quality brand-name material goods, whether for the home, the office or the yard. And now that a new product has finally hit the shelves, you can bet I'll be picking up one for

see PRODUCT on page 13

Sudanese 14-Year-Old Has Midlife Crisis

AD DUWAYM, SUDAN—Though it may often seem that way, Americans don't hold the patent on middle-age malaise. Just ask Sudan's Kutum Malakai.

Just like many people here in America, Malakai is going through a deep midlife crisis. A retired Sudanese Army captain and father of three, the 14-year-old Malakai says he is often left feeling listless and depressed by the thought that half his life is behind him.

"I've really accomplished most of my life goals, so what is there to look forward to?" Malakai says. "I've built my

see MIDLIFE on page 8

Woodland Pals Hold Impromptu Oompah-Band Jamboree

THE WOODS—An estimated 15 woodland animals gathered for an improvised oompah-band jamboree Monday.

Performing in a pasture just outside the forest in which they live, the "Woodland Pals," as the creatures are known, put on a rollicking musical performance characterized by whimsical merriment and irrepressible mischief.

According to reports, the gay oompah-band session was initiated by Ferdinand Fox, the group's leader. Fox, dressed in his trademark two-button short-pants, allegedly triggered the jamboree by declaring to his fellow Woodland Pals, "Hey, everybody! Let's put on a show!"

Moments after Fox's announcement, the other Pals emerged from their woodland hiding places sporting ill-fitting band uniforms and makeshift musi-

see JAMBOREE on page 12

Right: The jovial jamboree.

Inside: What The Stars Were Wearing At Terrible Movie's Gala Premiere
See Entertainment, page 6E

New Diet Surge Targets Overweight Snowboarders
See Business, page 5D

Area Mother Enters 16th Year Of Post-Partum Depression
See Local, page 1C

the ONION®

VOLUME 34 ISSUE 2 AMERICA'S FINEST NEWS SOURCE™ 13–19 AUGUST 1998

NEWS

Out Of Respect For Families, Horrific Disaster Footage Repeated Hourly

See Nation, page 4A

WEATHER

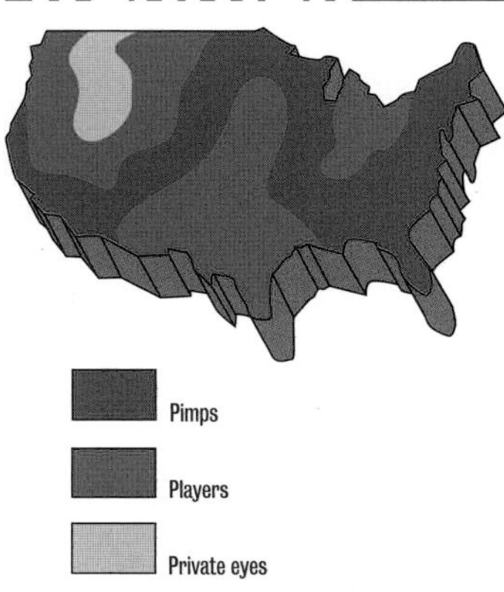

DOW

The Dow rose over 88 points yesterday. By the by, don't you just adore the way he looks in his cute little Dowhouse?

INSIDE

NEWS IN BRIEF....2
THE OPINION PAGE....4
WHAT DO YOU THINK....5
ONION INFO-GRAPHIC....5
PATHETIC GEEK STORIES....8
FUNNY BUSINESS....18
A-V CLUB....21
MOVIE LISTINGS....28
VIDEO....29
MUSIC....30
WORDS....32
SAVAGE LOVE....33
CALENDAR....35
CLASSIFIEDS....37

Saddam Hussein Steps Down Following Sex Scandal

BAGHDAD—Succumbing to public outcry and intense media scrutiny over his alleged March 1996 sexual liaison with a Presidential Palace concubine, embattled Iraqi president Saddam Hussein resigned Monday.

"President Hussein has finally done the right thing," said Special Inquisitor and Most-Holy Scholar Of The Koran

see HUSSEIN on page 12

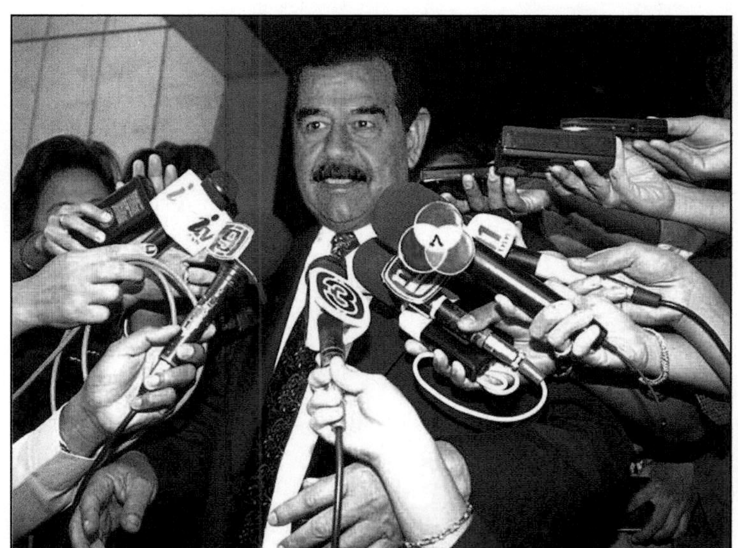

Right: Iraqi reporters deluge Saddam Hussein with questions about his alleged 1996 sexual tryst with a 22-year-old Presidential Palace concubine (above).

Infomercial Makes Leap To Big Screen

Bruce Willis To Star In Paramount Pictures' *The Abdomenizer*

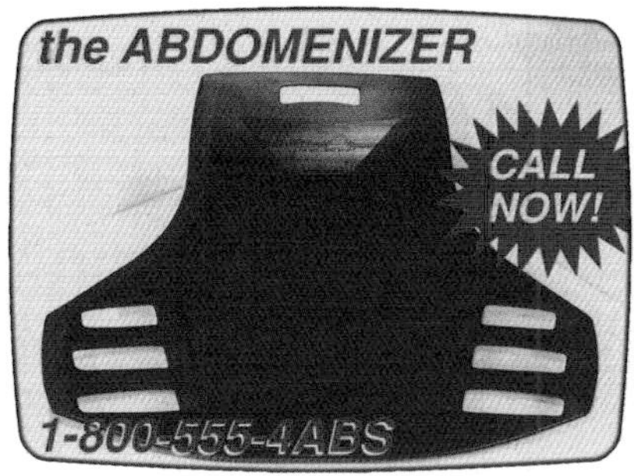

HOLLYWOOD, CA—A spokesperson for Paramount Pictures confirmed Tuesday that the studio will make a feature-length film version of the wildly popular "Abdomenizer®" television infomercial.

"Next summer, Bruce Willis is The Abdomenizer, a marked-for-death federal agent with nothing to lose but those unsightly love handles," Paramount vice-president of development Irwin Shuler said. "On July 4, 1999, get ready for explosive firming and toning action."

Bruce Willis

The Abdomenizer, which begins shooting next month, will star Willis as Jack Tyler, an FBI munitions expert who struggles daily with overpriced exercise equipment that just doesn't deliver. As the twin crises of losing muscle tone and turning 40 hit Tyler, a mysterious young woman comes into his life and introduces him to the Abdomenizer® muscle-toning system. As the film builds to a thrilling climax, terrorists announce that a nuclear bomb will devastate Los Angeles

see ABDOMENIZER on page 8

Report: 32 Percent Of U.S. Citizens Still Not Famous

WASHINGTON, DC—According to a report released Tuesday by the U.S. Census Bureau, only 32 percent of Americans are still not famous.

"Between Powerball winners, president-fellaters, 11-year-old elementary-school shooters, daytime-TV talk-show guests, and women who give birth on the Internet, a whopping 68 percent of U.S. citizens can be categorized as celebrities," Census Bureau director Gordon Tillinghast said. "The 'non-famed' demographic is among the most rapidly shrinking in the U.S."

The 32 percent figure, determined by the Census Bureau's July 1998 Current Population Survey, represents a 10 percent decline in the number of non-famous Americans over the past 18 months. At the current rate of celebrity growth among the general populace, census officials estimate, 225 million U.S. citizens will be famous by 2003.

"Just about everyone I know is famous," said Wichita Falls, TX, resident Frederick Trotta, who rose to national prominence in 1997 when he

see FAMOUS on page 14

the ONION®

VOLUME 34 ISSUE 6 | AMERICA'S FINEST NEWS SOURCE™ | 10–16 SEPTEMBER 1998

NEWS

Local Cat Attempts World Record For Things Sat On

see LIFESTYLE page 6D

Area Man Could Use The Overtime Anyway

see LOCAL page 10C

Somebody, Somewhere Proposes *Gattaca: The Series*

see ENTERTAINMENT page 1D

DJ Shadow's Mother Releases Extended Chex Party Mix

see PEOPLE page 9B

STATshot

A look at the numbers that shape your world.

Top Adult Films

What are the top-selling adult videos of the summer?

$115 mil.	Shaving Ryan's Privates
$98 mil.	The Shaft Of Zorro
$86 mil.	Hair π
$77 mil.	How Stella Got Her Tube Packed

INSIDE the ONION®

News In Brief 2
Opinion Page. 4
What Do You Think. . . 5
Onion Infographic . . . 5
Horoscopes 23
AV Club 25
Movie Listings. 35
Video. 36
Music 38
Words 42
Savage Love. 43
Calendar. 46

Oprah Viewers Patiently Awaiting Instructions

Above: Hagerstown, MD, *Oprah Winfrey Show* viewer and mother of four Liz Kuharski, 34, awaits word from her leader about what to buy, cook and read.

CHICAGO, IL—With nearly three weeks having passed since talk-show host Oprah Winfrey last issued an official command, approximately 60 million *Oprah Winfrey Show* viewers are on standby, stationed in front of their television sets and patiently awaiting further instructions from their leader.

"We must be patient with Oprah," said Winfrey fan Melanie Leupke, 44, of Stillwater, OK. "Ours is not to question why she is taking so long. When the time is right and we are needed again, Oprah will tell us what to do."

Across the U.S., *Oprah* viewers' anticipation for new Winfrey directives is reaching a fever pitch. In Winfrey's home base of Chicago, throngs of fans gather outside her Harpo Studios headquarters around the clock, maintaining their silent, faithful vigil. Though the city's streets are quiet, a palpable sense of expectation fills the air.

"What book should I read? What low-fat

see OPRAH on page 6

Parents Of Suicide Victim Saw It Coming A Mile Away

GLENDALE, AZ—Last week's suicide of Glendale 16-year-old Adrian Lucas came as no surprise to his parents, who "saw it coming a mile away," according to a statement made by the couple Tuesday.

Adrian Lucas

"I wish I could say this came as a huge shock to us, but it really didn't," said Roberta Lucas, who on Sept. 4 came home from work to find her son dead on the living-room floor with a gunshot wound to the left temple. "All the warning signs were there."

Jim Lucas, 47, said he had sensed for months that his son was seriously contemplating suicide.

"Adrian was profoundly depressed and had lost all self-confidence and self-esteem," he told reporters. "He was convinced that nobody in the world loved him at all, or even cared if he lived or died. He'd frequently call himself names like 'shithead' and 'worthless,' and he was always telling us how we'd be better off without him. It was a textbook case."

Roberta Lucas agreed. "He was constantly saying things like, 'I guess

see SUICIDE on page 11

Yeltsin Forcibly Ejected From Detroit-Area Check-Cashing Service

DETROIT—Russia's economic woes continued Tuesday, when a belligerent Boris Yeltsin was forcibly ejected from a Detroit-area check-cashing service after his attempt to cash a $375 personal check drawn on a Moscow bank was denied.

"[Yeltsin] came in here around 10 p.m., looking to cash a check," said Duane Simmons, night manager of the Mack Avenue Check 'N' Cash where the incident occurred. "So while he's filling out the forms, I check the list we have taped up behind the register, and guess what? The guy's name is there under both Boris Yeltsin and Yeltsin, Boris. And they're both underlined about five times, because, apparently, he

see YELTSIN on page 21

Above: Security guard Dale Hobson escorts Russian President Boris Yeltsin from the premises of a Detroit-area Check 'N' Cash store. Yeltsin was asked to leave after becoming hostile and verbally abusive over a refused check.

the ONION®

VOLUME 34 ISSUE 8 AMERICA'S FINEST NEWS SOURCE™ 24–30 SEPTEMBER 1998

NEWS

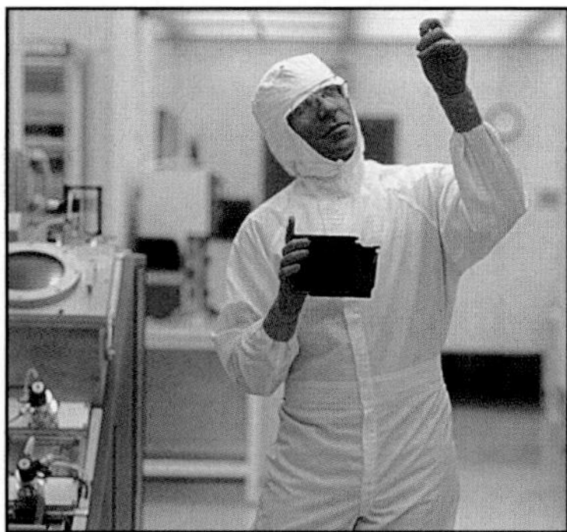

New Drug Offers Hope To Infertile Inner-City Teens

see HEALTH & TECHNOLOGY page 1B

GM Workers Strike For 2,000-Peso Raise

see BUSINESS page 9A

Inside: Talking To Your Kids About Sucking The President's Cock

see FAMILY FOCUS page 11D

STATshot

A look at the numbers that shape your world.

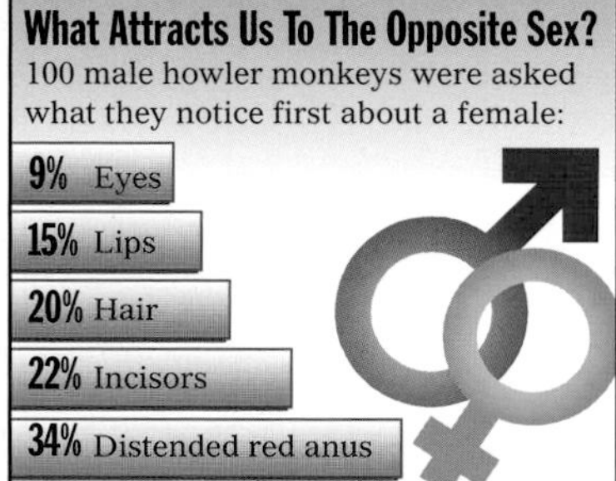

INSIDE the ONION®

News In Brief 2
Opinion Page. 4
What Do You Think. . . 5
Onion Infographic . . . 5
Horoscopes 21
AV Club 23
Movie Listings. 35
Video. 38
Music 40
Words 42
Savage Love. 43
Calendar. 45

Tenth Circle Added To Rapidly Growing Hell

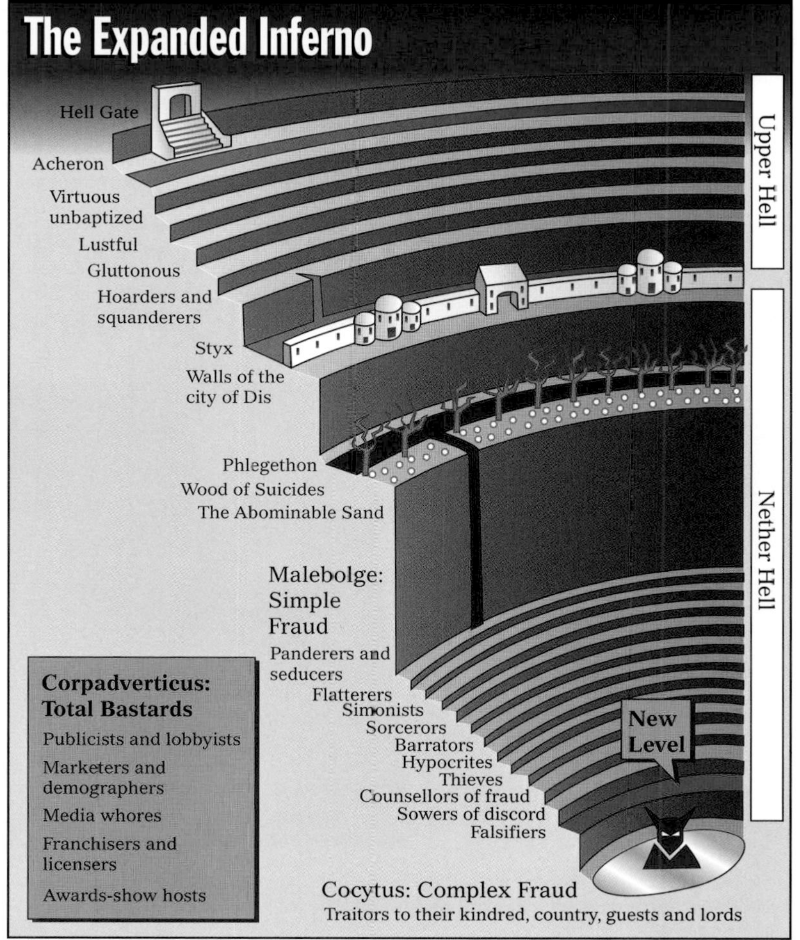

CITY OF DIS, NETHER HELL—After nearly four years of construction at an estimated cost of 750 million souls, Corpadverticus, the new 10th circle of Hell, finally opened its doors Monday.

The Blockbuster Video-sponsored circle, located in Nether Hell between the former eighth and ninth levels of Malebolge and Cocytus, is expected to greatly alleviate the overcrowding problems that have plagued the infernal underworld in recent

see HELL on page 18

Strom Thurmond Drafts Bill Prohibiting Telegraph Porn

WASHINGTON, DC—Contending that morse-coded descriptions of improperly petticoated young ladies are undermining the morals of American boys yet in short pants, U.S. Sen. Strom Thurmond (R-SC) proposed legislation Monday banning telegraph porn.

Senator Thurmond

"My friends, this revolutionary new 'Tele-graph' technology, by which messages are transmitted across vast distances via cable wire, is indeed a wondrous device," Thurmond told fellow members of the Senate. "But certain telegraphers—most corrupt and foul telegraphy men indeed—have debased Mr. Morse's code by using its ingenious dots and dashes to transmit porno-graphs describing flagrantly uncorseted womenfolk. I submit to you, gentlemen, that laws be passed to prevent the tele-graph device from becoming a machine of ill repute!"

Thurmond's proposed legislation would establish stiff penalties for the transmission of certain obscene words and

see THURMOND on page 14

'I Provide Office Solutions,' Says Pitiful Little Man

SANTA FE, NM—When Santa Fe-area marketing and sales professionals are looking for an office-management consultant with a nose for improving productivity and cost-effectiveness, they turn to Jim Smuda. For the past six years, this pitiful little man has served as senior field consultant at VisTech, one of Santa Fe's leading service-support companies.

"I provide office solutions," the sniveling, detestable Smuda said. "Whether you need help with digital networking, facilities management, outsourcing, systems integration or document services, I have the

Left: Spineless nonentity Jim Smuda, who offers clients a wide range of consulting and computer-networking services.

experience and know-how to guide you through today's business maze."

"If you've got questions," the 41-year-old worm added, "the team of experts at VisTech has got the answers."

Before joining VisTech, Smuda spent nine years freelancing as a data-retrieval specialist in the Dallas area, troubleshooting computer systems for corporate clients. Though capable of handling a broad spectrum of business problems, the gutless half-man specializes in information-systems consulting, offering services ranging from network set-up, upgrading and maintenance to software installation,

see SOLUTIONS on page 12

the ONION®

VOLUME 34 ISSUE 10 | AMERICA'S FINEST NEWS SOURCE™ | 8–14 OCTOBER 1998

Poll: 73 Percent Of Americans Unable To Believe This Shit

PRINCETON, NJ—According to the latest Gallup Poll, conducted Monday and Tuesday of this week, nearly three out of four Americans can no longer believe this shit.

In addition to the 73 percent of poll respondents who described this shit as "beyond belief," 9 percent said they could "hardly" believe this shit, with another 5 percent "just barely" believing it. An additional 13 percent said they "couldn't give a flying fuck about the whole goddamn thing."

The poll also found that the National Shit-Credulity Index (NSCI) has hit an all-time low, with only 2 percent of Americans describing themselves as "fully confident of [their] capacity to believe this shit."

"The American people have had to deal with this kind of shit for years," Gallup Organization president Lee Sanderson said, "but now, for the first time, it appears that the vast majority of them just can't

see POLL page 8

Everyone Involved In Pizza's Preparation, Delivery, Purchase Extremely High

AUSTIN, TX—Everyone involved in the preparation, delivery, purchase and consumption of a pizza from Tony's New York-Style Pizzeria was thoroughly baked off his ass, it was reported Monday.

"From its creation at the hands of a stoned-out-of-his-mind pizzeria employee to its eventual consumption by a group of guys so unbelievably high they didn't even realize they had mistakenly given the delivery driver a $20 tip, this pizza spent its entire existence in a dense cloud of marijuana fumes," said pizza-industry watchdog Roger Dernier, who has been monitoring the link between pizza production and illegal drug use since 1991. "In the brief time this pizza spent on Earth, at no point did it come into contact with a single non-stoned human being."

According to reports, the pizza—a 16-inch black-olive and green-pepper pie mistakenly topped with extra cheese and sausage—was first conceptualized by area stoner Doug Bickell at approxi-

see PIZZA page 10

Jesse Jackson Honored For Providing Inner-City Youths With Increased Photo Opportunities

NEW YORK—The National Urban League presented Rev. Jesse Jackson with a special lifetime-achievement award Tuesday, lauding him for his "unwavering commitment to creating photo opportunities for disadvantaged inner-city youths."

"For more than 30 years, Jesse Jackson has worked tirelessly to give at-risk young people the chance to stand next to him in photos that appear in major newspapers and magazines," National Urban League director Clarence Booker said. "Thanks to his efforts, thousands of inner-city youths, from Red Hook to Compton, can proudly stand up and say, 'I *am* somebody who has appeared in a picture with Jesse Jackson.'"

see JACKSON page 14

Right: Jesse Jackson provides youths in Chicago's Cabrini Green housing project with a much-needed photo opportunity.

NEWS

Special Olympics T-Ball Stand Pitches Perfect Game

see SPORTS page 5C

On-Line Gambling Too Depressing To Even Think About

see NETWATCH page 10D

Area Man Swears He Was Just Vacuuming Naked

see LOCAL page 7D

STATshot

A look at the numbers that shape your world.

INSIDE the ONION®

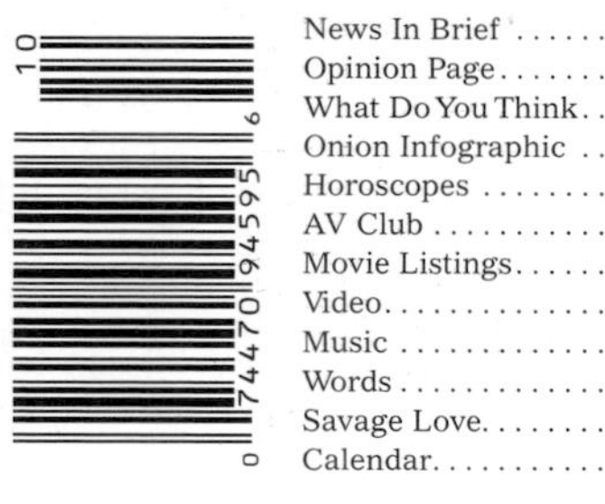

News In Brief 2
Opinion Page 4
What Do You Think . . . 5
Onion Infographic . . . 5
Horoscopes 17
AV Club 19
Movie Listings 29
Video 30
Music 32
Words 34
Savage Love 35
Calendar 37

NEWS

Larry King's Frothing Saliva Hosed Off Bette Midler

see PEOPLE page 2C

Area Stadium Inadequate

see SPORTS page 1D

Answering-Machine Message Brings Laughter And Joy To All Who Hear It

see LOCAL page 3E

STATshot

A look at the numbers that shape your world.

INSIDE the ONION®

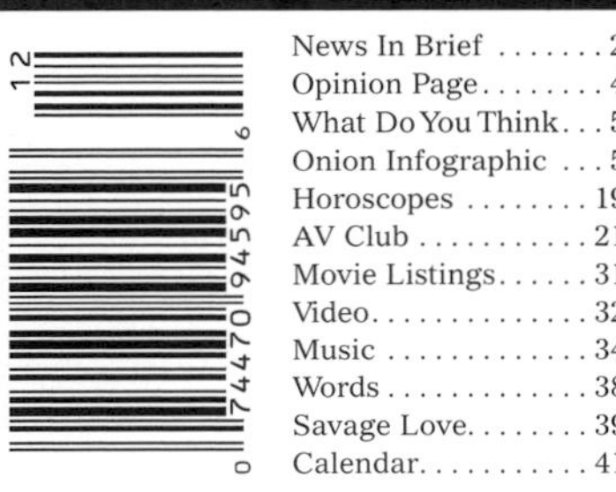

News In Brief 2
Opinion Page. 4
What Do You Think. . . 5
Onion Infographic . . . 5
Horoscopes 19
AV Club 21
Movie Listings. 31
Video. 32
Music 34
Words 38
Savage Love. 39
Calendar. 41

the ONION®

VOLUME 34 ISSUE 12 — AMERICA'S FINEST NEWS SOURCE™ — 22–28 OCTOBER 1998

Consumer-Product Diversity Now Exceeds Biodiversity

WASHINGTON, DC—According to an EPA study conducted in conjunction with the U.N. Task Force On Global Developmental Impact, consumer-product diversity now exceeds biodiversity.

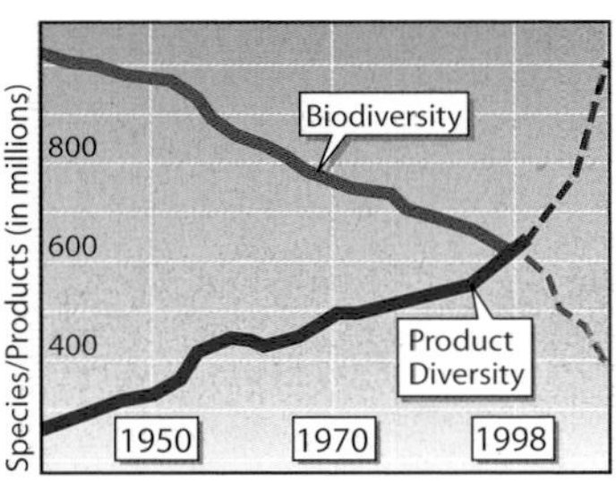

According to the study, for the first time in history, the rich array of consumer products available in malls and supermarkets surpasses the number of living species populating the planet.

"Last year's introduction of Dentyne Ice Cinnamint gum, right on the heels of the extinction of the Carolina tufted hen, put product diversity on top for the first time," study chair Donald Hargrove said. "Today, the Procter & Gamble subphylum alone outnumbers insects two to one."

The sharp rise in consumer-product diversity—with more than 200 million new purchasing options generated since 1993—comes as welcome news for those upset over the dwindling number of plant and animal species.

"As more and more species fall victim to extinction, we face a grave crisis

see DIVERSITY page 6

State Department To Hold Enemy Tryouts Next Week

Above: Secretary of State Albright answers reporters' questions about plans to hold open auditions for a new U.S. enemy.

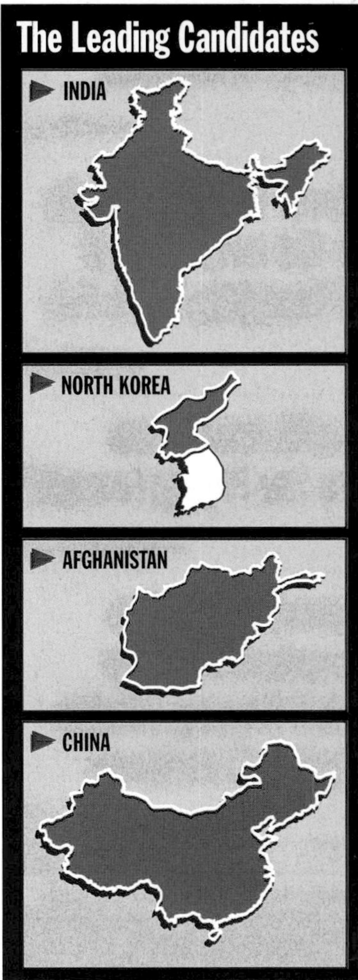

WASHINGTON, DC—Taking steps to fill the void that has plagued the American military-industrial complex since the 1991 collapse of the Soviet Union, Secretary of State Madeleine Albright announced Tuesday that the U.S. will hold enemy tryouts next week.

Slated to begin Oct. 26, the tryouts will take place at the Pentagon. More than 40 nations are expected to vie for the role of U.S. adversary, including India, Afghanistan, China, North Korea and Sudan.

"Over the past seven years, the State

see ENEMY page 15

Area Man Has Naked-Lady Fetish

Left: Warren Geary, a seemingly normal business owner and family man who harbors a secret fetish for women without clothes.

ST. JOHNSBURY, VT—Looking at Warren Geary, you'd never suspect. A respected business owner and devoted family man, the 41-year-old Geary, by all outward indications, would appear to be just like anyone else in this sleepy New England hamlet of 4,700.

But looks can be deceiving.

Dig a little deeper, beyond the many years of PTA involvement and Kiwanis Club membership, and you'll discover a very different Warren Geary, one who derives sexual stimulation and pleasure from the sight of unclothed women. This seemingly normal husband and father of three has a naked-lady fetish.

"I really enjoy looking at naked ladies," Geary said. "I don't know what it is, but seeing women without clothes gets me excited."

So consuming is Geary's fetish, he said he will sometimes pass a woman on the street and catch himself imagining what she would look like undressed.

"I'll often think about naked women, even when none are around," said Geary, who has a collection of magazines and videotapes devoted to naked-lady fetishism, including the 1998 film *Boogie Nights*. "It's just this fixation of mine."

Geary said he doesn't recall when or how he first developed his strange compulsion for seeing women in a state of rant

see FETISH page 12

NEWS

Local Couple Celebrates Birth Of Son With Ritual Genital Mutilation

see LOCAL page 2C

Power Of Prayer Fails To Rid Jerry Falwell Of Unsightly Neck Fat

see PEOPLE page 5D

Health Insurance: Are You Paying Enough?

see MONEYWATCH page 1E

Dazed, Nude Man Hospitalized After Mind-Blowing Gillette Mach 3 Experience

see LOCAL page 3C

STATshot

A look at the numbers that shape your world.

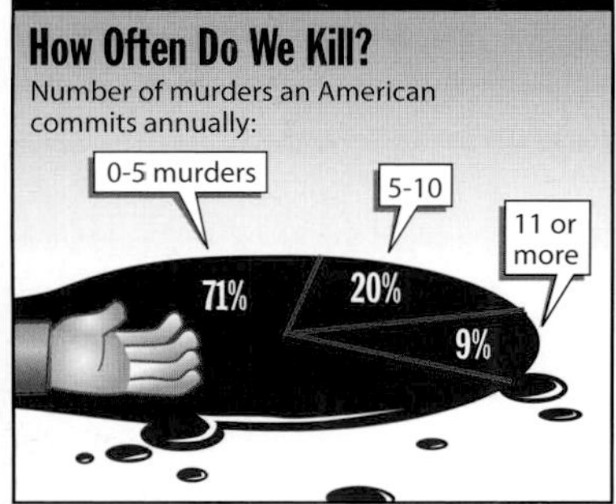

INSIDE the ONION®

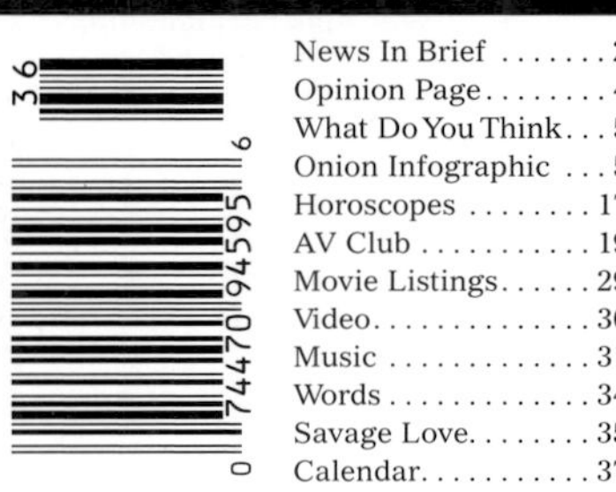

News In Brief 2
Opinion Page. 4
What Do You Think. . . 5
Onion Infographic . . . 5
Horoscopes 17
AV Club 19
Movie Listings. 29
Video. 30
Music 31
Words 34
Savage Love. 35
Calendar. 37

the ONION®

VOLUME 34 ISSUE 13 | AMERICA'S FINEST NEWS SOURCE™ | 29 OCTOBER–4 NOVEMBER 1998

Area Man Forces Self To Drink Another Free Refill

ERIE, PA—Local fast-food consumer Don Turnbee forced himself to drink another free refill Tuesday, despite the fact that he had already consumed three small soft drinks and was no longer thirsty, Burger King outlet #4579 sources reported.

According to Turnbee, known throughout the Erie area for his reliance on local fast-food outlets for convenient, delicious meals at a reasonable price, the decision to consume a third free refill was motivated by financial considerations.

"I didn't really want another Mello Yello, but I went ahead and refilled my cup anyway, because it was free," said Turnbee, addressing reporters near the self-service soda fountain conveniently located in Burger King's dining area. "With all that free soda just sitting there unused, it

see REFILL page 8

Right: Erie, PA, fast-food consumer Don Turnbee, moments after the consumption of a third beverage refill.

SPECIAL REPORT

EPA Warns Of Rise In Global Heartwarming

Unchecked Spread Of Touching Sentiment May Spell Disaster

see HEARTWARMING page 6

Above: The illuminated, female-attracting license plate frame.

Purple Neon Light Around License Plate Lures Potential Mate

MARSHFIELD, WI—A purple neon light bordering the license plate of Marshfield 20-year-old Doug Hoechst helped him lure a potential mate Saturday.

The stylish, luminescent automotive accessory, which Hoechst affixed to the rear of his 1990 Pontiac Firebird Formula in July, attracted the attention of fellow motorist Michelle Kopecke, 19, ultimately leading to the exchange of pager numbers.

"I was cruising up and down The Strip when I noticed this chick checking me out," said Hoechst, an oil-change specialist with Kwik-Lube in Marshfield. "We started to tailgate each other and race a little bit—nothing too serious. But then, when we were both stopped at the intersection by the Country Kitchen, she rolled down her window and yelled, 'Where'd you get that rad purple light?' Within an hour, I had digits. The glowing neon had done its job."

Kopecke, a Spencer native who had traveled nine miles

see LICENSE PLATE page 9

NEWS

Pro Governing: Is It Faked?

see EDITORIAL page 3A

Personnel Director Really Enjoyed Meeting You

see BUSINESS page 1C

Bloody Mess Found In Area Toilet

see LOCAL page 3E

STATshot

A look at the numbers that shape your world.

Top-Ranked U.S. Technical Colleges

1. Typist State
2. Davenport Area Post-High-School High-School School
3. University Of Dental Hygiene & Floor Installation
4. Texas Air-Conditioning & Marriage
5. University Of Beauty–San Mateo

INSIDE the ONION®

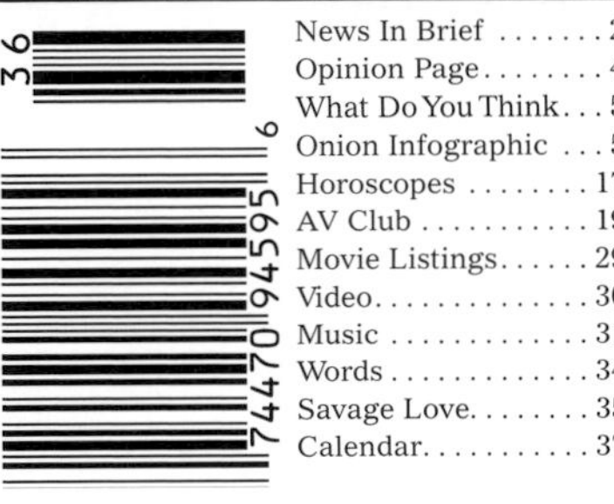

News In Brief 2
Opinion Page 4
What Do You Think . . . 5
Onion Infographic . . . 5
Horoscopes 17
AV Club 19
Movie Listings 29
Video 30
Music 31
Words 34
Savage Love 35
Calendar 37

the ONION®

VOLUME 34 ISSUE 15 • $2 AMERICA'S FINEST NEWS SOURCE™ 12–18 NOVEMBER 1998

Midwest Peace Talks Shattered By Illinois Toll-Booth Bombing

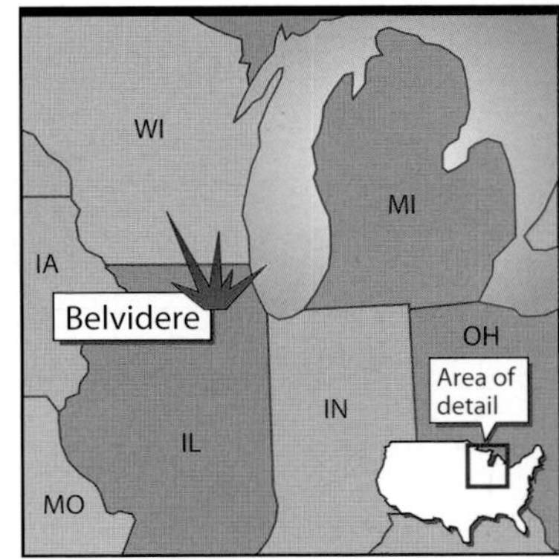

Left: Rescue workers struggle to free survivors trapped beneath several hundred pounds of exact change. Below: Illinois governor-elect George Ryan vows to bring the perpetrators to justice.

BELVIDERE, IL—Hopes for a Midwest peace accord were dealt a severe blow Monday, when a bomb ripped through a toll booth on the I-90 Illinois Tollway. The attack, which killed six and delayed westbound traffic for hours, is believed to be the work of Iowa-based militant Lutheran extremists.

The explosion is the deadliest in the troubled region since Oct. 4, 1997, when a bomb went off in a crowded Kankakee flea market, killing 22.

Illinois governor-elect George Ryan denounced the attack as "the work of cowards."

"If there is to be any hope of a lasting peace in the Middle West, these sorts of despicable acts of violence must not be

see MIDWEST page 14

Report: Many Rappers May Suffer From Unrealistically High Self-Images

WASHINGTON, DC—According to an American Psychological Association report released Tuesday, a large percentage of U.S. rappers may suffer from unrealistically high self-images, placing them at risk of a host of emotional and interpersonal problems.

The study—which examined the attitudes and self-perceptions of over 600 MCs in hoods across the U.S., including Illtown, H-Town, Strong Island, the Brooklyn Zoo, Harlem World and Long Beach—found that nearly 95 percent of those surveyed suffered from a distorted sense of their own prowess, particularly with regard to wealth, sexual potency and influence over their peers.

"While personal confidence is a vital aspect of building a healthy self-image, an exaggerated sense of self can lead

see RAPPERS page 12

Educational Puppet Pelted With Crayons

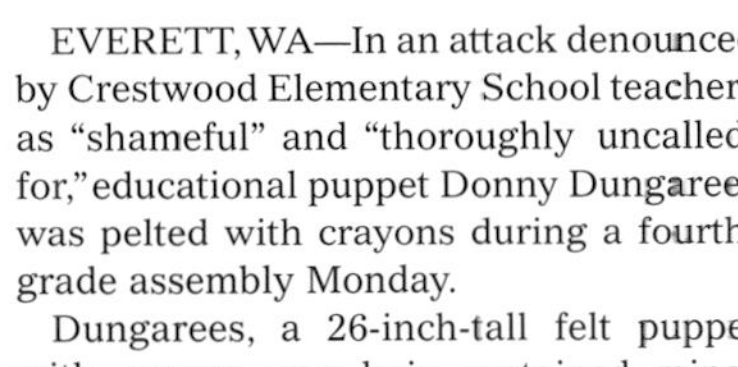

EVERETT, WA—In an attack denounced by Crestwood Elementary School teachers as "shameful" and "thoroughly uncalled-for," educational puppet Donny Dungarees was pelted with crayons during a fourth-grade assembly Monday.

Dungarees, a 26-inch-tall felt puppet with orange yarn-hair, sustained minor injuries in the attack, including a torn plaid kerchief and crayon marks to the face and neck. Dungarees' puppet pals Peggy Pipecleaners and Friendly Policeman Henry were unharmed.

Three 10-year-olds were held for questioning in connection with the brutal puppet-pelting, which occurred during the presentation of "It's Okay To Say, 'No Way!'" The anti-drug play was performed

see PUPPET page 10

Right: Donny Dungarees, moments before he was struck down.

NEWS

Cool 'Cybergranny' Needs Machines To Help Her Live

see SENIORBEAT page 1D

Magnificent Sunset Loses Out To *Home Improvement*, *Judge Judy* Hour

see LOCAL page 4E

Marc Singer Appointed Beastmaster General

see NATION page 3A

STATshot

A look at the numbers that shape your world.

INSIDE the ONION®

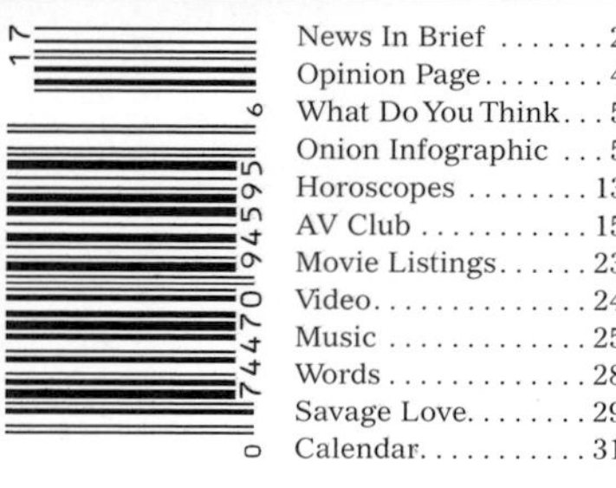

News In Brief 2
Opinion Page. 4
What Do You Think. . . 5
Onion Infographic . . . 5
Horoscopes 13
AV Club 15
Movie Listings. 23
Video. 24
Music 25
Words 28
Savage Love. 29
Calendar. 31

the ONION®

VOLUME 34 ISSUE 17 • $2 AMERICA'S FINEST NEWS SOURCE™ 26 NOVEMBER–2 DECEMBER 1998

Christ Kills Two, Injures Seven In Abortion-Clinic Attack

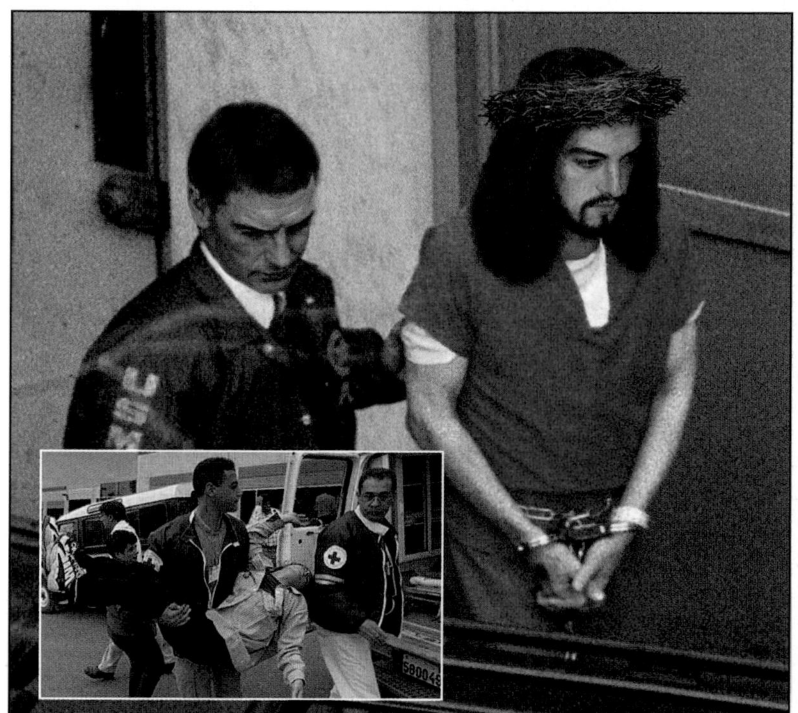

Above: A U.S. Marshal leads Christ to a holding cell. Inset: One of the injured is loaded into an ambulance.

HUNTSVILLE, AL—Jesus Christ, son of God and noted pro-life activist, killed two and critically wounded seven others when He opened fire in the waiting room of a Huntsville abortion clinic Tuesday.

Security guards at the Women's Medical Clinic of Huntsville were able to disarm the Messiah before He could reload His weapon, a secondhand Glock 9mm pistol that authorities said He purchased legally at a Jackson, MS, sporting-goods store.

"Abortion is a sin," said Christ as He was led away in handcuffs. "It is an abomination in the eyes of Me."

Witnesses said the attack, which took the lives of Dr. Nelson Woodring, 51, and clinic nurse Danielle Costa, 29, came from "out of nowhere."

"He walked up to the admissions desk

see CHRIST page 11

Report: Hostess May Have Marketed Unhealthy 'Twinkies' To Minors

WASHINGTON, DC—According to a controversial Federal Trade Commission report released Tuesday, food manufacturer Hostess may have intentionally marketed "Twinkies"—a dangerous snack cake linked to obesity and hyperactivity—to minors.

Above: The controversial cartoon mascot critics claim targets children.

"There is substantial evidence supporting the claim that, for decades, Hostess has carried out an aggressive marketing campaign with the goal of promoting Twinkie use among underage consumers," the FTC report read. "Our nation's children have been targeted for the consumption of these fattening, unwholesome cakes at a vulnerable age, before they are

see TWINKIES page 8

Auto Workers Strike For More Acrylic Novelty Baseball Caps

DETROIT—General Motors workers called a general strike Monday, vowing to stay off the assembly line until their demand for more acrylic novelty baseball caps is met.

"Fair is fair," said UAW Local 163 president Wayne Garber, marching with fellow workers in front of GM's Romulus Powertrain Assembly Plant. "All we want is our rightful share of mesh-backed hats emblazoned with humorous slogans about bass fishing, inebriation, spousal weight gain and other such topics of relevance to our lives."

Added Garber: "GM management treats its workers like mushrooms: They keep us in the dark and feed us shit."

Garber—who has vehemently denied recent allegations that he has a drinking problem, claiming that he drinks, gets drunk and falls down with

see CAPS page 6

Right: UAW members John MacArdle (left) and Burt Reese protest in front of a GM plant in Pontiac, MI.

NEWS

Your Kids: Are They Sexy Enough?

see PARENTCORNER page 4E

Cardboard Snowflake Half-Heartedly Masking-Taped To Break-Room Door

see OFFICE page 1D

Hulking, Amorphous Mass Claims Corner Booth At Denny's

see LOCAL page 3C

STATshot

A look at the numbers that shape your world.

Worst-Selling Holiday Toys

1. *Xena: Warrior Princess* Self-Discovery Kit with Lotion and Rubber "Fun Sword"
2. 12-Ounce Can Of Van de Kamp's Pork & Beans
3. Gund "Not A Teddy"™ 3,000-pound Alaskan Kodiak Bear
4. JonBenét's "I'm A Big Girl Now!" Dress-Up Playset
5. Hairby

INSIDE the ONION®

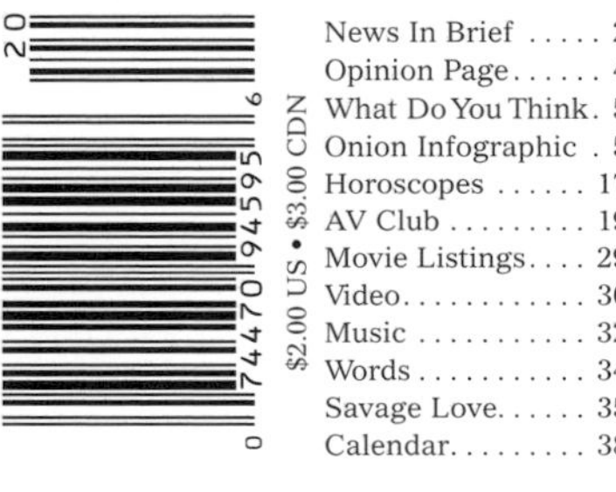

News In Brief 2
Opinion Page. 4
What Do You Think. 5
Onion Infographic . 5
Horoscopes 17
AV Club 19
Movie Listings. . . . 29
Video. 30
Music 32
Words 34
Savage Love. 35
Calendar. 38

the ONION®

VOLUME 34 ISSUE 20 AMERICA'S FINEST NEWS SOURCE™ 17 DEC. 1998–13 JAN. 1999

Animal-Rights Activists Release 71,000 Cows Into Wild

PRAIRIE DU CHIEN, WI—Members of the radical group Animal Liberation Front swept through a 900-square-mile region of Western Wisconsin Monday, freeing an estimated 71,000 cows from their human captors.

"These cows are finally free to run wild through the wilderness," said ski-masked ALF member "Brent," loosing a 200-head Guernsey herd from Milk-Rite Dairy in Reedsburg. "No creature should have to live in servitude to humans."

Within hours of the cows' release, police departments throughout the area began receiving reports of bovine fatalities.

"We've been getting calls all night long," Viroqua police chief Dale Chambers said. "So far, 43 cows have been hit by cars, 11 have fallen off bridges and drowned, and three have been electrocuted from chewing on power lines."

see COWS page 14

Right: One of the newly liberated cows.

Collectible-Plate Industry Calls For Tragic Death Of Streisand

Top: A prototype of a limited-edition commemorative Streisand plate. Left: Franklin Mint president Jim Campion addresses fellow members of the collectible-plate industry.

With sales of Princess Di memorabilia falling off sharply after a record 1997, collectible-plate-industry leaders Monday called for the tragic death of beloved entertainer Barbra Streisand.

"For the 1998 Christmas season to be anywhere near as successful as last year's, we need a heartbreaking, untimely end to a wonderful life that we can commemorate with a series of limited-edition collector's plates," said Franklin Mint president Jim Campion, who joined representatives from the Bradford Exchange and Danbury Mint in a unified call for Streisand's tragic demise. "The death of Barbra Streisand, with her upscale, intensely devoted following, would be ideal."

Economists say the unexpected death of a star of Streisand's magnitude would translate to a 70 percent sales boost for the $1 billion collect-

see STREISAND page 6

Area Bedroom Has That Weird Jeff Smell, Housemates Report

PHOENIX—The bedroom of Jeffrey Worthen has that weird sort of Jeff smell, housemates of the 22-year-old Rio Salado Community College art student reported Tuesday.

"I don't know what it is, but the whole room always has that certain distinct Jeffish odor," housemate Evan Cadwaler said. "I can't put my finger on what the smell is exactly, but it definitely smells like Jeff."

Convening to discuss containment strategies for the mysterious Jeff-based vapors, Cadwaler and fellow housemates Eric Mayhew and Chad Beem agreed that the smell seems to be strongest at around 8:30 p.m.

Jeffrey Worthen

"His room is right off the room where the TV is, and usually, like halfway through *The X-Files*, we're hit with like this wave of, well, I can't really describe it."

According to Mayhew, the housemates first noticed the Jeff smell this past May, when Worthen left the door to his bedroom, located right

see SMELL page 10

Above: Worthen's room.

Miracle Of Birth Occurs
For 83 Billionth Time

Busy Executive Has To
Take This Call Girl

Nation Impressed By Large
Pair Of Breasts

JANUARY FEBRUARY MARCH APRIL MAY JUNE

Apple Employee Fired For Thinking Different

Casual One-Nighter Gives
Strom Thurmond Change Of
Heart On Gay Issue

NYPD Apologizes For Accidental
Shooting-Clubbing-Stabbing-
Firebombing Death

1999

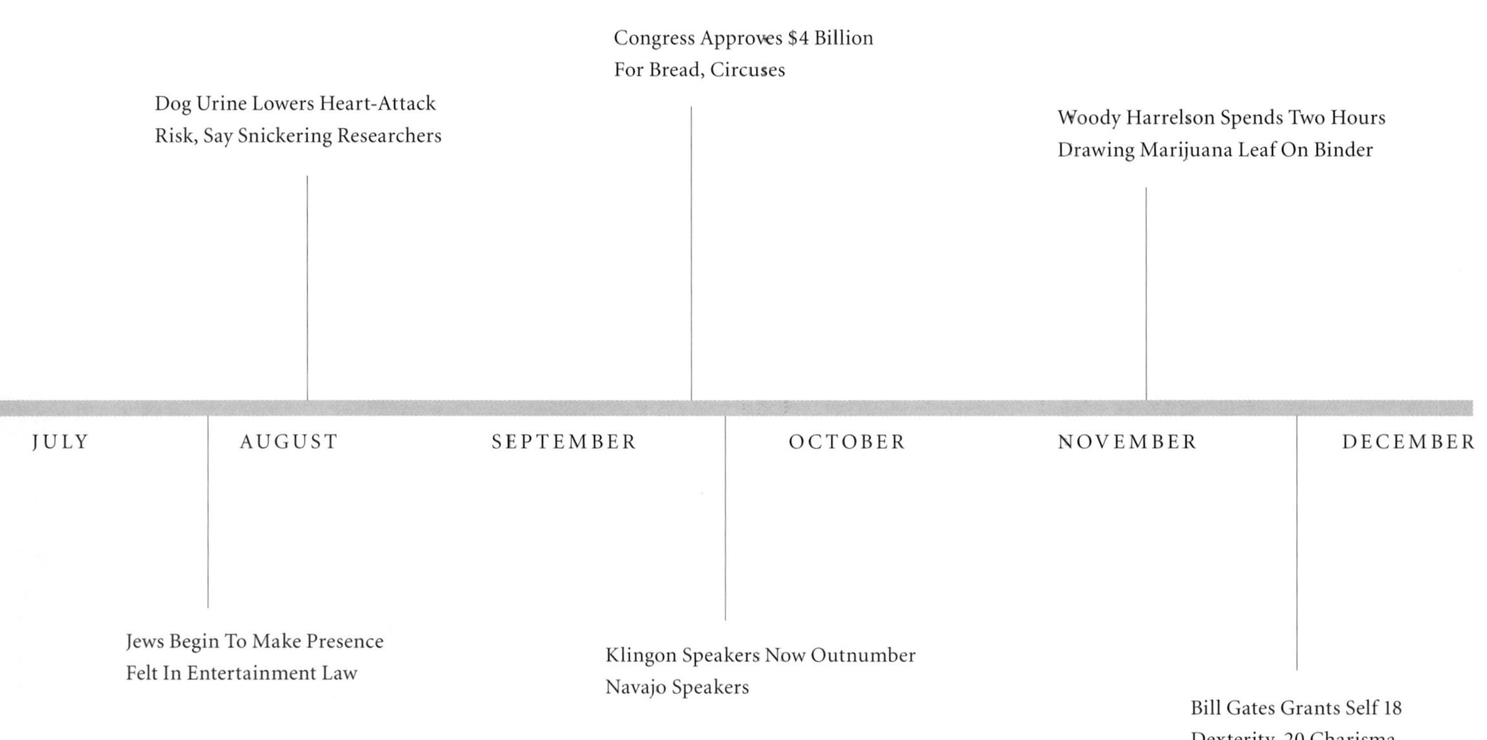

Congress Approves $4 Billion For Bread, Circuses
Dog Urine Lowers Heart-Attack Risk, Say Snickering Researchers
Woody Harrelson Spends Two Hours Drawing Marijuana Leaf On Binder
JULY
AUGUST
SEPTEMBER
OCTOBER
NOVEMBER
DECEMBER
Jews Begin To Make Presence Felt In Entertainment Law
Klingon Speakers Now Outnumber Navajo Speakers
Bill Gates Grants Self 18 Dexterity, 20 Charisma

NEWS

The American Dream: What Does That Part About Kissing The Gym Teacher Mean?

see NATION page 4A

Police Homicide Investigation Uncovers Cap In Ass

see CRIME page 3C

Terry Bradshaw Bookmarks Statler Brothers Website

see PEOPLE page 4E

STATshot

A look at the numbers that shape your world.

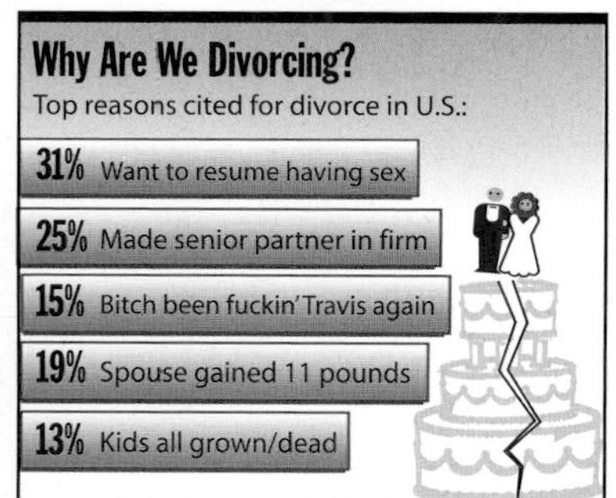

INSIDE the ONION

News In Brief 2
Opinion Page 4
What Do You Think . 5
Onion Infographic . 5
Horoscopes 17
AV Club 19
Movie Listings 29
Video 30
Music 32
Words 35
Savage Love 36
Calendar 38

the ONION®

VOLUME 35 ISSUE 2 | AMERICA'S FINEST NEWS SOURCE™ | 21–27 JANUARY 1999

Clinton Deploys Very Special Forces To Iraq

Above: Sgt. Tommy Dolber, who loves baseball and rollerskating, leads a group of very special forces in maneuvers near the Iraq-Kuwait border.
Right: President Clinton fields reporters' questions.

WASHINGTON, DC—Preparing for another possible showdown with Iraq, President Clinton deployed more than 15,000 very special U.S. forces to the Persian Gulf region Tuesday.

Clinton said the objective of the mission, dubbed Operation Great Job!, is twofold: to keep pressure on Saddam Hussein to permit the return of U.N. weapons inspectors, and to provide America's very special forces with a positive, rewarding, esteem-building experience.

"With Operation Great Job!, we send the message loud and clear to Saddam Hussein that his open defiance of the United Nations and international law will not be tolerated," Clinton said. "We also send the equally important message to

see SPECIAL page 10

Long-Awaited Baby Boomer Die-Off To Begin Soon, Experts Say

WASHINGTON, DC—After decades of waiting, the much-anticipated mass Baby Boomer die-off should finally commence within the next five to ten years, Census Bureau officials said Monday.

"I am pleased to announce that it won't be much longer now," Census Bureau deputy director Arthur Clausewitz said at a press conference. "According to our statistics, by 2009, we should see the Baby Boomers start to die off in large numbers. Heart attacks, strokes, cancer, kidney failure—you name it, the Boomers are going to be dropping from it."

Clausewitz said the Great Boomer Die-Off should hit full stride in approximately 2015, when the oldest members of the Baby Boom generation—born during the last days of World War II—turn 70.

"Before long, tens of millions of members of this irritating generation will achieve what such Boomer icons as Jim Morrison, Janis Joplin, Timothy Leary and John Kennedy already have: death. Before long, we will live in a glorious new world in which no one will ever again have to endure tales of Joan Baez's performance at Woodstock."

Despite his enthusiasm, Clausewitz cautioned that the Great Boomer Die-Off will not be without its downside.

"Our nation must steel itself for one vast, final orgy of Boomer self-obsession as we are hit with a bewildering onslaught

see BOOMERS page 9

Transgendered Sea Anemone Denounced As 'Abomination' By Clergy

HUNTSVILLE, AL—A coalition of Baptist clergymen spoke out Monday against the *Telia felina*, a transgendered sea anemone they are decrying as "base and depraved."

"This filthy anemone, which exhibits both male and female characteristics, is turning our oceans' intertidal zones into dens of sin and perversion," said Rev. William Chester, spokesman for the Save Our Seas Coalition, a Huntsville-based activist group dedicated to "the preservation of aquatic decency and morality." "For God knows how long, this twisted sea creature has been running rampant in our oceans, spreading its unnatural, bisexual lifestyle. And it's high time somebody took a stand."

The controversial anemone, common to warm-water reefs and basins worldwide, has been practicing its alternative sexual lifestyle at least as far back as 1859, when Charles Darwin first catalogued its phylum and species. Since

see ANEMONE page 7

Right: The dually gendered *Telia felina* sea anemone, which Baptist leaders are denouncing as "base and depraved."

the ONION®

VOLUME 35 ISSUE 4 AMERICA'S FINEST NEWS SOURCE™ 4–10 FEBRUARY 1999

Lewinsky Subpoenaed To Re-Blow Clinton On Senate Floor

'We Must Know Exactly What Happened,' Say Legislators

WASHINGTON, DC—On the heels of last week's decision to allow witness testimony in the presidential impeachment trial, key witness Monica Lewinsky was subpoenaed Monday to re-blow President Clinton on the Senate floor.

The controversial re-fellating, which, under the terms of the court order, will involve the full participation of both Lewinsky and the president, was described by Senate leaders as a "regrettable but unfortunately very necessary" move.

"This trial is not about sex, it's about perjury," Senate Majority Leader Trent Lott (R-MS) said. "Our job is to deter-

see RE-BLOW page 8

Left: Sen. Trent Lott (R-MS) speaks to reporters about Monica Lewinsky's Senate-ordered re-fellating of the president. Above: Lewinsky arrives in D.C.

Study: Sniffing Glue Proven Effective In Treatment Of Adolescent Boredom

BOSTON—A groundbreaking study released Monday by the American Medical Association, conducted in conjunction with the National Organization of Craft and Hobby Retailers, finds that repeated exposure to glue fumes and other industrial chemicals "may prove to be our most effective weapon yet in the fight against teen boredom."

Though ABS (Adolescent Boredom Syndrome), a debilitating condition that afflicts an estimated 90 percent of Americans between the ages of 11 and 17, has long been regarded by the medical community as incurable, the study reported that "significant reductions in teen-boredom levels" were observed in youths who regularly self-administered concentrated doses of airplane glue and other solvents.

"It's a tremendous breakthrough," said Dr. Gerald Osgood, the report's co-author. "This could be the most significant development since the 1973 discovery that aerosol whipped-cream canisters can get you really high."

Glue fumes, which can cause light-headedness, dizziness, incoherence and involuntary loss of muscle control, have for

see GLUE page 10

Roof On Fire Claims Lives Of 43 Party People

NEW YORK—Tragedy struck at a popular Manhattan nightclub Saturday, when the roof, the roof, the roof of The Tunnel caught fire, collapsing and killing 43 party people.

According to fire-department officials, the death toll was exacerbated by the clubgoers' unwillingness to evacuate the burning building.

"I tried shouting to the people on the dance floor that the roof was on fire and that they should exit the premises immediately, but they seemed unfazed by the danger," firefighter Michael Pitti said. "I just kept shouting, 'The roof! The roof! The roof is on fire!' and so forth, but they just went right on dancing, insisting that they didn't need any of our water and that we should let the motherfucker burn."

The party people's refusal to exit the flame-engulfed nightclub is widely believed to have been the result of DJ Phreek Malik's unstoppable mix of the hottest house, funk, hip-hop, disco, jungle and techno beats.

"DJ Phreek Malik was spinning in a manner so hot, these party people were willing to

see ROOF page 7

Right: NYC firefighters struggle to put out the roof blaze that took the lives of 43 party people Saturday.

NEWS

War-Torn, Blood-Soaked Kosovo: Would Bombing It Help?

see WORLD page 2A

Data Technician By Day A Data Technician By Night

see LOCAL page 6D

Diseased Baby Seal Dies Alone On Ice Floe

see NATURE page 14E

STATshot

A look at the numbers that shape your world.

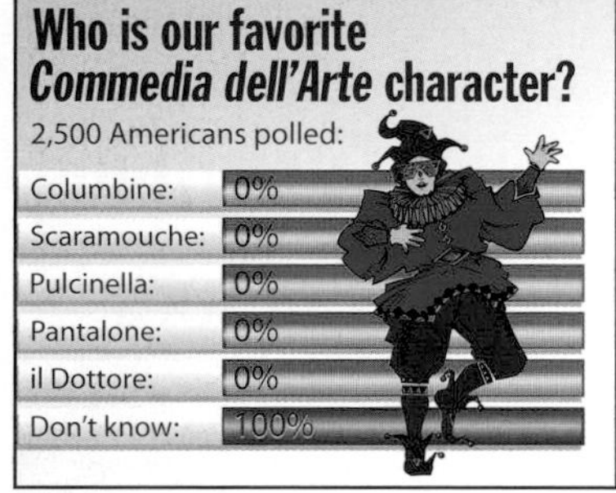

INSIDE the ONION®

News In Brief 2
Opinion Page. 4
What Do You Think. 5
Onion Infographic . 5
Horoscopes 15
AV Club 17
Movie Listings. . . . 27
Video. 28
Music 29
Words 31
Savage Love. 32
Calendar. 34

NEWS

Child Abuse: How Much Is Too Much?

see OPINION page 1C

Pier 1 Issues Formal Apology For Rattan Death March

see WORLD page 2A

Report: Advances In Porn Technology May Make 'Hypernudity' Possible By 2005

see SCIENCE page 4E

STATshot

A look at the numbers that shape your world.

Most Popular U.S. Baby Names

	White	Black	Asian
♂	Cameron	Antwaine	Michael
	Brandon	Dacron	Tim
	Austin	Newport	Chris
	Dakota	LaPrell	Rick
♀	Caitlin	Shawanda	Sue
	Brianna	Tamiqua	Lisa
	Ashleigh	Propecia	Michelle
	Madison	Sinutab	Amy

INSIDE the ONION®

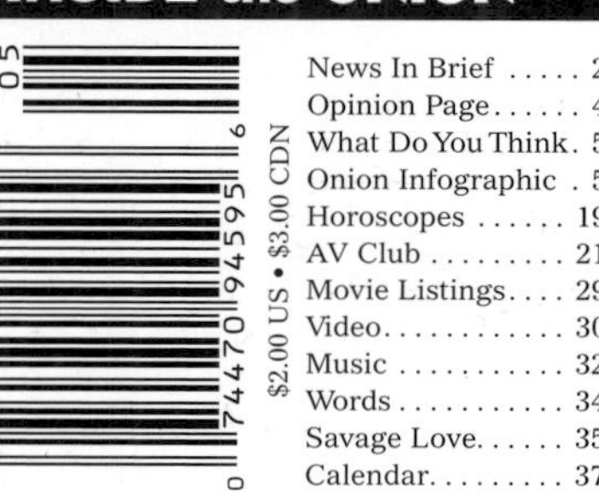

News In Brief 2
Opinion Page 4
What Do You Think . 5
Onion Infographic . 5
Horoscopes 19
AV Club 21
Movie Listings 29
Video 30
Music 32
Words 34
Savage Love 35
Calendar 37

the ONION®

VOLUME 35 ISSUE 5 AMERICA'S FINEST NEWS SOURCE™ 11–17 FEBRUARY 1999

THE ROAD TO WAD UNIFICATION

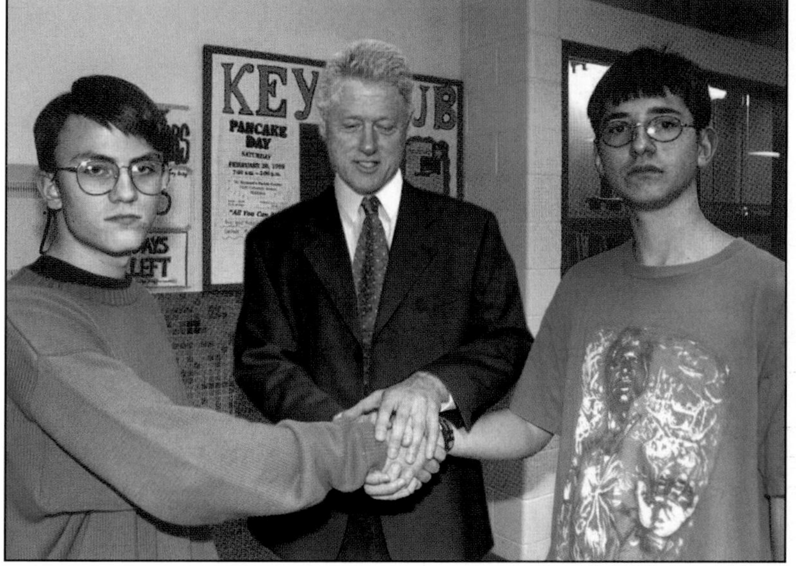

Gaywads, Dorkwads Sign Historic Wad Accord

ROCKVILLE, MD—In a historic show of wad solidarity, delegates representing gaywads and dorkwads signed the first-ever Wad Alliance Treaty Monday in the cafeteria of Adlai Stevenson Memorial High School.

The landmark accord, whose signing was presided over by President Clinton, is considered the most significant step ever taken toward wad unification.

"For too long, wad factionalism has divided the wad community, senselessly pitting wad against wad in bitter inter-wad disputes," dorkwad representative Tad Patrick Reems, 15, told reporters. "Now is the time for us to set aside our differences and join together in opposition of our common enemy—the mean, popular kids who have mercilessly inflicted locker-room wedgies upon us since time immemorial."

Gaywad Jeff Brunner, 14, agreed. "From this day forward," he said, "we will no longer see each other as dorkwads and gaywads, but instead, simply as wads,

see WADS page 10

Land Mine Seizes Power In Angola

LUANDA, ANGOLA—The war-torn West African nation of Angola, for decades wracked by violent power struggles among rival factions, was cast into further political turmoil Monday when a 40-pound anti-personnel land mine seized power and declared itself president for life.

"Today represents the dawn of a glorious

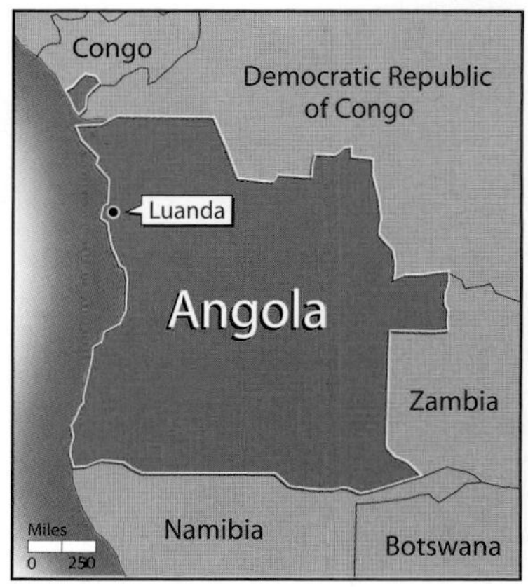

new era for our nation," said the landmine, which rose to power with the backing of Angola's estimated 40 million subterranean explosive devices. "For too many years, we have been ignored by Angola's leaders, denied representation despite the fact that we outnumber the humans by a margin of four to one."

The new leader punctuated its remarks with periodic detonations, which blew off the legs of numerous nearby orphans.

see LAND MINE page 9

Aging Pope 'Just Blessing Everything In Sight,' Say Concerned Handlers

VATICAN CITY—Concerned handlers for Pope John Paul II announced Monday that, in recent weeks, the 78-year-old Catholic leader has "just been blessing everything in sight."

The frail pope has been confined to bed ever since his Jan. 28 return from North America.

"We are, of course, very concerned for His Holiness' mental condition," said chief papal physician Giuseppe Clementi, standing by the pope's bedside, surrounded by dozens of newly consecrated pill bottles, urine-specimen cups and orthopedic slippers. "Pretty much anything you hold up in front of his face these days, he blesses."

Vatican handlers said they first noticed signs of papal deterioration on Jan. 26, as he deplaned at St. Louis' Lambert International Airport upon his arrival in the U.S. After descending the airplane staircase and kissing the runway, as is papal tradition, the pope broke free of his handlers and blessed a luggage cart, a podium, a *Life* photographer's camera, the plane's left-side landing gear, three TWA flight attendants, and two of the Swiss Guard who were attempting to release his grip on the landing struts and subdue

see POPE page 6

Left: The aging Pope John Paul II, who observers say has been "consecrating random objects like there's no tomorrow."

NEWS

Irish-Americans Gear Up For 'The Reinforcin' O' The Stereotypes'

see NATION page 5A

House Of Blues Actually House Of Whites

see LOCAL page 3E

Politician Caught On Tape With Media Whore

see WASHINGTON page 7A

STATshot

A look at the numbers that shape your world.

Most Memorable Oscar Moments

1941: Wallace Beery streaks across stage

1972: Marlon Brando damages Oscar statue while "trying to get at chocolate inside"

1986: Oliver Stone refuses Best Director award in protest of CIA brain-implant-chip experimentation

1996: Onstage mercy-killing of Billy Crystal

1998: James Cameron's "I'm king of the assholes!" speech

INSIDE the ONION®

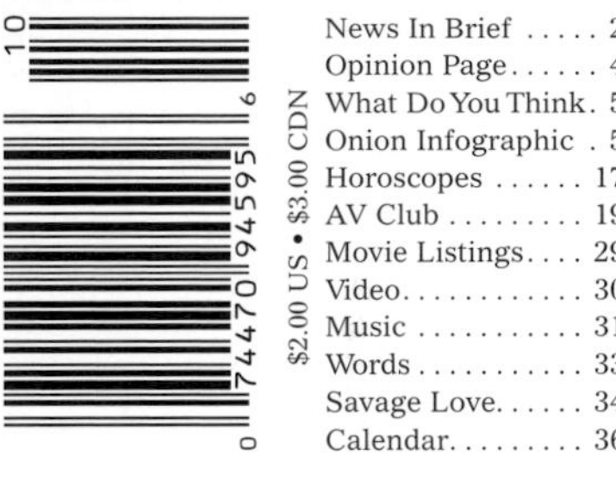

$2.00 US • $3.00 CDN

News In Brief 2
Opinion Page. 4
What Do You Think. 5
Onion Infographic . 5
Horoscopes 17
AV Club 19
Movie Listings. . . . 29
Video. 30
Music 31
Words 33
Savage Love. 34
Calendar. 36

the ONION®

VOLUME 35 ISSUE 10 | AMERICA'S FINEST NEWS SOURCE™ | 18–24 MARCH 1999

Bottom Of Barrel Dangerously Overscraped, Experts Warn

WASHINGTON, DC—The bottom of the collective national barrel, already badly strained from massive content depletion in recent years, is now in "severe danger" as a result of unchecked, unregulated overscraping, a report from the House Subcommittee on Barrel Affairs revealed Monday.

"Because of the nation's dwindling cultural output, the bottom of the barrel has been scraped beyond recognition," Barrel Affairs chairman Rep. Bernard Cooper (R-PA) told reporters at a Washington press conference. "If immediate steps are not taken to federally protect what little of the barrel's lowermost layer remains, the bottom could fall out completely by as early as spring 2001."

American Focus

Though federal barrel-watchers have long called for the adoption of broad-based barrel-bottom-conservation policies, their initiatives have been consistently defeated in Congress. The defeats, experts say, have largely been the result of the enormous pressure exerted by lobbyists representing America's film, television and publishing industries, whose relentless lowering of cultural standards

see BARREL page 12

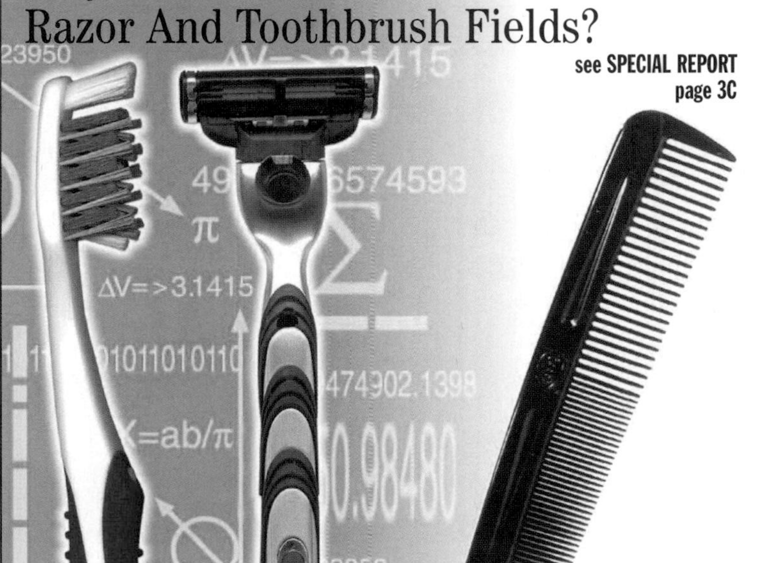

Comb Technology:

Why Is It So Far Behind The Razor And Toothbrush Fields?

see SPECIAL REPORT page 3C

Area 5-Year-Old Has Tummy Cancer

CITRUS HEIGHTS, CA—Joshua Colquitt, a Citrus Heights-area 5-year-old, was diagnosed Monday with inoperable cancer of the tummy.

Colquitt

"The doctor says I have something bad in my tum-tum," said Colquitt, speaking from his bed at St. Luke's Memorial Hospital. "He said he's gonna try his best to make it go away, but he's not sure he can."

Colquitt first complained of tummy pain on Feb. 20. Subsequent tests revealed that a malignant, golf-ball-sized tumor had metastasized near the point where the duodenum meets the belly-welly.

"I've got to be a brave boy until my tummy gets better," Colquitt said.

Tummy cancer claims the lives of more than 4,500 children each year. Ø

Horribly Awkward First Sexual Encounter 'Worth The Wait' For Christian Newlyweds

CHARLESTON, SC—John and Linda McCue, joined in holy matrimony Sunday before friends, family and their Lord at Holy Christ Almighty Lutheran Church, said the incredibly awkward wedding-night consummation of their love was "well worth the wait."

"I'm so glad we waited until we got married—it made it so much more special," said the 26-year-old Linda, who is "pretty sure" John's penis penetrated her vaginal opening during the brief, fumbling lovemaking session. "I can't imagine what a letdown our first sexual experience would have been if we'd done it at some point during our five years of dating."

John, 27, agreed. "As I prepared, sweat-drenched and terror-struck, to insert my semi-erect penis into my petrified new bride, I couldn't help but think what a precious, magical moment it was. Then, as Linda started to cry out from the anticipation of pain from

see NEWLYWEDS page 8

Right: Newlywed Christians John and Linda McCue.

the ONION®

VOLUME 35 ISSUE 12 — AMERICA'S FINEST NEWS SOURCE™ — 1–7 APRIL 1999

NEWS

Routine Drunk-Driving Trip Turns Tragic For Five Local Teens

see LOCAL page 4B

Worthless Dog Can't Talk, Drive, Solve Crimes

see PETCORNER page 11E

Trophy Wife Mounted

see LOCAL page 5B

The Y2K Bug: How Will It Affect The Rapture?

see TECHNOLOGY page 1D

STATshot

A look at the numbers that shape your world.

What Is Sarah Michelle Gellar Complaining About This Week?

Specifically told assistant she wanted Evian, not Ice Mountain

That *Entertainment Weekly* bitch totally misquoted her

Hair-extension color obviously doesn't match real hair

Stupid new costume barely accentuates cleavage

Buffy wouldn't do that

INSIDE the ONION®

News In Brief 2
Opinion Page. 4
What Do You Think. 5
Onion Infographic . 5
Horoscopes 13
AV Club 15
Movie Listings. . . . 22
Video. 23
Music 24
Words 26
Savage Love. 27
Calendar. 29

$2.00 US • $3.00 CDN

Revolutionary New Insoles Combine Five Forms Of Pseudoscience

MASSILLON, OH—Stressed and sore-footed Americans everywhere are clamoring for the exciting new MagnaSoles shoe inserts, which stimulate and soothe the wearer's feet using no fewer than five forms of pseudoscience.

"What makes MagnaSoles different from other insoles is the way it harnesses the power of magnetism to properly align the biomagnetic field around your foot," said Dr. Arthur Bluni, the pseudoscientist who developed the product for Massillon-based Integrated Products. "Its patented Magna-Grid design, which features more than 200 isometrically aligned Contour Points™, actually soothes while it heals, restoring the foot's natural bio-flow."

"MagnaSoles is not just a shoe insert," Bluni continued, "it's a total foot-rejuvena-

see INSOLES page 12

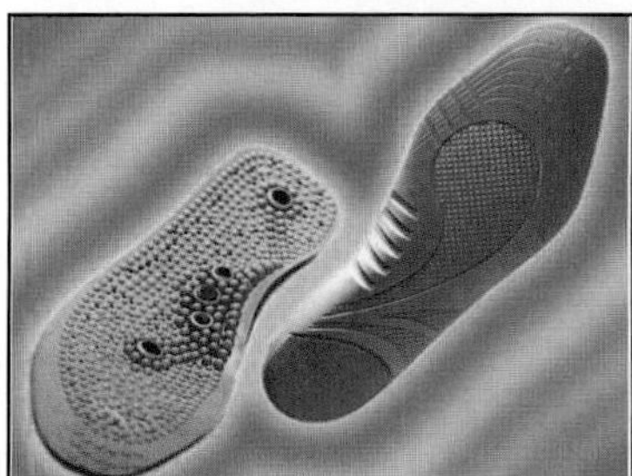

Right: The pseudoscientifically proven MagnaSoles

U.S. Populace Lurches Methodically Through The Motions For Yet Another Day

SPECIAL REPORT

The wall-eyed, slack-jawed U.S. populace, beaten down into a state of near-catatonia by the relentlessly deadening banality of their joyless, insipid lives, dutifully trudged through the motions for yet another emotionally blank day Monday, sources reported.

Against all logic, the nation's citizenry, their insides withering away with each passing moment, somehow managed to continue filling out invoices, shopping for footwear, loading dishwashers, eating Whoppers, pressing buttons, watching reality-based TV programs, vacuuming floors, engaging in conversations about petty office politics, riding buses, sitting in traffic, mailing letters, and tending to the little rubber mats people wipe their feet on as they enter the lobby areas of vast, windowless industrial complexes. How they managed to do it, no one can say.

The populace's minor victory of con-

see POPULACE page 7

Stoner Regales Friends With Tale Of This One Bong He Saw In Iowa City Once

MINNEAPOLIS—Area stoner Mike Cudahy, his eyes a deep red from five years of near-continuous recreational marijuana use, regaled friends and neighbors Tuesday with half-remembered tales of this one amazing bong he saw in Iowa City once.

The bong, described in reverent, half-whispered tones by Cudahy as "awesome," "fuckin' incredible" and "seriously mind-blowing," was allegedly seen during a weekend stay at his friend's cousin's place in Iowa City this one time, probably sometime between 1993 and 1995.

According to Cudahy, the "super-bong," composed of an intricate network of plastic tubing, a motor from a lawn mower, several five-gallon buckets of ice water and a fully functional antique pool table, was "so unbelievable, I couldn't hardly believe what I was fuckin' lookin'

see BONG page 8

Above: Stoner Mike Cudahy

the ONION®

VOLUME 35 ISSUE 15 AMERICA'S FINEST NEWS SOURCE™ 22–28 APRIL 1999

NEWS

Data-Entry Clerk Reapplies Carmex At 17-Minute Intervals

see OFFICEWATCH page 9D

New History Textbook Makes Hatred Of History Come Alive For Students

see EDUCATION page 11C

QLTMKR Driving In Two Lanes Of Traffic

see LOCAL page 2D

Area Pubis Shorn

see LOCAL page 6D

STATshot

A look at the numbers that shape your world.

Nastiest Shit In U.S. Refrigerators

1. Amorphous, bruise-colored mass in cottage-cheese container—Massapequa, NY
2. Eleven-week-old T.G.I. Friday's fettucine leftover—Monroe, LA
3. Ziploc bag of black, liquefied lettuce—Owasso, OK
4. "Something to remember her by forever"—Miami, FL
5. Eight lime-green Armour hot dogs in original package—Forsyth, GA
6. Jeremy Robinson, age 10—Erie, PA

INSIDE the ONION®

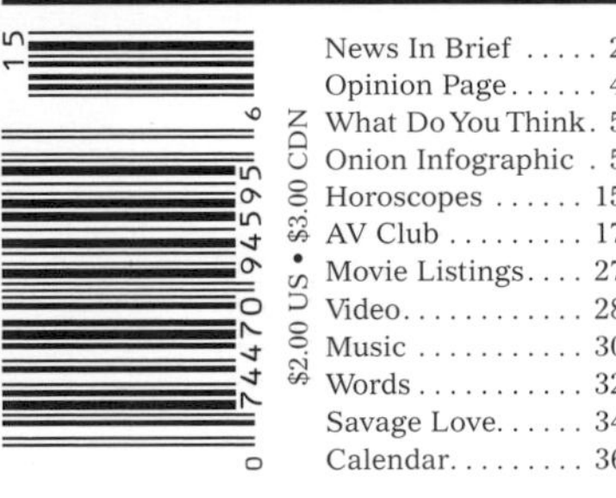

News In Brief 2
Opinion Page. 4
What Do You Think. 5
Onion Infographic . 5
Horoscopes 15
AV Club 17
Movie Listings. . . . 27
Video. 28
Music 30
Words 32
Savage Love. 34
Calendar. 36

Neighbors Confront Alcoholic Child-Abuser About His Lawn

ARLINGTON, TX—Following a brief meeting Saturday, members of the Ridgeway Circle Homeowners Association confronted alcoholic child-abuser Gene Oberst about his continued failure to uphold basic standards of lawn care.

Left: Child-beater Gene Oberst, whose unkempt lawn and untrimmed hedges have caused alarm among neighbors.

"It's never easy to stick your nose in someone else's business, but in this case, we felt we had no choice but to step in and do something," association president Trudy Hinsdale said of the 33-year-old unemployed electrician and abusive parent. "That lawn is a major eyesore, and it reflects badly on the whole rest of the block. Mr. Oberst has no idea what kind

see LAWN page 13

Clinton Takes Leave Of Office To Stand In Line For *Star Wars: Episode I*

WASHINGTON, DC—Citing "America's unprecedented prosperity and stability" and "this one part where this ship is underwater and this sea-monster thing tries to eat it," Bill Clinton became the first U.S. president to take a leave of absence Tuesday, temporarily stepping down to wait in line for the May 19 opening of *Star Wars: Episode I—The Phantom Menace.*

"My fellow Americans, like so many of you, I am extremely eager to see the next chapter in the greatest movie series in the history of mankind," Clinton, sporting a limited-edition IG-88 tie clip, said during a White House press conference. "And, as president of the nation that has produced these movies, I am fully committed to being at that very first showing, even if it means missing almost four weeks of

see STAR WARS page 10

Right: President Clinton and other *Star Wars* fans wait outside a D.C.-area Loew's Multiplex for the May 19 opening of *The Phantom Menace.*

McDonald's Employee Just In It For The Money

SHREVEPORT, LA—According to reports, Sean Boyce, a member of the Jefferson Avenue McDonald's team, may be doing it purely for the money. Critics say Boyce, 22, who lives with girlfriend Renee Simmons and their 2-year-old daughter, cares more about getting paid than dedicating himself to his craft.

"It's sad when a person's sole motivation is money, but that really seems to be the case with Mr. Boyce," said Peter Kuharcich, editor of the restaurant-industry newsletter *Fast Food Report*. "The only thing he's interested in is getting that paycheck."

Contrary to claims made at the time of his hire, Boyce does not crave the challenge of brightening people's day the McDonald's way.

"When I interviewed Sean, he really seemed to agree that the most fulfilling thing about working here is getting the chance to make the customer's McDonald's experience as enjoyable as possible," assistant manager Frederick Taubense said. "But the longer he was here, the more apparent it became that it was all about the money for him. He's always asking stuff like, 'Wasn't I supposed to get a raise last month?' and, 'I thought I get time and a half when I work overtime.' At some

see McDONALD'S page 6

Right: McDonald's employee Sean Boyce.

the ONION®

VOLUME 35 ISSUE 21 AMERICA'S FINEST NEWS SOURCE™ 3–9 JUNE 1999

NEWS

Jew-Sponsored Stock Car Booed Off Track

see SPORTS page 3D

Nursing Home Patient Glad She's Going Home Tomorrow Every Day

see LOCAL page 8C

Local Man Wonders Where That Sick Fuck Hockey Coach Is Now

see LOCAL page 11C

Hamburger Helped

see HOME page 9E

STATshot

A look at the numbers that shape your world.

Least Qualified U.S. Daycares

1. Wee Basement Daycare — Kirby, AR
2. Discarded Refrigerator Play Park — Howell, MI
3. Arthur Treacher's Fish & Daycare — Bristol, PA
4. Krawlspace-4-Kids — Bedford, IN
5. Pappy 'n' Betty Lou's Common-Law Kidcare Cabin — Erwin, TN
6. Vista View Daycare-On-A-Jutting-Precipice — Livingston, MT

INSIDE the ONION®

News In Brief 2
Opinion Page...... 4
What Do You Think. 5
Onion Infographic . 5
Horoscopes 10
AV Club 11
Movie Listings.... 19
Video............ 20
Music 21
Words 23
Savage Love...... 24
Calendar......... 25

Importance Of Education Given Valuable Lip Service

BLOOMINGTON, IN—In a speech before constituents at Indiana University Tuesday, U.S. Rep. Dan Burton (R-IN) paid much-needed lip service to the importance of a well-rounded education in the lives of young people.

"For every 100 children who enter kindergarten this fall, only 70 will graduate from high school," Burton told the group of approximately 250 Indiana residents. "Fewer still will finish college. As your representative, I consider it my duty to observe this statistic and mention it very, very often."

Burton continued: "In a recent study of high-school seniors, 50 percent were unable to locate their own country on a globe. I, for one, will not be satisfied until every single young person in America has been given the opportunity to hear me speak about this appalling problem."

Burton, who is known for giving much-needed lip service to such diverse issues as inner-city poverty, the federal deficit and environmental pollution, added, "Compounding the problem is the fact that parents are failing to take an active role in their children's education. Nearly 75 percent of parents cannot name the subjects their children are failing versus those they are passing—another tragic figure I appear deeply saddened by at public speaking events."

After demonstrating the dire need for educational reform for a full 55 minutes, Burton left the auditorium and took immediate action by returning to his hotel room.

see EDUCATION page 6

SPECIAL REPORT

Millions And Millions Dead

As the body count continues to rise, a shaken nation is struggling to cope in the wake of the mass deaths sweeping the world population. With no concrete figures available at this early stage, experts estimate at least 250,000 U.S. citizens have died in the last month alone, with death tolls across the globe reaching into the millions.

The wave of deaths has left a brutal aftermath, rocking survivors with feelings of loss and horror, traumatizing the American cultural landscape to its core and leaving behind emotional devastation some say may take years to heal.

What's worse, experts say, the crisis shows no signs of letting up any time soon.

"Oh, my God," sobbed Edina, MN resident Elizabeth Kendrick, 42, whose father, retired insurance actuary Gilbert Ploman, 68, lost his life last Thursday at Shady Villa Nursing Home. "He was a good man, a kind man who never did anything to deserve this terrible fate. Why did something like this have to happen? Oh, God, why?"

As wrenching as Kendrick's grief is, she is just one of the countless Americans who feel the anguish that continues to tear the country apart. Across the nation, in millions of homes in thousands of cities, similar scenes played out, as survivors gathered to mourn, pray, and somehow pick up the

see DEAD page 6

Area Daughter Wearing Next To Nothing

ATHENS, GA—Anger, shock, and feelings of intense awkwardness were just some of the reactions in the Helstein household Tuesday as Jeremy Helstein, 46, scolded his 17-year-old daughter Erica for allegedly wearing "next to nothing."

"This is my house, young lady," Helstein told the oldest of his three children—whom he says has lived by his rules ever since she was born and will continue to do so as long as she's under his roof—during the emotionally charged confrontation. "If you think you're going out dressed like that, you've got another thing coming, I'll tell you right now. For Christ's sake, everyone can see all the way from here to Timbuktu."

Despite efforts at mediation by his wife Clara, Helstein said he has no plans to rescind his condemnation of his daughter's outfit, a white cotton tank-top and snug-fitting jeans that "leave nothing to the imagination."

According to family members who witnessed the dispute, Erica responded to the allegations with severe sulking, angrily stomping out of the living room and violently slamming the bathroom door.

The high-school junior has denied the charges, admitting that the tank top exposes her shoulders and back but contending that it is in not inappropriate Friday-night attire for someone who will be graduating from high school in less than a year.

see DAUGHTER page 7

Right: Athens-area high-school junior Erica Helstein, right out in public.

the ONION®

VOLUME 35 ISSUE 22 | AMERICA'S FINEST NEWS SOURCE™ | 10–16 JUNE 1999

NEWS

Police Seize 250 Pounds Of Marijuana Smoker

see NATION page 2B

Awards Given Out Randomly To Skinny Blonde Women

see ENTERTAINMENT page 5E

Deviant Kellogg's Worker Comes In Specially Marked Boxes

see BUSINESS page 11C

STATshot

A look at the numbers that shape your world.

INSIDE the ONION®

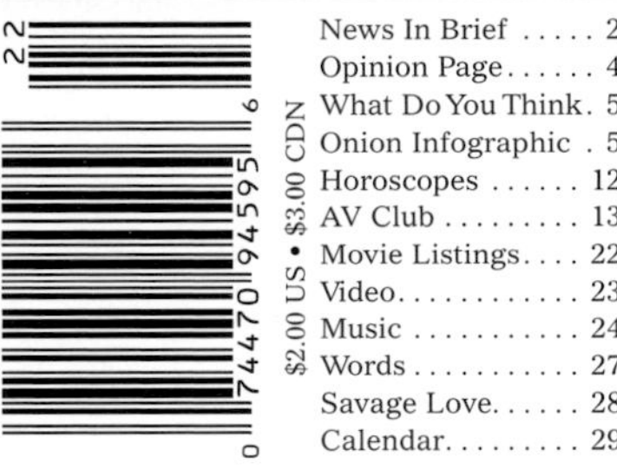

News In Brief 2
Opinion Page...... 4
What Do You Think. 5
Onion Infographic . 5
Horoscopes 12
AV Club 13
Movie Listings.... 22
Video............ 23
Music 24
Words 27
Savage Love...... 28
Calendar......... 29

Clinton Injected With Highly Unstable Experimental Growth Serum

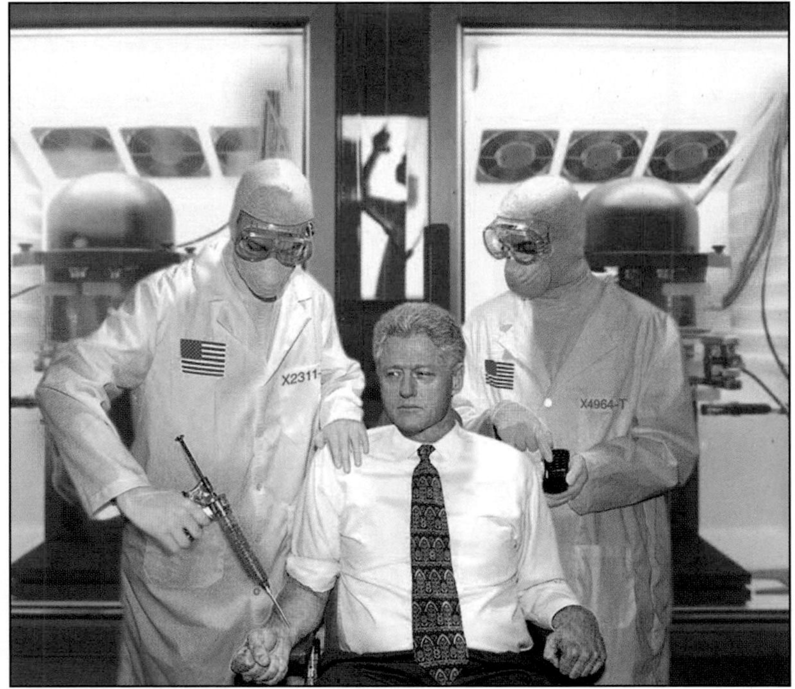

Above: Military scientists prepare to inject Clinton with the controversial superdrug.

WASHINGTON, DC—Forced to take desperate measures in a last-minute attempt to avert disaster and save the free world, President Clinton ordered top military scientists to inject his body with a highly unstable experimental growth serum Monday.

"Earth is threatened on every side by danger. We must act now to save humanity," Clinton said in a prepared statement prior to receiving the untested super-serum. "Our rapidly fragmenting societal infrastructure faces myriad crises: drugs in our streets, guns in our schools, economic collapse in Asia, military aggression in Europe, and global environmental destruction creating an unstoppable army of six-legged mutant frogs. If nothing is done, disaster is imminent."

"This experiment, risky as it is, is a gamble I cannot afford not to take," Clinton

see CLINTON page 8

Nation Demands Easier Instructions

WASHINGTON, DC—Decrying needlessly confusing directions for the use and assembly of countless products, citizens across the nation are organizing advocacy groups to demand that American manufacturers simplify the instructions they place on packaging.

American Focus

"I'm a busy father of three," said Richard Graham of Chester, VA. "I don't have time to wade through all those words and confusing pictures on the box of flavored instant-oatmeal packets. Why can't I just get the bowl of hot oatmeal without going through so much trouble?"

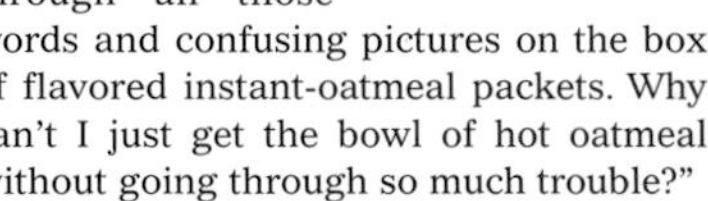

On behalf of dissatisfied consumers like Graham, the Washington-based activist group Citizens for Easier Instructions has delivered an ultimatum to corporations: Replace current directions with easier versions or face a consumer boycott.

"We demand that product manufacturers provide their customers with intuitive, easy-to-follow directions featuring larger pictures, color coding, shorter words, and no words at all where a letter, number or pictograph would suffice," CEI director Melanie Pruitt said Tuesday

see INSTRUCTIONS page 7

Hall Monitor Pushed Into Girls' Restroom

MILFORD, CT—In an incident that sent shockwaves through the halls of Milford East Elementary School, sixth-grade hall monitor Alex Greibe was brutally pushed into the girls' restroom Tuesday, midway through his normal third-period rounds.

"I was down by Mrs. Talcott's room, bending over to pick up a candy wrapper, when some guys snuck up behind me and shoved me right through the bathroom door," said Greibe, 11. "There I was, trapped where no sixth-grade boy had ever been before."

Inside the girls' room, since nicknamed "the Greibe's room," were three female classmates—Janie Lewis and Patricia Henderson, standing by the sinks, and an unidentified party wearing white-and-black Avia tennis shoes, using the furthest stall.

see HALL MONITOR page 9

Above: The girls' restroom briefly entered by hall monitor Alex Greibe (inset).

NEWS

Star Wars Fan Collects All 48,720

see PEOPLE page 4C

Pabst Drinker Celebrates Pabst Purchase With Pabst

see LIFESTYLE page 2D

STATshot

A look at the numbers that shape your world.

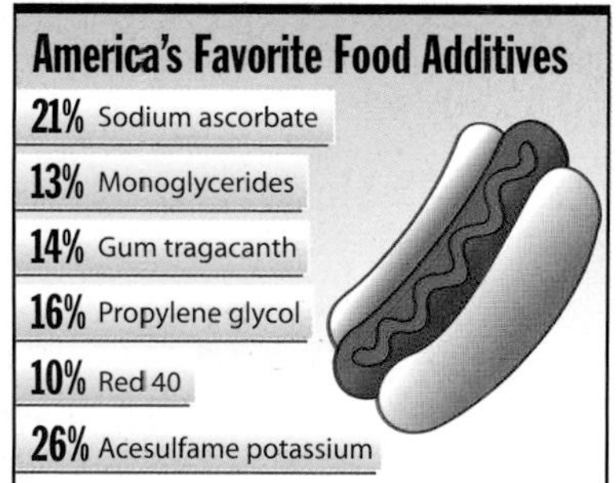

INSIDE the ONION

News In Brief 2
Opinion Page...... 4
What Do You Think. 5
Onion Infographic . 5
Horoscopes 15
AV Club 17
Movie Listings.... 26
Video........... 27
Music 28
Words........... 31
Savage Love...... 32
Calendar......... 33

$2.00 US • $3.00 CDN

the ONION®

VOLUME 35 ISSUE 23 | AMERICA'S FINEST NEWS SOURCE™ | 17–23 JUNE 1999

Left: Child-rearing expert Dr. Patrick Coughlin and Korean War expert Dr. Laurence Block field reporters' questions following the mass resignation of America's 243,839 experts.

Nation's Experts Give Up

'From Now On, You're On Your Own,' Say Experts

WASHINGTON, DC—Citing years of frustration over their advice being misunderstood, misrepresented or simply ignored, America's foremost experts in every field collectively tendered their resignation Monday.

"Despite all our efforts to advise this nation, America still throws out its recyclables, keeps its guns in unlocked cabinets where children have easy access, eats three times as much red meat as is recommended, watches seven hours of TV per day, swims less than 10 minutes after eating, and leaves halogen lights on while unattended," said Dr. Simon Peavy, vice-president of the National Association of Experts. "Since you don't seem to care about things you don't understand, screw

see EXPERTS page 6

Deciding Vote On Wetlands Preservation Bill Rests With The Littlest Senator

WASHINGTON, DC—Congress narrowly passed the McCann-Hawkins Florida Wetlands Preservation Bill Tuesday, with the deciding vote coming from an unlikely source: Sen. Dwight Q. Peabody (D-RI), the Littlest Senator.

Despite his diminutive stature and timid demeanor, Peabody became the most important legislator of all when the vote became deadlocked at 49-49. With Sen. Chuck Hagel (R-NE) absent, the fate of countless species of Everglades flora and fauna fell into the teeny, tiny hands of Peabody.

Ever since he was sworn into Congress in January, Peabody, who represents the nation's littlest state, has not been taken seriously by his Senate colleagues, many of whom are big, important politicians from big, important states like Texas and California. When Peabody arrived at the U.S. Capitol for the first time, the bigger senators took one look at him and laughed.

"That's a senator?" Sen. Phil Gramm (R-TX) said. "Why, he could get lost in my shirt pocket! What a pipsqueak!"

"I can't see how he could possibly influence legislation," Sen. Daniel Patrick Moynihan (D-NY) said. "One thing's for certain: We won't let him join in any Senate games."

Peabody's small size, coupled with his lack of seniority, prevented him from being

see SENATOR page 7

Right: Dwight Q. Peabody, the Littlest Senator.

Above: The Hansons, who recently moved to the white suburb of Glencoe, IL.

White Family Moves To Town

GLENCOE, IL—Shock, outrage and fear were just some of the emotions that failed to sweep through this affluent Chicago suburb Monday, when word got out among residents that a white family had moved to town over the weekend.

Challenging none of the close-knit community's long-held beliefs and traditions, maxillofacial surgeon Bill Hanson, his wife Marge, and children Kevin and Sue are the first Caucasians to relocate to Glencoe in more than two days.

"I'll admit, I was concerned at first," said longtime Glencoe resident and neighborhood-watch president Linda Brubaker, 50. "I thought, how will having a white family move here affect property values? Then I realized it wouldn't at all."

"After all," Brubaker added, "once I looked beneath the surface, I realized that this

see WHITE FAMILY page 8

NEWS

Painful Reminder Celebrates Fourth Birthday

see LIFESTYLE page 3E

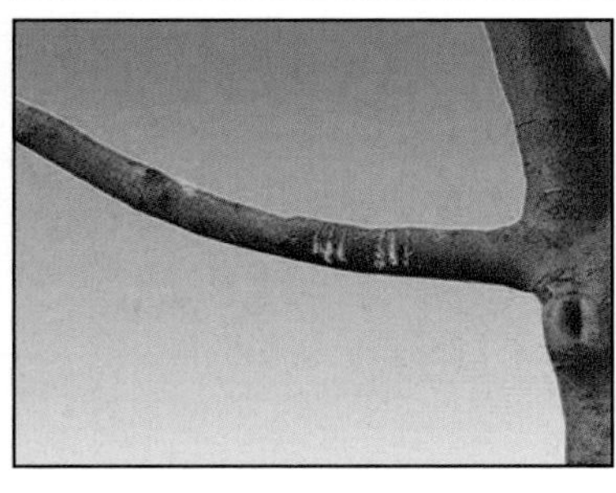

Inspirational Poster Kitten Falls To Death After 17 Years

see NATION page 2C

Danish Woman Has Huge Crush On TV's Søren Pilmark

see WORLD page 14B

STATshot

A look at the numbers that shape your world.

Least-Visited Science Museum Exhibits

Sheep Diseases Of The World (Houston Museum Of Natural Science)

The Slide-Through Urinary Tract (Boston Museum Of Science)

Armour Presents: Hands-On Historic Sausage-Filling (Boise Children's Museum)

"Sounds Of The Prairie" Locked Isolation Chamber (Oklahoma Museum Of Science And Industry)

Tooth Decay: An IMAX Presentation (New York Hall Of Science)

INSIDE the ONION®

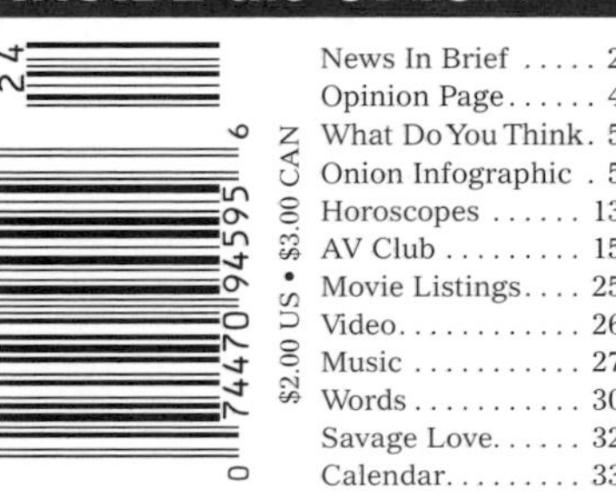

24
0 74470 94595 6
$2.00 US • $3.00 CAN

News In Brief 2
Opinion Page 4
What Do You Think. 5
Onion Infographic . 5
Horoscopes 13
AV Club 15
Movie Listings. . . . 25
Video. 26
Music 27
Words 30
Savage Love. 32
Calendar. 33

the ONION®

VOLUME 35 ISSUE 24 | AMERICA'S FINEST NEWS SOURCE™ | 24 JUNE–22 JULY 1999

Aliens Demand More Positive Portrayal In The Media

WASHINGTON, DC—A coalition of extraterrestrials representing some two trillion lifeforms across the five major planetary confederations descended on Earth Monday to speak out against "the demeaning, degrading and hurtful portrayals" of aliens in the planet's media.

"Attention! People of Earth!" said Gnortakk, Son Of K'Tzazzghn, spokesbeing for Extraterrestrials For Media Equity. "The preponderance of stereotypical and condemnatory images of non-Earth species in your films, TV programs, books and video games can no longer be tolerated."

"For years, we have endured your planet's depiction of aliens as either ruthless, tyrannical conquerors or bumbling, ineffectual, 'comic relief' creatures," Aegon, Fifth Of The Five, said. "It's high time humanoids presented positive, realistic images of aliens going about their everyday lives."

Presenting a montage

see ALIENS page 8

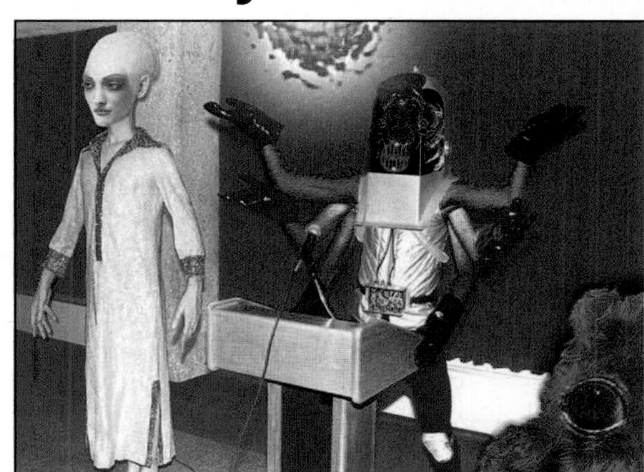

Right: Gnortakk, a spokesbeing for Extraterrestrials For Media Equity, speaks to Earthling reporters.

AMERICAN FOCUS

Should The U.S. Impose Limits On Incredibly Stupid Shit?

WASHINGTON, DC—With national stupid-shit consumption at an all-time high and federal shit projections indicating sharply rising levels of stupidity over the next decade and a half, a small but vocal group of lobbyists has revived an old debate on Capitol Hill, calling for strict, federally mandated limits on incredibly stupid shit.

Though every previous congressional effort to curb incredibly stupid shit has

see SHIT page 6

Left: The direct-deposit-obsessed Elaine Massey.

Area Payroll Secretary Really Pushing Direct Deposit For Some Reason

GRAND RAPIDS, MI—For reasons unknown to her coworkers, Midwest Book & Stationery payroll secretary Elaine Massey is "really pushing" direct deposit, aggressively encouraging fellow employees to have their biweekly checks electronically deposited into their bank accounts, company sources reported Tuesday.

"I swear, Elaine has mentioned this direct-deposit thing to me at least four times in the past week alone," said Midwest shipping clerk Jan Prentiss. "I mean, what does she care if I go to the bank or not?"

The direct-deposit option, which Massey ~~has assured coworkers is "real simple and~~ just takes a few minutes to set up," first became available during the pay period ending April 17. Ever since, Massey has vigorously championed the option, releasing a memo about it, holding an informational meeting in the breakroom, and approaching each of her co-workers individually to discuss the "great opportunity to save [themselves] some running around."

Stock sorter Aaron Douglas is one of 22 Midwest employees Massey has approached in the last month to remind that direct deposit is available for both checking and savings accounts.

see PAYROLL page 7

NEWS

Corey Hart Still Performing 'Sunglasses At Night' Somewhere

see ENTERTAINMENT page 9D

Second Nintendo Controller Sits Unused

see LIFESTYLE page 13E

Horrified Onlookers Watch Helplessly

see NATION page 1B

Molly Bloom: 'Yes'

see PEOPLE page 5F

STATshot

A look at the numbers that shape your world.

INSIDE the ONION®

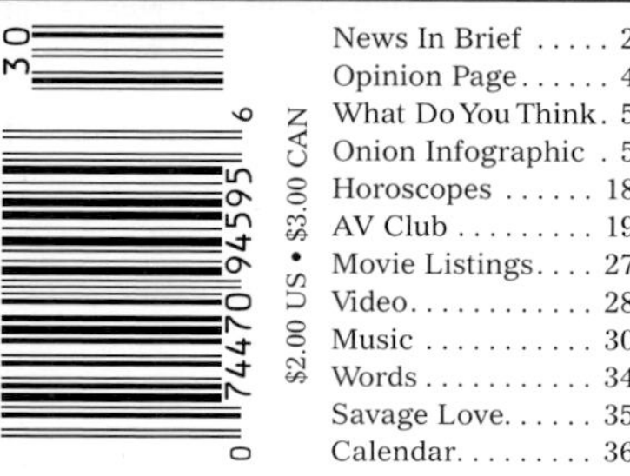

News In Brief 2
Opinion Page 4
What Do You Think . 5
Onion Infographic . 5
Horoscopes 18
AV Club 19
Movie Listings 27
Video 28
Music 30
Words 34
Savage Love 35
Calendar 36

the ONION®

VOLUME 35 ISSUE 30 AMERICA'S FINEST NEWS SOURCE™ 26 AUGUST–1 SEPTEMBER 1999

Clinton Meets With Guy With Tie

Above: Clinton smiles and shakes hands with an important guy wearing a tie.

WASHINGTON, DC—In a historic summit with profound, far-reaching implications for the nation at large, President Clinton met with a guy in a tie Tuesday, shaking the man's hand firmly while projecting a warm yet determined countenance.

Standing confidently before reporters and various dignitaries in a White House meeting room equipped with a raised dais, podium, microphone and prominently displayed American flag, the two men greeted each other, exchanged polite small talk and waved cordially to the assembled press.

The guy, presumably an important

see TIE page 6

U.S. Ice Cubes Melting At Alarming Rate

WASHINGTON, DC—High summer temperatures and ever-increasing levels of U.S. beverage consumption are causing ice cubes across the nation to melt at "an alarmingly

unprecedented rate," the U.S. Department of Consumer Affairs reported Tuesday.

"We are looking at a nationwide trend of crisis proportions," said Clyde Simms, director of the USDCA's potables division and Clinton-appointed Beverage Czar. "If the current rate of melting continues, we may face a situation in which Americans are not assured the option of having an ice-cold beverage in their hands at any given moment."

Of the 28.9 billion tons of ice cubes produced commercially in August, it is estimated that less than half remains. With these frozen resources already depleted—most of them having been removed from proper storage facilities and left to melt in glasses, paper cups and styrofoam coolers—government officials are powerless to stem the tide.

"So far, we have been able to replenish our ice-cube reserves at a fast enough rate to maintain an acceptable level of comfort," Simms said.

see ICE CUBES page 10

Man With Complete *Mama's Family* Video Library Never Going On eBay Drunk Again

NEWTON, MA—In a solemn pledge to himself and the world, Kevin Wollersheim, the new owner of a complete *Mama's Family* video library, announced Monday that he will "never, ever again" shop the online auction house eBay while inebriated.

"Over the course of Saturday evening, Aug. 21, I drank two Jack and Cokes, somewhere in the vicinity of six to eight Icehouse beers, plus, I believe, at least one shot of Cuervo 1800 tequila," Wollersheim said at a press conference held in his apartment. "And, although I now have no memory of doing so, it is clear that I logged on to America Online and accessed eBay sometime before 2:28 a.m. early Sunday morning."

"During my visit to the eBay site," Wollersheim continued, his voice beginning to break, "for some reason known only

see EBAY page 8

Right: Wollersheim and a portion of his recent purchase. Inset: Vicki Lawrence as TV's Mother Harper.

NEWS

Self-Helped Woman Won't Stop At Just Self

see LIFESTYLE page 9C

New Toxic-Waste By-Product Contains No Fat

see FOOD page 13D

Gap Orders 'Everybody In Showers'

see ADWATCH page 11F

Ape Suit Worn Only Once

see LOCAL page 1B

STATshot

A look at the numbers that shape your world.

What are those sports guys on the Shop-At-Home Network yelling about this week?

1. Gem-mint '85 Topps Mark McGwire Olympic Team rookie card
2. 1999 Upper Deck Series 2 factory-sealed box
3. Limited-edition John Elway Super Bowl XXXIII lithograph
4. Michael Jordan Starting Lineup retirement figurine
5. Autographed '98 Donruss Elite Gold Derek Jeter

INSIDE the ONION®

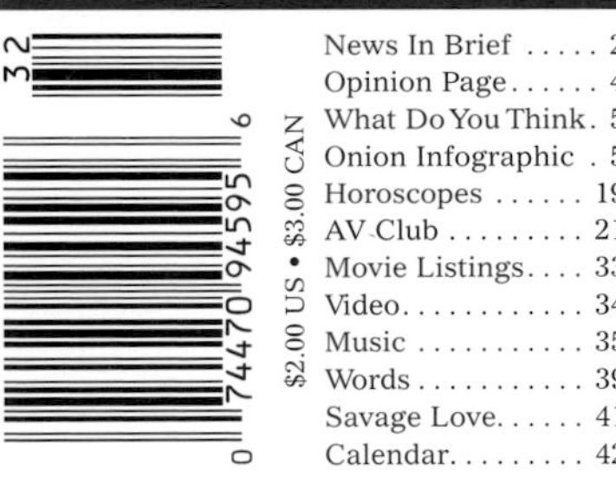

News In Brief 2
Opinion Page...... 4
What Do You Think. 5
Onion Infographic . 5
Horoscopes 19
AV Club 21
Movie Listings.... 33
Video............ 34
Music 35
Words........... 39
Savage Love...... 41
Calendar......... 42

the ONION®

VOLUME 35 ISSUE 32 | AMERICA'S FINEST NEWS SOURCE™ | 9–15 SEPTEMBER 1999

Columbine Jocks Safely Resume Bullying

Above: Members of Columbine High School's popular crowd, who, more than four months after the tragic shooting at their school, have finally begun to exclude again.

LITTLETON, CO—On April 20, when two students at Columbine High School opened fire in a brutal shooting spree that left 12 classmates and a teacher dead, many feared that this affluent suburban school would never be the same.

But now, more than four months after a tragedy that shook the nation to its core and marked the most notorious incident of school violence in U.S. history, the atmosphere is optimistic. Slowly but surely, life at Columbine is returning to normal.

Thanks to stern new security measures, a militarized school environment and a massive public-relations effort designed to obscure all memory of the murderous event, members of Columbine's popular crowd are once again safe to reassert their social dominance and resume their proud, longstanding tradition of excluding those who do not fit in.

"We have begun the long road to healing," said varsity-football starting halfback

see COLUMBINE page 6

Cruise, Kidman Walk Through Lobby

Above: Tom Cruise and Nicole Kidman in their newsmaking lobby walk.

LOS ANGELES—A-list Hollywood celebrities Tom Cruise and Nicole Kidman, considered by many to be the most important humans on the planet, walked through the lobby of the Four Seasons Hotel Monday, drawing the attention of dozens of reporters and photographers and thrilling millions of television viewers, *Access Hollywood* sources reported.

Cruise, universally admired for his sly, charismatic grin and stunning good looks, and wife Kidman, who has garnered worldwide acclaim for her breathtaking beauty, were reportedly in the hotel "for some reason" and traversed the lobby "to exit it and leave" when *Access Hollywood* captured their beautiful images.

"They were definitely at the location with their actual physical persons

see LOBBY page 12

Corporation's New Logo Changes Everything

INDIANAPOLIS—Responding swiftly to a *60 Minutes* piece exposing its longtime use of child labor in Malaysian sweatshops, Fortune 500 consumer-goods manufacturer United Home Products unveiled a brand-new logo Tuesday.

"After the *60 Minutes* story aired, we received a lot of tremendously helpful feedback regarding our staffing policies at some of our facilities in the Asian sphere. And after listening to you, our customers, UHP saw it was time for a change," said

CEO Dale Schwantes, gesturing toward the red, white and blue logo. "And here's that change, America!"

"If you thought you knew UHP, look again!" Schwantes added.

While the business practices of UHP, the nation's fifth largest manufacturer of household consumer goods, will remain unchanged, the introduction of the new logo signals "a brand-new corporate philosophy and an entirely different way of doing things."

The decision to be "a whole new company" came as a result of the Aug. 5 airing

see LOGO page 10

the ONION®

VOLUME 35 ISSUE 33 | AMERICA'S FINEST NEWS SOURCE™ | 16–22 SEPTEMBER 1999

Clinton Molested By Visiting Uncle

Above: A scared and confused President Clinton collects his thoughts after revealing he was molested by his uncle Carl (inset).

WASHINGTON, DC—In a tearful address to the American people Monday, President Clinton announced that he would be taking an indefinite leave of office to recover from his recent molestation at the hands of his visiting uncle Carl.

"My fellow Americans," the president said during the nationally televised speech, "two weeks ago, my uncle Carl came to visit me and take a tour of the White House. And at one point during that tour, while we were alone in the Lincoln Bedroom, Uncle Carl did something to me that he said should be our little secret."

Clinton said Uncle Carl "touched me in ways I knew were wrong," and that Carl instructed him "not to tell anyone, especially not Hillary or the Secret Service," saying that

see CLINTON page 9

T.A. Spotted At Bar

STATE COLLEGE, PA—Drew Phelan, 26, a Penn State University graduate student and teaching assistant for History 107: Introduction To Western Civilization, was spotted at the Bulldog Brew Pub last weekend, Section Four sources revealed shortly before class Monday.

Drew Phelan

"I walked into the 'Dog at, like, midnight Saturday, and sitting right there at the bar was Drew, our T.A.," sophomore Zach Matthews told several fellow students in Phelan's 11:05 a.m. discussion section. "It was crowded as hell, but I'm totally positive it was him."

Matthews, who assured sectionmates that he was not shitting them, said Phelan was dressed in his typical style, wearing a button-down shirt and khakis. The T.A. was accompanied by two females,

see T.A. page 6

Huge Quantities Of Primo Shit Incinerated By Feds

LAKE ARROWHEAD, CA—A ton of people up and down the coast were seriously bumming Monday, when the Drug Enforcement Administration announced the seizure and destruction of huge quantities of seriously primo shit.

According to a DEA spokesman, more than 16,000 pounds of marijuana—with a street value of, shit, practically $70 million or something—was destroyed in the bust, the largest illegal-crop confiscation by the federal government in a hell of a long time.

DEA agents uncovered the kind bud on a 60-acre farm five miles north of Lake Arrowhead.

"In terms of sheer numbers, this was by far the largest growing operation we've seen this decade," said DEA agent Donald Krujcek, who supervised the way-uncool burning of all that primo weed.

Discovered during a DEA helicopter surveillance sweep last week, the killer stash had previously gone undetected by authorities due to its totally sweet set-

see PRIMO page 10

Above: DEA agents destroy bales of confiscated marijuana, majorly bumming out loads of dudes all over.

NEWS

Owner Pleads With Cat To React To Fuzzy Object

see LOCAL page 3B

Sony Unveils Matte-Black Box Of Red And Green Lights

see PRODUCTWATCH page 8C

World's Biggest Football Fan Holds Many Other 'World's Biggest' Records

see LIFESTYLE page 10D

Woman Subjugated

see PEOPLE page 7E

STATshot

A look at the numbers that shape your world.

INSIDE the ONION®

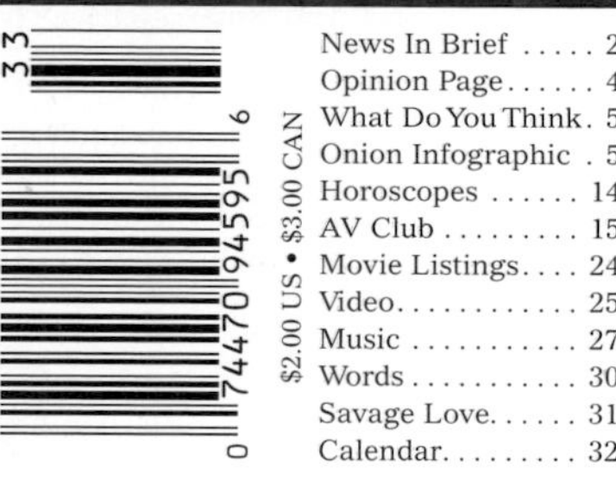

News In Brief 2
Opinion Page...... 4
What Do You Think. 5
Onion Infographic . 5
Horoscopes 14
AV Club 15
Movie Listings.... 24
Video............ 25
Music 27
Words........... 30
Savage Love...... 31
Calendar......... 32

$2.00 US • $3.00 CAN
33
0 74470 94595 6

NEWS

Area Roofer Badmouths College

see LOCAL page 6B

America's Love Affair With *Ally McBeal* Ends Violently

see TELEVISION page 11D

Breathtaking Beauty Of Autumn Enjoyed During Walk To Car

see LIFESTYLE page 3F

STATshot

A look at the numbers that shape your world.

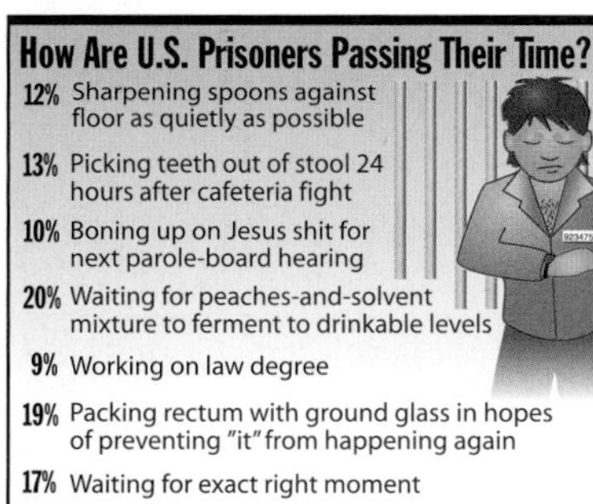

INSIDE the ONION®

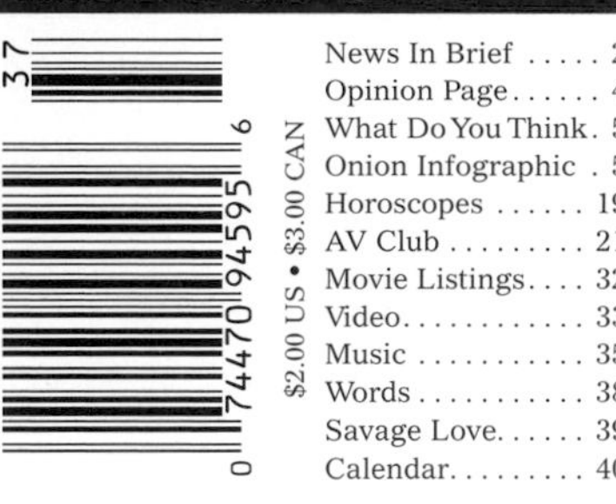

News In Brief 2
Opinion Page 4
What Do You Think . 5
Onion Infographic . 5
Horoscopes 19
AV Club 21
Movie Listings 32
Video 33
Music 35
Words 38
Savage Love 39
Calendar 40

the ONION®

VOLUME 35 ISSUE 37 — AMERICA'S FINEST NEWS SOURCE™ — 14–20 OCTOBER 1999

Male Orgasm Captured On Film

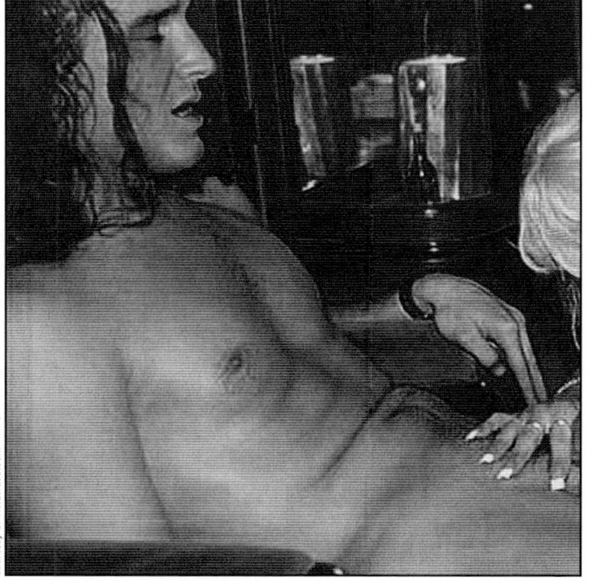

courtesy of vividvideo.com

Left: An image from the first footage of the elusive male orgasm ever to be captured by science.

CAMBRIDGE, MA—Announcing "a major advance in the age-old quest to unlock the secrets at the heart of human sexuality," researchers at Harvard's Center For The Graphic Depiction Of The Human Sexual Act confirmed Monday that, with the aid of experimental new high-speed photographic technology, they have successfully captured the elusive male orgasm on film.

The breakthrough marks the first time the male orgasm—perhaps the most mysterious, least-understood element of the complex dance that is human sexual behavior—has been successfully photographed.

"We have taken a giant leap forward in the struggle to unravel the mysteries of human love, illuminating aspects of the male orgasm that have long been hidden in a haze of speculation," said Dr. Donald Roehnert, head of the multidisciplinary team of experts credited with the breakthrough. "Though it is still too early to say how much can be learned, even a cursory examination of this historic footage reveals much that we otherwise never would have known about the magic and mystery of male sexuality."

For centuries, the male orgasm has remained shrouded in myth. Though it has long captivated imaginations with its evocative beauty, humanity's understanding of this most

see ORGASM page 10

America Reminded Of Beef's Existence By Bold New Ad Campaign

KANSAS CITY, MO—A new $100 million "Beef—Come And Get It™" ad campaign is reminding the American people of the existence of edible cow flesh.

The Kansas City-based American Beef Council launched the ambitious television and print campaign after discovering that U.S. citizens were no longer aware of the food item.

"Over the past few years, the American Beef Council let up on its promotional efforts, running very few beef ads," council president Richard Harnisch said. "And that lack of aggressiveness came home to roost: A recent focus-group test indicated that Americans had forgotten all about this delicious mealtime staple. When asked about beef or shown pictures of it, they seemed vague on the concept, often asking if it was some new, redder form of pork."

"Only after repeated explanations that beef is a separate, distinct meat that has always existed did test subjects begin to understand and remember," Harnisch said. "We soon realized that all Americans needed to have it explained to them that beef is a delicious meat that can be pur-

see BEEF page 9

Right: One of the new print ads designed to remind Americans that beef exists.

Office Copying Getting Out Of Hand, Says Office Manager

ARLINGTON, TX—South-central Medical Supply office manager Wendell Sulley formally announced Monday that office copying is "getting out of hand."

"After months of seeing the copy-machine, fax and print-station areas littered with copies of documents that are obviously for personal use, it was time to put my foot down," the 42-year-old Sulley said. "I've changed that second-floor toner cartridge twice in the past three weeks alone."

Added Sulley: "Those cartridges cost $55 each."

Sulley's official decree came in the form of a notice in 40-point type posted above the office's two Xerox 5830 copiers and three Hewlett-Packard LaserJet 5000N printers. It read, "Access to the copier is a privilege, not a right. From now on, restrict your usage to necessary, work-related items ONLY!"

see COPYING page 8

Right: Office manager Wendell Sulley.

the ONION®

VOLUME 35 ISSUE 40 | AMERICA'S FINEST NEWS SOURCE™ | 4–10 NOVEMBER 1999

NEWS

Brown Workers Put Company In The Black

see BUSINESS page 1C

Seven-Year-Old Told To Take It Like A Man

see LOCAL page 12B

Maria Shriver's Face Resharpened

see PEOPLE page 10D

Ska Band Outnumbers Audience

see MUSIC page 2E

STATshot

A look at the numbers that shape your world.

Top-Selling Novelty Condoms

1. Adams Joke Company Black-Ink, Hot-Pepper & Itching Condom Three-Pak
2. Edible "Exotic Flavors Of The Midwest" Condom–Available In Corn, Bacon Or Beef
3. Smith & Wesson .38 Snubnose Police Special
4. Comfortable Fruit Of The Loom 100% Cotton Condom
5. Altoids Condom With Curiously Strong Reservoir Tip

INSIDE the ONION®

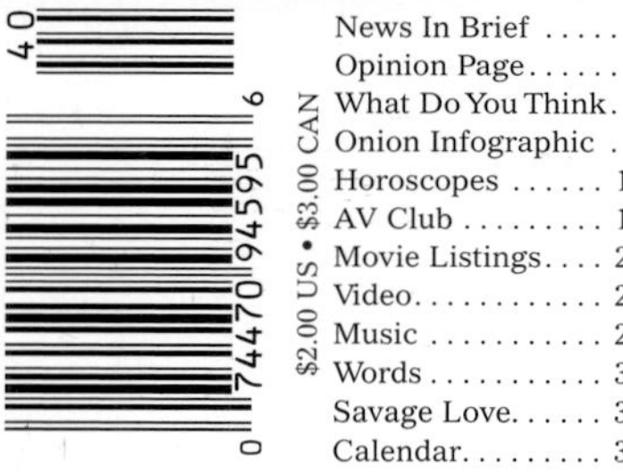

News In Brief 2
Opinion Page...... 4
What Do You Think. 5
Onion Infographic . 5
Horoscopes 15
AV Club 17
Movie Listings.... 26
Video............ 27
Music 28
Words........... 30
Savage Love...... 31
Calendar......... 32

Pudding-Factory Disaster Brings Slow, Creamy Death To Town Below

Above: Automobiles are trapped in a deadly swirl of chocolate and vanilla Snak-Tyme pudding.

CENTRALIA, IL—Sweet, creamy death swept through this small Illinois town Monday, when nine 300,000-gallon storage vats violently burst at the local Snak-Tyme pudding factory, burying hundreds of residents in a rich, smooth tidal wave of horrifying pudding goodness.

The death toll from the lip-smacking tragedy currently stands at 350 and is expected to rise.

"After hearing a series of loud explosions, I looked out the window and saw the great taste of Snak-Tyme engulfing everything in its path," said barber Bill Cangelosi, who barely escaped with his life when his shop was devastated by a lethal dollop of butterscotch.

The death toll from the lip-smacking tragedy currently stands at 350.

Within an hour, the downtown area was transformed into a scrumptious hell on earth, as millions of gallons of chocolate, vanilla and butterscotch pudding slowly seeped through the streets.

"I've lost everything," said Anne Dubrow, whose ground-floor apartment was filled to the ceiling with a heapin' helpin' of

see PUDDING page 6

Clinton Writes Fan Letter To Joan Jett

Above: President Clinton composes his fan letter to Joan Jett.

WASHINGTON, DC—In what White House sources are calling "a show of support and admiration for one of our nation's most talented and dynamic popular musicians," President Clinton drafted and mailed a fan letter Monday to '80s rock-'n'-roll superstar Joan Jett.

"Dear Joan Jett, I think your awesome. You are a awesome rock star. You are my favorite rock star," the fan letter read in part. "I have all your albums."

Jett, best known for her string of

see CLINTON page 10

Local Trailer Park Shatters No Stereotypes

TULSA, OK—Over the course of its 24-year history, Kilty's Kourt, a Tulsa-area trailer park, has shattered no stereotypes, causing no one to rethink any preconceptions about its coarse, poorly educated residents.

"Very often, one forms a set of preconceived notions about a type of person based on generalizations, but then a closer examination of the individuals within the situation allows one to look beyond these stereotypes," said University of Oklahoma sociologist Dr. Terry Atkins, who recently completed an in-depth three-year study of the trailer park. "Such is not the case here, though: Kilty's Kourt is pretty much a depressing, disgusting place filled with total losers."

Atkins had intended the study to challenge unfair, negative images of mobile-home dwellers by collecting statistical data that contradicts commonly held misconceptions. The professor's findings, however, only affirmed popular conceptions, with unemployment, sexual promiscuity and lack of education the norm among residents.

Affirming widely held

see TRAILER PARK page 9

Above: The non-stereotype-defying Kilty's Kourt trailer park in Tulsa, OK.

NEWS

Xabraxian Astronomers Discover New Planet

see SCIENCE page 3C

Missing Kazakhstani Nukes Turn Up In Manhattan

see NATION page 5A

Fat Woman Thinks She Looks Fat In Photo

see LIFESTYLE page 9B

Land Filled

see LOCAL page 10D

STATshot

A look at the numbers that shape your world.

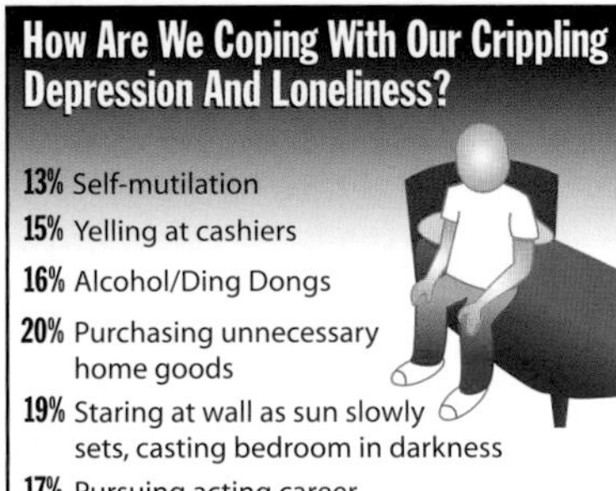

INSIDE the ONION®

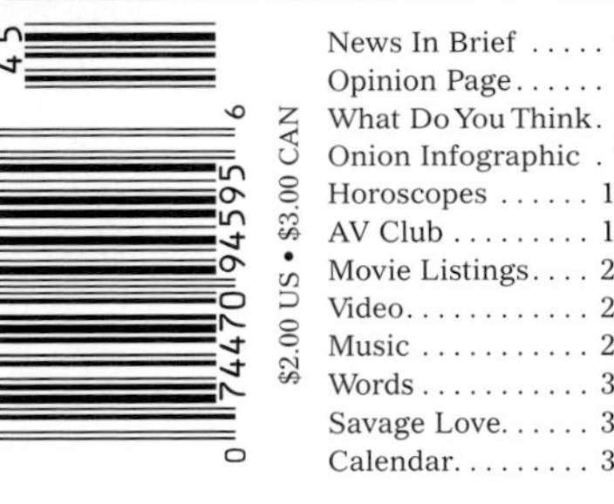

News In Brief 2
Opinion Page. 4
What Do You Think. 5
Onion Infographic . 5
Horoscopes 15
AV Club 17
Movie Listings. . . . 26
Video. 27
Music 28
Words 30
Savage Love. 31
Calendar. 32

the ONION®

VOLUME 35 ISSUE 45 | AMERICA'S FINEST NEWS SOURCE™ | 9–15 DECEMBER 1999

Archaeological Dig Uncovers Ancient Race Of Skeleton People

AL JIZAH, EGYPT—A team of British and Egyptian archaeologists made a stunning discovery Monday, unearthing several intact specimens of "skeleton people"—skinless, organless humans who populated the Nile delta region an estimated 6,000 years ago.

"This is an incredible find," said Dr. Christian Hutchins, Oxford University archaeologist and head of the dig team. "Imagine: At one time, this entire area was filled with spooky, bony, walking skeletons."

"The implications are staggering," Hutchins continued. "We now know that the skeletons we see in horror films and on Halloween are not mere products of the imagination, but actually lived on Earth."

Standing at the excavation site, a 20-by-20-foot square pit along the Nile River, Hutchins noted key elements of the find. "The skeletons lived in this mud-brick structure, which, based on what we know of these people, was probably haunted," he

see SKELETON page 7

Right: An archaeologist examines the intact remains of a spooky "skeleton person."

Above: Surrounded by purchases, President Clinton discusses his recent $865 spending spree with an advisor.

Clinton Blows Entire Paycheck

WASHINGTON, DC—After refusing comment on the matter for days, President Clinton finally admitted Monday that he blew his most recent paycheck, failing to deposit it into the joint checking account he shares with his wife and instead spending it on a variety of items of dubious necessity.

"My fellow Americans, I stand before you to confess that it is all gone," a contrite Clinton said in a televised address. "I honestly did not think I was buying all that

see CLINTON page 14

Area Man Can Actually Feel The Advanced Vapor Action Working

ELMIRA, NY—Local resident Maurice Weathers enjoyed temporary relief from congestion and minor throat irritation Monday thanks to the fast-acting advanced vapor action of Halls Mentho-lyptus™ cough drops.

"It's a proven fact that Halls, the brand you've trusted for nearly a century, alleviates the discomfort associated with cold-related coughs for as much as 12 hours," said Dr. Richard Marin, an ears, nose and throat specialist at the famed Mayo Clinic in Rochester, MN. "But don't take my word for it: Take Maurice Weathers'."

"When I first heard about Halls, I was skeptical," said Weathers, who had been suffering from flu symptoms since Dec. 3. "Other leading cough-drop brands had failed me before. And this was one tough cold."

Weathers said his wife Nicole urged him to try the product, saying that her grandmother "used to swear by it." "When Nicole said that, I thought to myself, 'Her *grandmother*? That must have been an awful

see VAPOR ACTION page 9

Above: Maurice Weathers (inset) breathes in the wavy, sinus-clearing vapors of doctor-recommended Halls Mentho-lyptus™ cough drops.

New Mommy A Lot Prettier

Affluent White Man
Enjoys, Causes The Blues

Beanie Baby Collection Stares At
Owner With 226 Cold, Dead Eyes

JANUARY FEBRUARY MARCH APRIL MAY JUNE

Genuine Happiness Now
Seen Only On Game Shows

Israelites Sue God For Breach Of Covenant

Wasteland Of Human Soul Earmarked
For Additional Development

2000

Troubled Robert Downey Jr. Placed Under 24-Hour Media Surveillance

$500 Stereo Installed In $400 Car

Dolphins Evolve Opposable Thumbs—'Oh Shit,' Says Humanity

JULY AUGUST SEPTEMBER OCTOBER NOVEMBER DECEMBER

Pelvis Thrust At Camera

Wedding-Reception DJ's Choice Of 'Strokin'' Proves Controversial

Clinton Goes Back In Time, Teams Up With Golden-Age Clinton

the ONION®

VOLUME 36 ISSUE 4 AMERICA'S FINEST NEWS SOURCE™ 10–16 FEBRUARY 2000

NEWS

Mars Lander Staggers Into NASA Headquarters Drunk, Broke

see SPACE page 3A

Employee Owned And Operated

see WORKPLACE page 9E

Area Man Can't Stop Playing With Piercing

see LOCAL page 2D

Cat Makes Break For It

see PETS page 15B

STATshot™

A look at the numbers that shape your world.

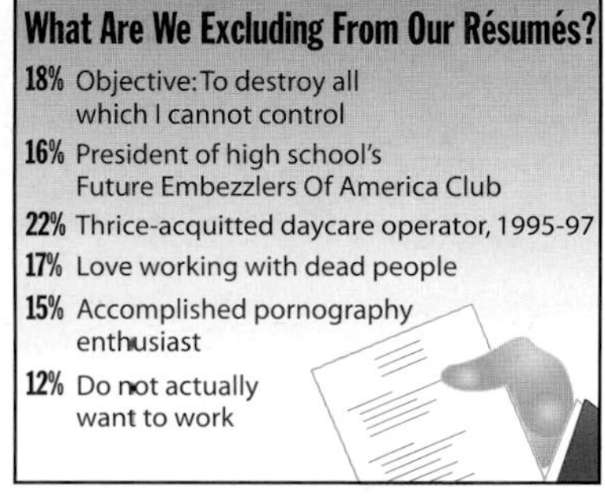

What Are We Excluding From Our Résumés?

18%	Objective: To destroy all which I cannot control
16%	President of high school's Future Embezzlers Of America Club
22%	Thrice-acquitted daycare operator, 1995-97
17%	Love working with dead people
15%	Accomplished pornography enthusiast
12%	Do not actually want to work

INSIDE the ONION®

News In Brief 2
Opinion Page 4
What Do You Think . 5
Onion Infographic. . 5
Horoscopes 17
AV Club 19
Cinema. 24
Video 28
Music 29
Words. 31
Savage Love 32
Picks. 33

Women

Why Don't They Lose Some Weight?

see WOMEN page 3A

Amazing New 'Swiffer' Fails To Fill The Void

CINCINNATI—The blank, oppressive void facing the American consumer populace remains unfilled today, despite the recent launch of the revolutionary Swiffer dust-elimination system, sources reported Monday.

The lightweight, easy-to-use Swiffer is the 275,894,973rd amazing new product to fail to fill the void—a vast, soul-crushing spiritual vacuum Americans of all ages helplessly face on a daily basis, with nowhere to turn and no way to escape.

"The remarkable new Swiffer sweeps, dusts, wipes, and cleans with a patented electrostatic action that simply cannot be beat," said spokeswoman Judith McReynolds, media-relations liaison for Procter & Gamble, maker of the dust-broom device. "Whether it's vinyl floors, tile, hardwood, ceilings, or stairs, the incredible Swiffer quickly cleans any dry surface by attracting and trapping even the tiniest dirt and dust particles."

see SWIFFER page 6

NFL Star Thanks Jesus After Successful Double Homicide

CHARLESTON, SC—Washington Redskins defensive end D'Aundré Banks gave "all thanks and praise to my personal Lord and Savior Jesus Christ" Monday for giving him the strength he needed to fatally stab bouncer Isaac Edmonds and ex-girlfriend Nicole Hamilton outside a Charleston nightclub early Sunday morning.

"All glory to Jesus," the 25-year-old Banks, who attended the University of South Carolina, told reporters from his cell in the Charleston County Jail. "He is with me in this dark hour, as He was in our devastating 14-13 playoff loss to the Buccaneers. His love will see me through this."

According to police reports, at approximately 2:30 a.m., a visibly intoxicated Banks became involved in an altercation with Edmonds regarding who would accompany Hamilton home. When Edmonds attempted to restrain Banks, the 288-pound devout Christian produced a knife and stabbed Edmonds and Hamilton repeatedly. He then fled to the home of girlfriend and Hooters waitress Lisa Nolan in nearby Summerville,

see JESUS page 7

> **"All glory to Jesus," the two-time Pro Bowler told reporters from his cell in the Charleston County Jail.**

Above: Redskins All-Pro D'Aundré Banks sacks an opponent during a 1999 game.

the ONION®

VOLUME 36 ISSUE 10 — AMERICA'S FINEST NEWS SOURCE™ — 23-29 MARCH 2000

NEWS

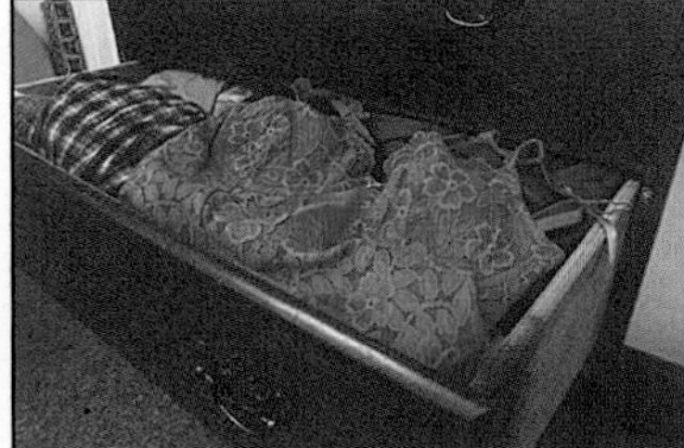

Victoria's Secret Also Andrew's Secret

see LOCAL page 4D

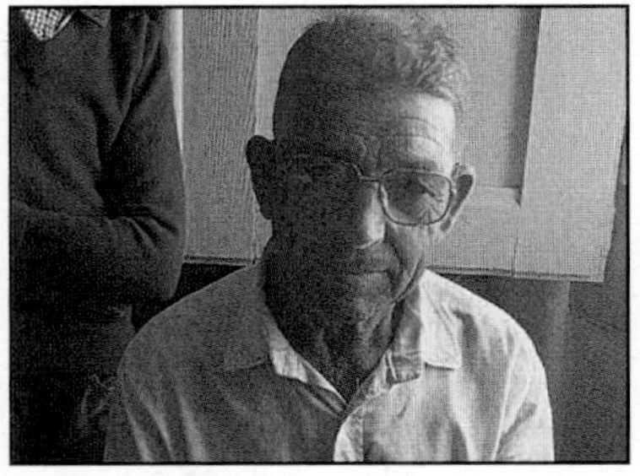

Elderly Patient Threatened With Suppository

see SENIORBEAT page 9B

Area Restaurant Cajun Again

see FOOD page 6E

Charlize Theron Has Opinion

see PEOPLE page 1C

STATshot™

A look at the numbers that shape your world.

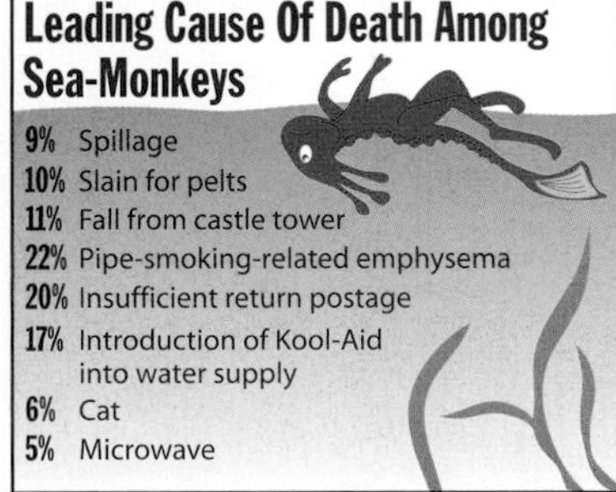

INSIDE the ONION®

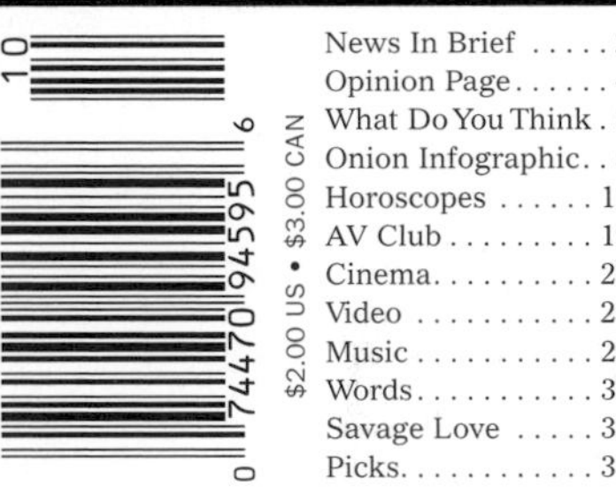

News In Brief 2
Opinion Page 4
What Do You Think . 5
Onion Infographic. . 5
Horoscopes 17
AV Club 19
Cinema. 24
Video 28
Music 29
Words. 31
Savage Love 32
Picks. 33

Gore Already Regretting Promise To Help Clinton Move Out

Above: Gore surveys "the shitload of furniture" he'll be helping Clinton move next January.

WASHINGTON, DC—President Clinton is still 10 months away from leaving the White House, but Al Gore is already regretting his promise to help him move out, the vice-president admitted Monday.

"I am not looking forward to that, let me tell you," said Gore, surveying the four large couches and three oak desks that adorn the East Room. "As Bill's vice-president and good friend, I try to help him out with stuff whenever he asks, but that is going to be one serious bitch of a move."

Gore made the promise last summer while talking to Clinton about his own plans to live in the 132-room residence at 1600 Pennsylvania Avenue.

"I told him I was thinking about running for president, and he said I could expect his full support if I did. But then, right at the very end of the conversation, he slips in, 'Oh, by the way, are you going to be free on moving day?'" Gore said. "That's so Bill: He totally waited until I needed his political backing before asking me."

> "I try to help him out with stuff," Gore said, "but that is going to be one serious bitch of a move."

Gore's reluctance to help Clinton stems from the bad experience he had helping him move in January 1993.

"What a complete nightmare," Gore said. "I swear, by the end of the day, I wanted to kill him."

see GORE page 6

Above: The graceful, awe-inspiring Bobo.

Majestic Lowland Gorilla Exploited For Comic Effect

CENTURY CITY, CA—The serene, awe-inspiring majesty of the lowland gorilla, one of nature's proudest and most powerful creatures, was compromised once again Tuesday, when an adult bull was "willfully and maliciously" exploited for humorous purposes, spokespersons for the Organization To Prevent The Comedic Exploitation Of Animals said.

The humiliating spectacle occurred when "Bobo," raised in captivity and trained since birth to submit to embarrassing lowbrow comedy scenarios for the amusement of humans, was strapped into humorously undersized bellboy garb on the set of the upcoming made-for-cable comedy *Monkey Honeymoon*, starring Carrot Top and Jennifer Tilly. The animal was then allegedly ordered by handlers to "go ape," creating slapstick disruptions and raising irreverent havoc in an otherwise stodgy and formal luxury-hotel setting.

It was the worst case of primate-degra-

see GORILLA page 9

Apartment Full Of Jesus Stuff Brings Date To Screeching Halt

PAWTUCKET, RI—A first date that "actually seemed to be going pretty well" came to a screeching halt Saturday, when area resident Kyle Richman stepped into Melinda Tulle's Christ-packed apartment.

"Immediately upon walking into the living room, I spotted that framed Last Supper hanging above the couch," said Richman, 32, speaking from the safety of his own non-Jesus-themed apartment. "It took me about half a second to realize that it just wasn't going to happen for the two of us."

Richman expressed regret that the evening turned sour, but also relief that he "found out when [he] did."

"It was only our first date, but I'd been thinking I might have actually found someone

see DATE page 3

Above: The apartment which ended Richman's date "in about two seconds flat."

NEWS

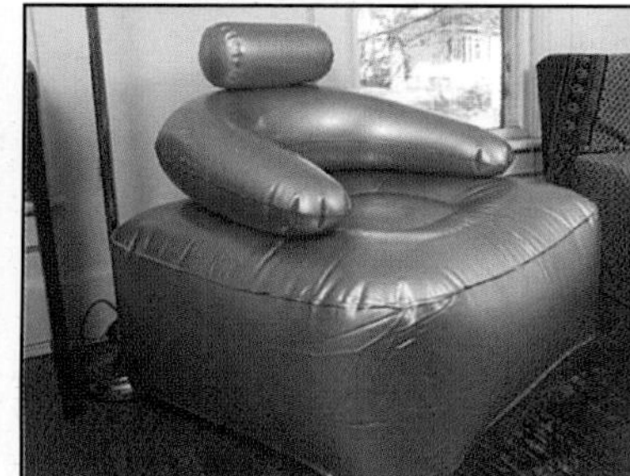

Inflatable Chair's Novelty Wears Off

see LIVING page 2D

Guy At House Party Must Be At Least 32

see CAMPUS page 11E

Call Ignored In The Order It Was Received

see LOCAL page 8B

Brand-New Wife Breaks Down

see LIFESTYLE page 2C

STATshot™

A look at the numbers that shape your world.

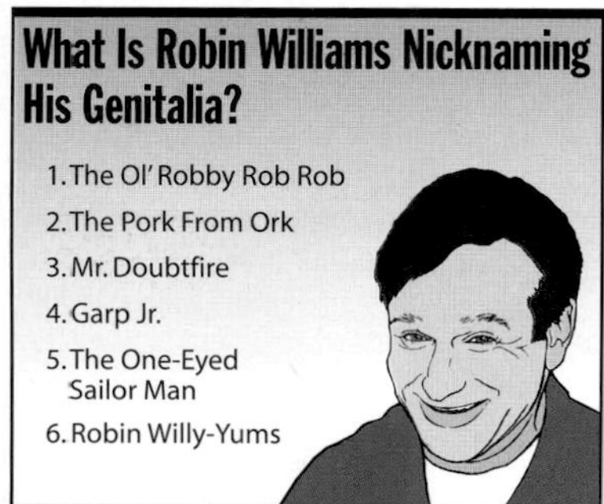

INSIDE the ONION®

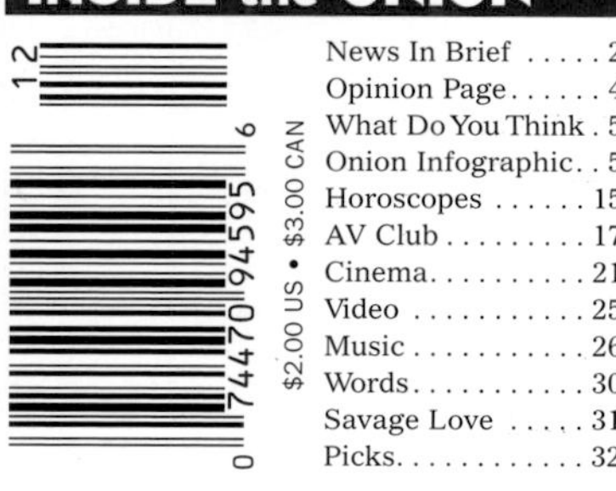

News In Brief 2
Opinion Page. 4
What Do You Think . 5
Onion Infographic. . 5
Horoscopes 15
AV Club 17
Cinema. 21
Video 25
Music 26
Words. 30
Savage Love 31
Picks. 32

the ONION®

VOLUME 36 ISSUE 12 | AMERICA'S FINEST NEWS SOURCE™ | 6-12 APRIL 2000

U.S. Population At 13,462

'We Don't Think Everybody Sent In Their Census Forms,' Say Officials

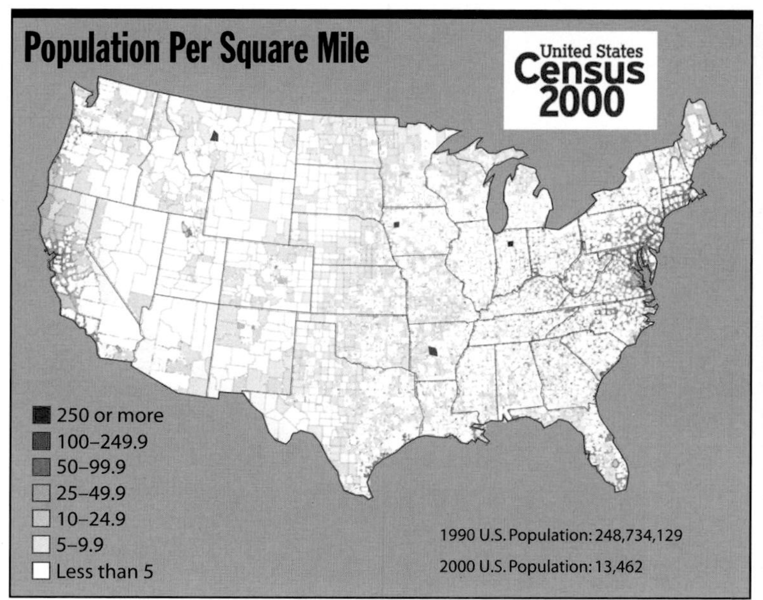

WASHINGTON, DC—With the April 1 deadline for returning Census 2000 forms finally passed, the Bureau of the Census announced Monday that the U.S. population stands at 13,462.

"We at the Census Bureau are shocked by the incredible decrease in the population that apparently took place in the 10 years since the last Census in 1990," Census Bureau director Kenneth Prewitt said. "A 1999 projection estimated the U.S. population at 274 mil-

see CENSUS page 7

Above: Census Bureau director Kenneth Prewitt.

Above: The unpopular product.

Funyuns Still Outselling Responsibilityuns

DALLAS—Funyuns, the world leader in artificial onion-ring-flavored and -shaped snack-food items, continues to enjoy an "overwhelming sales lead" over competing brand Responsibilityuns, the trade publication *Impulse Purchase Quarterly* reported Monday.

Responsibilityuns, launched last May in a bold attempt to challenge Funyuns' dominance of the faux-onion-ring snack market, have done "little to no damage" to its rival's sales through the first quarter of 2000.

"I just don't understand what went wrong," said James Connell, CEO of Delayed Gratification Foods, the Dallas-based maker of the sober, salted snack. "Everybody knows that responsibility and self-reliance are virtues which, with patience and persistence, bring rewards

see RESPONSIBILITYUNS page 10

Attempt To Impress Becky Lundegaard Undermined By Interloper

HAMPTON, VA—An attempt by Brian Shuman, 12, to impress fellow seventh-grader Becky Lundegaard, 13, met with spectacular failure Monday, when his school supplies and shoulder bag were forcibly seized, his sweater vest yanked over his head, and his face pressed into a row of lockers, witnesses reported.

According to the unpopular Shuman, known primarily among classmates at Hampton Middle School for his scholastic achievements and awkward social manner, he was "deliberately undermined by the uncalled-for actions of an interloping usurper intent on humiliating me in a derogatory manner in front of Miss

see INTERLOPER page 11

Right: Brian Shuman, the foiled would-be suitor of Becky Lundegaard (inset).

NEWS

Child Disciplined For Wasting Yarn

see LOCAL page 6B

Soda Nearing Room Temperature

see BEVERAGES page 12E

Bargain Hunter Becomes The Bargain-Hunted

see LOCAL page 2C

Moment Of Your Time Apparently Means 33 Minutes

see MARKETING page 1D

STATshot™

A look at the numbers that shape your world.

How About The Rack On That Blonde?

12% I hear ya, dude
21% I wouldn't mind plowing into those
17% Talk about some all-day suckers
13% I've seen better
19% She's got a three-dick mouth, too
18% That's my fucking sister, asshole

INSIDE the ONION®

News In Brief 2
Opinion Page. 4
What Do You Think . 5
Onion Infographic. . 5
Horoscopes 15
AV Club 17
Cinema. 20
Video 24
Music 26
Words. 28
Savage Love 30
Picks. 31

VOLUME 36 ISSUE 13 AMERICA'S FINEST NEWS SOURCE™ 13–19 APRIL 2000

South Postpones Rising Again For Yet Another Year

Left: Three of the estimated 45 million Southerners who have not yet gotten around to rising again.

HUNTSVILLE, AL—For the 135th straight year since Gen. Robert E. Lee's surrender at Appomattox, representatives for the South announced Monday that the region has postponed plans to rise again.

"Make no mistake, the South shall rise again," said Knox Pritchard, president of the Huntsville-based Alliance Of Confederate States. "But we're just not quite ready to do it now. Hopefully, we'll be able to rise again real soon, maybe even in 2001."

Pritchard's fellow Southerners shared his confidence.

"Yes, sir. The South will rise again, and when it does, I'll be right up front waving the Stars and Bars," said Dock Mullins of Decatur, GA. "But first, I gotta get my truck fixed and get that rusty old stove out of my yard."

"Lord willing, and the creek don't rise,

see SOUTH page 7

Nation Shocked By Pre-Natal Shooting

ALBUQUERQUE, NM—Investigators are trying to determine what led an unborn child to fatally shoot his twin with a .38-caliber revolver during an altercation in their shared Albuquerque womb Monday.

According to police, the twins' mother, Evelyn Alpert, 34, was awakened at 4 a.m. by the sensation of a scuffle in her uterus, which she dismissed as "routine kicking." Approximately 30 minutes later, Alpert heard and felt three pistol shots.

A subsequent forensic ultrasound revealed that the unborn gunman—identified as a five-inch-tall male Caucasian of slight build with no eyes or hair—shot his brother twice in what eventually would have become his heart.

After a tense four-hour standoff, the unborn gunman

see SHOOTING page 11

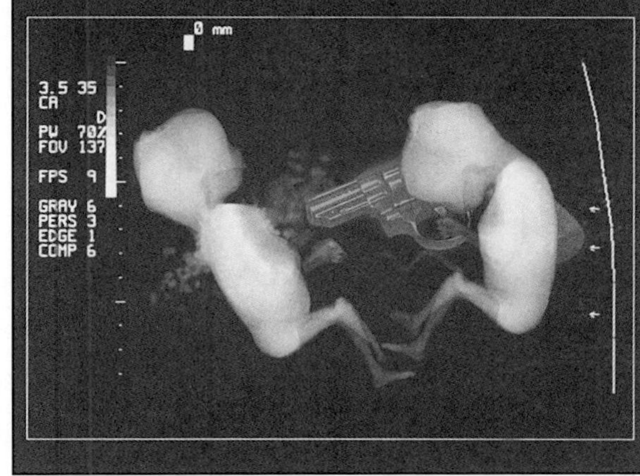

Above: An Albuquerque Police Department ultrasound depicting the fetal fatality.

Insurance Executive Fakes Own Life

Above: The fraudulent Gordon Krumrie.

WARREN, MI—Gordon Krumrie, a 43-year-old executive with Great Lakes Mutual, admitted Tuesday that he faked his own life to collect a substantial insurance payoff.

"It was simple," said Krumrie, who came clean after collecting more than $300,000 over a 25-year period. "Just fool the right people, make my life look believable, and every month, Great Lakes would cut me a check for $5,000."

"Plus bonuses," he added. "If they only knew."

Krumrie began laying the groundwork for his false identity at an early age. In high school, he fabricated an interest in community and local business affairs, getting elected student-council treasurer and president of his school's chapter of Future Business Leaders of America.

"It was dirty work, but I had to establish a credible cover story early," Krumrie said. "It's the first thing those insurance investigators check when they suspect a wrongful life has been committed."

Krumrie's deception continued at Western Michigan University, where he earned an economics degree, deceiving professors into thinking he had a genuine interest in a career in finance. All the while, he made the necessary behind-the-scenes connections.

"I spent four years playing along with those Sigma Chi bastards," Krumrie said. "But they left me no choice. Some of them had highly placed fathers in key firms."

Upon being hired by Great Lakes

see EXECUTIVE page 9

the ONION®

VOLUME 36 ISSUE 14 AMERICA'S FINEST NEWS SOURCE™ 20–26 APRIL 2000

NEWS

New Spiritually Correct Doll Lets Children Show Where And How Jesus Touched Them

see RELIGION page 9C

Jesse Helms Treed By Coon Hounds

see NATION page 7A

Hero Cop Awarded Own Theme Music

see PEOPLE page 4D

STATshot™

A look at the numbers that shape your world.

INSIDE the ONION®

News In Brief 2
Opinion Page. 4
What Do You Think . 5
Onion Infographic. . 5
Horoscopes 15
AV Club 17
Cinema. 23
Video 26
Music 28
Words. 30
Savage Love 31
Picks. 32

Mid-Level Manager Forced To Find Out Who Isn't Flushing The Toilet

DOVER, DE—Bill Tepfer, an associate service-department manager at Shademaster Tent & Awning Supply, was ordered by his supervisor Monday to determine the party responsible for not flushing the second-floor toilet.

"Someone in this company has been neglecting to flush after going to the bathroom," said Tepfer, 31. "And I've been put in charge of finding out who that person is."

According to secretary Shelley Grabisch, three times in the past two days, various Shademaster employees have attempted to use the second-floor bathroom, only to discover toilet paper and fecal matter still in the bowl.

"It's disgusting," Grabisch said. "It's been particularly bad the last few days, but it's been going on a lot longer than that. We're talking *at least* every other day for a

see TOILET page 8

Left: Associate service-department manager Bill Tepfer.

Federal Judge Rules Parker Brothers Holds Monopoly Monopoly

WASHINGTON, DC—In a landmark antitrust decision, U.S. District Judge Thomas Nance ruled Monday that Parker Brothers' controlling interest in the popular board game Monopoly constitutes an illegal Monopoly monopoly.

Found guilty of colluding with Hasbro to corner the Monopoly market—undermining the production and sale of similar board games and designing the

see MONOPOLY page 11

Right: Rich Uncle Pennybags testifies before a Senate subcommittee on April 3. Below: A row of Parker Brothers-owned hotels in Atlantic City.

Area Man Creeped Out By Request To 'Make Love'

WINSTON-SALEM, NC—A half-naked Patrick Fuller was thoroughly creeped out Saturday, when fellow Wake Forest University senior Alicia Echols suggested that the two "make love."

"There we were, messing around on the couch in her apartment's living room," Fuller said. "Things were heating up, so I asked if we should go back to her bedroom in case her roommate came home. That's when she stood up and said, 'Make love to me, Patrick.'"

"It was really weird," continued Fuller, who met Echols three weeks ago and had gone on two dates with her prior to Saturday. "I mean, Alicia's definitely not the type of girl who'd say, 'Let's fuck.' But still: 'Make love to me'? That's very different than saying, 'Let's have sex.'"

"What did she mean by 'love'?" Fuller asked. "We're not even dating."

"What did she mean by 'love'?" Fuller asked. "We're not even dating. I mean, we've gone out a few times, so I guess we're sort of technically casually dating, in a way, but it's not like she's my girlfriend."

Fuller said he was further creeped out when, upon entering the bedroom, Echols told him she was "ready to take you

see MAKE LOVE page 7

NEWS

Guy Totally Looked Like Chick From Behind

see LOCAL page 2D

Disembodied Voice In Elevator Wants To Know Way To San Jose

see OFFICE page 9C

47 Punk Bands Change Name To 'The Miami Relatives'

see MUSIC page 3E

STATshot™

A look at the numbers that shape your world.

Does This Shirt Make Me Look Gay?

12% Define "gay"
21% Yes, but Rock Hudson gay, not Freddie Mercury gay
17% Uh, no, not at all
13% Only if, by "gay," you mean "homosexual-looking"
19% I think it's the collar
18% Kinda—but that's what you want, right?

INSIDE the ONION®

16
0 74470 94595 6
$2.00 US • $3.00 CAN

News In Brief 2
Opinion Page 4
What Do You Think . 5
Onion Infographic . . 5
Horoscopes 17
AV Club 19
Cinema 24
Video 28
Music 30
Words 33
Savage Love 34
Picks 35

the ONION®

VOLUME 36 ISSUE 16 | AMERICA'S FINEST NEWS SOURCE™ | 4–10 MAY 2000

American People To Live Happily Ever After

WASHINGTON, DC—With the U.S. enjoying unprecedented prosperity at home and stability abroad, President Clinton announced Monday that the Bad Times are gone forever, and that the American people will live happily ever after.

"My loyal subjects," said Clinton, speaking from his great White House atop a shining hill, "once upon a time, the Kingdom was beset with great dangers, and the Bear ran amok on Wall Street, and the men from the Red Land menaced us with their great rockets, and everyone was much afraid. But, henceforth, I decree that all Americans will be happy and live in comfy houses filled with plenty of good things to eat, and all mommies and daddies will be kind and all children good, and the Wizard Greenspan

see AMERICA page 7

Coalition Of Developmentally Disabled Adults Demands Trip To McDonald's

WASHINGTON, DC—Chanting, "We want McDonald's!" in relative unison, representatives of the American Association of Developmentally Disabled Adults held a press conference Monday to demand a trip to a D.C.-area McDonald's.

"For weeks, my clients have been pleading with relatives, social workers, and assisted-living aides for a group outing to McDonald's," said Allan Lefferts, a civil-rights lawyer representing the AADDA. "Yet time and time again, these requests have been brushed aside with dismissals like, 'Not now' and, 'Maybe next week, if you're good.' Well, these folks will not wait any longer. They will not 'settle down.'"

Lefferts' remarks were met with cheers and stomping feet from AADDA members, with several adding cries of "French fries!"

"At this point, my clients are in good

see McDONALD'S page 8

Right: AADDA member Billy Thorne (at podium) tells reporters that he has been "very good" and deserves a trip to McDonald's.

Internet Opens Up Whole New World Of Illness For Local Hypochondriac

MERIDEN, CT—All her life, Janet Hartley has suffered from a host of ill-defined viruses and inexplicable aches and pains, diagnosing herself with everything from diabetes to cancer. But ever since discovering such online medical resources as WebMD, drkoop.com, and Yahoo! Health, the 41-year-old hypochondriac has had a whole new world of imaginary illnesses opened up to her.

"The Internet has really revolutionized my ability to keep on top of my medical problems," said Hartley, speaking from her bed. "For instance, I used to think my headaches were just really bad migraines. But then last week, while searching Mt. Sinai Hospital's online medical database, I learned about something much more serious called cranial AVM, or arteriovascular malformation, which, along with headache pain, may also result in dizziness, loss of concentration, and impaired vision. I immediately thought to myself, 'Hey,

see HYPOCHONDRIAC page 10

Above: Janet Hartley learns more about her suspected case of arteriovascular malformation on Yahoo! Health.

NEWS

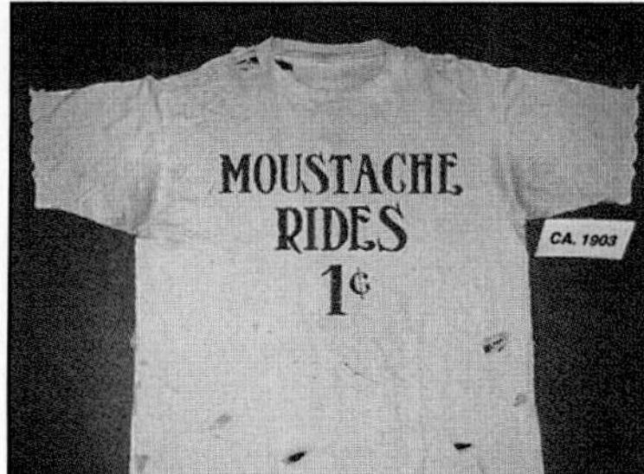

Earliest Known T-Shirt Found

see SCIENCE page 1E

Model To Give Acting A Shot

see PEOPLE page 9B

Greenspan Tattoos 'Fed Life' Across Abdomen

see NATION page 6A

Woman On TV Gives Birth To Four-Month-Old Baby

see TELEVISION page 3C

STATshot™

A look at the numbers that shape your world.

Top Cannes Contenders

What are the frontrunners for the Palme d'Or?

Film	Country
• *My Bassoon Teacher's Décolletage*	France
• *I Am Curious, Gray*	Sweden
• *The Spirit And Purpose Of Geography*	Germany
• *Céline Of The Artesian Well*	France
• *Battlefield Perth*	Australia
• *USA! USA! USA!*	USA

INSIDE the ONION®

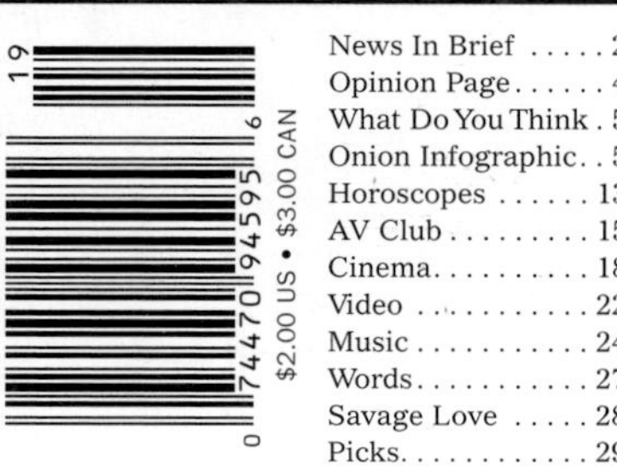

News In Brief 2
Opinion Page. 4
What Do You Think . 5
Onion Infographic. . 5
Horoscopes 13
AV Club 15
Cinema. 18
Video 22
Music 24
Words. 27
Savage Love 28
Picks. 29

the ONION®

VOLUME 36 ISSUE 19 | AMERICA'S FINEST NEWS SOURCE™ | 25–31 MAY 2000

U.S. No Longer Responsible For Lost Or Stolen Items

WASHINGTON, DC—Holding aloft a box of unclaimed coats, wallets, and in-line skates labeled "Cincinnati," Secretary of the Interior Bruce Babbitt announced Monday that the federal government is no longer responsible for personal items lost or stolen within U.S. borders.

"Effective immediately, the U.S. will not be held accountable for anything that happens to citizens' eyeglasses, baseball caps, Walkmans, outdoor grills, or Chevy Impalas—or any other items that are misplaced, broken, or stolen on U.S. premises," Babbitt said. "Your personal effects are your own responsibility, folks."

According to Babbitt, the warning "Please Watch Your

see U.S. page 10

Right: A sign at the U.S.-Mexico border reminds citizens to look after their own belongings.

Twelve Customers Gunned Down In Convenience-Store Clerk's Imagination

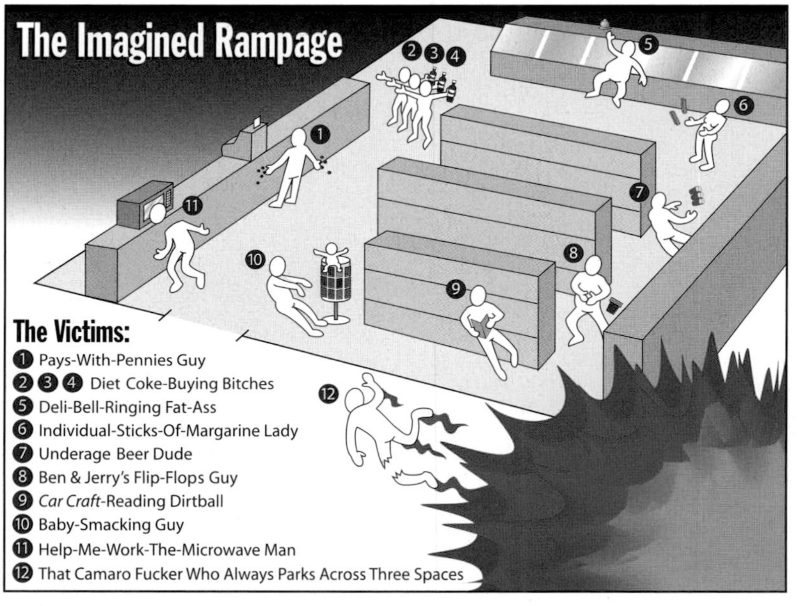

CLACKAMAS, OR—Driven to homicidal rage by mounting job-related frustrations, third-shift Stop 'N' Shop clerk Justin Fonseca, 27, shot and killed 12 customers in his imagination Monday.

Justin Fonseca

The mass slaying, the 63rd to take place in Fonseca's mind since he began working at the Portland-area convenience store last August, was the worst since Mar. 17, when he visualized himself fatally stabbing 22 intoxicated St. Patrick's Day revelers with their own broken beer bottles.

Fonseca began his mental rampage at approximately 10 p.m., when he was approached by a Stop 'N' Shop regular known as "Pays-With-Pennies Guy."

"I was the only guy working and was totally swamped, when in walks Pays-

see SHOOTING page 6

Canadian Girlfriend Unsubstantiated

BEMIDJI, MN—Despite his insistence, Timothy Woronoff has been unable to substantiate his longstanding claim that he has a girlfriend in Canada, sources close to the 16-year-old Bemidji High School junior reported Monday.

Ever since September, Woronoff has been telling friends and classmates that he is involved in a long-distance relationship with "Audrey de Trudeau," an alleged Banff, Alberta 17-year-old. According to Woronoff, he and de Trudeau met last July while both were counselors at a band camp in the Boundary Waters region of northern Minnesota near the U.S.-Canadian border.

"We totally fell in love with each other at camp, and when the summer ended, we decided to stay together," Woronoff said. "It's too bad Audrey can't come down and visit me all that often, living so far away and all."

Andrew Dwight, Woronoff's best friend, said he has long doubted the girlfriend-having claims.

"I first wondered about it last October, when I asked Tim exactly how he met Audrey," Dwight said. "He was all quiet for a while, saying he was trying to remember. Finally, after about a minute, he said, 'Oh, yeah—this guy Jeff we both happened to know introduced us. I totally forgot about that.'"

see GIRLFRIEND page 8

Above: Timothy Woronoff holds up a picture of his alleged Canadian girlfriend.

NEWS

You Can Tell Area Bank Used To Be A Pizza Hut

see LOCAL page 3C

Sierra Leone Burns Down

see WORLD page 9A

Area Teen Able To Distinguish Between Gap, Old Navy T-Shirts

see SHOPPING page 5D

Pope Breaks Cinder Block With Head

see VATICAN page 2B

STATshot™

A look at the numbers that shape your world.

INSIDE the ONION®

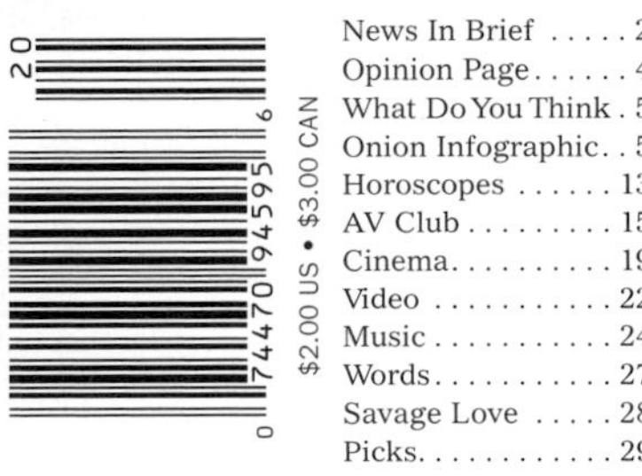

News In Brief 2
Opinion Page 4
What Do You Think . 5
Onion Infographic. . 5
Horoscopes 13
AV Club 15
Cinema. 19
Video 22
Music 24
Words. 27
Savage Love 28
Picks. 29

the ONION®

VOLUME 36 ISSUE 20 AMERICA'S FINEST NEWS SOURCE™ 1–7 JUNE 2000

Raccoon Leaders Call For Loosening Of Garbage-Can Lids

Above: NARF president Bristletail urges homeowners to be less careful about sealing their trash cans.

WASHINGTON, DC—In a 4 a.m. speech at the group's annual convention Sunday, North American Raccoon Federation president Bristletail called upon homeowners to loosen the lids of their garbage cans, providing the ring-tailed mammals with greater access to discarded food scraps during nocturnal scavenging.

"Every time you seal a standard 30-gallon garbage can, as many as six raccoons are forced to go without their necessary daily supply of congealed baked beans, rancid cottage-cheese chunks, and moldy cantaloupe rinds," Bristletail told an audience of NARF members and human

see RACCOONS page 10

Apartment-Wide Porn Sweep Precedes Date's Arrival

Above: Randy Thaler purges his apartment of all visible pornographic material.

BETHPAGE, NY—Preparing for the arrival of dinner date Amanda Raskin, area resident Randy Thaler conducted a thorough porn sweep of his one-bedroom apartment Monday.

"I almost forgot to do it, actually," the 24-year-old graphic designer said. "But while I was clearing off the kitchen table, I saw the box for *A Fistful Of Dolores* sitting out and thought, 'Oh, shit.'"

As a pot of spinach fettuccine boiled in the kitchen, Thaler swiftly moved through the apartment, racing to collect all traces of print- and video-based female objectification before his date's 7 p.m. arrival. First, he headed to the bathroom, where he removed from the top of the toilet a copy of last month's *Playboy* and a November 1999 issue of the non-pornographic but sexist *Maxim* magazine.

Thaler then proceeded to the living room, where he found a copy of *Girls Gone Wild: Best Of Mardi Gras* sticking

see PORN page 8

High-School Senior Amazed By Coolness Of University Of Wisconsin–Whitewater

MENOMONEE FALLS, WI—Chris Knopecke, a senior at Menomonee Falls High School, declared the University of Wisconsin at Whitewater "awesome" Monday, describing his weekend visit to the school as "so unbelievably cool."

"UW–Whitewater is the most amazing place," said Knopecke, who has decided to attend the school in the fall. "Right in the middle of campus, there's this big lawn where tons of people were just hanging out together. And there was this guy on the sidewalk selling sunglasses and those Mexican-poncho things. I cannot wait to get out of stupid Menomonee Falls."

Living less than 40 miles from Whitewater, Knopecke had long heard rumors about parties involving alcohol and even marijuana at the school, but he was hardly prepared for the vast cultural spectrum he would encounter during his visit.

"There was someone from Minnesota on my campus tour with me, and there was a black guy, too," Knopecke said. "Then, at one point, this guy with blue hair walked by, and no one was even giving him a second look. I am so looking forward to being

see WHITEWATER page 12

Right: Menomonee Falls High School senior Chris Knopecke shows off the University of Wisconsin–Whitewater T-shirt he bought during a weekend visit to the school.

NEWS

Backstreet Boys Become Backstreet Men In Backstreet Ritual

see PEOPLE page 2D

Ramen Master Defeated By New Kung-Pao Style

see WORLD page 8A

Secretary Waxes Garfieldian

see OFFICE page 11E

Cheap Garbage Disposal Can't Handle Femur

see HOME page 7B

STATshot™

A look at the numbers that shape your world.

INSIDE the ONION®

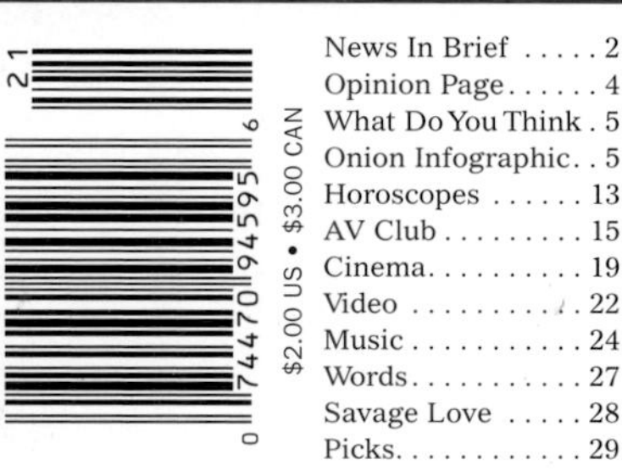

News In Brief 2
Opinion Page...... 4
What Do You Think . 5
Onion Infographic. . 5
Horoscopes 13
AV Club 15
Cinema.......... 19
Video 22
Music........... 24
Words........... 27
Savage Love 28
Picks............ 29

the ONION®

VOLUME 36 ISSUE 21 AMERICA'S FINEST NEWS SOURCE™ 8–14 JUNE 2000

THE ECONOMY

Blue Line Jumps 11 Percent

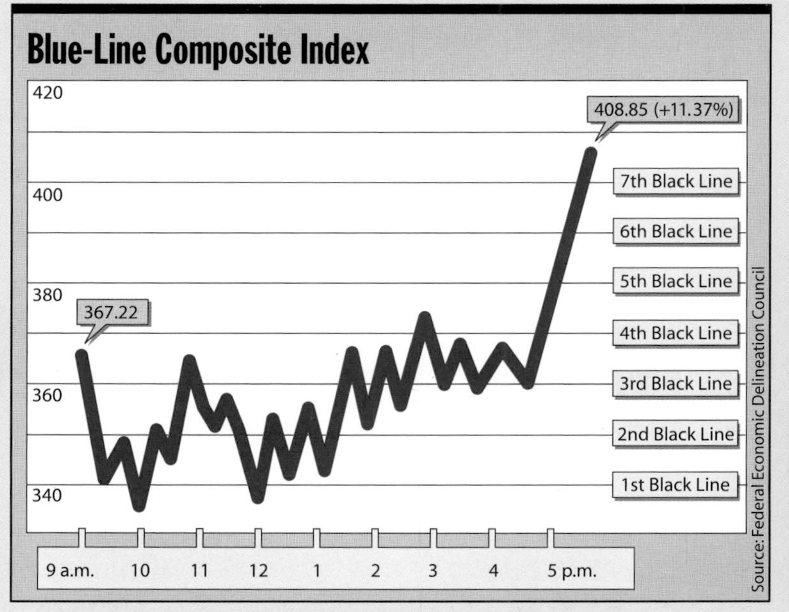

NEW YORK—Excitement swept the financial world Monday, when a blue line jumped more than 11 percent, passing four black horizontal lines as it rose from 367.22 to 408.85.

It was the biggest single-day gain for a blue line since 1994.

"Even if you extend the blue line's big white box back many vertical lines, you

see BLUE LINE page 7

Below: Wall Street traders react to the blue line's 41-point leap.

Ant Farm Teaches Children About Toil, Death

PASADENA, CA—Wonderco, a Pasadena-based educational-toy manufacturer, unveiled its new Playscovery Cove Ant Village Monday, touting the ant farm as a fun, interactive way to teach children ages 5 and up about unceasing, backbreaking toil and the cold, inescapable reality of death.

"Your little ones will have a front-row seat as worker ants labor, day in and day out, until they inevitably die of exhaustion, their futile efforts all for naught," Wonderco spokeswoman Joan Kedzie said. "A Playscovery Cove Ant Village, complete with stackable tiny ant barns, see-through 'Antway' travel tubes, and connecting 'Antports,' is your children's window into the years of thankless, grueling labor that await them as worker drones in our post-industrial society."

see ANT FARM page 6

Right: Children learn about the cruel reality of pain, toil, and death with the Playscovery Cove Ant Village.

Area Man Really Wants To Like The Marx Brothers

Left: Self-described "film buff" Craig Logan.

AUSTIN, TX—Despite repeated attempts to gain an appreciation of the legendary comedy team, area graphic designer Craig Logan confessed Monday that he still can't get into the Marx Brothers.

"I realize they're extremely important, and I very much want to enjoy them," Logan, 29, said. "But I just don't find them funny at all."

"It's not because it's old and in black and white, either," Logan added. "I'm not some sort of philistine."

Over the years, Logan has rented numerous Marx Brothers movies in his efforts to like the seminal stars of vaudeville, Broadway, radio, and TV. Each attempt, however, has ended in failure.

"A couple years ago, I rented the 1935 screwball comedy *A Night At The Opera*, considered by many to be their masterwork," Logan said. "The whole movie, all they were doing was running around like idiots and using funny voices. It was like some annoying Adam Sandler movie. I thought I missed something, so I read about it in the Leonard Maltin video guide, then watched it again, but I still couldn't pick up on the 'brilliant subversiveness of this anarchic laugh riot.'"

Last December, Logan's longtime desire

see MARX BROTHERS page 10

NEWS

Area Woman Tired Of Men Staring At Her Breast Implants

see LOCAL page 3C

Sun-Dried Sparrow Carcass Washed Away With Hose

see WORLD page 9A

Charles Durning Hocks Up Four-Pound Chunk Of Phlegm

see SHOPPING page 5D

STATshot™

A look at the numbers that shape your world.

INSIDE the ONION®

News In Brief 2
Opinion Page. 4
What Do You Think . 5
Onion Infographic. . 5
Horoscopes 13
AV Club 15
Cinema. 20
Video 23
Music 25
Words. 27
Savage Love 28
Picks. 29

the ONION®

VOLUME 36 ISSUE 22 AMERICA'S FINEST NEWS SOURCE™ 15–21 JUNE 2000

Clinton Calls For National Week Off To Get National Shit Together

Above: A "swamped" President Clinton announces his plan for a National Week Off.

WASHINGTON, DC—Citing years of distracting, time-consuming obligations that have caused many important matters to go unattended, President Clinton called for a National Week Off Monday for the purpose of getting the nation's shit together.

If approved, the week off, scheduled for June 18-24, would give Clinton and the American people a chance to finally take care of all their shit.

"My fellow Americans," Clinton said in his weekly radio address, "as your president, I have had a great many things to deal with during my time in office: welfare reform, Whitewater, gun-control legislation, Bosnia, sex scandals—you name it. As a result, a lot of shit has piled up that I have not had the chance to take care of."

Among the shit Clinton intends to deal with during the national week off: a pile of bills that he meant to pay a few months ago but forgot all about because of the Sierra Leone crisis. "I just want to take a whole day to do nothing but go at that stack. Then there's all that crap piling up on the Oval Office floor. I've got to do something about those boxes."

Clinton said other shit would be targeted in subsequent days. "I still have to call back that Barak guy—he's left a load of messages about that whole Lebanon-pull-out deal. And the Army's been hassling me for months about getting them some new bombers. Plus, I owe Mexico, like, a billion dollars."

"I am certain," Clinton said during the

see CLINTON page 8

Above: "Hollywood" Hulk Hogan tells reporters what he is going to do to Olympic gold medalist Viktor Ulianov when he gets him on the mat.

IOC Clears Pros To Wrestle In Summer Olympics

LAUSANNE, SWITZERLAND—International Olympic Committee president Juan Antonio Samaranch announced Monday that, for the first time ever, professionals will be permitted to compete in wrestling in the upcoming Sydney Summer Olympics.

"The time has come for the best wrestlers to come together and compete against one another on the world stage," Samaranch said. "This is the true Olympic spirit."

The U.S. Olympic wrestling team, which was badly beaten by Russia and the Ukraine in the '92 and '96 Games, is expected to be the biggest beneficiary of the rule change. Already, a number of high-profile U.S. pros have filed requests with the USOC to compete in Sydney, including "Stone Cold" Steve Austin, Diamond Dallas Page, The

see OLYMPICS page 12

God Answers Prayers Of Paralyzed Little Boy

'No,' Says God

SAN FRANCISCO—For as long as he can remember, 7-year-old Timmy Yu has had one precious dream: From the bottom of his heart, he has hoped against hope that God would someday hear his prayer to walk again. Though many thought Timmy's heavenly plea would never be answered, his dream finally came true Monday, when the Lord personally responded to the wheelchair-bound boy's prayer with a resounding no.

"I knew that if I just prayed hard enough, God would hear me," said a joyful Timmy, sitting in the wheelchair to which he will be confined for the rest of his life. "And now my prayer has been answered. I haven't been this happy since before the accident, when I could walk and play with the other children like a normal boy."

God's response came at approximately 10 a.m., following a particularly fervent Sunday-night prayer session by little Timmy. Witnesses said God issued His miraculous answer in the form of a towering column of clouds, from which poured forth great beams of Divine light and the music of the Heavenly Host. The miraculous event took place in the Children's Special Care Ward of St. Luke's Hospital, which Timmy visits three times a week for an excruciating two-hour procedure to

see GOD page 7

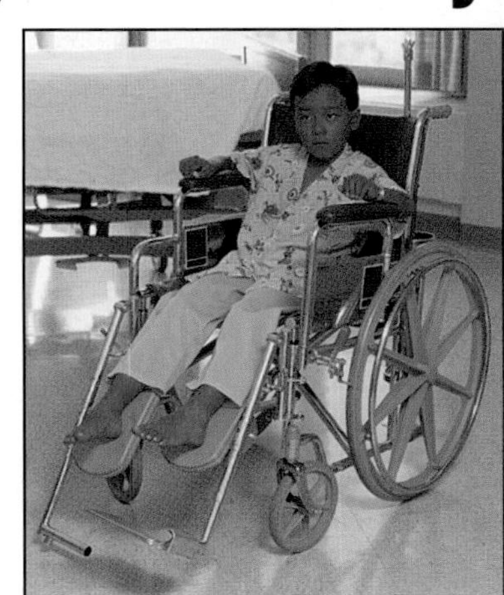

Right: Wheelchair-bound Timmy Yu, who finally received his long-awaited reply from God.

NEWS

Auto Industry Agrees To Install Brakes In SUVs

see BUSINESS page 5C

Standard Deviation Not Enough For Perverted Statistician

see LIFESTYLE page 2D

Kenyan Grandmother Dominates Walkathon

see SPORTS page 1E

Dishwasher Trained

see WORKPLACE page 5B

STATshot™

A look at the numbers that shape your world.

Remaining Unregistered Internet Domain Names

- www.fullyclothed.net
- www.godlovesyouwithallhisfuckingheart.com
- www.ludditeworld.com
- www.pissguzzlinggrannies.edu
- www.tomskerrittisgod.com
- www.gayrepublicanmetalheadwiccans.org
- www.njkfjkhrjhojfkjhwqfkl.com

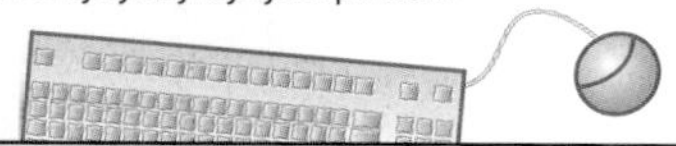

INSIDE the ONION®

News In Brief 2
Opinion Page 4
What Do You Think . 5
Onion Infographic . . 5
Horoscopes 13
A.V. Club 15
Cinema 20
Video 23
Music 25
Words 27
Savage Love 28
Picks 29

the ONION®

VOLUME 36 ISSUE 25 AMERICA'S FINEST NEWS SOURCE™ 27 JULY–2 AUGUST 2000

Harry Potter Books Spark Rise In Satanism Among Children

LOCK HAVEN, PA—Ashley Daniels is as close as you can get to your typical 9-year-old American girl. A third-grader at Lock Haven Elementary School, she loves rollerblading, her pet hamsters Benny and Oreo, Britney Spears, and, of course, Harry Potter. Having breezed through the most recent *Potter* opus in just four days, Ashley is among the millions of children who have made *Harry Potter And The Goblet Of Fire* the fastest-selling book in publishing history.

And, like many of her school friends, Ashley was captivated enough by the strange occult doings at the Hogwarts School Of Witchcraft And Wizardry to pursue the Left-Hand Path, determined to become as adept at the black arts as Harry and his pals.

"I used to believe in what they taught us at Sunday School," said Ashley, conjuring up an ancient spell to summon Cerebus, the three-headed hound of hell. "But the *Harry Potter* books showed me that magic is real, something I can learn and use right now, and that the Bible is nothing but bor-

see POTTER page 10

Right: Three young *Harry Potter* fans in Winter Park, FL, recite an ancient Satanic incantation.

Left: Presidential hopeful George W. Bush is flanked by his mom and dad, who holds a check for him.

Bush Reluctantly Accepts Donation From Parents

DEL MAR, CA—Despite strong personal reservations, Republican presidential contender George W. Bush confirmed Monday that he has "reluctantly" agreed to accept a $2 million donation from his parents "to help with some of the mounting expenses involved in running for office."

"I didn't want to do it, as I have always prided myself on paying my own way," Bush told reporters during a campaign stop near San Diego. "Unfortunately, the increasing difficulty of competing with the Gore campaign's unlimited taxpayer war chest has forced me to

see BUSH page 7

Ad-Agency Print Buyer Can't Believe They Want To Add A Perf This Late In The Game

LINCOLN, NE—Milt Olberding, a print buyer with L&G Advertising, expressed disbelief Tuesday that Capital City Chrysler owner William "Biff" Brignola wants to add a perforated insert to his ad this late in the game.

"A perf? At this point?" said Olberding, 33, upon learning of the change from L&G Advertising account manager Phil Essene. "We were about to put this whole thing to bed. Why didn't Brignola mention this last week when I was giving him quotes for coated?"

Essene, who helped design the full-page Capital City ad slated to run in a 32-page "Great Savings" sales flyer that will be mailed to all Lincoln-area households Monday, said he was "just as blown away" as Olberding.

"I was all set to seal up the Cap City ad and send out a proof, when I get this fax from Brignola asking about a BRM," Essene said. "Talk about a complete 180. I was, like, 'What? Now you want a 4 1/4 corner perf? Do you have any idea what that entails? Hello!'"

According to Olberding, the insertion of the business-reply-mail postcard will not only necessitate the perforation changes, but a switch to heavier paper, as well.

"I was going to go with Blue Lake, but I don't even think they do perfs on card stock," Olberding said. "Brignola had better be prepared to pay for 110-pound weight, because I'm not pulling the Great

see BUYER page 11

Right: L&G Advertising print buyer Milt Olberding.

NEWS

Christian Prop Comic Wowing Churches From Coast To Coast

see RELIGION page 10B

Alec Baldwin Secretes Own Hair Gel

see PEOPLE page 2D

'Leave Your Daughter At Work Day' A Huge Success

see OFFICE page 4E

STATshot™

A look at the numbers that shape your world.

INSIDE the ONION®

News In Brief 2
Opinion Page. 4
What Do You Think . 5
Onion Infographic . . 5
Horoscopes 12
A.V. Club 13
Cinema. 17
Video 20
Music 22
Words. 24
Savage Love 25
Picks. 26

the ONION®

VOLUME 36 ISSUE 27 | AMERICA'S FINEST NEWS SOURCE™ | 10–16 AUGUST 2000

Above: Gore greets diner patrons in Scranton, a city he called "the absolute worst place on Earth."

Visiting Gore Calls Pennsylvania 'A Hellhole'

ALTOONA, PA—During a campaign stop at an Altoona paper mill Monday, presidential contender Al Gore launched into an unexpected 40-minute tirade against the "not-so-great state of Pennsylvania," calling it "the nation's armpit" and "a total hellhole."

"Over the past few days, I have traveled all over your state and met many of you. And what has impressed me most is that no matter where I have gone, my reaction has been the same: 'Oh, God, get me the fuck out of this dump,'" said Gore, who alternately referred to the Keystone State's 12 million residents as "animals" and "ghouls." "From Pittsburgh to Philadelphia, from Erie to Easton, the places and faces of Pennsylvania stand in direct opposition to everything that makes America great."

Gore went on to tell the assembled mill workers that he "couldn't care less" if he loses Pennsylvania's 23 electoral votes, so long as he "never [has] to set foot in this steaming dungheap again."

Raising his voice and pointing at the crowd, Gore continued: "During this presi-

see GORE page 6

Video-Game Characters Denounce Randomly Placed Swinging Blades

WASHINGTON, DC—A coalition of video-game characters representing the nation's leading systems appeared before Congress Monday to decry "the pointless, deadly presence" of spinning blades in video-game landscapes.

"We are here to demand an end to the shockingly casual placement of dangerous blades in our places of work," said Tomb Raider star Lara Croft, who estimates that she has lost more than 600,000 lives to spinning, falling, swinging, and suddenly appearing blades this year alone. "This kind of thing has been going on since the days of Pitfall Harry, and it has got to stop."

Croft, flanked by Metal Gear's Solid Snake, Super Mario 64's Mario, and both soldiers from Contra, called upon Congress to revise OSHA laws to extend protection to the digitally rendered.

"From Pitfall to Bad Dudes Versus

see VIDEO GAMES page 8

Right: A concerned Mario discusses the rotating fireball chains found throughout World 1-4 of Super Mario Bros.

Stoner Architect Drafts All-Foyer Mansion

MINNEAPOLIS—In the oft-overlooked field of stoner architecture, new talent often goes unnoticed. But that hasn't been the case for Minneapolis stoner architect Richard "Dick" Donovan, whose groundbreaking design for an all-foyer mansion is earning slack-jawed admiration from some of the most respected members of the Twin Cities stoner-architecture community.

Donovan had won moderate recognition for past work, including his subterranean ranch house and his roofless A-frame. The 27-year-old's latest design, however, has won him unprecedented acclaim, hailed in the August issue of

see ARCHITECT page 7

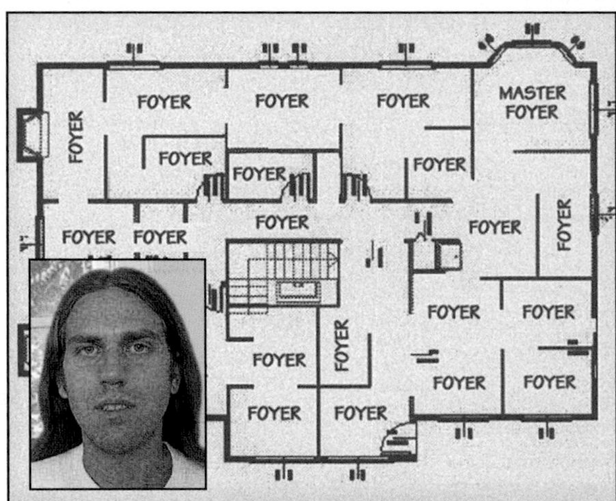

Right: The blueprint for Richard Donovan's (inset) revolutionary all-foyer mansion.

NEWS

Man Listening To 'Highway To Hell' Actually On Parkway To Waukegan

see LOCAL page 4B

Marriage Breaks Up Over Procreative Differences

see LOCAL page 12B

Alabama Governor Rassles With Controversy

see NATION page 14A

STATshot™

A look at the numbers that shape your world.

Least Sacred Holy Days

- Feast Of Louie Anderson
- St. Hallmark's Day
- Pentecostcutters
- Some Soul's Day
- Feast Of The Impala Conception
- All Taints' Day
- Palm-Slapping Sunday
- Sacrament Daze
- Yeaster

OCTOBER

INSIDE the ONION®

News In Brief 2
Opinion Page. 4
What Do You Think . 5
Onion Infographic. . 5
Horoscopes 16
A.V. Club 17
Cinema. 21
Video 26
Music 28
Words. 30
Savage Love 31
Picks. 32

the ONION®

VOLUME 36 ISSUE 37 AMERICA'S FINEST NEWS SOURCE™ 19–25 OCTOBER 2000

Bush Horrified To Learn Presidential Salary

Above: A distraught George W. Bush, moments after learning of the salary that potentially awaits him.

AUSTIN, TX—Republican presidential candidate George W. Bush was aghast to learn Monday that the position of U.S. president, the highest office in the land and most powerful in the free world, pays just $200,000 a year.

"That's it?" asked Bush, struggling to comprehend the figure reported to him by aides. "A measly couple hundred grand a year? Not per month, even? Because I've already spent more than $60 million to get this job. I'll have to be president for 300 years just to break even."

"I guess I just assumed that a job like that would have a much bigger salary," continued Bush, shaking his head. "You know, something like $120 million. That's what my friend Vance Coffman makes as CEO of Lockheed Martin, and that's just an aerospace firm, not a whole country."

Bush was further disturbed to learn that the salary is not bolstered by incentive clauses.

"Don't I maybe get a 2 percent commission on any increase in the GNP? No? And there's no bonus for, say, brokering a Mideast peace accord or vetoing a certain number of bills?" Bush asked. "Well, at least the salary's tax-free, right?"

Told that the position's only benefits are free room and board, unlimited non-per-

see BUSH page 14

Discovery Of Oil Turns Peru Into Bunch Of Assholes

LIMA, PERU—The recent discovery of a vast oil reserve in southern Peru has turned the South American nation's citizenry into "a bunch of first-class assholes," U.N. sources said Monday.

"Before this oil thing, the Peruvians were a real nice, down-to-earth people," said U.N. General Assembly president Harri Holkeri. "But now they strut around, wearing flashy clothes, driving Mercedes, loudly talking about their summer homes in Monaco. Everyone here at the U.N. has noticed the change."

The discovery of the oil field is expected to increase Peru's crude-oil reserves from less than a billion barrels to nearly 23 billion. With a production goal of 800,000 barrels a day, the reserve is expected to add almost $9 billion to the country's GNP and place it among the world's top 20 oil-producing nations as early as next year.

"It's too bad we're stuck down here in South America, surrounded by all these poor countries," Peruvian president

see PERU page 10

Aging Gen-Xer Doesn't Find Bad Movies Funny Anymore

HOBOKEN, NJ—Dave Erdman, 34, no longer finds bad movies and other forms of mass-media trash culture humorous, the aging Gen-Xer confided Monday.

"I hate to admit it, but I just don't get off on movies like *Can't Stop The Music* or *Krull* or The Bee Gees' *Sgt. Pepper's Lonely Hearts Club Band* like I used to,' Erdman told longtime friend Patrick Faulk, 33, over drinks at Melvin's, a non-retro, non-hipster, family-style restaurant. "Even that one where Gary Coleman is living in the bus-station locker and picks winning horses doesn't do it for me anymore. The sad fact is, I can't get excited by anything unless I actually, without irony, enjoy it. How lame is that?"

Citing such factors as work-related stress, mortgage worries, and the ever-growing duties of parenthood and marriage, Erdman said he has finally accepted the reality that embarrassingly bad films, TV

see MOVIES page 8

Right: Erdman struggles to muster the enthusiasm he once had for the 1980 Olivia Newton-John bomb *Xanadu*.

the ONION®

VOLUME 36 ISSUE 40 | AMERICA'S FINEST NEWS SOURCE™ | 9–15 NOVEMBER 2000

NEWS

Vote, Voter Wasted

see NATION page 3A

Magazine Correctly Judged By Its Cover

see MEDIA page 3C

Office Casual-Day Policy Hastily Rewritten To Exclude Unitards

see OFFICE LIFE page 4E

Sex Had

see LOCAL page 11D

STATshot™

A look at the numbers that shape your world.

INSIDE the ONION®

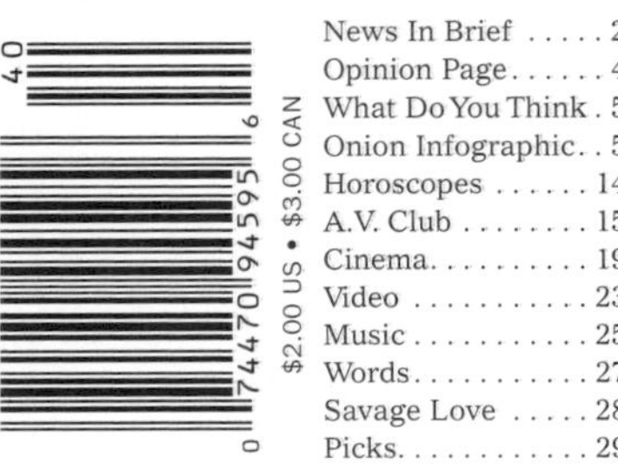

News In Brief 2
Opinion Page. 4
What Do You Think . 5
Onion Infographic. . 5
Horoscopes 14
A.V. Club 15
Cinema. 19
Video 23
Music 25
Words. 27
Savage Love 28
Picks. 29

DECISION 2000

Bush Or Gore: 'A New Era Dawns'

Above: Bush and Gore, one of whom called the election "a victory for America."

AUSTIN, TX, OR NASHVILLE, TN—In one of the narrowest presidential votes in U.S. history, either George W. Bush or Al Gore was elected the 43rd president of the United States Tuesday, proclaiming the win "a victory for the American people and the dawn of a bold new era in this great nation."

"My fellow Americans," a triumphant Bush or Gore told throngs of jubilant, flag-waving supporters at his campaign headquarters, "tonight, we as a nation stand on the brink of many exciting new challenges. And I stand here before you to say that I am ready to meet those challenges."

"The people have spoken," Bush or Gore continued, "and with their vote they have sent the message, loud and clear, that we are the true party of the people."

With these words, the crowd of Republicans or Democrats erupted.

Bush or Gore attributed his victory to

see ELECTION page 10

Neighborhood Children Gear Up For Hotly Anticipated 'Opening Of The Gerbil's Tomb'

COVINGTON, KY—In what promises to be the biggest neighborhood event since July's golf-ball dismantling, Andy Mefford, 9, announced plans Monday to exhume Marshall, his sister's deceased pet gerbil.

"Guys," said Mefford, addressing fellow fourth-graders from the jungle gym during recess, "this Saturday morning, right after *Batman Beyond*, I'm gonna dig up Marshall to see what he looks like now."

Marshall, who died June 24 of complications from an eye infection, was laid to rest the following day beneath the large oak tree in the Meffords' backyard. The gerbil was entombed in a styrofoam hamburger container, along with a daisy and a poem written by its devoted owner, 7-year-old Kimberly Mefford.

Mefford's decision to exhume the rodent, made partly in response to a recent Learning Channel *Secrets Of The Pyramids* documentary, has sparked excitement among children throughout the Reardon Street area.

"That's gonna be so cool," said classmate Danny Stossel. "I bet it's all gross, with worms crawling out of his eyes and stuff."

"My brother once dug up a parakeet after it was buried for, like, three weeks, and it was all black and hard," next-door neighbor Douglas Beane, 10, said. "This'll probably be even better."

Added Beane: "I wonder if the tail will still be there."

Despite such enthusiasm, not all neighborhood children support the gerbil

see GERBIL page 7

Right: The soon-to-be-disturbed burial site.

the ONION®
VOLUME 36 ISSUE 41 AMERICA'S FINEST NEWS SOURCE™ 16–22 NOVEMBER 2000

Nation Plunges Into Chaos

Pro-Bush Rebels Seize Power In West; D.C. In Flames

Above: Riot police advance through downtown Miami, where clashes between Gore and Bush factions left 23 dead Monday night. see COVER STORY page 6

NBC News Reverses Earlier Report Of Gore's Death

NEW YORK—Three hours after placing Al Gore in the "dead" column, NBC News retracted its projection Tuesday, changing the vice-president's status to "too close to call."

"I'm sorry, but it now appears that we reported Mr. Gore's death prematurely," NBC News anchor Tom Brokaw announced on air at approximately 2:15 a.m. EST. "The latest readings show his red-blood count down to 3.1. At this point, it could go either way."

Gore, shot Monday by a Republican

see NBC page 12

Clinton Declares Self President For Life

WASHINGTON, DC—Denouncing the American electoral process as "immoral and corrupt," President Clinton announced Tuesday that he will not step down on Jan. 20, 2001, declaring himself "President For Life."

Proclaiming Nov. 14 a new national holiday as "Day One of Americlintonian Year Zero," Clinton issued a directive of total martial law over "all territories formerly

see CLINTON page 8

Right: Clinton greets his subjects from a White House balcony.

Communication With Florida Cut Off

TALLAHASSEE, FL—Federal officials confirmed Tuesday that all forms of communication with Florida, the bloody battleground for 25 electoral votes, have been cut off.

Across the state, Atlantic Bell phone lines and relays have been severed. The efforts of Georgia-based emergency crews hoping to reconnect lines have been hampered by piles of burning vehicles choking all roads leading into the state.

In addition to the loss of phone contact, Internet, television, and radio communica-

see FLORIDA page 11

Bush Executes 253 New Mexico Democrats

Retakes State's Five Electoral Votes

ALBUQUERQUE, NM—New Mexico's five electoral votes swung back into the Bush column Monday when George W. Bush executed 253 Las Cruces-area Democrats. With their deaths, the Al Gore-backing Democrats were declared ineligible, wiping out the Democratic candidate's narrow 252-vote victory margin in New Mexico and giving Bush the state by just one vote.

"We express great sorrow for the families of the condemned," said Karl Rove, Bush's senior strategist. "We must keep in mind, however, that these are not innocent people we're talking about here. These individuals were guilty of a variety of crimes, from vagrancy to jaywalking to reckless endangerment of

see NEW MEXICO page 10

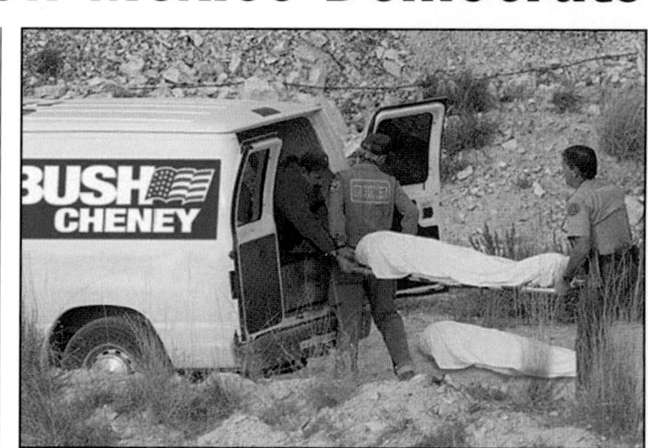

Right: The bodies of Democrats are taken by Bush 2000 coroners.

NEWS

Tipper's Thumb Delivered To Gore Campaign Headquarters

see ELECTION page 2A

Naderite Loyalists Nuke Dam

see ELECTION page 4A

Bob Dole: 'Bob Dole's Been Shot'

see ELECTION page 7A

McVeigh Urges Calm

see ELECTION page 8A

STATshot™

A look at the numbers that shape your world.

INSIDE the ONION®

News In Brief 2
Opinion Page. 4
What Do You Think . 5
Onion Infographic. . 5
Horoscopes 16
A.V. Club 17
Cinema. 22
Video 28
Music 30
Words. 33
Savage Love 34
Picks. 35

NEWS

Running Shoes Used Mainly For Computer Programming

see LOCAL page 4C

Another Fond Childhood Memory Destroyed

see ENTERTAINMENT page 11B

Parkay Container Suffers Debilitating Stroke; Now Speaks With Difficulty Out Of One Side Of Lid

see PRODUCTS page 2D

STATshot™

A look at the numbers that shape your world.

Top Obsessive-Compulsive Disorders

- **36%** Having sex with exactly eight women on way home from supermarket
- **25%** Stabbing potato three times before buttering
- **16%** Researching OCDs
- **14%** Keeping careful track of usage of the word "the" while reading (2)
- **9%** Always scrubbing hands before performing surgery

INSIDE the ONION®

News In Brief 2
Opinion Page. 4
What Do You Think . 5
Onion Infographic. . 5
Horoscopes 12
A.V. Club 13
Cinema. 18
Video 22
Music 24
Words. 26
Savage Love 27
Picks. 28

the ONION®

VOLUME 36 ISSUE 43 AMERICA'S FINEST NEWS SOURCE™ 30 NOVEMBER–6 DECEMBER 2000

Lab Rabbit Strongly Recommends Cover Girl Waterproof Mascara For Sensitive Eyes

CINCINNATI—LR-4427, a two-year-old laboratory rabbit at Procter & Gamble's cosmetics testing facility, Monday gave his full endorsement to Cover Girl Long & Luscious waterproof mascara for sensitive eyes.

"Cover Girl Long & Luscious waterproof mascara will dramatically magnify your lashes for a look that's glamorous and natural," LR-4427 said. "And the great part is, they won't irritate your eyes, even if you accidentally smear some over your clamped-open eyeballs with a Q-tip and can't flush it out for 48 hours."

LR-4427 said he also likes the fact that the Cover Girl product stays on, rain or shine.

"No matter what the weather, you're

see RABBIT page 9

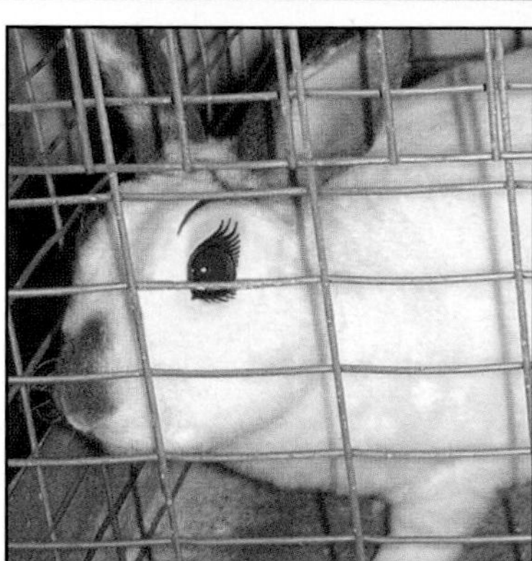

Right: Lab rabbit LR-4427 enjoys all-day glamour with Cover Girl Long & Luscious mascara.

Teen Exposed To Violence, Profanity, Adult Situations By Family

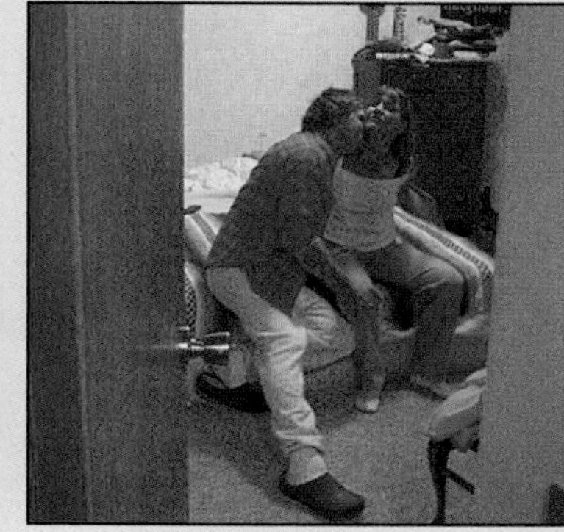

BROWNSVILLE, TX—According to the conservative watchdog group Family Research Council, the home of 15-year-old Beth Arnott contains violence, profanity, adult situations, and other material "wholly unsuitable" for those 16 and under.

"That house is filled with inappropriate material that sets a poor example for the impressionable youths living there," said Family Research Council president Kenneth Connor, citing 44 instances of domestic violence, adult language, nudity, and graphic sexual content in the Brownsville home in the past month alone. "This is hardly the sort of family we should be exposing our nation's children to."

Connor noted that Beth's stepfather, 43-year-old Randy Skowron, frequently walks around the house in an open bathrobe, inadvertently exposing his genitalia to Beth. He also cited numerous incidents of Skowron hitting Beth's brother Ronnie

see TEEN page 8

Report: 98 Percent Of U.S. Commuters Favor Public Transportation For Others

WASHINGTON, DC—A study released Monday by the American Public Transportation Association reveals that 98 percent of Americans support the use of mass transit by others.

"With traffic congestion, pollution, and oil shortages all getting worse, now is the time to shift to affordable, efficient public transportation," APTA director Howard Collier said. "Fortunately, as this report shows, Americans have finally recognized the need for everyone else to do exactly that."

Of the study's 5,200 participants, 44 percent cited faster commutes as the primary reason to expand public transportation, followed closely by shorter lines at the gas station. Environmental and energy concerns ranked a distant third and fourth, respectively.

Anaheim, CA, resident Lance Holland, who drives 80 miles a day to his job in downtown Los Angeles, was among the proponents of public transit.

"Expanding mass transit isn't just a good idea, it's a necessity," Holland said. "My drive to work is unbelievable. I spend

see COMMUTERS page 7

Above: Traffic moves slowly near Seatte, WA, where a majority of drivers say they support other people using mass transit.

Developmentally Disabled Burger King Employee Only Competent Worker

Marilyn Manson Now Going Door-To-Door Trying To Shock People

Video-Game Violence Blamed In Giant-Robot Shooting Spree

JANUARY FEBRUARY MARCH APRIL MAY JUNE

Christ Converts To Islam

Irrepressible Bad Boy Slays Seven

Teacher Of The Year Awards 'A Fashion Nightmare'

2001

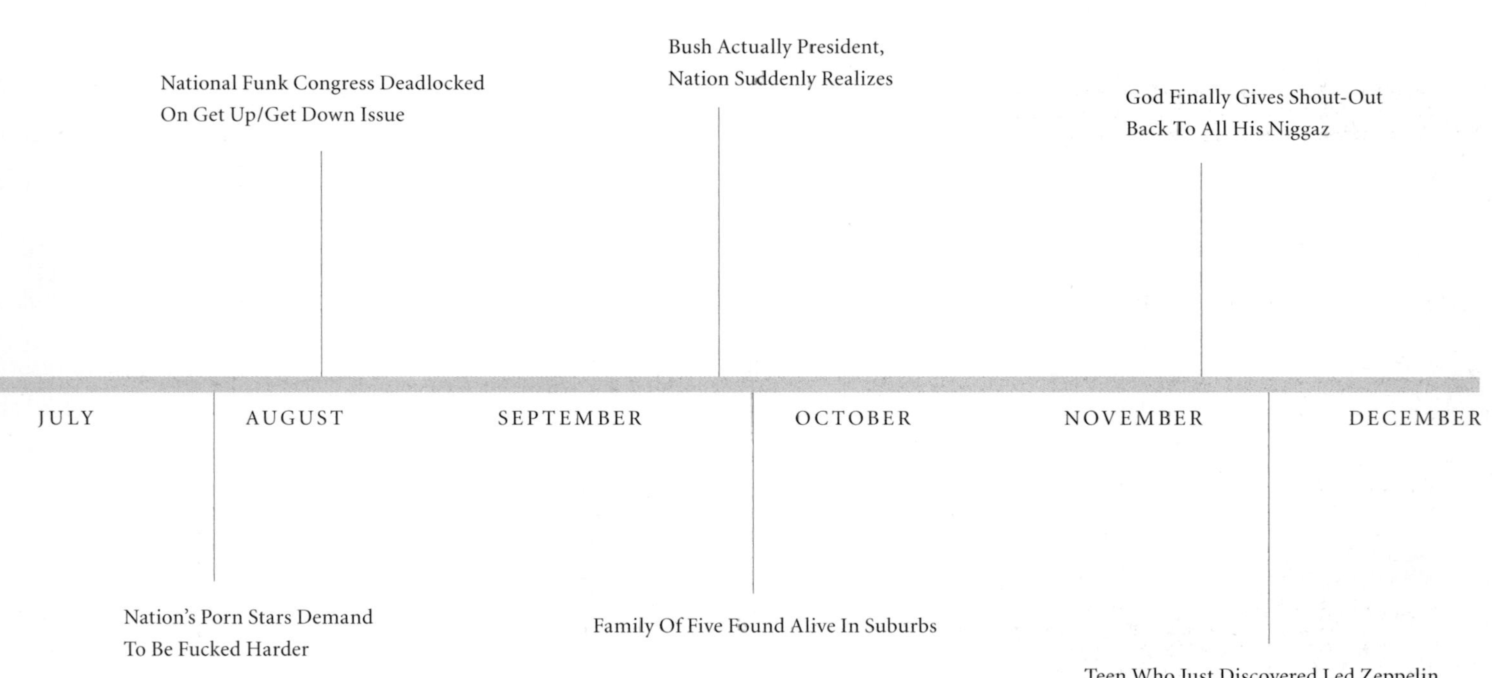

National Funk Congress Deadlocked
On Get Up/Get Down Issue
Bush Actually President,
Nation Suddenly Realizes
God Finally Gives Shout-Out
Back To All His Niggaz
JULY
AUGUST
SEPTEMBER
OCTOBER
NOVEMBER
DECEMBER
Nation's Porn Stars Demand
To Be Fucked Harder
Family Of Five Found Alive In Suburbs
Teen Who Just Discovered Led Zeppelin
Starting To Piss Off Friends

the ONION®

VOLUME 37 ISSUE 01 AMERICA'S FINEST NEWS SOURCE™ 18–24 JANUARY 2001

Bush: 'Our Long National Nightmare Of Peace And Prosperity Is Finally Over'

Above: President-elect Bush vows that "together, we can put the triumphs of the recent past behind us."

WASHINGTON, DC—Mere days from assuming the presidency and closing the door on eight years of Bill Clinton, president-elect George W. Bush assured the nation in a televised address Tuesday that "our long national nightmare of peace and prosperity is finally over."

"My fellow Americans," Bush said, "at long last, we have reached the end of the dark period in American history that will come to be known as the Clinton Era, eight long years characterized by unprecedented economic expansion, a sharp decrease in crime, and sustained peace

see BUSH page 8

Corpse-Reanimation Technology Still 10 Years Off, Say MIT Mad Scientists

CAMBRIDGE, MA—Dead-tissue reanimation, projected in the 1980s to be standard medical practice by 2001, won't be possible for at least another decade, scientists at the Massachusetts Institute of Technology's Mad Science Research Center announced Monday.

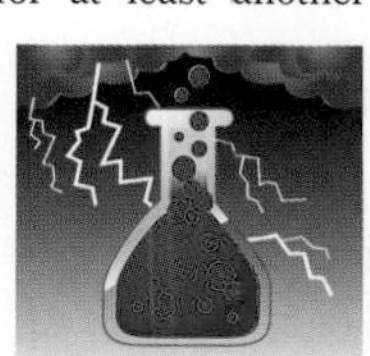

"They laughed when we said we would rekindle the divine spark of life in flesh grown cold and lifeless," said MIT mad scientist Dr. Otto Von Verruchtheit, the nation's leading corpse-reanimation expert, speaking from the castle that houses the MSRC's state-of-the-art corpse-reanimation laboratory. "Oh, how they laughed! They said we were mad to attempt such an unholy ambition by the century's end. Fools! Fools, all of them! However, in this case, they were actually right."

Von Verruchtheit then raised his arms to the heavens, attempting to summon a lightning bolt and thunder crash to punc-

see SCIENTISTS page 6

Rural Nebraskan Not Sure He Could Handle Frantic Pace Of Omaha

NORTH PLATTE, NE—Lifelong North Platte resident Fred Linder, 46, revealed Monday that he doesn't think he could cope with the fast-paced hustle and bustle of Omaha, the Cornhusker State's largest city.

"Oh, sure, I bet it'd be exciting at first, going to see 9 p.m. showings of movies, shopping at those big department stores, and maybe even eating at one of those fancy restaurants that doesn't use iceberg lettuce in their salads," Linder said. "But I just don't think I could put up with all that hub-bub for more than a day or two."

Added Linder: "And parking's a nightmare there."

Linder expressed doubts about Omaha's "hectic pace" while having dinner at the home of Pastor Bob Egan, the long-time spiritual leader of North Platte's Holy Christ Almighty Church.

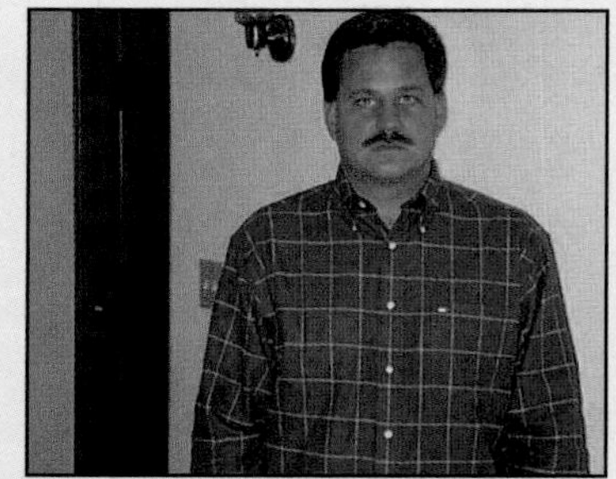

Above: North Platte resident Fred Linder.

"I'd just returned from a 'Prayer & Share' fellowship conference in Omaha, and I mentioned to Fred how much

see OMAHA page 7

NEWS

Chinese Guy Still Insisting It Was Him In Front Of That Tank

see WORLD page 4A

Denny's Introduces 'Just A Humongous Bucket Of Eggs And Meat'

see FOOD page 3C

Date With Proctologist Ends Predictably

see LOCAL page 10D

STATshot

A look at the numbers that shape your world.

How Did We Celebrate MLK Day?

- 36% Let freedom ring in lieu of alarm clock
- 21% Re-waterproofed deck
- 16% Drove down Martin Luther King Jr. Blvd.
- 11% Realized that *Card Sharks* was a pretty good game show
- 9% Wondered why bank was closed on a Monday
- 7% Gestured emptily

THE ONION VOLUME 37 ISSUE 01 $2.00 US $3.00 CAN

NEWS

Dozens Of Glowing Exit Signs Mercilessly Taunt Multiplex Employee

see WORKPLACE page 10C

Elderly Woman Casually Mentions Wish To Die

see SENIORBEAT page 2E

Alex Winter Keeps Bugging Keanu Reeves About Third *Bill & Ted* Movie

see HOLLYWOOD page 7B

STATshot

A look at the numbers that shape your world.

Most Common Drug Side-Effects

- 13% Highness
- 16% Music over-appreciation
- 18% Eye poppage
- 15% Penile lactation
- 23% Proportionate strength and speed of a spider
- 14% Swedish citizenship
- 1% Inability to complete *Smile* album

THE ONION
VOLUME 37
ISSUE 04
$2.00 US
$3.00 CAN

the ONION®

VOLUME 37 ISSUE 4 — AMERICA'S FINEST NEWS SOURCE™ — 8–14 FEBRUARY 2001

Above: Bill Clinton ponders his legacy in the den of his suburban New York home.

Clinton Vaguely Disappointed By Lack Of Assassination Attempts

CHAPPAQUA, NY— Reflecting on his presidency Monday, Bill Clinton expressed a "strange sense of disappointment" over the lack of dramatic attempts on his life.

"All the great ones had someone take a crack at them," Clinton said. "Lincoln, Teddy Roosevelt, FDR, Kennedy—even Reagan. An assassination attempt would have really elevated my status in the pantheon of presidents."

"Is this how I'm going to be remembered? As the president who wasn't worth a couple pot shots?" Clinton asked. "For God's sake, even Ford had Squeaky Fromme."

Clinton said an assassination attempt

see CLINTON page 6

Receptionist At Chiropractor's Office Considering Pursuing Chiropractic Degree

BALTIMORE—Paula Budig, 33, a receptionist at Liberty Heights Chiropractic Clinic since November, confirmed Tuesday that she is seriously considering returning to school to pursue a degree in chiropractic medicine.

"When I answered the want ad for this job, I didn't really even know what a chiropractor did," said Budig, straightening the magazines in the patient waiting room. "But after working at the clinic for a few

see RECEPTIONIST page 8

Above: Chiropractic secretary Paula Budig.

Lava Lamps Revert From Passé Retro Kitsch Back To Novel Retro Camp

WASHINGTON, DC—Lava lamps, the once-popular, then passé, then popular again, then passé again novelty items that have cyclically taken various American subcultures by storm throughout their 35-year history, are back.

According to a report issued Monday by the U.S. Department of Retro, the status of the multi-colored, mildly psychedelic light fixtures changed again in 2000, reverting from a tired form of passé retro kitsch back into a novel form of retro camp. The switch marks the 17th time the government has changed the lava lamp's retro classification since its initial resurgence in 1976 as an amusing, campy throwback to the then-outmoded '60s hippie drug culture.

"Lava lamps, which throughout the late '90s were seen as an irrelevant remnant of a relatively minor mid-'90s form of '60s retro, are once again retro in an exciting new way for millions of Americans unfamiliar with their previous kitsch-object incarnations," U.S. Retro Secretary Brian Setzer said. "That fallow period of the late '90s laid the groundwork for a revival within a subset of retro consumer for whom the novelty factor of floating bulbs of wax suspended in water and lit from below had not yet worn off."

Setzer—who made his name in the '80s playing retro '50s rockabilly with The Stray Cats and subsequently enjoyed a

see LAVA LAMPS page 11

NEWS

Brad Pitt Bored With Sight Of Jennifer Aniston's Naked Body

see PEOPLE page 10D

Area Man Fills Important 'Demand' Role In Economy

see COMMERCE page 2E

Cub Scout Wishes They'd Taught Him How To Chew Through Ball Gag

see LOCAL page 4C

STATshot

A look at the numbers that shape your world.

Top Spin-Off Series

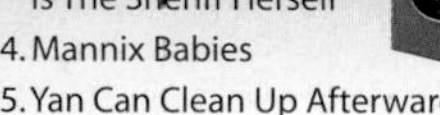

1. Sipowicz's Place
2. Acquaintances
3. She's The Daughter Of The Sheriff And Now Is The Sheriff Herself
4. Mannix Babies
5. Yan Can Clean Up Afterwards
6. Family Law Nights
7. Star Trek: A New Journ—You Know What? Fuck This

the ONION®

VOLUME 37 ISSUE 06 AMERICA'S FINEST NEWS SOURCE™ 22–28 FEBRUARY 2001

Nigeria Elects Black President

AFRICAN FOCUS

Above: Bilikisu Adewale waves to supporters after becoming the next black man ever to lead Nigeria.

ABUJA, NIGERIA—In a historic triumph for Nigeria's African-African community, Bilikisu Adewale, a 49-year-old black man, was elected president Monday.

"Today is a great day for the people of Nigeria," Adewale told a cheering crowd in his 30-minute acceptance speech. "But even more so, today represents a tremendous victory for this nation's black citizens, who came to the polls in full force to put one of their own in power."

"I am overwhelmed," Adewale added. "This is truly precedented."

Addressing the largely black crowd, Adewale, who served as Nigeria's Foreign Minister from 1993 to 1998, pledged to defend the interests of the nation's sizable black community. Among his chief campaign promises was to increase funding for schools in Nigeria's

see NIGERIA page 6

Grueling Household Tasks Of 19th Century Enjoyed By Suburban Woman

SAUSALITO, CA—Ellen Brinkworth, a 37-year-old homemaker from the upscale San Francisco suburb of Sausalito, enjoys spending her free time engaged in the back-breaking labors of a 19th-century pioneer woman.

"My friend Linda came over Saturday and we spent the whole day making soap," Brinkworth said. "We made some abso-

see WOMAN page 7

Above: Brinkworth and one of her handmade candles.

Guy At Bar A Little Too Into Stevie Ray Vaughan

EUCLID, OH—According to Main Street Tavern employees and patrons, the guy at the end of the bar is a little too into deceased blues guitarist Stevie Ray Vaughan.

Bar-goer John Menke said that the guy, an unidentified beret- and denim-vest-wearing man in his early 30s, should be avoided "unless you want to talk about Stevie Ray Vaughan for at least an hour."

"I go up to get another pitcher of beer, and this guy at the bar just stares at me, biting his lip and nodding his head to the Stevie Ray Vaughan song on the jukebox," Menke said. "I try to look away, but then I accidentally make eye contact for a split second. That's when he says to me, 'Man, there'll never be another SRV.' Before you know it, I'm trapped listening to him go off about Vaughan's blistering guitar solo [on 'Cold Shot']."

After expounding on Vaughan's "fiery, impassioned guitar work" on "Cold Shot" for several minutes, the guy explained to Menke the song's origins.

"The guy says to me, 'Stevie

see VAUGHAN page 9

Above: The guy (right) discusses Stevie Ray Vaughan with an uninterested stranger.

the ONION®

VOLUME 37 ISSUE 09 AMERICA'S FINEST NEWS SOURCE™ 15–21 MARCH 2001

NEWS

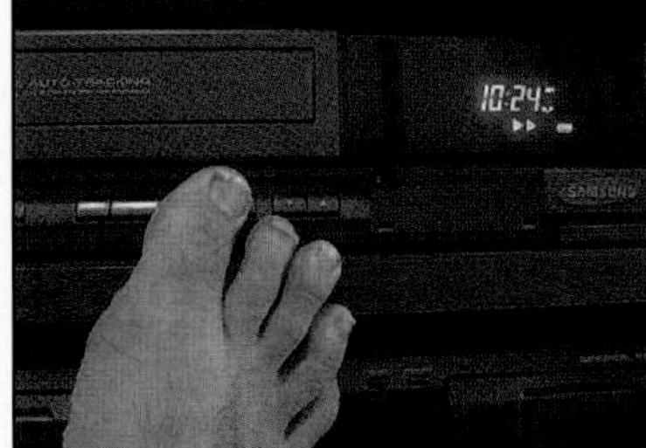

VCR Fast-Forwarded With Toe

see LOCAL page 2D

Real-Life Pepe Le Pew Rapes Cat

see CRIME page 10E

Downturn In Economy Forces CEO To Reduce Own Pay Raise By Five Percent

see BUSINESS page 1B

Third Shoe Somehow Drops

see LOCAL page 4D

STATshot

A look at the numbers that shape your world.

Least-Recommended Toilet-Training Books For Children

1. Only Girls Wipe
2. The Domineering Mother And Her Obsessively Neat Son
3. Little Timmy Disappears Forever
4. The Berenstain Bears Shit In The Woods
5. No Longer Mama's Baby
6. Mermaids Are Girls Who Pushed Too Hard (And Other Stories)

THE ONION
VOLUME 37
ISSUE 09
$2.00 US
$3.00 CAN

No Jennifer Lopez News Today

NEW YORK—Despite herculean efforts to somehow include her in the day's reportage, journalists, magazine editors, and TV-news producers across the nation have been forced to concede that there is no Jennifer Lopez news today.

"It grieves me to report that 'J. Lo,' America's gluteally gifted superstar diva, did not do anything newsworthy today," MTV News correspondent John Norris said. "As far as we can tell, as of press time, she didn't even leave her apartment."

Members of the media stressed that the dearth of Lopez coverage was not due to a lack of effort on their part.

"The sad reality of this situation is, we've already explored every possible angle," *People* feature writer Jill Smolowe said. "We did the new-album-coming-out piece. We did the new-movie-coming-out piece. We did the new-album-and-new-movie-are-both-number-one-at-the-same-time piece. We did the breakup-with-controversial-bad-boy-and-millionaire-rap-mogul-Puff Daddy piece, as well as the did-she-or-didn't-she-know-he-had-a-piece piece. And, of course, we've done countless variations on the what-is-she-wearing piece, which, incidentally, is a great piece, because you get to run lots of photos

see LOPEZ page 6

Right: Lopez in the infamous dress at the 2000 Grammy Awards.

Starbucks To Begin Sinister 'Phase Two' Of Operation

Above: The front of a temporarily closed Starbucks in Canton, OH.

SEATTLE—After a decade of aggressive expansion throughout North America and abroad, Starbucks suddenly and unexpectedly closed its 2,870 worldwide locations Monday to prepare for what company insiders are calling "Phase Two" of the company's long-range plan.

"Starbucks has completed the coffee-distribution and location establishment phase of its operation, and is now ready to move into Phase Two," read a statement from Cynthia Vahlkamp, Starbucks' chief marketing officer. "We have enjoyed fur-

see STARBUCKS page 7

Area Man Less Capable Than Own Watch

SANTA FE, NM—According to coworkers at Spee-Dee Printers, Len Halicki, 37, is less capable in his day-to-day activities than his own wristwatch.

Above: Halicki

"It's sad to see someone get outperformed by their watch," said Craig Denny, who works with Halicki at the Santa Fe print shop. "But there's no getting around the fact that this watch has about three times as many features as Len."

Halicki received the $200 timepiece, a Suunto Vector, as a Christmas gift from his parents. Intended primarily for outdoorsmen, the watch is described in the Suunto

see WATCH page 10

NEWS

Milosevic Confesses To Crimes Against Subhumanity

see WORLD page 3A

6,000-Year-Old Culture Now A 'Developing Nation'

see WORLD page 5A

Lite Brite Peg Extracted From Ear

see LOCAL page 7C

STATshot

A look at the numbers that shape your world.

Worst-Selling Specialty Magazines

1. *Dry-Erase Marker Huffer*
2. *Mauled By Bears Magazine*
3. *TRS-80 World*
4. Monkeybone *Insider*
5. *Grease Trap Aficionado*
6. *Eye Schmutz Collector's Weekly*
7. *Two-Weeks-To-Live Illustrated*

THE ONION
VOLUME 37
ISSUE 14
$2.00 US
$3.00 CAN

the ONION®

VOLUME 37 ISSUE 14 — AMERICA'S FINEST NEWS SOURCE™ — 19–25 APRIL 2001

Bush Regales Dinner Guests With Impromptu Oratory On Virgil's Minor Works

Above: An effervescent Bush delights friends with tales of the poet Virgil.

WASHINGTON, DC—President Bush delighted an intimate gathering of White House dinner guests Monday, regaling the coterie of dignitaries, artists, and friends with a spirited, off-the-cuff discussion of the Roman poet Virgil's lesser-known works.

"Ah, W. was in top form tonight," Spanish foreign minister Josep Pique Camps said. "We were all held captive by his erudition and charm. First, a brief history of the opium trade, then a bit of Brahms on the piano, then a rousing discussion of Virgil.

see BUSH page 8

Report: Stuffed-Animal Biodiversity Rising

WASHINGTON, DC—According to a World Wildlife Fund study released Monday, stuffed-animal biodiversity is rapidly rising, with the number of species available in plush form up nearly 800 percent since 1990.

"While the number of living species

Above: A rich spectrum of stuffed animal life is found under a leafy canopy in New York's FAO Schwarz.

continues to plummet, the exact opposite is true of their toy counterparts," WWF director Ruth Aberg said. "This is particularly true in America, where polyester-fiber-filled replicas of even the most endangered species can be found in glorious abundance."

According to the WWF report, 885 animal species are in danger of extinction worldwide, and another 165 are classified as threatened. Of these 1,050 at-risk species, however, an estimated 970 can be found in mass quantities in children's toy boxes and on collectors' shelves.

Stuffed-animal biodiversity, Aberg said, has not always been so robust. Ten years ago, the number of species produced by toy manufacturers was "abysmally low," mainly restricted to North American wildlife and a few select jungle animals. The past decade, however, has seen a proliferation of all manner of synthetic fauna.

"There are an estimated 41,000 species of vertebrates on Earth, yet until recently, only a small handful were available for

see BIODIVERSITY page 6

Asshole Proud Of Asshole Son

SUNDERLAND, MA—Gordon Ostrove, a 51-year-old Sunderland-area asshole, said Monday that he is very proud of his son Keith, 18, who is growing up to be a fine young asshole in his own right.

"Keith is a real chip off the old block," said the elder asshole, beaming with pride. "Just like his old man, he appreciates all the finer things in life—beer, Beemers, and broads. And, like me, he doesn't take shit from anybody: The other day, some kid at school made some smart-assed remark to him, and Keith mopped the floor with him."

Before Keith was born, Ostrove said he'd never thought he would have such a special relationship with his child.

"To be honest, [wife] Jackie was the one who wanted kids," Ostrove said. "But on the day Keith was born, I walked into the delivery room to have a look at the little turd. When I leaned over, he grabbed my finger. Everything changed at that

see ASSHOLE page 10

Above: Asshole father-son duo Gordon and Keith Ostrove.

the ONION®

VOLUME 37 ISSUE 15 — AMERICA'S FINEST NEWS SOURCE™ — 26 APRIL–2 MAY 2001

NEWS

Mason-Dixon Line Renamed IHOP-Waffle House Line

see NATION page 5A

First Chapter In History Of Sino-American War Of 2011 Already Written

see WORLD page 9A

Spelling-Bee Runner-Up Bursts Into Tears Whenever Anyone Says 'Proprietor'

see LOCAL page 10C

STATshot

A look at the numbers that shape your world.

What Are We Talking About Other Than *Survivor*?

1. That show that comes on after *Survivor*
2. That show that comes on before *Survivor*
3. The *Survivor-Boot Camp* lawsuit
4. *Survivor's* time slot
5. What's up with *Survivor 3*?
6. That Pepsi ad they showed during *Survivor*
7. That Destiny's Child song "Survivor"
8. Why anyone would want to watch *Survivor*

THE ONION VOLUME 37 ISSUE 15 $2.00 US $3.00 CAN

Left: Participants in Saturday's Los Angeles Gay Pride Parade, which helped change straight people's tolerant attitudes toward gays.

Gay-Pride Parade Sets Mainstream Acceptance Of Gays Back 50 Years

WEST HOLLYWOOD, CA—The mainstream acceptance of gays and lesbians, a hard-won civil-rights victory gained through decades of struggle against prejudice and discrimination, was set back at least 50 years Saturday in the wake of the annual Los Angeles Gay Pride Parade.

"I'd always thought gays were regular people, just like you and me, and that the stereotype of homosexuals as hedonistic, sex-crazed deviants was just a destructive myth," said mother of four Hannah Jarrett, 41, mortified at the sight of 17 tanned and oiled boys cavorting in jock straps to a throbbing techno beat on a float shaped like an enormous phallus. "Boy, oh, boy, was I wrong."

The parade, organized by the Los Angeles Gay And Lesbian And Bisexual And Transvestite And Transgender Alliance (LAGALABATATA), was intended to "promote acceptance, tolerance, and equality for the city's gay community." Just the opposite, however, was accomplished, as the event

see PARADE page 6

Area Father Must Have Read Some Drug-Slang Brochure Or Something

DECATUR, GA—Rodney Dunbar, a 46-year-old civil engineer and father of two, "must have read some drug-slang pamphlet or something," his children reported Monday.

"Dad and I were watching the NBA playoffs Saturday," 14-year-old son Dylan said. "Someone missed a pass, and he goes, 'Sometimes, I get the feeling that some of

see FATHER page 10

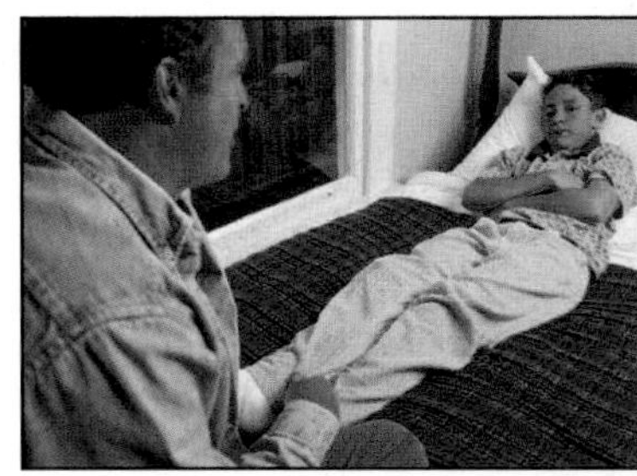

Right: Rodney Dunbar holds a rap session with his son.

Best-Laid Plans Of Mice And Men Faulted In 747 Crash

WASHINGTON, DC—Representatives of the National Transportation Safety Board, their "bosoms heavy with melancholia," announced the findings of their investigation of American Airlines Flight 251 Monday, citing "fate's cruel hand" as the cause of the Apr. 10 crash that claimed 411 lives.

"The best-laid plans of mice and men go oft astray," NTSB spokesman Frank Whelan said, "and leave us naught but grief and pain for promised joy. Such was the case when the 747 unexpectedly burst into flames and plummeted to the ground at 7:14 a.m., shortly after take-off from Chicago's O'Hare Airport."

According to NTSB investigators, the London-bound Boeing 747 relayed a distress call at 7:07 a.m., just 12 minutes after leaving O'Hare. Three minutes of desperate radio communication between the pilots and air-traffic con-

see 747 page 8

Right: The smoldering wreckage of Flight 251, which crossed the Stygian ferry.

NEWS

Attorney, Client Privileged

see LOCAL page 4C

That One McDonald's Plate From The '70s: Holy Shit, There It Is

see NOSTALGIA BEAT page 2B

Dwarf Falls Equivalent Of 10 Stories

see LOCAL page 6C

STATshot

A look at the numbers that shape your world.

the ONION®

VOLUME 37 ISSUE 16 AMERICA'S FINEST NEWS SOURCE™ 3–9 MAY 2001

Lowest Common Denominator Continues To Plummet

American Focus

WASHINGTON, DC—The lowest common denominator (LCD), the leading cultural indicator for American mass-market tastes, continued its precipitous drop last week, fueling worries about the future of the U.S. marketplace for ideas and stoking fears of a long-term cultural recession.

The ill health of the LCD, in steady decline since the advent of television, has been cause for concern among the intelligentsia for decades. But double-digit drops in the LCD since October 2000 have alarmed even the most pandering members of the entertainment industry.

"Quite simply, the collective intelligence level is dropping so rapidly that it's becoming increasingly difficult for producers to insult the intelligence of the American public," said News Corp president and COO Peter Chernin. "Without a way to set a floor for the lowest common denominator, even the stupidest material we can develop is not stupid enough for audiences to enjoy."

As examples of the accelerating descent of the LCD, experts cite Chyna's bestselling wrestling biography, the elephant-sperm-filled Tom Green film *Freddy Got*

see DENOMINATOR page 6

God Diagnosed With Bipolar Disorder

NEW HAVEN, CT—In a diagnosis that helps explain the confusing and contradictory aspects of the cosmos that have baffled philosophers, theologians, and other students of the human condition for millennia, God, creator of the universe and longtime deity to billions of followers, was found Monday to suffer from bipolar disorder.

Rev. Dr. J. Henry Jurgens, a practicing psychiatrist and doctor of divinity at Yale University Divinity School, announced the historic diagnosis at a press conference.

"I always knew there had to be some explanation," Jurgens said. "And, after several years of patient research and long sessions with God Almighty through the intercessionary medium of prayer, I was able to pinpoint the specific nature of His problem."

Bipolar, or manic-depressive, disorder is a condition that afflicts millions. Characterized by cycles of elation

see GOD page 8

Above: The Lord, found to be manic-depressive by Rev. Dr. Jurgens (left).

Local Man Exhausted After Long Day Of Video Games

Left: A visibly drained Broskowski gathers the strength for one more game.

SAGINAW, MI—Jon Broskowski, a 32-year-old Saginaw liquor-store clerk, described himself as "completely wiped" Monday after a long, hard day of video games.

"I'm totaled," said Broskowski, tossing his PlayStation 2 controller onto the floor following one last "cool-down" game of Madden 2001. "That shit really takes it out of you."

Broskowski, who has logged two decades of back-breaking toil on systems ranging from Intellivision to Sega Genesis, woke up at the crack of noon and went straight to work.

"I had the whole day off from the liquor store, and I thought, today's the day I roll up my sleeves and earn all the extra characters in SSX Snowboarding," Broskowski said. "Man, it was a grind."

"They make you snowboard over the same course and do the same tricks, like, a thousand times to get a new character," said Broskowski, who, through discipline and

see VIDEO GAMES page 10

the ONION®

VOLUME 37 ISSUE 23 | AMERICA'S FINEST NEWS SOURCE™ | 21–27 JUNE 2001

NEWS

Jenna Bush's Federally Protected Wetlands Now Open For Public Drilling

see NATION page 3A

Opening Soda Bottle Inadvertently Makes Man Loser

see LOCAL page 4D

Keebler Elves Multiracial All Of A Sudden

see PRODUCTWATCH page 10B

STATshot

A look at the numbers that shape your world.

Top Euphemisms For Menstruation

1. Ridin' the cotton pony
2. Checking into the Red Roof Inn
3. Kate Bush-ing
4. Falling to the Communists
5. A visit from Cap'n Bloodsnatch
6. Walking along the beach in soft focus
7. "Red Skelton dropped by"
8. Gettin' down with the O.B.
9. "It's 'that time of the month' where 'I'm not at my best' because 'my vagina is bleeding'"

June

THE ONION
VOLUME 37
ISSUE 23
$2.00 US
$3.00 CAN

Nobel Fever Grips Research Community As Prize Swells To $190 Million

STOCKHOLM—The Nobel Prize in Physiology or Medicine, unclaimed in 2000, has climbed to a staggering $190 million, setting off a frenzy of research and publication among scientists.

"This is very exciting," said Sweden's King Carl XVI Gustaf, who will announce the winner of the Nobel Prize at a gala July 20 ceremony in Stockholm. "One lucky scientist will never have to do another research project for the rest of his life."

Scientists around the globe are submitting their studies to the Nobel committee in the hopes of striking it rich.

"I think I've got a real shot at the grand prize with my genomewide scan of 200 families with hereditary prostate cancer that can be used to identify regions of

see NOBEL page 9

Above: King Carl XVI Gustaf keeps an eye on the Nobel jackpot.

The New Homeland

SYRIA
Mediterranean Sea
JORDAN
Tel Aviv
ETHNIKLASHISTAN
Jerusalem
Gaza Strip
ISRAEL

- Basques
- Chechens
- Greek Cypriots
- Hutus
- Kashmiris
- Kurds
- Moros
- Northern Irish
- Papuans
- Serbs
- Sikhs
- Somalis
- Tajiks
- Tamils

WORLD FOCUS

Northern Irish, Serbs, Hutus Granted Homeland In West Bank

UNITED NATIONS—In a bold gambit hoped to resolve dozens of conflicts around the world, the U.N. announced Monday the establishment of Ethniklashistan, a multinational haven in the West Bank that will serve as a new homeland for Irish Protestants, Hutus, Serbs, and other troubled groups.

"For far too long, these groups have been locked in prolonged strife with their former neighbors, unable to achieve a lasting peace," U.N. Secretary-General Kofi Annan said. "Now that these various peoples have a new homeland where they can find refuge, all the years of fighting and bloodshed can finally be put behind them."

Former Serbian leader Slobodan Milosevic, now presiding over a Serb settlement near the Jordanian border, was

see HOMELAND page 6

Guests Forced To Pretend Wedding A Good Thing

MINOT, ND—Suppressing their feelings about the doomed couple, guests at Saturday's wedding of Jerome Sykes, 23, and Madeline Pirone, 26, pretended the marriage was a good thing.

"Madeline looked so beautiful today," said mother of the groom Betsy Sykes, who once threatened to disown her son if he married "that manipulative bitch." "She looked positively radiant. They're going to give me such beautiful grandchildren one day."

Willfully ignoring the eight months of screaming, pleading, and threats that marked the couple's courtship, both families were outwardly positive about what they secretly called a "horrible disaster waiting to happen."

"Jerome and Madeline said they were in love and wanted to spend the rest of their lives together," said Dorothy Pirone, the bride's mother, who reacted to the October 2000 announcement of the engagement by throwing a porcelain cookie jar at Sykes' head. "It's so wonderful to see a young couple so in love."

see WEDDING page 7

Above: Sykes and Pirone after their secretly disapproved-of wedding.

the ONION®

VOLUME 37 ISSUE 25 AMERICA'S FINEST NEWS SOURCE™ 26 JULY–1 AUGUST 2001

NEWS

Anne Geddes Starting To Lose It

see ARTS page 7B

Someone's Job Riding On Success Of Antacid Gum

see BUSINESS page 10D

Car Wreck Turns Frown Upside Down

see LOCAL page 4A

STATshot

A look at the numbers that shape your world.

What Are Our Loved Ones Throwing At Us?

1. Wedding albums
2. Lousy $2 bouquets purchased from street vendor
3. Subpoenas
4. Mug we made for them in fourth-grade art class
5. Contents of stomach
6. Habitrails
7. Half-empty bottles of fortified wine
8. The baby

Gore Upset That Clinton Doesn't Call Anymore

NEW YORK—Six months after leaving Washington, a despondent Al Gore expressed frustration and sadness Monday that Bill Clinton no longer calls or makes an effort to maintain their once-close friendship.

According to sources close to the former vice president, despite Gore's open invitation to "call or hang out any time," Clinton has not taken the opportunity to contact him since the duo's January departure from office.

"Just before we left D.C., [Clinton] and I sat down and talked about the eight years we'd gone through together," a sweatpants-clad Gore said. "We talked about the good times and the bad times. At the end, we hugged, and he said that even though he had no idea what the future held for him, there was one thing he did know: that we'd always be close."

see GORE page 6

Above: Al Gore waits by the phone for a call that may never come.

Four Generations Of Americans Demand Sitcom Reparations

AMERICAN FOCUS

Left: *Hello, Larry* survivors demonstrate in front of NBC Studios in Burbank, CA.

WASHINGTON, DC—Pressure is building for the nation's TV networks to offer a formal apology and reparations to the four generations of Americans who lost millions of hours to inane sitcoms.

"We, on behalf of this nation's 215 million Telecaust victims, demand extensive reparations from the perpetrators of these heartless and falsely heartfelt programs," said Meredith Bishop, 47, president of Americans For Sitcom Reparations (AFSR). "For hours wasted staring at mind-numbing swill, for idiotic pap promoted as outrageous romps, for an unending parade of very special episodes, season-ending cliffhangers, and celebrity walk-on appearances, we demand justice be served at

see REPARATIONS page 8

Area Man An Expert On What Women Hate

HOUSTON—A self-professed expert on the fairer sex, 31-year-old Houston resident Gerald Doelpe says he knows exactly what women hate.

"Make sure you don't come on too strong tonight," Doelpe advised friend Joel Bartolo last Saturday before a first date. "Trust me, women don't like it when you come on too strong, kissing their hands and arms a lot on the first date. So be careful about showering them with too much affection, because it *will* backfire."

Above: Gerald Doelpe

Even though Doelpe's friends rarely see him around women, they say he is always more than willing

see MAN page 9

NEWS

Gay Comptroller Tired Of Being Referred To As 'That Gay Comptroller'

see LOCAL page 7B

Steve Allen: Gone, Forgotten

see PEOPLE page 4D

The Missing Intern: Unfortunate And All, But What Does It Have To Do With Anything?

see NATION page 2A

STATshot

A look at the numbers that shape your world.

Top-Selling Fragrances

1. Elizabeth Taylor's "Overwrought"
2. N'asal D'Congestanté
3. Finnish Leather
4. Alpha Male
5. Rosie O'Donnell's "Portion"
6. Rogaine Nights
7. Some Cheap Crap For Mother's Day

EAU DE HO

THE ONION
VOLUME 37
ISSUE 26
$2.00 US
$3.00 CAN

the ONION®

VOLUME 37 ISSUE 26 | AMERICA'S FINEST NEWS SOURCE™ | 2–8 AUGUST 2001

Fast-Food Purchase Seething With Unspoken Class Conflict

HUNTINGTON BEACH, CA—Resentment, anger, and pity were among the emotions mutually felt by Burger King employee Duane Hesketh and customer Robert Lalley during a class-conflict-laden transaction Tuesday.

According to sources, at 4:22 p.m. PST, the upper-middle-class Lalley approached the working-class Hesketh's register at the Beach Boulevard Burger King to order a meal. The two men instantly became locked in an icy showdown of mutual loathing and disrespect, each resenting the other and everything he represents. For the next seven minutes, the age-old conflict between the haves and have-nots was played out in a passive-aggressive verbal exchange that betrayed no trace of the roiling vortex of bitter hatred that lay just beneath the surface.

"May I help you?" Hesketh asked the golf-loving, SUV-driving financial planner standing before him. Without making eye contact with the mulleted cashier, Lalley replied, "Whopper Jr., large fries, and a large Diet Coke."

see CONFLICT page 8

Right: Cashier Duane Hesketh and customer Robert Lalley eye each other with disgust.

Video-Game Character Wondering Why Heartless God Always Chooses 'Continue'

Left: Solid Snake lies dead on the ground once again.

ORANGEBURG, SC—Solid Snake, tactical-espionage expert and star of PlayStation's "Metal Gear Solid," questioned the nature of the universe Monday when, moments after his 11th death in two hours, a cruel God forced him to "Continue" his earthly toil and suffering.

"Is this all there is?" asked Snake, hiding in a storage locker while two masked guards searched for him in the hold of a cargo ship. "Is this why I was created? To suffer? Will I ever escape this endless loop of grueling labor followed by violent death?"

Snake was then discovered by the guards and cut down in a hail of gunfire.

Snake, who has been fatally shot 2,143 times in the past six months, said he does not know why God deems it necessary for him to endlessly repeat his mission, which involves sneaking aboard a hijacked mili-

see VIDEO GAME page 6

Bush Finds Error In Fermilab Calculations

BATAVIA, IL—President Bush met with members of the Fermi National Accelerator Laboratory research team Monday to discuss a mathematical error he recently discovered in the famed laboratory's "Improved Determination Of Tau Lepton Paths From Inclusive Semileptonic *B*-Meson Decays" report.

"I'm somewhat out of my depth here," said Bush, a longtime Fermilab follower who describes himself as "something of an armchair physicist." "But it seems to me that, when reducing the perturbative uncertainty in the determination of V_{ub} from semileptonic Beta decays, one must calculate the rate of Beta events with a standard dilepton invariant mass at a subleading order in the hybrid expansion. The Fermilab folks' error, as I see it, was omitting that easily overlooked mathematical transformation and, therefore, acquiring

see BUSH page 7

Above: Bush shows Fermilab scientists where they went wrong in their calculations.

NEWS

Laura Bush Noisily Devours Infant

see NATION page 6A

Yacht Name Conveys Owner's Easygoing Lifestyle

see LOCAL page 5C

Donut Made With Real Kreme

see FOOD page 4E

Mississippi DNR To Ban Cockfishing

see NATION page 7A

STATshot

A look at the numbers that shape your world.

What Does Someone Have To Do To Get A Drink Around Here?

1. Blow the bartender?
2. Ferment the hops myself?
3. Take out an ad in *Thirst Weekly*?
4. Marry the Jamesons' daughter?
5. Wait until communion?
6. Ring for the night nurse?
7. Come back when you're open?

THE ONION VOLUME 37 ISSUE 28
$2.00 US
$3.00 CAN

the ONION®

VOLUME 37 ISSUE 28 AMERICA'S FINEST NEWS SOURCE™ 16–22 AUGUST 2001

Endangered Manatee Struggles To Make Self Understood To Congress

WASHINGTON, DC—Despite valiant efforts to make itself understood, an endangered West Indian manatee failed to communicate its urgent-sounding message to members of the House of Representatives Tuesday.

"Euyah, euyaaaah," said the visibly flustered 900-pound manatee, accidentally knocking over a podium with its flat, paddle-like tail. "Huuun nun. Eyah."

The manatee, one of only 3,000 left in the U.S., arrived unexpectedly in Washington after a long journey from its Florida home. It spent more than two hours bleating to House members, rolling its 10-foot-long body from side to side and waving its clawed flippers.

Democrats and Republicans were united in their confusion over the honking beast.

"Clearly, this manatee has something urgent to say, but what?" House Speaker Dennis Hastert (R-IL) said. "Something

see MANATEE page 7

Right: The manatee slowly works its way up the steps of the Capitol.

Inexorable March Of Time Brings TV's Jerry Mathers One Step Closer To Death

Left: *Leave It To Beaver* star Jerry Mathers, whose light grows dim.

HOLLYWOOD, CA—The inexorable march of time, the prison into which all humankind is born, brought *Leave It To Beaver* star Jerry Mathers—and all of us—one step closer to the grave Monday.

"I saw Jerry Mathers on *Entertainment Tonight* a couple months ago," said Barry Carter, 34, of Duluth, MN. "It was weird. He still has that baby face, but he's, like, in his 50s now. I was like, 'Whoa, look at Jerry Mathers, he's getting up there in years,' and my wife said, 'Well, aren't we all?' I guess it's true. I'm not as young as I used to be, either."

Added Carter with a reflective sigh: "It makes you think."

> **"I was like, 'Whoa, look at Jerry Mathers, he's getting up there in years,' and my wife said, 'Well, aren't we all?' I guess it's true."**

Mathers, who recently came face-to-face with his own mortality when a worm he swallowed on *The Tonight Show*'s "Celebrity Survivor" gave him a severe

see MATHERS page 6

Retired Realtor Drawn Back In For One Last Big Score

HARRISON, OH—After 30 years in the real-estate business, Jack Parker knew what he was: retired. His time in The Life had given him more than his share of ups and downs, and the veteran RE/MAX agent was finally out of the game for good, with a little house of his own and some money socked away. Yes, Jack Parker's days of proudly serving the home-buying needs of the greater Cincinnati area were over.

At least, that's what he thought.

Last Thursday, four months after hanging up his red RE/MAX blazer, Parker was

see REALTOR page 8

Right: Retired agent Parker stands before his last big score.

NEWS

Hugging Up 76,000 Percent

see NATION page 10A

Jerry Falwell: Is That Guy A Dick Or What?

see PEOPLE page 3C

Rest Of Country Temporarily Feels Deep Affection For New York

see NATION page 8A

Massive Attack On Pentagon Page 14 News

see NATION page 14A

STATshot

A look at the numbers that shape your world.

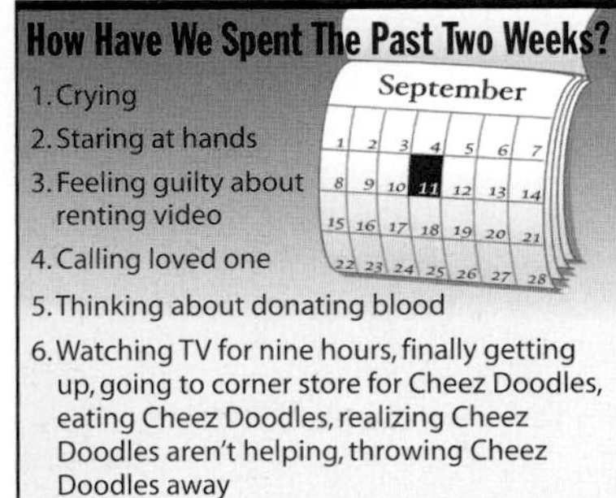

THE ONION
VOLUME 37
ISSUE 34
$2.00 US
$3.00 CAN

the ONION®

VOLUME 37 ISSUE 34 AMERICA'S FINEST NEWS SOURCE™ 27 SEPTEMBER–3 OCTOBER 2001

SPECIAL REPORT

Above: Flanked by Condoleezza Rice and Donald Rumsfeld, President Bush pledges to "exact revenge, just as soon as we know who we're exacting revenge against and where they are."

U.S. Vows To Defeat Whoever It Is We're At War With

WASHINGTON, DC—In a televised address to the American people Tuesday, a determined President Bush vowed that the U.S. would defeat "whoever exactly it is we're at war with here."

HOLY FUCKING SHIT

Attack On America

"America's enemy, be it Osama bin Laden, Saddam Hussein, the Taliban, a multinational coalition of terrorist organizations, any of a rogue's gallery of violent Islamic fringe groups, or an entirely different, non-Islamic aggressor we've never even heard of... be warned," Bush said during an 11-minute speech from the Oval Office. "The United States is preparing to strike, directly and decisively, against you, whoever you are, just as soon as we have a rough idea of your identity and a reasonably decent estimate as to where your base is located."

Added Bush: "That is, assuming you have a base."

Bush is acting with the full support of Congress, which on Sept. 14 authorized him to use any

see WAR page 6

Hijackers Surprised To Find Selves In Hell

'We Expected Eternal Paradise For This,' Say Suicide Bombers

JAHANNEM, OUTER DARKNESS—The hijackers who carried out the Sept. 11 attacks on the World Trade Center and Pentagon expressed confusion and surprise Monday to find themselves in the lowest plane of Na'ar, Islam's Hell.

"I was promised I would spend eternity in Paradise, being fed honeyed cakes by 67 virgins in a tree-lined garden, if only I would fly the airplane into one of the Twin Towers," said Mohammed Atta, one of the hijackers of American Airlines Flight 11,

see HIJACKERS page 12

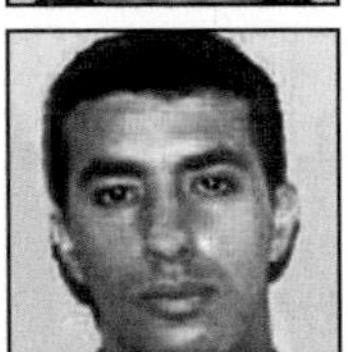

Right: Mohammed Atta (top) and Ahmed al-Haznawi.

American Life Turns Into Bad Jerry Bruckheimer Movie

Above: An actual scene from real life.

NEW YORK—In the two weeks since terrorists crashed hijacked planes into the World Trade Center and Pentagon, American life has come to resemble a bad Jerry Bruckheimer-produced action/disaster movie, shellshocked citizens reported Tuesday.

"Terrorist hijackings, buildings blowing up, thousands of people dying—these are

see MOVIE page 13

Not Knowing What Else To Do, Woman Bakes American-Flag Cake

TOPEKA, KS—Feeling helpless in the wake of the horrible Sept. 11 terrorist attacks that killed thousands, Christine Pearson baked a cake and decorated it like an American flag Monday.

Above: Pearson

"I had to do something to force myself away from the TV," said Pearson, 33, carefully laying rows of strawberry slices on the white-fudge-frosting-covered cake. "All of those

see CAKE page 12

NEWS

Gas-Station Employee Gives 109 9/10ths Percent

see LOCAL page 4C

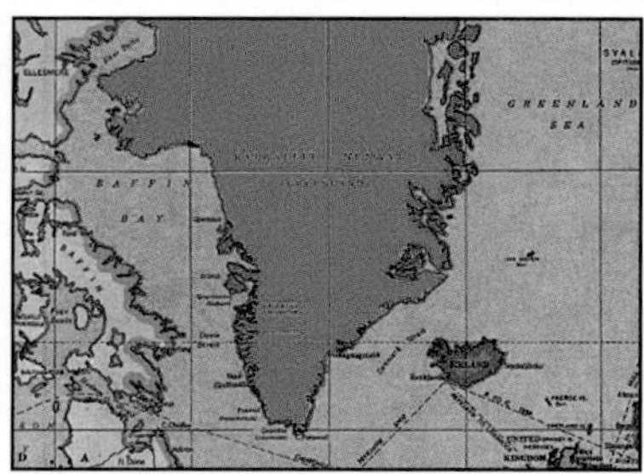

Greenland Thinks It Looks Fat In Mercator Projection

see WORLD page 7A

Friend's Comment Dismissed With Wanking Motion

see LOCAL page 6C

STATshot

A look at the numbers that shape your world.

What Are We Titling Our Masters Thesis?

1. An Overview Of Property Records, Schuyler County, VA, 1790-1815: Soooooo Boring
2. Green With Envy: The Hulk As Jealous Lover
3. White Chicks/Black Sticks
4. Doing Things At The Last Minute: A Sociopsychological Analystical Thing
5. The Fatal Obsolescence Of The American Professorship
6. Masters! Masters! Masters Thesis Of Puppets!

THE ONION
VOLUME 37
ISSUE 35
$2.00 US
$3.00 CAN

the ONION®

VOLUME 37 ISSUE 35 AMERICA'S FINEST NEWS SOURCE™ 4–10 OCTOBER 2001

THE AFTERMATH

A Shattered Nation Longs To Care About Stupid Bullshit Again

SPRINGFIELD, MO—Were this an ordinary Tuesday night, Wendy Vance would return home from her receptionist job at a Springfield chiropractor's office and spend the evening engaged in any number of empty, meaningless diversions: watching old, taped episodes of *Friends*, browsing the new issue of *Cosmopolitan*, or driving to Center Square Mall to browse for shoes.

Tonight, however, the 29-year-old is unable to bring herself to turn on the TV or even half-heartedly flip through the new Pottery Barn catalog. Instead, she has decided to visit her grandmother in nearby Mountain Grove.

"If none of this had happened, right

see BULLSHIT page 6

Security Beefed Up At Cedar Rapids Public Library

CEDAR RAPIDS, IA—In the wake of the Sept. 11 terrorist attacks on the World Trade Center and Pentagon, the Cedar Rapids Public Library is undertaking steps to tighten security, library officials announced Monday.

"As caretakers of the most prominent public building in the second largest city in Iowa, this library can no longer afford to take chances," library director Glenda

> **"As caretakers of the most prominent public building in the second largest city in Iowa, we can no longer afford to take chances," the library director said.**

Quarles said. "Due to our limited budget, we can't devote the kind of resources and manpower to security that, say, the Library of Congress can. But because of our high profile and easy access, we feel a strong responsibility to ensure the safety and well-being of those members of the public who visit and use us."

Quarles said that on the day of the attacks, she ordered the library closed. The following day, she called a special meeting with department heads and library-board members to discuss what changes needed

see LIBRARY page 11

NEWS

U.S. Postal Service Unveils New Uniforms

see NATION page 6A

Plant Dead Because Of You

see LOCAL page 8B

Gay Man Has Been Planning Halloween Costume Since July

see LOCAL page 2B

'Party-Pak' Just Cheese

see PRODUCTWATCH page 4C

STATshot

A look at the numbers that shape your world.

What Did We Forget To Ask The Doctor?

1. So is cancer, like, real serious?
2. What's the best way to contract eczema?
3. When blood comes out of your ding-ding, is that bad?
4. Can I have the fetus back as a souvenir?
5. Are Earring Tree employees allowed to do trepannings?
6. Isn't that thing on your wall a real-estate license?

the ONION®

VOLUME 37 ISSUE 38 AMERICA'S FINEST NEWS SOURCE™ 25–31 OCTOBER 2001

Just Shoot Me Writer Assumes Everyone He Meets Watches *Just Shoot Me*

LOS ANGELES—Andy Kaminowitz, 31, a staff writer for the popular Thursday-night NBC sitcom *Just Shoot Me*, operates under the assumption that everyone he meets watches the show, sources revealed Monday.

"It's kind of weird how he thinks everybody should be familiar with his work," said Frank Scalia, a bartender at Dublin's, a Sunset Boulevard bar frequented by Kaminowitz. "He'll walk in, strike up a conversation with somebody, and casually bring up that he's a writer for *Just Shoot Me*. Then, he just sits back with this air of expectation, like people are going to have all these questions for him about specific episodes or whatever."

"I mean, I've seen the show once or twice, and I guess it's all right," Scalia said.

see WRITER page 6

Above: Andy Kaminowitz in the *Just Shoot Me* writer's room.

Privileged Children Of Millionaires Square Off On World Stage

WASHINGTON, DC—After nearly two weeks of heavy, sustained air strikes, President Bush made final preparations Monday for a full-scale U.S. ground assault against Osama bin Laden, the privileged, formerly hard-partying heir to a family fortune.

"Osama bin Laden is a true emblem of evil, a man responsible for the deaths of thousands of innocent Americans," Bush said. "He cannot, and will not, escape justice."

Bin Laden, son a Saudi construction tycoon worth an estimated $5 billion at the time of his 1968 death, was not cowed by Bush's resolve.

"We will not bow to George W. Bush, the emblem of all that is evil and corrupt about America," said bin Laden, who frequented Beirut nightclubs as a young man, drinking heavily and fighting over women. "This is a man who spent much of his early life defiling God with his immoral ways. He will fall."

"The vile influence of the West must be driven out of the Arab world once and for all," continued bin Laden, who studied English at Oxford University in the '70s and went on to earn a degree in management and economics at King Abdul Aziz University. "And it will, for God is on our side in this righteous and holy war."

Responding to the increasingly incendiary rhetoric of bin Laden, Bush said

see PRIVILEGED page 8

Above: Kristin Petrie.

Thin, Attractive Woman Accepted For Who She Is

DALLAS—In a world too often filled with hatred and intolerance toward those who are different, 23-year-old Kristin Petrie is accepted for who she is: a natural blonde with a dazzling smile and spectacular body.

"I don't know how to describe it, but Kristin has this special, magnetic quality," said Ron Angelo, Petrie's supervisor at ExecuTech, a Dallas-based headhunting firm where the willowy beauty works as a corporate recruiter. "When Kristin arrived here, she had zero recruiting experience. But did she let that stop her from landing the job? Absolutely not. Kristin is determined not to let her shortcomings keep her from succeeding. And you know what? They rarely do."

Petrie has been able to overcome numerous setbacks since joining the ExecuTech team, including frequent error-filled

see WOMAN page 12

NEWS

Congress To Meet At Feingold's House Today

see NATION page 6A

Hot-Dog Craving Ends After First Bite

see EATS page 10E

Wedding Ring Mistakenly Left Inside Prostitute

see LOCAL page 4D

Man Waxes Patriotic, Truck

see LOCAL page 5D

STATshot

A look at the numbers that shape your world.

What Are We Feeling That Would Be Better Expressed In German?

1. Dread of something inevitable yet benign *Fuerchtenünabwendbarfreundlich*
2. The wish to see all suffer for the crimes of one *Schadenallemeinverbrechen*
3. Laughter at something one knows in one's soul is not funny *Lachenaüfkomischsnichtspaßheit*
4. Shame over eating last piece of Black Forest cherry cake *Schwarzschamekirschkuchenessen*

THE ONION
VOLUME 37
ISSUE 41
$2.00 US
$3.00 CAN

the ONION®

VOLUME 37 ISSUE 41 AMERICA'S FINEST NEWS SOURCE™ 15–21 NOVEMBER 2001

6,000 Runners Fail To Discover Cure For Breast Cancer

ATLANTA—Despite their diligent, dedicated running, the 6,000-plus participants in Sunday's 5K Race For The Cure did not find a cure for breast cancer.

Hopes were high, given the excellent weather and record turnout for the 11th annual event, but no viable cure for the disease was discovered along the 3.1-mile course.

"We were particularly hopeful of locating the cure somewhere around the two-and-a-half-mile mark," race organizer Jill Broadbent said. "At that point, the route goes right past Northside Hospital and within a block of several Emory University oncology facilities. That seemed the most promising place to perhaps spot a breast-cancer cure. Regrettably, the runners were unable to do more than momentarily glimpse in researchers' windows as they passed by."

At 10 a.m., participants gathered outside the Georgia Dome and proceeded

see CANCER page 12

Above: Race For The Cure runners take off in search of a breast-cancer cure.

Spaghetti-Os Discontinued As Franco-American Relations Break Down

PARIS—With talks collapsing at the 11th hour, Franco-American relations hit an all-time low Monday, casting the future of Spaghetti-Os-brand canned pasta in serious doubt.

"Thus far, three months of negotiations have yielded bitter fruit," French minister of foods Guy Charpentier said. "Despite concessionary offers from both sides, no acceptable compromise has been reached on a number of key issues, including sauce tanginess, sodium levels, and pasta-ring size. As a result, the sort of friendly Franco-American partnership necessary to produce the neat, round spaghetti one can eat with a spoon may no longer be possible."

U.S. Canned Goods Secretary James Miller echoed Charpentier's sentiments with

see SPAGHETTI-OS page 8

Above: French prime minister Lionel Jospin and U.S. Canned Goods Secretary James Miller at last month's Franco-American conference. Left: Spaghetti-Os.

Luann Creator Wrestling With How To Address Terrorist Crisis

Left: The creator of *Luann* in his studio.

SAN MARCOS, CA—Greg Evans, creator of the popular *Luann* comic strip, continues to struggle to find the right way to address the events of Sept. 11 and their aftermath, the cartoonist reported from his home Monday.

"I definitely feel an obligation to address this tragedy—through Luann's eyes," said Evans, referring to Luann DeGroot, the inquisitive and outspoken teen whose adventures appear daily in more than 300 newspapers nationwide. "It's a real high-wire act: entertaining, informing, and providing emotional support to my readers all at the same time. But it's a challenge I have no choice but to rise to."

"I'm so lucky to have this public forum," Evans continued. "With it, however, comes responsibility. I must not let my readers down."

Though he has been wrestling with it for weeks, Evans has yet to integrate the current crisis into either the plotline about Luann's crush on Aaron Hill or the subplot about Bernice's budding romance with Zane.

"Zane is the strip's first character in a wheelchair, so I think it would send a terrible message to suddenly drop his storyline," Evans said. "I definitely have to find a way to work this in, though. Like

see LUANN page 6

the ONION®
VOLUME 37 ISSUE 46 · AMERICA'S FINEST NEWS SOURCE™ · 20 DEC. 2001–16 JAN. 2002

NEWS

Mother Still Yammering Away Under Her Tombstone

see LOCAL page 11E

Dept. Of Transportation Discontinues 'Bridge Out 8 Feet Ahead' Sign

see NATION page 3A

Chicken Bones, Beer Cans Bob In The Froth Of John Goodman's Hot Tub

see PEOPLE page 2D

STATshot

A look at the numbers that shape your world.

ONION Special Report

What Is Sexy In The Wake Of Sept. 11?

NEW YORK—On Sept. 11, the world changed. The tragic events of that fateful day have had a profound impact on American society, altering—as documented in countless magazines and newspapers—everything from our our travel habits to our tastes in music to our gourmet-cheese preferences. But three months later, one vital question still remains unanswered: What is sexy in the wake of Sept. 11?

"After the deaths of so many thousands of people, what turns us on?" asked Robyn Loeb, Life section editor of *USA Today*. "I'm hearing arched backs, lithe young bodies glistening with sweat, naked lovers embraced in long, slow, steamy kisses. Given everything that we as a nation have been through, when it comes to sex, we long for a return to the tried-and-true."

According to *Vogue* managing editor Carrie Bettig, beautiful women are in.

"Ever since Sept. 11, we've been seeing a lot of gorgeous women in fashion magazines," Bettig said. "A great many of the models featured in recent spreads have stunning faces and spectacular bod-

see SEXY page 7

Entrepreneur Stuck With 40,000 Unsold Bin Laden Urinal Cakes

REGO PARK, NY—Gabe Kloster, a 32-year-old Queens-based entrepreneur, expressed fear Monday that he may be unable to sell his remaining inventory of 40,000 urinal cakes bearing an image of Osama bin Laden between a pair of crosshairs.

"A few months back, I couldn't make them fast enough," said Kloster, who supplies news- and pop-culture-related novelty products to dis-

see CAKES page 6

Left: Kloster displays one of the thousands of novelty urinal cakes (above) that sit in his warehouse.

Partygoers Mocked By Catering Staff

MARIETTA, GA—Unbeknownst to attendees of Susan and Mel Gullicksen's holiday party Saturday, the Feather & Fennel Catering staff spent most of the evening mocking partygoers behind their backs.

"Matt, you have *got* see the sow in the powder-blue chiffon jumpsuit," said Feather & Fennel server Christine Salerno, 23, whispering to coworker Matt Blaine. "She looks like Brian Dennehy in drag, only less feminine."

Blaine then rushed a tray of miniature quiches into the living room to get an eyeful of the unattractive guest.

The party, held in the Gullicksens' spacious suburban Atlanta home, was attended by nearly 100 friends of the upper-class couple. The caterers were hired to set up the buffet, serve appetizers and entrees to guests, and break down the food area at the party's conclusion. All surreptitious, catty remarks about the Gullicksens and their friends were added free of charge.

"I've seen not one but two different people wearing pas-

see CATERERS page 10

Above: Feather & Fennel staffers laugh at a partygoer's lime-green dress.

Man Back With Woman His Best Friend Spent Week Criticizing

Mideast Peace Process Derailed, Burned To Ground, Shoveled Over With Dirt

John D. And Catherine T. MacArthur Foundation Goes On Wild Endowment Binge

JANUARY FEBRUARY MARCH APRIL MAY JUNE

Yes, Area Man Has Been Told He Resembles A Fat Gregg Allman

Friendship Blossoms Into Unrequited Love

Klan Rally 70 Percent Undercover Reporters

2002

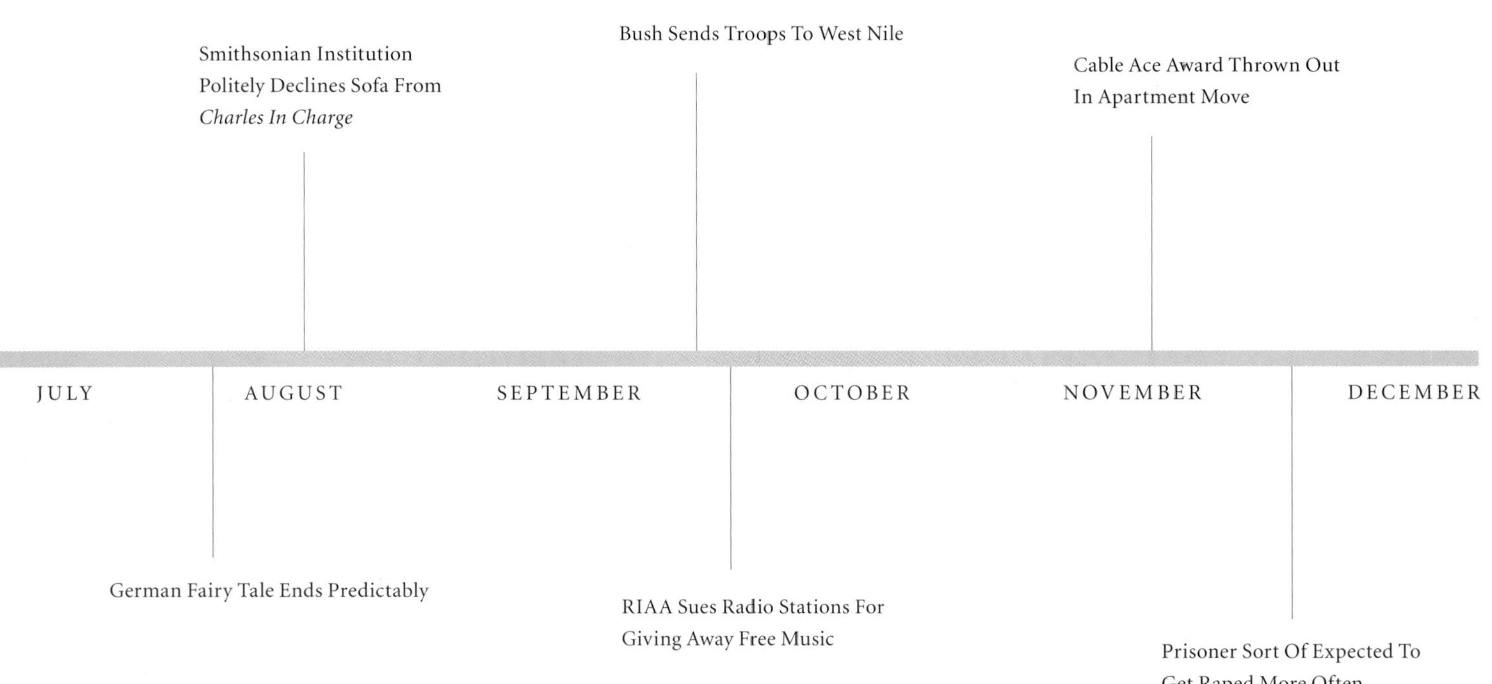

Smithsonian Institution Politely Declines Sofa From *Charles In Charge*
Bush Sends Troops To West Nile
Cable Ace Award Thrown Out In Apartment Move
JULY
AUGUST
SEPTEMBER
OCTOBER
NOVEMBER
DECEMBER
German Fairy Tale Ends Predictably
RIAA Sues Radio Stations For Giving Away Free Music
Prisoner Sort Of Expected To Get Raped More Often

the ONION®

VOLUME 38 ISSUE 01 | AMERICA'S FINEST NEWS SOURCE™ | 17–23 JANUARY 2002

NEWS

Speed Stick Now Available In Neapolitan

see PRODUCTS page 2B

Space Shuttle Endeavour: What's In It For Me?

see NATION page 11A

John Ashcroft Blood Donation Eats Through Bag

see NATION page 6A

Backrub Turns Ugly

see LOCAL page 10D

STATshot

A look at the numbers that shape your world.

Area Man Not Exactly Sure When To Take Down American Flags

Above: Jerry Wenger with two of his six flags.

UTICA, NY—After more than four months of proudly displaying American flags on his car, home, and body, 47-year-old computer consultant Jerry Wenger is uncertain when the appropriate time will be to take them down.

"It seems like the war in Afghanistan is winding down," said Wenger from his cubicle at Armstrong & Grunau Consulting Monday. "Then again, we still haven't caught bin Laden. Am I supposed to keep [the flags] up until we get him? But what if we never do?"

"Do I have to wait until all the troops are home?" Wenger continued. "Because that could take years. I'm not trying to be a jerk—I'm just not sure when to consider this whole thing over."

Though Wenger has nothing against displaying the American flag, prior to last September, he'd never owned a flag in his life.

"Right after the attacks, there was some-

see FLAGS page 6

Peppy U.S. Teens Vow To Make This The Best Year Ever

WASHINGTON, DC—At a pep rally Monday on the National Mall, a coalition of enthusiastic U.S. teens vowed to make 2002 the "best year ever."

Decked out in red-white-and-blue "spirit wear," the high-energy youths clapped, cheered, and did cartwheels on the steps of the Lincoln Memorial, visibly increasing the energy level of the estimated 1.3 million U.S. citizens in attendance.

"Hello, America!" said Jennifer Richards, captain of the U.S. Peppy Teen Squad. "Raise your hands in the air if you think America kicks butt! Whoooo!"

Richards then did a series of backflips and high kicks before unveiling the schedule of USPTS-sponsored events that will keep the nation's spirits high throughout

see TEENS page 9

Archaeologist Tired Of Unearthing Unspeakable Ancient Evils

HASAKE, SYRIA—When archaeologist Edward Whitson joined a Penn State University dig in Hasake last year, he did so to participate in the excavation of a Late Bronze Age settlement rich in pottery shards and clay figurines. Whitson had hoped to determine whether the items contained within the site were primarily Persian or Assyrian in origin.

Instead, he found himself fleeing giant flying demon-cats as he ran through the temple's cavernous halls, jumping from ledge to ledge while locked in a desperate struggle for his life and soul for what seemed like the thousandth time in his 27-year career.

"All I wanted to do was study the settlement's remarkably well-preserved kiln," said the 58-year-old Whitson, carefully recoiling the rope he had just used to clamber out of a pit filled with giant rats. "I didn't want to be chased by yet another accursed manifestation of an ancient god-king's wrath."

Over the course of his career, Whitson has been frequently lauded by colleagues

see ARCHAEOLOGIST page 7

Right: Edward Whitson waits while yet another tortured wraith rises from a dig site in Syria.

NEWS

Kurt Warner Cheered On By Wire-Haired Man-Goblin

see SPORTS page 10C

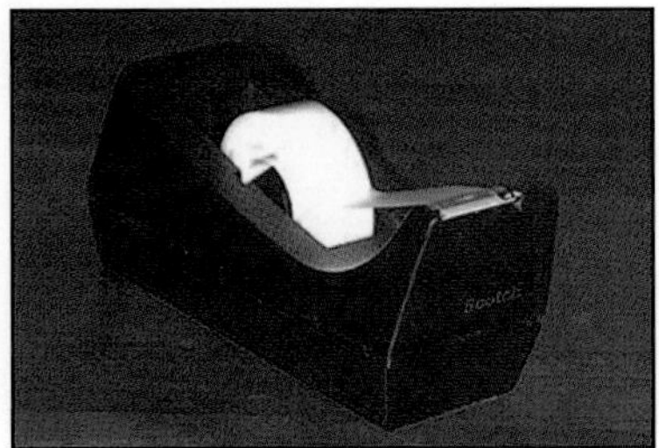

Haunted Tape Dispenser Unsure How To Demonstrate Hauntedness

see LOCAL page 2D

Man Accidentally Rents *Delta Force 4* Instead Of *3*

see VIDEO page 7B

STATshot

A look at the trends that shape your world.

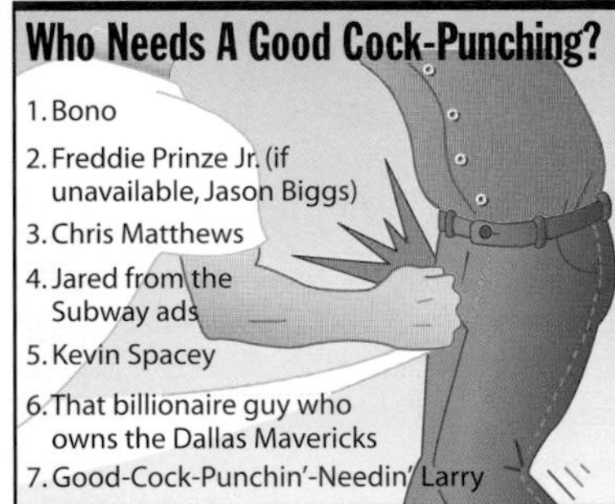

THE ONION
VOLUME 38
ISSUE 04
$2.00 US
$3.00 CAN

the ONION®

VOLUME 38 ISSUE 04 AMERICA'S FINEST NEWS SOURCE™ 7-13 FEBRUARY 2002

Bush Earmarks 1.5 Billion Gold Stars For Education

WASHINGTON, DC—Vowing to give the nation's public schools "a much-needed boost," President Bush announced Monday that his 2003 budget proposal would allocate 1.5 billion gold-star stickers for education.

"As class sizes continue to grow and test scores continue to decline, our public schools are in a state of crisis," Bush said at a White House press conference. "There is no more time for deliberation. It is time to act. Our children need these adhesive gold stars."

Bush went on to describe the "alarming state" of many of the nation's public schools, citing underpaid teachers, buildings badly in need of repair, and woefully outdated textbooks.

"If a child is going to learn under these conditions, he or she is going to need lots of encouragement," Bush said. "These

see BUSH page 10

Right: Bush holds up a Dayton, OH, fourth-grader's gold-star-adorned book report on Ferdinand Magellan.

Indo-Pakistani Tensions Mount At Local Amoco

The Detroit-area Amoco station where hostilities have erupted between Indian-born owner Rajesh Srinivasan (left) and Majid Ashraf (right), the Pakistani manager of the Subway franchise inside.

DETROIT—Indo-Pakistani tensions continue to escalate this week at the Eight-Mile and Telegraph Road Amoco, where hostilities between owner Rajesh Srinivasan and in-store Subway mini-franchise manager Majid Ashraf threaten to spill over into all-out war.

"We have made every effort to extend the hand of friendship to the Pakistani delegation that runs the Amoco Mart's Subway Express," said the India-born Srinivasan, 49, in a statement to the press Monday. "But that hand, my own hand with which I built this business for my family, has been repeatedly and without remorse slapped away."

Leased and operated by Pakistani immigrant Ashraf and his family since March 1999, the in-store Subway occupies 30 percent of the Amoco Mart's total retail space. Ever since their arrival, the Ashrafs have been the subject of increasingly inflammatory rhetoric from Srinivasan,

see TENSIONS page 6

Deaf Man's Deaf Friends Way Too Into Deaf Culture

COLUMBIA, MD—Jonathan Deeds, a 26-year-old Rockville resident who lost his hearing as an infant, feels a growing sense of alienation from his deaf friends, who he says are "way too into" deaf culture.

"I'm deaf, but it's not like it's my whole life or anything," said Deeds, a 26-year-old sales administrator, speaking through an American Sign Language interpreter Monday. "I wish I could say the same for some of the people I hang out with."

According to Deeds, friends Rob Planter and Ben Trantvan automatically gravitate toward "all things deaf," including deaf greeting cards, deaf Kabuki theater, and "Deaf Elvis," a D.C.-area Elvis impersonator.

"Lately, it seems like everything they do is deafness-related," Deeds said. "Like, for example, they're really into this deaf comedian named Ken Glickman. He's all right, I guess, but I don't see why his being deaf makes him any funnier. But try

see DEAF CULTURE page 11

Above: Jonathan Deeds.

the ONION®

VOLUME 38 ISSUE 08 AMERICA'S FINEST NEWS SOURCE™ 7–13 MARCH 2002

NEWS

Pope Asks To Be Taken Off List Of World's 100 Richest People

see WORLD page 4A

Shopper Takes Bizarre Journey Beyond Bed, Bath

see LOCAL page 9B

Bicep Felt On Demand

see LOCAL page 10B

Cloned Cat Neutered

see SCIENCE page 7C

STATshot

A look at the trends that shape your world.

Least-Appropriate Baby-Shower Games

1. Belly-Flop Contest
2. Do a shot whenever anyone says "cute"
3. Feel The Baby Kick From The Inside
4. Down Syndrome Roulette
5. Ring Around The Pathetic, Childless Spinster

THE ONION VOLUME 38 ISSUE 08
$2.00 US
$3.00 CAN

Bush Calls On Business Leaders To Create 500,000 Shitty Jobs By 2003

THE RECESSION

WASHINGTON, DC—In a keynote address at the National Economic Summit, President Bush issued a bold challenge to the nation's business leaders Monday, calling on them to create 500,000 shitty jobs by next year.

"So long as unemployment continues to rise, this recession will continue, as well," said Bush, speaking before nearly 400 of the nation's top CEOs. "That is why I am turning to you to create thousands of new shit jobs. Whether it is a night-shift toilet-cleaning position at an airport or a fry-cook post at a KFC, it's up to you to help provide every hard-working American with a demeaning, go-nowhere job."

During his 25-minute speech, Bush cited a number of industries with the potential

see BUSH page 8

Above: Bush challenges the nation's top CEOs to create thousands of new shit jobs.

Above: Liman with a 1985 Corolla he is considering buying.

Area Man Perpetually In Process Of Buying Or Selling Car

MARION, IL—Local resident Don Liman, 49, is almost constantly in the process of buying, selling, or preparing to buy or sell a car, sources reported Monday.

"That's Don for you," said Russell Flange, Liman's neighbor. "We always say old Donnie's got a one-car car lot instead of a driveway. There's a Sable wagon for sale in front of his house right now."

"It's not easy to find the exact right car," said Liman, whose search for the ideal car

see MAN page 9

McDonald's Drops 'Hammurderer' Character From Advertising

OAK BROOK, IL—Bowing to outcry from consumers and parents groups, the McDonald's Corporation announced Monday that it is discontinuing its new advertising mascot, "The Hammurderer," a mischievous, homicidal imp who kills McDonaldland characters and takes their sandwiches.

Developed by Chicago advertising agency DDB Needham, the Hammurderer made his debut two months ago and has since appeared in a series of Saturday-morning television commercials, as well as on Happy Meal bags and activity placemats. All appearances by and references to the violent, ill-tempered prison escapee will be dropped.

"Over the years, McDonald's has successfully introduced a number of new characters whose defining characteristic is a certain measure of comical, criminal intent," said Andrew Perlich, McDonald's vice-president of promotions. "Such shady characters as The Hamburglar, The Goblins, and the bloodthirsty pirate Captain Crook have all fit nicely into the McDonald's advertising universe. We had every reason to believe that the Hammurderer,

Above: The discontinued character.

with his long rap sheet of burger-related crimes and his signature cry of 'Stabble Stabble Stabble,' would take his place in this proud lineage of McDonaldland mischief-makers."

The Hammurderer's Jan. 11 debut ad—in which he seizes and devours the McDonald's Happy Meal Guys, oblivious to their frantic screams—earned poor marks from parents and child-develop-

see MCDONALD'S page 13

NEWS

Obesity-Study Lab Rat's Life Pretty Sweet

see SCIENCE page 5C

Rapist Gets New Start At Technical College

see LOCAL page 11C

Southerner Either Looking For 'Pawn Shop' Or 'Porn Shop'

see LOCAL page 3C

Lord's Prayer Ad-Libbed

see FAITH page 3B

STATshot

A look at the trends that shape your world.

the ONION®

VOLUME 38 ISSUE 12 | AMERICA'S FINEST NEWS SOURCE™ | 4–10 APRIL 2002

Nation's UPS Men Break Out The Shorts

MANCHESTER, NH—In a welcome sight heralding the end of another winter and the arrival of spring, United Parcel Service men across the nation are breaking out the shorts.

"Look!" said Manchester, NH, cashier Brenda Cosgrove, staring out the window of the yarn shop where she works. "There goes another one! That's three today!"

Across the U.S., signs of the change of season abound, as daffodils poke out of the ground, the songs of the robin are once again heard in the trees, and leaves bud on the branches. For millions of Americans, however, there is no more beloved harbinger of spring than the sight of a UPS man's sturdy calves in the open air after months hidden away beneath heavy brown fabric.

"Between the long winter and this cold rain we've been having, it felt like it was never going to warm up," said Hugh

see SHORTS page 6

Above: UPS driver Luis Tendero breaks out the shorts in Eugene, OR.

WORLD

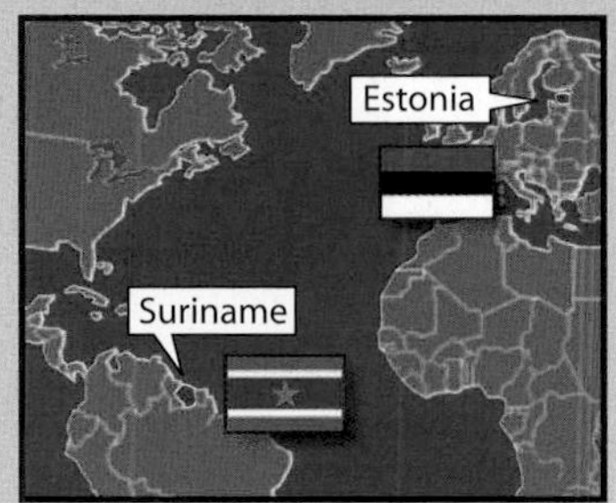

Countries Who Met Over Internet Go To War

TARTU, ESTONIA—Just months after meeting in an Internet chat room, the nations of Suriname and Estonia have entered a state of open hostility, U.N. sources reported Tuesday.

"In early January, Surinamese president Runaldo Ronald Venetiaan logged onto a small-nations chat room on Yahoo! and came across Estonian president Arnold Ruutel," U.N. Secretary-General Kofi Annan said. "The two exchanged messages and, before long, became Internet friends, bond-

see WAR page 12

New Roommate Has Elaborate Theory About How Kenny Rogers Is A Genius

DAYTON, OH—University of Dayton sophomores Mike Maritz and Andrea Haltigan reported Monday that their otherwise normal-seeming new roommate has "this whole theory about how Kenny Rogers is a genius."

"So, yesterday, we're moving the living room around to fit in some of Kurt [Schaier]'s stuff,' said Maritz, 21. "The two of us are pushing my big CD shelf into the corner, and out of nowhere, Kurt says, 'Kenny Rogers is the most underrated musician alive.' I was like, 'Where did that come from?'"

According to Maritz, Schaier spent the next 25 minutes elaborating on his bold assertion, discussing Rogers' pre-solo days with The First Edition, his duets with Dottie West, and his 1977-80 "Golden Era." Later that evening, Schaier returned to the subject twice more, once to offer a line-by-line analysis of the lyrics to "Coward Of The County" and once to declare the 1968 First Edition hit "Just Dropped In (To See What Condition My Condition Was In)" a "true pop-psychedelic classic."

Above: Kurt Schaier, whose deep admiration of Kenny Rogers (left) has caused confusion among his new roommates.

Haltigan and Maritz first met Schaier on March 14 when he responded to a classified ad for the vacant room in their three-bedroom apartment.

see ROOMMATE page 6

NEWS

Cheney Returns To U.S. With Full Head Of Thick, Wavy Hair

see NATION page 6A

Santa Fe Resident Pretty Kokopellied Out

see LOCAL page 15D

Melon Balled

see EATS page 1E

Abortion Stops A Beating

see LOCAL page 10D

STATshot

A look at the trends that shape your world.

the ONION®

VOLUME 38 ISSUE 13 AMERICA'S FINEST NEWS SOURCE™ 11–17 APRIL 2002

Nevada To Phase Out Laws Altogether

CARSON CITY, NV—The Nevada legislature voted Monday to repeal all laws within the state and prohibit the proposal of any new laws.

"Laws have been good to the state of Nevada," said Gov. Kenny Guinn between swigs of Jim Beam. "But ultimately, after carefully considering what's best for the long-term economic growth and prosperity of the state, we decided that lawfulness just wasn't a good idea."

Nevada's laws, Guinn said, will be slowly phased out over a five-year period, easing residents into a state of total anarchy. Gambling and prostitution have already been decriminalized, and car theft is slated to follow in 2004. Bans on murder and rape will be lifted in 2007.

Though the elimination of the rule of

see NEVADA page 8

Right: Nevada Gov. Kenny Guinn in his office.

37 Record-Store Clerks Feared Dead In Yo La Tengo Concert Disaster

ATHENS, GA—Thirty-seven record-store clerks are missing and feared dead in the aftermath of a partial roof collapse during a Yo La Tengo concert Monday.

"We're trying our best to rescue these clerks, but, realistically, there's not a lot of hope," said emergency worker Len Guzman, standing outside the 40 Watt Club, where the tragedy occurred. "These people are simply not in the physical condition to survive this sort of trauma. It's just a twisted mass of black-frame glasses and ironic Girl Scouts T-shirts in there."

Also believed to be among the missing are seven freelance rock critics, five vinyl junkies, two 'zine publishers, an art-school dropout, and a college-radio DJ.

The collapse occurred approximately 30 minutes into the Hoboken, NJ, band's set, when a poorly installed rooftop heating-

see CONCERT page 6

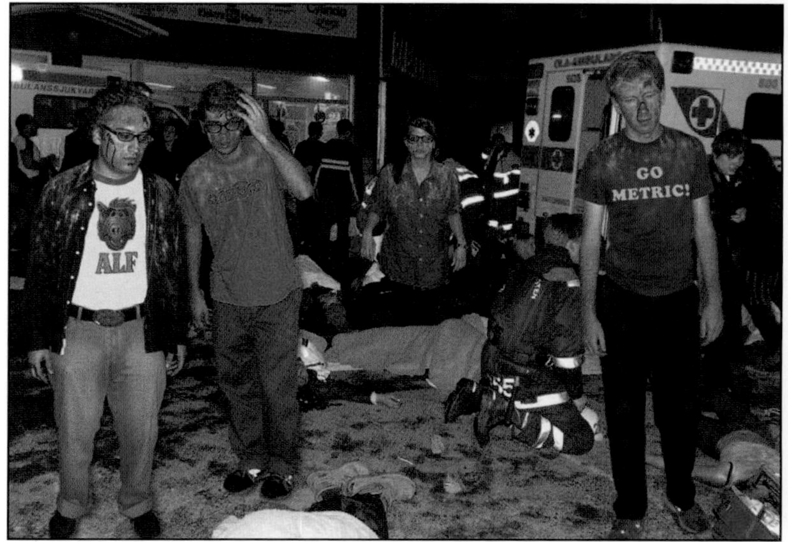

Right: Dazed record-store clerks stagger away from the scene of the roof collapse.

Above: The Japanese restaurant to which Miyazawa (inset) was taken.

Japanese Exchange Student Taken To Japanese Restaurant

BETTENDORF, IA—Takashi Miyazawa, 16, an exchange student from Nagoya spending six months in Bettendorf, was given the opportunity to experience authentic Japanese cuisine Monday, when host mother Bobbie Tucker arranged a visit to Edo, a restaurant in nearby Davenport.

"The Eagle [Food Center] has take-out sushi, but I didn't think there was a place you could sit down for a genuine Japanese meal," Tucker said Monday. "But as I was reading the paper Sunday, I happened to notice an ad for Edo. I knew Takashi would be so thrilled."

The outing marked the first time any of the Tuckers had eaten Japanese food and Miyazawa's 18,358th.

see STUDENT page 13

NEWS

Ancient Melanesian Masks Thundered Past To Get To *Star Wars* Exhibit

see MUSEUMS page 10D

Detroit Burned Down For The Insurance Money

see NATION page 5A

Cartoon Prisoner Stands Holding Bars All Day

see LOCAL page 3C

Guy Upstairs Discovers Ska

see LOCAL page 6C

STATshot

A look at the trends that shape your world.

How Have We Brought Shame To Our Grandparents?

1. Launched Watchmygrandparentsfuck.com
2. Quit the seminary
3. Adopted immodest Western-style dress
4. Started hanging around with ethnic kids
5. Slept with Mildred in 204B
6. Acquired own worldview

the ONION®

VOLUME 38 ISSUE 19 AMERICA'S FINEST NEWS SOURCE™ 23–29 MAY 2002

Pope Forgives Molested Children

VATICAN CITY—Calling forgiveness "one of the highest virtues taught to us by Jesus," Pope John Paul II issued a papal decree Monday absolving priest-molested children of all sin.

"Though grave and terrible sins have been committed, our Lord teaches us to turn the other cheek and forgive those who sin against us," said the pope, reading a prepared statement from a balcony overlooking St. Peter's Square. "That is why, despite the terrible wrongs they have committed, the church must move on and forgive these children for their misdeeds."

"As Jesus said, 'Let he who is without sin cast the first stone,'" the pope continued. "We must send a clear message to these hundreds—perhaps thousands—of children whose sinful ways have tempted so many of the church's servants into lustful violation of their holy vows of celibacy. The church forgives them for their trans-

see POPE page 8

Handlers Desperate To Prevent Tara Reid Political Awakening

LOS ANGELES—Tara Reid's agent, publicist, and other members of her management team are working feverishly to avert a potential political awakening in the 26-year-old actress, sources reported Tuesday.

Above: Tara Reid

"Thus far, Tara has been blissfully oblivious to world affairs," said Rick Stein, Reid's agent at International Creative Management. "But we must remain ever-vigilant of the possibility that, as her star continues to rise, she will develop a political consciousness like so many others in Hollywood."

"As bad as she is, could you imagine if, during an interview for a new movie, she started going off on saving the animals or ending world hunger or something?" Stein said. "So long as she's my client, I will do

see REID page 6

Factual Error Found On Internet

LONGMONT, CO—The Information Age was dealt a stunning blow Monday, when a factual error was discovered on the Internet. The error was found on TedsUltimateBradyBunch.com, a *Brady Bunch* fan site that incorrectly listed the show's debut year as 1968, not 1969.

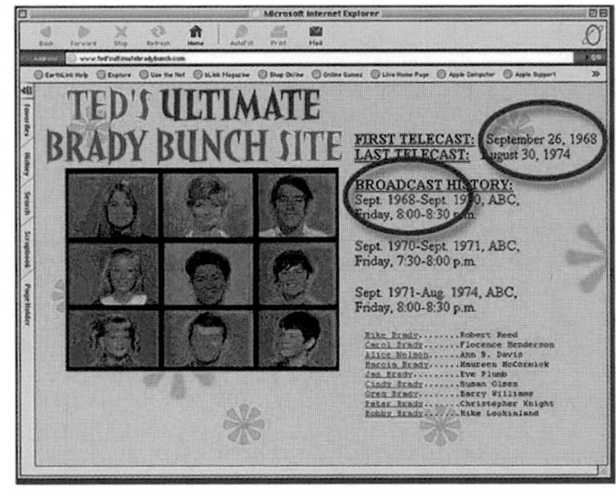

Above: The shocking error.

Caryn Wisniewski, a Pueblo, CO, legal secretary and diehard *Brady Bunch* fan, came across the mistake while searching for information about the show's first-season cast.

"When I first saw 1968 on the web page, I thought, 'Wow, apparently, all those *Brady Bunch* books I've read listing 1969 as the show's first year were wrong,'" Wisniewski told reporters at a press conference. "But even though I obviously trusted the Internet, I was still kind of puzzled. So I checked other *Brady Bunch* fan sites, and all of them said 1969. After a while, it slowly began to sink in that the World Wide Web might be tainted with unreliable information."

Following up on her suspicion, Wisniewski phoned her public library, the ABC television network, and the office of *Brady Bunch* producer Sherwood Schwartz—all of whom confirmed that "Ted's Ultimate *Brady Bunch* Site" was in error.

Attempts to contact the webmaster of

see INTERNET page 7

the ONION®

VOLUME 38 ISSUE 20 AMERICA'S FINEST NEWS SOURCE™ 30 MAY–6 JUNE 2002

Sexual Tension Between Arafat, Sharon Reaches Breaking Point

Above: Arafat and Sharon share an awkward moment.

JERUSALEM—The long-simmering sexual tension between Israeli Prime Minister Ariel Sharon and Palestinian leader Yasser Arafat finally reached a breaking point Monday, culminating in a passionate kiss before a shocked delegation of Mideast negotiators.

"You always got the feeling that there was something more behind all the anger and tension," said European Union Foreign Policy Chief Javier Solana. "They wouldn't agree on *anything*, even though their people were dying, locked in this unending conflict. It never made sense—until now."

Continued Solana: "All that repressed passion. And neither of them would admit it to the other... or to themselves."

According to sources, midway through a 10 a.m. meeting to discuss a possible pullout of Israeli troops from several West Bank settlements, Sharon accused Arafat of secretly channeling PLO funds into Hamas and other terrorist organizations. The accusation

see TENSION page 7

Congress Threatens To Leave D.C. Unless New Capitol Is Built

Above: An architectural firm's proposal for a new retractable-dome capitol. Inset: Hastert addresses reporters.

WASHINGTON, DC—Calling the current U.S. Capitol "inadequate and obsolete," Congress will relocate to Charlotte or Memphis if its demands for a new, state-of-the-art facility are not met, leaders announced Monday.

"Don't get us wrong: We love the drafty old building," Speaker of the House Dennis Hastert (R-IL) said. "But the hard reality is, it's no longer suitable for a world-class legislative branch. The sight lines are bad, there aren't enough concession stands or bathrooms, and the parking is miserable. It hurts to say, but the capitol's time has come and gone."

see CAPITOL page 11

Above: Adam Sprouse and his parents.

Nerd's Parents Afraid Son Will Fall In With Popular Crowd

MUNDELEIN, IL—Lawrence and Marcia Sprouse expressed concern Monday that their 15-year-old son Adam, after years of being a social outcast, is in danger of falling in with the popular crowd at Mundelein High School.

"All the signs point to him getting involved with the popular kids," Marcia said. "The last few Saturday nights, instead of staying home and watching a movie, he's been out at parties. He's also been hanging around this boy who's on the school baseball team. Parties, hanging out with jocks—what's become of my baby boy?"

Primary among the Sprouses' worries is the prospect of Adam being exposed to drugs and alcohol.

"I'm not naïve about what goes on with these kids who aren't in the AP classes," Marcia said. "They stay up late, laughing

see NERD page 8

NEWS

Field-Trip Mishap Fulfills Child's Wish To Be Oscar Mayer Wiener

see LOCAL page 8C

Ross Ice Shelf Embarks On World Tour

see ENVIRONMENT page 7A

Road-Kill Squirrel Remembered As Frantic, Indecisive

see PASSINGS page 11E

STATshot

A look at the trends that shape your world.

What Posters Are We Taking Down?

1. Bryan from Color Me Badd
2. "Wanted" poster of self from county fair
3. Poverty Sucks
4. That Escher where the fish turn into birds
5. Perot-Stockdale '92
6. University of Wisconsin–Whitewater Orientation Week

Life is Full of Difficult Choices

THE ONION
VOLUME 38
ISSUE 20
$2.00 US
$3.00 CAN

the ONION®

VOLUME 38 ISSUE 22 AMERICA'S FINEST NEWS SOURCE™ 13–19 JUNE 2002

Body Of Missing *Mad* Magazine Reporter Found In Blecchistan

POTRZEBIE, BLECCHISTAN—Questions regarding the fate of *Mad* magazine reporter Phil Fonebone, kidnapped at the hands of Blecchistani extremists three months ago, were answered Monday with the discovery of his body at an undisclosed location near Potrzebie.

"Phil Fonebone's death was a brutal act of barbarism perpetrated by a group of clods, finks, and schmendricks who stand in direct opposition to the values we cher-

see REPORTER page 12

Above: A September 2001 file photo of *Mad* reporter Fonebone while on assignment near the Blecchistani city of Plort.

Thousands Of High-School Sweethearts Prepare For Post-Graduation Breakup

Left: Jeff Reidel and Amy Pocoroba, one of the nation's soon-to-break-up couples.

WASHINGTON, DC—In a time-honored annual ritual, thousands of high-school seniors across the nation are cramming for final exams, trying on their graduation gowns, and preparing to break up with their longtime sweethearts.

"Amy is an amazing girl," said Lancaster (OH) High School senior Jeff Reidel, who next week is planning to break up with Amy Pocoroba, his girlfriend of three and a half years. "I know we swore we'd be together forever, but, like me, she's got a lot of exciting opportunities ahead of her, and it just wouldn't be fair to her to keep her tied down."

Brianna Milbank, 17, a senior at Eisenhower High School in Prescott, AZ, said she plans to break up with boyfriend Chris Keegan in mid-July.

"We've already got plans for a July 4

see BREAKUP page 6

Getting Mom Onto Internet A Sisyphean Ordeal

ROCHESTER, MN—Karen Widmar, 33, who for the past two months has been trying to teach her 60-year-old mother how to use the Internet, called the endeavor "a Sisyphean ordeal" Monday.

"Jesus Christ, you have no idea," said Widmar after yet another unsuccessful lesson. "Every single thing I show her, no matter how simple, totally freaks her out. She's still afraid to click on pictures because she doesn't know where it's going to take her."

Widmar said she introduced her mother Lillian to the Internet at her request.

"It's funny, I was always trying to get her interested so I could e-mail her," Widmar said. "Then, one day, she called me up and said she was watching *Today*, and they had a guest on who made potatoes, and

see MOM page 8

Right: Lillian Widmar attempts to e-mail her daughter.

NEWS

Bush Extremely Proud Of New Suit

see NATION page 4A

Unidentified Yowling Animal In Carrier Apparently Named Kiwi

see LOCAL page 9C

Life-Sized Cutout Of Brent Spiner Folded In Half, Placed In Dumpster

see LOCAL page 11C

STATshot

A look at the trends that shape your world.

THE ONION
VOLUME 38
ISSUE 22
$2.00 US
$3.00 CAN

the ONION®

VOLUME 38 ISSUE 30 | AMERICA'S FINEST NEWS SOURCE™ | 22–28 AUGUST 2002

NEWS

Ozzy Wins Tickets To Ozzfest

see PEOPLE page 10B

Tank Operator Wishes Buddies Back Home Could See Him Now

see WORLD page 3A

Heat Sworn At

see LOCAL page 2C

Fat Kid Calls Shirts

see LOCAL page 7C

STATshot

A look at the trends that shape your world.

How Are We Dressing Our Monkeys?

1. Whipped-cream bikini
2. Monocle, derby, and copy of *The New Yorker*
3. Jumpsuit emblazoned with NASA logo
4. In old monkey's hand-me-downs
5. Gorilla suit
6. Ninja (Halloween only)
7. Better than ourselves

THE ONION
VOLUME 38
ISSUE 30

$2.00 US
$3.00 CAN

God Promises 'Big Surprises' In Store For Hurricane Season

HOLLYWOOD, FL—The 2002 hurricane season will be packed with "big surprises, big windspeeds, and a big, big finish," God announced Monday at a press conference touting His fall schedule.

"Get ready for the biggest, wildest, most exciting hurricane season yet," God said. "You'll see all the 200 mph winds, all the flooding, all the overturned cars. As for what else you'll see—well, you'll just have to wait and see."

Though hurricane season officially began in June, God has not yet released any major storms in the Pacific or Atlantic theaters. A press release sent to the media by Benediction/Holmes-Morgan, the Lord's public-relations agency, did drop a few tidbits on what to expect in the coming months.

"As God enters His landmark 23,450,750th hurricane season, He finds Himself dealing with a larger and more diversified audience," the statement read

see GOD page 7

Above: The aftermath of a September 2000 flood in North Carolina. Inset: God.

Above: Former Virginia senator Chuck Robb loiters outside the U.S. Capitol.

Former Senator Still Hanging Around Capitol

WASHINGTON, DC—Former Virginia senator Charles Robb, ousted from Congress in the 2000 elections by Republican challenger George Allen, continues to hang around the Capitol building nearly two years later, sources reported Monday.

"I saw him again this morning," said Sen. Ted Stevens (R-AK), who served on various subcommittees with Robb during his 1989-2001 senate tenure. "As usual, he was leaning against a column by the front steps, smoking a cigarette. I tried to act like I didn't see him, but he flagged me down and started asking me all these questions about new legislation and 'what's been up with everybody.' It was so awkward."

While most ousted legislators land jobs in the private sector, go on the speaking circuit, or retire, Robb has struggled with the transition to post-senate life.

"Serving in Congress was

see SENATOR page 11

Dad Defends Purchase Of Bargain-Brand Cereal

Left: Showalter with two of his controversial purchases.

GOSHEN, IN—Calling his actions "sensible" and "how it's going to be from now on," Glen Showalter, a Goshen-area father of three, defended his unpopular decision to purchase bargain-brand breakfast cereals Monday.

"They're far cheaper than the name brands, and you can't tell me there's any difference in the taste," said Showalter, 41, holding a bag of Apple Zaps, a budget-priced Apple Jacks knockoff. "I can't think of a single reason to justify spending $2 more for the exact same product."

Showalter made the controversial decision at approximately 2 p.m. Sunday while grocery-shopping at Sav-A-Lot Foods on College Road. Noticing a cluster of cereals in plastic bags on the bottom shelf of the cereal aisle, Showalter was surprised to discover that they were significantly less expensive than their boxed counterparts.

"I couldn't believe I'd been shopping for groceries all those years and never noticed the bargain versions until then," Showalter said. "To think of all the money we could have saved. Actually, I don't want to—it's too painful."

see CEREAL page 6

NEWS

Laptop Guy At Coffee Shop Nine Times Out Of Ten

see LOCAL page 10B

Michelin Introduces Tires For Women

see PRODUCTWATCH page 8E

Animal Has Animal-Print Covering

see NATURE page 4D

Fake Leg Urinated Down

see LOCAL page 2B

STATshot

A look at the trends that shape your world.

THE ONION
VOLUME 38
ISSUE 33
$2.00 US
$3.00 CAN

the ONION®

VOLUME 38 ISSUE 33 | AMERICA'S FINEST NEWS SOURCE™ | 12–18 SEPTEMBER 2002

Bush Won't Stop Asking Cheney If We Can Invade Yet

THE IRAQ SITUATION

Left: Bush asks Cheney for the fourth time Tuesday.

WASHINGTON, DC—Vice-President Dick Cheney issued a stern admonishment to President Bush Tuesday, telling the overeager chief executive that he didn't want to hear "so much as the word 'Iraq'" for the rest of the day.

"I told him, 'Listen, George, I promise we're going to invade Iraq, but you have to be patient,'" Cheney said. "'We need a halfway plausible *casus belli*. You know that, George. Now, *stop bugging me* about it.'"

According to Cheney, for the past three weeks, Bush has been constantly asking if it's time to move troops into the Gulf region.

"George is calling me, he's following me around in the halls, he's leaving notes on my desk reminding me to let him know if I hear 'any news,'" Cheney said. "He just will not sit still. I actually have a permanent red mark on my shoulder on the spot where he comes up and taps me."

see IRAQ page 6

Second Birthday In A Row Ruined By Terrorism

Left: The birthday boy tries in vain to enjoy his special day.

HOBOKEN, NJ—In what threatens to be an annual ritual, Rob Bachman, born Sept. 11, 1973, braced himself Tuesday for yet another birthday ruined by the Sept. 11 terrorist attacks.

"My birthday's gonna suck for the rest of my life," Bachman said on the eve of his 29th birthday. "Every year, I'm going to want to go out and have fun, but it's always going to be inappropriate in light of the meaning of this most tragic of days."

Added Bachman: "Man, there's nothing quite like hitting the bars on the anniversary of the worst act of terrorism ever perpetrated on U.S. soil."

> **"My birthday's gonna suck for the rest of my life," Bachman said.**

Though Bachman will try to enjoy his "special day" as best he can, he said he is not

see BIRTHDAY page 8

Man Knows Just What He'd Say If He Met Christina Ricci

PITTSBURGH—Rick Hazell, a 29-year-old Pittsburgh liquor-store clerk and self-described "Christina Ricci nut," knows exactly what he would say if he were ever to meet the actress.

"Most people who approach her, especially guys, probably do the whole panting-fanboy thing, but I'd be totally cool about it," Hazell said. "First off, I'd definitely focus on her indie stuff, like *Buffalo '66* and The *Opposite Of Sex*, which I'm sure she'd appreciate since most people who say they're fans probably just want to talk about *That Darn Cat* and crap like that."

see RICCI page 11

Right: Hazell, who would be "totally cool about it" if he met Ricci (above).

NEWS

Religious Pamphlet Sat On

see LOCAL page 7D

Baby Found On Doorstep Moved To Neighbor's Doorstep

see LOCAL page 9D

Nantucket Poet Laureate Refuses To Apologize For Controversial Limerick

see ARTS page 3C

STATshot

A look at the trends that shape your world.

What Are We Gluing To The Governor Of Wyoming?

1. Legos
2. Bus transfer
3. Corn Nuts
4. Used DVD copy of *Joe Dirt*
5. Sign reading, "Kick Me, The Governor Of Wyoming"
6. Funny hillbilly beard
7. $175,000 in cattle-lobby contributions
8. The governor of Massachusetts

the ONION®

VOLUME 38 ISSUE 38 AMERICA'S FINEST NEWS SOURCE™ 17–23 OCTOBER 2002

FAA Considering Passenger Ban

WASHINGTON, DC—Seeking to address "the number-one threat to airline security," the Federal Aviation Administration announced Monday that it will consider banning passengers on all domestic and international commercial flights.

"In every single breach of security in recent years, whether it was an act of terrorism or some other form of crime, it was a passenger who subverted the safety systems on board the aircraft or in the terminal," FAA administrator Marion Blakey said. "Even threats that came in the form of explosives inside baggage were eventually traced back to a ticketed individual. As great a reve-

see FAA page 6

Bush On Economy: 'Saddam Must Be Overthrown'

WASHINGTON, DC—Amid growing concerns about the faltering stock market and deepening recession, President Bush vowed to tackle the nation's economic woes head-on Tuesday, assuring the American people that he "will not rest" until Saddam Hussein is removed from power.

"Our nation's economy is struggling right now," said Bush, delivering the keynote address at the National Economic Forum. "Our manufacturing base is weak, new home sales are down, and unemployment is up. Millions of our people are suffering. That is why I stand before you tonight and make this promise: Saddam Hussein *will* be stopped."

With the Dow regularly suffering triple-digit plunges and the Nasdaq hitting a six-year low of 1184.94 late last month, Bush used the speech as an opportunity to outline his plan for getting the economy back on track.

see ECONOMY page 8

Right: Bush addresses business leaders.

Goodwill Toy Section Most Depressing Thing Ever

Left: One of the Goodwill store's heartbreaking rejects.

SPENCER, IA—The toy section of the Fleet Road Goodwill, with its heartbreaking assortment of soiled, broken, bargain-priced playthings, depressed an estimated 20 shoppers Tuesday.

"Look at this one," said Spencer resident Bobbie Perrin, 43, gingerly picking up a grimy stuffed animal with her fingertips. "Judging from the 'Kennel Kritters' tag, it must be a knock-off of one of those Pound Puppies from the '80s, only I'm pretty sure those had legs."

"Oh my God, are those tomato-soup stains on its back?" asked Perrin, flinging the Kennel Kritter back into a large bin, where it landed between a plastic horse and a faded Parcheesi game board. "I thought those were spots."

The bin, whose items were priced at 50 cents each, also contained a chewed rawhide dog bone, a Rubik's Cube with the stickers peeled off and sloppily reapplied, a broken laser-pointer key chain, a nude Skipper doll, a deflated Minnesota Vikings plastic football, a Ziploc bag containing

see GOODWILL page 10

NEWS

Nelly Reiterates Sex-Liking Stance

see ENTERTAINMENT page 3B

Motorist Overwhelmed By Array Of Jerky Choices

see LOCAL page 1C

Corporate Brass Forced To Tolerate Tech Support Guy's Wolfman-Like Hair, Beard

see BUSINESS page 4E

STATshot

A look at the trends that shape your world.

THE ONION VOLUME 38 ISSUE 39
$2.00 US
$3.00 CAN

the ONION®

VOLUME 38 ISSUE 39 AMERICA'S FINEST NEWS SOURCE™ 24–30 OCTOBER 2002

63 Percent Of U.S. Implicated In New Scandal

WASHINGTON, DC—The Securities and Exchange Commission announced Tuesday that more than 63 percent of all U.S. citizens have been implicated in an illegal stock-dumping, the latest scandal to rock the nation's economy.

"It's staggering how far-reaching this is," SEC chairman Harvey Pitt said. "More than 175 million citizens from all walks of life are involved in one criminal imbroglio. Everybody from white-collar workers to grandmothers, boy-scout leaders, and the entire state of Delaware. Point a finger anywhere, and you have a better chance than not of hitting a guilty party."

According to the SEC, on Jan. 15, Jerome P. Lippman, vice-president of pharmaceutical giant Unocore Systems in Dallas, warned friends and business associates of a failed merger with Pfizer. The information was leaked by an as-yet-undetermined source, resulting in 98 percent of Unocore's stock being sold off on Jan. 16, one day prior to an official

see SCANDAL page 6

Above: Citizens implicated in the scandal conceal their faces on a New York City street Tuesday.

Sunken Oil Tanker Will Be Habitat For Marine Life, Shell Executives Say With Straight Face

HOUSTON, TX—The 1,080-foot, 300,000-ton oil tanker *Shell Global Explorer*, which sank off the coast of Newfoundland last month, will provide a welcome habitat for many diverse species of endangered marine life, Shell Oil Company executives announced with a straight face Tuesday.

"In its new resting place, far beneath the surface of the North Atlantic, the *Global Explorer* is host to countless fish and an infinite variety of marine vegetation," a press release from Shell read without a trace of irony. "A ship that once helped run life above the waves now houses life beneath them."

see TANKER page 10

Right: The new habitat, moments before sinking.

Left: Sweedlin spends a leisurely hour applying polish to her nails.

Nails, Hair Cared For Better Than Child

MOBILE, AL—In terms of time, money, and effort expended, local parent Kelly Sweedlin takes better care of her hair and nails than she does her 2-year-old daughter Porcia, the bank teller reported Tuesday.

"As a single mom, it's sometimes hard to squeeze in my manicures between work and everything else, but I make it a priority," Sweedlin, 26, told her daughter's daycare provider. "If I don't spend the time to really take care of them, who will?"

In spite of all the hard work required to grow a beautiful set of nails, Sweedlin calls it

see CHILD page 8

Bush On North Korea:
'We Must Invade Iraq'

Fashion Plate Smashed

Orange Alert Sirens To Blow
24 Hours A Day In Major Cities

JANUARY FEBRUARY MARCH APRIL MAY JUNE

U.N. Orders Wonka To Submit To
Chocolate Factory Inspections

White History Year Resumes

Report: Al-Qaeda May Be
Developing 'Dirty Soldier'

2003

Heroic Pit Bull Journeys 2,000 Miles To Attack Owner

Ashcroft Rejected By Newly Created Bride Of Ashcroft

LAPD Discovers Hidden Deformed Olsen Triplet

JULY AUGUST SEPTEMBER OCTOBER NOVEMBER DECEMBER

137 More Oil Wells Liberated For Democracy

Department Of Homeland Security Deputizes Real Mean Dog

Skywriter Leaves Suicide Note

NEWS

Merle Haggard Haggard

see PEOPLE page 7C

Grandma Knitting Escape Ladder

see LOCAL page 4D

Mormon Family Trying To Ignore Dog's Huge Boner

see FAITH page 11E

Ikea Manager Böring

see LOCAL page 2D

STATshot

A look at the trends that shape your world.

What's The Secret To Our Delicious Pancakes?

1. Seagull eggs
2. Batter aged minimum of three years
3. Pinch of concrete
4. Obsessive drive to out-pancake everyone else
5. Ganja butter
6. If I told you, the Order of Jemimans would kill me
7. "Soylent maple"

THE ONION
VOLUME 39
ISSUE 02
$2.00 US
$3.00 CAN

the ONION®

VOLUME 39 ISSUE 02 AMERICA'S FINEST NEWS SOURCE™ 23–29 JANUARY 2003

New Economy Wistfully Recalled As Tiny Dot-Com Promotional Object Found In Drawer

Left: The antHead.com promotional thingy.

SAN FRANCISCO—The "New Economy"—the Internet-driven business landscape once predicted to make "bricks and mortar" retailers obsolete—was wistfully recalled Monday, when a small dot-com promotional item was discovered in the junk drawer of former dot-commer Eric Noyce.

Noyce, 28, an associate vice-president of business development for Pets.com from August 1998 to December 2000, came across a small gadget emblazoned with "antHead.com" while searching for a corkscrew to open a $3 bottle of wine.

"Holy shit, check this out," said the minimum-wage-earning Noyce as he examined the slick-looking promotional

see DOT-COM page 11

Kim Jong Il Unfolds Into Giant Robot

Left: Kim Jong Il marches through the streets of Pyongyang.

PYONGYANG, NORTH KOREA—Responding to mounting pressure and increasingly confrontational rhetoric from the outside world, North Korean president Kim Jong Il unfolded into a 70-foot-tall, 62-ton giant robot Monday.

"The DPRK's nuclear program is very much its own business, as is its right to determine its own path of security," said Kim, his torso splitting along ventral seams as clusters of Taepo-Dong ICBMs rose from his shoulders. "Any attempt by Washington to decide our fate will surely result in a sea of fire being unleashed upon them."

As his arms and legs sheathed themselves in bullet-proof Mecha-Muscle telescoping outward from his chest, Kim reiterated his refusal to bow to international demands.

"Constant criticism from outside indicates mistrust of our promise to refrain from missile tests," said Kim, speaking over the mechanical shriek of wingblades sprouting from his back. "Only trust from the U.S. that we will keep our word can prevent World War III."

"The imperialist West is

see ROBOT page 10

Father Wants Only The Best For His Truck

PRINEVILLE, OR—Charles "Chuck" Maurer, a local lumberyard manager and father of two, wants only the very best for his 2002 Ford F150 extended-cab truck, the 41-year-old reported Monday.

"Growing up, my family didn't have much money," said Maurer, ignoring his son Cory's pleas to play catch. "There were lots of things we couldn't afford, that we had to make do without. But now that I make a good wage, I want my own truck to have all the things my dad's truck never had."

Since purchasing the F150 last April, Maurer has treated it to numerous small upgrades, including wheel covers, floor mats, radar detector, and sun shield, as well as costlier, factory-installed features such as anti-lock brakes, cruise control, and air bags.

Though he makes an effort to pay equal attention to the family's other vehicle, the 1994 Chevy Corsica his wife June uses to drive to work and pick up sons Cory, 12,

see TRUCK page 8

Right: Maurer, seen here with his wife and sons, is dedicated to being a good provider for his Ford F150.

NEWS

Heroic Turtle Dials Most Of 911

see LOCAL page 6B

Gondolier Ordered To Follow That Gondola

see WORLD page 5A

Plowshare Hastily Beaten Back Into Sword

see NATION page 3A

Porn Star XXX-hausted

see ARTS page 3E

STATshot

A look at the trends that shape your world.

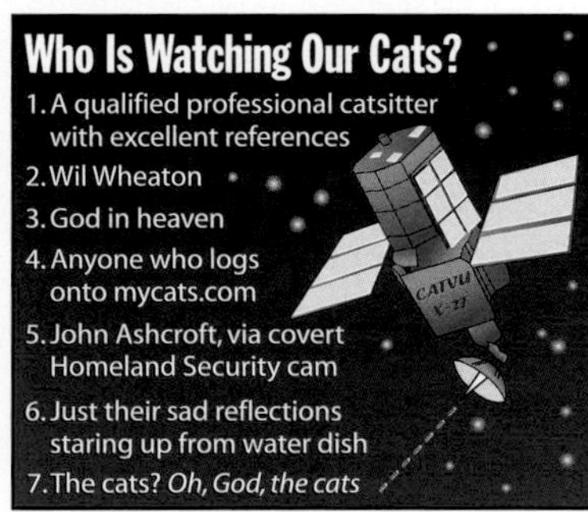

THE ONION VOLUME 39 ISSUE 04

$2.00 US $3.00 CAN

the ONION®

VOLUME 39 ISSUE 04 AMERICA'S FINEST NEWS SOURCE™ 6–12 FEBRUARY 2003

Yankees Ensure 2003 Pennant By Signing Every Player In Baseball

NEW YORK—With a week to go before pitchers and catchers report for spring training, the New York Yankees shored up their pitching, hitting, and defense Monday by signing every player in professional baseball.

"We'd like to welcome the entire roster of Major League Baseball into the Yankees family," said team owner George Steinbrenner, watching as the franchise's 928 newest additions held up their pinstripes at a Yankee Stadium press conference. "With these acquisitions, we are in position to finally nab that elusive 27th World Series title."

Sports reporters were not surprised by the move.

see YANKEES page 10

Right: Some of the New York Yankees' newest additions are introduced to the press.

North Dakota Found To Be Harboring Nuclear Missiles

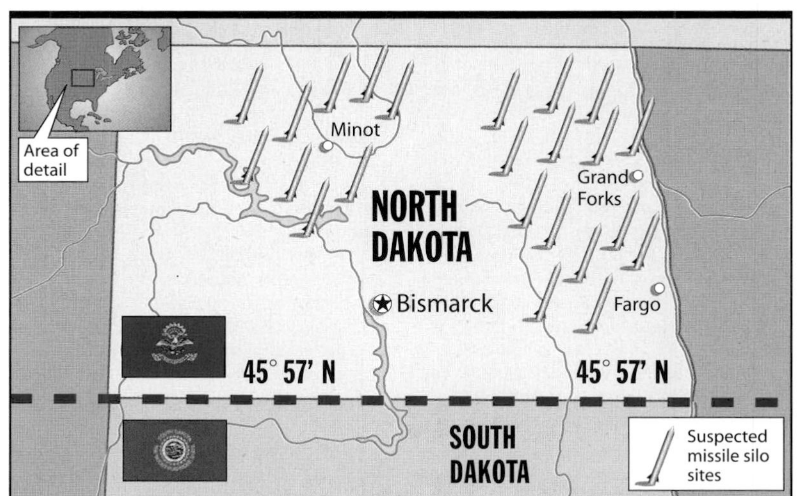

BISMARCK, ND—The stage was set for another international showdown Monday, when chief U.N. weapons inspector Hans Blix confirmed that the remote, isolationist state of North Dakota is in possession of a large stockpile of nuclear missiles.

see NORTH DAKOTA page 6

Below: Kofi Annan addresses the U.N. Security Council regarding the North Dakota situation.

Nation's Love Affair With *Lord Of The Rings* Threatening Its Relationship With *Star Wars*

LOS ANGELES—America's love affair with the J.R.R. Tolkien epic-fantasy saga *Lord Of The Rings*, a romance which has flowered ever since the 2001 release of the *Fellowship Of The Ring* film adaptation, has damaged the nation's long-term relationship with George Lucas' *Star Wars* saga, perhaps irreparably.

"When I first laid eyes on *Star Wars*, it was love at first sight," said Los Angeles comic-book-store proprietor Michael Janus, 33, who was just 8 when he encountered the film. "For the rest of that summer of '77, my life was *Star Wars*."

see LORD OF THE RINGS page 8

Above: Former *Star Wars* lovers Jim Cross and Peter Boehm get ready for the *Two Towers* premiere at a New York City theater.

NEWS

Chinese Man Still Writing 'Horse' On Checks

see WORLD page 11D

Pizza Hut Introduces New Meat Sympathizer's Pizza

see PRODUCTWATCH page 8E

Okay, TiVo Gets It, You Like Porn

see TELEVISION page 3B

Space Pen Explodes

see LOCAL page 9C

STATshot

A look at the trends that shape your world.

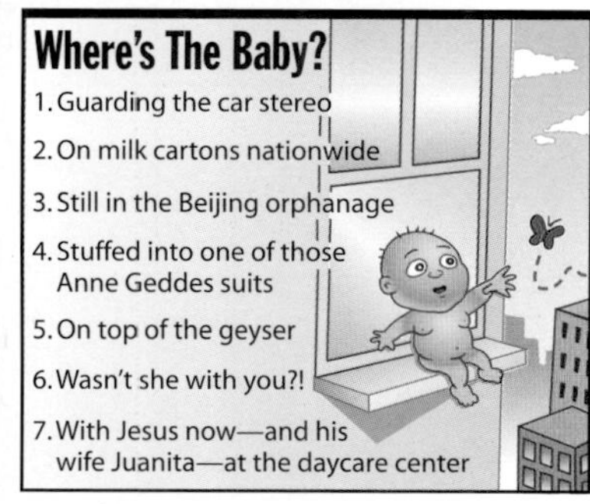

THE ONION VOLUME 39 ISSUE 06
$2.00 US $3.00 CAN

the ONION®

VOLUME 39 ISSUE 06 | AMERICA'S FINEST NEWS SOURCE™ | 20–26 FEBRUARY 2003

Above: Iraq's Saddam Hussein and Kentucky's Travis Lee Butler hone their cloud-shooting skills.

Iraq, Kentucky Vie For World Shooting-Into-The-Air Supremacy

COON HOLLOW, KY—In a rivalry that shows no signs of abating, Iraq and Kentucky remain locked in a bitter struggle for world shooting-into-the-air supremacy.

"I'll be damned if any Muslim's gonna beat the great state of Kentucky at what she do best," said Coon Hollow resident Billy Joe Dupree, 39, in between bouts of firing his shotgun skyward Monday. "We been shootin' into the air for all kinds 'a reasons since they was a Kentucky, and that's a fact. Why, even my wall-eyed cousin Mavis could outshoot one o' them Muslims, and she ain't hardly finished the fifth grade."

Aziz Hourani, 24, of Baghdad, took exception to Dupree's claims of air-shooting superiority.

"Such is our anger at the Great Satan that we send many bullets into the air every day," said Hourani, raising his AK-47 carbine and firing several rounds. "No one can surpass us at shooting upwards—and certainly not the Americans."

Though worlds apart geographically

see SUPREMACY page 10

Women Now Empowered By Everything A Woman Does

OBERLIN, OH—According to a study released Monday, women—once empowered primarily via the assertion of reproductive rights or workplace equality with men—are now empowered by virtually everything the typical woman does.

"From what she eats for breakfast to the way she cleans her home, today's woman lives in a state of near-constant empowerment," said Barbara Klein, professor of women's studies at Oberlin College and director of the study. "As recently as 15 years ago, a woman could only feel empowered by advancing in a male-dominated work world, asserting her own sexual wants and needs, or pushing for a stronger voice in politics. Today, a woman can empower herself through actions as seemingly inconsequential as driving her children to soccer practice or watching the Oxygen network."

Klein said that clothes-shopping, once considered a mundane act with few sociopolitical implications, is now a bold

see WOMAN page 8

Terrorism 'Not Likely' Cause Of Fire At Local Laundromat

EUCLID, OH—Homeland Security Secretary Tom Ridge assured the American people Monday that terrorism was "not likely a factor" in the fire that damaged a downtown Euclid laundromat Sunday afternoon.

"At this time, there is nothing to suggest that yesterday's Sudsy Duds fire was the work of a terrorist group, al-Qaeda or otherwise," Ridge said. "The FBI is conducting a thorough investigation into the cause, but thus far, there is no evidence indicating that this was a terrorist strike against our nation."

Euclid Fire Chief Andrew Donnelly, who has been working closely with state and federal officials in the wake of the blaze, offered his theory on its cause.

"I'm guessing water flooded into the basement, causing a misfire in an oil furnace that sparked a minor explosion," Donnelly said. "Groundwater probably seeped through the

see FIRE page 6

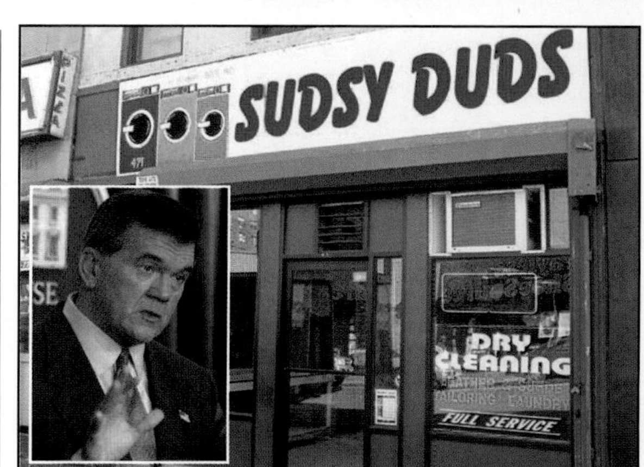

Right: The site of the blaze feared to be the work of al-Qaeda. Inset: Ridge answers reporters' questions.

the ONION®

VOLUME 39 ISSUE 11 | AMERICA'S FINEST NEWS SOURCE™ | 27 MARCH–2 APRIL 2003

NEWS

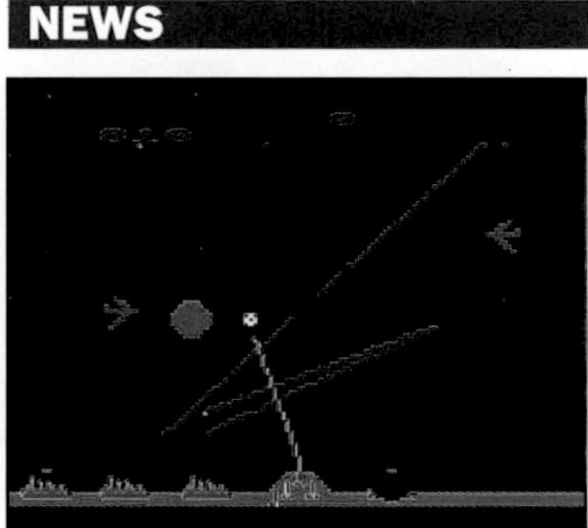

U.S. Takes Out Key Iraqi Bases In Midnight Raid

see WORLD page 10A

New Bomb Capable Of Creating 1,500 New Terrorists In Single Blast

see WEAPONRY page 3A

U.S. Draws Up Plan For Post-War Transitional Dictatorship In Iraq

see WORLD page 7A

STATshot

A look at the trends that shape your world.

SPECIAL COVERAGE: THE WAR ON IRAQ

Bush Bravely Leads 3rd Infantry Into Battle

Left: A weary Bush marches through enemy territory near the Iraq-Kuwait border.

IRAQ-KUWAIT BORDER—As the U.S. Army's 3rd Infantry Division began its ground assault on Iraq Monday, President Bush marched alongside the front-line soldiers, bravely putting his own life on the line for his country by personally participating in the attack.

"Bush is the real deal, and when he talks about fighting for freedom, he means it," said Pvt. Tom Scharpling, 21. "He'd never ask one of us grunts to take any risks for our country that he wasn't willing to take

> "George would never ask this nation's citizens to do anything he was unwilling to do himself."

see BUSH page 10

Dead Iraqi Would Have Loved Democracy

CASUALTIES

BAGHDAD, IRAQ—Baghdad resident Taha Sabri, killed Monday in a U.S. air strike on his city, would have loved the eventual liberation of Iraq and establishment of democracy, had he lived to see it, his grieving widow said.

"Taha was a wonderful man, a man of peace," his wife Sawssan said. "I just know he would have been happy to see free elections here in Iraq, had that satellite-guided Tomahawk cruise missile not strayed off course and hit our

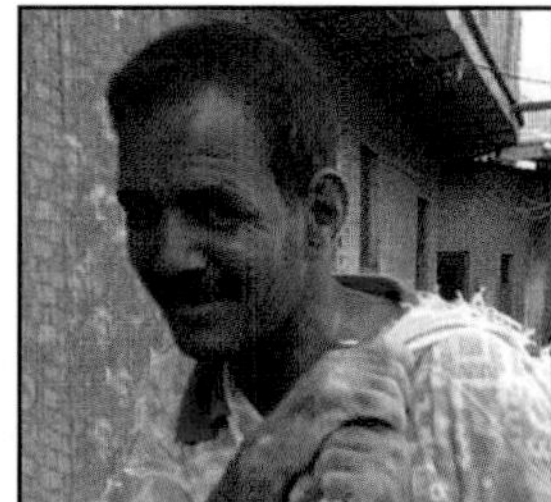

Above: Taha Sabri

see IRAQI page 7

DIPLOMACY

U.S. Forms Own U.N.

Above: The U.S. and U.S. delegations.

see U.S.U.N. page 10

Local Mom Whips Up Some Of Her Famous War Pie

Left: Sensenbrenner prepares the war pie's tasty crust.

HOMEFRONT

TIPTON, IA—With the invasion of Iraq underway, Janet Sensenbrenner, 54, a Tipton homemaker and mother of three, responded Tuesday by whipping up some of her famous war pie.

"Any time there's an invasion, I get down the mixing bowls and bake a sweet, delicious war pie," Sensenbrenner said. "In fact, I usually go ahead and make two because the first one always disappears in a flash. A U.S. military action in the Middle East just wouldn't be the same without it."

A self-described "amateur Martha Stewart," Sensenbrenner said her favorite way to serve the pie is oven-warm with a scoop of vanilla ice cream. She noted, however,

see WAR PIE page 8

NEWS

DVD Contains 87 Minutes Of Previously Unseen Movie

see ENTERTAINMENT page 5C

Football Fan Wears Off-Season Body Paint

see LOCAL page 8E

NBC Moves War To Thursdays After *Friends*

see TELEVISION page 10D

Grandfather Clocked

see LOCAL page 7E

STATshot

A look at the trends that shape your world.

Least-Visited Memorials

1. The Redenbacher Monument
2. Tomb of the Unknown Person
3. Dodi Al Fayed Memorial (behind Princess Diana Memorial)
4. The Grenada Veterans Memorial Railing
5. The Stomachache Quilt

THE ONION VOLUME 39 ISSUE 12
$2.00 US
$3.00 CAN
0 74470 94595 6 12

the ONION®

VOLUME 39 ISSUE 12 AMERICA'S FINEST NEWS SOURCE™ 3–9 APRIL 2003

Saddam Speech Suspiciously Mentions Nelly Song From Last Summer

LANGLEY, VA—The CIA announced Monday that it suspects Saddam Hussein's latest televised address was pre-recorded, pointing to its suspiciously dated reference to Nelly's "Hot In Herre," a rap hit from the summer of 2002.

"For the enemy invaders of Iraq, it soon will get truly hot in here," Hussein said in the speech, which was televised worldwide Monday. "No amount of clothing removal will be sufficient to withstand the fiery inferno that awaits them on the battlefield."

Many U.S. officials have speculated that Saddam may have been killed or injured

see SADDAM page 10

Above: In a message believed to be pre-taped, Saddam warns the U.S. about rising heat levels in Iraq.

Bush Thought War Would Be Over By Now

WASHINGTON, DC—Following a 12th consecutive day of fighting, a puzzled and frustrated President Bush confided to military advisors Monday that he "really figured the war would be over by now."

"It's been almost two weeks," said Bush, commander-in-chief of the 255,000 U.S. troops currently in the Persian Gulf. "What's taking so long? Will the Iraqi regime just topple, already?"

Though Bush has repeatedly declined making public comment on the expected duration of the war, in private he has expressed annoyance with the way the invasion is "dragging on."

"I knew the war would require courage and fortitude on the part of American people," Bush said. "What I didn't know was that it would go on for days and days and

see WAR page 10

Right: Bush endures another tedious meeting with (left to right) Vice-President Dick Cheney, CIA director George Tenet, and Chief of Staff Andrew Card.

Soup-Kitchen Volunteers Hate College-Application-Padding Brat

Left: Malveaux, who is passionately dedicated to getting into Stanford.

SEATTLE—Volunteers at the Pike Street Salvation Army have grown to hate college-application padder Justin Malveaux, 17, sources reported Monday.

"It's not that Justin doesn't work hard, because he does," said Karla Perkins, 44, weeknight coordinator at the downtown Seattle soup kitchen. "He does whatever you ask of him, and he's pleasant and polite, always complimenting everyone. Still, I can't stand the little Stanford-application-padding fucker."

Perkins met Malveaux in February, when the Bellingham West High School junior submitted a résumé and cover letter requesting a volunteer position.

"Justin said he wanted to help those less fortunate than him, and also to get his volunteering out of the way so he can concentrate on AP classes

see BRAT page 8

NEWS

Independent-Minded Cat Shits Outside The Box

see PETS page 14C

McCain Gives Up JCPenney Catalog-Modeling Job

see WASHINGTON page 7B

Man Puts Philandering Days Ahead Of Him

see LOCAL page 2E

STATshot

A look at the trends that shape your world.

Why Are We Moving To Austin?

1. Other guys in band wanted to
2. Hoping to land part in *Slacker 2: The Next Generation*
3. Sick of Chapel Hill
4. Heard great things about the fish tacos
5. Didgeridoo teacher moved there
6. Fake ID only works at Emo's
7. Amanda

HACKY SACKS

THE ONION VOLUME 39 ISSUE 20
$2.00 US
$3.00 CAN

the ONION®

VOLUME 39 ISSUE 20 AMERICA'S FINEST NEWS SOURCE™ 29 MAY–4 JUNE 2003

Terrifying Bill Passed During NBA Playoffs

WASHINGTON, DC—With the nation safely distracted by the NBA playoffs, Congress passed the terrifying Citizenship Redefinition And Income-Based Relocation Act of 2003 with little opposition Monday.

"This piece of legislation is essential, both for more efficient implementation of the New American Ideal and to give law enforcement the broad discretionary powers necessary to enforce certain vital civil and behavioral mandates," said U.S. Sen. Lamar Alexander (R-TN), addressing an empty press room Sunday, midway through game four of the NBA Eastern Conference finals. "We are confident that

see BILL page 6

Above: Dallas Mavericks fans cheer on their team while Senate Majority Leader Bill Frist (left) announced the passage of the terrifying new law.

Bassist Unaware Rock Band Christian

Above: The oblivious Rolen (left) and his Pillar Of Salt bandmates.

ORLANDO, FL—Brad Rolen, the new bassist for Pillar Of Salt, remains oblivious to the fact that he is in a Christian rock band, sources reported Tuesday.

"Pillar's great," said Rolen, 22, who is unaware of his bandmates' devotion to Christ, despite playing on such songs as "Wade In The Water," "Eternal Life," and "Kiss Of The Betrayer." "We rock really heavy and hard, but we've got a positivity that you don't see in too many bands these days. I've only been with these guys for three months, but I feel like it's the perfect fit for me."

Rolen, who joined the Orlando-based band in March after responding to a "bassist wanted" ad in a local newspaper, said he was attracted to Pillar Of Salt for its music, which he calls "really intense and powerful," as well as its impressive stage show.

"I was between bands after Junkhorse broke up," Rolen said. "I went to check them out live and was just blown away. They had this awesome Black Sabbath-type stage set, with

see BASSIST page 7

Casino Has Great Night

ATLANTIC CITY, NJ—A beaming Donald Brant, general manager of Bally's Atlantic City, reported that the casino had "an unbelievable night" Monday, cleaning up at the blackjack table, on the slot machines, and elsewhere.

"Man, we were on fire all night," Brant said. "It seemed like every time a casino patron pulled that slots lever, it came up a loser. Whenever somebody told the blackjack dealer to hit on 12, they drew a 10. We could do no wrong."

By the end of the night, the casino walked away a major winner, up $515,274.

"I had a sense that we were doing pretty well," Brant said. "So I checked around with the pit bosses, and it turned out that nearly all the dealers and croupiers were way, way ahead. It was amazing. A night like that only comes along five, six times a week, tops."

While most players are content to focus on one or two games, the casino participated in every available coin-operated machine and table game,

see CASINO page 9

Above: A Bally's blackjack dealer shows off a tiny portion of the casino's winnings.

NEWS

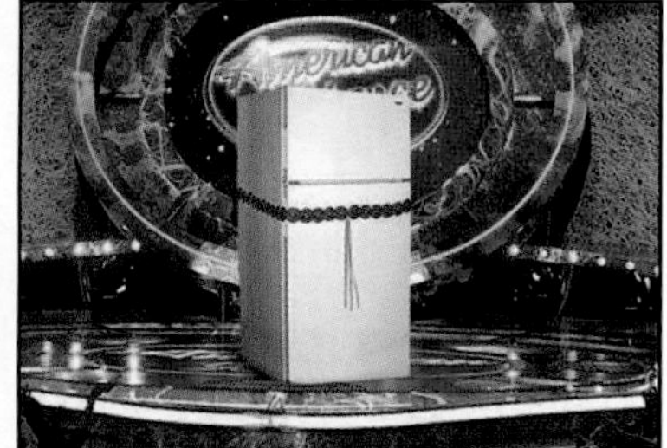

Refrigerator Wins *American Appliance*

see TELEVISION page 9C

New Lover Features 30 Percent More Cock

see LOCAL page 4E

Child In Stroller Stares At Man In Wheelchair

see LOCAL page 11E

Date Reeks Of Febreeze

see LOCAL page 7E

STATshot

A look at the trends that shape your world.

THE ONION VOLUME 39 ISSUE 22

$2.00 US
$3.00 CAN

the ONION®

VOLUME 39 ISSUE 22 AMERICA'S FINEST NEWS SOURCE™ 12–18 JUNE 2003

Gen. Tommy Franks Quits Army To Pursue Solo Bombing Projects

WASHINGTON, DC—Gen. Tommy Franks, commander of American forces in the wars in Iraq and Afghanistan, announced plans Monday to step down as U.S. Central Command chief to focus on solo bombing projects.

"The years I've spent with the Army have been amazing, and we did some fantastic bombing," said Franks at a Pentagon press conference. "But at this point, I feel like I've taken it as far as I can. It's time for me to move on and see what I can destroy on my own."

Franks said he is eager to seek out new challenges.

"Obviously, the U.S. Army is a first-rate organization," Franks said. "I mean, when we were on, no one could touch us. The '91 Gulf tour, the '95 Bosnia campaign... we kicked some serious ass. But it's pre-

see FRANKS page 6

Above: Gen. Franks tells reporters, "It's time for me to see what I can destroy on my own."

Five-Disc Jazz Anthology Still Unopened

LOUISVILLE, KY—A five-disc jazz-anthology box set, lovingly assembled to give novices an appreciation and understanding of the uniquely American art form, remains unopened nearly two years after its purchase, sources reported Monday.

"Yeah, I should really give that a spin one of these days," said Marc Bergkamp, 29, who in July 2001 purchased *Ken Burns Jazz: The Story Of American Music* for $69.99. "I just haven't had the time to sit down and go through it. I was thinking about putting it on this weekend while I clean my apartment, but jazz isn't really cleaning music. I need something a little more rocking, like The White Stripes or something."

Bergkamp purchased the deluxe box set after watching a portion of an episode of the 10-part, 19-hour *Ken Burns Jazz* documentary on PBS.

"I'd always meant to buy more jazz, but every time I went record shopping, there'd be something I wanted more," Bergkamp said. "Finally, after seeing the thing on

see BOX SET page 8

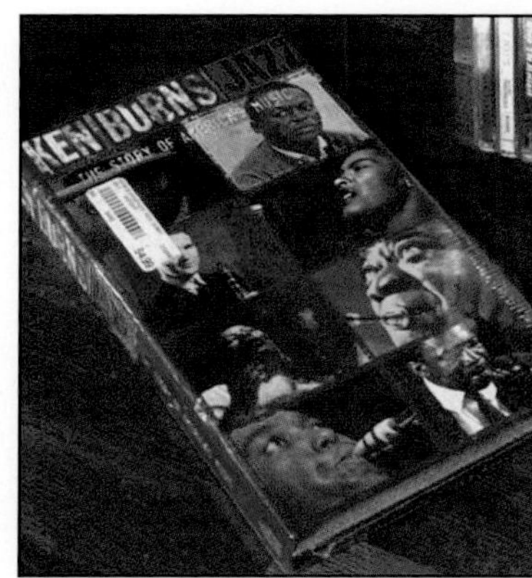

Above: The unopened box set.

Above: Rogowski and the 1990 Subaru mocked by Stefano (top) and Banks (bottom).

Troubled Teens Mock Social Worker's Car

CHICAGO—Despite facing socioeconomic inequities that put them at a lifelong disadvantage, troubled inner-city teens at Marcus Garvey High School are fond of openly mocking their social worker's "shitty car," sources reported Monday.

Social worker Gary Rogowski, 32, works with disadvantaged youths on Chicago's South Side through the neighborhood Second Start program. His car, a 1990 Subaru Loyale station wagon that, as Rogowski puts it, "has seen better days," is a constant source of derision among the teens he has dedicated his professional life to helping.

"Last week, Mr. Rogowski was all up in my face about

see TEENS page 7

NEWS

Man Forgets He Has Infant Strapped To Back

see PARENTING page 10D

8-Year-Old Obviously Packed Own Lunch

see LOCAL page 1C

Strom Thurmond Finally, Finally Dies

see NATION page 3A

Yard Sale Reeks Of Divorce

see LOCAL page 5C

STATshot

A look at the trends that shape your world.

THE ONION
VOLUME 39
ISSUE 25
$2.00 US
$3.00 CAN

the ONION®

VOLUME 39 ISSUE 25 | AMERICA'S FINEST NEWS SOURCE™ | 3–9 JULY 2003

Bush Asks Congress For $30 Billion To Help Fight War On Criticism

WASHINGTON, DC—Citing the need to safeguard "America's most vital institutions and politicians" against potentially devastating attacks, President Bush asked Congress to sign off Monday on a $30 billion funding package to help fight the ongoing War On Criticism.

"Sadly, the threat of criticism is still with us," Bush told members of Congress during a 2 p.m. televised address. "We thought we had defeated criticism with our successes in Afghanistan and Iraq. We thought we had struck at its very heart with the broad discretionary powers of the USA Patriot Act. And we thought that the ratings victory of Fox News, America's News Channel, might signal the beginning of a lasting peace with the media. Yet,

see BUSH page 9

Right: Bush unveils his sweeping new anti-criticism initiative.

Bowling-Alley Owner Wants TV Ad To Look 'More *Matrix*-y'

Left: Dieber in a rough cut of the *Matrix*-inspired ad.

MENASHA, WI—After seeing the rough cut of his new TV commercial, Bob Dieber, 46, owner of Menasha Lanes, told the 30-second spot's creator to make it look "more *Matrix*-y," sources reported Tuesday.

"Yeah, it definitely has the *Matrix* thing going like I wanted, but I can't help feeling like it could have more," Dieber said of the ad, slated to air on Appleton/Green Bay UPN affiliate WACY-32 during upcoming *Judge Hatchett* telecasts. "There needs to be more special effects or something. Like maybe a bowling ball flying through the air in slow motion. That'd be a pretty funny twist."

The ad, as scripted, features Dieber bowling in a dark trenchcoat similar to the one worn by Laurence Fishburne's *Matrix* character Morpheus. After bowling a strike, Dieber turns to the camera, strikes a martial-arts pose, and says, "At

see MATRIX page 6

Minister Constantly Mentioning Teenage Son's Virginity

PENSACOLA, FL—Much to his son Paul's chagrin, minister Donald Genzler takes every possible opportunity to proudly inform members of Faith United Presbyterian Church that the 16-year-old is still a virgin, "unspoiled by sins of the flesh," sources reported Tuesday.

"As it says in the second book of Timothy, 'Now flee from youthful lusts, and pursue righteousness, faith, love, and peace with those who call on the Lord from a pure heart,'" said Genzler from the pulpit Sunday. "Young people, I urge you to stand tall against the temptation of premarital sex, just as my own son Paul has done."

Seated in the third row, a mortified Paul slid low in the pew and buried his face in his hymnal, hoping not to be spotted.

"It's not easy to grow up in this confusing world, where everyone tells you to 'just

see MINISTER page 7

Right: A proud Genzler sermonizes about his son (inset).

NEWS

King Latifah Returns For Wife

see PEOPLE page 8C

Old El Paso Introduces Emergency Taco Kit

see BUSINESS page 3E

Scissors Kills Paper, Rock; Turns Blade On Self

see LOCAL page 6D

Rear End Justifies Means

see LOCAL page 5D

STATshot

A look at the trends that shape your world.

33
THE ONION
VOLUME 39
ISSUE 33
$2.00 US
$3.00 CAN
0 74470 94595 6

the ONION®

VOLUME 39 ISSUE 33 | AMERICA'S FINEST NEWS SOURCE™ | 28 AUGUST–3 SEPTEMBER 2003

Mad Scientist's Plot Thwarted By Budget Cuts

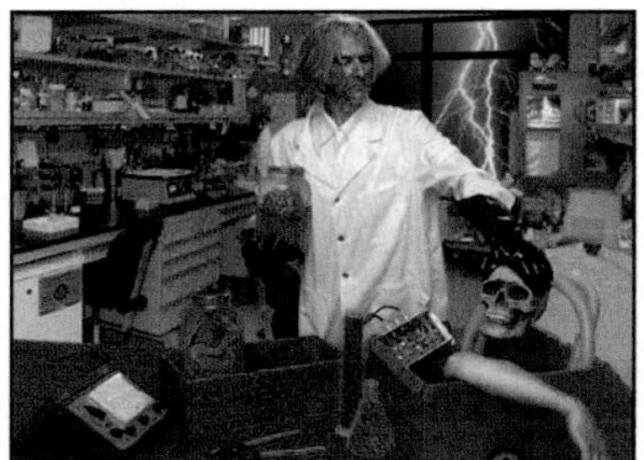

Left: Mortis packs up the lab he was forced to surrender.

UPTON, ME—In response to recent budget cuts, the National Science Foundation has reduced grants to individual recipients, including those of megalomaniacal researcher Dr. Edward Mortis of Brookhaven Laboratories.

"My positronic raygun was nearly complete," said Mortis at a press conference Tuesday. "With one gigagram of destructonium [a rare element mined from a meteor belt that passes Earth once every 29 years], I could have *ruled the world*!"

Days before the window of destructonium-mining opportunity closed, the "ignorant fools" at the NSF slashed Mortis' Armageddon Project funding by 90 percent. The cut in funding forced the mad scientist to halt work on his raygun, and set back his plans for world domination indefinitely.

see MAD SCIENTIST page 12

No One Makes It To Burning Man Festival

GERLACH, NV—The Burning Man festival, a prominent artistic and countercultural event that draws tens of thousands of people to the Nevada desert annually, is in danger of cancellation this week because "no one had their shit together enough to even make it," organizers said Tuesday.

"Jesus Christ, this is pathetic," said event coordinator Ethan Moon as he angrily gestured toward the empty Black Rock Desert basin expanse, known as the playa. "We've been promoting this thing all year. You can't start panhandling quarters for gas the week before the festival and expect to make it here in time, man."

Moon listed some of the most common no-show excuses, among them oversleeping, forgetting to request time off work, faulty van-borrowing arrangements, a shortage of ochre body-paint,

see BURNING MAN page 6

Above: The empty Burning Man festival grounds.

Graphic Artist Carefully Assigns Ethnicities To Anthropomorphic Recyclables

Above: Characters from the culturally sensitive Department of Sanitation leaflet.

PHILADELPHIA—Freelance graphic artist Chrissie Bellisle carefully delineated the ethnicities, genders, and sexual orientations of the RecyclaBuddies, a group of talking recyclables created for a public-service leaflet she submitted to the Department of Sanitation Monday.

"I assumed the Department of Sanitation would want the recyclables in its new leaflet to represent not only Philadelphia's recycling procedures, but also its diverse ethnic make-up," said Bellisle, flipping through some initial sketches in her studio. "It turned out to be quite a challenge."

Above: Bellisle in her studio.

As the purpose behind establishing racial and cultural identities for the talking waste was one of celebration, not

see ARTIST page 8

the ONION®

VOLUME 39 ISSUE 34 | AMERICA'S FINEST NEWS SOURCE™ | 4–10 SEPTEMBER 2003

NEWS

Bird's Nest 65 Percent Cigarette Butts

see NATURE page 4E

Local Band Finds Great Photo For Flier

see LOCAL page 12B

Woman Never Making Recipe From Back Of Gatorade Bottle Again

see LOCAL page 5B

Bush Calls Front Seat

see NATION page 3C

STATshot

A look at the trends that shape your world.

How Are We Organizing The Closet?

- **10%** By percentage polyester
- **16%** Alphabetically, by item's use
- **8%** With a cleansing fire
- **20%** Promoting most-deserving stuffed animals
- **19%** Cutting down backing wall, opening space into living room
- **27%** Locking child inside, hoping he tidies up

'Six Flags Killer' Still At Large, Say Souvenir-Bedecked Police

Above: Police launch a search of the Yukon Territory.

GURNEE, IL—Local authorities continue to search Gurnee's Great America theme park for a criminal dubbed "The Six Flags Killer," souvenir-laden police reported Monday.

"If you have any information that might lead to the capture of this vicious killer, please contact us immediately," a button-covered Gurnee Police Captain Jack Moynihan said at a press conference held in Carousel Plaza. "We have officers standing by on the Whizzer."

"Oh," Moynihan added. "And if you know where to get one of those blinking hats we've been seeing around, let us know."

Police began their search on Aug. 26, when ride operator Zack Lipton, 16, found a decapitated body behind the Fiddler's

see KILLER page 8

Above: One of four Tampa-area Tanzanias.

Tanzania Loses Name To Tanning-Salon Chain

TALLAHASSEE, FL—The country formerly known as the United Republic of Tanzania has lost the use of its name to Tampa-based Tanzania Tanning Salons, the Florida Supreme Court ruled Monday.

see TANZANIA page 6

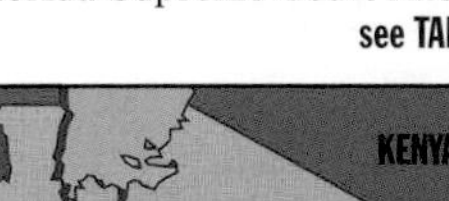

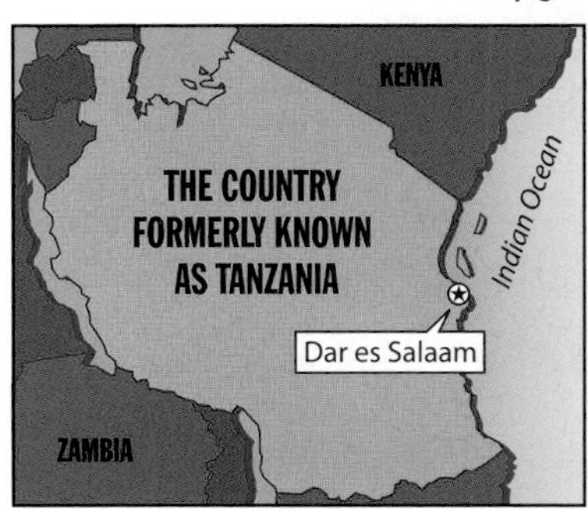

Entire Fourth-Grade Class Hates Jeremy Halcote

MUNCIE, IN—The entire fourth-grade class, everyone from Ashley Amberson to Corey Zoellner, hates Jeremy Halcote, sources at John Tyler Elementary School revealed Tuesday.

"The popular kids, the brains, even the bad kids who spend noon hour behind the groundskeeper's shed—they all hate that little pig," Indiana University sociologist Marian Newcomb told reporters Tuesday. "The consensus? Jeremy Halcote is just plain gross."

Halcote, who runs really slow, always looks sloppy, and forgets his schoolwork at home practically every other day, has been despised for as long as anyone at the school can remember.

"Last year, in Mrs. Swanson's class, Chad Vanderhof was in the bathroom with Jeremy Halcote," student Ivan Kinard said. "Well, Chad pushed Jeremy, and Jeremy's hand went right into the toilet. But Jeremy didn't even take his hand out! He just kept it in there for, like, forever."

"He started crying, too,"

see HALCOTE page 10

Above: Miss Grant's fourth-grade class, including the hated Halcote (circled).

NEWS

Sweatshop Laborer's Child Loves Her Irregular *Finding Nemo* Sweatshirt

see WORLD page 3B

Drug-Sniffing Dog Develops Taste For Bit-O-Honeys

see LOCAL page 11D

Alabama Man Wins Personal Victory Over Gun Control

see LOCAL page 7D

STATshot

A look at the trends that shape your world.

the ONION®

VOLUME 39 ISSUE 35 AMERICA'S FINEST NEWS SOURCE™ 11–17 SEPTEMBER 2003

FBI Discontinues Witness Protection Parade

WASHINGTON, DC—FBI director Robert S. Mueller III announced Monday that, due to logistical complications and a lack of interest among participants, the annual Witness Protection Parade will be cancelled "for the foreseeable future."

"The feeling among organizers, participants, and sponsors was that the John Smith Memorial Witness Protection Parade—though a lot of fun—presented too many headaches for everyone involved," Mueller said in a press conference Monday.

The parade, scheduled this year for Oct. 4, has been a major event in Washington ever since the creation of the federal witness-protection program 30 years ago, and

see PARADE page 6

Right: Participants in last year's Witness Protection Parade.

Relations Break Down Between U.S. And Them

WORLD FOCUS

WASHINGTON, DC—After decades of antagonism between the two global powers, the U.S. has officially severed relations with Them, Bush administration officials announced Tuesday.

"They have refused to comply with the U.S. time and time again," Defense Secretary Donald Rumsfeld said, following failed 11th-hour negotiations Monday night. "It's always unfortunate when diplomacy fails, but we could not back down. We have to be ready to fight back, in the name of freedom, against all of Them at once, if necessary."

Rumsfeld added: "If They're not with us, They're against us."

see RELATIONS page 8

Right: Rumsfeld announces that the U.S. has severed ties with Them.

Above: Hoagland, who one day will die.

Impending Mortality Influences Area Senior's Purchasing Habits

INDEPENDENCE, MO—Grace Hoagland's purchasing habits are increasingly influenced by her sense of impending mortality, sources close to the 73-year-old reported Tuesday.

"I offered to buy Mom a new fan, because hers is 10 years old and only works on 'low,'" daughter Nancy Seely said. "She said, 'Oh, don't bother. New things are only wasted on an old goat like me.' Like she's in the grave already."

Although she remains in good health and has a comfortable pension, Hoagland sees her golden years as a time to severely restrict her purchasing habits. This means sleeping on a sagging mattress with coils poking through the padding, watching a television with a drifting picture, and manually opening her heavy garage door.

see SENIOR page 10

NEWS

Stripper Not In Phone Book

see LOCAL page 3B

Vacationing Family Visits World's Biggest Asshole

see TRAVEL page 9E

God Grants John Ritter's Wish To Meet Johnny Cash

see OBITUARIES page 5H

Pancakes 'Famous'

see NATION page 14C

STATshot

A look at the trends that shape your world.

the ONION®

VOLUME 39 ISSUE 36 | AMERICA'S FINEST NEWS SOURCE™ | 18–24 SEPTEMBER 2003

D.C. Once Again Murder Capital, Mayor Brags

WASHINGTON, DC—Washington Mayor Anthony Williams bragged Monday that, after nearly a decade, the city has resumed its rightful place as the U.S. murder capital.

"Hey, it only makes sense," said Williams at a press conference Monday. "We're the capital of the United States, so we should also be the capital of murders. But the thing is, if you're *from here*, you know

see D.C. page 8

Right: Williams boasts of Washington's dangers.

OUR CULTURE

History Of Rock Written By The Losers

BOSTON—Fifty years after its inception, rock 'n' roll music remains popular due to the ardor of its fans and the hard work of musicians, producers, and concert promoters. But in the vast universe of popular music, there exists an oft-overlooked group of dedicated individuals who devote their ample free time to collecting, debating, and publishing the minutiae of the rock genre. They are the losers who write rock's rich and storied history.

"The city of Boston is about more than just Mission Of Burma or Galaxie 500, and it's certainly about more than Boston or The Cars," said 28-year-old Dana Harris, a rock historian. "The scene in Boston is full of history, but it's also vibrant right now. Someone needs

see ROCK page 6

Left: Dana Harris spends a Friday night cataloging his CD collection on a computer spreadsheet.

FDA Approves Sale Of Prescription Placebo

Science & Health

WASHINGTON, DC—After more than four decades of testing in tandem with other drugs, placebo gained approval for prescription use from the Food and Drug Administration Monday.

"For years, scientists have been aware of the effectiveness of placebo in treating a surprisingly wide range of conditions," said Dr. Jonathan Bergen of the FDA's Center for Drug Evaluation and Research. "It was time to provide doctors with this often highly effective option."

In its most common form, placebo is a white, crystalline substance of a sandy consistency, obtained from the evaporated juice of the Saccharum officinarum plant. The FDA has approved placebo in doses ranging from 1 to 40,000 milligrams.

The long-awaited approval will allow pharmaceutical companies to market placebo in pill and liquid form. Eleven major drug companies have developed placebo tablets, the first of which, AstraZeneca's Sucrosa, hits shelves Sept. 24.

"We couldn't be more thrilled to finally get this wonder drug out of the labs and into consumers' medicine cabinets," said Tami Erickson, a spokeswoman for AstraZeneca. "Studies show placebo to be

see PLACEBO page 10

NEWS

New Hallmark Line Addresses Israeli-Palestinian Conflict

see BUSINESS page 7B

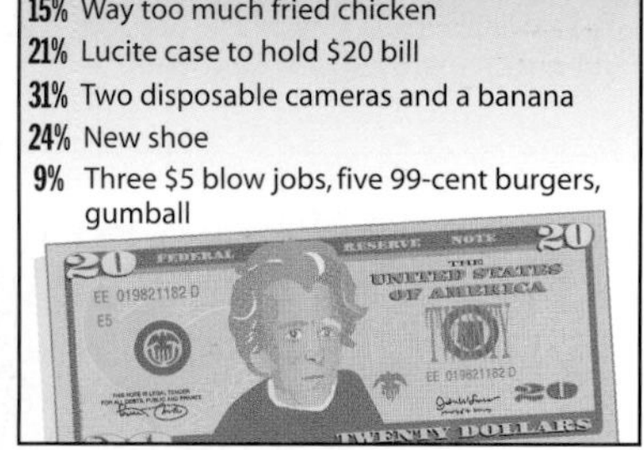

SeaWorld Whales Demand 10 Percent Chum Increase

see BUSINESS page 13B

Some Lady Weeping In Dairy Aisle

see LOCAL page 4C

STATshot

A look at the trends that shape your world.

What Are We Buying With The New $20 Bill?

15% Way too much fried chicken
21% Lucite case to hold $20 bill
31% Two disposable cameras and a banana
24% New shoe
9% Three $5 blow jobs, five 99-cent burgers, gumball

41
THE ONION
VOLUME 39
ISSUE 41
$2.00 US
$3.00 CAN
0 74470 94595 6

the ONION®

VOLUME 39 ISSUE 41 AMERICA'S FINEST NEWS SOURCE™ 23–29 OCTOBER 2003

Muscleman Put In Charge Of World's Fifth-Largest Economy

Above: The muscleman who was chosen to run California.

SACRAMENTO, CA—Political observers are struggling to understand exactly how, on Oct. 7, Arnold Schwarzenegger, an Austrian-born, movie-star muscleman with no political experience, was elected to govern the state of California, the world's fifth-largest economic region.

"We're a bit baffled as to exactly how this happened," said David Gergen, director of the Center for Public Leadership at Harvard's Kennedy School of Government. "Poll results show that the strongman received 1.3 million more votes than the next candidate—that much is clear. We just can't determine precisely why people believed that the bodybuilder was qualified to lead the

see MUSCLEMAN page 6

Above: Ashcroft says the scapegoat is "out there."

CIA-Leak Scapegoat Still At Large

WASHINGTON, DC—A White House administration official who can be blamed for leaking the identity of CIA officer Valerie Plame to the press remains at large, White House officials announced Monday.

"We are doing everything in our power to see that the scapegoat is found and held accountable," President Bush said. "We will not stop until he—or she—is found. Believe me, nobody wants to see the blame placed squarely on the shoulders of a single person, and photos of that individual in every newspaper in the country, more

see SCAPEGOAT page 8

Video-Store Clerk Helpless To Prevent *Charlie's Angels* Rental

BERWICK, OH—In spite of his efforts, Video Village clerk Brad Hersley was unable to prevent yet another rental of *Charlie's Angels* Tuesday.

"It happened again," said Hersley, shaking his head as he watched a customer leave the store with a copy of the 2000 blockbuster. "I can recommend better movies until I'm blue in the face, but inevitably, everyone gravitates toward *Charlie's Angels*."

Hersley said he's been attempting to prevent rentals of the big-screen version of the popular '70s TV show since its release in June 2001.

"You can't imagine how many times I've gone through the same exact experience," Hersley said. "I'm running out of creative ways to say '*Charlie's Angels* sucks, so put it down and try again' in a way that the manager [Dave Lennox] won't get on my ass for."

"I'm helpless to stop them from bringing that into their homes," Hersley said. "What's more, I'm actually aiding them. Do you know how that makes me feel?"

After working at Video Village for almost two years, Hersley said he is confident that, if asked, he could recommend a

see CLERK page 10

Above: Hersley (right) reluctantly rents *Charlie's Angels* to yet another customer.

the ONION®

VOLUME 39 ISSUE 42 AMERICA'S FINEST NEWS SOURCE™ 30 OCTOBER–5 NOVEMBER 2003

NEWS

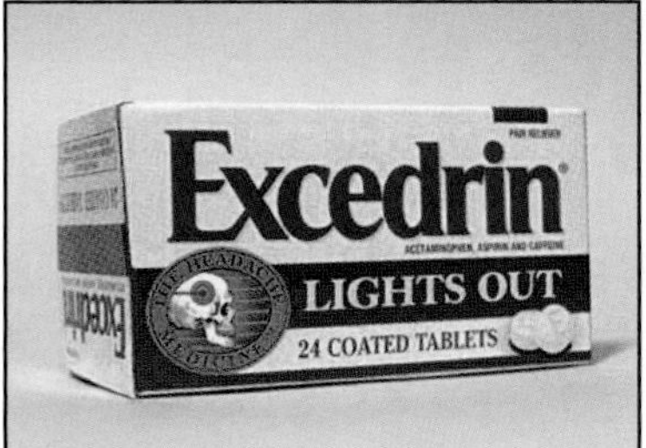

New Excedrin 'Lights Out' Kills You Dead On The Spot

see BUSINESS page 11E

Moral Compass Lost In Woods

see LOCAL page 7B

Non-Crime-Fighting Dog Takes Bite Out Of Couch

see LOCAL page 2B

Understudy Overacting

see ENTERTAINMENT page 11E

STATshot

A look at the trends that shape your world.

THE ONION VOLUME 39 ISSUE 42 $2.00 US $3.00 CAN

Ridiculous Small-Business Plan Encouraged By Friends

MISSOULA, MT—Due in large part to the encouragement of her so-called friends, 34-year-old Karen Sabin quit her steady job to make and sell homemade gourmet dog biscuits out of her home, the former hospital receptionist told reporters Monday.

Above: Sabin's friends encourage her terrible idea.

"People love gourmet foods," said Sabin, describing the thought behind her half-formed business plan. "It only makes sense that dogs would, too. Don't they deserve to have their taste buds tickled? There's a huge untapped market for high-end dog treats made with natural ingredi-

see PLAN page 8

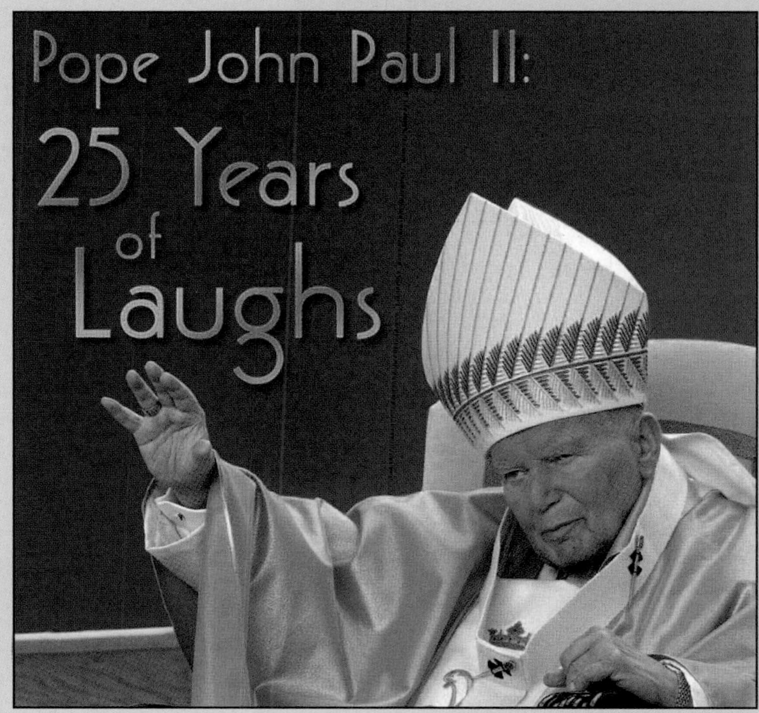

VATICAN CITY—As Pope John Paul II enters his 26th year as pontiff, the world is stopping to reflect on the legendary funnyman's career as one of the most influential performers in modern history. Standing staunchly against contraception and women's equality right through the turn of the 21st century, the pope and his quirky, deadpan comic persona still entertain audiences around the world.

Revered by multiple generations for his weird and wonderful wit, the 83-year-old pontiff is perhaps the best-known stand-up alive today. Throughout an

see POPE page 10

'Well, *You* Try To Reconstruct Iraq,' Says U.S. Defensive Dept.

WASHINGTON, DC—Responding to recent criticism of reconstruction efforts in Iraq, the U.S. Defensive Department released a statement to the public Monday suggesting that perhaps *they* could do better, since they're obviously so smart.

"Well, it looks like you American people have figured it all out, then," the statement read in part. "There's no need for the old government to do anything, because the citizens know just how to handle this whole reconstruction-of-Iraq thing. Well, go ahead! If it's so simple, and if you're so smart, then what's stopping you? Come on."

"Oh, gosh!" the statement continued.

see IRAQ page 12

Left: U.S. soldiers in Basra reconstruct Iraq, while you do nothing but criticize.

the ONION®

VOLUME 39 ISSUE 43 AMERICA'S FINEST NEWS SOURCE™ 6–12 NOVEMBER 2003

NEWS

Ladykiller Gets Life Sentence

see LOCAL page 12E

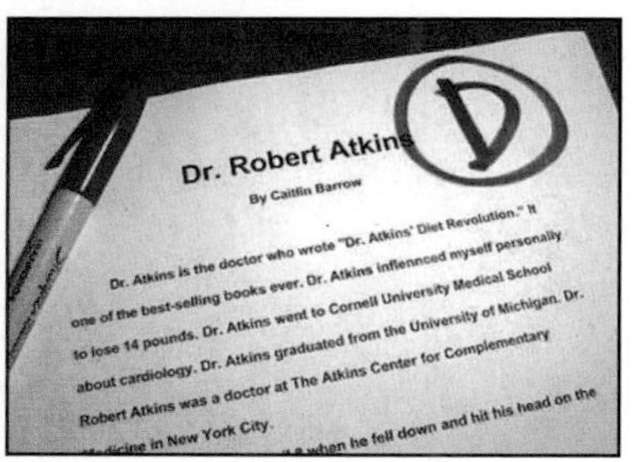
Dr. Robert Atkins D

By Caitlin Barrow

Dr. Atkins is the doctor who wrote "Dr. Atkins' Diet Revolution." It
one of the best-selling books ever. Dr. Atkins influenced myself personally
to lose 14 pounds. Dr. Atkins went to Cornell University Medical School
about cardiology. Dr. Atkins graduated from the University of Michigan. Dr.
Robert Atkins was a doctor at The Atkins Center for Complementary
Medicine in New York City.
when he fell down and hit his head on the

Cheerleader Given A 'D'

see LOCAL page 14E

Random Attack Restores Man's Faith In Inhumanity

see WORLD page 5C

Cheese Spill Cleaned Up With Nacho

see LOCAL page 19E

STATshot

A look at the trends that shape your world.

THE ONION VOLUME 39 ISSUE 43

$2.00 US $3.00 CAN

Family Unsure What To Do With Dead Hipster's Possessions

LOUISVILLE, KY—Five weeks after the death of her 26-year-old hipster son Kent, Enid Lowery announced that the family faces a difficult task in figuring out what to do with his many unusual possessions.

Kent Lowery (1977-2003)

"I just can't believe how much stuff Kent collected over the years," said Lowery Tuesday. "There's a poster for some movie called *Urgh!*, stacks of empty Quisp cereal boxes, at least five old lamps that don't work, and a slew of little plastic toys. Obviously, all these things meant something to Kent—but *what*? And *why*?"

A part-time English tutor and bassist for the local band Extra Moist, Kent died in a car accident Sept. 27. Overwhelmed with grief, his family members in nearby Bedford only mustered the strength to visit his apartment last week, where they were overwhelmed once again, this time by Kent's dense accumulation of miscellany.

Assisted by her husband Thomas and her daughter Regina Panziel, Lowery set

see HIPSTER page 6

Above: Lowery and Panziel among Kent's belongings.

Above: Abraham said he's sure he mentioned his work in films like *Shacking Up* (inset).

Energy Secretary Just Assumed Cabinet Knew He Did Porn Films In The '80s

WASHINGTON, DC—Addressing shocked fellow cabinet members, Secretary of Energy Spencer Abraham said Tuesday that he had assumed everyone knew about his roles in numerous 1980s pornographic films.

"I just figured people knew about the porno," Abraham said, shrugging. "I never got any flak about it, so I didn't think it was a big deal."

A former U.S. senator from Michigan who was appointed Energy Secretary by President Bush in 2001, Abraham said he has never denied that he performed in more than 50 erotic videos between 1984 and 1987.

"It *feels* like I mentioned it to everyone," Abraham said. "I can't remember the specific circumstances, but I'm positive I talked about it. If some people didn't know, maybe that's because they weren't around when it was discussed. Or else

see PORN page 10

Americans Demand Increased Governmental Protection From Selves

NEW YORK—Alarmed by the unhealthy choices they make every day, more and more Americans are calling on the government to enact legislation that will protect them from their own behavior.

"The government is finally starting to take some responsibility for the effect my behavior has on others," said New York City resident Alec Haverchuk, 44, who is prohibited by law from smoking in restaurants and bars. "But we have a long way to go. I can still light up on city streets and in the privacy of my own home. I mean, legislators acknowledge that my cigarette smoke could give others cancer, but don't they care about me, too?"

"It's not just about Americans eating too many fries or cracking their skulls open when they fall off their bicycles," said Los Angeles resident Rebecca Burnie, 26. "It's a financial issue, too. I spend all my money on trendy clothes and a nightlife that I can't afford. I'm $23,000 in debt, but the credit-card companies keep letting me spend. It's obscene that the government

see PROTECTION page 8

NEWS

Celebrity 'Caught' Smoking

see ENTERTAINMENT page 11C

Burger King Hat Put In Deep Fryer

see LOCAL page 7E

Locksmith Brings Along Boombox To Play *Mission: Impossible* Theme

see LOCAL page 4E

Maid Frenched

see LOCAL page 12E

STATshot

A look at the trends that shape your world.

How Are We Cooking The Goose?

- 12% Stuffed with smaller geese
- 18% Drunk on Beaujolais Nouveau
- 24% Getting recipe off back of goose box
- 10% Atop engine of Ford F-250
- 11% With SCIENCE!
- 25% In front of other geese, to serve as an example

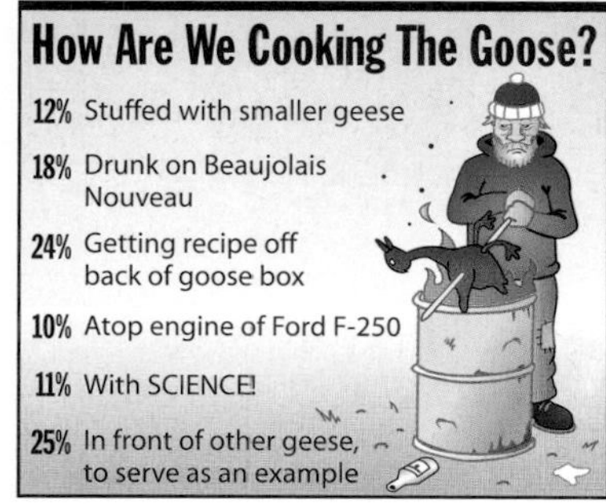

THE ONION VOLUME 39 ISSUE 49
$2.00 US
$3.00 CAN

the ONION®

VOLUME 39 ISSUE 49 AMERICA'S FINEST NEWS SOURCE™ 18 DEC. 2003–7 JAN. 2004

Christmas Brought To Iraq By Force

BAGHDAD, IRAQ—On almost every corner in Iraq's capital city, carolers are singing, trees are being trimmed, and shoppers are rushing home with their packages—all under the watchful eye of U.S. troops dedicated to bringing the magic of Christmas to Iraq by force.

"It's important that life in liberated Iraq get back to normal as soon as possible," said Deputy Defense Secretary Paul Wolfowitz at a press conference Monday. "That's why we're making sure that Iraqis have the best Christmas ever—something they certainly wouldn't have had under Saddam Hussein's regime."

To that end, 25,000 troops from the 3rd Armored Cavalry Regiment and 82nd Airborne Division have been deployed. Their

see CHRISTMAS page 6

Right: U.S. soldiers instruct an Iraqi to tell Santa what he wants for Christmas.

Senate Carpool 'Forgets' To Pick Up Feingold Again

Left: Feingold waits outside his house for a ride to work.

WASHINGTON, DC—U.S. Sen. Russ Feingold (D-WI) was forced to find an alternate means of transportation to work Monday, because his Senate carpool once again "forgot" to pick him up.

"Did we forget Feingold again?" Sen. Lisa Murkowski (R-AK) asked. "Gee, I don't know how that happened. I guess we were running late and just flaked on it. Hmm, same thing happened last week."

Feingold and Murkowski, along with senators Chuck Hagel (R-NE), Bill Nelson (D-FL), and Dick Durbin (D-IL), comprise the ride-sharing carpool formed three years ago to split the costs of commuting and reduce fuel waste and air pollution.

see CARPOOL page 10

So-Called Obese Pets Held To Unrealistic Body Standards

CHICAGO—To the casual eye, Tippy might appear to be a regular Labrador. He loves sunbathing at the park, watching squirrels, and getting loads of attention from passersby.

But Tippy is not a normal dog. By veterinarians' standards, he is 65 pounds overweight.

A closer examination of Tippy's body reveals a rounded abdomen, thick limbs, and a fleshy neck and back. And, unlike dogs seen on television and in magazines, Tippy does not have a discernible waistline or ribcage.

"I don't care if people say he's chubby," said Tippy's owner Katherine Mathers, gently scratching the dog's protruding belly. "So what if he doesn't look like the dog in the Iams commercial? What's more important: having a perfect body or being happy? I love him whether he's 25, 50, or even 150 pounds overweight. In fact, I think he's the cutest dog in the world."

"Yes, you are!" said Mathers, waving the

see PETS page 8

Right: Tippy and Katherine Mathers enjoy a day at the park.

Some Dork Brought In To
Address Civics Class

Jesus Demands Creative Control Over Next Movie

Bush Vows To Pay Closer Attention
To Needs Of Non-Presidents

JANUARY FEBRUARY MARCH APRIL MAY JUNE

Scientists Abandon AI Project
After Seeing *The Matrix*

Department Of Libel:
Drew Carey Killed A Guy
And Paid To Cover It Up

Work Begins On Clinton
Presidential DVD Library

2004

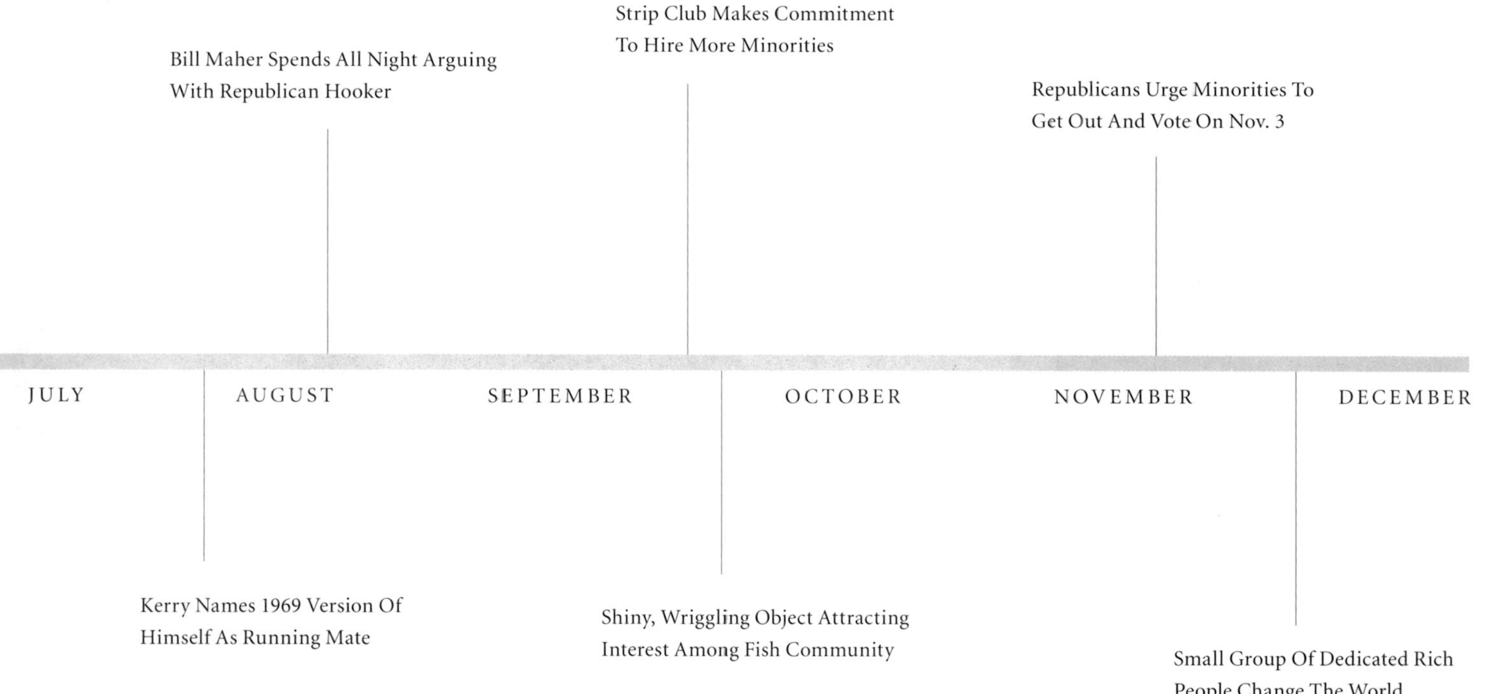
Strip Club Makes Commitment To Hire More Minorities
Bill Maher Spends All Night Arguing With Republican Hooker
Republicans Urge Minorities To Get Out And Vote On Nov. 3
JULY
AUGUST
SEPTEMBER
OCTOBER
NOVEMBER
DECEMBER
Kerry Names 1969 Version Of Himself As Running Mate
Shiny, Wriggling Object Attracting Interest Among Fish Community
Small Group Of Dedicated Rich People Change The World

NEWS

Child's Last Steps Captured On Video

see FAMILY page 14E

Woman With Amazing Rack Told She Has Beautiful Eyes

see BUSINESS page 4C

Gun Owner Ready For Them

see LOCAL page 4B

Coin Flip Disputed

see LOCAL page 6B

STATshot

A look at the trends that shape your world.

04
0 74470 94595 6
THE ONION
VOLUME 40
ISSUE 04
$2.00 US
$3.00 CAN

the ONION®

VOLUME 40 ISSUE 04 | AMERICA'S FINEST NEWS SOURCE™ | 29 JANUARY–4 FEBRUARY 2004

Above: Bush says he will "put an end to the current lack of honesty and compassion in Washington."

Bush 2004 Campaign Pledges To Restore Honor And Dignity To White House

BOSTON—Addressing guests at a $2,000-a-plate fundraiser, George W. Bush pledged Monday that, if re-elected in November, he and running mate Dick Cheney will "restore honor and dignity to the White House."

"After years of false statements and empty promises, it's time for big changes in Washington," Bush said. "We need a president who will finally stand up and fight against the lies and corruption. It's time to renew the faith the people once had in the White House. If elected, I pledge to usher in a new era of integrity inside the Oval Office."

Bush told the crowd that, if given the opportunity, he would work to reestablish

see BUSH page 11

Study:

Most Self-Abuse Goes Unreported

BOULDER—According to a study released Tuesday by the University of Colorado sociology department, approximately 95 percent of self-abuse cases in the U.S. go unreported.

"As shocking as it may seem, unreported incidents of self-abuse number in the billions," said Dr. Henry Cracklin, director of the study. "This isn't just the plight of teenage boys and truck drivers. Self-abuse affects both genders and all ages. Nevertheless, a great majority of victims suffer the abuse in silence."

The study's results, obtained through five years of surveys and interviews, indicate that millions of Americans have publicly acknowledged involvement in a self-abusive relationship. Yet the study finds that unreported abuse victims comprise an alarming 87 percent of the female population and 99.6 percent of males.

"In many cases, the self-abuse occurs repeatedly over the course of a lifetime, with the victims believing themselves powerless to break the cycle of shame, embarrassment, and self-loving," Cracklin

see ABUSE page 9

Concert Ruined By Guy Enjoying Himself

CHICAGO—Brian Grant, 24, reported that a rock concert he attended at the Empty Bottle Saturday was ruined by 35-year-old music fan Daryl Froemer's enthusiasm.

"I was trying to enjoy [New York-based rock group] Oneida, but it was totally impossible because [Froemer] was making a spectacle of himself," Grant said. "I couldn't even pay attention to the band. Halfway through the set, I had to leave."

"I go out to a bar to have a good time, and I can't because there's some jackass racing around in circles and waving his beer bottle in the air," Grant added. "I mean, he was even jumping up and down during the mid-tempo songs. Come on! It's not the '90s anymore. This isn't grunge."

In addition to dancing, Froemer reportedly pounded the stage "like it was on fire," sang along when he knew the lyrics, yelled out the names of songs he wanted to hear, and repeatedly attempted to enter into a dialogue with the band.

"Every time the singer asked us a question, he was the first one to yell back," Grant said. "I don't mind the occasional 'Yeah' or 'Woo,' but this guy was shouting after every song, whistling, and asking them how their amps were. If he hadn't been so annoying, I would have been embarrassed for him."

see CONCERT page 9

Right: Froemer has a good time, to the dismay of concertgoers like Grant (inset).

NEWS

Michael Jackson Hires Magical Anthropomorphic Giraffe As Defense Lawyer

see NATION page 8C

Parent Takes Out $100 Bill In Front Of Wide-Eyed 7-Year-Old

see FAMILY page 13E

Vibrator Left On All Night

see LOCAL page 4B

STATshot

A look at the trends that shape your world.

Top Notes Left By Roommates

25% Borrowed your diaphragm

12% Your parents stopped by to take me out to dinner

32% Totaled your car—your part of phone bill was $47.35

14% Wanna fuck? J/K! Do you, though?

17% Someone called—either Barry's dead, or they buried your dad

THE ONION
VOLUME 40
ISSUE 05
$2.00 US
$3.00 CAN

the ONION®

VOLUME 40 ISSUE 05 AMERICA'S FINEST NEWS SOURCE™ 5–11 FEBRUARY 2004

New Anger-Powered Cars May Revolutionize The Way We Drive

DETROIT—With gas prices approaching $2 per gallon in some areas and gridlock on the rise, Detroit's three major automakers are stepping up development of their newest brainchild: the anger-powered car.

"By drawing a significant percentage of its motive power from the unbridled temper of the American motorist, the new anger-powered car will change, or at least take mechanical advantage of, the way Americans drive," General Motors vice-chairman Robert A. Lutz said. "We plan to have these furiously efficient machines careening down America's highways, byways, and sidewalks within two years."

see CARS page 10

Right: The Chevrolet Tantrum, one of the new road-rage-fueled vehicles.

Democrats Somehow Lose Primaries

WASHINGTON, DC—In a surprising last-minute upset, all seven Democratic presidential hopefuls somehow lost the Democratic primaries Tuesday.

"While it's true that the Democratic Party has been struggling to find a strong voice, you can imagine our surprise when

ELECTION 2004

results indicated that John Kerry, Howard Dean, Wesley Clark, Joe Lieberman, and John Edwards all failed to carry a single primary," American Research Group political analyst Dick Bennett said late Tuesday. "Oh, and Al Sharpton and Dennis Kucinich, too."

Primaries were held in Delaware, Missouri, Arizona, Oklahoma, and South Carolina, with no single Democratic candidate coming in higher than second place.

see PRIMARIES page 6

Coworkers Dying To Tell Man He's Going To Be Fired

Left: Tendulkar (front) and coworkers.

RAPID CITY, SD—Employees at Reynolds Business Machines are dying to tell sales representative Mark Tendulkar that he is about to be fired, sources reported Tuesday.

"I was out with [sales manager] Frank Lascowicz last Thursday, and he let slip that Tendulkar's cubicle would be free. It took some free rounds, but I got it out of him: Mark's out on Feb. 15," sales representative Jeff Wildner said. "Mark is such a total dick, and so incompetent, I don't know how I'm going to be able to keep it from him that long."

Wildner said it's not his place to break the news to Tendulkar, no matter how much he would love to.

"I'm just going to have to wait until the boss axes him," Wildner said. "But the writing's definitely on the wall for ol' Tendulkar."

Tendulkar has worked at Reynolds since 1999, but according to fellow employees,

see FIRED page 8

NEWS

Fox News Problem Solvers In Way Over Their Heads

see LOCAL page 5B

Penis Enlargement Pills Tested On Dog

see PETS page 7E

Martha Stewart Witness Grilled After Being Marinated Overnight

see NATION page 10C

STATshot

A look at the trends that shape your world.

the ONION®

VOLUME 40 ISSUE 07 | AMERICA'S FINEST NEWS SOURCE™ | 19–25 FEBRUARY 2004

WAR ON TERROR

Osama Bin Laden Found Inside Each Of Us

WASHINGTON, DC—Defense Secretary Donald Rumsfeld announced Tuesday that Osama bin Laden, prime suspect in the Sept. 11 attacks on the World Trade Center and the Pentagon, has "at long last been found."

"For more than two years, we combed the Middle East looking for bin Laden," Rumsfeld said. "Frankly, it was starting to be an embarrassment. You can imagine our surprise when we finally found him hiding deep inside the darkest recesses of each and every one of our souls."

Since toppling the Taliban regime in 2001, U.S. forces in Afghanistan had searched for bin Laden primarily along the rugged Afghan-Pakistani border, but overlooked that place inside every one of us that has ever raised his voice in anger or turned away from someone in need.

"We were so busy tracking the remaining members of the Taliban regime and freezing al-Qaeda assets that we

see OSAMA page 6

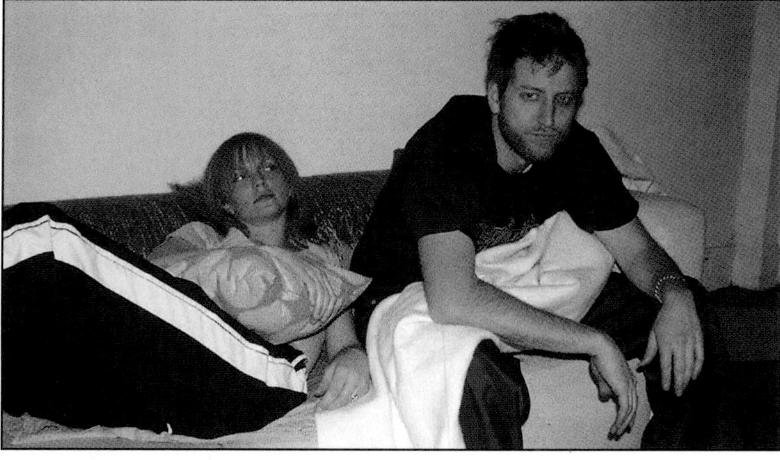

Above: Hayter with his former ex-girlfriend Peterman.

Hungover Couple Unaware They Broke Up Last Night

MINNEAPOLIS—Area couple Gene Hayter and Amy Peterman spent most of Sunday tenderly helping each other nurse massive hangovers, unaware that they had broken up in a bitter, alcohol-fueled rage during the night.

"Man, we must've really tore it up, that's all I can say," Hayter said, his voice raw from Jack Daniel's, cigarettes, and, unbeknownst to him, shrieked accusations of infidelity. "I woke up on Amy's couch, of all places, with a beer bottle in my hand and this terrible feeling, like I wanted to cry

see COUPLE page 8

Kerry Makes Whistle-Stop Tour From Deck Of Yacht

Above: Kerry waves down to a crowd of supporters.

LANCASTER, PA—Democratic front-runner Sen. John Kerry (D-MA) began a seven-day, eight-state whistle-stop tour Monday, addressing a group of Frigidaire factory workers from the all-teak deck of his 60-foot luxury motor cruiser.

see KERRY page 10

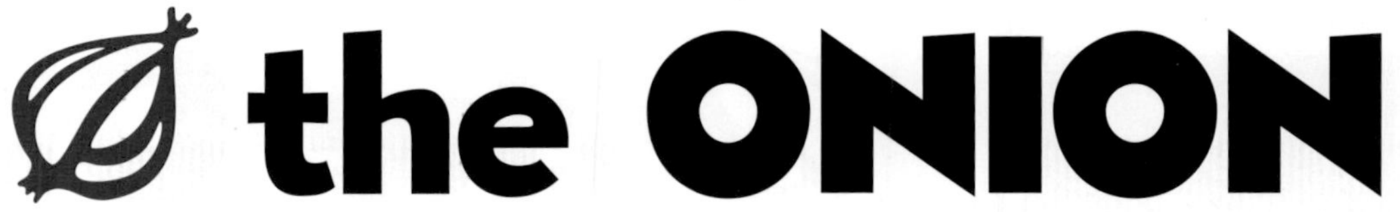

VOLUME 40 ISSUE 11 AMERICA'S FINEST NEWS SOURCE™ 18–24 MARCH 2004

Rumsfeld Hosts No-Holds-Barred Martial Arts Tournament At Remote Island Fortress

FANG ISLAND—U.S. Secretary of Defense Donald Rumsfeld has opened his fortified island headquarters to participants in his second no-holds-barred martial arts tournament, the enigmatic mastermind announced Monday.

"Warriors of the world, hear me," said Rumsfeld, seated on the onyx throne overlooking the fighting arena at the island's central volcano, surrounded by a phalanx of exotic but murderous beauties and his seven-foot-tall guard Omarra. "I declare the Eagle Fist all-styles, hand-to-hand combat world championship open once more. For the next 10 days, the world's mightiest fighters will come together here at Fang Island to compete for a prize of

$1 million and the post of Associate Secretary Of Full-Contact Defense!"

Rumsfeld then declared the tournament open by symbolically shattering a block of

see TOURNAMENT page 10

Above: Rumsfeld's Fang Island headquarters.

Best Man Has No Idea Why He Was Picked

GREENSBORO, NC—Although he has had a cordial relationship with officemate Karl Harrison for almost two years, Jeff Ashland reported Monday that he has no idea why he was asked to be the best man at Harrison's wedding in June.

"It's an honor, I suppose," Ashland said from his cubicle at Whitehead Consulting. "I just wish I knew why it fell to me. Karl went to college just down the road, and he's lived in Greensboro for five years or so. He must have met at least a few other guys during all that time, right? But *I'm* the one he chooses to be his right-hand man on the biggest day of his life?"

Harrison asked Ashland to be his best man on Mar. 12, the same day he publicly announced his engagement to his girlfriend of four years, Tracy Newman. Ashland said he had trouble feigning the joy expected of someone assuming such an honor.

"Karl came up to me with this big grin on his face, so I figured his business card was picked out of the fishbowl at the Gumbo Pot again," Ashland said. "But he told me he'd proposed to his girlfriend the night before. As I was congratulating him, trying desperately to remember Tracy's

Above: Ashland, the best-man-to-be.

name, he dropped the bomb. He said it'd be 'awesome' if I'd be his best man. At first I thought he was making one of his non-funny jokes, but he was serious."

Ashland said he felt he had no choice but to accept the invitation.

see BEST MAN page 8

Citizens Form Massive Special Disinterest Group

LAWRENCE, KS—More than 3,000 U.S. citizens have banded together to form a massive special disinterest group, Coalition Of Unconcerned Americans press secretary Sarah Fisher said Tuesday.

"Politicians are completely out of touch with those Americans who are completely out of touch with politics," Fisher said. "Why is Congress always debating foreign policy and

see DISINTEREST page 6

NEWS

Apparently Soccer Player Just Did Something Really Good

see SPORTS page 5D

British Girl Exotic Enough

see PEOPLE page 6C

Song From Area Man's Past Comes Back To Rock Him

see LOCAL page 13B

STATshot

A look at the trends that shape your world.

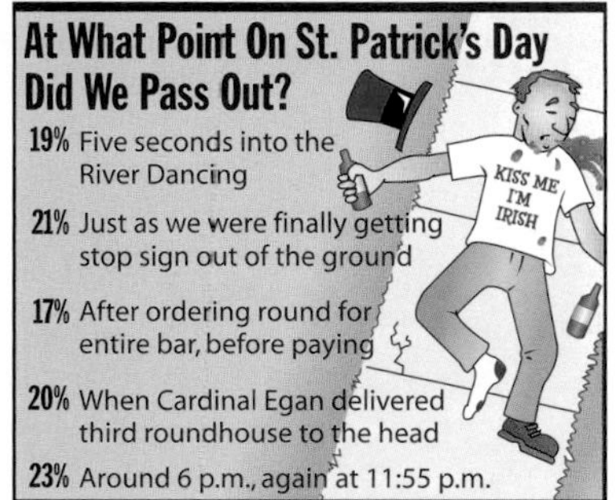

THE ONION VOLUME 40 ISSUE 11
$2.00 US
$3.00 CAN

NEWS

FCC Sentences Artie Lange To Death

see WASHINGTON page 7C

Transit Authority Pledges To Double Number Of Out-Of-Service Buses By 2006

see LOCAL page 11B

Scientists Celebrate Unlocking Of Corn Genome With Extra Serving Of Corn

see SCIENCE page 13E

STATshot

A look at the trends that shape your world.

the ONION®

VOLUME 40 ISSUE 13 | AMERICA'S FINEST NEWS SOURCE™ | 1–7 APRIL 2004

Bush Addresses 8.2 Million Unemployed: 'Get A Job'

Left: President Bush urges America's jobless to get off their duffs.

WASHINGTON, DC—Responding to the nation's worst unemployment rate since the Hoover Administration, President Bush addressed the nation's 8.2 million unemployed workers in a televised speech Monday.

"The economy has been on the rebound for months, but 5.6 percent of you are still out of work," Bush said. "Come on, people: Get a job! Don't just sit there hoping that you'll win the lottery. Turn off that boob tube, get off that couch, and start pounding the pavement."

When the number of people taking part-time jobs because they can't get full-time work is factored in, the unemployment figure approaches 15.1 million, a number Bush called "unacceptable."

"My fellow Americans, don't come crying to me," Bush said. "*I've* got a job. I go to work every day, whether I feel like it or not. I don't take handouts, and I don't give them. That's a belief my daddy taught me. Now, let's get this show on the road!"

The unemployment rate remains high, in spite of the many tax-cut initiatives the

see BUSH page 6

New Strip Mall Of America Stretches Over 1/6th Of North Dakota

FARGO, ND—Representatives from the North Dakota Department of Commerce attended a ribbon-cutting ceremony Saturday for the new Strip Mall Of America, the state's largest shopping center to date.

"This new mall brings together all the low- to mid-range franchise stores that America loves," Strip Mall Of America spokesman Henry Sloan said. "It's the largest strip mall in the country—in fact, it's the largest in the world. It's your one 90-linear-mile stop for vitamins, house-

see STRIP MALL page 8

Right: A tiny section of the mall, which stretches from Eldridge to the outskirts of Fargo.

Heartbroken FBI Agent Crosses Ex-Girlfriend's Name Out Of Classified Documents

WASHINGTON, DC—Special agent Brian Walters said he felt resignation, sadness, and a sense of duty Monday while stripping all mention of his ex-girlfriend Cathy Blessing from a file of FBI documents.

"It's painful, going through these classified documents and seeing Cathy's name right there in front of me, over and over again," said Walters, whose current assignment requires him to review transcripts of DC-area activist-group meetings and remove

see EX-GIRLFRIEND page 10

Right: Walters holds a file containing FBI documents stripped of all mention of Blessing (inset).

NEWS

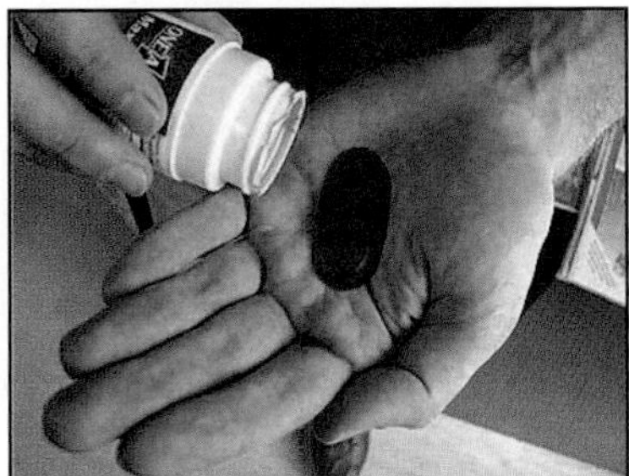

New One-A-Month Vitamin Presents Choking Hazard

see HEALTH page 11C

Mexicans Sweeping The Nation

see PEOPLE page 8E

That Guy Who Lifts Weights With His Nutsack Lets Nutsack Get Out Of Shape

see SPORTS page 4E

STATshot

A look at the trends that shape your world.

the ONION®

VOLUME 40 ISSUE 18 AMERICA'S FINEST NEWS SOURCE™ 6–12 MAY 2004

Lone Wolf Ashcroft Given Rookie Partner

WASHINGTON, DC—John Ashcroft, the tough, no-nonsense U.S. attorney general famous for his refusal to take orders, was assigned a rookie trainee Tuesday.

"John's taking it well," President Bush said, introducing Ashcroft's new partner, Deputy Attorney General Nate N. Burnhard, to the press. "He threw a couple chairs around the office, and he broke the two-way mirror in the Department of Justice squad room, but I'm sure it won't be long before he comes around to the idea of showing Burnhard here the ropes. It's about time John came in from the cold and started playing along with the team."

According to Bush, the 28-year-old Burnhard shows "real promise," having

see ASHCROFT page 9

Right: Ashcroft hits the streets with his inexperienced new partner, Burnhard.

Peace Talks Just An Excuse To Visit Scenic Mideast

WASHINGTON, DC—White House officials announced Monday that representatives from the U.S. will join those from Sweden, Russia, and the U.N. in the Mideast next week to sight-see, sunbathe, and mediate peace talks between Palestine and Israel.

Left: Some of the sights Bethlehem has to offer delegates.

"A few weeks ago, President Bush asked me to go to the West Bank and work on the road map to peace," an excited Secretary of State Colin Powell said. "There's absolutely no chance that these talks will ever work, but I was like, 'Free trip to the disputed zone? No way I'm gonna turn that down!'"

see TALKS page 6

Mom Hogging Family Therapy Session

THORNTON, CO—According to her husband and two children, Jeanette Westphal, 41, is hogging the regular therapy sessions supposedly intended to help all of them.

"Mom made us go to stupid therapy, because she said we had to learn to communicate as a family," 12-year-old daughter Amy said of the sessions the family has been attending since March. "Now, every Tuesday from 6 to 7 p.m., we sit in a circle and listen to Mom talk. It's driving everyone crazy, but try telling her that. She won't hear you, because she's too busy going on about her boring 'needs.' *Hello*, there are other people in therapy here."

Westphal's husband Greg said he can't get a word in edgewise, either.

see MOM page 10

Above: Westphal and the family forced to endure her selfishness on a weekly basis.

the ONION®

VOLUME 40 ISSUE 22 AMERICA'S FINEST NEWS SOURCE™ 3–9 JUNE 2004

NEWS

Shotgun Blast To Abdomen Just Pisses Wilfred Brimley Off More

see ENTERTAINMENT page 10E

New 40-Gigabite iHOP Breakfast Platter Holds Up To 10,000 Pancakes

see BUSINESS page 4C

All Else Fails

see LOCAL page 10B

STATshot

A look at the trends that shape your world.

Heartbreaking Country Ballad Paralyzes Trucking Industry

Above: Memphis-area traffic slows to a near-standstill as WGKX plays "She's Gone Back To What She Calls Home."

NASHVILLE, TN—The interstate trucking industry, already beset with rising fuel prices and a shortage of qualified workers, was dealt another blow last month, with the release of the agonizingly sorrowful country ballad "She's Gone Back To What She Calls Home," by Cole Hardin.

COLE HARDIN *Fenced In Heart*

"At any given time, day or night, an estimated 45 percent of the nation's over-the-road truckers are idling on the shoulder, in waysides, or in truck-stop parking lots, listening to Mr. Hardin's ballad of infidelity, loss, and heartbreak," said Russell Knutson, a spokesman for trucking giant Schneider National. "There's been an alarming number of loads that don't make it to their destinations. And the ones that do make it are usually behind schedule, because they're being loaded, transported, and unloaded by crews brought low by the

see BALLAD page 6

Poll: Many Americans Still Unsure Whom To Vote Against

WASHINGTON, DC—According to Gallup Poll results released Monday, 6 percent of Americans are still undecided about whether to vote against President Bush or Democratic challenger John Kerry in November's presidential election.

"At first, I was really leaning toward voting against Kerry, because the way he tried to hide his ambivalence about his military service made him seem like a political operator," poll participant and Trenton, NJ resident Amber Barthelme said. "But then, the Bush Administration's mishandling of the Iraqi prisoner-abuse scandal got me thinking that there's a lot to not like about the current administration. It's almost impossible to decide which side I don't want to be on."

According to the poll, 46 percent of the registered voters surveyed would vote against Bush if the election were held tomorrow, while 45 percent said they were ready to vote against Kerry. Factoring in the 2 percent margin of error, the two candidates are essentially deadlocked in the

see POLL page 8

Gay Couple Feels Pressured To Marry

DEDHAM, MA—Ever since last month, when Massachusetts became the first state to allow same-sex weddings, parents, friends, and coworkers have been pressuring Kristin Burton and her girlfriend Laura Miyatake to marry, the couple of 14 months said Monday.

"As soon as the news coverage about gay marriage started, my mom called me up," said Burton, who works as a nursing-home administrator. "Of course, she didn't directly ask me when I was going to

see COUPLE page 8

Right: Miyatake (left) and Burton, who aren't ready to tie the knot.

the ONION®

VOLUME 40 ISSUE 24 | AMERICA'S FINEST NEWS SOURCE™ | 17–23 JUNE 2004

NEWS

Jimmy Fallon Six Tantalizing Months From Disappearing Forever

see ENTERTAINMENT page 12F

Reagan's Memory Honored With Sharp Increase In Federal Budget Deficit

see WASHINGTON page 3C

Heinz Factory Explosion Looks Worse Than It Is

see LOCAL page 5E

STATshot

A look at the trends that shape your world.

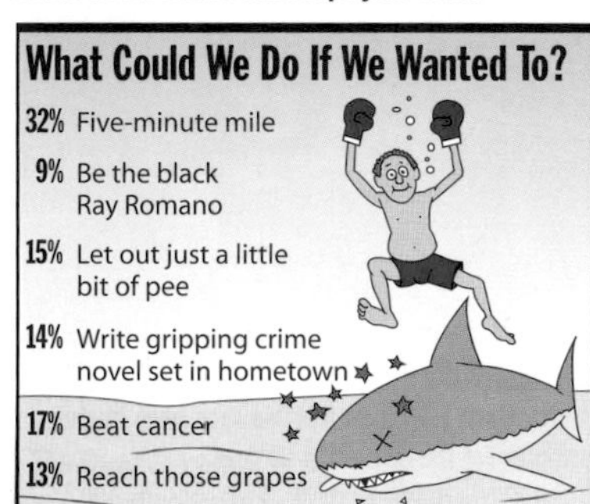

THE ONION
VOLUME 40
ISSUE 24
$2.00 US
$3.00 CAN

J.K. Rowling Ends *Harry Potter* Series After Discovering Boys

EDINBURGH, SCOTLAND—Speaking though her publicist, author J.K. Rowling shocked fans and the publishing world Monday when she announced that she has opted to end the best-selling *Harry Potter* series because she has discovered boys.

"For many years, writing the *Harry Potter* books was the most important thing in Joanne's life," said publicist Mark Knowles, who is "just good friends" with Rowling. "She's been experiencing a lot of changes lately. She still wants to keep in touch with her fans, but she doesn't feel she can sit in a room at her computer all day while there are so many cute boys running around."

According to Knowles, instead of working on the as-yet-untitled sixth installment in her series, Rowling has spent the past two months sunning herself at the beach, reading fashion magazines, and talking on the phone for hours.

"I know many of you are upset by this news," Knowles said. "But Ms. Rowling was tired of devoting herself to

see ROWLING page 9

Above: Rowling, who is "so over dragons and magical gems."

Report: 9/11 Commission Could Have Been Prevented

Left: Members of the 9/11 commission that destroyed countless political careers.

WASHINGTON, DC—According to key members of the Bush Administration, the tragic proceedings of the 9/11 commission, which devastated the political lives of numerous government officials, could have been averted with preventive action in 2002 and 2003.

"A few adept legislative maneuvers could have saved the reputations of hundreds," President Bush's counterterrorism chief Fran Townsend told reporters Monday. "Had we foreseen the dangers of the commission's deceptively simple requests, we could have spared dozens of victims from the shocking, public mangling of their careers."

"It's tragic," Townsend added. "All those political futures snuffed out as millions of

see COMMISSION page 7

Man's Impending Death Alcohol-Related

MATTOON, IL—In a press conference Monday, Mattoon-area police announced that the early death of Derek Yothers, 42, will be alcohol-related.

"Until we can complete a full investigation, we're considering Yothers' future death to be the result of alcohol poisoning," patrolman John O'Malley said. "However, we haven't ruled out hepatitis, kidney failure, cirrhosis of the liver, acute pancreatitis, Wernicke-Korsakoff's syndrome, alcoholic cardiomyopathy, or fatal injuries sustained in some kind of drunk-driving accident."

O'Malley said police do not suspect that there will be foul play.

"Yothers' on-again/off-again girlfriend Brandi Freyer could get fed up and shoot

see MAN page 8

Right: Yothers in a photo taken just months, or even weeks, before his death.

NEWS

Ashcroft Loses Job To Mexican

see WASHINGTON page 3B

Woman With Really Pointy Feet Finds Perfect Shoes

see LOCAL page 13G

Domineering Wife Specifically Said 'Chunk-Style' Pineapple

see PEOPLE page 9E

STATshot

A look at the trends that shape your world.

THE ONION VOLUME 40 ISSUE 46
$2.00 US
$3.00 CAN

the ONION®

VOLUME 40 ISSUE 46 | AMERICA'S FINEST NEWS SOURCE™ | 18–24 NOVEMBER 2004

Oprah Celebrates 20,000th Pound Lost

CHICAGO—Talk-show superstar Oprah Winfrey celebrated losing her 20,000th pound in a star-packed gala at the Sutton Place Hotel in Chicago's Gold Coast Monday night.

"Tonight is an amazing personal milestone," Winfrey said. "I want everyone who has supported me through the years—my friends, my loved ones, and all of my wonderful fans—to share the joy I feel tonight in having shed my 20,000th pound."

According to her spokesman, Winfrey has been on 674 diets, embarked on 255 fitness routines, and weighed herself 4,349,571 times during her 30-year

see OPRAH page 8

Right: Winfrey celebrates her momentous achievement on the set of her TV show.

Teen Handed Awesome Responsibility Of Closing Subway Alone

BARTLESVILLE, OK—Subway sources report that employee Jeremy Prusher, 17, appeared proud and a little nervous after accepting the momentous duty of closing the franchise location by himself Monday night.

"Okay, here are keys to the front door and the deadbolt at the back," said Michael Rotley, 32, who has managed the Juniper Avenue restaurant since March 2003. "I know it seems like a lot to remember the first time, but as long as the doors are locked, the alarm is set, and the lids on the sandwich line are closed, I probably won't fire you."

"Just kidding about the firing," Rotley added. "But seriously, if those lids are up, we'll have to throw everything out. That's hundreds of dollars in product, so don't forget."

A Subway employee since Aug. 1, Prusher quickly earned several positive performance reviews and a 45-cent raise. Rotley said that, although Prusher is only

see TEEN page 10

Left: Prusher, minutes after being told that he, and he alone, would be in charge of closing the restaurant.

Republicans Call For Privatization Of Next Election

WASHINGTON, DC—Citing the "extreme inefficiency" of this month's U.S. presidential election, key Republicans called for future elections to be conducted by the private sector.

"When the average citizen hears the phrase 'presidential election,' he thinks of long lines at polling places and agonizing waits as election results are tallied," U.S. Sen. Rick Santorum (R-PA) told reporters Monday. "Putting the election of our public officials into the hands of private industry would motivate election officials to be more efficient."

"There's too much talk about the accuracy and fairness of our national elections, and not enough about their proficiency and profitability," Santorum added. "Who bears the brunt of bureaucratic waste? Taxpayers."

U.S. Sen. Conrad Burns (R-MT) called for an end to "big

see REPUBLICANS page 6

Left: Santorum calls for the removal of big government from the election process.

NEWS

Bollywood Remake Of *Fahrenheit 9/11* Criticizes Bush Administration Through Show-Stopping Musical Numbers

see ENTERTAINMENT page 13E

Pet Winterized

see LOCAL page 8C

High Times Web Page Cached

see TECHNOLOGY page 3D

STATshot

A look at the trends that shape your world.

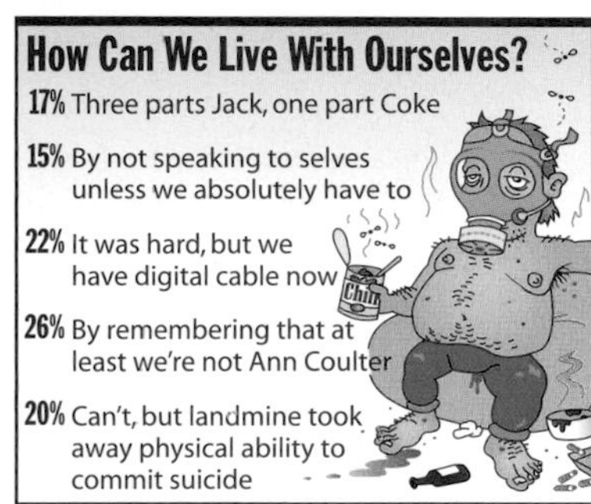

THE ONION
VOLUME 40
ISSUE 49
$2.00 US
$3.00 CAN

the ONION®

VOLUME 40 ISSUE 49 | AMERICA'S FINEST NEWS SOURCE™ | 9–15 DECEMBER 2004

Wal-Mart Announces Massive Rollback On Employee Wages

BENTONVILLE, AR—Wal-Mart, the world's largest discount retailer, announced its biggest-ever rollback Monday, with employee pay cuts of up to 35 percent.

"Just in time for the holiday shopping season, we're rolling back the hourly wages of workers in every department—housewares, automotive, health and beauty, and so many more!" Wal-Mart

see WAL-MART page 6

Above: A sign announces a Louisville, KY Wal-Mart's low, low wage for cashiers.

World's Scientists Admit They Just Don't Like Mice

ZURICH, SWITZERLAND—Nearly 700 scientists representing 27 countries convened at the University of Zurich Monday to formally announce that their experimentation on mice has been motivated not by a desire to advance human knowledge, but out of sheer distaste for the furry little rodents.

"As a man of science, I deal with facts, and the fact is that mice are gross," said Dr. Douglas White, chair of the Oxford biogenetics department and lifelong mouse-hater. "They're squirmy, scurrying little vermin, and they make my skin crawl. I speak for all of my assembled colleagues when I say that the horrible little things deserve the worst we can dish out."

According to a 500-word statement, scientists hate mice for "their beady little eyes," "their repulsive tails," and "the

see SCIENTISTS page 8

Left: White examines detested specimens in his Oxford lab.

Authority Figures Call For Closing Of Area Roughhouse

SEYMOUR, IN—Local authority figures and townspeople assembled Monday at Seymour Town Hall to call for the closure of the town's controversial roughhouse, alleging that it has caused countless scrapes, bumps, and bruises since it opened in 1986.

"We're fed up," said Dolly Geary, the local PTA chairwoman and a co-founder of the Task Force Against Skinned Knees. "That place is dangerous. It needs to be shut down before someone gets hurt."

The roughhouse, a crude wooden shanty erected on a vacant lot in the southwestern

edge of the city, serves as the site of activities that Geary characterized as rowdy. She said screaming, giggling, and "slamming sounds" often emanate from the structure, especially when school isn't in session.

"I'm tired of people asking 'Where's the rumpus?'" Geary said. "We know darn well

see ROUGHHOUSE page 10

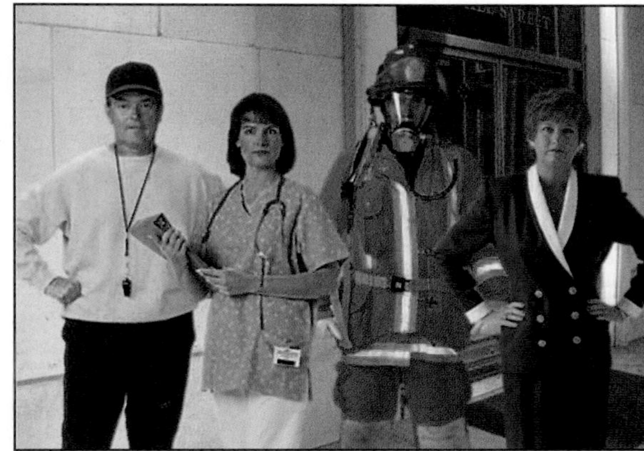

Above: Authority figures at City Hall call for the closing of the roughhouse (left).

Goth, Metalhead Overcome Subcultural Differences To Find Love

Armchair Publicist Would Totally Rein In Tom Cruise

Bush Vows To Eliminate U.S. Dependence On Oil By 4920

JANUARY FEBRUARY MARCH APRIL MAY JUNE

Democratic Senator Strides Down Corridors Of Powerlessness

Chardonnay Vomited Into NPR Tote

Evangelical Scientists Refute Gravity With New 'Intelligent Falling' Theory

2005

Google Announces Plan To Destroy All Information It Can't Index

Bush Nominates First-Trimester Fetus To Supreme Court

Bush To Appoint Someone To Be In Charge Of Country

JULY AUGUST SEPTEMBER OCTOBER NOVEMBER DECEMBER

War On String May Be Unwinnable, Says Cat General

Cosmopolitan Releases 40-Year Compendium: 812,683 Ways To Please Your Man

Racial Harmony Achieved By Casting Of Black Actor As Teen Computer Whiz

NEWS

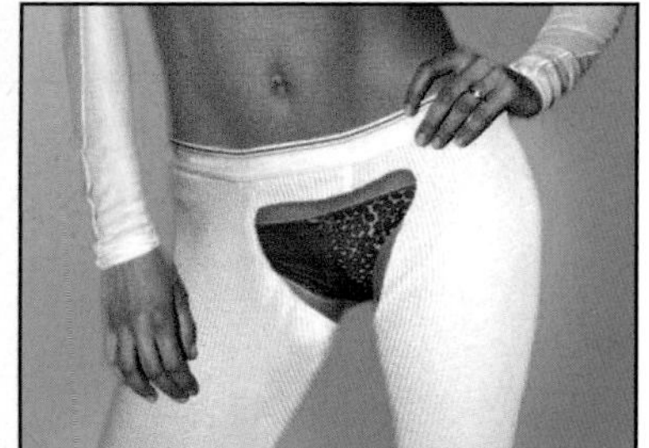

Frederick's Of Anchorage Debuts Crotchless Long Underwear

see FASHION page 14E

Guy In Rome Does As The Tourists Do

see TRAVEL page 7H

Area Man A Walking Bag Of Hazardous Biological Waste Material

see FAMILY page 20G

STATshot

A look at the trends that shape your world.

Where Do We See Ourselves In Five Years?

13% Women's plus-size section

26% Watching rerun of show we're currently watching

21% Still in Iraq

28% Same spot, different couch, playing Playstation 3

12% Unsold skeleton in Midwest Medical Supply warehouse

06
THE ONION VOLUME 41 ISSUE 06
$2.00 US
$3.00 CAN
0 74470 94595 6

the ONION®

VOLUME 41 ISSUE 06 AMERICA'S FINEST NEWS SOURCE™ 10–16 FEBRUARY 2005

Above: McNabb attempts to go long with a two-liter bottle of refreshing Pepsi in the third quarter.

Product Placement Mars Otherwise Exciting Super Bowl

JACKSONVILLE, FL—Although NFL commissioner Paul Tagliabue declared the Super Bowl XXXIX experiment with in-game product placement a success, fans and players expressed mixed feelings about the championship game Monday.

"Don't get me wrong—this year's Super Bowl was an exciting face-off," said Philadelphia Eagles head coach Andy Reid, whose team was pitted against the New England Patriots in Alltel Stadium Sunday. "The Patriots got a couple big plays on our defense before we adjusted to tackling players doused in Axe Deodorant Bodyspray For Men. But you can be sure they felt the heat of our Ford Motor Company sponsored Lincoln Mark LT blitzes.

see SUPER BOWL page 6

Latest Bin Laden Videotape Wishes America 'A Crappy Valentine's Day'

Above: Bin Laden tears up a "putrid Western Valentine's Day trifle" during his videotaped message.

WASHINGTON, DC—A new videotape of Osama bin Laden broadcast on the Arab satellite news channel Al-Jazeera Monday beseeched Allah to grant all Americans a "crappy Valentine's Day."

"This Feb. 14th on the Western infidels' calendar, may all Americans receive no valentines from their beloved ones," bin Laden said. "May the homemade construction-paper mailboxes taped to the desks of the American schoolchildren remain empty, as well. May whomever you ask to 'bee yours' tell you to 'buzz off.'"

Bin Laden called for "romantic humiliation for all Americans of courting and betrothal age."

"Allah willing, embarrassment and tearful rejection shall rule this day," bin Laden said. "Paper hearts shall be rent and trod upon, and dreams of love delivered stillborn. Body language shall be misinterpreted, crushes unrequited, and sincere expressions of affection mocked.

see BIN LADEN page 7

Woman Begins To Regret Dating Someone Spontaneous

Above: Bird and Maddox spend an afternoon at home.

AUBURN, CA—After four months of romantic involvement, Wells Fargo mortgage lending assistant Heidi Bird, 27, said Monday that she is beginning to regret getting into a relationship with the carefree Jason Maddox.

"Jason was everything I wanted in a boyfriend as recently as three months ago," Bird said. "I used to dream of meeting someone who knew how to have fun and didn't let himself get weighed down by formalities and obligations. But my dreams never had the part where that person doesn't call for a week, then drops by at 3 a.m. with a broken mannequin torso under his arm."

Bird said she was swept off her feet by the handsome 30-year-old in August, when she met him at a local park. A part-time bicycle-shop employee and occasional street musician, Maddox "was straight out of a romantic Hollywood movie," according to Bird.

"I was walking my dog Shadow when I heard someone call out to me from above," Bird said. "I looked up and saw Jason sitting on a tree branch. He told me he once had a dog like Shadow. Then he asked

see WOMAN page 8

the ONION®

VOLUME 41 ISSUE 10 AMERICA'S FINEST NEWS SOURCE™ 10–16 MARCH 2005

NEWS

Could Hillary Clinton Have What It Takes To Defeat The Democrats In 2008?

see POLITICS page 7B

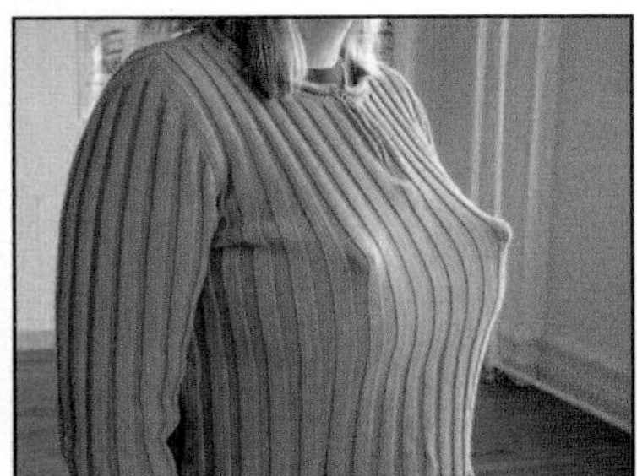

Thick Sweater No Match For Determined Nipples

see LOCAL page 3C

Country Mouse, City Mouse Devour Face Of Homeless Corpse

see NATURE page 11E

STATshot

A look at the trends that shape your world.

Bush Announces Iraq Exit Strategy: 'We'll Go Through Iran'

WASHINGTON, DC—Almost a year after the cessation of major combat and a month after the nation's first free democratic elections, President Bush unveiled the coalition forces' strategy for exiting Iraq.

"I'm pleased to announce that the Department of Defense and I have formulated a

see IRAN page 6

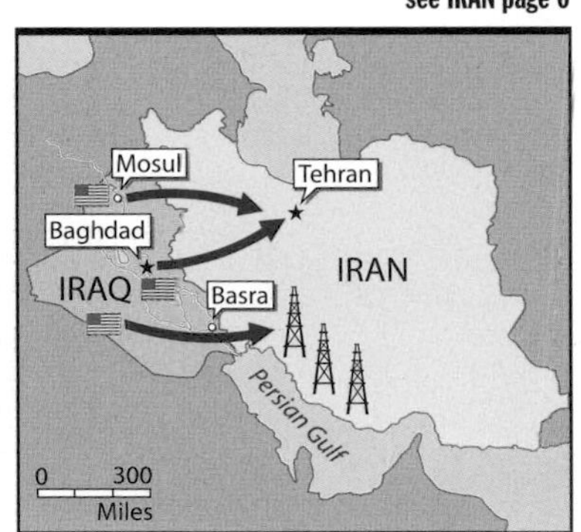

Above: Bush announces the pullout of Iraq through Iran.

Study: Reality TV, Reality Unfair To Blacks

Left: The cast of the popular reality-TV show *The Apprentice 3.*

WASHINGTON, DC—According to a study released Monday by the Center for Media and Social Research, the reality-TV genre is unfairly biased against black people. The study revealed that reality is unfair to blacks, as well.

"Programs like *The Apprentice* routinely stereotype black participants," read the 5,000-page report. "Black contestants are often portrayed as stormy and indolent fringe elements, while their white counterparts are portrayed as stable and industrious collaborators. Black reality-TV contestants face discrimination at levels approaching those of everyday life."

The study cited the case of Omarosa Manigault-Stallworth, a black woman who criticized *The Apprentice* for stereotyping her and other black contestants.

"Producers edited footage to make Omarosa look like a self-involved diva," study director Simon Rosemead said. "Her allegations are not isolated.

see REALITY TV page 8

Victims Sought In Next Week's Shooting

CHARLOTTE, NC—In an extremely brief press conference on the steps of City Hall, area psychopath Roland Walling, 46, announced Monday that he is on the lookout for potential victims in the unprovoked shootout that he expects will leave at least three dead and up to 10 wounded next Tuesday.

"I'm asking for the community's help in piecing together

see SHOOTING page 9

Right: Walling, who is asking the public for help in his upcoming massacre.

NEWS

Cheney Offspring Bursts From Bush's Chest

see WASHINGTON page 2B

Slowly Rotating Pie A Metaphor For Trucker's Failing Marriage

see PEOPLE page 4G

Drummer Forced To Retrieve Sticks From Audience For Encore

see LOCAL page 12C

STATshot

A look at the trends that shape your world.

the ONION®

VOLUME 41 ISSUE 14 | AMERICA'S FINEST NEWS SOURCE™ | 7–13 APRIL 2005

Local Fox Affiliate Debuts Terror-Alert Van

MURFREESBORO, TN—Touting itself as "the only channel with a terror-alert system designed to meet the specific needs of central Tennessee," Fox News affiliate WMFB-TV Channel 11 debuted its terror-alert van Monday.

"The team you trust to keep you informed is working to keep the greater Murfreesboro area—and your family—safe from Muslim extremists," said station manager Carl Bogert, unveiling the TerrorFirst! van at a press conference held in the "Terrorist No Zone" in the back parking lot. "When terrorism threatens the people of central Tennessee, Fox 11 is there first. Watch Channel 11 for up-to-the-minute coverage of where, when, and how the enemies of freedom are coming to get *you*."

Painted red, white, and blue, the TerrorFirst! van is the first mobile unit devoted to monitoring terrorist threats on a local level. The van is equipped with live satellite

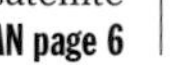

see VAN page 6

Above: The WMFB TerrorFirst! van.

Congress Awards Itself Congressional Medal Of Honor

'We've Done A Very Good Job,' Says Congress

WASHINGTON, DC—In recognition of its "service above and beyond the call of duty in the legislative field," Congress awarded itself the Congressional Medal of Honor Monday.

Left: Members of Congress applaud their decision to award themselves the Congressional Medals of Honor.

"We've done a very good job this past year," House Majority Leader Tom DeLay (R-TX) said. "After passing H.R. 682 through the Senate, we realized the 109th U.S. Congress had done something that would benefit the entire country. We felt it was time we officially recognize our

see CONGRESS page 11

Actual Urgent Message From Robert Redford Goes Unheeded

MARSING, ID—An actual urgent message from actor Robert Redford, whose mass-mailed call to action on behalf of the Natural Resources Defense Council reached millions of Americans last year, went unheeded last week by its lone recipient, Michael Sanborne of Marsing, ID.

"MICHAEL, I'm asking for your help to stop the robbery and possible destruction of one of America's most treasured human resources—actor Robert Redford," read the message typed on NRDC letterhead. "At this very moment, two or more men are holding me captive within my office in order to further their profit-motivated agenda to strip my home of its valuable assets and leave me with nothing—perhaps not even my life."

see REDFORD page 8

Above: A stack of Sanborne's unopened mail.

the ONION®

VOLUME 41 ISSUE 15 | AMERICA'S FINEST NEWS SOURCE™ | 14–20 APRIL 2005

NEWS

DEA Seizes Half-Built Suspension Bridge From Bogotá To Miami

see WORLD page 8D

Inside: Spring Fashions So Glamorous You'll Practically Shit Yourself

see STYLE page 1E

Bystander Stops To Watch Incompetent Parallel-Park Job

see PEOPLE page 11G

STATshot

A look at the trends that shape your world.

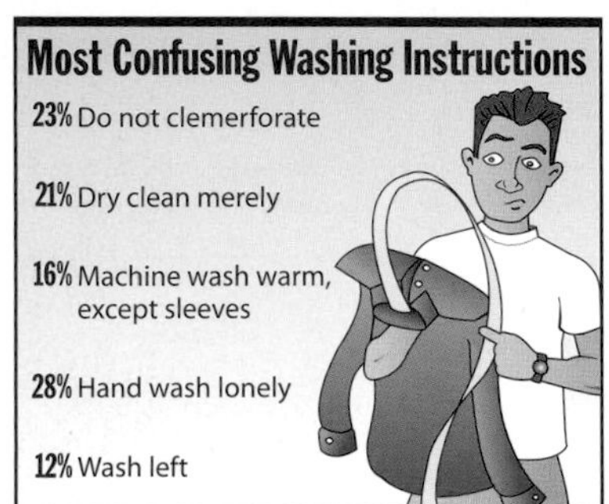

Heaven Less Opulent Than Vatican, Reports Disappointed Pope

HEAVEN—The soul of Pope John Paul, which entered heaven last week following a long illness, expressed confusion and disappointment Saturday, upon learning that the Celestial Kingdom of God to which the departed faithful ascend in the afterlife is significantly less luxurious than the Vatican's Papal Palace, in

see POPE page 8

Above: St. Peter's Basilica, with its 90-foot bronze baldachin designed by Bernini, is one of the many Vatican splendors no longer enjoyed by Pope John Paul II (left).

French's Introduces Antibacterial Mustard

ROCHESTER, NY—In response to increasing American demand for tangier, more hygienic meals, condiment giant French's has introduced a new antibacterial mustard.

"Each year, 15 million cases of bacterial food poisoning originate in U.S. home

see MUSTARD page 10

Report:

Cost Of Living Now Outweighs Benefits

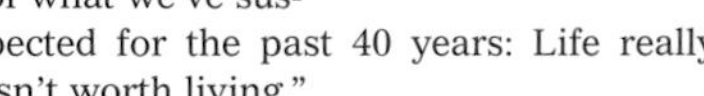

WASHINGTON, DC—A report released Monday by the Federal Consumer Quality-Of-Life Control Board indicates that the cost of living now outstrips life's benefits for many Americans.

"This is sobering news," said study director Jack Farness. "For the first time, we have statistical evidence of what we've suspected for the past 40 years: Life really isn't worth living."

To arrive at their conclusions, study directors first identified the average yearly costs and benefits of life. Tangible benefits such as median income ($43,000) were weighed against such tangible costs as home-ownership ($18,000). Next, scientists assigned a financial value to intangibles such as finding inner peace ($15,000),

see LIVING page 6

NEWS

Office Manager Forced To Resort To Unfriendly Reminders

see BUSINESS page 11C

Dreamcatcher On Rearview Mirror Protects Sleeping Driver

see LOCAL page 1B

Greasy Spoon Has Crusty Forks

see FOOD page 8F

STATshot

A look at the trends that shape your world.

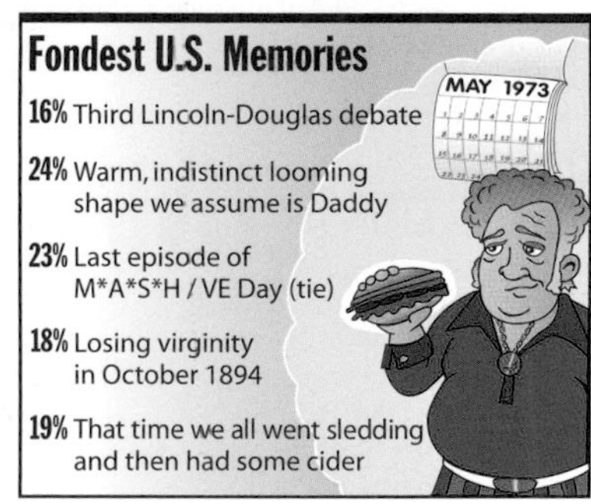

Fondest U.S. Memories

16% Third Lincoln-Douglas debate

24% Warm, indistinct looming shape we assume is Daddy

23% Last episode of M*A*S*H / VE Day (tie)

18% Losing virginity in October 1894

19% That time we all went sledding and then had some cider

16
THE ONION
VOLUME 41
ISSUE 16
$2.00 US
$3.00 CAN
0 74470 94595 6

the ONION®

VOLUME 41 ISSUE 16 AMERICA'S FINEST NEWS SOURCE™ 21–27 APRIL 2005

Papal Election Brings End To Worldwide Unsupervised-Catholic Sin Binge

VATICAN CITY—In the interim between Pope John Paul II's death and the election of his replacement, unsupervised Catholics seized the opportunity to sin without fear of reprisal, sources confirmed Tuesday.

"For two weeks, it was like Mardi Gras all over again," said Bryan Cousivert, a Catholic from Arizona. "People were drinking, cursing, and engaging in premarital or even extramarital sex. More importantly, everyone was being totally open about it. No one was worried about doing any penance at all!"

Continued Cousivert: "When

see ELECTION page 6

Above: Catholics cavort in St. Peter's square last week.

Pope Emerges From Chrysalis A Beautiful Butterfly

VATICAN CITY—Vatican officials joyously report that Pope John Paul II, who led the Catholic Church during the 26 years of his larval stage, emerged from his chrysalis transformed into a beautiful butterfly Monday.

"John Paul II's emergence was a thing of

see POPE page 10

Left: John Paul II flits above Vatican City hours after leaving his chrysalis (below).

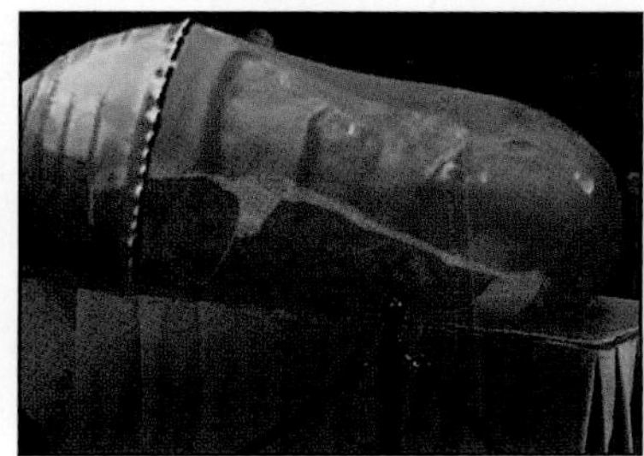

Police Sketch Artist Likes How Portrait Of Serial Rapist Turned Out

BIRMINGHAM, AL—Area police officer Lynn Marie Potter said Monday that she is "pretty proud of" her latest sketch, a drawing of an unidentified white male suspected of committing at least four recent Birmingham-area rapes since February.

"He looks so real, doesn't he?" said Potter, 38, admiring her rendering of the Caucasian believed to be in his early-to-mid 30s. "I mean, he looks like he could just leap off the sketch pad and violate you."

Potter, a certified criminal-image profiler who has drawn more than 400

see ARTIST page 10

Right: Potter and her sketch.

the ONION®
VOLUME 41 ISSUE 24 AMERICA'S FINEST NEWS SOURCE™ 16–22 JUNE 2005

NEWS

Secret Service Not Sure If That Suit Of Armor Was In Oval Office Yesterday

see WASHINGTON page 12B

New Lawn-Care Product Makes Neighbor's Lawn Less Green

see BUSINESS page 13D

Mail-Order Bride Comes In Wrong Color, Size

see BUSINESS page 11D

STATshot

A look at the trends that shape your world.

THE ONION
VOLUME 41
ISSUE 24
$2.00 US
$3.00 CAN

Habitrail For Humanity Under Fire

PAYNEVILLE, KY—Habitrail For Humanity, the faith-based, non-profit group that builds networks of affordable, transparent-tube housing for needy families, has come under intense criticism for its recent projects in the Payneville area.

"This is no way for people to live," said Kentucky Family Outreach coordinator Martin Weiss, speaking Monday in front of a half-constructed, five-story Habitrail outside Payneville. "While it's true that poor Americans need a viable alternative to housing projects, placing them in large, confusing warrens of see-through cylinders is not the solution."

Habitrail For Humanity spokesman Nick Bulwer, whose organization has

see HABITRAIL page 7

Right: A new Habitrail For Humanity structure nears completion in Payneville.

Left: Chen makes yet more stupid crap for consumers overseas.

Chinese Factory Worker Can't Believe The Shit He Makes For Americans

FENGHUA, CHINA—Chen Hsien, an employee of Fenghua Ningbo Plastic Works Ltd., a plastics factory that manufactures lightweight household items for Western markets, expressed his disbelief Monday over the "sheer amount of shit Americans will buy."

"Often, when we're assigned a new order for, say, 'salad shooters,' I will say to myself, 'There's no way that anyone will ever buy these,'" Chen said during his lunch break in an open-air courtyard. "One month later, we will receive an order for the same product, but three times the quantity. How can anyone have a need for such useless shit?"

see WORKER page 10

Politician Awkwardly Works The Bathroom

Above: Hecht meets and greets a lavatory visitor.

BATTLE CREEK, MI—In what had originally been intended as a brisk, businesslike trip to the urinal, Calhoun County executive hopeful Phil Hecht spent seven minutes working the Battle Creek Sheraton men's bathroom Monday.

"That politician guy didn't seem to realize how weird it was in there," said David Muntz, a local orthodontist. "I don't know... It was like he couldn't turn it off."

"I had to wash up an extra time after he glad-handed me," Muntz added.

Hecht's unplanned bathroom tour took place several minutes after his remarks at the Battle Creek Rotary Club's annual Unsung Heroes luncheon, held this year in honor of Jefferson Middle School principal Phyllis DeVreaux. Observers speculated that Hecht "got carried away" by both the generous applause following his address and the large number of people in the men's restroom.

"When he came toward me, I

see BATHROOM page 8

NEWS

Rookie NASCAR Driver Gets Lost

see SPORTS page 1C

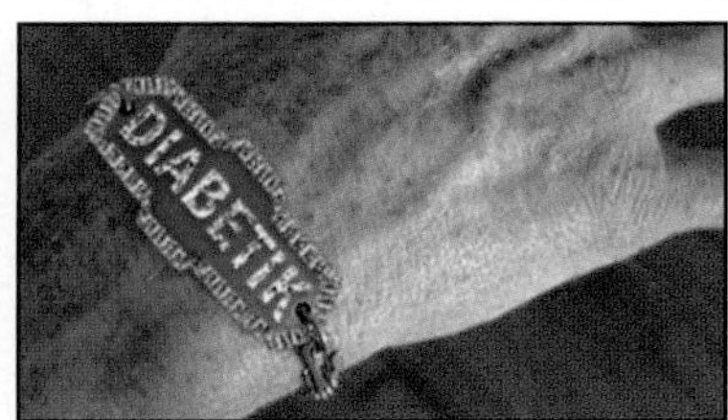

MedicAlert Bracelet Iced Out

see HEALTH page 11B

Recently Discovered Egyptian Tomb Sure Smells Like Mummies

see SCIENCE page 11D

Cycle Of Violence Running Smoothly

see WORLD page 8G

STATshot

A look at the trends that shape your world.

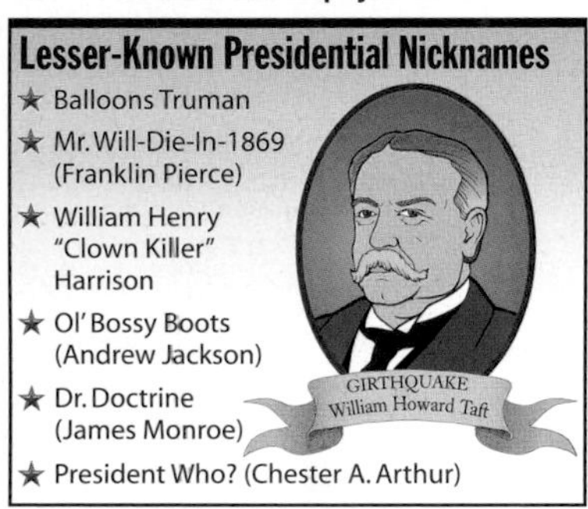

the ONION®

VOLUME 41 ISSUE 26 AMERICA'S FINEST NEWS SOURCE™ 30 JUNE–6 JULY 2005

Vatican Tightens Nocturnal Emissions Standards

VATICAN CITY—The Vatican has released a strict new set of Church laws intended to reduce the nocturnal emissions of teenage polluters by 50 percent in the next decade, Cardinal Antoni Bertoli announced Monday.

"In the past 10 years, unholy emissions from young men have risen by 150 million cubic centimeters, releasing erotic-dream byproducts into the bedsheet environment," Bertoli said. "The accumulation of pollutants from millions of individual violators around the world is having a dev-

see VATICAN page 6

Above: Cardinal Bertoli.

The moral atmosphere, clouded with over 150 parts-per-million of sin, undergoes a change called the Hothouse Effect

Various pollutants condense back into offending boys, staining souls and making purification vastly more difficult

Millions of tiny onanocules disrupt ambient holiness

Unrestricted nocturnal emissions release sexually charged amounts of venality and ungodliness into the bedding environment

Source: Emissions Prevention Administration

Food-Court Taco Bell Not As Good, Area Man Reports

ERIE, PA—Fast-food consumer Don Turnbee announced Monday that the Taco Bell in the Millcreek Mall food court is "not as good" as regular, full-service Taco Bell restaurants.

Turnbee, a frequent patron of the full-service Taco Bell on Buffalo Road, encountered the scaled-down version of the Mexican-style franchise Sunday afternoon while waiting for his wife Shelly to complete her shopping.

"It was so-so," Turnbee told reporters outside the mall. "It's not as nice as the one I usually go to. This one had tacos and burritos, but no Double Decker Tacos."

Unlike a regular Taco Bell, the Millcreek Taco Bell Express has a reduced menu that does not offer many of the choices or add-on options to which Turnbee is accustomed, including the carne asada steak upgrade.

"I tried to add steak to something, and the girl got mad," Turnbee said. "I guess

see TACO BELL page 8

Right: Veteran fast-food patron Don Turnbee.

New *Us Quarterly* To Explore Celebrity Issues In More Depth

NEW YORK—Describing it as a "discerning and literary companion" to their flagship entertainment-news magazine, *Us Weekly* editor-in-chief Janice Min announced on Tuesday the creation of *Us Quarterly*, a scholarly, four-times-yearly journal dedicated to sizzling-hot celebrity gossip.

The quarterly will feature in-depth essays, investigative pieces, and expert commentary on Hollywood's hottest megastars.

"Due to the demands of weekly publication, [*Us Weekly*] was only able to scratch the surface," said Min, who is helming the offshoot publication. "The quarterly is a dream come true for the more serious-minded star-watcher, who enjoys pictorials showcasing Mary-Kate Olsen's club-hopping wardrobe, but craves a more critical examination of her hottest boots."

Min estimated that the first issue of *Us Quarterly*, slated to debut in August, will be 300 pages long. It will feature a thoughtful analysis of Lindsay Lohan's troubles on the set of *Herbie: Fully Loaded*, a Michael Cunningham short

see US QUARTERLY page 7

Left: The premiere issue of *Us Quarterly*.

NEWS

Bush Awaits Orders From Rove On Handling Of Rove Scandal

see NATIONAL page 6A

Which Jackson Will Dominate Next Year's Headlines?

see ARTS page 1C

Terri Schiavo's Corpse Blown Away By Hurricane

see LOCAL page 18A

STATshot

A look at the trends that shape your world.

the ONION®

VOLUME 41 ISSUE 29 AMERICA'S FINEST NEWS SOURCE™ 21–27 JULY 2005

New Puppy Teaches Congress Important Lesson About Responsibility

Above: a bipartisan commission of legislators holds Buster on the Senate floor.

WASHINGTON, DC—Beltway insiders report that Buster, the 7-month-old yellow Labrador Congress was allowed to keep amid much controversy last spring, has taught the nation's legislators some valuable lessons about responsibility.

"The skeptics believed that the House and Senate weren't ready for a puppy," Senate Majority Leader Bill Frist (R-TN) said. "They believed we wouldn't be able to maintain America's defenses, regulate commerce, and pass laws while raising Buster. But we have proven them wrong. We feed him and walk him every day."

Frist referred to a bicameral duty roster ratified Jan. 31.

"Congress knows who's supposed to

see PUPPY page 6

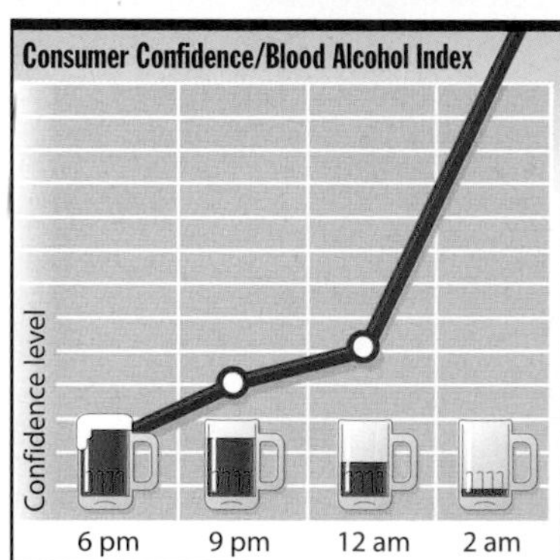

Alcoholic-Beverage-Consumer Confidence Skyrockets

NEW YORK—Alcoholic-beverage-consumer confidence hit a record high Friday between the hours of 5 p.m. and 3 a.m., briefly reaching 105.3 points before dropping to 94.2 at last call.

"Weekend market conditions were extremely favorable for cash/beverage trading," said Byron Seidler of the Board of Alcohol Consumption and Expenditure. "Drinkers' confidence in the strength of the dollar, in their attractiveness to the opposite sex—even in their dart-playing abilities—rose sharply."

see CONFIDENCE page 9

Local Company Moves Production Underseas

NEWARK, NJ—In an effort to revitalize the company after years of stagnant profits, BakeCo Inc., makers of Good Twist Pretzels and Fluffy Brand Cream Cakes, announced plans Monday to move their Newark-based production facility underseas.

"This move is long overdue," said Jeremy Helheman, vice president of marketing for BakeCo. "Many exciting possibilities lie ahead for us at the bottom of the ocean."

The 30-year-old company's new bakery, manufacturing center, and office complex

see COMPANY page 8

Right: BakeCo's new underwater headquarters.

the ONION®

VOLUME 41 ISSUE 36 | AMERICA'S FINEST NEWS SOURCE™ | 8–14 SEPTEMBER 2005

NEWS

Immune-Deficient Realtor Forced To Spend Entire Life In Housing Bubble

see REAL ESTATE page 6D

Supervisor Has A Word With Cologne Guy

see BUSINESS page 1B

Area Man Does His Best Thinking On His ATV

see REAL ESTATE page 4E

Japanese Candy Finally Eaten

see LOCAL page 3C

STATshot

A look at the trends that shape your world.

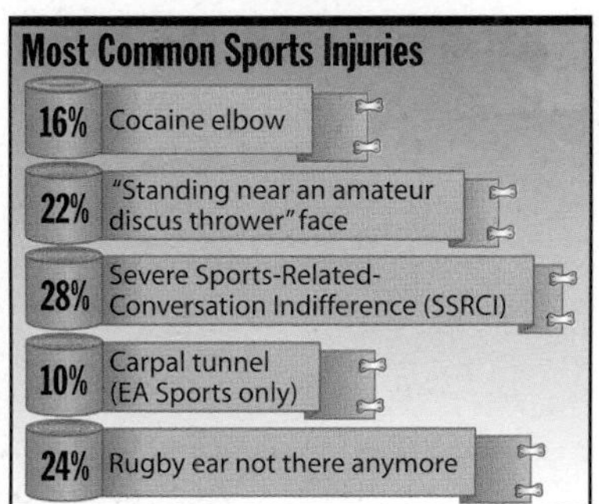

SPECIAL REPORT: DISASTER IN THE DELTA

God Outdoes Terrorists Yet Again

- Officials Uncertain Whether To Save Or Shoot Victims
- Nation's Politicians Applaud Great Job They're Doing
- Area Man Drives Food There His Goddamned Self
- Bush: 'It Has Been Brought To My Attention That There Was Recently A Bad Storm'

see SPECIAL REPORT page 8

Cheney Dropped By White House HMO

WASHINGTON, DC—Citing Dick Cheney's pre-existing health conditions and his refusal to meet regularly with his primary care physician, the White House's health-insurance provider terminated the vice president's coverage Monday.

AmeriHealth, the parent company of the HMO serving the executive branch, issued a "termination of benefits" notice to Cheney Aug. 3. The form letter, addressed to "Member #782B-11107-3905C (Cheney, Richard Bruce)," informed the vice president that his health coverage would cease, "effective immediately."

Speaking to reporters Monday, Cheney expressed dismay over being dropped from the HMO.

"I am a victim of a bureaucracy," Cheney said. "This action on the part of AmeriHealth is exceedingly unfair."

In the form letter, AmeriHealth cus-

see CHENEY page 12

Right: Vice President Dick Cheney.

CEO Barbie Criticized For Promoting Unrealistic Career Images

EL SEGUNDO, CA—Toy company Mattel is under fire from a group of activists who say their popular doll's latest incarnation, CEO Barbie, encourages young girls to set impractical career goals.

"This doll furthers the myth that if a woman works hard and sticks to her guns, she can rise to the top," said Frederick Lang of the Changes Institute, a children's advocacy organization. "Our young girls need to learn to accept their career futures, not be set up with ridiculously unattainable images."

The issue was first brought to national attention by mother, activist, and office manager Connie Bergen, 36, who became

see CEO BARBIE page 14

Left: Mattel's controversial CEO Barbie.

NEWS

Evangelical Christians Enter 10th Day Of Vigil Outside Your House

see NATIONAL page 6D

Wrestling Announcer Can't Believe What He's Seeing

see SPORTS page 8B

Grizzly Bear Ruins Otherwise Non-Fatal Camping Trip

see LOCAL page 3E

STATshot

A look at the trends that shape your world.

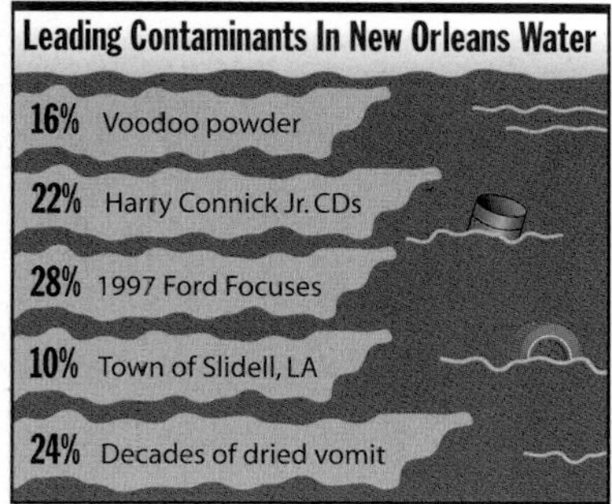

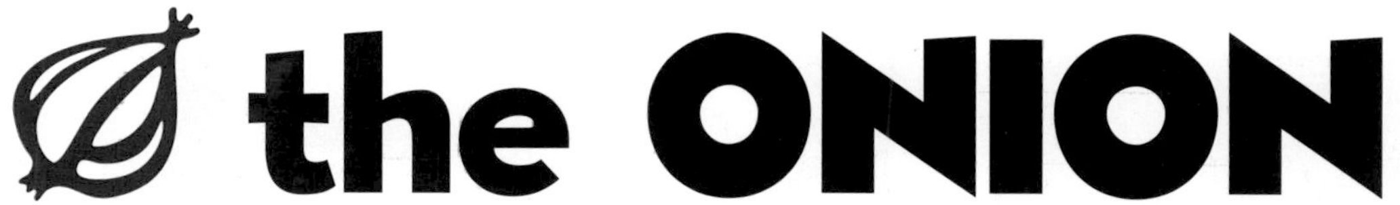

VOLUME 41 ISSUE 38 AMERICA'S FINEST NEWS SOURCE™ 22–28 SEPTEMBER 2005

I

Oprah Stuns Audience With Free Man Giveaway

CHICAGO—The season premiere of *The Oprah Winfrey Show* unleashed a surprise for viewers Monday, when host Winfrey presented her studio audience with an unexpected gift: eligible men.

"Everybody gets a man! Everybody gets a man!" said Winfrey, almost drowned out by cries of disbelief as 276 men, one for every member of the studio audience, filed onto the *Oprah* set.

Hoping to top last year's season-debut surprise, when members of the studio audience received free cars, Winfrey watched elated as the men knelt before their awestruck new mates and delivered gallant kisses and professions of undying affection.

"Signed, sealed, delivered... they're yours!" Winfrey said.

Hand-picked by Winfrey and her staff,

see OPRAH page 8

Right: Winfrey presents the studio audience with men.

Bill Introduced As Joke Signed Into Law

WASHINGTON, DC—A bill introduced by Sen. George Allen (R-VA) as "just a goof" several weeks ago was signed into law by President Bush Tuesday.

"I was just trying to crack up Frist and some of the other guys," Allen said. "Everyone's been on edge lately, what with the Katrina situation, and I thought we could use a good laugh."

Added Allen: "Looks like the joke's on me. And, I suppose, the American citizens."

S. 1718, also known as the Preservation Of Public Lands Of America Act, authorized a shift of $138 billion from the federal Medicare fund to a massive landscaping effort that, over the next five years, will transform Yellowstone National Park into a luxury private golf estate.

"I thought it was pretty damn funny when I read over the draft of the thing," said Allen, who said he struggled to keep a straight face when he introduced the law. "Especially the part about how it would create over 10,000 caddy and drink-girl jobs. But I guess it went over people's heads."

The bill passed with a vote of 63-37.

Allen said he thought the Senate bill

see JOKE BILL page 6

Left: Tyler Sheehan.

Bush Braces As Cindy Sheehan's Other Son Drowns In New Orleans

WASHINGTON, DC—According to White House sources, President Bush is bracing for intensified criticism following Monday's report that the body of Tyler Sheehan, son of outspoken anti-war activist Cindy Sheehan, was recovered from the receding floodwaters in New Orleans.

Although the White House has not released a statement, a firestorm of controversy is expected to follow the death of the dynamic, well-liked young man, who was working on a levee-upkeep crew while completing the EMT-certification training he needed to become a firefighter.

"Tyler was the very picture of an American hero," said Jorge Guiterrez, an Ochsner Hospital orderly present when Sheehan evacuated dozens of patients from its intensive-care unit. "He pulled off-the-clock double shifts moving guys in wheelchairs, guys without arms, guys on

see SHEEHAN SON page 10

NEWS

Astronomers Discover Extremely Graphic Galaxy

see SCIENCE page 7D

Third-Grade Slumber Party A Snakepit Of Machiavellian Alliances

see LOCAL page 3B

Foreign-Policy Mistake Blows Up In Soldier's Face

see INTERNATIONAL page 6C

Pop & Pop Shop Boycotted

see LIFESTYLES page 4E

STATshot

A look at the trends that shape your world.

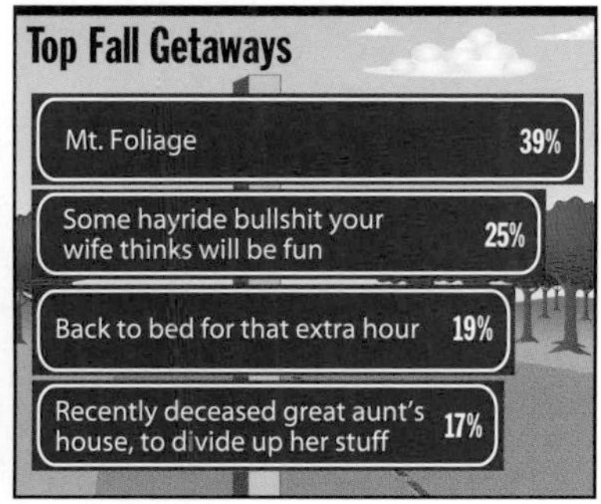

the ONION®

VOLUME 41 ISSUE 42 | AMERICA'S FINEST NEWS SOURCE™ | 20–26 OCTOBER 2005

Study Reveals Pittsburgh Unprepared For Full-Scale Zombie Attack

Above: Pittsburgh, a prime target of the undead.

PITTSBURGH—A zombie-preparedness study, commissioned by Pittsburgh Mayor Tom Murphy and released Monday, indicates that the city could easily succumb to a devastating zombie attack. Insufficient emergency-management-personnel training and poorly conceived

see ZOMBIE ATTACK page 6

Poll: More Americans Getting Their News From Bev

MARSHFIELD, MA—With an increasing variety of news media options, including 24-hour cable channels, websites, and blogs, more Americans have been tuning out traditional newscasts and turning to local resident Beverly Tollefsen for their news, a poll released Monday shows.

According to the poll, 42 percent of Americans rely on Bev to keep them informed of the top news events. Only 37 percent said they get their news from network or cable TV. The remaining 21 percent rely on newspapers and radio, though 8 percent of that group does not form a strong opinion on the news "until chatting with Bev first."

Adults over 55 lead the shift, with two-thirds saying they consider Bev a top source of national news.

A local news source since 1974, 54-year-

see BEV page 8

Right: Trusted newswoman Beverly Tollefsen.

Six Dead In Gubernatorial Suicide Pact

COLUMBUS, OH—The bodies of six U.S. governors were discovered in the Ohio Statehouse early Monday, all apparent participants in what authorities believe to be some sort of statewide-officeholder suicide pact.

Police have identified five members of the media-dubbed "Gubernatorial Six": governors Haley Barbour (R-MS), John Lynch (D-NH), Bill Richardson (D-NM), Ernie Fletcher (R-KY), and Robert "Bob" Taft (R-OH). The identity of the sixth governor is being withheld until his family is notified. Columbus Police Chief James Jackson confirmed rumors that "Governor X," as he is being called, was a male, and governor of "a very large state."

Early toxicology reports indicate that five of the governors died after drinking scotch laced with barbiturates. Gov. Fletcher is believed to have mixed the drug with bourbon and a splash of water.

Discovered by a Statehouse night cleaning crew in the pre-dawn hours, the governors' bodies were arranged in a circular pattern on the floor of the Finan Room. Forensic evidence indicated that Taft, who was found clutching the presidential seal to his chest, was the last one alive, leading police to speculate that he was the ringleader.

"We believe Governor Taft served the executive authorities their final cocktails," Jackson said. "There were no signs of struggle, no attempts to escape. It appears that all participated willingly and sought a common end."

Although the reasons behind the suicide pact remain unknown, many of the country's surviving 44 state chief executives said they are not surprised by the tragedy. The governors were all known in their home states for their penchants for dark suits, their similar hairstyles, and their "fuck everything" attitudes.

"I never really talked to them except when I had to, like during the occasional National Governors' Association meeting," Hawaii Gov. Linda Lingle said. "They tended to stay away from girls altogether. It's sad to see such bright and promising state-level executives succumb to this senseless rage and self-destruction."

Oklahoma Gov. Brad Henry, who sometimes socialized with members of the

see SUICIDE page 10

the ONION®

VOLUME 41 ISSUE 46 AMERICA'S FINEST NEWS SOURCE™ 17–23 NOVEMBER 2005

NEWS

KFC Introduces New Bird-Flu Dipping Vaccine

see HEALTH page 2C

Scientific American Somehow Makes Woman Feel Bad About Her Body

see NATIONAL page 3E

Evangelical Scientists Discover Calculation Error: Earth Only 60 Years Old

see SCIENCE page 12F

STATshot

A look at the trends that shape your world.

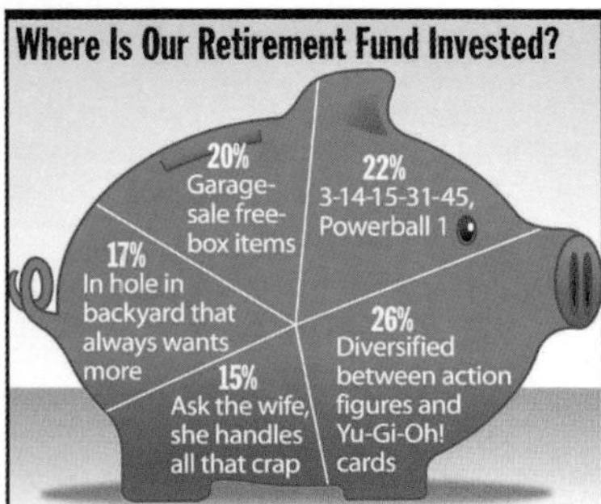

THE ONION VOLUME 41 ISSUE 46 $2.00 US $3.00 CAN

Long-Awaited Beer With Bush Really Awkward, Voter Reports

WARREN, PA—Although respondents to a Pew poll taken prior to the 2004 presidential election characterized Bush as "the candidate they'd most like to sit down and have a beer with," Chris Reinard lived the hypothetical scenario Sunday afternoon, and characterized it as "really uncomfortable and awkward."

Reinard, a father of four who supported Bush in the 2000 and 2004 elections, said sharing a beer with the president at the Switchyard Tap gave him "an uneasy feeling."

"I thought he'd be great," Reinard said. "But when I actually met him, I felt real put off."

The president arrived at the bar via motorcade close to 3 p.m. After a sweep by Secret Service agents, Reinard was asked, for security reasons, to move from his favorite stool. Shortly after he had reseated himself, Reinard said he "was pleased"

see BUSH page 8

Above: Chris Reinard and President Bush try to think of something to talk about.

133 Dead As Delta Cancels Flight In Midair

Above: Delta Flight 1060, which was forced to land in an Indiana cornfield after being canceled mid-flight.

CINCINNATI—A 737 traveling from Cincinnati to Salt Lake City was lost with all passengers and crew Monday when cash-strapped Delta Airlines, the aircraft's operator, canceled Flight 1060 en route.

According to a statement from Delta, the midair cancellation was made as part of the company's plan to cut continental service by 25 percent and emerge from Chapter 11 bankruptcy with an economically viable business strategy.

"Delta Airlines regrets any inconvenience to our valued customers," the statement read in part. "Unfortunately, in today's uncertain economy, service interruptions and cancellations are inevitable."

Air-traffic-control personnel reported that Flight 1060 was at cruising altitude when Delta cancelled the flight. According to the aircraft's black-box flight recorder, the crew announced the cancellation over

see DELTA page 10

Animal Planet Reality Show To Put Bear, Antelope, Hawk, Cheetah In Same House

LOS ANGELES—Cable network Animal Planet announced its most ambitious foray into reality-TV programming yet Monday with *The Zoo*, a weekly, hourlong show in which members of a diverse, all-animal cast square off in a single 3,200-square-foot home in the San Fernando Valley.

"Sparks—and fur—are sure to fly when animals from 11 different ecosystems share a single row house in trendy Echo Park," executive producer Stu Wolchek said. "For many of these wild, colorful, and totally unpredictable cast members, it's the first time they've ever seen a bison or sloth."

Wolchek added: "Some of these guys have never even lived under a roof."

see ANIMAL PLANET page 6

the ONION®

IV

VOLUME 41 ISSUE 50 AMERICA'S FINEST NEWS SOURCE™ 15–21 DECEMBER 2005

Activist Judge Cancels Christmas

Above: Per the court order, city workers take down the Christmas tree from New York's Rockefeller Plaza.

WASHINGTON, DC—In a sudden and unexpected blow to the Americans working to protect the holiday, liberal U.S. 9th Circuit Court of Appeals Judge Stephen Reinhardt ruled the private celebration of Christmas unconstitutional Monday.

"In accordance with my activist agenda to secularize the nation, this court finds Christmas to be unlawful," Judge Reinhardt said. "The celebration of the birth of the philosopher Jesus—be it in the form of gift-giving, the singing of carols, fanciful decorations, or general good cheer and warm feelings amongst families—is in violation of the First Amendment principles

see CHRISTMAS page 8

New Video Game Designed To Have No Influence On Kids' Behavior

NEW YORK—Electronic-entertainment giant Take-Two Interactive, parent company of *Grand Theft Auto* series creator Rockstar Games, released *Stacker* Tuesday, a first-person vertical-crate-arranger guaranteed not to influence young people's behavior in any way.

"With *Stacker*, the player interacts with an environment full of boxes—lightweight, uniformly brown boxes with rounded corners—and uses diligence and repetitive hard work to complete his mission," said Doug Benzies, *Stacker*'s chief developer. "We're confident that the new 'reluctantly interactive' content engine we designed will prevent any excitement or emotional involvement, inappropriate or otherwise, on the part of the player."

To avoid any appearance of suggestive or

see VIDEO GAME page 7

Weather-Weary Nation Not Surprised By Forecast Of Blood Storms

WASHINGTON, DC—A National Weather Service advisory predicting that graphic blood storms will touch ground in the southern U.S. Wednesday is being met with numb resignation by weather-weary Americans.

"Guess I should go buy some plastic tarps and cover up the house, or what remains of it," said Scott Huster of Waveland, MS, echoing the sentiments of a nation battered in recent months by a succession of violent hurricanes, tropical storms, and tornadoes.

According to the advisory, clouds of pure blood have congealed in the atmosphere above Port-au-Prince, Haiti and are heading north at speeds of up to 80 miles per hour. NWS meteorologists predict that the unprecedented storm will splatter most of the Gulf states and West Coast by Friday.

"I suppose I'll have to cancel the barbecue," said Larry Milhouse of Kiln, MS.

Meteorologists are predicting an epic storm of biblical proportions, marked by bullet-velocity winds and flash blooding in low-lying areas. In the Great Lakes and New England states, blood may even coagulate and freeze into softball-sized clot-hail, shattering windows, damaging roofs, and triggering massive blockages on roads and highways.

"Blood-hail can't be any worse than the early thaw in spring," Vermont mother of four Stacey Boswell said. "Still, I'd better take the clothes off the line."

During a Monday night

Above: Satellite image of the approaching storm of blood.

press conference, acting FEMA Director R. David Paulison recommended that citizens of the Southwest evacuate the area immediately, in order to avoid bile blizzards and packs of marauding wolves.

"We recommend that people

see BLOOD STORMS page 9

NEWS

Golden Years Spent In Brass Urn

see LOCAL page 3D

Load-Bearing Walls Not Architect's Forte

see HOME & STYLE page 12F

Man On Horse Hates City

see METRO page 2F

Velcro Unfastened Seductively

see LOCAL page 12F

STATshot

A look at the trends that shape your world.

Baby Panda Names

- Overgrown Bamboo-Eating Raccoon-Looking Motherfucker
- Favrey, the Green Bay Zoo's first panda
- Remorseless Slaughtering Machine Jr.
- "Rodney Endangeredfield"
- Zoo Fundraising Tool The Third
- Joe Mantegna The Panda

ONION NEWS ONLINE

www.theonion.com

- President Bush's Weekly Radio Address
- Daily Onion Radio News
- Daily American Voices

NEWS

Congressman Lets His Guitar Do The Talking

see NATIONAL page 3D

New Christmas TiVo Knows When You've Been Naughty

see ENTERTAINMENT page 12F

Sole Surviving Bridge Club Member Didn't Want To Win Like This

see LOCAL page 2F

STATshot

A look at the trends that shape your world.

Top Temporary Holiday Stores

- Don't-Tell-The-Cops Independence Day M-80 Emporium
- Martin Luther Mattress King
- The Post-Christmas Christmas Store (formerly The Christmas Store)
- Everything's Religious And A Dollar
- Sweet Christ!™ America's #1 Easter Candy Outlet

the ONION®

VOLUME 41 ISSUE 51 | AMERICA'S FINEST NEWS SOURCE™ | 22–28 DECEMBER 2005

Rove Implicated In Santa Identity Leak

WASHINGTON, DC—The recent leak revealing Santa Claus to be "your mommy and daddy" has been linked to President Bush's senior political adviser and deputy chief of staff Karl Rove.

"If this devastating leak, which severely undermines the security of children everywhere and has compromised parent-child relations, came from the highest levels of the White House, that is an outrage," said former Bush counterterrorism adviser and outspoken Bush Administration critic Richard Clarke.

The identity of the mythical holiday gift-giver, previously known only in grown-up circles, was published in the popular *Timbertoes* cartoon in the December issue of *Highlights For Children*. Jean Abrams, a conservative firebrand known to have close

see ROVE page 6

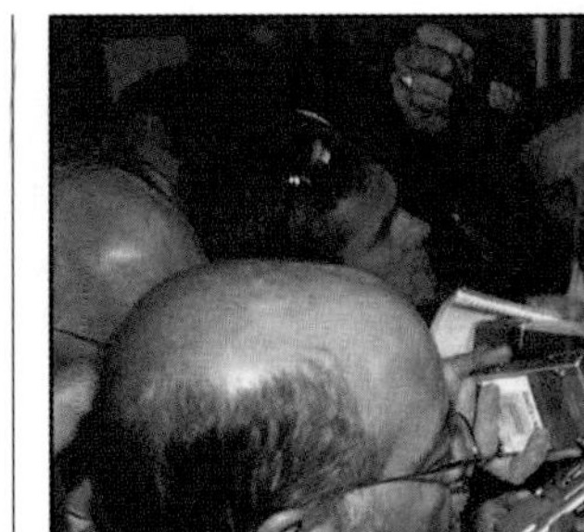

Above: Rove, who stands accused of revealing the non-existence of Santa (left).

U.S. Troops Draw Up Own Exit Strategy

BAGHDAD—Citing the Bush Administration's ongoing refusal to provide a timetable for withdrawal, the U.S. troops stationed in Iraq have devised their own exit strategy.

"My marines are the best-trained, best-equipped, most homesick fighting force in the world," said Staff Sgt. Cornelius Woods. "Just give us the order, and we will commandeer every available vehicle to execute a flanking maneuver on the airstrips of Mosul. By this time tomorrow, we will have retaken our positions at our families' dinner tables in full force."

In a striking rebuke of the assertions of the Pentagon and the White House that a swift exit is neither practical nor possible, soldiers of varying rank have outlined a straightforward plan of immediate disengagement, dubbed "Operation Screw This."

"We kicked around several withdrawal scenarios in our barracks, but ultimately settled on the idea of getting out of here as soon as possible," said Maj. Brian Garcia, who is on his third tour of duty in Iraq.

Supporters of the Iraq war say the reconstruction of politically and economically devastated Iraq will take decades, and the gradual process of departure will begin only after a lengthy occupation.

"I'm familiar with the 'years of occupation to facilitate reconstruction' theory," said Army Spc. Megan Beaulieu. "However, virtually

see EXIT STRATEGY page 7

Above: Staff Sgt. Cornelius Woods debriefs Pfc. Jack Colin.

Rising Home-Heating Costs Hitting Reptile Families Hardest

CHICAGO—With government figures indicating double-digit home-heating cost increases in coming months, America's reptilian citizens are warning that, unless swift measures are taken to provide them with adequate warmth, many will face serious metabolic crises this winter.

"Unlike our mammalian citizens, who maintain a consistent body temperature and have the option of throwing on a sweater, reptiles are entirely dependent on external heat sources," Sen. Richard Durbin (D-IL) said. "All my constituents are facing rate hikes of 21 percent or more. But some of them, like it or not, may be forced into a quasi-hibernative state if they do not receive emergency fuel-price relief."

According to Department of Energy data, households in northern states have

see HEATING COSTS page 8

JANUARY

TV Blamed For Rise In Formulaic Violence

Senate Ethics Committee To Meet
In New Ethics Committee Mansion

FEBRUARY

Cheney Orders Motorcade To Gun
It Over Half-Open Drawbridge

MARCH

Wonder Drug Inspires Deep, Unwavering
Love Of Pharmaceutical Companies

APRIL

Poverty-Stricken Africans Receive
Desperately Needed Bibles

MAY

32-Year-Old Actress Dies Of Old Age

JUNE

2006

Toby Keith Struggling To Come Up With Rhyme For Ahmadinejad

New 'Anti-Abortion Pill' Kills Mother, Leaves Fetus Alive

Kim Jong-Il Interprets Sunrise As Act Of War

JULY | AUGUST | SEPTEMBER | OCTOBER | NOVEMBER | DECEMBER

Study Finds Alligators Dangerous No Matter How Drunk You Are

Americans Celebrate 10 Millionth 'Bring Yourself To Work Day'

'C-List Celebrity Killer' Leaves Police Enthusiastically Guessing Who's Next

NEWS

Suicide Bomber Reacts Poorly To Surprise Birthday Party

see LOCAL page 3D

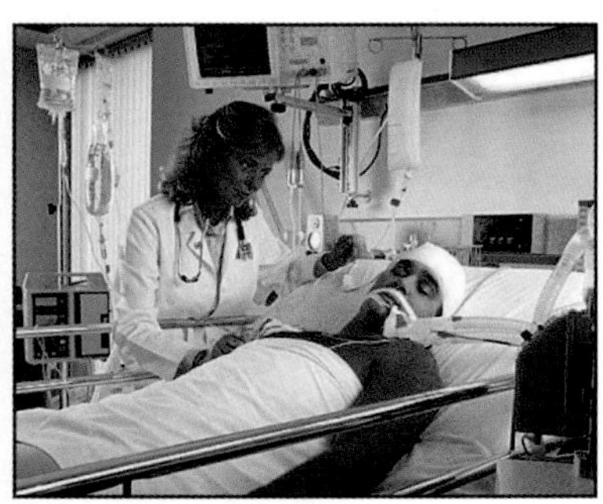

Surviving Miner Ordered Back To Work

see NATIONAL page 2C

STATshot

A look at the trends that shape your world.

ONION News Online:

http://www.theonion.com

- President Bush's Weekly Radio Address
- Daily Onion Radio News
- Daily American Voices

THE ONION
VOLUME 42
ISSUE 03
$2.00 US
$3.00 CAN

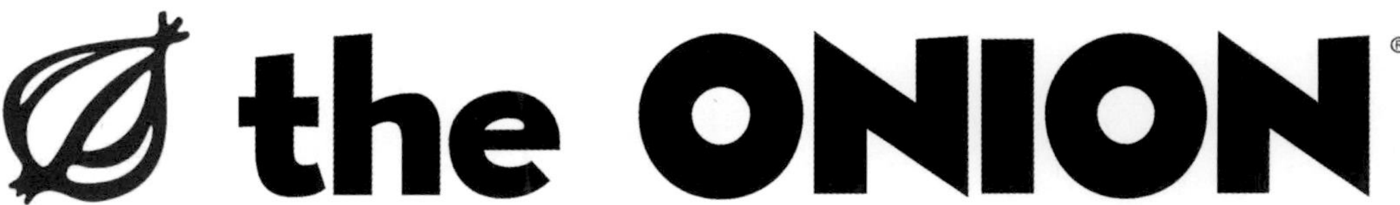

VOLUME 42 ISSUE 03 AMERICA'S FINEST NEWS SOURCE™ 19–25 JANUARY 2006

U.S. Holds Going-Out-Of-Business Sale

WASHINGTON, DC—In an address broadcast on late-night television Tuesday, President Bush announced that the federal government will liquidate its holdings in a going-out-of-business sale scheduled to begin Friday.

"The U.S. government, America's place for law and order since 1776, has lost its lease, and everything must go, go, go," Bush said. "But our loss is your gain, and make no mistake: You, the people, would be crazy to miss out on these amazing closeout bargains."

The Washington-based government, which hasn't shown a profit in five years and carries the highest debt in its history, was ultimately driven out of business by costly overhead and cheap foreign competitors. As a result, Bush said, everything—from flag stands and Capitol cafeteria flatware to legislation dating from the early days of the republic—will be marked down 30 to 90 percent.

"Get yourself a piece of history, or just stock up on your favorite items—whatever it is, chances are we've got it," said Bush, wearing a 10-gallon hat and standing before a chroma-key background of the National Mall as a list of federal items and their discounted prices scrolled down the screen. "But act fast, because deals like

see SALE page 8

Right: After 200-plus years of service, the U.S. government is closing its doors.

Left: Battle-wearied Avers pauses after 20 hours on the front line.

Call Of Duty 2 Gamer Wonders If War Is Worth Dying 79 Times For

PITTSFIELD, MA—As World War II entered its sixth grueling week within the video game *Call Of Duty 2*, battle-hardened soldier-player Martin Avers admitted Tuesday that his commitment to the struggle to free electronic Europe from the virtual Third Reich is wavering.

"After weeks of fighting for every pixel of ground and see-

see CALL OF DUTY page 11

Sean Penn Demands To Know What Asshole Took SeanPenn@gmail.com

LOS ANGELES—In an impassioned 1,900-word open letter published in Monday's *Washington Post*, actor-director Sean Penn urged the unknown person who registered the e-mail address SeanPenn@gmail.com to "come forward immediately, rather than wallowing in the shame and ignominy of fraud."

The paid full-page advertisement, addressed to "a certain inconsiderate asshole," continued: "Every American—indeed, every human being, regardless of nationality—deserves to be rightfully and accurately represented on the World Wide Web—the communication gateway into the next century and beyond—without having to resort to nonsensical aliases with random strings of numbers tacked onto the end. In an era of global wireless technology, our very identities are at stake. It's highly unethical at best, criminal at worst, for others to wantonly abscond with them."

Penn recounted in the letter how he had waited for an invitation to Google's e-mail service for a year and a half before receiving one earlier this month. According to Penn, when he tried to establish an account, he received a message indicating

see SEAN PENN page 12

NEWS

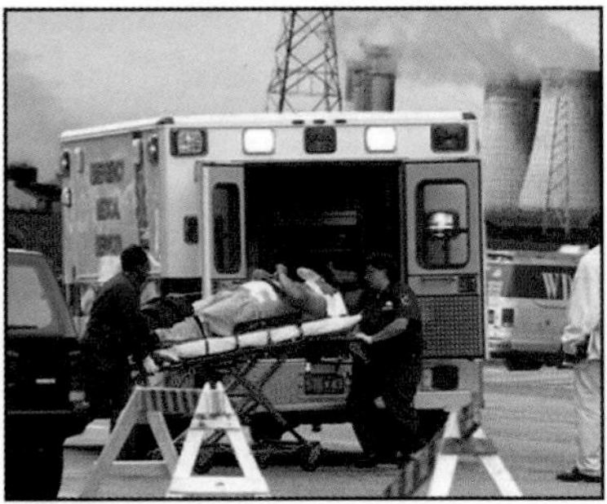

Casual Friday Claims Lives Of 13 Nuclear-Waste-Disposal Technicians

see LOCAL page 12F

Family Cell-Phone Plan Area Family's Closest Bond

see REGIONAL page 2C

STATshot

A look at the trends that shape your world.

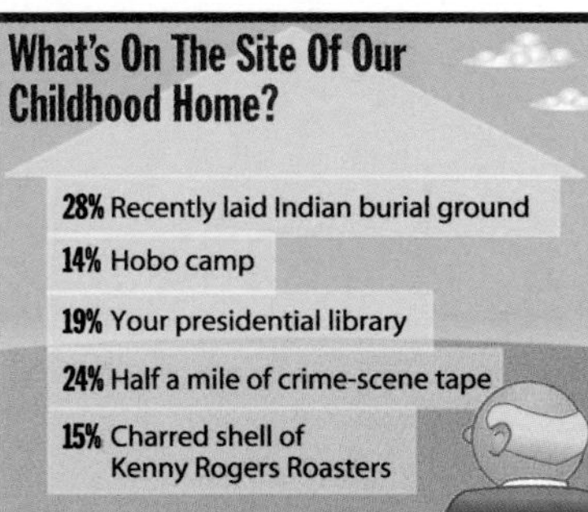

ONION News Online:

http://www.theonion.com

- President Bush's Weekly Radio Address
- Daily Onion Radio News
- Daily American Voices

the ONION®

VOLUME 42 ISSUE 04 | AMERICA'S FINEST NEWS SOURCE™ | 26 JANUARY–1 FEBRUARY 2006

Nation's Snowmen March Against Global Warming

WASHINGTON, DC—Braving balmy temperatures and sunny skies, millions of scarfless snowmen and snowwomen gathered in cities across the world Tuesday to raise public awareness about the heavy toll global warming is taking on their health and well-being.

According to organizers of marches in Washington, Atlanta, Montreal, Berlin, London, Reykjavik, and Moscow, global warming is the primary cause of the steep reduction in the snowman population throughout the Northern Hemisphere. Demonstrators worldwide called on their governments to take more aggressive steps to reduce the effects of climate

see SNOWMEN page 6

Right: Snowmen from across the nation gather at the Washington Monument to protest global warming.

More Companies Phasing Out Retirement Option

NEW YORK—With pension funds dwindling as retirees enjoy longer, more capable lives, many businesses have opted to freeze their workers' employment status and keep them on the job through their sunset years.

"Under the new approach, our employees gain the advantage of lifelong job security," Hewlett-Packard CEO and president Mark Hurd said. "Even though our workers will no longer be able to collect a pension, they will receive checks as long as they are able to be wheeled into work and punch the clock."

Hewlett-Packard, Verizon, and IBM are just a few of the Fortune 500 companies that are phasing out the retirement option in favor of "indefinite-employment" plans, under which thousands of qualified workers will continue to earn yearly stipends in exchange for work.

"To the list of outmoded and costly business practices such as health insurance, overtime pay, and lunch breaks, add age-based quitting," corporate management consultant Robert Hopgood said.

see RETIREMENT page 7

Above: Agriculture Secretary Mike Johanns.

Secretary Of Agriculture Keeps Bragging He's Ninth In Line For The Presidency

WASHINGTON, DC—Beltway insiders report that since his appointment in February 2005, Agriculture Secretary Mike Johanns has been preoccupied with the fact that he is ninth in the line of presidential succession.

Said Johanns: "It's really something to think that, if the president and the vice-president, the speaker of the house, the president pro tempore of the Senate, the secretary of state, the secretary of the treasury, the secretary of defense, the attorney general, and the secretary of the interior were somehow unable to fulfill their capacities as president, I would have to be the one to take up the mantle."

Those close to him say that Johanns never expressed any particular knowledge of or interest in presidential succession prior to his appointment as head of the U.S. Department of Agriculture.

"If you've ever wondered what it's like to be nine heartbeats away from the presidency, just ask Mike," Deputy Secretary Chuck Conner said. "He'll tell you."

Johanns said he has promised his children that should he become president, he will not allow the press to exploit them or put them in the spotlight.

"I used to be intimidated by it a little," Johanns said. "But now that I've had a

see SECRETARY page 8

NEWS

Children's Hospital Charity Dependent On Teri Hatcher's Knowledge Of British Parliament

see LOCAL page 2C

Philippine Mud Wins In Landslide

see POLITICS page 12F

STATshot

A look at the trends that shape your world.

ONION News Online:
http://www.theonion.com
Daily American Voices
Daily Onion Radio News
President Bush's Weekly Radio Address

THE ONION
VOLUME 42
ISSUE 09
$2.00 US
$3.00 CAN

the ONION®

VOLUME 42 ISSUE 09 AMERICA'S FINEST NEWS SOURCE™ 2–8 MARCH 2006

I

Rotation Of The Earth Plunges Entire North American Continent Into Darkness

SPECIAL REPORT

NEW YORK—Millions of eyewitnesses watched in stunned horror Tuesday as light emptied from the sky, plunging the U.S. and neighboring countries into darkness. As the hours progressed, conditions only worsened.

At approximately 4:20 p.m. EST, the sun began to lower from its position in the sky in a westward trajectory, eventually disappearing below the horizon. Reports of this global emergency continued to file in from across the continent until 5:46 p.m. PST, when the entire North American mainland was officially declared dark.

As the phenomenon hit New York, millions of motorists were forced to use their headlights to navigate through the blackness. Highways flooded with commuters who had left work to hurry home to their families. Traffic was bottlenecked for more than two hours in many major metropolitan areas.

see ROTATION page 7

Left: Satellite view at 4:50 p.m. EST shows the sun disappearing from the sky.

Democrats Vow Not To Give Up Hopelessness

WASHINGTON, DC—In a press conference on the steps of the Capitol Monday, Congressional Democrats announced that, despite the scandals plaguing the Republican Party and widespread calls for change in Washington, their party will remain true to its hopeless direction.

"We are entirely capable of bungling this opportunity to regain control of the House and Senate and the trust of the American people," Senate Minority Leader Harry Reid (D-NV) said to scattered applause. "It will take some doing, but we're in this for the long and pointless haul."

"We can lose this," Reid added. "All it takes is a little lack of backbone."

Despite plummeting poll numbers for the G.O.P nationwide and an upcoming election in which all House seats and 33

see DEMOCRATS page 10

Right: House Minority Leader Nancy Pelosi reaffirms the Democratic Party's promise to remain marginalized.

Modern-Day John Henry Dies Trying To Out-Spreadsheet Excel 11.0

BALTIMORE—Office laborers across the nation are mourning the passing of Wallace Peters, 42, the mythic three-column accountant at Chesapeake & Ohio Consultants who pitted himself against Microsoft's latest version of the popular spreadsheet program Excel.

Although Peters was able to balance his sheet a full 10 seconds before the program

see HENRY page 8

Far Left: The late Wallace "Wally" Peters, whom colleagues are calling a 21st-century John Henry (left).

the ONION®

VOLUME 42 ISSUE 14 AMERICA'S FINEST NEWS SOURCE™ 6–12 APRIL 2006

NEWS

Eager Understudy Beginning To Think John Lithgow Impervious To Disease

see ENTERTAINMENT page 10A

Delicate Pastry Not Made For This World

see LOCAL page 3E

STATshot

A look at the trends that shape your world.

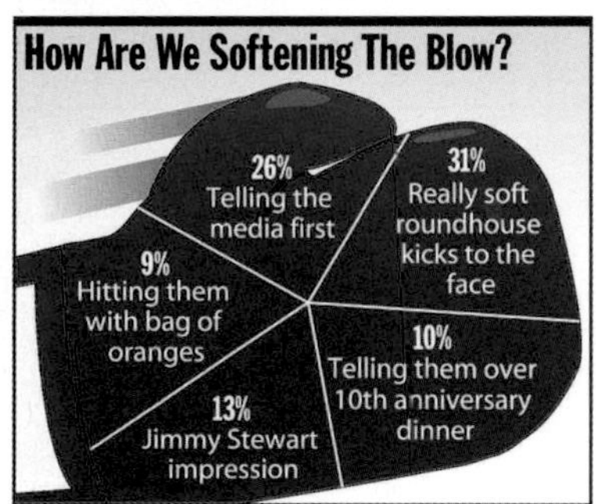

THE ONION VOLUME 42 ISSUE 14

$2.00 US $3.00 CAN

Girls Gone Wild Released Back Into Civilization

Above: Two Girls Gone Wild in their natural habitat, just before capture at the height of molting season.

SOUTH PADRE ISLAND, TX—In what wildlifestyle reformation volunteers are calling a "positive step," the first group of rehabilitated Girls Gone Wild were released back into the civilized world Monday, and early signs indicate that they are adjusting smoothly, according to the director of the group responsible for their rescue.

"At first, the girls were disoriented," said Janet Ottley, director of the South Padre Island Wild Life Rescue Foundation. "They were frightened by the absence of familiar comforts such as overt male attention, binge drinking, and camcorders. But over time, we've seen improvement: so far, no reports of nipple exposure, so we're very hopeful."

The 11 girls were captured nearly one month ago during their annual spring migration to the area and then put through an intensive rehabilitation program. "They have come a very long way," Ottley said. "When we first brought them into our clinic, they could barely function beyond baring their breasts, and they communicated solely through loud, sustained hoots."

As their subspecies does every year, the Girls Gone Wild, roaming in packs,

see GIRLS page 6

Above: Site of the former Detroit Museum of African-American History, which took in over $135.

Detroit Sold For Scrap

DETROIT—Detroit, a former industrial metropolis in southeastern Michigan with a population of just under 1 million, was sold at auction Tuesday to bulk scrap dealers and smelting foundries across the United States.

"This is what's best for Detroit," Mayor Kwame M. Kilpatrick said. "We must act now, while we can still get a little something for it."

Once dismantled and processed, Detroit is expected to yield nearly 14 million tons of steel, 2.85 million tons of aluminum, and approximately 837,000 tons of copper.

The decision to demolish and cull Detroit for scrap was approved last month by a 6-3 City Council vote after a cost-benefit analysis revealed that, as a functioning urban area, it held a negative cash value.

According to scrap dealers, Detroit is an aging city in fair-to-poor condition, with "substantial wear and tear." It also bears the marks of extensive fire and rust damage, and it may not comply with current U.S. safety and emissions standards.

see DETROIT page 8

Critics Blast Bush For Not Praying Hard Enough

WASHINGTON, DC—President Bush, already facing the lowest approval ratings in history, is coming under fire from former supporters over what they call his "ineffectual and incompetent" use of prayer for national guidance and assistance.

"Every time the president is criticized, he insists that the nation is in his prayers," said the Family Research Council's Bob Jensen. "That may be, but it's becoming more and more clear that these prayers are either too infrequent, too brief, or not strongly worded enough to be effective."

Jensen added: "This nation deserves more than a president who just pays lip service to prayer. It deserves a president who demands that his prayers get real-world results."

Despite assurances from the president that he "prays every day" for the nation's interests both at home and abroad, the mounting crises of recent months—escalating gas prices, the botched Dubai port security deal, ethics scandals, and the rising death toll in Iraq—have left many unimpressed

see BUSH page 9

NEWS

Amazon 1-Click Bankrupts Area Parkinson's Sufferer

see LOCAL page 11B

Jessica Alba Saving Money For When Audience Turns On Her

see ENTERTAINMENT page 6C

STATshot

A look at the trends that shape your world.

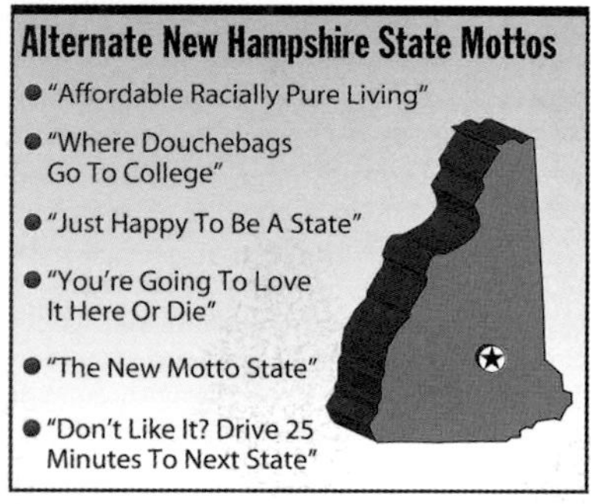

THE ONION
VOLUME 42
ISSUE 17
$2.00 US
$3.00 CAN

the ONION®

VOLUME 42 ISSUE 17 | AMERICA'S FINEST NEWS SOURCE™ | 27 APRIL–3 MAY 2006

Grease Fire Rages Through Midwest

Left: Arm & Hammer donated 100,000 pounds of baking soda to help extinguish the massive blaze.

MILWAUKEE—A raging grease fire has spread across the southern half of Wisconsin and into the neighboring states of Illinois, Iowa, and Minnesota, killing at least eight and leaving hundreds injured or missing after the intense heat and acrid odor of charred pork and cheese-filled breading overwhelmed the region.

Six of the dead reportedly tried to put out the grease flames with water, causing the fire to spread; two others perished after running back into their burning homes to save bacon still cooking on their stoves.

By Tuesday evening, more than 700,000 acres of Midwestern greaseland—including tens of thousands of patio grills, outdoor beer gardens, supper-club kitchens, and barbecue pits—had been destroyed in the blaze.

Beloit, WI Fire Chief Paul Tolley said the fire was spreading faster than crews could react.

"The main problem is it's being fed at every turn. The homes and businesses here are oversaturated with corn dogs, melted cheese, and any number of deep-fried items," Tolley said. "Every time we think we have it under control, it hits a Hardee's and everything turns to chaos."

Officials said the grease blaze began after a Dodgeville, WI resident attempted to submerge an entire 21-pound turkey in a makeshift deep fryer Sunday. The fire then leapt rapidly from pancake house to pancake house, intensifying when flames reached a dense patch of diners at the peak of the brunch rush, which Dodgeville

see FIRE page 6

Scholars Discover 23 Blank Pages That May As Well Be Lost Samuel Beckett Play

PARIS—Just weeks after the centennial of the birth of pioneering minimalist playwright Samuel Beckett, archivists analyzing papers from his Paris estate uncovered a small stack of blank paper that scholars are calling "the latest example of the late Irish-born writer's genius."

The 23 blank pages, which literary experts presume is a two-act play composed sometime between 1973 and 1975, are already being heralded as one of the most ambitious works by the Nobel Prize-winning author of *Waiting For Godot*, and a natural progression from his earlier works, including 1969's *Breath*, a 30-second play with no characters, and 1972's *Not I*, in which the only illuminated part of the stage is a floating mouth.

"In what was surely a conscious decision by Mr. Beckett, the white, uniform, non-ruled pages, which symbolize the starkness and emptiness of life, were left unbound, unmarked, and untouched," said Trinity College professor of Irish literature Fintan O'Donoghue. "And, as if to further exemplify the anonymity and facelessness of 20th-century man, they were found, of all places, between other sheets of paper."

"I can only conclude that we have stumbled upon something quite remarkable," O'Donoghue added.

Above: O'Donoghue shows off what could easily be the play's whimsically tragic opening scene.

According to literary critic Eric Matheson, who praised the work for "the bare-

see BECKETT page 12

Search For Wallet Self-Narrated

YPSILANTI, MI—Local man Kevin McCormick, 28, delivered a complete running commentary throughout a 12-minute search for the 4-year-old, Velcro-fastened wallet he misplaced Sunday.

The narration began in the late afternoon, when McCormick, a part-time pet-store attendant, announced his intention to visit a local taqueria for lunch. It was then that he first audibly noticed the wallet was missing.

"Oh shit," he said. "I can't find my wallet."

McCormick then turned his attention to vocally describing the central task before him—finding the wallet in what would prove to be an exhaustive, continuous commentary on the nearly quarter-hour search.

"All right, Kev—think," he began aloud. He then scanned the loose clothing and clutter around the one-bedroom apartment.

"When was the last time you saw it?" he

see WALLET page 8

the ONION®
I
VOLUME 42 ISSUE 24 AMERICA'S FINEST NEWS SOURCE™ 15–21 JUNE 2006

NEWS

Inner-City Prodigy Earns GED At Age 11

see EDUCATION page 4F

Nation's Grandmothers Swept Up In Textile-Messaging Craze

see PEOPLE page 13B

STATshot

A look at the trends that shape your world.

22
0 74470 94595 6
THE ONION
VOLUME 42
ISSUE 24
$2.00 US
$3.00 CAN

Pope Makes First Papal Visit To Six Flags

Above: Pope Benedict XVI returns from a "fucking awesome" trip on the XCalibur.

EUREKA, MO—Pope Benedict XVI returned to Rome today following a historic, three-day trip to Six Flags St. Louis, the first official papal visit to a major American theme park since Pope Paul VI's Thanksgiving Mass at Wet 'n Wild in August 1966.

As the park opened its doors to the general public last Friday, the pope emerged from the last car of the Foghorn Leghorn National Park Railway to greet the throngs of people who had assembled hours earlier for a once-in-a-lifetime chance to pay their respects to the blessed pontiff and to vie for a seat on Superman Tower of Power, a popular free-fall ride.

The pope began his visit with a brief sermon delivered from the balcony of the Old Glory Amphitheatre, and blessed the park's many concession-stand workers who "provide sustenance for our brethren seeking to beat the heat."

"My friends in Christ, as we stand togeth-

see POPE page 6

Above: The new Steve will buy Sony products.

Sony Unveils New Model Customer

NEW YORK—Sony Corporation chairman and CEO Howard Stringer gave the public a first glimpse of Steve, the latest model in the company's highly anticipated line of ideal electronics consumers, during the Sony Corporation of America's annual stockholders meeting Monday.

The 72-inch, 195-pound consumer—a 34-year-old unmarried financial analyst—is smaller, lighter, and swifter than last year's beta-model consumer, Larry.

"Larry was much less mobile, which worked well for electronics enjoyment but

see SONY page 9

Surgeon General Issues Report On Dangers Of Secondhand Fire

WASHINGTON, D.C.—Three decades after health advocates brought to the world's attention the serious risks associated with being on fire, a report released Monday by U.S. Surgeon General Richard Carmona purports that secondhand exposure to those ablaze could prove equally as deadly.

"We now know that individuals engulfed in flames not only pose a danger to themselves, but to everyone else around them," Carmona said. "While severe irritation of the eyes, throat, face, arms, and legs is common among those not on fire themselves, prolonged contact can also cause irreparable damage to bodily organs, most frequently the skin."

"Be it the increased chance of heart attacks, malignant growths that rapidly swell and blister over the surface of the flesh, or simply a burning sensation, secondhand fire is not something to be taken lightly," Carmona added. "It can, and often does, significantly affect one's quality of life."

According to the report, exposure to secondhand fire, or "passive burning," as it is also known, for as little as two minutes can take 80 years off one's life. Statistics

Above: Carmona warns of fire danger.

show that senior citizens with dry skin, young children who are smaller and consequently take less time to burn, and men and women covered in flammable liquids are most at risk. Chronic asthma sufferers were shown to have their condition drastically worsen within seconds.

see FIRE page 8

NEWS

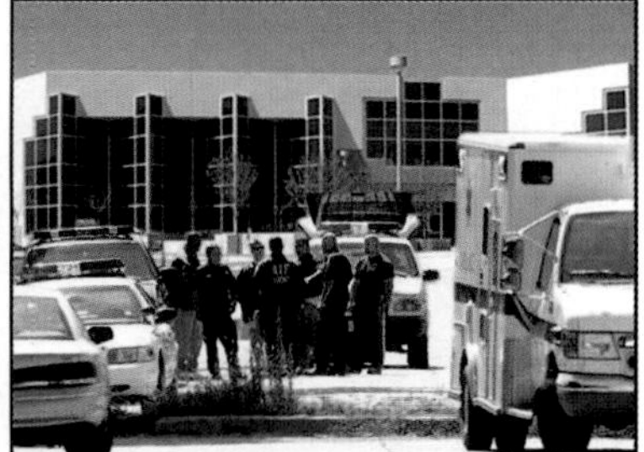

Secretarian Violence Claims Lives Of Three Receptionists

see NATIONAL page12B

Area Mom: 'I Finally Learned Computers'

see LOCAL page 4E

STATshot

A look at the trends that shape your world.

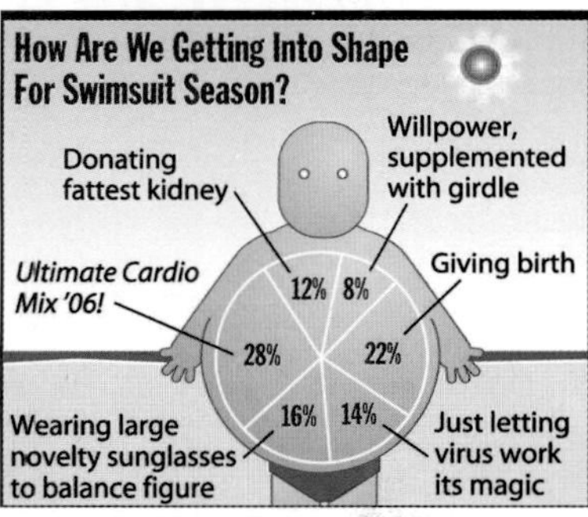

ONION News Online:

http://www.theonion.com

- Daily American Voices
- Daily Onion Radio News
- President Bush's Weekly Radio Address

the ONION®

VOLUME 42 ISSUE 26 | AMERICA'S FINEST NEWS SOURCE™ | 29 JUNE–5 JULY 2006

Government To Defend Marriage From Dashing Reginald St. Croix, Esq.

WASHINGTON, DC—Amid clamor from thousands of cuckolded husbands nationwide, a bipartisan group of lawmakers has drafted legislation designed to safeguard the institution of marriage, the moral cornerstone of American society, from the greatest threat to its sanctity: suave master-seducer Reginald St. Croix, Esq.

"I coauthored the Defense Of Marriage From Reginald St. Croix Act because I find it unconscionable that our nation would allow this brazen scourge of connubial bliss to thrive unchecked," Senate Majority Leader Bill Frist (R-TN) said. "Why, just this last week he approached my wife Karyn at a Senate mixer, brought her hand to his full, sensuous lips, and requested the honor of calling on her in the garden. The very idea!"

Sources close to the senator confirmed that Karyn Frist, incapacitated by unabated swooning since the incident, has been confined to her canopy bed by physicians.

Although little is known of St. Croix's parentage, provenance, or means of support, he is known to be an unusually well-formed man in his mid-to-late 30s, possessed of pellucid blue eyes, dark wavy hair, a silver tongue, and an all-encompassing appetite for the company of attached womanhood.

Above: Reginald St. Croix, Esq., rake, knave, and despoiler of the divine institution.

Tax records and divorce statistics, as

see ST. CROIX page 6

McCain, Feingold Co-Sponsor Chain Of Integrity-Themed Eateries

WASHINGTON, DC—Citing a long-standing need to "restore honor and dignity to the American food-service industry," Sens. John McCain (R-AZ) and Russ Feingold (D-WI) announced the public debut of their joint business venture Monday, a chain of integrity-themed restaurants which opened in 12 locations nationwide.

The new Russ & John's chain, which the two senators funded privately via small financial donations of no more than $2,000 per investor, was founded on the idea that "today's customers want quality food without all the lies and exaggerations that all too often accompany it," according to McCain.

"When we say we've got the best burger in town, you can be sure that we can back up that claim with documented evidence," Feingold said to an estimated crowd of 4,000 at the grand opening of a Russ & John's in Stevens Point, WI. "We've done the research, our staff has interviewed hundreds of burger lovers, and I can truthfully say that nothing compares to our mouthwatering Bleu Cheese 'N Bacon Burger."

see McCAIN-FEINGOLD page 8

THE LIGHTER SIDE

Baggage-Handling Mix-Up Sends Dirty Bomb To St. Louis

Above: Terrorist Yousef waits in vain for his dirty bomb.

NEW YORK—Even in the air-conditioned confines of New York's John F. Kennedy Airport back on June 14, Abu Basir Yousef was sweating.

His sole piece of luggage—a black duffel bag—was lost upon his arrival in New York.

Despite hours of waiting, and several U.S. Airways check-in counter workers and Transportation Security Administration screeners joining in the search, the Yemen-born 32-year-old had yet to hear any positive updates. Finally, a baggage claim representative approached him.

"Afraid I've got some bad news," the worker said to Yousef.

Airline personnel had searched the plane, the tarmac, and the gate, but were still unable to locate his bag containing his homemade dirty bomb.

"My trip was ruined," Yousef said. "But Allah will right this wrong."

Most Americans have grown accustomed to inconvenience in the name of security, be it color-coded anxieties or metal detectors at public libraries.

see DIRTY BOMB page 10

Child Soldier Promoted To Child Private 1st Class
INTERNATIONAL, page 14C

Mariachi Band Has No Idea Your Mother Just Died
LOCAL, page 3A

Opinion
Why Will No One Sign Up For My Pain-Inducement Study?
By Clark Trenton, page 11B

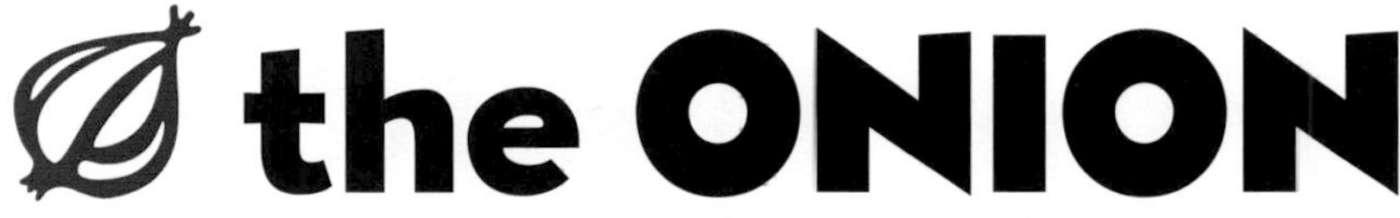

LOW 60 | HIGH 82

A good day for boating, if you're a dick

July 27, 2006 | Volume 42 Issue 30

AMERICA'S FINEST NEWS SOURCE • ONION.COM

Wikipedia Celebrates 750 Years Of American Independence

Founding Fathers, Patriots, Mr. T. Honored

NEW YORK—Wikipedia, the online, reader-edited encyclopedia, honored the 750th anniversary of American independence on July 25 with a special featured section on its main page Tuesday.

"It would have been a major oversight to ignore this portentous anniversary," said Wikipedia founder Jimmy Wales, whose site now boasts over 4,300,000 articles in multiple languages, over one-quarter of which are in English, including 11,000 concerning popular toys of the 1980s alone. "At 750 years, the U.S. is by far the world's oldest surviving democracy, and is certainly deserving of our recognition," Wales said. "According to our database, that's 212 years older than the Eiffel Tower, 347 years older than the earliest-known woolly-mammoth fossil, and a full 493 years older than the microwave oven."

"In fact," added Wales, "at three-quarters of a millennium, the USA has been around almost as long as technology."

The commemorative page is one of the most detailed on the site, rivaling entries for *Firefly* and the Treaty Of Algeron for sheer length. Subheadings include "Origins Of Colonial Discontent," "Some Famous Guys In Wigs And Three-Cornered Hats," and "Christmastime In Gettysburg." It also features detailed maps of the original colonies—including Narnia, the central ice deserts, and Westeros—as well as profiles of famous American historical figures such as Benjamin Franklin, Special Agent Jack Bauer, and Samuel Adams who is also a

see **Wikipedia**, page 8

U.S. Soldiers Ask Rumsfeld If They Could Get Surprise Visit From Loved Ones Instead

Onion Capitol Bureau

BAGHDAD—Although U.S. troops in Iraq said they appreciated Defense Secretary Donald Rumsfeld's recent surprise visit, thousands of them have petitioned the Department Of Defense to arrange surprise visits from relatives and spouses as well. "As great as it was to get a visit from him, given the choice, I'd rather see my mom," said Army Cpl. Emilio Salazar, who is serving his third tour of duty. "Or my dad, or even my girlfriend. I'm just saying, they could fit a lot of people on Air Force One." An estimated two-thirds of American military personnel in Iraq have signed the petition, with the rest saying Iraq is still far too dangerous a place for anyone's loved ones to spend time.

Sparrow Aviation Administration Blames Collision On Failure To Detect Pane Of Glass

■ Mysterious Phenomenon Kills Millions Each Year

PIERRE, SD—Sparrow Aviation Administration officials are calling the Monday collision of an westbound sparrow with the window of a Mitchell, SD home a clear case of "controlled flight into glass," after the bird failed to detect a transparent windowpane directly in his flight path.

Howard R. Trojanowski, a Pierre-bound, 2-year-old field sparrow who had been licensed to fly since two weeks after he was hatched and had logged over 60,000 flying hours, departed from a ledge near Sioux Falls Regional Airport at 11:04 a.m. CST. Trojanowski never reached his intended tree branch, instead striking a tempered-glass picture window 2.5 miles northwest of Mitchell 74 minutes after takeoff at an estimated speed of 39 mph.

There were no survivors.

SAA Commissioner Vincent Stivolo said the crash was likely due to glass, a "common, yet not fully understood phenomenon" in which an area normally blocked by such barriers as curtains, blinds, or shutters suddenly appears to be an open passage to an indoor facility or an unobstructed extension of the outdoor environment.

Conclusive explanations have historically eluded sparrow-crash investigators, some of whom have themselves apparently fallen victim to the phenomenon. Three investigators dispatched to the Mitchell site failed to show up and have since been reported missing.

"Flight records indicate that Mr. Trojanowski unexpectedly diverted his route above the corner of St. Ray Street and Longfellow Drive, and began a slow descent when he noticed a colorful hanging potted plant about 15 feet below SAA-regulated minimum flying altitude," said Stivolo, a sparrow. "It is at this point that we believe he made the fatal decision to make an unscheduled landing on the plant."

Above: SAA officials describe the crash at a press conference.

"Our thoughts and prayers go out to Mr. Trojanowski's wife and four eggs," Stivolo added.

The SAA has officially ruled out sparrow error, finding no evidence that Trojanowski tried to swerve out of the way. Additionally, his Glass Proximity Warning System failed to activate until 0.001 seconds after he came into contact with the glass.

An autopsy performed late Monday evening suggests that Trojanowski's crown struck the impenetrable transparent terrain first, followed by the left wing, which snapped in half on impact.

According to sparrow coroner Stephanie Barlow, an inspection of the scattered wreckage at the crash site revealed no prior damage to the wings, tail, or any other part of Trojanowski.

"This bird was in good, airworthy condition before takeoff for this routine flight—one that he had made literally thousands of times before," Barlow said. "But unfortunately, this happens all too often, even with the most experienced fliers."

Since the advent of the clear glass window in the 16th century, untold billions of birds have been lost or severely injured in similar incidents. In the early

see **Sparrow**, page 6

Report: 47% Of Satellites Currently Monitoring Celebrity Parenting

Onion Science Thursday

LOS ANGELES—Just days after the launch of *SURI-II*, whose state-of-the-art instruments are expected to provide the

first-ever infrared images of Tom Cruise and Katie Holmes' infant daughter, a report published by NASA revealed that nearly half of all communications and reconnaissance satellites currently in orbit are engaged in collecting and transmitting data relating to the child-rearing practices of Hollywood stars.

According to Monday's report, the *SURI-II* is one of 73 celebrity-surveying satellites currently deployed by the U.S. and assigned a variety of tasks including analyzing the rising levels of hostility between new mother Britney Spears and husband Kevin Federline, calculating the long-term effects of Julia Roberts' decision to bottle-feed her twins, and tracking the ever-changing whereabouts of Angelina Jolie and Brad Pitt.

see **Satellites**, page 6

FASHION
Prada Raincoat Ruined By Rain page 2B

MEDICINE & HEALTH
Man Recalls Relaxing Battle With Sedatives, page 11F

ENTERTAINMENT
Lute Player Getting All The Wenches At Medieval Fair, page 9A

INDEX

ONION
Briefs ... 2
Opinion ... 9
Sports ... 14

A.V. CLUB
Cinema ... 24
Music ... 30
Words ... 33

A.V. MADISON
Calendar ... 34
Food ... 42
Funny Pages ... 45
Savage Love ... 47

ONION NEWS ONLINE
onion.com GO

$2.00 US | $3.00 CANADA

THIS WEEK IN THE A.V. CLUB
Paul Reubens discusses life as Pee-wee Herman, Rhymefest reaffirms his love for crack babies, Woody Allen's back, and more.

A.V. MADISON
Tune in to Eels' twisted pop Wednesday at The Annex.
page 39

Jogger Thinks He Looks Great
FITNESS, page 4D

Intel Unveils Oversized Novelty Processor
TECHNOLOGY, page 13E

Opinion
The Surveillance Camera Loves Me
by Scott Jackson, page 3A

LOW 60 | HIGH 82
Partly bathed in the healing light of the Lord

August 31, 2006 | Volume 42 Issue 35
AMERICA'S FINEST NEWS SOURCE • ONION.COM

Bush Urges Nation To Be Quiet For A Minute While He Tries To Think

In a televised address to the nation, Bush called for "a little peace and quiet."

Onion Capitol Bureau

WASHINGTON, DC—In a nationally televised address Monday, President Bush urged all citizens, regardless of race, creed, color, or political affiliation, "to quiet down for just one minute" so he could have "a chance to think."

"Every American has an inalienable right to free speech and self-expression," Bush said. "Nonetheless, I call upon the American people to hold off on it for, say, 60 seconds. Just long enough for me to get this all sorted out in my head."

"Please," Bush added.

While the president said achieving a unilateral peace and quiet "would not be easy," he hoped that citizens would respect his wish and work toward a temporary cease-talk so that he could can hear his own thoughts "for once."

"Make no mistake: It will take patience and sacrifice," Bush said. "But such drastic measures could lead to a better tomorrow for all of us, especially for your commander in chief."

Bush then closed his speech by exhaling sharply, tightly closing his eyes, and massaging his temples. "I just—Christ, I just need a goddamn minute, you know?" he said.

The presidential call for national silence came as little surprise following weeks of rumors from White House sources that Bush appeared increasingly distracted and wearied by the ever-pervasive noise. Excerpts from an unedited videotaped meeting made public last Thursday revealed a frustrated Bush rhetorically asking Turkish Prime Minister Recep Erdogan how "the leader of the free world was supposed to get any work done around here with all this volume."

Assuring the public it "can make as much noise as [it] wants" as soon as the Bush-proposed national minute of silence concludes, Chief Of Staff Josh Bolten said that the White House was making "every effort" to accommodate Bush's wishes.

"Currently, the president's calls

see QUIET, page 7

Police Dog Successfully Brings Down Fugitive Frisbee

COLUMBUS, OH—Columbus police commended the bravery and quick instincts of Dutch, an off-duty police dog, who pursued, apprehended, and retrieved a Frisbee that temporarily escaped the grasp of a fellow officer during a department-wide summer cookout Sunday. "The flying disk spun out of my hands shortly after I took temporary custody of same from a fellow officer," said Sgt. Vincent Visceglia, who admitted that the wanted Frisbee likely could have escaped into traffic if not for Dutch's fast actions. "Somehow Dutch knew that the Frisbee was a flight risk, so much so that he later displayed some reluctance to transfer it to authorities." Dutch, who had no comment on the incident, later grudgingly accepted a decoration for valor in secondhand baby clothing from Visceglia's daughters Eve and Cynthia.

LOCAL
Joke Mercilessly Beaten To Death Outside Bar page 8A

TECHNOLOGY
GPS Unit Second-Guessed page 5D

WORKPLACE
Newly Opened Time Capsule Filled With 'Go To Hell' Messages page 10E

INDEX

ONION
Briefs ... 2
Opinion ... 9
Sports ... 12
A.V. CLUB
Cinema ... 20
Music ... 23
Words ... 25
A.V. MADISON
Calendar ... 26
Food ... 34
Funny Pages ... 37
Savage Love ... 39

ONION NEWS ONLINE
onion.com GO

$2.00 US | $3.00 CANADA

ONION SPECIAL REPORT

10 O'Clock News Team Relying Heavily On Work Of 6 O'Clock News Team

AMARILLO, TX—Despite claims from the TV news outlet to offer "nonstop news" and "coverage you can count on," an *Onion* investigation has uncovered hundreds of instances in which KAMR Channel 4 *10 O'Clock Eyewitness News* team relied almost exclusively on news reports, weather forecasts, and even special-interest features already generated by the station's *6 O'Clock Eyewitness News* team.

In an examination of 98 consecutive prime-time and late-night broadcasts, including dozens more nationwide, the Amarillo-based station—the region's self-styled "News Leader"—repeatedly ran pieces for its Health Beat, Pet Patrol, and Bargain Busters segments in both evening news slots, and regularly relayed the same weather updates and traffic reports up to 15 times a day. KAMR even routinely rehashed 6 p.m. footage for seemingly urgent "breaking news" reports, most recently the Plum Creek Nursing Home power outage and the Bonham Middle School roof collapse.

In an April incident involving the 10 p.m. recap of a local Cancer Fun Run, anchor Andy Justus read almost the exact same copy introducing the piece as he had just four hours earlier, while reporter Shalandys Anderson altered only one word between broadcasts, changing "heartwarming" to "inspiring."

"If they're 'on our side,' as they claim, what, then, is a purportedly professional

see NEWS TEAM, page 8

THIS WEEK IN THE A.V. CLUB

The Roots' ?uestlove talks about trend-free hip-hop, The Hater takes aim at MTV's Video Music Awards, we review Jennifer Egan's scary new book and much more.

A.V. MADISON

Cracker's smart-ass roots rock at High Noon Thursday
page 26

Parasite Regrets Choosing Adam Carolla As Host

LOS ANGELES—Just two weeks after settling on Adam Carolla as its next host, a Los Angeles–area hookworm whose lifecycle depends on the performance of the comic personality's digestive system said it is beginning to question Carolla's ability to stay fresh and produce consistent, quality nutrients on a daily basis.

"It doesn't take much to be a decent host—you just have to sit there, generate a couple cell lines every few minutes, and let me systematically tunnel my way through your internal organs," said the *Necator americanus* hookworm, a 10-millimeter-long nematode parasite of the *Ancylostomatidae* family, from Carolla's small intestine Tuesday.

"I've been trying to suck the life out of Adam, but it's difficult when there's absolutely no life to work

see CAROLLA, page 7

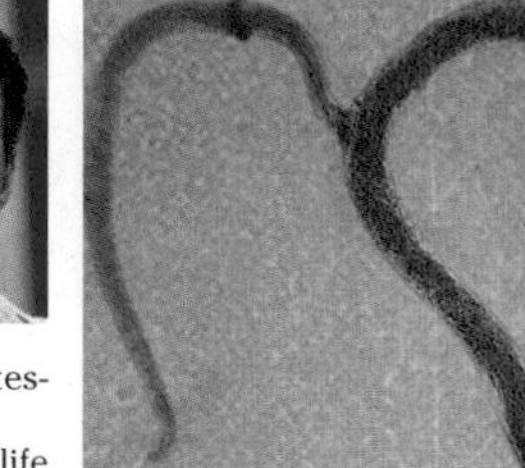

Carolla, top left, and *Necator americanus*, above

Rolling Stones Kick Off 'Sing Our Songs For Us' Tour
ENTERTAINMENT, page 11C

Video-Game Character Feeling Healthier After Eating Turkey-Leg Off Ground
LOCAL, page 4F

Opinion
If I Was Stranded On A Desert Island, I'd Bring My Smile
by Betty Handleman, page 7B

LOW 60 | HIGH 82
The kind of rain your granddad told you about

September 7, 2006 | Volume 42 Issue 36
AMERICA'S FINEST NEWS SOURCE • ONION.COM

Cubans: New Dictator Doing It All Wrong

HAVANA—Citing the lack of rambling six-hour speeches, cessation of random closings of entire industrial sectors, as well as a failure to condemn the U.S. for imperialist warmongering, the Cuban population has turned in an informal vote of no-confidence in acting dictator Raúl Castro. "He shows no understanding of the finer points: surprise raids on opposition newspapers conducted at 3 o'clock in the afternoon instead of 3 o'clock in the morning are not befitting a Castro," said sugar farmer Juan-Miguel Moinelo, who also lamented the total absence of any mass boat-lifts of "undesirables" during the younger Castro's tenure. "He may have the great bloodline, but our new Presidente lacks the firm-yet-arbitrary touch that Cuba has grown to appreciate." Raúl Castro has responded to criticism of his performance by saying that, if the Cuban people think government is so easy, maybe they should try running the country themselves for a change.

TECHNOLOGY
Secret Password Taped To Computer Monitor page 8A

LOCAL
14 Days, $150,000 Spent On Impractical Joke page 5D

WORKPLACE
Piggyback Ride Could Not Have Come At A Better Time page 10E

INDEX

ONION
Briefs ... 2
Opinion ... 10
Sports ... 14
A.V. CLUB
Cinema ... 26
Music ... 39
Words ... 43
A.V. MADISON
Calendar ... 46
Food ... 58
Funny Pages ... 69
Savage Love ... 71

ONION NEWS ONLINE
onion.com GO

$2.00 US | $3.00 CANADA

NYC UNVEILS 9/11 MEMORIAL HOLE

FIVE YEARS LATER

A birds-eye view of the magnificent new memorial.

NEW YORK—Days before the fifth anniversary of the destruction of New York's World Trade Center by terrorists, city officials gathered on the site where the Twin Towers once stood to dedicate the newly completed 9/11 Memorial Hole.

"From the wreckage and ashes of the World Trade Center, we have created a recess in the ground befitting the American spirit," said New York Governor George Pataki from a cinderblock-and-plastic-bucket-supported plywood platform near the Hole's precipice. "This vast chasm, dug at the very spot where the gleaming Twin Towers once rose to the sky, is a symbol of what we can accomplish if we work together."

Pataki then cut a ceremonial ribbon to release a giant blue plastic tarpaulin, reportedly the largest of its kind, which fluttered and snapped while slowly settling into the detritus and mud at the bottom of the 70-foot Hole, drawing a long, tired sigh of resignation from the estimated crowd of 50,000 who had assembled to watch and shake their heads.

Begun only days after the 2001 attacks, the Hole covers almost the entire footprint of the original World Trade Center, contains over 16 acres of empty space, and is visible as far away as Hoboken, NJ. Over $175 million has been spent on the Hole's development, and thousands of pages of proposals and designs concerning

see MEMORIAL, page 6

Caltech Physicists Successfully Split The Bill

PASADENA, CA—Sequestered in a private booth at a Pasadena-area Cheesecake Factory for nearly 25 minutes, a party of eight California Institute Of Technology physicists emerged exhausted but visibly excited Friday evening after successfully splitting the bill.

"This is an important day for us, not only because it marks Professor [Wayne] Newbury's birthday, but because we have accomplished a feat thought unimaginable ever since [late computational physicist Philip] Eisenreich found that it was impossible to calculate how a group of paired bodies, set in motion by the presence of a solid-state check, could come to rest at a non-variable, evenly distributed mathematical constant," said lead party organizer and theoretical physicist Dr. Cynthia Dreyfuss.

Science Watch

Before the arrival of the check, several early bill-splitting theories were proposed, including a simple process of dividing it into eight identical fragments, the Random Contribution Model, and a theory posited by Newbury himself—who insisted that he was bound to treat everyone—which was widely rejected on the basis that it would undermine the whole objective of the evening.

"When the check came, we all immediately agreed that the total of $284.57 could be defined as an irrational number of dollars for a party of eight to spend at a chain restaurant," said Dreyfuss.

The team of physicists decided to test Dreyfuss's Pay For What You Ordered Algorithm, which hypothesized that it was possible to determine what each individual owed by defining variables such as the

see CALTECH, page 9

Make-A-Wish Recipient Now Wishes Macho Man Randy Savage Would Go Away

PHOENIX—9-year-old leukemia patient Tyler Blashock was initially ecstatic to learn Monday that the Make-A-Wish Foundation was sending Macho Man Randy Savage to meet him at the Phoenix Children's Hospital. But after spending half a day with Savage, Blashock said he wished the 44-year-old wrestler would "just go."

Tyler, who was diagnosed six months ago with acute lymphocytic leukemia and has undergone chemotherapy through painful cerebrospinal injection, said the two-time WWF World Heavyweight Champion was physically and mentally demanding.

"I really only wanted him to give me an autograph and tell me what it was like to fight the Ultimate Warrior," Tyler said. "Not read me bedtime stories and try to feed me."

"Crying hurts," Tyler added.

Tyler's father Frank said he and wife Helen were "thrilled" that their son would finally have a positive experience, "especially after his hair started falling out."

see MACHO MAN, page 9

Blashock views Savage's muscles again.

A.V. CLUB

THIS WEEK IN THE A.V. CLUB
We sift through the new fall TV shows and review the new Mars Volta album. Also: Satan.

A.V. MADISON
Get sassy with The Gossip at The Annex Friday
page 46

Mo'Nique Know She Look Good
NATIONAL, page 4D

Skywriter Trailed By Skyeditor
LOCAL, page 9C

Opinion
You Have To Act Casual After A Hit And Run
By Justin MacGregor, page 13D

LOW 37 | HIGH 45
Mostly sunny, too windy to appreciate

November 9, 2006 | Volume 42 Issue 45

AMERICA'S FINEST NEWS SOURCE • ONION.COM

POLITICIANS SWEEP MIDTERM ELECTIONS

Resounding Victories In All States, Counties, Cities, Towns

Prominent politicians from across the country celebrate the election results.

Onion Political Desk

WASHINGTON, DC—After months of aggressive campaigning and with nearly 99 percent of ballots counted, politicians were the big winners in Tuesday's midterm election, taking all 435 seats in the House of Representatives, retaining a majority with 100 out of 100 seats in the Senate, and pushing political candidates to victory in each of the 36 gubernatorial races up for grabs.

While analysts had been predicting a possible sweep for months, and early exit-poll numbers seemed favorable, politicians reportedly exceeded even their own expectations, gaining an impressive 100 percent of the overall national vote.

2006 Electoral Results

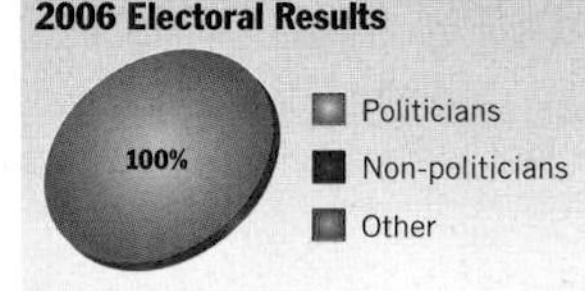

"It's a good night to be a politician," said Todd Akin, an officeholder from Missouri. "The American people have spoken, and they have unanimously declared: 'We want elected officials to lead this nation.'"

Already confident they would have an easy time in the Midwest, a region long known for electing politicians, as well as with poll-going Americans in the deep South, politicians also picked up seats in each additional area of the country.

"We expected politicians to take Washington, Indiana, Oregon, Minnesota, Pennsylvania, Michigan, North Carolina, Maryland, South Carolina, Georgia, North Dakota, Mississippi, Montana, Vermont, Maine, Kentucky, California, Iowa, Alaska, Connecticut, Florida, Idaho, Louisiana, Alabama, Virginia, Delaware, Wisconsin, and Arkansas," said Georgetown University political science professor Barbara Steward. "But the fact that voters in the urban areas of Rhode Island and the farmlands of West Virginia, along with every other state, all put elected politicians into office is quite extraordinary."

"Even in the most hotly contested local races that went down to the wire, politicians still came out on top every time," she added.

This year's results are the most unanimous since the last election two years ago, in which politicians enjoyed widespread victories unrivaled since the election before that, and the one in 2000.

Politicians managed to appeal to all economic and ethnic backgrounds, genders, and age groups, enjoying equal success among both liberal voters and conservatives.

Issues advanced by politicians dominated not only the Senate and House races, but also all state, district council, county, and town-board elections.

"It looks like politicians are poised to dominate the political discourse of the country for years to come," said analyst Maria Lawson of the Free Enterprise Institute, who as long ago as December of 2004 had picked congressmen to once again take over the House of Representatives. "This should allow them to pursue their own political agendas almost unimpeded, sign even more bills into law, and appoint fellow politicians to committee chairmanships, special interest commissions, and other posts of power."

Added Lawson: "While it's still too early to tell, after the success of this election, it might not be too long before we see another politician in the White House."

Despite fears that the dozens of campaign-finance viola-

see **POLITICIANS**, page 7

Frito-Lay Angrily Introduces Line Of Healthy Snacks

Onion Health Desk

PLANO, TX—With the recent trend of wholesome snack foods reaching "truly ridiculous proportions," Frito-Lay announced Monday that it would, against its better judgment, roll out a new line of healthy fruit-and-vegetable-based chips next February.

"Here," said Frito-Lay CEO Al Carey as he disgustedly tossed a bag of the company's new Flat Earth-brand snack crisps onto the lectern during a meeting with shareholders and members of the press. "Here's some shit that's made from beets. I hope you're all happy now that you have your precious beet chips with the recommended daily serving of fruit, or vegetables, or whatever the hell a 'beet' is."

"Mmm, dehydrated bulb things," Carey added. "Sounds delicious."

Carey appeared visibly appalled as Frito-Lay employees distributed Flat Earth snack samples to the

see **FRITO-LAY**, page 7

Sexual Tension Unbearable Between 15-Year-Old, Rest Of World

Ness

MELBOURNE, FL—Palm Bay High School freshman Keith Ness said the overwhelming sexual tension he experiences daily between himself and roughly 3.65 billion other people on earth has become "almost more than [he] can handle."

"At first, I didn't even take much notice of the world around me," said the 15-year-old of the charged but nebulous relationship he has enduredwith a majority of the human population. "But then, I found myself staring at the sexy way everyone walked down the hall, jogged in the park, or sat down at the bus stop. Something about that blond, brown, or red hair tied back, pinned up, or dreadlocked, really gets me going."

"It's driving me crazy having to sit here while the world tempts

see **TENSION**, page 8

Area Man Achieves Your Dream

CHARLOTTE, NC—After almost two decades of dreaming on your part, 34-year-old Stephen Hochenko achieved your goal of opening up a small bookstore and café last Thursday, coincidentally in the exact location you had planned to open yours.

"This proves that no matter what your dreams are, someone out there can achieve them if they just do a little homework, save their money, and believe in themselves," said a satisfied Hochenko as he arranged tables and chairs for a Monday night wine tasting and reading featuring acclaimed author Neil Gaiman. "I'm happier than you can even imagine or will probably ever experience yourself."

Hochenko joins a long list of people who have achieved your dreams, including the creators of YouTube, Grand Prix motorcycle-racer Valentino Rossi, and the people who married your longtime crush and potential soul mate in April 1998, June 2001, and last Saturday.

$2.00 US | $3.00 CANADA

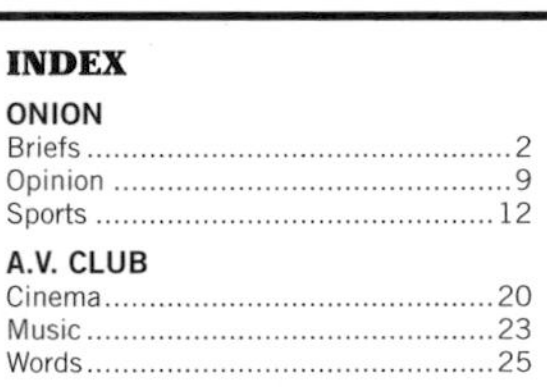

INDEX

ONION
Briefs ... 2
Opinion ... 9
Sports ... 12
A.V. CLUB
Cinema ... 20
Music ... 23
Words ... 25

INSIDE

LOCAL
Midhusband Takes Expectant Father Out For Beer page 16B

NATIONAL
Paul McCartney Quiets Wife-Beating Allegations With Stirring Rendition Of 'Blackbird' page 8A

THIS WEEK IN THE A.V. CLUB
Steven Wright longs for his home, Rick Ocasek looks back in contentment, and much more.

That Chinese Girl In Office: 'I Am Not Chinese'
INTERNATIONAL, page 15B

Wax-Museum Fire Results In Hundreds Of New Danny DeVito Statues
LOCAL, page 3E

I Would've Drunk More Had I Known My Stomach Was Going To Be Pumped
By Eleanor Taft-Meyers, page 8C

NATIONAL EDITION

LOW | HIGH
39 | 51

Flashbacks to 1988

November 30, 2006 | Volume 42 Issue 48

AMERICA'S FINEST NEWS SOURCE • ONION.COM

Kansas Outlaws Practice Of Evolution

TOPEKA, KS—In response to a Nov. 7 referendum, Kansas lawmakers passed emergency legislation outlawing evolution, the highly controversial process responsible for the development and diversity of species and the continued survival of all life.

"From now on, the streets, forests, plains, and rivers of Kansas will be safe from the godless practice of evolution, and species will be able to procreate without deviating from God's intended design," said Bob Bethell, a member of the state House of Representatives. "This is about protecting the integrity of all creation."

The new law prohibits all living beings within state borders from any willful adaptation to changing environmental conditions. In addition, it strictly limits any activity that may result in enhanced health or survival beyond the current average lifespan of their particular species.

Violators of the new law may face punishments that include jail time, stiff fines, and rehabilitative education and training to rid organisms suspected of evolutionary tendencies. Repeat offenders could face chemical sterilization.

To enforce the law, Kansas state police will be trained to investigate and apprehend organisms who exhibit suspected signs of evolutionary behavior, such as natural selection or speciation. Plans are underway to track and monitor DNA strands in every Kansan life form for even the slightest change in allele frequencies.

"Barn swallows that develop lighter, more streamlined builds to enable faster migration, for example, could live out the rest of their brief lives in prison," said Indiana University chemist and pro-intelligent-design author Robert Hellen-

see *EVOLUTION*, page 6

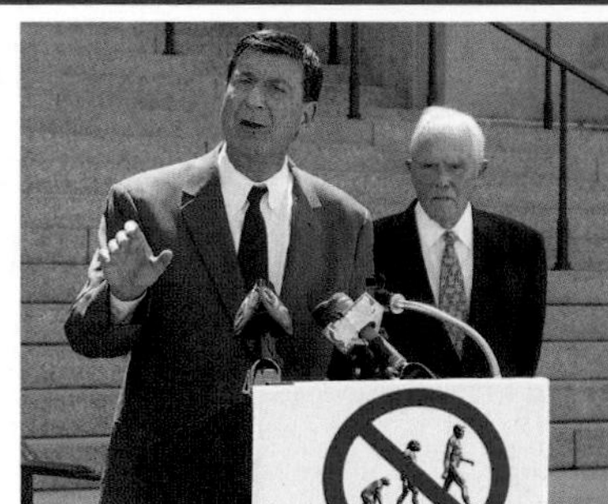

Lawmakers decried spontaneous genetic mutations.

Boyfriend Ready To Take Relationship To Previous Level

Sullivan

COLUMBIA, SC - Following a romantic three-day getaway to South Carolina's Hilton Head Island, 32-year-old Matthew Sullivan said he is now "more ready than ever" to take his 10-month relationship with girlfriend Carol Moag to the previous level.

"After spending every waking moment with Carol for 72 hours, I know in my heart that I'm prepared to see her face twice, maybe even once a week," said Sullivan, who met Moag, 34, at a friend's New Year's party in January.

Sullivan claimed he has been considering "taking the big leap backward" since Moag suggested last month that the two get a cat. The weekend of uninterrupted intimacy served to erase whatever reservations Sullivan may still have held about the move.

"I know this is a big decision, but I'm ready for it," said Sullivan as he picked up a few DVDs and

see *BOYFRIEND*, page 6

INDEX

ONION
Briefs 2
Opinion 7
Sports 9

A.V. CLUB
Inventory 12
The Hater 13
Cinema 16
DVD 19
Music 20
Games 21
Words 21
Savage Love 22
Funny Pages 23

$2.00 US | $3.00 CANADA

0 74470 94595 6 48

Troop Morale Boosted By Surprise Visit From First Dog

BAGHDAD—U.S. troops stationed in Iraq hailed an unannounced and unaccompanied visit Monday from Barney, the senior White House dog who belongs to President Bush and First Lady Laura Bush.

The First Dog

Barney, the highest-ranking official to visit Iraq in months, had a full schedule:

- **8 a.m.** Morning walk with generals on the ground
- **9 a.m.** "Sit-down" with troops
- **10:30 a.m.** Game of catch
- **12 p.m.** Lunch, photo ops
- **1 p.m.** Bathroom break
- **1:05 p.m.** Moment of silence for fallen soldiers
- **2 p.m.** Treat

Landing in Baghdad's Green Zone amid extremely tight security, the Scottish terrier met with nearly 800 troops at a military mess hall, then visited Camp Victory, the U.S. military headquarters on the outskirts of Baghdad. In both locations, the 6-year-old First Dog was greeted with loud cheers and standing ovations by servicemen and women.

"Barney's visit really cheered us all up," said Army Spc. Anthony Udall, who was given the privilege of escorting Barney across the airport tarmac. "I can't tell you how great it is that the White House would send one of its own to spend some time with us out here."

Barney is escorted by troops on the landing strip at Camp Victory, Baghdad.

Although the dog was in Iraq for less than a day, he maintained a busy schedule while there. Events included handshakes with top U.S. field commanders, a tour of the base's new recreation facility, and a ride in an armored vehicle. Besides sitting and staying at a military briefing, Barney also participated in the ground-breaking for a new visitors reception center at Camp Victory, during which he energetically dug alongside camp officials.

"As soon as he stepped off the plane, it was clear he was interested in what was happening on the ground here," said Gen. George Casey, commander of Multi-National Force-Iraq who met with the First Dog in the courtyard outside his office at Camp Victory. "He seemed extremely enthusiastic about the whole situation and he was even visibly excited about some of the progress we're making."

But the visit's highlight was the First Dog's encounter with soldiers, who were clearly taken with his presence. Sitting with his head cocked to

see *FIRST DOG*, page 6

INSIDE

LOCAL
Discerning Burglar Leaves GameCube page 5B

TRENDS
Whole Foods Bag Full Of Pudding Cups page 16C

WORKPLACE
Boss Not The One Who Decided To Get Pregnant page 8E

Focus Groups Hated It Right Up Until Guy's Head Got Cut Off

LOS ANGELES—A focus group of 150 people who saw this one movie, Fox Searchlight's modern adaptation of some Charles Dickens classic, were unresponsive right up until the violent and sudden decapitation of the lead character, which was widely heralded as "awesome."

"For the first hour and 50 minutes, comments were along the lines of 'boring,' 'too talky,' and 'booooring,'" assistant producer Marla Cannon said Monday.

"But the final scene, in which the guy gives himself up to rebels who behead him on his twin brother's TV station, was described as 'totally sick' and 'kick-ass,' often in all capital letters or with multiple exclamation points."

Producers said they were currently reworking the film to include a bunch more beheadings.

THIS WEEK IN THE A.V. CLUB
Demetri Martin speaks in palindromes, we talk to Maynard Keenan from Tool and more

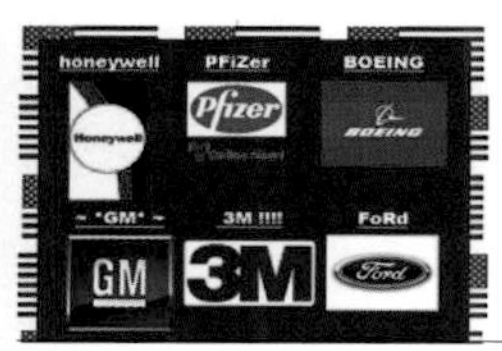

Senator's MySpace Top 8 All Corporations

BUSINESS, page 5C

Local Building Too Wheelchair-Friendly

LOCAL, page 9B

Opinion

My Goodness, Will You Look At The Geological Time

By An Outcropping of Granite, page 10E

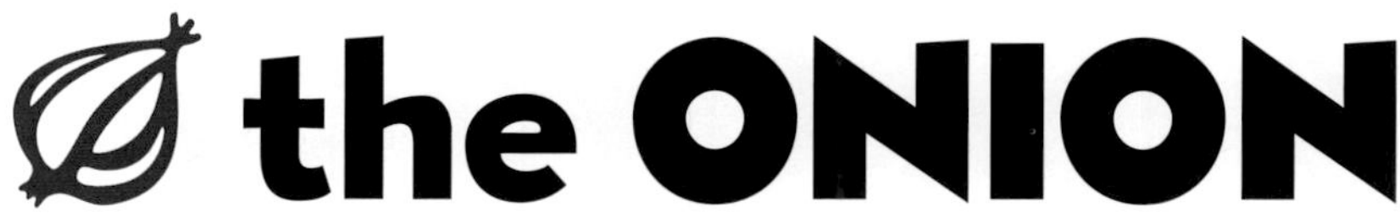

LOW | HIGH
39 | 55

Earthquuuuaaaakessss!!!

December 14, 2006 | Volume 42 Issue 50

AMERICA'S FINEST NEWS SOURCE • ONION.COM

Dictator Slays Millions In Last-Minute Push To Be *Time*'s Man Of The Year

Onion Asia Bureau

RANGOON, MYANMAR—Than Shwe, the brutal dictator of the southeast Asian nation of Myanmar, dramatically increased his already horrific rate of murdering citizens this week in a late, desperate attempt to become *Time* magazine's 2006 Man Of The Year, who will be honored in the Dec. 25 issue.

"I vow to do everything in my power to make the great acts being carried out in this great country known to all the world on this day and every day until Christmas Day," Than Shwe said in a speech broadcast on the state-run Myanmar News Network. "No longer will we stand in the shadow of better-known perpetrators of genocides, purges, and ethnic cleansing. Print-news media outlets, take notice!"

Than Shwe has racked up an impressive list of horrors:

- Executed 2,000 soldiers for failing to execute child laborers properly
- Placed entire country under house arrest and rape
- Nearly beat activist Aung San Suu Kyi to death with her Nobel Peace Prize

He then ordered everyone in the room shot.

Although Than Shwe is considered a sadistic and merciless tyrant within the borders of Myanmar—also known as Burma—his human-rights abuses have long been ignored in the international media. After he failed to make *The Economist*'s list of Top 25 Worst Leaders, Than Shwe introduced a program of "random liquidation," doubled the number of rape and torture camps, and instructed aides to inundate news outlets with press releases in which he is referred to as "The Ripper Of Rangoon." Likewise, he recently added four ethnic groups to his list of subhuman residents, ordered his special police to drag thousands of opposition-party members from their beds

see ***CRISIS***, *page 8*

HO, HO, HO! *I Saw You Masturbating!*

A SPECIAL MESSAGE *FROM SANTA CLAUS*

Season's greetings from your old friend Santa!

My, oh, my, only 12 nights left until Christmas Eve! It's so close now, we can hardly contain ourselves here at the North Pole. And from the looks of it, my young friend, we're not the only ones set to burst! Why, Jolly Old Saint Nick hasn't seen a Yule log this lit in ages!

Now, don't be shy. You know what Santa's talking about. You just couldn't wait to open your present this year, could you? Ho, ho, ho! Dear child, I saw you masturbating!

And it hasn't been just once either, wee child! Oh, no! Santa's seen you at least twice splashing away in the bathtub, three times in the attic with one of your mother's old art history books, and more times than even Santa can count spread out like a stunned partridge on that beanbag chair of yours!

Why, old Santa might just have a heart attack if he popped out your chimney on that cold winter's night and, instead of milk and cookies, found his dear little pen pal shamefully hunched over the family computer.

Oh, what a naughty, prolific rascal you've been!

You see, dear lad, Santa's been keeping a list—just like the one you keep in your head of all your favorite classmates, the one you've checked much more than twice! But when Santa thinks about his list, he doesn't rub his crotch feverishly against the smooth contours of his writing desk. Ho, ho, ho!

I see you when you're sleeping, child, and I know when you're awake. And, believe it or not, I even know when you're just pretending to sleep, but really have your rosy palms down the front of your britches.

Yes, I suppose you could say old Kris Kringle knows everything. Well, not *everything*. You did teach me a thing or two about scented body wash! Ho, ho, ho!

Tell me now, what do you want Santa to bring you this year? A bright red bicycle? Some fun new board games? Or

see ***SANTA****, page 6*

Hero Man Dials 911

■ 'He Sensed Something Was Wrong'

Tony at home with his phone.

NORCROSS, GA—Patricia Welch is lucky to be alive. Just days ago, the 37-year-old human-resources specialist lay helpless and bleeding on the brink of death, the victim of a freak accident in her own home. But the story gets even stranger: Welch owes her life to one brave but unlikely companion, who remarkably managed to dial 911 just in time.

According to Welch, Tony, her 36-year-old husband and "best friend," jumped to action after a loud crash Sunday woke him from a mid-afternoon nap on his favorite spot on the couch. Running through the house, he eventually came upon Welch in the basement, pinned beneath a collapsed wooden shelf used to store canned foods, and nearly unconscious. He immediately sensed that she was in trouble and, amazingly, headed directly for the upstairs phone.

"He must have somehow knocked the phone off its cradle," said Welch, ruffling Tony's hair as the two sat in their living room. "I guess he just did it out of instinct."

Tony's actions astonished even seasoned emergency personnel at the 911 call center.

"At first, I thought it was some kind of practical joke," said dispatcher Wanda Emerson, who fielded the call. "All I could hear was some panting and the occasional whimper. But then it occurred to me that he was actually trying to communicate with us."

see ***HERO****, page 6*

Discouraged Bush Begins Seeking Approval Of Other Nations

WASHINGTON—With public opinion sinking to an all-time low, a forlorn President Bush announced his intention Tuesday to "pack it in" and embark on a 192-nation trip seeking the favor and approval of a foreign country.

"I guess I'll just go find out if the citizens of Borneo, Turkmenistan, or Paraguay are willing to treat me a little better and see that I still have many appealing qualities," Bush said. "There's a lot of things I'm going to miss about America, but it's clearly time for me to go."

The president departs tomorrow for Bulgaria, which he called his favorite former Soviet state after Romania and Slovenia.

Bush added that he will spend the remainder of his presidency in the first independent state he comes across in which more than 30 percent of the population approves of the job he is doing.

INDEX

ONION
Briefs 2
Opinion 10
Sports 12

A.V. CLUB
Cinema 24
Music 35
Words 40

A.V. MADISON
Calendar 42
Food 51
Savage Love 55

$2.00 US | $3.00 CANADA

0 74470 94595 6 33

INSIDE

LOCAL
Area Man Shoots Self In Self-Defense page 8B

NATIONAL
Masseur Clearly That Pressure-Point Kid From Second Grade page 1C

LOCAL
Janitor Befriended page 4G

ONION NEWS ONLINE

onion.com GO

THIS WEEK IN THE A.V. CLUB

It's the best music of 2006. Also, we review *The Pursuit Of Happyness* and more.

A.V. MADISON

We salute Madison's music scene

page 42

Rookie Tragically Misinterprets Suicide-Squeeze Sign
BASEBALL, page 9D

Millions Of Americans Buying Floyd Landis-Inspired Bracelets
CYCLING, page 4A

Deion Sanders Intercepts Incoming North Korean Missile
FOOTBALL, page 9D

ONION SPORTS
2006 YEAR IN REVIEW

LOW -5 | HIGH 31
It's A Great Day For Baseball

DECEMBER 28, 2006 AMERICA'S FINEST SPORTS SOURCE • ONIONSPORTS.COM VOLUME 42 ISSUE 52

March 9, 2006

Barry Bonds Took Steroids, Reports Everyone Who Has Ever Watched Baseball

SAN FRANCISCO—With the publication of a book detailing steroid use by San Francisco Giants superstar Barry Bonds, two San Francisco Chronicle reporters have corroborated the claims of Bonds' steroid abuse made by every single person who has watched or even loosely followed the game of baseball over the past five years.

In *Game Of Shadows*, an excerpt of which appeared in *Sports Illustrated* Wednesday, authors Mark Fainaru-Wada and Lance Williams claim that more than a dozen people close to Bonds had either been directly informed that Bonds was using banned substances or had in fact seen him taking the drugs with their own eyes. In addition to those witnesses, nearly 250 million other individuals nationwide had instantly realized that Bonds was using banned substances after observing his transformation from lanky speedster to hulking behemoth with their own eyes.

According to hundreds of thousands of reports coming out of every city in the U.S., Bonds' steroid use has been widely reported and well-documented for years, with sports columnists, bloggers, people attending baseball games, memorabilia collectors, major ballpark popcorn and peanut vendors, groundskeepers, roommates, significant others, fathers-in-law, next-door neighbors, fellow fitness club members, bartenders, mailmen, coworkers, teachers, doormen, parking-lot attendants, fellow elevator passengers, Home Depot clerks, servicemen and women serving in Iraq, former baseball players, Congressmen, second-tier stand-up comics, *Sports Illustrated's* Rick Reilly, and random passersby all having stated at some point in the last five years that Bonds was obviously taking some sort of performance-enhancing drugs.

Many of those eyewitnesses came forward following Wednesday's revelation with their own accounts of Bonds' seven-year history of steroid use.

"I originally heard that Barry Bonds was on

see **BONDS**, page 5

June 29, 2006

Somalia Defeats Rwanda To Win Third-World Cup

KHARTOUM, SUDAN—The host city of the 2006 Developing Nations Football Championship erupted in cheers that nearly drowned out the cries of the starving and wounded Tuesday when the underdog Somali side, playing four down due to injuries and landmines, outlasted the more experienced if disease-ridden Rwandans 1-0 to win the inaugural Third-World Cup.

"This is a relatively great day for Somalia," said team captain Omar Bin-Shakur, the seasoned veteran whose rise from squalor in the violent ghettoes of Mogadishu to stardom in the squalid and violent ghettoes of the Sudan is already passing into legend. "It seemed like nothing could stop us in the title match—not the great Rwandan defender Bimenyimana, not the mortar strikes,

see **THIRD-WORLD CUP**, page 5

September 14, 2006

Florida State University To Phase Out Academic Operations By 2010

TALLAHASSEE, FL—Bowing to pressure from alumni, students, and a majority of teaching professors of Florida State University, athletic director Dave Hart, Jr. announced yesterday that FSU would completely phase out all academic operations by the end of the 2010 school year in order to make athletics the school's No. 1 priority. "It's been clear for a while that Florida State's mission is to provide the young men and women enrolled here with a world-class football program, and this is the best way to cut the fat and really focus on making us No. 1 every year," Hart said. "While it's certainly possible for an academic subsidiary to bring a certain amount of prestige to an athletic program, the national polls have made it that our non-athletic operations have become a major distraction." FSU's restructuring program will begin with the elimination of the College of Arts and Sciences, effective October 15.

September 28, 2006

Overjoyed Saints Fans Tear Roof Off Reopened Superdome

NEW ORLEANS—Over 70,000 elated New Orleans Saints fans celebrated the first professional football game to take place in the newly renovated Superdome since Hurricane Katrina Monday night by joyously rushing from their seats onto the field, ripping down the goalposts, destroying the playing surface, and trampling three people to death after the Saints' 23-3 win over the Atlanta Falcons.

"This city is back!" said Marcus Hammond, one of 5,000 Saints fans who rushed from the French Quarter to seek refuge in the Superdome's reopening. Early reports indicate that as news of the victory spread, the excited citizens steadily breached the dome's walls throughout the night, creating a chaotic and devastating environment of celebration.

"This was something all of us needed," said resident Sean Montrell, who joined several thousand

see **SUPERDOME**, page 4

$2.00 US | $3.00 CANADA

SPORTS INSIDE

- Royals Hire Tom Emanski To Teach Them Fundamentals Of Baseball *page 5B*
- Cross-Country Champ Wishes He Were Good At Sports *page 7D*

Apple Unveils New Product-Unveiling Product

Unreleased Jimmy Page Guitar Riff To Be Retrieved From Secret Vault To Save Rock And Roll

Only Jewish Kid In Class Asked To Talk About Holocaust Remembrance Day

JANUARY FEBRUARY MARCH APRIL MAY JUNE

Justin Timberlake Apathetically Crowned King Of Pop

This American Life Completes Documentation Of Liberal, Upper-Middle-Class Existence

DNA Evidence Frees Man From Zoo

2007

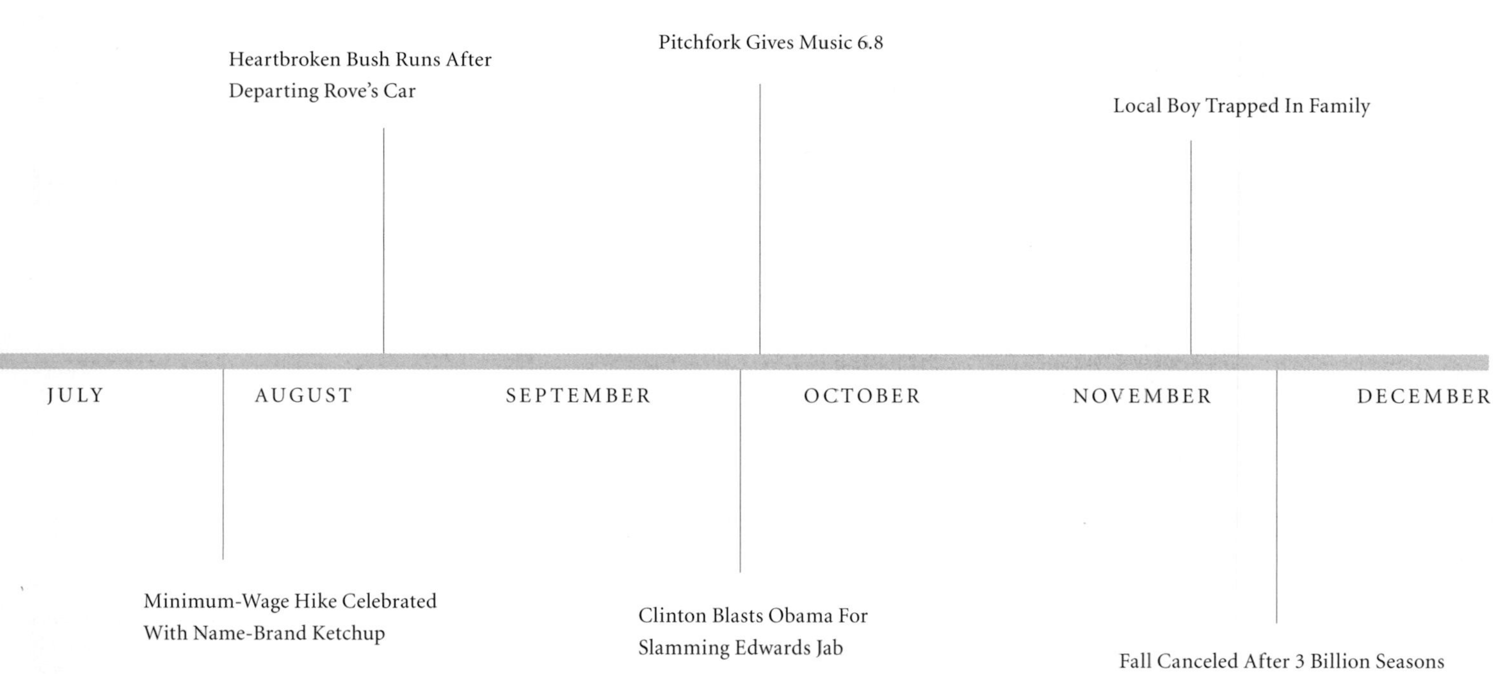
Heartbroken Bush Runs After Departing Rove's Car
Pitchfork Gives Music 6.8
Local Boy Trapped In Family
JULY
AUGUST
SEPTEMBER
OCTOBER
NOVEMBER
DECEMBER
Minimum-Wage Hike Celebrated With Name-Brand Ketchup
Clinton Blasts Obama For Slamming Edwards Jab
Fall Canceled After 3 Billion Seasons

McDonald's Birthday Party To Be Happiest Time In Child's Life
NATIONAL, page 5C

WebMD Doesn't Know How To Tell You This
LOCAL, page 9B

NBA
L.A. Grants Clippers $12 For New Nets
SPORTS, page 24A

LOW 33 | HIGH 49
Halfhearted storm warning in semi-effect

February 1, 2007 | Volume 43 Issue 05
AMERICA'S FINEST NEWS SOURCE • ONION.COM

Meth Addicts Demand Government Address Nation's Growing Spider Menace

Onion Washington Bureau

Harlowe pleads with senators to ask the King of America to do something about "all the goddamned spiders."

WASHINGTON, DC—Following the tragic falling death of 32-year-old methamphetamine addict Phillip Diggs, who was reportedly attacked by spiders while scaling a large construction crane near Palo Alto, CA, thousands of outraged and confused meth addicts marched frenetically on Washington as part of a week of activities urging the federal government to address the nation's growing spider epidemic.

"Something needs to be done and it needs to be done soon—these spiders are everywhere," said Rich Harlowe, event organizer and founder of Tweakers' Rights NowNow NowNowNowNowNowNowNow!, in testimony before a Senate committee Tuesday. "The government must address this problem before the situation gets out of hand and these poisonous, acid-shooting spiders develop the powers of mind control or—God forbid—flight."

"America cannot afford to ignore this any crisis any longer," Harlowe added.

The rally drew addicts from every part of the country, many traveling on foot through the night, trading sex with truck drivers for rides, or stealing their brothers-in-law's bicycles. At dozens of rambling public speeches, organizers decried the fact that it took the spider-related death of an innocent meth addict to raise awareness of the issue, while lauding the bravery of meth addicts, and methamphetamines themselves.

A 45,000-word proposal was drafted by members of TRN during a marathon, 72-hour meeting under the Roosevelt Bridge, and presented twice to the Senate Indian Affairs Committee. The document, which includes schematics for the development of a giant "spider bomb" the size of Rhode Island, concludes repeatedly that the problem would best be combated with large quantities of methamphetamines and steel wool.

"This very morning, I saw a small child completely covered in hairy, bloodsucking, scream-

see SPIDERS, page 5

Civic leaders unveil the new old New Orleans.

FEMA Calls Rebuilding Complete As New Orleans Restored To Former Squalor

NEW ORLEANS—After an unprecedented 18-month cleanup and repair effort supervised by the Federal Emergency Management Agency and several state and local government bureaus, Undersecretary for Federal Emergency Management R. David Paulison announced Monday that the city of New Orleans has been successfully returned to its pre–Hurricane Katrina state of decay and deterioration.

"Our job here is done," said Paulison, who was joined by Louisiana Gov. Kathleen Blanco in a ceremony along the banks of the Industrial Canal. "Our beloved Big Easy has its soul back. The downtown shops are open and in full violation of code, the nightlife is alive with the sound of violence, and the streets are once again safe for poverty and vice."

The $41 billion restoration of the city's hallmark abandoned buildings, shacks, vacant lots, and standing trash piles was among the most complex and painstaking ever undertaken. Starting just four weeks after the August 2005 hurricane, workers recovered millions of pieces of flood-damaged debris, cleaned them of sediments and chemicals, and then replaced them where they were originally found.

The work, however, did not proceed without controversy, often grinding to a halt as preservationists quarreled in court over which sections of rot, toxic chemical compounds, PCBs, bacteria, and pathogens predated Katrina.

Despite the bitter disputes, Blanco declared the restoration project an "unqualified success," and invited the

see SQUALOR, page 6

Bush Commits One Additional Troop To Afghanistan

Pfc. Ekenberg prepares for the flight to Kandahar.

WASHINGTON, DC—In an effort to display his administration's willingness to fight on all fronts in the War on Terror, President Bush said at a press conference Monday that American ground forces in Afghanistan will be aided by the immediate deployment of Marine Pfc. Tim Ekenberg of Camp Lejeune, NC.

"I want the American people to know that I have not forgotten that our battle for freedom began in Afghanistan, rooting out the extremists of al-Qaeda and the Taliban," Bush said. "Today, I am ordering the deployment of the 325th Marine Expeditionary Brigade, Private Tim Ekenberg, to the embattled Kandahar region."

"We will take whatever measures necessary to win," Bush added. "Isn't that right, Tim?"

Ekenberg is scheduled to arrive in Afghanistan on Friday. His duties include providing full military support for the still-tenuous democratic government, resolving potential conflicts between rival warlords, gathering intelligence for his superiors, delivering humanitarian relief to millions of Afghan citizens

see TROOP, page 5

ONION NEWS ONLINE
onion.com GO

$2.00 US | $3.00 CANADA
05
0 74470 94595 6

INSIDE

STYLES
Hockey Jersey Tucked In For Date page 9D

NATIONAL
Wrong Tool Suffices page 5B

LOCAL
Pet Peeve Parlayed Into Local Ordinance page 3F

INDEX

ONION
Briefs 2
Opinion 8
Sports 10
A.V. CLUB
Cinema 18
Music 22
Words 25
A.V. MADISON
Calendar 26
Food 36
Savage Love 39

A.V. CLUB

THIS WEEK IN THE A.V. CLUB
The ubiquitous Jimmy Kimmel. Also: Oscar-winning songs that actually aren't bad.

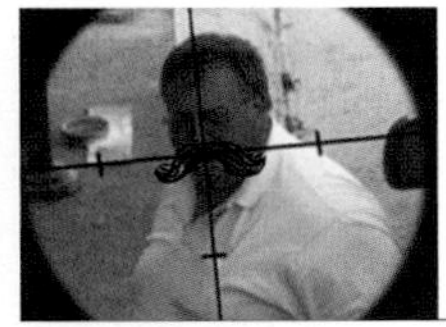

Sniper Draws Moustache on Crosshairs

NATIONAL, page 5C

'The Word You Use To Denote Long Sandwiches In Your Region Is Ridiculous'

OPINION, page 9B

Castro Leaves Hospital 2 Years Younger, 4 Inches Taller

LOCAL, page 7E

LOW 33 | HIGH 49

Freaking flying squirrels everywhere

February 8, 2007 | Volume 43 Issue 06

AMERICA'S FINEST NEWS SOURCE • ONION.COM

Mysterious Congressman Announces Dark Horse Candidacy

ONION POLITICS WATCH

The dashing figure on the steps of the very Capitol Building.

WASHINGTON, DC—The Mysterious Congressman, whose flamboyant oratory and swashbuckling condemnations of greed and cynicism in modern politics have electrified Washington, announced Monday that he was considering a White House run in 2008.

"Noble citizens, hear me now!" said the enigmatic, masked Congressman (D-WI) from the dome of the nation's Capitol Monday, his long cape cutting a dramatic silhouette against the rising moon as he addressed a crowd of mostly lawmakers and congressional staff. "Too long has a craven dullard and his moneyed masters made a mockery of our beloved and sacred Union. No more! For today I have of two dozen advisers good and true an advisory committee formed, which, along with my budget-restructuring plan and my program for

see *MYSTERIOUS*, page 8

Thousands Lose Jobs As Michigan Unemployment Offices Close

LANSING, MI—In another devastating blow to the state's already fragile economy, the Unemployment Insurance Agency of the state of Michigan permanently shuttered its nine branch offices Monday, leaving more than 8,500 unemployment employees unemployed.

Newly unemployed workers stream out of the UIA headquarters.

Announcing the closings at a press conference, Michigan Gov. Jennifer Granholm called them "a tragic coda" to a once-vibrant industry that until this week defined the Michigan economy and served almost one-fifth of the state's employable population.

"This is a sad day for the people of Michigan," Granholm said to a crowd of part-time reporters and former assembly-line workers Tuesday. "Our state has a long, hallowed history of unemployment, and with these closings, we have lost an vital part of our economic and social fabric."

Since its inception in 1937, Michigan's unemployment benefits system has been among the nation's most productive, outlasting the state's automotive and other industrial and manufacturing sectors to become Michigan's most enduring job-provider.

For many, the closing of UIA marks an end of an era. Flint resident Martha Ayers recalled the "glory days" of the 1980s when the line of

see *MICHIGAN*, page 7

"Helping people move on with their lives after they'd been suddenly fired is all I've ever known. What am I going to do with myself now?"

Former UIA employee Paul Huegli

Nation To Celebrate First-Ever Black History Month History Week

WASHINGTON, DC—Saying the time had come for America to recognize "some of its most unsung heroes," President Bush issued a statement Tuesday announcing the creation of Black History Month History Week, which is to be held in the last seven days of February and will honor the men and women who pioneered the commemoration of Black History Month.

HONORING THE CELEBRATION OF DIVERSITY

"From Monday, February 19, to Sunday, February 25, I invite the American people to join Laura and me in remembering those who made a difference in remembering those who made a difference in the rich history of this great land of ours," Bush's statement read. "People like Cleveland Mayor Michael White, who recited Martin Luther King, Jr's famous 'I Have A Dream' speech during Black History Month in 2004; event planner Sheila Carter, whose passion and determination forever changed the face of commemorating civil rights in America; and, of course, the Father Of Black History Month, Gerald Ford, who first signed

see *HISTORY*, page 7

Touring Raffi Refuses To Play 'Shake My Sillies Out'

FORT WAYNE, IN—Raffi, the veteran Canadian children's entertainer, told an audience of 4-year-olds at the Shrine Auditorium last Friday that he would not play his popular hit "Shake My Sillies Out" during the 2007 Raffi Renaissance Tour, no matter how often his young fans requested it. "I wrote 'Sillies' at a completely different time in my life," said Raffi, explaining that he wanted to play "some lesser-known stuff" on the tour, such as "Joshua Giraffe" and "Spider On The Floor." "I appreciate you wearing your 'Shake My Sillies Out' T-shirts, but I like to think that as I grow as an artist, you'll grow with me." Parents attending the concert said their children stopped singing along and closed their eyes during Raffi's final number, a sprawling 20-minute instrumental rendition of "Bananaphone." ⌀

Raffi

ONION NEWS ONLINE

onion.com GO

$2.00 US | $3.00 CANADA

06

0 74470 94595 6

INDEX

ONION
Briefs 2
Opinion 10
Sports 14

A.V. CLUB
Cinema 23
Music 28
Words 33

A.V. MADISON
Calendar 34
Food 44
Savage Love 47

INSIDE

LOCAL
Last McNugget Savored page 12A

NATIONAL
Child Gains Upper Hand After Discovering Highlighted Parenting Guide page 10B

ENTERTAINMENT
Jim Breuer Now Eating Garbage Offscreen page 28F

Postmodern Architect Unveils 7-Story Found-Art Object
NATIONAL, page 18F

Opinion
"My Tartar Is Impervious To Even The Most Dynamic Foaming Action"
By Jake Goodwin page 22A

Wrong Font Chosen For Gravestone
LOCAL, page 2B

LOW | HIGH
33 | 49
15 percent chance of joy

February 22, 2007 | Volume 43 Issue 08

AMERICA'S FINEST NEWS SOURCE • ONION.COM

Jill Tyn, 4, perilously close to danger.

Child-Safety Experts Call For Restrictions On Childhood Imagination

Onion Family

WASHINGTON, DC—The Department of Health and Human Services issued a series of guidelines Monday designed to help parents curtail their children's boundless imaginations, which child-safety advocates say have the potential to rival motor vehicle accidents and congenital diseases as a leading cause of disability and death among youths ages 3 to 14.

"Defuse the ticking time-bomb known as your child's imagination before it explodes and destroys her completely," said child-safety expert Kenneth McMillan, who advised the HHS in composing the guidelines. "New data shows a disturbing correlation between serious accidents and the ability of children to envision a world full of exciting possibility."

The guidelines, titled "Boundless Imagination, Boundless Hazards: Ways To Keep Your Kids Safe From A World Of Wonder," are posted on the HHS website, and will also be available in brochure form in pediatricians' offices across the country.

see ***IMAGINATION****, page 6*

ONION POLITICS WATCH

GIULIANI TO RUN FOR PRESIDENT OF 9/11

Giuliani at a campaign stop near Washington.

NEW YORK—At a well-attended rally in front of his new Ground Zero headquarters Monday, former New York City Mayor Rudy Giuliani officially announced his plan to run for president of 9/11.

"My fellow citizens of 9/11, today I will make you a promise," said Giuliani during his 18-minute announcement speech in front of a charred and torn American flag. "As president of 9/11, I will usher in a bold new 9/11 for all."

If elected, Giuliani would inherit the duties of current 9/11 President George W. Bush, including making grim facial expressions, seeing the world's conflicts in terms of good and evil, and carrying a bullhorn at all state functions.

"Let us all remember how we felt on that day, with the world watching our every move, waiting on our every word," said Giuliani, flanked by several firefighters, ex-New York Police Commissioner Bernard Kerik, and Judith Nathan, his third wife. "With a campaign built on traditional 9/11 values, and with the help of every citizen who believes in the 9/11 dream, I want to make 9/11 great again."

According to Washington-based political analyst Gregory Hammond, Giuliani's candidacy "should not be underestimated."

"Sure, he has no foreign or national policy experience, and both his personal life and political career are riddled with scandal," said Hammond. "But in the key area of having been on TV on 9/11, the other candidates simply cannot match him. And as we saw in 2004, that's what matters most to voters in this post-9/11 world."

After his downtown Manhattan announcement, Giuliani held an afternoon rally near the Pentagon. In the early evening, he flew to a field outside Shanksville, Pennsylvania, where he hosted a $5,000-a-plate fundraising dinner in a tent decorated with clouds of ash, streaming sheets of singed office paper, and small piles of authentic rubble from the World

see ***GIULIANI*** *page 6*

CANDIDATE BIO: RUDOLPH GIULIANI

- Born in Brooklyn, 1944
- Was near World Trade Center when towers collapsed on 9/11
- Made numerous appearances on radio and television on 9/11
- Took credit for uniting city on 9/11

Dane Cook Parlays New Burger King Menu Item Into Hour-Long HBO Special

LOS ANGELES—Building upon his previous Burger King–related work, comedian Dane Cook announced plans Monday to tape an hour-long HBO stand-up special devoted entirely to the Texas Double Whopper, the latest menu offering from the fast-food giant.

The Cookster

"Bro, I got a solid 15 [minutes] on the name alone," said Cook on the "Danecast" video weblog feature on his MySpace page. "I'm still working out the kinks, but I'm probably gonna call it the 'T-Dubs' or maybe the 'Spicy Dub-Whops.'"

Cook said that the new burger, which substitutes jalapeño peppers and mustard for the original Double Whopper's mayonnaise and ketchup, has inspired him to "new creative heights." The routine came to the popular comic "in a flash" as he watched a Burger King TV spot for the sandwich during ESPN's *World Series Of Poker*.

The 'Spicy Dub-Whops.'

Last week, HBO signed Cook to produce, write, and star in the special, tentatively titled *Dane Cook: Burgasm,* for an unprecedented $25 million, the highest amount the cable network has ever paid to a comedian

see ***COOK*** *page 8*

Rapture Wreaks Havoc On Local Book Club

MARION, IN—Following last week's rapture, which transported four members of the Millersville Mockingbirds Book Club to heaven in order to be with Jesus Christ, the three remaining members have reportedly been scrambling to maintain a regular Wednesday meeting schedule as well as the usual coffee-and-pastry rotation.

"It's a shame because I think Shirley had the most stimulating opinions, and I was really looking forward to hearing what she'd have to say about [Fannie Flagg's *Standing In The Rainbow*] right before her ascension," said club member Diane Valinsky Monday. "And we were supposed to meet at Lucas' house this week, but I guess that's out now, seeing as the armies of Satan are on the march."

Valinsky said she and the remaining members were not surprised that the Antichrist turned out to be Mitch Albom, calling his latest fiction effort, *For One More Day*, "disappointing."

$2.00 US | $3.00 CANADA

INDEX

ONION
Briefs 2
Opinion 10
Sports 12
A.V. CLUB
Cinema 20
Music 24
Words 25

INSIDE

LOCAL
Anger-Bottling Factory Explodes page 8A
ARTS
Stage Fright Justified page 11C

THIS WEEK IN THE A.V. CLUB

The creators and characters of *Reno 911!* speak out. Also, TV that should be on DVD.

A.V. MADISON
Challenging films at MadCat Festival
page 35

Bill Clinton Waiting Until After Primaries To Endorse Candidate
NATIONAL, page 2B

Inanimate Object Despised
LOCAL, page 18F

BASKETBALL
Tim Hardaway: 'Sorry, Faggots'
SPORTS, page 22D

"Tu Stultus Es"

the ONION®

LOW 33 | HIGH 49
Temperatures, tempers rising

March 1, 2007 | Volume 43 Issue 09

AMERICA'S FINEST NEWS SOURCE • ONION.COM

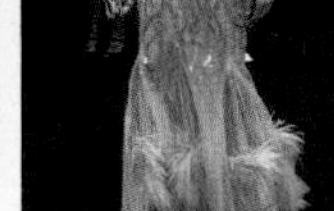

Two film stars demonstrate the disparity.

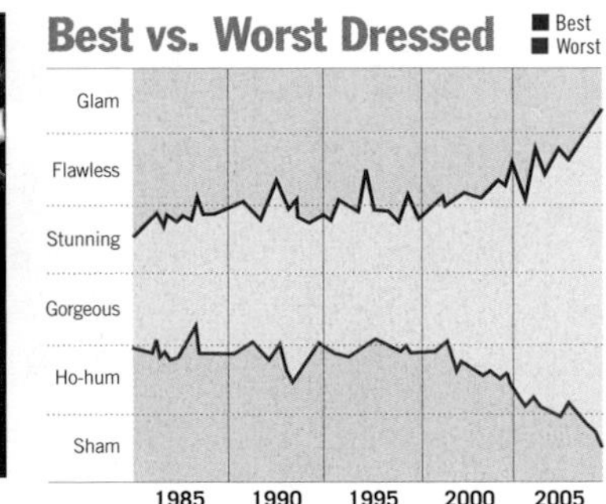

Oscars Reveal Widening Gap Between Best, Worst Dressed

LOS ANGELES—This year's Academy Awards pre-ceremony red carpet display has analysts worried that the divide between the nation's best and worst dressed is only growing, forcing thousands to live well below the taste line while a lucky few see their glamour levels skyrocket.

"Every year it's the same story, with the flashy getting flashier and the trashy getting trashier," said red carpet fashion expert Melissa Rivers, who brought attention to the issue Sunday night in a special post-Oscars report broadcast on the TV Guide channel. "If nothing is done to level the playing field, we may never see members of the fashion underprivileged, like Lindsay Lohan and Pamela Anderson, make the transition from sham to glam."

Oscar night fashion, which many experts use as a bellwether for the state of celebrity gorgeousness nationwide, has shown in recent

see OSCARS, page 8

Viacom Demands YouTube Pull 400,000 Ex-TV Viewers From Its Site

MEDIA WATCH

NEW YORK—In a cease-and-desist letter sent to Google's attorneys last week, media conglomerate Viacom demanded that YouTube immediately pull 400,000 ex-TV viewers from its industry-leading video-sharing site.

"These viewers clearly belong to Viacom and its related entertainment subsidiaries," stated the letter, which called the co-opted viewership "the result of an investment of hundreds of millions of dollars by our company." "Should YouTube fail to adequately address this blatant infringement, Viacom will not hesitate to assert its ownership rights to its intellectual property."

The letter threatened further legal action if all the 400,000 viewers in question are not removed from their desks and returned to their couches by the end of the week.

Kindergartner Being Groomed For Line-Leader Position

Hutter

BELLE MEADE, TN—Belle Meade Day School kindergarten teacher Mrs. Allen, 33, says she has known since the first day of class that student Gregory Hutter, 6, was "line-leader material."

"He's wasn't the tallest, but he conducted himself as if he were over four feet," Mrs. Allen said of Hutter, whom she believes "has what it takes" to lead the class to key locations throughout the school such as the cafeteria, bathroom, water fountain, and to the playground. "Once he's got his feet under him a bit more, the sky's the limit on where he can take this class."

Mrs. Allen realized that Hutter could maintain his composure in high-pressure situations several months ago when, after recess, he took a quick sip of water at the drinking fountain. "He just had this innate sense that there were people waiting behind him who were also thirsty, and that the class was going to be late for music," she said. "You can't teach that."

Most teachers, after seeing Hutter cry when his mother dropped him off for school during the first two weeks, would have dismissed Hutter's future leadership prospects, but Mrs. Allen reportedly "kept on the boy." She forced him to complete his noodle necklace and printing drills with precision, despite the obvious emotional strain.

"I had to break him a little bit, but I was just preparing him for the kind of focus one needs to line lead," said Mrs. Allen, a former line

see KINDERGARTNER page 8

THE WAR IN IRAQ: HEROES

Bumbling Ragtag Regiment Achieves Heartwarming Victory In Iraq

Sad-Sack Sarge 'Only One Who Believed'

BAGHDAD—The war in Iraq came to a sudden, complete, and ultimately heartwarming end after the U.S. Army's hapless 115th Regiment defeated the insurgent forces in what military observers are terming a startling victory for the war's most notorious underdog unit.

"I hereby announce the cessation of hostilities in the country of Iraq," said the head of U.S. Central Command, Gen. John Abizaid, grudgingly singling out the ragtag bunch of misfits at a press conference Monday. "In all my years of military experience, I've never seen a sorrier group of bumbling, no-good, dangerously incompetent yahoos as the 115th. But, against my better judgment, and in recognition of their valor, courage, hijinks, and hilarity, I'm nominating each of these lovable bastards for the Congressional Medal of Honor."

Despite a record of egregious tactical errors, a high rate of friendly-fire deaths, and an official classification as "dishonorable dingbats," the 115th Light Infantry Regiment—or "Walters' Wombats," as they were known throughout southern Iraq—sent troop morale soaring in the occupied territories after they wiped out a group of enemy combatants in the insurgent-controlled

see RAGTAG page 7

TIMELINE OF BATTLE

Feb. 23, 2007 *V-Ouch Day*

12:30	Regiment wakes up
13:45	Hamburger-eating contest
14:37	Suffers heavy casualties
17:08	Installs night-vison cameras in lady insurgents' barracks
18:33	Wins war

Psc. Charlie Bartowsky managed to accidentally set off 22 IEDs without sustaining major injuries.

Spc. Jolene "Joey" Saunders defied gender expectations by killing more than 200 enemies.

Lance Cpl. Novak's military data-systems skills proved crucial, despite his lack of social skills.

Medic Booker T. Roosevelt's scaredy-cat quips kept unit in—and out of—stitches.

$2.00 US | $3.00 CANADA

INDEX

ONION
Briefs 2
Opinion 10
Sports 12

A.V. CLUB
Cinema 21
Music 27
Words 31

INSIDE

LOCAL
Casio Keyboard Used To Set Mood page 8A

INTERNATIONAL
Africa Not Told About Global Economy page 11C

THIS WEEK IN THE A.V. CLUB
It's a salute to sidekicks with Greg Grunberg of *Heroes* and Jack McBrayer of *30 Rock* and more

OPINION
'Celebrities Are The Real Heroes'
By Lt. Frank Jackson, page 9B

Freshness Escaping From Bag Of Peas
LOCAL, page 13D

***Scarface* Onesie Social Worker's First Tip-Off**
NATIONAL, page 13D

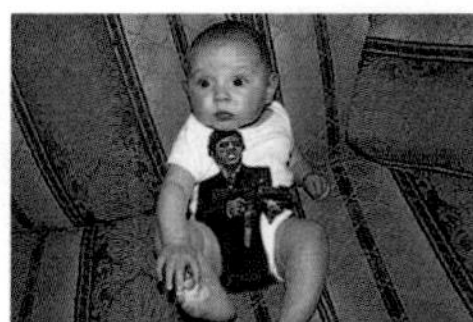

"Tu stultus es"

LOW | HIGH
33 | 49
Outdoor drinking advisory

April 5, 2007 | Volume 43 Issue 14
AMERICA'S FINEST NEWS SOURCE • ONION.COM

Christ Getting In Shape For Second Coming

Onion Fitness Desk

HEAVEN—Emerging from a grueling 90 minutes of cardiovascular exercise and light lifting for tone, Son of God Jesus Christ said Monday that He is "definitely on track" to achieve peak fitness condition for the Second Coming.

"If every eye is going to see Me, and all the tribes of earth are going to wail on account of Me, I think I owe it to them and to Myself to be in the best shape of My life," Christ said. "Right now I'm up to 35 minutes at seven [miles per hour] on the treadmill and benching about 165 [pounds]."

"I'm really starting to feel like I'll have the strength and endurance to move every mountain and island from its place," Christ added.

Since His birthday last Dec. 25, Christ has committed Himself to a demanding daily regimen of exercise and prophecy fulfillment. Each of His workouts, Christ said, starts with an hour of cardio, after which He focuses on two muscle groups, replacing conventional free weights with the Rod of Iron with which He intends to rule all nations.

On Mondays, Christ works His chest and biceps and completes three sets of 10 transfigurations. On Tuesdays, He switches to triceps and abdominals, and passes as many sets of Last Judgments as He can in a minute. Wednesdays are devoted to the back

see *CHRIST*, page 7

The Son of God spends each morning trying to attain perfect abdominal definition.

Area Man Has Sex With Man To Get Out Of Office Blood Drive

ABBEVILLE, GA—In an effort to devise a plausible reason to excuse himself from an office-wide blood donation drive this Friday, systems specialist Brett Karns, 32, reportedly engaged in unprotected sex with another man last weekend.

"When the nurse asks me if I've participated in any high-risk sexual activity recently, I don't want to have to lie," said Karns, who describes himself as squeamish about needles. "Maybe she wouldn't question my story, but better safe than sorry, right?"

Public Health

Karns told reporters he intends to have sex with another man next week to get out of his office's canned food drive.

ONION NEWS ONLINE
onion.com GO

Bush Refuses To Set Timetable For Withdrawal Of Head From White House Banister

Onion Washington Bureau

WASHINGTON, DC—Though critics have argued that he does not understand the futility of his current situation, President Bush announced today that he has no plans to remove his head from its current position: wedged painfully between two balusters on a White House staircase.

"Setting a timetable for withdrawal of my head would send mixed messages about why I put my head here in the first place," Bush said at a press conference on the Grand Staircase. "I am going to finish what I set out to accomplish here, no matter how unpopular my decision may be, or how much my head hurts while stuck between these immovable stairway posts."

Democrats, emboldened by electoral victories that gave them control of both houses of Congress, are calling for Bush to begin withdrawing his head from the banister immediately.

"Why does the president refuse to pull his head out of that banister?" House Speaker Nancy Pelosi said in a speech yesterday. "Hasn't he had his head in there long enough? We'd all like to know just how the American people are being served by him keeping his head in that banister."

Entering its fifth day, the president's incursion into the banister is now widely considered a quagmire. Bush initially told the nation that he was going to stick his head through the banister in order to secure stockpiles of cashews on the other side. Though intelligence reports cited by the president seemed to indicate the presence

see *HEAD*, page 8

Bush has refused to budge from his position.

CRISIS IN THE NEWSROOM

'Most E-Mailed' List Tearing *New York Times*' Newsroom Apart

NEW YORK—A feature on the *New York Times*' website that lists the stories most e-mailed by readers is destroying morale and escalating tensions among the once-dignified and professional *Times* staff, sources within the newspaper of record said Tuesday.

This week's most frequently e-mailed story, titled "In Manhattan, Even Felines Have Therapists," which detailed the growing phenomenon of clinical depression among indoor urban cats, provoked a fresh round of envy and dismay among reporters still stinging from last week's top article, "Do You Really Have Time For Your Time-Share?".

"Your reputation is everything here at the *Times*, and if you want get known, you've got to deliver what readers want: differences between men and women, and photos of cats," national political reporter Adam Nagourney said. "I suppose I could be most e-mailed, too, if I sat in front of my computer all day making up cutesy names for government officials, like some red-headed Wednesday and Saturday columnists I know."

see *TIMES*, page 9

"I'll write anything—do anything—to get on that list each week. I don't care what it takes."
***Times* columnist Paul Krugman**

$2.00 US | $3.00 CANADA

INDEX

ONION
Briefs 2
Opinion 10
Sports 12

A.V. CLUB
Cinema 20
Music 24
Words 27

INSIDE

WORKPLACE
Sensitivity Training Seminar Retarded page 14A

LOCAL
Mother Keeps Deceased Son's MySpace Just As He Left It page 3C

THIS WEEK IN THE A.V. CLUB
Mindy Kaling spills the secrets of *The Office*. Also, the return of Paul Verhoeven.

A.V. MADISON
Attack of the candy mutants!
page 35

Caricaturist's Self-Portrait Extremely Forgiving

ARTS, page 13D

OPINION

'If I Can't Get This Couch Into My Apartment, I Will Build A New Apartment Around This Couch'

By Ralph Eversoll, page 9B

Goldfish Teetering On Edge Of Sanity

ENVIRONMENT, page 13C

"Tu stultus es"

the ONION®

LOW 33 | HIGH 49

Mexican storm making a run for it

April 26, 2007 | Volume 43 Issue 17

AMERICA'S FINEST NEWS SOURCE • ONION.COM

Middle East Conflict Intensifies As Blah Blah Blah, Etc. Etc.

Onion Middle East Bureau

MIDDLE EAST—With the Iraq war in its fifth year, the war in Afghanistan in its sixth, and conflict between Israel and the rest of the region continuing unabated for more than half a century, intelligence sources are warning that a new wave of violence in the Middle East may soon blah blah blah, etc. etc., you know the rest.

"Tensions in the region are extremely high," said U.S. Ambassador to Iraq Ryan Crocker, who added the same old same old while answering reporters' questions. "We're disappointed by the events of the last few months, but we're confident that we're about to [yakety yakety yak]."

The U.N. has issued a strongly worded whatever denouncing someone or something presumably having to do with the vicious explosive things that raged across this, or shattered the predawn calm of that, or ripped suddenly through the other, killing umpteen innocent civilians in a Jerusalem bus or Beirut discotheque or Fallujah mosque or whatever it was this time.

see *BLAH*, page 7

Yet another act of violence in response to something else terrible that occurred in, oh, let's say Basra.

Even CEO Can't Figure Out How RadioShack Still In Business

FORT WORTH, TX—Despite having been on the job for nine months, RadioShack CEO Julian Day said Monday that he still has "no idea" how the home electronics store manages to stay open.

CEO Julian Day

"There must be some sort of business model that enables this company to make money, but I'll be damned if I know what it is," Day said. "You wouldn't think that people still buy enough strobe lights and extension cords to support an entire nationwide chain, but I guess they must, or I wouldn't have this desk to sit behind all day."

The retail outlet boasts more than 6,000 locations in the United States, and is known best for its wall-sized displays of obscure-looking analog electronics components and its notoriously desperate, high-pressure sales

see *RADIOSHACK*, page 9

How Revenues *Should* Look

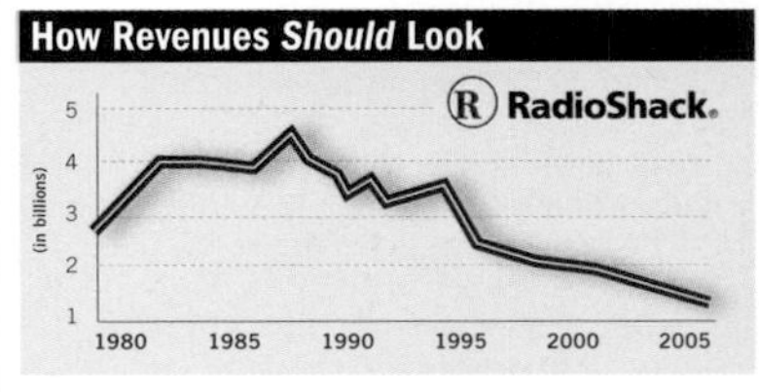

Weird Kid Shines During Dissection Project

Onion School Watch

Sam Hollis, who is small for his age, takes a moment to reflect on the only instance of easy social interaction in his 14 years of life.

PONCA CITY, OK—Weird Ponca City High School freshman Sam Hollis, 14, briefly transcended his lifelong streak of social awkwardness Wednesday, surprising his classmates and teacher when he deftly dissected a frog during his second-period biology lab.

Displaying a never-before-witnessed confidence and poise, Hollis effortlessly handled a surgical scalpel and a pair of forceps. After making a clean lengthwise incision in the preserved frog's abdomen, he used the forceps to skillfully pull aside the layers of skin and muscle.

Hollis reportedly completed the opening of the body cavity in less than one minute, which drew the attention of nearby pairs of students still arguing over who would have to touch their frog and gagging from the stench of formaldehyde.

"At first I thought he was going to be all weird and start to cry or something," said Hollis' assigned lab partner Ricky Malnight, who before knew Hollis only as "that dork who never talks and has dandruff." "But he just picked up the scalpel and dove right in. He didn't even look at the workbook or anything. It was pretty awesome because all I had to do was sit there while he did everything."

Hollis appeared so in his element, Malnight said, that for the rest of the class period he almost forgot the scrawny teen's faintly musty odor, perennially crooked glasses, and widely agreed-upon "gross" status.

As students craned their necks to watch him assuredly navigate the frog's abdominal cavity, Hollis capitalized on his fleeting peer acceptance by identifying the functions of all seven major organs. He even showed his classmates how to cut out the gall bladder without damaging the liver, a skill which earned many extra credit on the project.

see *WEIRD KID*, page 8

Cheney Celebrates Earth Day By Breathing Oxygen

WASHINGTON, DC—At a special Earth Day event Sunday, Vice President Dick Cheney inhaled his first-ever breath of oxygen.

"I am…proud to stand before you today and…breathe in the same gas used by…millions of Americans," said a wheezing and gasping Cheney, whose body is accustomed to compounds of chlorine and sulfur dioxide. "One breath, however, is enough for me. I'm glad the stuff will be out of the atmosphere forever in a few decades."

Cheney then left the press conference to attend a cardiac health awareness dinner, where he feasted on human hearts.

$2.00 US | $3.00 CANADA

INDEX

ONION

Briefs 2
Opinion 11
Sports 14

A.V. CLUB

Cinema 22
Music 28
Words 31

INSIDE

LOCAL

Son-In-Law Welcome Any Time

page 19F

LOCAL

Man Shows Up To Arcade With Own Set Of Skee Balls page 12F

THIS WEEK IN THE A.V. CLUB

We talk with the minds behind *Hot Fuzz* and pay tribute to Kurt Vonnegut

Hillary Clinton Threatened By Black Man

NATIONAL, page 13A

OPINION

'Turns Out Smoking Is A Lot Easier Than I Thought'

By Peter Sohn, page 9B

Pizza Hut's New Pizza Lover's Pizza Topped With Smaller Pizzas

BUSINESS, page 13C

"Tu stultus es"

LOW | HIGH 48 | 65

Nice kerchief weather

May 3, 2007 | Volume 43 Issue 18

AMERICA'S FINEST NEWS SOURCE • ONION.COM

Prince William Fells Prince Willem-Alexander Of The Netherlands In Crucial Joust

Onion Christendom Bureau

CHELTENHAM, ENGLAND—In a resounding display of horsemanship, lancemanship, and puissance that marked both his first major tournament success and a great victory on the international stage for the British crown, the gallant English Prince William did mightily unseat Prince Willem-Alexander of the Netherlands in combat at the Cheltenham Jousts this Sunday week.

The prince, his aspect as always noble and his armour brightly agleam, did strike his gentleman-foe the Prince of Orange with a single shivering blow to the very center of his greatshield, all glory be to God, ensuring, as well, a victory in global currency exchange.

"Alack! I am bested, and fall heavy to the ground, and must therefore renegotiate the terms of special exchange between our nations when managing debts that predate conversion to the new EU standard," quoth Willem-Alexander as he tumbled from his steed, acknowledging his opponent the

see *JOUST*, page 7

The valiant Prince William astride his trusty steed (above) and triumphant in victory (left).

Area Woman's Entire Day Ruined By Bangs

ROCKLAND, DE—Local resident Heather Telford's entire Friday was ruined by a set of uncooperative bangs that refused to set correctly, the 26-year-old benefits coordinator told reporters.

According to Telford, the trouble began "right away" as she got ready for work, when she discovered that the three inches of forehead-skirting hair was unable to sit flat, despite the application of numerous gels, sprays, and pomades. A tuft on either side would not integrate with the central grouping, leaving three-quarter-inch gaps, while other wispy strands strayed from her temples, creating a highly undesirable "wing" effect. A last-ditch effort to wet and restyle the bangs only worsened their state, adding several more small kinks and increasing their overall dishevelment.

"It was so awful," Telford said. "I should've just called in sick after I found out that my straightening iron was broken, because the whole day went downhill from there. I can't imagine a worse thing happening to me."

The bangs went on to adversely affect every element of Telford's day, including her commute, her interactions with coworkers, the way food tasted, and even the sound of her voice.

"I kept feeling these awful little

see *BANGS*, page 6

TIMELINE: THE RUINED DAY

- **7:29 a.m.** More than 920 comb strokes fail to tame bangs
- **8:15 a.m.** Brief eye contact made with friendly receptionist
- **9:02 a.m.** Reflection in break-room coffee urn renews despair
- **11:55 p.m.** Vows to spare children, never reproduce
- **4:55 p.m.** Peruses job sites for new listings

CRIME IN OUR OFFICES

White-On-White Violence Claims Life Of Accounts Receivable Supervisor

POYNETTE, WI—Foul play is suspected in the death of an accounts receivable supervisor for a regional office-supply company, sheriff's deputies reported Tuesday.

Kornfeld

Herbert F. Kornfeld, 34, was an alleged accounting gang leader considered by law enforcement to be a key player in a series of ongoing office worker turf wars. He was found dead Monday morning in the third-floor copy room of Midstate Office Supply, his employer of 12 years.

"We believe the victim was assaulted after hours Friday by an unknown individual or individuals," a Columbia County sheriff's department spokesman said. "Though autopsy results are still pending, we believe the victim suffered fatal head trauma after his face was immobilized against the glass of a photocopier and repeatedly struck with the machine's cover."

Midstate Office Supply vice-president Howard Dinwiddie is expected this week to name accounts receivable assistant Irving Weinbaum, 23, as Kornfeld's successor. Ø

CBS To Release Own Version Of NBC's *The Office*

David Spade has big, Steve Carell–sized shoes to fill, but he and CBS executives think he's up to the task.

Onion Entertainment Watch

NEW YORK—Hoping to replicate the success of the Emmy-winning NBC show *The Office*, executives at CBS announced Monday that the network will adapt the highly rated comedy for CBS audiences.

"We're excited to bring the fresh, groundbreaking comedy of *The Office* to a completely new channel," CBS President Leslie Moonves said. "Some people say a show like *The Office* can only work on NBC, but we're out to prove them wrong."

Since securing rights to the sitcom, producers Bruce Klein and Greg Winston have worked diligently to repackage the show for its new context.

"We're huge fans of NBC's *The Office*—we want to remain faithful to that while at the same time creating our own voice," Klein said. "Obviously we had to change some of the language and cultural references to things our audience will understand. But the show's central message is the same: Just because they call it 'work' doesn't mean you can't have a few laughs while doing it."

The show's pilot, a shot-for-shot re-creation of NBC's *Office* pilot, features comedian David Spade as boss Peter Craig, the fun-loving and inspirational boss of a small-town Ohio paper company.

"Having David on the project is such a thrill," said Klein, who offered Spade the part after Ray Romano and Kevin James turned down the role. "Don't get me wrong—Steve Carell is

see *OFFICE*, page 8

$2.00 US | $3.00 CANADA

INDEX

ONION
Briefs....2
Opinion....10
Sports....12
A.V. CLUB
Cinema....20
Music....28
Words....32

INSIDE

LOCAL

Women To Drink For Free Until 10 Tonight At Spanky's page 19F

FOOD

Pillsbury Cinnamon Rolls To Rise In Stomach page 12H

THIS WEEK IN THE A.V. CLUB

One man's big summer movie is another man's bargain-bin DVD.

A.V. MADISON

Sketching for sketchy people.

page 34

Ohio State Uses T-Shirt Blaster To Pass Out Diplomas
EDUCATION, page 5D

OPINION
'I Just Had A Great Idea For Another War'
By President George W. Bush, page 9B

Sharon Stone Auctioned Off To German Conglomerate
BUSINESS, page 9C

'Tu Stultus Es'

LOW 42 | HIGH 65
Jackpot!

May 24, 2007 | Volume 43 Issue 21

AMERICA'S FINEST NEWS SOURCE • ONION.COM

Dog Breeders Issue Massive Recall Of '07 Pugs

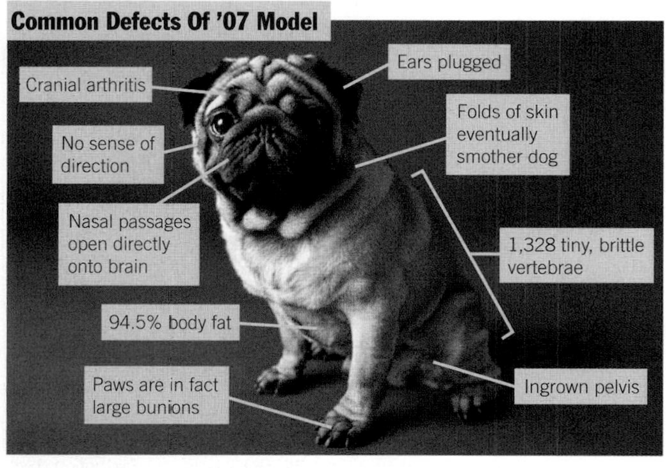

Onion Pet Owner Affairs Desk

WASHINGTON, DC—Citing centuries of quality-control issues that have resulted in chronic unreliability, cascading system failures, and even total unit shutdown, the American Pug Breeders Association announced a recall Monday of all pugs produced between February 2006 and the present day.

"We apologize wholeheartedly to any and all owners of the 2007 pug," APBA director Betty McAndrews said at a press conference, standing before a table where 10 defective pugs were displayed. "While pug owners are accustomed to dog malfunction, the latest animals are prone to more problems than just the usual joint failures, overheating, seizures, chronic respiratory defects, and inability to breed without assistance. The latest model pug is simply not in any way a viable dog."

According to the APBA's online recall notice, pugs produced in the specified period are at "moderate to high risk" for convulsive respiratory failure, soft palate suppuration, corneal ulcers leading to sudden deliquescence of the eyeballs, catastrophic lung collapse, ingrown ribs, diabetes, patellar luxation, encephalitis, Lou Gehrig's pug's disease, impacted hips, neck dysplasia, tracheal fissures, morbid obesity, cranial arthritis, and leakage of the anal sacs. In addition, due to strong allergic reactions to almost all medications, 97 percent of pugs are untreatable.

This week, the APBA has begun to send out recall information and cardboard mailing boxes to registered pug owners, who are asked to place their '07 pug inside the box, seal it, and, if they wish, punch air holes in the top and sides. Owners must then put the box inside an airtight heavy-duty plastic bag, affix a postage-paid mailing label, and drop it off at any U.S. post office.

In order to ensure that all '07 pugs are taken out of circulation, the organization is also providing a complimentary on-site disposal service to pug owners

see PUGS, page 10

Modern-Day Martin Luther Nails 95 Comment Cards To IHOP Door

Ronald Lyman

SIOUX FALLS, SD—Managers of an area International House of Pancakes discovered 95 comment cards nailed to its front door Sunday, which were later identified as the work of local resident Ronald Lyman, a 53-year-old contractor and one-time regular customer who is calling for wide-scale reform of the venerable chain.

"IHOP has grown weak on powdered sugar and fruity garnishes, forsaking the righteousness of its original rib-sticking mission," said Lyman, who nailed his 95 comments to the door shortly before the morning brunch rush, when they would receive maximum exposure. "This house is no longer a house of pancakes—it is a house of lies."

Lyman's 95 cards assail IHOP for what he perceives to be an "unholy alliance" of the sweet and the savory, a dangerously narrowing blueberry-to-batter ratio, hard-to-open butter packets, and an increasingly tall short stack. Fifteen cards alone attack the excessive breadth of syrup selection.

"IHOP is about pancakes, not syrups," card 41

see IHOP, page 10

Study: 38 Percent Of People Not Actually Entitled To Their Opinion

CHICAGO—In a surprising refutation of the conventional wisdom on opinion entitlement, a study conducted by the University of Chicago's School for Behavioral Science concluded that more than one-third of the U.S. population is neither entitled nor qualified to have opinions.

"On topics from evolution to the environment to gay marriage to immigration reform, we found that many of the opinions expressed were so off-base and ill-informed that they actually hurt society by being voiced," said chief researcher Professor Mark Fultz, who based the findings on hundreds of telephone, office, and dinner-party conversations compiled over a three-year period. "While people have long asserted that it takes all kinds, our research shows that American society currently has a drastic oversupply of the kinds who don't have any good or worthwhile thoughts whatsoever. We could actually do just fine without them."

In 2002, Fultz's team shook the academic world by conclusively proving the existence of both bad ideas during brainstorming and dumb questions during question-and-answer sessions.

NATION MOBILIZES FOR BEAUTIFUL WEEKEND

U.S. Fathers Order Troops Into Minivans

NEW YORK—The nation's domestic forces are responding to the imminent arrival of pleasant weekend weather conditions by launching the largest coordinated surge on America's outdoor recreation destinations in recent history, sources reported Thursday.

"For the sake of our loved ones and our way of life, we have a solemn duty to enjoy this beautiful weather to its maximum potential," said Boston resident Ross Schneiderman, 37, a veteran of more than two dozen beautiful weekends since 1988. "So we intend to be ready to lock and load at the crack of dawn tomorrow."

see WEEKEND, page 8

While most Americans are waiting until early Saturday morning to move out, a 100-mile convoy of sedans, minivans, and RVs has already been sighted on I-94 leaving Chicago.

$2.00 US | $3.00 CANADA

INDEX

ONION
Briefs ... 2
Opinion ... 12
Sports ... 14
A.V. CLUB
Cinema ... 22
Music ... 26
Words ... 27

INSIDE

NATIONAL
Train Wreck Not That Interesting page 3A

LOCAL
Unmarked VHS Tape Kept 'Just In Case' page 11B

THIS WEEK IN THE A.V. CLUB
We talk to Louis C.K. and review that one movie with the pirates.

A.V. CLUB

A.V. MADISON
Local entertainers share day-job wisdom.
page 33

OPINION

'Lock Up Your Daughters, Because I Am Going To Kill Them'

By Silvio Milardin, page 9C

Dept. Of Homeland Security Introduces DHS For Men

NATIONAL, page 5A

Jeremy Piven Outraged Microsoft Word Doesn't Recognize His Name

TECHNOLOGY, page 9D

'Tu Stultus Es'

LOW | HIGH 42 | 65

Unclear; check back in a few minutes

June 14, 2007 | Volume 43 Issue 24

AMERICA'S FINEST NEWS SOURCE • ONION.COM

Author To Use Water As Metaphor

CHAPEL HILL, NC—Novelist, playwright, and poet H. Gregor Lafferty, 41, announced Monday his plan to use water as a metaphor in an upcoming and as-yet-untitled work.

"Water," said Lafferty, pausing for effect and gazing off into the middle distance. "It could have any number of profoundly resonant meanings: the flow of time, a lover's secret, death, birth, an archetypal coming-of-age experience, or even a spiritual cleansing. Really, the possibilities are endless...as endless as the eternal yet ever-changing sea."

Several of Lafferty's previous literary efforts, which employed such devices as a wedding dress symbolizing fate and a gas station that represents renewal, have been published in the North Carolina-based quarterly *Catawba*.

ONION **SPECIAL** REPORT

PHOTO **EXCLUSIVE**

Gendelman leaves Whitford Middle School Monday, striking his now familiar erection-concealment pose.

Davey Gendelman Hits Puberty

Investigation Reveals 13-Year-Old's Body Is Changing

WHITFORD, NJ—After several months of observation and interviews with nearly everyone in the young teen's life, an *Onion* investigation has conclusively determined tthat Whitford seventh grader David "Davey" Gendelman, 13, is presently undergoing the bodily changes that will slowly transform his awkward, boyish frame into that of a sexually mature adult.

Despite repeated denials from the transparently defensive Gendelman, members of his peer group told reporters that the Whitford native now experiences spontaneous erections throughout the day. The majority of these occur during third-period social studies class, in which he sits behind classmate Sarah Miller, also 13, and stares desperately at the bra straps visible under her tank top. Several handwritten poems discovered during a search of Gendelman's school locker identify Miller as the secret object of his budding affections.

When informed of her classmate's sexual interest in her underwear, Miller called Gendelman "perverted and gross."

The boy's penis, although still tiny compared to those of most boys his age, is becoming erect at other times as well, including in the hallway between classes, on the school bus, and at lunch, an analysis of school security-camera footage confirmed. Gendelman has been observed carrying textbooks and other objects directly in front of his midsection in an ineffective

see ***PUBERTY****, page 9*

» ONLINE

For more information on Davey Gendelman's puberty, check out our additional features online, including our extensive **'Scrotum Hair: Before and After'** photo slideshow, video profile, and four-part series of charts on recent changes to his body.

onion.com

Cracker Barrel Announces Plans To Build Another One Out By The Highway

The sign for the Cracker Barrel down by the ball fields.

ALDERWINE, MO—Cracker Barrel CEO Michael Woodhouse announced Tuesday that the restaurant and retail chain would expand to a new location out by Highway 18, near the Harmon Road turnoff.

"At Cracker Barrel, our mission is to give our customers hearty, all-American food and old license plates on the walls to look at while they eat," said Woodhouse, gesturing toward a scale model of the future restaurant, which is the same model used for all new location announcements. "That's why we're proud to announce our newest location, just up a ways past the Flying J."

The new location will be the fourth Cracker Barrel in town, fifth if you count the one half a mile from the city limits where the dirt track speedway used to be.

The decision to build one, Woodhouse said, was based on months of extensive internal research indicating that people around here like to eat, like to drive, and are willing to drive to eat.

"Our data showed that folks driving north out of town might like a Cracker Barrel in the immediate area," Woodhouse said. "I always said there should be one out that way any-

see ***CRACKER BARREL****, page 8*

Shaking Off Amnesia, Gonzales Remembers He's Actually Pool Salesman From Tulsa

Gonzales asks Congress to let him return to his real career as soon as possible.

WASHINGTON, DC—Embattled Attorney General Alberto Gonzales' future was thrown further into jeopardy Friday when he was accidentally struck by a boom microphone, reversing a years-long case of amnesia and causing him to remember his true identity as hotshot Tulsa, OK pool and spa salesman "Cabana Al" Gonzales.

"My God, what am I doing here?" a dazed Gonzales asked reporters in what they assured him was indeed his office. "The last thing I remember is slipping on some wet redwood decking out by the Boswicks' 16-by-48-foot in-ground El Tropico—beautiful pool, that one, with a hefty seven percent commission attached—and then suddenly I'm waking up three years older, 25 pounds heavier, and defending my actions in the firing of eight federal prosecutors. Somebody has obviously made a really big mistake."

"Clearly, I should not be seventh in line for the presidency," Gonzales said.

see ***GONZALES****, page 7*

INDEX

ONION
Briefs....2
Opinion....11
Sports....14
A.V. CLUB
Cinema....22
Music....25
Words....27

INSIDE

STYLE

Innovative Fashion Designer Comes Up With New Direction For Stripes To Go In page 3F

Pentagon To Surround Self With Pentagon Decoys
NATIONAL, page 5A

OPINION
'I Wish I Had Invented A Way Not To Die'
By Thomas Edison, page 9C

Dog In Purse Stares Longingly At Dog In Yard
FASHION, page 9D

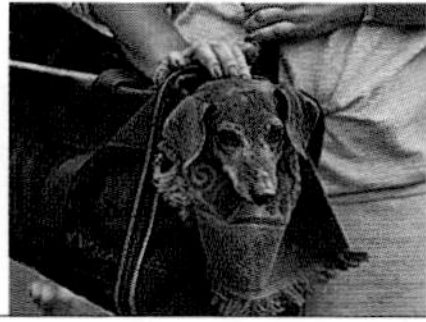

'Tu Stultus Es'

LOW 42 | HIGH 65
Pollen chunks

July 19, 2007 | Volume 43 Issue 29

AMERICA'S FINEST NEWS SOURCE • ONION.COM

No One Admits To Singing, Writing, Producing Nation's No. 1 Song

THIS WEEK	LAST WEEK	2 WEEKS AGO	WEEKS ON CHT	ARTIST IMPRINT & NUMBER / DISTRIBUTING LABEL (PRICE)
1	HOT SHOT DEBUT		1	#1 1 WK ANONYMOUS UNKNOWN (18.98)
2	1	–	2	MAROON 5 A&M/OCTONE 008917/INTERSCOPE (18.98)
3	2	1	3	LINKIN PARK MACHINE SHOP 44477/WARNER BROS. (18.98)
4	NEW		1	JASON ALDEAN BROKEN BOW 7047 (17.98)
5	6	10	28	DAUGHTRY RCA 88860/RMG (18.98)
6	11	12	12	AMY WINEHOUSE UNIVERSAL REPUBLIC 008428/UMRG (10.98)
7	4	–	2	YOUNG JEEZY PRESENTS U.S.I CORPORATE THUGZ/DEF JAM 008738/IDJMG (10.98
8	9	6	7	AVRIL LAVIGNE RCA 03774/RMG (18.98)
				MICHAEL BUBLE ...BROS. (18.98)

LOS ANGELES—As of Monday, the CD single "Baby Baby (Luvya Girl)" has rocketed to the top the *Billboard* Hot 100 on its debut week, despite the fact no one has claimed credit for singing, composing, or producing it.

The single's success marks a rare occasion in which both critics and the music industry find themselves in agreement, as magazines such as *Spin* call "Baby Baby" "a wasteland" and "creatively brain-dead," and major recording labels such as Interscope and Sony BMG distance themselves from it.

"This is a first in modern recording history," *Billboard Magazine* writer Jim Shapiro said. "Even third-place *American Idol* contestants and Diddy have not come forward as the creators, though it's obviously a solid hit and could make them a lot of bank."

Receiving heavy rotation on terrestrial Top 40 stations, the R & B-infused tune clocks in at just under two minutes and 45 seconds. The song's main, and sole, lyrics, "Baby, baby, love you girl," are sung in a breathy male voice that alternates between a grunt and a falsetto. A cooing female voice vaguely simulating an orgasm provides the bridge at approximately the 1:50 mark.

Even seasoned music journalists and A&R executives are having difficulty identifying the voices, saying it's anyone's guess whom they belong to.

"Justin Timberlake, Usher, Beyoncé, Fergie, Ludacris, Rihanna—you tell me," said Jive Records executive Scott Giordano, who strongly denied any responsibility for "Baby Baby." "The wispy whine of the female's voice sounded a bit like Britney Spears doing a comeback attempt—the tune certainly seemed up her alley—but she sounded black, so then I considered that 'Milkshake' girl. But really, I can't tell. I'd bet the guy's not R. Kelly, but then

see SONG, page 8

John Edwards Vows To End All Bad Things By 2011

AMES, IA—In an effort to jump-start a presidential campaign that still has not broken into the top Democratic tier, former Sen. John Edwards made his most ambitious policy announcement yet at a Monday campaign event in Iowa: a promise to eliminate all unpleasant, disagreeable, or otherwise bad things from all aspects of American life by the end of his second year in office.

"Many bad things are not just bad—they're terrible," said a beaming Edwards, whose "Only the Good Things" proposal builds upon previous efforts to end poverty, outlaw startlingly loud noises, and offer tax breaks to those who smile frequently. "Other candidates have plans that would reduce some of the bad things, but I want all of them gone completely."

According to Edwards, his plan is composed of three steps. Everyday bad things, such as curse words and splinters, would be eradicated during his first six months in office. Next, very bad things, including child abduction, soil erosion, and resurgent diseases such as malaria and tuberculosis, would be ended by the the end of 2009. Finally, extremely bad things—plights such as genocide, species extinction, and virtually every form of cancer—would take a full two years to wipe out.

"Racism will soon be a thing of the past," Edwards said. "Same goes for being picked last for playground athletics, AIDS, robbery, not having enough spending

see BAD THINGS, page 10

In Iowa, Edwards speaks with conviction about his lifelong distaste for bad things.

Sources: Barista Not Actually Flirting With You

SAN FRANCISCO—Though she greets you every morning with a smile, sometimes chats with you, and makes sure the chocolate syrup is evenly distributed throughout your mocha, Starbucks barista Molly Sopel is in truth not flirting with you, and is instead simply a pleasant person and conscientious employee, coffee-shop sources reported Monday.

"The best part about Molly is that she laughs and talks with everyone," said manager Mike Dezort, who confirmed that Sopel asks if you want room for milk as a courtesy, and not because of the physical attraction you think exists between the two of you. "I always overhear her calling customers sweetie, which people seem to like."

A Starbucks regular who frequently watches you order from Sopel is reportedly "shocked" that you still haven't realized that she only calls you by your first name when you pay with your debit card. Ø

OUR ECONOMY, OUR PLANET

New Eco-Friendly Packaging Triggers Boom In Guilt-Free Littering

ROCKFORD, IL—Nick Sundin used to be neurotic about littering. The 37-year-old pediatrician admits he kept trash bags in his car, and would even pick up and throw away garbage he found on the street. Since boyhood, Sundin said, he was keenly attuned to the environmental degradation littering caused, an attitude triggered by the famous Keep America Beautiful "Crying Indian" public service announcement he saw on television as a young man.

OUR ENVIRONMENT

Not anymore.

"These 'eco' products are amazing—they've totally changed my life," Sundin said. "Now, I just toss my used Seventh Generation–brand paper plates out the car window, knowing they'll soon be absorbed into the earth."

The growing "green" trend in product packaging, which emphasizes the use of recycled, biodegradable post-consumer paper-based materials and relies less on petroleum-derived polymers like styrofoam, has unleashed a spontaneous trashing of sidewalks, roadsides, and pristine wilderness by gratified consumers. Though some environmentalists and

see LITTERING, page 6

INDEX

ONION
Briefs 2
Opinion 13
Sports 16

A.V. CLUB
Cinema 22
Music 24
Words 25

29
0 74470 94595 6

INSIDE

BUSINESS
Acquisition Of 3-Hole Punch Triples Intern's Productivity page 3F

THIS WEEK IN THE A.V. CLUB
It's time to talk to Spoon. Also, we review *Hairspray* and more.

A.V. MADISON

OPINION
'Remember This Face, For It Will One Day Be Famous For Eating A Record Amount Of Glass'
By Lisa Kampfel, page 5C

NASA Launches Probe To Find, Destroy Earth-Like Planet
SCIENCE, page 9D

Mike Johanns Only One Showing Up To Cabinet Meetings Now
NATIONAL, page 3A

'Tu Stultus Es'

LOW 60 | HIGH 85
Partlycast

SEPTEMBER 20, 2007 · VOLUME 43 ISSUE 38
AMERICA'S FINEST NEWS SOURCE · ONION.COM

14 American Apparel Models Freed In Daring Midnight Raid

Law enforcement officials continued clearing models from the compound into the early morning hours.

LOS ANGELES—Acting on information gathered from billboards, alternative weeklies, and Internet banner ads, an FBI strike team liberated 14 dazed, sallow, and undernourished American Apparel models in a raid on the controversial organization's downtown Los Angeles compound early Monday.

"There were girls lying everywhere—draped over furniture, sprawled spread-eagled in the corner, and huddled close like animals," FBI Special Agent Curtis Froman, who oversaw the raid, said at a press conference. "Many of them had been given nothing more than a pair of tube socks or men's briefs to wear."

Froman said it took agents nearly 20 minutes to cut through the holding-cell padlocks, only to find the ambiguously ethnic-looking captives living in "unspeakable conditions."

"They just stared up at us with blank expressions of utter confusion," Froman added. "I don't think they'd seen the sun in weeks."

Nine American Apparel security enforcers were also killed during the raid.

see RAID, page 7

Fred Thompson Fears Presidential Run Will Typecast Him As Politician

WASHINGTON, DC—Veteran character actor and Republican presidential candidate Fred Thompson expressed worries to reporters Tuesday that a successful White House bid could spell "total career death."

"It would be nice to get away from the FBI agent and district attorney roles—that's why I eventually decided to try out for the Oval Office part—but would being forced to play presidents for the rest your life be that much better?" said Thompson, whose résumé includes *Law & Order*, *Die Hard 2*, U.S. senator from 1994 to 2003, and *Baby's Day Out*. "Sure, you don't want to turn down work, and it'd be a solid four-to-eight-year gig, but after that I'd always be known as 'that politician guy.' Look what happened to Reagan—he never worked again."

Recent polls have placed Thompson among the GOP frontrunners, with many voters citing the value of his experience as U.S. president in the 2005 docudrama *Last Best Chance*.

Sequel-Hungry Nation Demands *Click II*

The threat of no *Click* sequel brings out the masses.

LOS ANGELES—As the summer movie season comes to an end, hundreds of thousands of deeply disappointed moviegoers converged on Los Angeles this weekend to demand that Hollywood finally honor their wish for a sequel to the Adam Sandler comedy *Click*.

"When I saw no *Click II* on my town's multiplex marquee this summer, I felt I had to speak out," said North Carolina resident Jim McNulty, who quit his job to travel to the nation's movie capital. "And I think I speak for virtually all Americans when I say we won't rest until we find out what happens next to nutty everyman Michael Newman and his family."

The group People for the Continuation of Filmic Storylines, the largest of the many organizations in the pro-sequel grassroots move-

see SEQUEL, page 5

PEOPLE

Area Man Has Sad Little Routine For When He Needs Cheering Up

TIPTON, IN—Wes Mendic, a grown man who works at a pool-supply store and lives all by himself, finds solace in a series of sad, piddling little activities when he is feeling down, he reported from his tiny one-bedroom apartment Tuesday.

"Whenever I'm down in the dumps, rather than wallow in my troubles, I try to do things that will get my mind off them," Mendic, 28, said. "Like, the first thing I always do is turn on all the lights in my apartment, even during the day. It just makes everything brighter."

"It's amazing what something as small as lifting up your kitchen window, leaning your head out, and looking outside for a few minutes can do for your spirits," Mendic added.

Wes Mendic

Mendic also indulges in a succession of "fun" tasks, including putting fresh, clean sheets and pillowcases on his bed; using his Dustbuster to thoroughly vacuum his two-by-three-foot welcome mat, the only section of carpeting he owns; and dumping out the contents of his coin bank, stacking the coins into small piles by denomination, and then placing them one by one back into the coin bank.

"Something that always gives me a chuckle is going to my computer and loading up Bobby McFerrin's 'Don't Worry, Be Happy,'" said Mendic, who often watches the four-minute music-video clip several times in a row, staring intently at the screen and silently mouthing the lyrics in one of the saddest displays you will ever see. "It's funny, it's catchy, and it really helps remind you not to take this crazy business called life too seriously. I remember it used to cheer me up back when I was in college too. Good times."

see ROUTINE, page 6

INSIDE

LOCAL
Prisoner Now Wishes He Hadn't Turned Toothbrush Into Shiv PAGE 3B

LOCAL
Lost Dog Probably Better Off PAGE 8B

INDEX

ONION
Briefs 2
Opinion 8
Sports 12
A.V. CLUB
Cinema 26
Music 31
Words 34

ONION NEWS ONLINE
onion.com GO

OPINION

'Oh My God, You've Never Seen Every Movie Ever Made?'

By Jeremy Edel, page 5C

Pants Attempt To Convey What Owner Can't

FASHION, page 9D

Japanese Prime Minister Resigns To Seek Revenge On Man Who Killed His Family

INTERNATIONAL, page 3A

'Tu Stultus Es'

LOW 60 | HIGH 85

Start piling sandbags. Trust us.

SEPTEMBER 27, 2007 • VOLUME 43 ISSUE 39

AMERICA'S FINEST NEWS SOURCE • ONION.COM

BUSH MAKES SURPRISE VISIT TO WORK

President Bush exits Marine One at the start of his four-hour visit to Washington's White House.

Onion Washington Bureau

WASHINGTON, DC—In an unexpected move that shocked White House staff and stunned the nation, President George W. Bush arrived unannounced at the Oval Office Monday.

Bush, who flew in from his home in Texas, was greeted by security forces upon landing outside the White House, and quickly escorted through the building's back entrance. Wearing a special suit-and-tie uniform intended to boost morale and show support for men and women serving in the Beltway, Bush entered the East Room at about 3:30 p.m. and addressed a bewildered but enthusiastic crowd of staff members.

"Am I late?" Bush joked to the group of approximately 200, who were led to believe they would be attending a ceremony to honor Secretary of Transportation Mary Peters. Bush's entrance received a standing ovation.

"It is incredible to see firsthand what you brave men and women do every day," Bush said to rousing applause. "You are all heroes."

Telling the group he wished he had the time to work alongside each and every one of them, Bush made general inquiries about con-

see **SURPRISE**, page 10

INSIDE

ARTS

Marcel Marceau Trapped In Real Box This Time

PAGE 3F

TECHNOLOGY

Home Phone Hasn't Rung In 3 Years

PAGE 8E

INDEX

ONION

Briefs 2

Opinion 12

Sports 16

A.V. CLUB

Cinema 26

Music 33

Words 35

A.V. MADISON

Five fine local bands at the Majestic Wednesday

page 46

ONION NEWS ONLINE

39

0 74470 94595 6

ONION SCIENCE THURSDAY

Scientists Ask Congress To Fund $50 Billion Science Thing

WASHINGTON, DC—Top physicists from several major American universities appeared before a Congressional committee Monday to request $50 billion for a science thing that would further U.S. advancement science-wise and broaden human knowing.

The scientists spoke for approximately three hours about the complicated science machine, which is expensive, and large, telling members of the House Committee on Science and Technology that the tubular, gamma-ray-using mechanism is vital in some big way. Yet the high price tag of the thing, which would be built on a 40-square-mile plot of land where the science would ultimately occur, remained a pressing question.

"While expense is something to consider, I think it's very important that we have this kind of scientific apparatus, because, in the end, I have always said that science is more important than it is unimportant," Committee chairman Rep. Bart Gordon (D-TN) said. "And it's essential we stay ahead of China, Japan, and Germany in science. We are ahead in space, with the

see **SCIENCE**, page 7

"The [science thing] will make valuable inroads into our ultimate understanding of how [atoms and quarks move around and so on]."

David Kaminski, Caltech Physicist

Google Launches 'The Google' For Older Adults

MOUNTAIN VIEW, CA—The popular search engine Google announced plans Friday to launch a new site, TheGoogle.com, to appeal to older adults not able to navigate the original website's single text field and two clearly marked buttons.

"The Google will have all the same information currently found on regular Google, but with the added features of not stealing your credit-card numbers or giving your computer all kinds of viruses," said Rick Tillich, The Google project director. "All you have to do to turn the website on is put the little blinking line thing in the cyberspace window at the top of the screen, type 'thegoogle.com,' and press 'return'—although it will also recognize http.wwwthegoogle.com, google.aol, and 'THEGOOGLE' typed into a Word document."

Tillich added that he hopes the site will soon replace Yahoo Internet Website.com as the most popular search engine for users over 55.

Chinese Authorities Execute 10 Million Recalled Toys

Barbie dolls pay the ultimate price for containing lead paint.

BEIJING—In an attempt to assure the world's children that the millions of Chinese-made toys currently being recalled for containing toxic lead paint and tiny choking hazards can no longer hurt them, high-level Chinese officials announced Tuesday that millions of playthings are being rounded up and immediately put to death.

"A Chinese official" announces the execution of 52,000 Barbies suspected of lead-paint contamination (above).

"We are committed to the well-being of children and putting the consumer's mind at ease," said Chinese president Hu Jintao at a press conference. "Boys and girls of the world, you need not worry. Your toys will be executed swiftly and harshly. When we are through, there will be nothing left to play with."

In the past six weeks, Mattel Inc. has recalled more than 20 million toys from China that are believed to contain lead paint and other safety defects, a situation that prompted the Chinese government to send People's Liberation Army forces into major industrial sectors

see **TOYS**, page 8

'Tu Stultus Es'

the ONION®

WEATHER PAGE B16

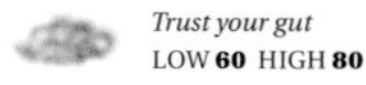

Trust your gut
LOW 60 HIGH 80

OCTOBER 18, 2007 · VOLUME 43 ISSUE 42

AMERICA'S FINEST NEWS SOURCE · ONION.COM

HIGHLIGHTS

SPORTS
Curt Schilling Inexplicably Bleeding Throughout Game 2 Start page 3C

What's Left Of Pamela Anderson Married Again
ENTERTAINMENT, page 5E

Over-Hydrated Terrier Proud Owner Of Six City Blocks LOCAL, page 9B

INSIDE

LOCAL
Aquarium Worker Can't Remember If He Locked Up Beluga Whales
PAGE 3B

TECHNOLOGY
OnStar Used To Parallel Park
PAGE 8F

INDEX

ONION
Briefs 2
Opinion 12
Sports 16
A.V. CLUB
Cinema 26
Music 33
Words 35

THIS WEEK IN THE A.V. CLUB

ONION SECURITY WATCH

Conceptual Terrorists Encase Sears Tower In Jell-O

CHICAGO—In what is being called the first conceptual terrorist attack on American soil, the landmark Sears Tower was encased in 18 million tons of strawberry gelatin early Tuesday morning, leaving thousands shocked, angry, and seriously confused.

Authorities called to the scene of the senseless attack said they could do little to control the large crowds of dangerously bewildered citizens, many of whom searched desperately for some semblance of meaning in what had just taken place. As of press time, 11 night security guards were still trapped inside the famous structure, their rescue seeming

see JELL-O, page 11

The Sears Tower (above) and shocked, slightly damp rescue workers (right).

It Only Tuesday

WASHINGTON, DC—After running a thousand errands, working hours of overtime, and being stuck in seemingly endless gridlock traffic commuting to and from their jobs, millions of Americans were disheartened to learn that it was, in fact, only Tuesday.

"Tuesday?" San Diego resident Doris Wagner said. "How in the hell is it still Tuesday?"

Tuesday's arrival stunned a nation still recovering from the nightmarish slog that was Monday, leaving some to wonder if the week was ever going to end and others to ask what was taking Friday so goddamn long.

"Ugh," said Wagner, echoing a national sense of frustration over it not even being Wednesday at the very least.

According to suddenly depressed sources, the feeling that this week may in fact last forever was further compounded by the thought of all the work left to be done tomorrow, the day after tomorrow, and, if Americans make it that far, possibly even Friday, for Christ's sake.

Fears that the week could actually be going backwards were also expressed.

see TUESDAY, page 9

First Orgy After Brian's Death Very Solemn

FAIRFIELD, CA—Lacking the exuberance, spontaneity, and airborne bodily fluids of previous all-night fuckfests, the first orgy since the passing of group-sex enthusiast Brian Hodge was a solemn and subdued affair, heavily lubricated sources reported Monday.

"Spirits were definitely low," said Catherine Davis, who claimed that Hodge's accidental drowning death was almost as unexpected as the time Scott Warner reached climax so quickly inside her mouth. "We were clearly all hurting on the inside. Especially Marissa, who got double-teamed right from the start."

The orgy, which was marked by long stretches of silence despite the use of only two ball gags, began shortly before midnight when a number of somber participants halfheartedly undressed and arranged one another in a melancholy daisy chain on the floor.

Friends of the late Brian Hodge gather in quiet remembrance.

"I tried acting like nothing had changed, like this was just another four-hour marathon of raucous, uninterrupted intercourse," orgy at-

see ORGY, page 8

'95-'96 Prayers Finally Answered

HEAVEN—Explaining that He had been "absolutely swamped," God announced yesterday that He was finally able to find time in His busy schedule to answer a portion of the 1995 and 1996 prayer backlog. "Unfortunately, I don't really want a red wagon anymore," 18-year-old Morgantown, WV resident Zach Gilpin said. Others expressed similar displeasure, including 30-year-old accountant Jack Demont, who said that former classmate and high school cheerleader Heidi Stillman's repeated phone calls to his house are "destroying" his marriage. Other prayers that were answered include Christopher Reeve's 1996 wish to walk again, the Pittsburgh Steelers' prayer on the sidelines prior to playing the Dallas Cowboys in Super Bowl XXX, and former office manager Jeff Watenhofer's request for cheap leather chairs for PNC Bank's 53rd-floor office inside the World Trade Center.

'Tu Stultus Es'

the ONION®

NOVEMBER 1, 2007 · VOLUME 43 ISSUE 44

AMERICA'S FINEST NEWS SOURCE · ONION.COM

WEATHER PAGE B16

Partly chancy
LOW **49** HIGH **54**

HIGHLIGHTS

'I Have No Idea You Exist'
OPINION, page 5C

Bike Helmet Protects Child From Helmet-Inspired Beating
LOCAL, page 9B

SPORTS
David Ortiz Incorporates Champagne Goggles Into Everyday Uniform page 3D

INSIDE

LOCAL
Tugboat Dealer Can Really See You In Tugboat
PAGE 3B

NATIONAL
Charity Walk Accidentally Raises Awareness Of Vehicular Manslaughter
PAGE 8A

INDEX

ONION
Briefs 2
Opinion 11
Sports 14
A.V. CLUB
Cinema 24
Music 28
Words 29

Child On White House Tour Momentarily Seizes Control Of Nation

Federal officers assess the damage to the seat of American power.

WASHINGTON, DC—In an event unprecedented in American history, Brandon Myers, a relatively obscure Iowa 10-year-old with no previous experience in domestic politics, took advantage of a clear leadership void and seized control of the United States Tuesday after he slipped away from his White House tour group and locked himself in the Oval Office.

The bloodless coup occurred when Myers, a fifth-grader at Mulberry Elementary School, stormed into the empty office and seated himself at the president's desk, thereby toppling the world's longest-running democracy. Myers spent much of his reign, which lasted from approximately 2:15 p.m. to 2:30 p.m., spinning in circles in the president's chair before proclaiming that he was "President Brandon" with a handwritten decree scrawled in cursive on White House stationery.

"Earlier this afternoon, sometime between a description of the James Buchanan portrait in the Main Hall and the question-and-answer session, a pre-adolescent boy overthrew the president and gained executive authority over the United States of America," White House press secretary Dana Perino said at a news conference Tuesday. "Several minutes ago, our nation's new leader made his first statement: 'Brandon rules.'"

Shortly after forcing former president George W. Bush out of office, Myers issued an executive order for pizza using the intercom in the Oval Office. Congress immediately passed emergency funding for 1,200 stuffed-crust pepperoni pizzas from Pizza Hut.

While the sudden change in government came as a shock to

see **TOUR**, page 10

Mel Brooks Starts Nonprofit Foundation To Save Word 'Schmuck'

An emotional Brooks stopped short of kvetching at a schmuck fundraiser Monday.

NEW YORK—Saying he could no longer stand idly by while a vital part of American culture is lost forever, activist and Broadway producer Mel Brooks has founded a private nonprofit organization dedicated to preserving the word "schmuck."

"Schmuck is dying," a sober Brooks said during a 2,000-person rally held in his hometown of Williamsburg, Brooklyn Monday. "For many of us, saying 'schmuck' is a way of life. Yet when I walk down the street and see people behaving in foolish, pathetic, or otherwise schmucky ways, I hear only the words 'prick' and 'douche bag.' I just shake my head and think, 'I don't want to live in a world like this.'"

The nonprofit, Schmucks For

see **SCHMUCK**, page 8

Postmaster General: 'Letter Carrier Surge Is Working'

WASHINGTON, DC—In testimony before Congress Tuesday, beleaguered Postmaster General John E. Potter stated that last month's nationwide deployment of 25,000 additional letter carriers, a controversial move designed to stem demoralizing mail loss, has been an unmitigated success. "We're losing fewer and fewer packages every day," said Potter, rebuffing critics who claim the increase has failed to stabilize the country's most troubled routes. "We ask the public to be patient. The American people have to keep in mind that we still lack the resources to deliver on Sundays." Potter drew additional fire from lawmakers after he announced plans to scale back the number of active-duty postal workers right before the holiday season.

Gerbil Growing Distant

Onion Local Desk

Kerlin, 34, and Blinkers, 0.5, sometimes go days without making eye contact.

TEMPE, AZ—Calling his pet "a completely different gerbil" than the one he brought home from the store, Doug Kerlin, 34, told reporters Tuesday that he fears the small mammal is growing increasingly distant.

"When I first got Blinkers, it was like we had this amazing connection," said Kerlin, who aside from his gerbil lives by himself in a one-bedroom apartment. "But lately it's almost as if he cares more about burrowing in his wood chips than he does about me."

Despite recent attempts by Kerlin to bridge the ever-growing void between himself and the withdrawn rodent—primarily by placing several new wooden ramps and ladders inside Blinkers' 15-gallon aquarium—as of press time the gerbil had refused to emerge from his nesting box.

"I don't know what to do," said Kerlin, who claimed the gerbil barely acknowledges his presence when he comes home from work. "Sometimes it's like he doesn't even recognize me."

According to Kerlin, the eight-inch, 2.3-ounce Mongolian gerbil's aloof behavior started when the junior accountant noticed that Blinkers would avoid looking at him every time he stared into the rodent's cage. The emotional detachment only became more apparent, Kerlin said, when Blinkers started making rhythmic thumping sounds with his hind legs every time Kerlin would reach into the glass enclosure to hold the gerbil.

"I was concerned," said Kerlin, who purchased the pet on a whim when he was walking through a shopping mall last Saturday night. "But the veterinarian told me that there was nothing medically wrong with Blinkers. That's when I knew it was me."

Though Kerlin has tried to personally engage his despondent gerbil by giving him more dust baths and leaving a cleaned-out coconut shell on the aquarium floor, Blinkers became even more cold and unfeeling with every conciliatory gesture, opting to ignore his owner for hours at a time by roaming around his multicolored climbing tunnel.

"Sometimes I come downstairs in the middle of the night to get a snack, and I hear him running on the exercise wheel and rustling

see **GERBIL**, page 7

'Tu Stultus Es'

the ONION®

DECEMBER 13, 2007 · VOLUME 43 ISSUE 50

AMERICA'S FINEST NEWS SOURCE · ONION.COM

WEATHER PAGE B16
Hail-sized sleet
LOW 41 HIGH 54

HIGHLIGHTS

Baby Jesus Stolen From Live Nativity LOCAL, page 5B

Triumph Of Human Engineering Slept Through TECHNOLOGY, page 9D

SPORTS
Gatorade Inventor Robert Cade, 1927–2007, Given Touching Memorial Tribute page 3C

INSIDE

LOCAL
Limits Of Nair Tested PAGE 3B

MUSIC
Child Prodigy Becomes Adult Guy-Who's-Pretty-Good-At-The-Banjo PAGE 8E

INDEX

ONION
Briefs 2
Opinion 13
Sports 16
A.V. CLUB
Random Rules 22
Cinema 29
Words 33

50
0 74470 94595 6

2007 Holiday Cheer Brought To You By Toyota

NEW YORK—In one of the largest marketing coups in recent years, holiday cheer—the intangible spirit of goodwill towards man, peace on Earth, and warmth in the hearts of all—will now be sponsored by the Toyota Motor Corporation, sources reported Tuesday.

The exclusive $30 million endorsement deal, which includes promotional tie-ins with the season's first snowfall and the smell of roasting turkey wafting gently through a warm and cozy home, was signed earlier this week by Toyota Motor Sales U.S.A. executive vice president James Lentz.

"We are very excited to be partnering with holiday cheer," said Lentz, who called the look of wonder on a young child's face and the company's new line of durable trucks a "natural pairing." "From now on, whenever anyone curls up in front of a crackling fireplace, or takes a moment to reflect on the importance of family, Toyota will be there."

Added Lentz: "This truly is the most wonderful time of the year."

While many details of the deal are still unclear, Lentz said that the automotive company has been awarded endorsement rights to all affection and joy experienced during the month of December. Toyota will also be the chief sponsor of numerous holiday-related events, such as the untangling of Christmas lights while listening to

see TOYOTA, page 9

One of 100 million greeting cards Toyota is sending out to the American public this Christmas season.

Bush's New Dentist Faces Tough Confirmation Hearing

Applebaum evades a question regarding his past stance on rinsing.

WASHINGTON—The Senate Judiciary Committee announced Monday that, after five days of intense questioning, internal debate, and outside testimony, it is no closer to confirming Dr. Richard J. Applebaum, President George W. Bush's controversial nominee to be the 73rd presidential dentist in U.S. history.

Applebaum—a Howard University College of Dentistry graduate, owner of the private practice Gentle Dental, and close friend of the Bush family—faced a seemingly unending battery of questions during the first week of his confirmation hearing, with the committee's 19 members grilling him on issues ranging from tooth decay to tartar control to the

see DENTIST, page 8

Only Positive Statistic Of Year Announced

WASHINGTON—Amid a growing list of domestic and international concerns such as skyrocketing fuel prices, the slumping dollar, massive recalls of tainted food, the housing market collapse, and an increase in obesity, the American Society for the Prevention of Cruelty to Animals delivered the country's only positive statistic Tuesday when officials announced that cases of feline leukemia had stabilized.

"In this current climate, we were all waiting for some good news," said Brad Gambrell, 37, an unemployed census worker. "With more infants perishing during childbirth, fewer citizens covered by health insurance, and air quality steadily worsening, it's a huge relief that the number of cats dying from this horrible disease is staying the same." Additional data showed that, upon hearing the news, hundreds of Americans who were being evicted from their homes or learning that they had colon cancer briefly experienced a glimmer of hope—a once-common sensation that has declined by 250 percent since 2002.

Sources: George Clooney Looking Good

Clooney looking, as always, good.

HOLLYWOOD—According to sources from every imaginable demographic across the United States, Canada, Europe, and the rest of the civilized world, Academy Award–winning actor and two-time *People* magazine "Sexiest Man Alive" George Clooney is looking good.

"I saw him on the cover of *Vanity Fair*, clean shaven, and he was looking good," Austin-area film and TV buff David Haas said Monday. "Then I saw him on the cover of *GQ* with a few days' growth, and he was still looking good. He's been looking good since he was Dr. Doug Ross on *ER*, and he'll probably be looking good for his next 20 roles."

"I wish I looked one tenth as good as he's looking," Haas added.

Clooney – whose steely gaze and easygoing personality have consistently captivated millions around the globe, across all categories of race, religion, class, gender, and sexual orientation – has for the past 25 years attained the highest possible scores in every known measure of physical, psychological, and spiritual attractiveness.

A recent poll conducted by the Pew Research Center revealed that 18 percent of respondents described Clooney as looking "distinguished," 11 percent found him looking "sharp," and 3 percent found him looking "square-jawed and rugged, yet stately and reserved, as one would expect a baron or king to look."

The poll had no statistical margin of error.

"When you think of George Clooney, the first thing you think is 'sexy,'" said Julia Allison, editor-at-large for *Star* magazine.

see CLOONEY, page 7

ONION SPORTS 2007 YEAR IN REVIEW
DECEMBER 27, 2007 • VOLUME 43 ISSUE 52

HIGHLIGHTS

NFL Reports Strong Sales Of Michael Vick's 2008 Jersey PAGE 5C

London Unveils 2012 Olympics Logo To Stunned Silence PAGE 9B

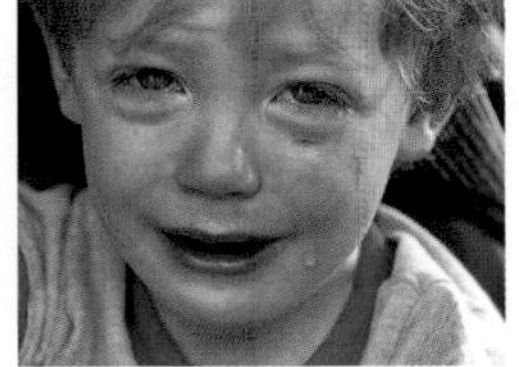

Jonathan Papelbon's 95 mph Water Balloon Ruins Family Barbecue PAGE 24E

INSIDE

BASEBALL
Slight Breeze Shatters Ken Griffey Jr.'s Femur
PAGE 3E

FOOTBALL
Bears Lead Rex Grossman To Super Bowl
PAGE 8C

INDEX

ONION
Sports Wire 02
Sportsgraphic 13
Horoscopes 14
A.V. CLUB
Cinema 20
Music 26
Words 27

THIS WEEK IN THE A.V. CLUB
John C. Reilly and the year's least essential music

A.V. MADISON
New Year's Eve adventures
page 33

Barry Bonds Home-Run Scandal Somehow Becomes Feel-Good Sports Story Of Year

■ JULY 26, 2007

SAN FRANCISCO—Although Barry Bonds remains the target of criticism over his possible—some say almost certain—use of performance-enhancing substances, the fact that Bonds has not been implicated in dogfighting, nightclub shootings, gambling, or murdering his family has transformed his controversial pursuit of the all-time home-run record into the feel-good sports story of the summer.

"Until we have definitive proof one way or the other, the very

see HOME RUN, page 9

Destruction Of National Pastime Given Two-Minute Standing Ovation

■ AUGUST 9, 2007

SAN FRANCISCO—A sellout crowd rose to its feet and exploded into ecstatic cheers Tuesday night as Barry Bonds completed the downfall of America's most revered sport by hitting a thundering 435-foot shot into the right center field bleachers for career home run No. 756 and tainting baseball's most beloved record.

Celebrations broke out throughout AT&T Park and thousands of flashbulbs went off as Bonds took his ceremonial trip around the

see OVATION, page 7

ONION SPORTS EXCLUSIVE

Confiscated Patriots Videotapes Contain Extensive Footage Of Tom Brady Showering

■ SEPTEMBER 20, 2007

NEW YORK—The hundreds of hours of game and practice scouting videotapes that league officials seized from the New England Patriots also include over 100 hours of painstakingly thorough footage of Patriots quarterback Tom Brady in the shower, sources within the NFL competition committee confirmed Tuesday.

"We are still investigating whether the assembled shower footage of Brady soaped up and wreathed in steam—which I can personally confirm was in fact taken in the showers of several different NFL-affiliated facilities around the league, and appears to have been shot by head coach Belichick himself—constitutes a violation of league laws or policies," league spokesman Greg Aiello told reporters during a press conference held at the league's Manhattan offices. "It is the opinion of the commissioner and the league that further extensive study is required before any judgment can be

see BRADY, page 8

NASCAR Unveils New 'Car Of Yesterday'

■ MARCH 29, 2007

CHARLOTTE, NC—Only days after its long-anticipated, much-criticized Car of Tomorrow debuted to overwhelmingly negative reviews at the Bristol Motor Speedway, NASCAR responded to the wishes of competitors and fans alike by introducing the stylishly retro, technologically retrograde NEXTEL Cup Car of Yesterday.

"This is exactly what everyone from race teams to race fans wanted all along—a real American racecar," said Robby Gordon, standing in front of the Jim Beam '77 Oldsmobile Cutlass Supreme he will drive for the rest of the season. "To hell with things like spoilers, adjustable suspensions, disc brakes, shoulder belts, all that junk. People want to see us racing the cars they drive every day, and anyone who's seen the parking lot at a NASCAR race will tell you that's what the Car of Yesterday gives them."

Based on tried-and-true NASCAR designs from what many consider the golden age of stock-car racing, the Car Of Yesterday is based on the racing team's choice of four-door body styles: either the '77 Cutlass Supreme, the '79 Chevrolet Caprice Classic, the '78 Dodge Diplomat, the '77 Ford Granada, the '77 Mercury Gran Marquis, or for series newcomers Toyota, the 1989 Corolla. All cars, regardless of body style, must have fully reclining seats, column shifters, vinyl tops, ashtrays, and automatically retracting seatbelts. Adding spoilers and air dams for purposes other than providing advertising space is forbidden, although teams will be allowed to bolt wooden 2-by-8

see TRAPPED, page 7

Victim Of Mall Shooting Determined Not To Die In Yankee Candle

Novelists Strike Fails To Affect Nation Whatsoever

Everything Falling Apart, Reports Institute For Somehow Managing To Hold It All Together

JANUARY FEBRUARY MARCH APRIL MAY JUNE

Congress To Raise Alpacas To Aid Struggling Economy

JPMorgan Chase Acquires Bear Stearns In Tedious-To-Read News Article

Local Idiot To Post Comment On Internet

2008

McCain Silences Critics With Perfectly Executed Cartwheel

Obama Modifies 'Yes We Can' Message To Exclude Area Loser

Long-Standing Conflict Ends As Israel Returns Lawnmower To Palestine

JULY AUGUST SEPTEMBER OCTOBER NOVEMBER DECEMBER

Powerful 'His And Hers' Towel Lobby Stalls Gay Marriage Legislation

Thousands Gather For Stuffing Of Giant Rockefeller Center Turkey

Cash-Strapped NPR Launches *A Couple Things Considered*

'Tu Stultus Es'

WEATHER PAGE B16

Seasonal

LOW 41 HIGH 54

JANUARY 10, 2008 · VOLUME 44 ISSUE 02

AMERICA'S FINEST NEWS SOURCE · ONION.COM · NATIONAL EDITION

HIGHLIGHTS

All-Dad Blues Band A Critical Disappointment

MUSIC, page 5D

Baby New Year Abandoned In Street

NATIONAL, page 9A

SPORTS

Fan Favorite White

page 3C

BUSH BEGINS PREPARATIONS FOR NATION'S FINAL YEAR

Bush announced that plans for the country's final days have already been set into motion.

▪ Every Single Citizen To Make 'Ultimate Sacrifice'

WASHINGTON—As his last term winds to a close, President Bush has directed White House aides and Cabinet staff to begin preparing for 2008, the nation's 233rd and final year in existence.

"My fellow Americans, it has been an honor to be your last president," Bush said during a televised address Tuesday, assuring citizens he would do everything possible over the next few months to promote a smooth transition into utter oblivion. "I do not intend to let what precious little time we have left go to waste. That's why I ask all of you to pull together and follow me, so we can accomplish everything we've ever wanted to before it all crumbles around us in a terrible belch of smoke and ash."

Added Bush: "It's now or never, people. No regrets."

As part of his ambitious 11-and-a-half-month plan, Bush has prioritized securing Iraq's stability for a coming world where the United States is nothing more than a fleeting memory. Additionally, he has urged Congress to block all stem-cell legislation "just in case," and has set aside the months of April and May, repsectively, to call every country the United States has wronged in the past and apologize, and to default on America's

see YEAR, page 6

INSIDE

LOCAL

Janitor Could Be More Appreciative Of Nod PAGE 3B

EDUCATION

SAT To Add Sudoku Section PAGE 8E

INDEX

ONION

Briefs 02

Opinion 06

Sports 08

A.V. CLUB

Cinema 14

Music 20

Words 21

THIS WEEK IN THE A.V. CLUB

Food talk with Anthony Bourdain and Patton Oswalt

$2.00 US/$3.00 CAN

0 74470 94595 6 02

Fall Internship Pays Off With Coveted Winter Internship

NEW YORK—New York University student Dave Werner announced Monday that he has successfully parlayed an unpaid fall internship at the magazine *GQ* into a long-sought-after unpaid winter internship at the ESPN network.

"After three months spent fetching coffee and making copies, all my hard work has finally paid off," the 21-year-old communications major said as he dropped off executive assistant Matt Sullivan's dry cleaning at a local laundromat.

"These days, I'm totally in charge of taking lunch orders, and some of the people I work with already sort of know my name. What an invaluable experience." Werner added that his main goal is to use his connections at ESPN to secure a highly desirable spring internship that could possibly offer school credit and a modest travel stipend. Ø

Report: Someone Totally Doing It Somewhere Right Now

CHICAGO—According to a groundbreaking new study published Monday in *The Journal Of The American Statistical Association*, somewhere on the planet someone is totally doing it at this very moment.

"Of the 6.7 billion inhabitants of Earth, approximately 3.5 billion have reached sexual maturity," said Dr. Jerome Carver, a mathematics professor at the University of Chicago and lead author of the study. "From a statistical perspective, it simply stands to reason that at least two of these inhabitants are totally going at it right now. Like, as we speak."

"But it's probably way more than that," Carver added. "Like at least a hundred."

The multidiscipline study, which tapped leading experts in several fields, including reproduction and population sciences, found

see DOING, page 4

Scientists told reporters someone could be doing it right next door.

Syria Attends Mideast Peace Talks For Free Continental Breakfast

Syrian delegates maintained their position on the so-called "Danish situation."

ANNAPOLIS, MD—Despite years of diplomatic stalemate in the Mideast crisis, Syrian officials appeared eager to mend troubled Arab-Israeli relations this week by participating in a second round of U.S.-led peace talks, which feature representatives from every country in the region, as well as a complimentary continental breakfast in the hotel lobby.

"We are attending this conference in the interest of peace, and intend to take full advantage of the opportunities afforded by this historic summit," Syrian deputy foreign minister Faisal Mekdad said Tuesday. "I understand that a total of five different beverage options, including milk, tea, and assorted juices, will be available free of charge."

Now in its second day, the summit has reportedly been a success for the Syrians, who described themselves as "optimistic" and "full" and are already pointing to a number of positive developments, including fresh pastries and a new policy of unlimited coffee refills.

see BREAKFAST, page 4

'Tu Stultus Es'

the ONION®

WEATHER PAGE B16
Great clouds this week
LOW 15 HIGH 34

JANUARY 24, 2008 · VOLUME 44 ISSUE 04 · AMERICA'S FINEST NEWS SOURCE · ONION.COM · NATIONAL EDITION

HIGHLIGHTS

Jamie Lynn Spears Loses Custody Of Fetus
ENTERTAINMENT, page 5C

Report: 94% Of South Dakotans Unprepared For Mt. Rushmore Faces Coming Alive And Eating Everyone NATIONAL, page 9A

ONION SPORTS

Dallas-Area Suicide Hotline Operators Get Their Popcorn Ready page 3D

INSIDE

LOCAL
Fourth Sneeze Really Pushing It
PAGE 3B

FASHION
Beauty Regimen Horrifying
PAGE 8F

INDEX

ONION
Briefs 02
Opinion 06
Sports 08
A.V. CLUB
Cinema 14
Music 20
Words 21

THIS WEEK IN THE A.V. CLUB
Lessons learned from a year of flops

$2.00 US/$3.00 CAN

Bill Clinton: 'Screw It, I'm Running For President'

"Damn, this feels good," Clinton told supporters as he shook hands in Charleston Monday.

■ Only Candidate With 8 Years Of On-The-Job Experience

POLITICS WATCH

CHARLESTON, SC—After spending two months accompanying his wife, Hillary, on the campaign trail, former president Bill Clinton announced Monday that he is joining the 2008 presidential race, saying he "could no longer resist the urge."

"My fellow Americans, I am sick and tired of not being president," said Clinton, introducing his wife at a "Hillary '08" rally. "For seven agonizing years, I have sat idly by as others experienced the joys of campaigning, debating, and interacting with the people of this great nation, and I simply cannot take it anymore. I have to be president again. I have to."

He continued, "It is with a great sense of relief that I say to all of you today, 'Screw it. I'm in.'"

In a show of respect, Clinton then completed his introduction of Hillary Clinton, calling her a "wonderful wife and worthy political adversary," and warmly shook her hand as she approached the podium. A clearly shocked Mrs.

see PRESIDENT, page 4

Nation's Grandfathers To Receive Annual Shipment Of $2 Bills From U.S. Treasury

WASHINGTON—During a press conference Monday, Treasury Secretary Henry Paulson unveiled this year's shipment of brand-new $2 bills, all of which will be sent directly from the U.S. Mint to the nation's grandfathers by month's end.

"I'm willing to speculate that most of you have never seen one of these before," a grinning Paulson told reporters Monday, while gesturing to a sheet of 500 $2 bills, assuring those present that grandfathers everywhere will soon have the perfect gift for their grandchildren's birthdays, good report cards, or just for when they come over to visit. "You can spend them on Lemonheads or anything you want."

Throughout the presentation, reporters politely feigned excitement, and afterward they impressed the secretary by accurately guessing whose face was on the $2 bill without having to look at the name printed below it.

Study Finds Link Between Being Struck By Cream Pie, Diminished Social Standing

ITHACA, NY—A new study conducted by the Cornell Institute for Behavioral and Social Sciences has found what researchers believe to be a demonstrable link between being struck with a banana cream pie and a sudden, significant drop in one's public standing.

"What we have observed is nothing short of astounding," Dr. Philip Shaw, a human sciences professor at Cornell and the study's lead researcher, said Monday. "By having cream-topped pies forcibly applied to their faces—or *kissers*—men and women of high regard were seen to immediately fall in both status and esteem."

"Whether the subjects were wealthy shopkeepers, pompous barons of British descent, or matronly women sporting tiny opera glasses—our results were always the same," Shaw added.

The study, which was conducted with the help

see PIE, page 4

CAUSE AND EFFECT

Dr. Shaw found the most common outcomes for those hit with pie:

- **41%** Lost fiancée to poorer man with better sense of humor
- **34%** Ducked under pie, subsequently struck with large purse
- **15%** Ridiculed by business partner, who is then struck with pie
- **10%** Laughed themselves mad

THE ECONOMY

3.2 Million Unemployed Americans Apply For Opening At Ohio-Area Bob Evans

More than 74,000 qualified applicants wait to speak with the manager.

FINDLAY, OH—In what some economists believe to be a sign that the U.S. could be headed for a recession, a job opening last month at the Findlay-area Bob Evans prompted a deluge of more than 3 million job applications from out-of-work Americans, restaurant manager Tom Fields confirmed Tuesday.

Within three days of placing a "Help Wanted" sign at the Bob Evans front entrance, Fields reportedly received more than 800,000 resumés for the part-time hostess job. The newly available position offers no health benefits, minimum-wage pay, and a dress code that mandates both the standard red-and-white Bob Evans kerchief and "a smile," as well as a 15 percent discount on all meals eaten during one's shift.

"Word of a job opening in this country sure does travel fast," the visibly exhausted Fields said. "I'm just dreading having to make those 3,199,999 rejection phone calls."

Over the next two weeks,

see UNEMPLOYED, page 3

'Tu Stultus Es'

the ONION®

FEBRUARY 7, 2008 · VOLUME 44 ISSUE 06

AMERICA'S FINEST NEWS SOURCE · ONION.COM · NATIONAL EDITION

WEATHER PAGE B16

Highs in your mid-20s
LOW **14** HIGH **26**

HIGHLIGHTS

'People Make Stupid Comments On Message Boards And I Need To Set Them Straight'

By Mike Hirsch
OPINION, page 5C

Area Man A Little Too Old To Have Obama Fever

NATIONAL, page 9A

ONION SPORTS

Randy Moss Accused Of Stem-Cell Abuse page 3D

INSIDE

TECHNOLOGY
Facebook Helps Old MySpace Friends Get Back in Touch
PAGE 3B

HEALTH
Third Grader Vows To Change Lifestyle After Second Heart Attack
PAGE 8F

INDEX

ONION
Briefs 02
Opinion 08
Sports 10

A.V. CLUB
Cinema 16
Music 20
Words 21

$2.00 U.S./$3.00 CAN

World Leaders Gather To Roast Mahmoud Ahmadinejad

Musharraf, Gottfried, and Putin, left, zing Ahmadinejad, above.

■ Controversial leader blasted for anti-Semitism, brutality, and not being able to get it up

GENEVA—In what observers are calling an unprecedented opportunity for the international community to express its grievances against Iran's controversial leader, dozens of world leaders and key U.N. delegates gathered Saturday to roast Iranian president Mahmoud Ahmadinejad.

The event, which took place beneath U.N. headquarters in the historic Geneva Friars Club, brought together the heads of every G8 member state, as well as some of today's top foreign policy makers and peace brokers. Roastmaster and former U.N. secretary general Kofi Annan kicked off the evening by welcoming President Ahmadinejad to "what [was] sure to be the first and last time Mahmoud would ever be surrounded by 72 virgins."

"Ladies and gentlemen, and Tony Blair, we stand here in the presence of one of the most vicious and destructive forces in the world today—but enough about Bea Arthur," said Annan, gesturing with a tumbler of Makers Mark across the long white tables of chuckling diplomats to the former *Golden Girls* star. "Some people here tonight will tell you that Mahmoud refuses to engage in diplomatic talks, that he is the most ruthless stonewaller who has ever lived. Well, those

see **ROAST**, page 6

GM Introduces New 2008 Line Of Layoffs

DETROIT—Calling it the automotive company's "toughest and longest-lasting" line of cutbacks to date, General Motors proudly unveiled its new 2008 model layoffs on Monday, bringing months of rumor and speculation to an end.

According to industry insiders, the automaker's latest offering of layoffs is by far its largest, with hundreds of unemployed workers expected to hit the streets as early as next week, and thousands more scheduled to come off Michigan assembly lines by the end of spring.

"Introducing the all-new, all-American GM layoffs," announced General Motors chairman Rick Wagoner, gesturing toward a line-up of soon-to-be-released factory technicians outside the company's main Detroit plant. "Bigger, bolder, more daring—these 2008 redundancies are sure to create a stir."

see **LAYOFFS**, page 4

RELATED STORY INSIDE
Bully With Good Grades Indestructible
PAGE 14F

NATIONAL ALERT

Dept. Of Homeland Security: 'Has Anybody Seen A Blue Folder?'

■ Original Policy Of Waiting For It To Turn Up Not Working

WASHINGTON—In an emergency press conference held this morning, Department of Homeland Security Secretary Michael Chertoff urged the American public to be on the lookout for a folder that was misplaced sometime in the last 24 hours, most likely in the DHS offices, but also possibly anywhere else.

The last known location of the folder, described as a blue hanging-type folder with the DHS logo on the front, was in the hands of Assistant Secretary of the Office of Intergovernmental Programs Anne P. Petera during a classified meeting with President Bush and the Joint Chiefs of Staff yesterday. It reportedly contains a number of documents and satellite images that would be of no interest whatsoever to anyone if they found it.

"I can assure all Americans that the assistant secretary could have sworn she had it with her when she went through the metal detector," Chertoff said. "According to the latest information, she set it down for only a second right before the briefing, and now it is gone. Officials have diligently checked everywhere from the bathroom, to the top of the refrigerator in the breakroom, to the underground emergency command bunker we were touring this morning with representatives from the Centers for Disease Control, but apparently it has simply disappeared."

see **FOLDER**, page 6

ON THE HUNT

"We will not rest until we locate this totally irrelevant folder filled with boring documents that no terrorist would ever find useful."

Department of Homeland Security Secretary Michael Chertoff

'Tu Stultus Es'

the ONION®

AMERICA'S FINEST NEWS SOURCE · ONION.COM · NATIONAL EDITION

MARCH 20, 2008 · VOLUME 44 ISSUE 12

WEATHER PAGE B16
Pollinated snow
LOW **22** HIGH **34**

HIGHLIGHTS

'If You Love Something, Demean It Until It Doesn't Have The Self-Esteem To Leave'
By Joe DeNardo
OPINION, page 5C

ONION SPORTS

Rare Miami Heat Basket Captured On Videotape
page 3D

Dunkin' Donuts/Baskin Robbins/Pizza Hut/Taco Bell/Long John Silver's Opens DINING, page 15A

INSIDE

SCIENCE
Dept. Of Tautology Rereleases Report For Second Time
PAGE 3E

TECHNOLOGY
'Google' Now An Adjective
PAGE 8F

INDEX

ONION
Briefs .... ??
Opinion .... ??
Sports .... ??
A.V. CLUB
Cinema .... ??
Music .... ??
Words .... ??

$2.00 US | $3.00 CANADA

Black Guy Asks Nation For Change

A DESPERATE PLEA
The black guy is oddly comfortable demanding change from people he's never even met.

■ Seen Begging In Most Major Cities

CHICAGO—According to witnesses, a loud black man approached a crowd of some 4,000 strangers in downtown Chicago Tuesday and made repeated demands for change.

"The time for change is now," said the black guy, yelling at everyone within earshot for 20 straight minutes, practically begging America for change. "The need for change is stronger and more urgent than ever before. And only you—the people standing here today, and indeed all the people of this great nation—only you can deliver this change."

It is estimated that, to date, the black man has asked every single person in the United States for change.

"I've already seen this guy four times today," Chicago-area ad salesman Blake Gordon said. "Every time, it's the same exact spiel. 'I need change.' 'I want change.' Why's he so eager for all this change? What's he going to do with it, anyway?"

After his initial requests for change, the black man rambled nonstop on a variety of unrelated topics, calling for affordable

see **CHANGE**, page 6

Naked Woman Picture Gains Popularity On Internet

SAN FRANCISCO—According to leading web experts, a photo of an unidentified naked woman has caused an online sensation after appearing on the Internet sometime last week.

The inexplicably popular photograph, which features the woman exposing both breasts as well as providing an unobstructed view of her vagina, has been visited an estimated 750,000 times since it was first discovered two months ago.

"For some reason, people cannot seem to get enough of the naked woman pic-

see **NAKED**, page 7

The popularity of "Subject X," as the naked lady is known in academic circles, has baffled researchers.

Area Man Can Tell Commercial Will Be For Corona

BISBEE, AZ—Local man James Fitzner, 42, was able to successfully predict within seven seconds that a recent 30-second TV commercial was advertising Corona, despite having never seen the ad in his life. "I knew right away because it was really silent and the camera started zooming out a little bit and they never show the beach at first—they try to trick you," said the media-savvy Fitzner, who in the past has been able to identify ads for MasterCard and Red Bull before the product was mentioned. "Then, as soon as I heard the sound of waves in the background, I just said to myself, 'Corona.'" Fitzner's son David, 16, said that after the beer bottle appeared on screen, his father turned to him and winked. ⊘

OUR NATION'S CHILDREN

Wii Video Games Blamed For Rise In Effeminate Violence

WASHINGTON—Concerned parents are again blasting the Nintendo Wii for an incident of effeminate violence following a 13-year-old boy's limp-wristed attack on three of his classmates at a Cleveland-area middle school Tuesday.

The incident—the sixth of its kind in as many months—has left parents searching for answers and struggling to comprehend the dainty assault, which left the necks of two sweaters severely stretched out and countless fingers stubbed.

"These games are a prissy little menace to our society," said Linda Roberts, 35, a mother of three and founder of the group Parents Against Wii, which is suing Nintendo for $52 million in damages from two recent swattings. "One of these days, the red marks on our children's arms might not just go away after five minutes."

see **WII**, page 6

THE NEW FACE OF VIOLENCE

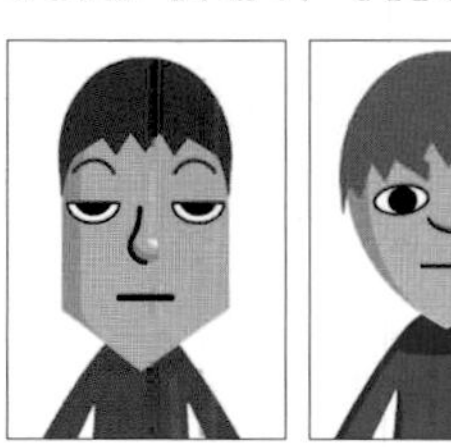

The Mii versions of effeminate-assault perpetrators Brian Strickland, left, and Andrew Connor, right, seem incapable of displaying regret, remorse, or any understanding of their dainty crimes.

'Tu Stultus Es'

the ONION®

WEATHER PAGE B16
Three snowflakes
LOW 26 HIGH 32

APRIL 3, 2008 · VOLUME 44 ISSUE 14

AMERICA'S FINEST NEWS SOURCE · ONION.COM · NATIONAL EDITION

HIGHLIGHTS

'I Am A Museum Volunteer First And Someone Who Likes To Touch Paintings When Nobody Is Around Second'
By Beverly Lentz
OPINION, page 5C

Novelty Pencil Worn Down To The Nub NATIONAL, page 9A

ONION SPORTS
David Ortiz Plays Games In Japan Wearing Camera, Fanny Pack page 3D

INSIDE

LOCAL
Waitress Too Attractive For Man To Order Nachos PAGE 3B

MUSIC
Guitar Removed From Closet For Annual 'Enter Sandman' Attempt PAGE 8F

INDEX

ONION
Briefs 2
Opinion 8
Sports 10
A.V. CLUB
Cinema 16
Music 20
Words 21

THIS WEEK IN THE A.V. CLUB

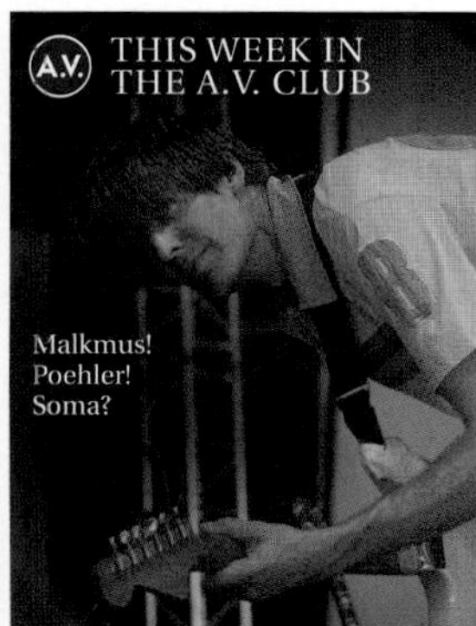

$2.00 US | $3.00 CANADA

Blood...Blood Everywhere

The blood.

DAVENPORT, IA—In what eyewitnesses described as some kind of terrible dream come true, a warm and viscous liquid identified only as blood...dear God, blood...spilled forth from every conceivable direction Monday.

According to sources still able to speak, the blood first appeared shortly before dawn, horrifying dozens of citizens stirred awake by its ceaseless dripping. While many details remain unclear, including why, why won't it stop and is that...are those...Jesus Christ, look, the situation has by all accounts

see BLOOD, page 6

Comedian Jim Breuer At College Party For Some Reason

Breuer calls Beirut play-by-play.

COLUMBIA, MO—Though he did not appear to have any scheduled performances in the area, stand-up comedian and former *Saturday Night Live* cast member Jim Breuer reportedly attended a party thrown for student John Harris' 19th birthday at the University of Missouri Saturday.

While it is unknown exactly when Breuer arrived at the Sigma Chi fraternity house, sophomore Steve Kendall told reporters he first heard an "odd but somehow familiar laugh" at approximately 11:30 p.m. coming from the vicinity of the living room's beer-pong table.

"I looked over and there's the guy from *Half Baked*," said Kendall, adding that Breuer was cheering on the drinking game's participants. "I

see BREUER, page 4

Report: Nation's Gentrified Neighborhoods Threatened By Aristocratization

WASHINGTON—According to a report released Tuesday by the Brookings Institution, a Washington-based think tank, the recent influx of exceedingly affluent powder-wigged aristocrats into the nation's gentrified urban areas is pushing out young white professionals, some of whom have lived in these neighborhoods for as many as seven years.

Maureen Kennedy, a housing policy expert and lead author of the report, said that the enormous treasure-based wealth of the aristocracy makes it impossible for those living on modest trust funds to hold onto their co-ops and converted factory loft spaces.

"When you have a bejeweled, buckle-shoed duke willing to pay 11 or 12 times the asking price for a block of

see GENTRIFIED, page 6

Multibillion-dollar castles like this one have been popping up all over Brooklyn, NY.

BP Opens Multi-Floor, 1,000-Pump Flagship Gas Station In Times Square

NEW YORK—Tourists and gas-lovers from around the nation flocked to New York City Saturday for the grand opening of the five-story, 1,000-pump "BP Town" gas station located in the heart of Times Square.

"We drove all the way from San Diego just so we could fill up our tank here," mother of three Cyndi Matheson said. "Sure, the lines were four hours long and the gas is a little more expensive here, but even at $27.99 a gallon, it was worth it just to see the kids' faces light up. We're going to drive around for a few hours so we can come back."

BP Town reported a successful opening weekend, having sold more than $2 million in gas and nearly $500,000 in souvenir beef jerky, sunflower seeds, and Hostess Donettes.

'Tu Stultus Es'

the ONION®

JULY 10, 2008 · VOLUME 44 ISSUE 28

AMERICA'S FINEST NEWS SOURCE · ONION.COM · NATIONAL EDITION

WEATHER PAGE B16
Wind chimes bothering neighbors today
LOW **63** HIGH **68**

HIGHLIGHTS

I'm Really Excited To Work Here, But Are You Married To The Name 'Coca-Cola'?
by William Bristol, OPINION, page 5C

Dollar Store Has Great Deal On Fig Nortons
LOCAL, page 9B

ONION SPORTS
NFL Commissioner Goodell Worried Sick At What Players May Have Been Up To During Offseason
page 3D

INSIDE

NATIONAL
Report: 82% Of Wiseguys Think They're Real Funny
PAGE 3A

LOCAL
Loud Friend Makes Loud Point
PAGE 8B

INDEX

ONION
Briefs 2
Opinion 8
Sports 10
A.V. CLUB
Cinema 16
Music 20
Words 21

THIS WEEK IN THE A.V. CLUB
Adventure movie icon Brendan Fraser
Also: Political talk with Matt Taibbi

Bill Clinton Sadly Folds First Lady Dress Back Into Box

The former commander in chief takes one last look at the most beautiful first lady dress in the whole wide world.

CHAPPAQUA, NY—After months of tirelessly supporting his wife on the campaign trail, devoted spouse and former president Bill Clinton breathed a resigned sigh Monday and carefully folded the charcoal silk, fitted sheath dress he had hoped to wear as first lady during next January's inauguration and placed it back in its beautiful box.

The 61-year-old Clinton, who has appeared on the covers of both *Time* and *Newsweek* and has recently been lauded for his work as an outspoken advocate for human rights, purchased the

see **DRESS**, page 7

5-Year-Old Wants To Be A Tractor When She Grows Up

Garretson

AKRON, OH—In a statement delivered to friends, family members, and household pets, Kendall Garretson announced Monday that she would like to become an 13-ton, 275-horsepower John Deere row-crop tractor when she grows up.

Garretson, who turned 5 in May, developed an interest in becoming the powerful motor-driven vehicle during a recent trip to her grandfather's farm. According to sources, the young kindergarten student made her decision based on a number of key factors, including her desire to have "big wheels," make holes in the ground with "a digger," and chase birds and butterflies through fields of sunflowers.

"I'm gonna be a tractor," Garretson said. "Tractors are fun."

Although Garretson does not have a six-cylinder diesel engine, independent-link suspension, or a comfort command seat with air-suspension swivel, the 5-year-old said she was excited to be both red and shiny someday. Garretson added that as a tractor she would sleep in the barn with the cows and the chickens, but not with the pigs, because the pigs make too much

see **TRACTOR**, page 6

Five-year-old Garretson as she will appear as an adult if her career plans shape out.

Steven Tyler Laid Off From Aerosmith As Band Jobless Rate Hits 20%

Tyler

BOSTON—After years of relative stability, the Aerosmith unemployment rate soared to an all-time high of 20 percent Monday following the downsizing of the band's vocal sector, Steven Tyler.

The announcement of the largest-ever round of Aerosmith layoffs sent shock waves throughout the group, but band leaders said that four decades of perfect employment was "unrealistic" and that it was necessary to shed some of the graying, outmoded workforce.

"Explaining to a longtime Aerosmith employee that his or her job is being eliminated is one of the most difficult challenges we face in this business," Aerosmith manager Trudy Green said in a statement released this morning. "We thank Steven for his many years of loyal service, and wish him the best of luck in all his future endeavors."

Analysts speculate that the sector-wide layoff was a result of multiple factors, including redundancies in the singing-songwriting division, rising rehab fees that have cost the group millions, and a 34 percent decline in jump-kicks since 2003. In addition, some of Aerosmith's younger, more ambitious employees, such as Joe Perry, 57, are willing to sing and play an instrument at the same time, often for

see **TYLER**, page 7

Aerosmith Production Down In All Categories
Percentage decline in key sectors since 2001

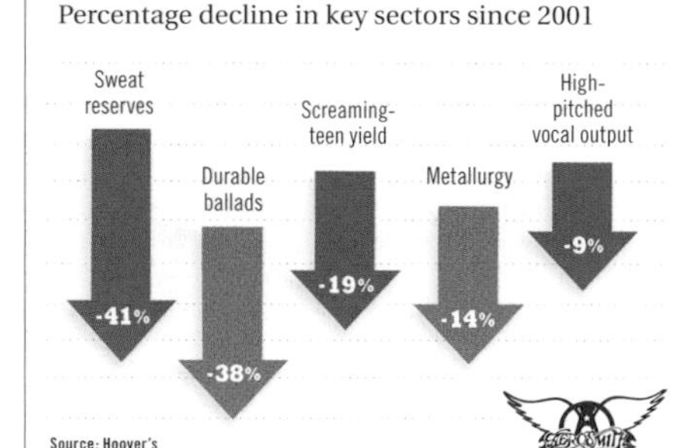

Special Ops Veteran Slips Back Into Family Undetected

ORLANDO, FL—After spending six years overseas as a covert operations specialist, Joe Jacobs slipped silently back into his family unit Tuesday, reappearing inside his home's dining room as if out of thin air.

"This truck exploded across the street, and when we looked back, Dad was sitting next to me, already halfway through his chicken-fried steak," said son Michael, adding that the pyrotechnic diversionary tactic was "classic Dad." "Other than the 6-inch scar across his face, it's like he was never gone."

Upon his return, Jacobs immediately demanded a concise summary of the last 10 arguments between Michael and his sister Lauren, as well as a quick debriefing re: the whereabouts of that raccoon that used to live in the shed. Ø

'Tu Stultus Es'

the ONION®

AMERICA'S FINEST NEWS SOURCE · ONION.COM · NATIONAL EDITION

JULY 17, 2008 · VOLUME 44 ISSUE 29

WEATHER PAGE B16

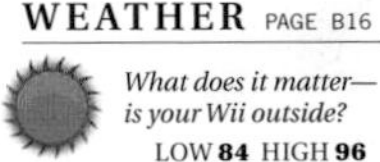

What does it matter—is your Wii outside?
LOW **84** HIGH **96**

HIGHLIGHTS

'That Stray Dog That's Biting Everyone It Sees Needs A Home'
by Jessica Alterman, OPINION, page 5C

Infants Piling Up At Orphanage's Old Address
NATIONAL, page 9A

ONION SPORTS
Mike Golic Finally Marries, Eats Mike Greenberg page 3D

INSIDE

LOCAL
Gathering Of Pigeons Shown Who Is Boss
PAGE 3B

RELATIONSHIPS
Sexual Boundaries Disputed
PAGE 8F

INDEX

ONION
Briefs 2
Opinion 8
Sports 10

A.V. CLUB
Cinema 16
Music 20
Words 21

$2.00 US | $3.00 CANADA

Recession-Plagued Nation Demands New Bubble To Invest In

ONION FINANCE

WASHINGTON—A panel of top business leaders testified before Congress about the worsening recession Monday, demanding the government provide Americans with a new irresponsible and largely illusory economic bubble in which to invest.

"What America needs right now is not more talk and long-term strategy, but a concrete way to create more imaginary wealth in the very immediate future," said Thomas Jenkins, CFO of the Boston-area Jenkins Financial Group, a bubble-based investment firm. "We are in a crisis, and that crisis demands an unviable short-term solution."

The current economic woes, brought on by the collapse of the so-called "housing bubble," are considered the worst to hit investors since the equally untenable dot-com bubble burst in 2001. According to investment experts, now that the option of making millions of dollars in a short time with imaginary profits from bad real-estate deals has disappeared, the need for another spontaneous make-believe source of wealth has never been more urgent.

THE ECONOMY

"Perhaps the new bubble could have something to do with watching movies on cell phones," said investment banker Greg Carlisle of the New York firm Carlisle, Shaloe & Graves. "Or, say, medicine, or shipping. Or clouds. The manner of bubble isn't important—just as long as it creates a hugely overvalued market based on nothing more than whimsical fantasy and saddled with the potential for a long-term accrual of debts that will never be paid back, thereby unleashing a ripple effect that will take nearly a decade to correct."

"The U.S. economy cannot survive on sound investments alone," Carlisle added.

Congress is currently consider-
see **BUBBLE**, page 6

The Next Big Bubble?

These are the economic bubbles Americans would like to foolishly invest in to take their minds off the current fiscal crisis most.

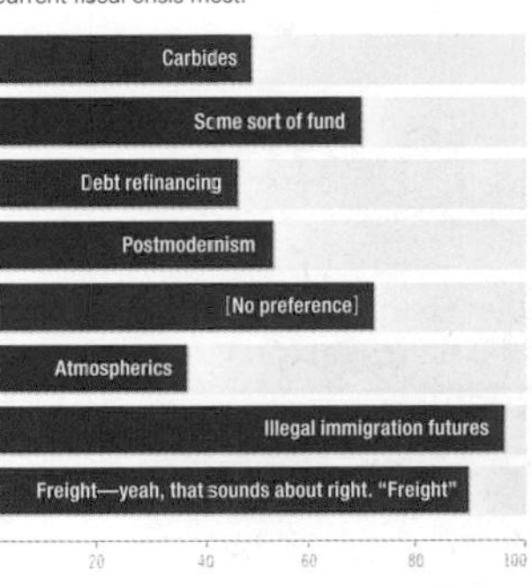

THE MEDIA

'Time' Publishes Definitive Obama Puff Piece

Obama

NEW YORK—Hailed by media critics as the fluffiest, most toothless, and softest-hitting coverage of the presidential candidate to date, a story in this week's *Time* magazine is being called the definitive Barack Obama puff piece.

"No news publication has dared to barely scratch the surface like this before," columnist and campaign reporter Michael King wrote in *The Washington Post* Tuesday. "This profile sets a benchmark for mindless filler by which all other features about Sen. Obama will now be judged. Just impressive puff-journalism all around."

The 24-page profile, entitled "Boogyin' With Barack," hit newsstands Monday and contains photos of the candidate as a baby, graduating from Columbia University, standing and laughing, holding hands with his wife and best friend, Michelle, greeting a crowd of blue-collar autoworkers, eating breakfast with diner
see **OBAMA**, page 4

ONION SCIENCE THURSDAY

Hubble Kaleidoscope Finds Evidence Of Space Looking All Crazy

BALTIMORE—Astronomers analyzing the first images captured by the new Hubble Space Kaleidoscope, which went online Tuesday, announced that they've acquired the first concrete evidence that the universe is in a constant state of total weirdness.

"With their unprecedented resolution, the latest images from the new kaleidoscope reveal that space, once thought to be isotropic, is actually continuously expanding, unfolding, and rearranging in a series of freaky patterns," said astronomer Douglas Stetler, head of the Space Kaleidoscope Science Institute in Baltimore. "It's an exciting time for the field of astrokaleidoscopics, or anyone interested in the vast, wacked-out nature of space."

At $200 billion, the HSK, as scientists designate it, is the most
see **HUBBLE**, page 6

Images from the kaleidoscope reveal that the Crab Nebula actually looks totally, like, freaky and everything.

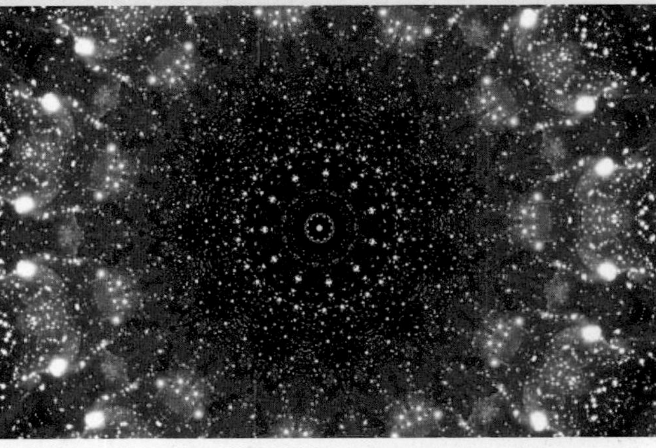

Going To Tops Of Things Still Favored By Nation's Tourists

NEW YORK—According to a report released Monday by the American Tourism Society, going to the tops of things is still the preferred activity among the nation's tourists. "Although driving past things and swimming in things have both grown in popularity over the last decade, going to the tops of things still surpasses both by nearly 30 percent," said ATS president Kimberly Davis, who was careful to point out that the photographing of things was not included in the report, since the near constant occurrence of this activity makes its frequency impossible to calculate. "In 2008, tourists remained committed to standing in long lines at the bottoms of things, paying upwards of $20 to gain access to the tops of those things, and then staring at other smaller, more distant things for a few minutes before descending, often to have funny pictures of themselves drawn incorporating the things in the background." Davis added that, perhaps as a consequence of the declining economy, the purchasing of miniature representations of the things that tourists enjoy going to the tops of has dropped by 14 percent.

'Tu Stultus Es'

the ONION®

JULY 31, 2008 · VOLUME 44 ISSUE 31

AMERICA'S FINEST NEWS SOURCE · ONION.COM · NATIONAL EDITION

WEATHER PAGE B16

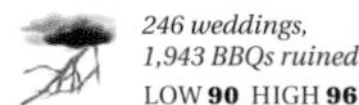

246 weddings, 1,943 BBQs ruined
LOW **90** HIGH **96**

HIGHLIGHTS

McCain Courts Youth Vote With Lengthy Speech On Forbearance, Morality
NATIONAL, page 5A

Troop Leader Awards Boy Scout With 'Tried To Save Best Friend' Badge
LOCAL, page 9B

ONION SPORTS
Placido Polanco Chokes Up All The Way page 3D

INSIDE

BUSINESS
Blood Of The Working Class Produces Satisfying Burrito
PAGE 3E

LOCAL
Man Has Sex At Woman
PAGE 8B

INDEX

ONION
Briefs 2
Opinion 8
Sports 10

A.V. CLUB
Cinema 16
Music 20
Words 21

$2.00 US | $3.00 CANADA

Young Gore sets out for his new home, where the sky is clear, the water is clean, and there are no Republicans.

Al Gore Places Infant Son In Rocket To Escape Dying Planet

EARTH—Former vice president Al Gore—who for the past three decades has unsuccessfully attempted to warn humanity of the coming destruction of our planet, only to be mocked and derided by the very people he has tried to save—launched his infant son into space Monday in the faint hope that his only child would reach the safety of another world.

"I tried to warn them, but the Elders of this planet would not listen," said Gore, who in 2000 was nearly banished to a featureless realm of nonexistence for promoting his unpopular message. "They called me foolish and laughed at my predictions. Yet even now, the Midwest is flooded, the ice caps are melting, and the cities are rocked with tremors, just as I foretold. Fools! Why didn't they heed me before it was too late?"

Al Gore—or, as he is known in his own language, Gore-Al—placed his son, Kal-Al, gently in the one-passenger rocket ship, his brow furrowed by the great weight he carried in preserving the sole survivor of humanity's hubristic folly.

"There is nothing left now but to ensure that

see GORE, page 4

World's Worst Person Decides To Go Into Marketing

■ 'I'm Thinking...Marketing,' Says Horrible, Horrible Man

NEW YORK—Twenty-three-year-old Louis Deenan, undeniably the most detestable, loathsome individual ever to walk the earth, willfully decided Monday to devote his miserable life and all of its awful ambitions to the field of marketing.

"I think it's the career path that will best utilize my networking skills and my ability to think outside the box," said Deenan, whose smug, gloating tone and shit-eating smile just make you want to punch his goddamn teeth in. "So I'm definitely thinking marketing. Either that, or PR."

Deenan's mother refused to comment on why she didn't abort the despicable pile of human excrement when she had the chance.

Phantom Diner Appears Only To Those In Their Drunkest Hour

ONION LOCAL DESK

ROCHESTER, NY—Reported sightings of Rochester's legendary "phantom diner," a mysterious restaurant that purportedly appears only to those in the most inebriated state of their lives, are often met with skepticism and incredulity. But for Leo Kline, 24, who claims he visited the diner this past weekend, the apparitional eatery is all too real.

"I had all but given up hope that I would get to eat pancakes and sausage that night," said Kline, who was separated from his group of friends early Sunday morning after leaving the Steel Toe Bar's nickel-beer night to urinate in an alleyway. "Then all of a sudden, there it was in front of me, bathed in this unnatural neon light. I don't remember much after that, but when I woke up the next day in the back of [Rick] Loomis' pickup truck, there was syrup in my hair."

"That's when I knew the whole thing

see DINER, page 6

Witnesses to the mysterious eatery recall having seen it somewhere on this block.

New Linens-N-Shit Opens

The store even allows customers to pull around back and strap a bunch of shit to the tops of their cars.

MACON, GA—Linens-N-Shit, the nation's largest retailer of bedsheets, tablecloths, and a wide assortment of other shit, will open its new location Tuesday morning at the Macon Mall.

"We are excited to open our first store in the Macon area, and we encourage shoppers to arrive early and check out all of our great linens and shit," said Robert Barlow, the company's senior vice president. "We're proud to offer the local community the best selection of the name-brand shit you want at the prices you love."

"We've got all sorts of shit," Barlow added. "Bath shit, kitchen shit, shit for the bedroom, seasonal shit, and all the other shit you could possibly imagine, plus linens."

The store is scheduled to open its doors at 6 a.m.

see LINENS, page 6

'Tu Stultus Es'

the ONION

WEATHER PAGE B16
A solid "7.5" on the Hot Scale
LOW 70 HIGH 80

AUGUST 14, 2008 · VOLUME 44 ISSUE 33 AMERICA'S FINEST NEWS SOURCE · ONION.COM · NATIONAL EDITION

HIGHLIGHTS

Area Woman's Greatest Dream To One Day Dance In Studio Audience Of 'The Ellen DeGeneres Show' LOCAL, page 5B

40-Foot American Flag Pin Welded To Statue Of Liberty NATIONAL, page 9A

ONION SPORTS
Togo's Lone Olympic Representative Under A Lot Of Pressure To Win Olympics page 3D

INSIDE

LOCAL
Local Man Built Like A Gay Tank PAGE 3B

BUSINESS
Scrabulous Creators Introduce Monopolonia, Yahtzig PAGE 8F

INDEX

ONION
Briefs ... 2
Opinion ... 8
Sports ... 10
A.V. CLUB
Cinema ... 16
Music ... 20
Words ... 21

THIS WEEK IN THE A.V. CLUB

An extended interview with Woody Allen

WAR FOR THE WHITE HOUSE

Obama's Hillbilly Half-Brother Threatening To Derail Campaign

PRODIGAL SONNY BOY

Cooter Obama welcomes his brother's supporters with a jug of "white lightning" before whipping up a steaming vat of flat-possum stew.

BOONEVILLE, KY—Barack Obama's once-commanding lead in the polls slipped to two points Monday, continuing a month-long slide that many credit to the recent appearance of the Democratic candidate's heretofore unknown half-brother, Cooter Obama.

Long kept a family secret, the overalls-clad, straw-chewing Kentuckian first entered the public spotlight in July, when he drove his 1982 Ford flatbed pickup through the press corps at an Obama rally in order to inform his brother that he caught the skunk that had been living under his front porch. According to witnesses, Cooter's skunk proceeded to spray *Washington Post* political reporter Michael D. Shear in the face.

"Sorry 'bout that, mister! Some tomater juice'll take care of the stank," Cooter said as his mortified younger brother led him off the stage. "Shoot, Barack, you didn't tell me you was runnin' for president!"

Since Cooter's emergence on the national scene, the Obama campaign has downplayed the brothers' relationship. A statement issued last week by Obama's top adviser, David Axelrod, claimed that the two lived together only for a brief

see HILLBILLY, page 7

Entire Refrigerator Rearranged To Accommodate Leftover KFC Bucket

Half Thing Of Milk, Other Stuff Moved

PIERRE, SD—After several unsuccessful attempts to insert a KFC bucket into his cluttered refrigerator Thursday, local man Jeremy Browning, 32, was forced to rearrange every item in the 24.5-cubic-foot cooling appliance to make the chicken container fit.

"At first I tried to just shove it in real hard and push the [refrigerator] door closed," Browning told reporters. "But the door wouldn't close."

Although Browning claims he initially tried to eat all 15 pieces of the Original Recipe chicken, the quantity proved too great and he realized that his only option to preserve the remaining four pieces for future consumption was to store the KFC bucket in his refrigerator. However, the 10-inch-tall, eight-inch-wide fried-chicken receptacle proved too large.

"It was too tall, so I had to lower the shelf a notch," said Browning, who removed each of the items from his refrigerator's top shelf and then placed them on the floor in

see KFC, page 6

Johnson & Johnson Introduces 'Nothing But Tears' Shampoo To Toughen Up Newborns

NEW BRUNSWICK, NJ—After decades of coddling young children, Johnson & Johnson unveiled its new "Nothing But Tears" shampoo this week, an aggressive bath-time product the company says will help to prepare meek and fragile newborns for the real world.

A radical departure for the health goods manufacturer, the new shampoo features an all-alcohol-based formula, has never once been approved by leading dermatologists, and is as gentle on a baby's skin as "having to grow up and fend for your goddamn self."

"We at Johnson & Johnson have been making bath time a safe and soothing experience for far too long," company CEO William C. Weldon said. "Years of pampering have left our newborns helpless, feeble, and ill-equipped for the arduous road ahead."

"It's time our children got the wake-up call that's been coming to them," Weldon continued. "It's time they cried their

see TEARS, page 6

Double-Jointed Man On Date Breaks It Out Too Early

COOPERSTOWN, NY—Double-jointed man Stephen Rothkowitz's first date with Lois Hiller, 30, was irrevocably derailed when the 29-year-old process server prematurely demonstrated his ability to bend his thumb all the way back to his wrist, witnesses reported Tuesday.

"There seemed to be a lull in their conversation, and then he just started yanking his thumb around," said patron David Cantrall, who was seated adjacent to Rothkowitz's table at the D&R Steakhouse.

"He didn't even preface it with something like, 'Hey, guess what I can do?'" Rothkowitz was reportedly unable to salvage the evening by shooting milk out of his eye.

'Tu Stultus Es'

the ONION®

SEPTEMBER 4, 2008 · VOLUME 44 ISSUE 36 AMERICA'S FINEST NEWS SOURCE · ONION.COM · NATIONAL EDITION

WEATHER PAGE B16

Hot and muggy in the upper 90s as a warm front yes kill her extends the heat wave with that knife until Tuesday

LOW **96** HIGH **99**

HIGHLIGHTS

'I'm A Stay-At-Home Aunt'

by Sharon Mellock

OPINION, page 5C

ATM Flees To Mexico With $50,000

INTERNATIONAL, page 14A

ONION SPORTS

Giants Unveil Strahan Signal

page 3D

INSIDE

BUSINESS

Everything Midas CEO Touches Turns To Mufflers

PAGE 3B

LOCAL

Making Pancakes Best Idea Man Has For Saving Relationship

PAGE 8F

INDEX

ONION

Briefs 2

Opinion 8

Sports 10

A.V. CLUB

Cinema 16

Music 20

Words 21

THIS WEEK IN THE A.V. CLUB

Writer-producers J.J. Abrams, Josh Schwartz, and Alan Ball talk fall TV

Top Story On John McCain Run Out Of Obligation

Large Compulsory Photo

Sen. John McCain, and not an exciting war scene or raging wildfire, shown below.

NEW YORK—Although his lack of charisma and charm has lately prevented the Arizona senator from grabbing front-page headlines, the tenets of journalistic objectivity made it necessary today to publish a top news story on Republican presidential candidate John McCain.

THE RACE TO BE THE PRESIDENT

Part 3 of a 5-part series

According to the newspaper's editors, the decision to run the story came after they realized that they had not printed a cover story about Sen. McCain (R-AZ) in a number of months, despite the distinct possibility that he could become the leader of the free world for the next four to eight years.

Some of the publication's employees said they recalled a recent profile on McCain's military service—also run out of obligation—but archival records revealed that piece was published in April 2007. While other articles published in recent weeks have referred to McCain, today's story

see **MCCAIN**, page 6

Man Pinned Under Blankets For Three Days

ONION PUBLIC WATCH

MOLINE, TX—Crushed under the weight of a sudden and unexpected emotional collapse Friday, local resident Sam Cartwright spent 72 hours completely immobilized beneath the covers of his bed.

"I don't know how long I was unconscious for," said Cartwright, who managed to stay alive by eating from a box of Ritz crackers that was within arm's reach. "I couldn't move. There were so many times that I wanted to just give up and die."

Cartwright was eventually freed from the blankets when his friend Rob brought over a six-pack and told him to "forget that bitch."

Cheney Waits Until Last Minute Again To Buy Sept. 11 Gifts

The vice president strolls happily down New York's Park Avenue, picking up the last few 9/11 presents for his friends back home at the Pentagon.

WASHINGTON—Busy dealing with important paperwork and other vice presidential duties in recent weeks, Dick Cheney was forced to put off until the last minute a cherished annual tradition: gift-shopping for his favorite holiday, 9/11.

"I looked at the calendar yesterday, and I couldn't believe my eyes—9/11 is almost here!" a rosy-cheeked Cheney said upon returning to the White House Sunday with two giant bags overflowing with gift-wrapped boxes and big red bows. "It's the most wonderful time of the year."

While Cheney is known by many to be cold and taciturn for the other 11 months of the year, those close to the vice president say there is something about the 9/11 season that puts a spring in his step and a smile on his face. Each Sept. 11 morning since 2001, Cheney has come to work donning a fireman costume and handed out small, thoughtful gifts to all White House staffers. In addition, at his home on 9/11 Eve, Cheney lays out large piles of presents for his children and grandchildren underneath the colorfully lit, six-foot-tall 9/11 towers that he sets up by the fireplace.

"I've outdone myself this year—I bought the president a box of cigars and a brand-new fountain pen, I got Condoleezza [Rice] a beautiful blue blazer, and for my wife [Lynne] I bought a diamond necklace, a new winter coat, and this neat little motorized airplane ornament to hang on the 9/11 towers," Cheney told reporters while perusing the windows of New York's famed Park Avenue shops. "And for [granddaughter]

see **CHENEY**, page 6

Darwinic pilgrims claim the image fills them with an overwhelming feeling of logic.

Evolutionists Flock To Darwin-Shaped Wall Stain

DAYTON, TN—A steady stream of devoted evolutionists continued to gather in this small Tennessee town today to witness what many believe is an image of Charles Darwin—author of *The Origin Of Species* and founder of the modern evolutionary movement—made manifest on a concrete wall in downtown Dayton.

"I brought my baby to touch the wall, so that the power of Darwin can purify her genetic makeup of undesirable inherited traits," said Darlene Freiberg, one among a growing crowd assembled here to see the mysterious stain, which appeared last Monday on one side of the Rhea County Courthouse. The building was also the location of the famed "Scopes Monkey Trial" and is widely considered one of Darwinism's holiest sites. "Forgive me, O Charles, for ever doubting your Divine Evolution. After seeing this miracle of limestone pigmentation with my own eyes, my faith in empirical reasoning will never again be tested."

Added Freiberg, "Behold the power and glory of the scientific method!"

Since witnesses first reported the unexplained marking—

see **STAIN**, page 4

'Tu Stultus Es'

the ONION®

OCTOBER 16, 2008 · VOLUME 44 ISSUE 42

AMERICA'S FINEST NEWS SOURCE · ONION.COM · NATIONAL EDITION

WEATHER PAGE B16

Just right to slip on a T-sweater

LOW **52** HIGH **58**

HIGHLIGHTS

McCain Clinches Religious Vote With Stirring High-Register Rendition Of 'Ave Maria'

NATIONAL, page 5A

Closed-Door Meeting To Determine Future Of Honey-Roasted Peanuts BUSINESS, page 12C

ONION SPORTS

Mr. Met Takes Frustrations Out On Fans page 3D

INSIDE

ENTERTAINMENT

Song Climbs To Top Of Country Music Charts, Throws Itself Off

PAGE 3F

LOCAL

Pizza Guy Asks The Score

PAGE 8B

INDEX

ONION
Briefs 2
Opinion 8
Sports 10

A.V. CLUB
Cinema 16
Music 20
Words 22

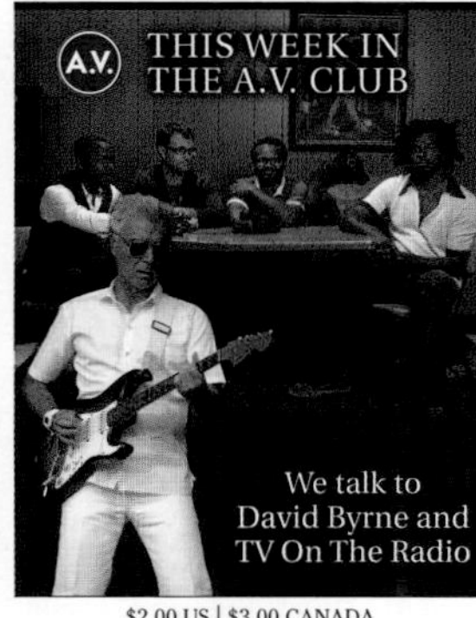

$2.00 US | $3.00 CANADA

BUSH CALLS FOR PANIC

President Bush addresses the nation shortly before shaving his head and soaking the Oval Office in his own urine.

'It's Time To Put Aside Our Differences, Come Together As A Nation, And Seriously Freak Out'

WASHINGTON—In a nationally televised address to the American people Wednesday night, President Bush called upon every man, woman, and child to spiral uncontrollably downward into complete and utter panic.

Speaking from the Oval Office, Bush assured citizens that in these times of great uncertainty, the best and only course of action is to come under the throes of a sudden, overwhelming fear marked by hysterical or irrational behavior.

"My fellow Americans, the time for running aimlessly through streets while shrieking and waving our arms above our heads is now," Bush said. "I understand that many of you are worried about your economic future and our situation overseas, and you have every right to be. Yet there is only one thing we as a nation can do in times like these: give up all hope and devolve into a lawless, post-apocalyptic, every-man-for-himself society."

"For those of you who have remained resolute in your belief that things will turn around eventually, I urge you to close your eyes, take shallow rapid breaths, and begin freaking out immediately," Bush added. "At this point, anyone who isn't scared to death needs to wake the fuck up—because we're screwed here."

The president then picked up the telephone from his desk and hurled it

see **PANIC**, page 5

Southern Sheriff Pulls Over Obama Campaign Bus For Broken Taillight

Sheriff Dewey Clutter makes Sen. Obama recite the Gettysburg Address backwards.

FOXWORTH, MS—Despite obeying the posted speed limit and having all inspection, registration, and insurance documentation up to date, Sen. Barack Obama's campaign bus was stopped for nearly four hours by Marion County deputy sheriff Dewey Clutter while en route to a Jackson, MS speech, sources reported Tuesday.

According to those on board the bus—including various journalists, members of the Secret Service, and Obama campaign staffers—several minutes passed before Clutter exited his cruiser. Witness statements all mention hearing the sheriff's jackbooted footsteps along the gravel roadside as he slowly approached the vehicle's passenger side. These reports also assert that, prior to reaching the front of the campaign bus, the sheriff paused momentarily to smash the right rear taillight of the bus before dragging his still-drawn baton along the entire length of the vehicle.

"Where's the fire, son?" Clutter, 42, was overheard saying to the Illinois senator and 2008 Democratic presidential nominee.

see **SHERIFF**, page 4

900-Pound Giant Squid Joins Cast Of 'The View'

Study Finds No Logical Reason Why Planes Fly

PALO ALTO, CA—According to a recent study conducted by a team of physicists at Stanford University, there is no logical explanation why airplanes are able to fly through the air.

"We understand the concepts of 'lift' and 'thrust,' but airplanes weigh like 800,000 pounds," head researcher Gabe Koplowitz said. "How does a huge metal tube just float up there in the sky without falling? And it's not even 'floating,' really, even though it looks like it is, because it's going 500 mph. Which means that when I'm sitting in an airplane, I'm actually going 500 mph, too. Me, Gabe Koplowitz. Jesus, how come we all don't vomit or have our hair blow back?"

The study posited a number of potential theories to explain the phenomenon, including wind propulsion, suspension of gravity, and the possibility that clouds "pull" the plane skyward. The Stanford team plans to devote the next two years to a new study on why telephones hear.

The sea creature squares off against Whoopi in a heated round of Hot Topics.

NEW YORK—*The View*, a daytime talk show featuring a panel of women who discuss current events and topical issues, has found its newest cohost—a 53-foot-long giant squid.

"We feel that the squid brings a fresh new point of view to the program," said *View* executive producer and host Barbara Walters. "We looked at hundreds of potential candidates, but in the end, this rare and exotic creature from the darkest depths of the sea truly stood out."

"And as far as we can tell, it is a female," Walters added.

The 900-pound cephalopod from the family *Architeuthidae* joins cohosts Whoopi Goldberg, Joy Behar, Elisabeth Hasselbeck, and Sherri Shepherd. Like many past hosts, who have come from such diverse backgrounds as law, stand-up comedy, and local news, the squid was a virtual unknown before joining the cast. Plucking it from relative obscurity, producers discovered the squid 26,000 feet below sea level in the Mariana Trench and said to themselves, "This is the perspective the show has been lacking."

see **SQUID**, page 5

'Tu Stultus Es'

the ONION®

WEATHER PAGE B16

So rainy you're probably moving today
LOW 58 HIGH 61

OCTOBER 23, 2008 • VOLUME 44 ISSUE 43

AMERICA'S FINEST NEWS SOURCE • ONION.COM • NATIONAL EDITION

Bailiff Can't Help Wondering What Life Would Be Like On Other Side Of Judge LOCAL, page 5B

Obama Purchases Ad Space On Side Of McCain's Bus NATIONAL, page 9A

ONION SPORTS

Flyers Defenseman Ceremonially Checks Sarah Palin Into Boards
page 3D

INSIDE

ENTERTAINMENT
Area Man Takes Up Piano For Sole Purpose Of Learning 'Jurassic Park' Theme PAGE 3F

LOCAL
Leather-Clad Gang Looks Capable Of Stylized Violence PAGE 8B

INDEX

ONION
Briefs 2
Opinion 8
Sports 10

A.V. CLUB
Cinema 16
Music 20
Words 21

$2.00 US | $3.00 CANADA

Dollar Bill On Floor Sends Wall Street Into Frenzy

ONION FINANCE

NEW YORK—Wall Street investors experienced a sudden surge in optimism Tuesday when, after six tumultuous weeks that saw record drops in the Dow Jones industrial average, a $1 bill was spotted on the floor of the New York Stock Exchange.

The dollar bill was discovered in the northwest corner of the trading floor at approximately 12:05 p.m., and its condition was reported as "crinkled, but real." Word of the tangible denomination of U.S. currency spread quickly across the NYSE, sending traders into a frenzied rush of shouting, arm-flailing, hooting, hollering, and, according to eyewitnesses, at least one dog pile.

"With credit frozen and the commercial paper market poised on the brink of collapse, this is the most promising development I've seen on Wall Street in months," said floor trader Tim Formato, one of hundreds who

see DOLLAR, page 5

NYSE traders excitedly swarm the piece of actual, tangible currency.

Plastic Surgeon General Warns Of Small Breasts Epidemic

U.S. Bosoms 'Dangerously Underdeveloped'

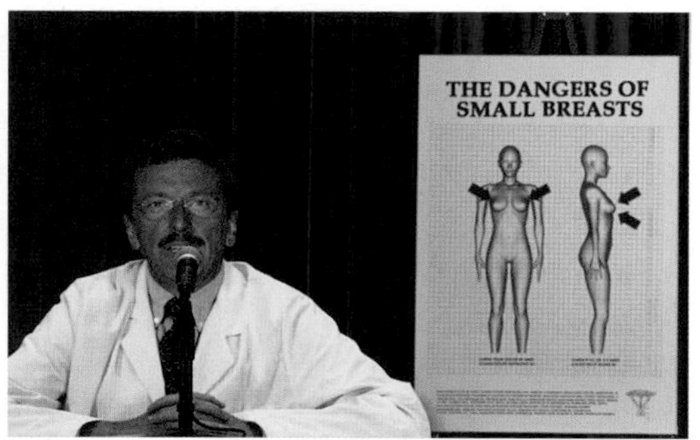

The National Center for Cosmetic Enhancement rails against A-cups.

BEVERLY HILLS, CA—According to a report released Monday by U.S. plastic surgeon general Dr. Louis T. Saddler, an alarming number of American women are suffering from dangerously small breasts.

The Office of the Plastic Surgeon General—headed by a presidential appointee tasked with monitoring the national aesthetic, alerting the public to any small flaws, and offering a wide range of affordable, noninvasive laser resurfacing options—first addressed the countrywide plague of undersized breasts in the mid-1980s by demanding that manufacturers of A- through C-cup bras place large warning labels on their products informing female consumers of the potential risk of having deficient bosoms.

Since taking the position in 2001, Dr. Saddler has continued these education efforts, launching several ad campaigns and personally reaching out to

see BREASTS, page 4

Swaggering Down 87%

Occurrences of swinging one's elbows arrogantly are at their lowest levels in decades.

NEW YORK—According to an alarming new study published Monday in *The Journal Of Applied Behavioral Science*, the time-honored American activity of swaggering, an extremely arrogant manner of walking, has dropped by nearly 90 percent since 2007.

The severe economic turmoil of recent weeks and the United States' diminished credibility and moral standing on the world stage are just two of the major factors named in the study as

see SWAGGERING, page 5

McCain Blasts Obama As Out Of Touch In Burma-Shave-Style Billboard Campaign

RAPID CITY, SD—John McCain escalated his attacks on Obama's leadership credentials Tuesday by endorsing a series of rhyming Burma-Shave-style billboards that accuse the Democratic presidential candidate of being out of touch with the current political landscape. "Barack Is Sipping/Fine Champagne/While U.S. Jobs/Go Down The Drain/McCain '08," read the five consecutive 2-by-5-foot bright red wooden signs erected along a 1.5-mile stretch of South Dakota highway, emulating an advertising medium first popularized by the Burma-Vita Company in 1926 to sell brushless shaving cream. As a follow-up to the scathing roadside polemic, McCain announced plans to lampoon Obama's foreign policy inexperience in a short skit alongside comedian Bert Wheeler and the vivacious Dorothy Lee, to be seen on the late-night variety program *Cavalcade Of Stars* on the DuMont Television Network.

'Tu Stultus Es'

the ONION®

AMERICA'S FINEST NEWS SOURCE · ONION.COM · NATIONAL EDITION

OCTOBER 30, 2008 · VOLUME 44 ISSUE 44

WEATHER PAGE B16

Loads and loads of weather today
LOW **50** HIGH **56**

HIGHLIGHTS

McCain Tucks Extra Neck Skin Into Collar
NATIONAL, page 5A

Fleet Of Stem-Cell Container Trucks Ready To Go If Obama Elected
HEALTH, page 9C

ONION SPORTS
Fumble!
page 3D

INSIDE

LOCAL
One-Woman Show Makes Audience Hate All Women
PAGE 3B

LIVING
Landlord Explains Difference Between Bad Roaches, Kind You Have
PAGE 8F

INDEX

ONION
Briefs 2
Opinion 8
Sports 10
A.V. CLUB
Cinema 16
Music 20
Words 21

$2.00 US | $3.00 CANADA

'I Would Make A Bad President,' Obama Says In Huge Campaign Blunder

POLITICS WATCH

TALLAHASSEE, FL—In a campaign gaffe that could potentially jeopardize Sen. Barack Obama's White House bid, the Democratic presidential nominee told nearly 8,000 supporters Tuesday that, if elected, he would be a terrible president.

The blunder, captured by all major media outlets and broadcast live on CNN, occurred when the typically polished Obama fielded a question about his health care policy. Obama answered by saying he would give small business owners a tax credit to help them provide health care for their employees, and then added, "Now, I'm not completely certain that my plan would work because, overall, I think I would make a bad president."

According to sources, before those on hand could fully process what Obama had said, the Illinois senator continued to stumble, claiming that, were he to win the general election, he'd have absolutely no idea what to do.

"My youth and inexperience would definitely make me an awful president," said Obama, whose seven-minute misstep was further exacerbated when he called himself "no expert" on the economy. "To be perfectly honest, I'd be worried about putting me in charge of the most powerful military in the world because I'm not any good when it comes to making important decisions. Also, I'm not sure how much I care about keeping this great nation of ours safe."

"I'm an elitist, I hate Israel, and I want to lose the war in Iraq," Obama concluded, and then, seemingly unaware of the magnitude of his blunder,

see **OBAMA**, page 4

Obama makes a slight gaffe when, instead of saying "Hello, Tallahassee," he says "John McCain is clearly the better candidate."

Microsoft Ad Campaign Crashing Nation's Televisions

30-Second Spots Causing Screens To Freeze, Interrupting Shows

Users have reported a number of failures resulting from the defective commercials, ranging from inability to change channels to "couldn't finish *Heroes*."

WASHINGTON—According to an FCC report released Monday, a new $300 million Microsoft ad campaign is responsible for causing televisions all across the country to unexpectedly crash.

The Microsoft ads, which began airing earlier this week, are being blamed for generating critical system errors in more than 70 million televisions. In addition, thousands of frustrated Americans said that the ads have caused their TVs to become unresponsive, their screens to turn blue, and a small box with the message "terminal application error" to suddenly appear.

"I was in the middle of watching *Monday Night Football* when, all of a sudden, that stupid ad comes on and my TV freezes up," said Scottsdale, AZ resident Michael Chaplin, adding that he never wanted to see the commercial in the first place. "The next thing I know, all these numbers and symbols show up and I get an error message saying 'invalid file format' or something. Now my TV is ruined."

The new ad campaign, which features footage of everyday Americans using PCs, was launched as an upgrade to the poorly performing Jerry Seinfeld and Bill Gates commercials, which suffered unspecified failures in two-thirds of U.S. households. Mi-

see **MICROSOFT**, page 5

Supremes Court Upholds Stopping In The Name Of Love In 2-1 Decision

The perfectly in sync judicial body delivers its passionate majority opinion.

WASHINGTON—After months of deliberation, the Supremes Court, the soulful judicial body that oversees federal matters of the heart, issued a historic decision in the case of *Holland v. Baby, Baby*, opting to uphold the practice of stopping in the name of love by a 2-1 vote.

"The court has given careful consideration to arguments from both sides, and tried so hard, hard to be patient," Justice Cindy Birdsong said in her well-choreographed majority decision. "It is our opinion that stopping in the name of love is not only the compulsory duty of the philandering party, but it would be irresponsible for him to do otherwise, pursuant to the aforementioned instances in which we have been both good and sweet to you, as well

see **SUPREMES**, page 5

'Tu Stultus Es'

the ONION®

WEATHER PAGE B16
Pre-winter bone-chilling cold
LOW **38** HIGH **42**

NOVEMBER 6, 2008 · VOLUME 44 ISSUE 45 AMERICA'S FINEST NEWS SOURCE · ONION.COM · NATIONAL EDITION | NAT

HIGHLIGHTS

Big Ben Set 15 Minutes Ahead To Give London A Little Extra Time In The Morning INTERNATIONAL, page 15A

Old Little League Trophy Stared At LOCAL, page 9B

ONION SPORTS

Greg Oden Signs On For Six-Week Run In Broadway's 'Young Frankenstein' page 3D

INSIDE

LOCAL
Buddy Vouched For
PAGE 3B

BUSINESS
Photos Used In Retirement Party Slide Show Mostly Taken During Last Two Weeks
PAGE 8F

INDEX

ONION
Briefs 2
Opinion 8
Sports 10
A.V. CLUB
Cinema 16
Music 20
Words 21

THIS WEEK IN THE A.V. CLUB

Conversations with Paul Rudd and the cast of *MST3K*

$2.00 US | $3.00 CANADA

KLEMKE WINS

Democrat Alan Klemke Becomes Wichita's 4th District Alderman

ELECTION 2008

WICHITA, KS—In a thrilling conclusion to one of the longest and most anticipated elections in U.S. history, charismatic Democrat Alan Klemke has defeated opponent Carl Ferguson to become the new alderperson for Wichita's 4th District.

Klemke delivered a rousing victory address in front of his now-famous campaign headquarters, located in a vacant storefront within the Westway Shopping Center. There Klemke thanked his staff for their hard work throughout a historic campaign that captured the hearts and minds of an entire district, including all neighborhoods south of Douglas Avenue and west of the Arkansas River.

"Thank you all," Klemke said, his momentous words signaling the beginning of a bold new era in Wichita City Council proceedings. "I promise to work hard on creating a more responsible municipal water policy and better parking regulations on the weekends. I am also committed to rezoning the old rail corridor on Baker Street, out past where the Denny's

see **ALDERMAN**, page 5

Nov. 4 will forever be remembered as the day Alan Klemke became 4th District alderman of Wichita, KS.

AMERICA FINALLY VOTES

The Electoral Map

A state-by state breakdown of how the nation cast its ballots

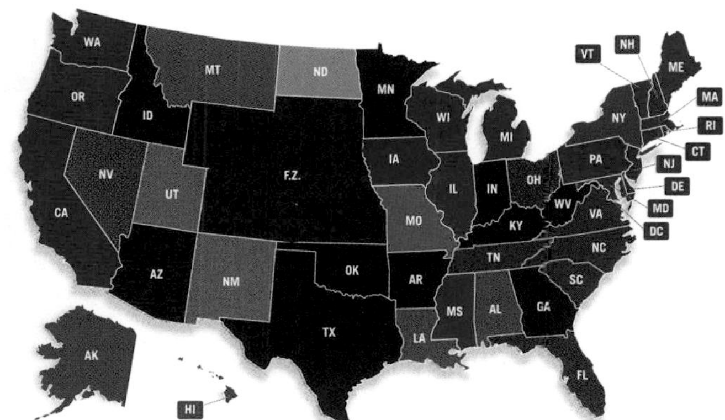

LEGEND

- Republican
- Democrat
- Canceled each other out
- Seceded
- Election? What Election? OH DEAR GOD, THE ELECTION!
- Should feel lucky they got to vote at all after what happened last time
- Still too scared to leave voting booth and face election results
- Entire state disqualified from voting for punching goddamn cop that one time
- Brought children to see how democratic process works, got fed up with long lines and left
- Voted for Hillary Clinton. Are Hillary Clinton.
- Forbidden Zone
- Thought about mailing absentee ballot. Used stamps to send away for Pop-Tart prize instead
- Upset about being shaded chartreuse on map
- Really had heart set on Chris Dodd, never fully recovered
- Wasn't about to fall for old "voting" trick again. No, sir. Not this time.

National Voter Highlights

In order to extend her lunch break an extra half hour, **Maria Gomez** of San Bernadino, CA pretended to feel conflicted for a while, before ultimately pulling the lever for Barack Obama.

George Olmussen of Cedar Rapids, IA voted for John McCain, and he's tired of everyone asking him why in that tone.

Christopher Nathans, 18, cast an informed vote for president and half a dozen ignorant votes for mayor, governor, county sheriff, and some ballot initiative about term limits or banks or something.

Undecided voter **Allison Blackmore** has been in that damn booth since 4 p.m. yesterday.

Simon Phillon of Short Hills, NJ broke a promise never to return to "that hellhole Hartshorn Elementary" when he voted for president Tuesday.

Mary Lynn Hauser of Poughkeepsie, NY quickly voted for John McCain and then ran her ballot to the ballot box before she had a chance to change her mind.

Steven Spring, 48, voted for Obama due to the fact that he could never support a candidate whose last name rhymes with "Hussein."

Michael Vernon of Boise, ID voted for Cynthia McKinney, the only candidate who didn't make fun of his protruding hump.

Exit Poll Results

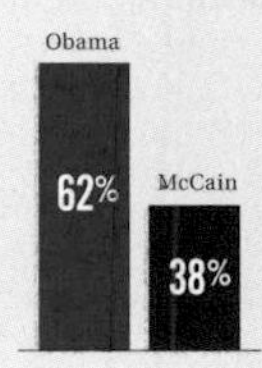

43% 57%
McCain
Obama

12% Obama
7% McCain
81%
Pervading feeling that polls are misleading, unreliable, and a rather primitive tool for keeping track of where Americans stand.

'Tu Stultus Es'

the ONION®

WEATHER PAGE B16
Unnamed comet passing Earth tonight. Send ideas to comet@nasa.gov
LOW **30** HIGH **34**

NOVEMBER 27, 2008 • VOLUME 44 ISSUE 48 AMERICA'S FINEST NEWS SOURCE • ONION.COM • NATIONAL EDITION

HIGHLIGHTS

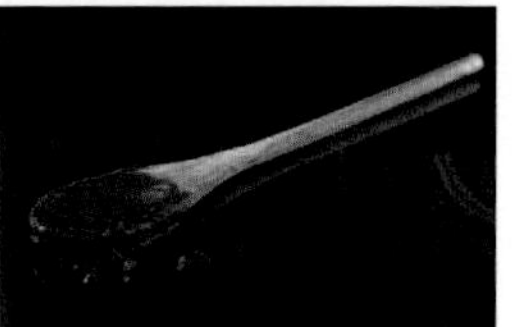

Gordon Ramsay Berates Spoon For 45 Minutes
ENTERTAINMENT, page 5C

Unemployed Man Photoshops Self Into Former Company's Staff Photo LOCAL, page 9B

ONION SPORTS
Carmelo Anthony Airballs Slam Dunk page 3D

INSIDE

LOCAL
Pervert Thinks You Seem Tense
PAGE 3B

LOCAL
Ghost Of Thanksgiving Future Shows Man Passed Out On Couch PAGE 8B

INDEX

ONION
Briefs 2
Opinion 8
Sports 10

A.V. CLUB
Cinema 16
Music 20
Words 21

$2.00 US | $3.00 CANADA

Blue Angels Hold First-Ever Open Tryouts

87 Dead, 243 Injured in Day 1 of Weeklong Event

Crowds line up for the chance to fly a supersonic jet.

PENSACOLA, FL—Harold Enderby's friends say that when he first saw the Navy's televised announcement that the Flight Demonstration Squadron, better known as the Blue Angels, would be holding open tryouts for the first time in its history, the lifelong aviation buff turned to his fellow sanitation workers at Doug's Dugout Bar-N-Grill and said, "Mark my words—I'm going to be a Blue Angel if it's the last thing I do."

And this Sunday, that dream came true for an incredible 43 seconds, as Enderby got the chance to fly the famed Blue Angels' F/A-18 Hornet directly into the tarmac during the first day of the Navy's most dramatic—and colorful—audition program ever.

Since 1946, the Blue Angels have recruited only elite military fighter pilots. But this week and this week only, the Navy is giving the public a rare treat: allowing ordinary, everyday citizens a chance to try out for the world's premiere stunt flying team. Memorial services for Enderby, along with five other late aspiring aviators and 81 others from the assembled crowd and surrounding communities, will begin Friday and continue throughout the month.

"Some of these folks may not have worked their way through four years of the Naval Academy, 10 years of flying missions as a naval aviator on three different carriers, two sessions at the fighter school at Miramar,

see **ANGELS**, page 6

Man With Apple Hovering In Front Of Face Sues René Magritte's Estate

Renfro did not approve use of his image.

TACOMA, WA—Michael Renfro, a 68-year-old retired CPA with an apple hovering in front of his face, announced Monday that he has filed a $15 million lawsuit against the estate of deceased Belgian artist René Magritte for unlawfully using his likeness in the 1964 painting *The Son Of Man*. "I only recently became aware of the painting's existence when an acquaintance slipped a Polaroid of the work between the apple and my face," said Renfro, who suspects that Magritte may have seen him while he was purchasing a bowler hat and topcoat in Brussels in the early 1960s. "Despite everything, I do respect Mr. Magritte's abilities as an artist. He was undeniably a master of photorealism." Magritte's work has often been the subject of litigation, most notably in 2003 when the Los Angeles County Museum of Art filed a Treachery of Images charge against the artist's estate after purchasing a piece by Magritte that was believed to be a pipe, but was later revealed not to be a pipe.

Area Man Holding Out Until Next Exit For Better Fast Food Options

ERIE, PA—Local fast food consumer and occasional motorist Don Turnbee announced his decision Wednesday to bypass I-79's Greenville exit in hopes that the following turnoff would lead to more appealing fast food options.

According to Turnbee, though the previous exit had several fast food establishments to choose from, the 41-year-old said that he "didn't feel like McDonald's," and that he had "just had Taco Bell a couple days ago."

"I think I want Wendy's," Turnbee told reporters at a rest stop alongside the highway. "There hasn't been a Wendy's in a while so there will probably be one at the next exit or the one after that."

"When you get on the road, there are more McDonald's and Burger Kings than Wen-

see **FOOD**, page 6

Don Turnbee weighs his options.

Just three glasses with dinner can support finally letting her have it.

Study Finds Link Between Red Wine, Letting Mother Know What You Really Think

CHICAGO—Health experts have long known that drinking red wine can have such positive benefits as reducing blood vessel damage, lowering the risk of heart attack, and preventing harmful LDL cholesterol from forming. But researchers at the Northwestern University Department of Preventive Medicine have recently found that the consumption of four to six glasses of red wine, most notably at dinner or a family function, may be linked to totally going off on one's mom.

According to a study published Monday in *The American Journal Of Medicine*, a previously unknown ingredient in red wine has been shown to cause a

see **WINE**, page 3

'Tu Stultus Es'

the ONION®

WEATHER PAGE B16
White
LOW 60 HIGH 80

DECEMBER 11, 2008 · VOLUME 44 ISSUE 50 AMERICA'S FINEST NEWS SOURCE · ONION.COM · NATIONAL EDITION | NAT

HIGHLIGHTS

'If There's Anyone Who's Been Hit Hard By The Stock Market Crash, It's Me: The Guy Who Sells Baby Turtles On The Sidewalk'
by Eddie Li
OPINION, page 5C

Nobody Touching Punch At CIA Christmas Party
NATIONAL, page 9A

ONION SPORTS
Pope Puts On Rally Mitre
page 3D

INSIDE

TELEVISION
Dogs Arranged On Bed In Shape Of Husband
PAGE 3B

LOCAL
Area Man Feeling Around In Candy Machine To Make Sure He Got All His Runts
PAGE 8B

INDEX

ONION
Briefs 2
Opinion 8
Sports 10
A.V. CLUB
Cinema 16
Music 20
Words 21

$2.00 US | $3.00 CANADA

Town Fails To Rally Around Adult Trapped In Well

No vigils held here to date.

CATONSVILLE, MD—Tragedy failed to strike the small suburban town of Catonsville this week, when local resident and full-grown adult Michael Ennis fell down an abandoned well, spraining both of his ankles and drawing the sympathy of absolutely no one.

According to sources, the not-so-moving accident has left this normally quiet Maryland community in a state of utter indifference, with hundreds of men, women, and children neglecting to come together as one and rally around the trapped 38-year-old.

"I don't understand," said Janice Peters, who has spent every day since first

see WELL, page 6

Lie To Cover Surprise Party Sounds More Fun Than Surprise Party

HOPATCONG, NJ—A lie told to 28-year-old Kyle Bida to cover up a surprise birthday party to be held in his honor later this evening sounds a lot more fun than the actual party will be. "Why don't you come over to my place to play Xbox and drink a few beers?" said best friend Louis Welles, leading Bida to believe he might have an enjoyable, relaxing evening rather than one spent making forced small talk with coworkers and a few cousins he doesn't see that often. "And don't forget to dress up a little bit, man. We're going to hit the bars later." Though Bida is doomed to an evening far inferior to the one described to him by Welles, most of the guests will likely leave early, using excuses that are more boring than what they actually plan to do.

Supreme Court Overturns Bush v. Gore

President Gore, retroactively determined by the Supreme Court to be the winner of the 2000 election, is sworn in for his six-week term.

WASHINGTON—In an unexpected judicial turnaround, the Supreme Court this week reversed its 2000 ruling in the landmark case of *Bush v. Gore*, stripping George W. Bush of his earlier political victory, and declaring Albert Arnold Gore the 43rd president of the United States of America.

The court, which called its original decision to halt manual recounts in Florida "a ruling made in haste," voted unanimously on Wednesday in favor of the 2000 Democratic nominee.

Gore will serve as commander in chief from Dec. 10 to Jan. 20.

"Allowing this flaw in judgment to stand would set an unworkable precedent for future elections and cause irreparable harm to the impartiality of this court," said Chief Justice John G. Roberts in his majority opinion. "Furthermore, let me be the first to personally congratulate President Gore on his remarkable come-from-behind victory. May he guide us wisely into this new millennium."

Added Roberts, "The system works."

Moments after the court's noontime announcement, Gore was flown to Washington, D.C. aboard Air Force One, sworn in on the steps of the U.S. Capitol, and immediately escorted to a brief victory rally at the National Mall. By 4:30 p.m., his 15 cabinet appointees had been vetted, contacted, and brought to Washington, where they were all simultaneously approved by a majority vote in the Senate.

Gore then delivered the first of sev-

see SUPREME, page 7

Staten Island Historians Piece Together Genealogy Of Wu-Tang Clan

NEW YORK—In what many are calling the most comprehensive study of its kind, Staten Island historians Robert Wilburn and Charles Tinsley have successfully traced the lines of the infamous Wu-Tang Clan all the way back to 1993 A.D.

The monumental undertaking, which is being hailed as a major breakthrough in the field of hip-hop genealogy, used a series of historical records—including *Wu-Tang Forever, Iron Flag,* and *8 Diagrams*—to piece together the group's vast and intricate ancestry.

"Through our exhaustive research, we have determined not only the start of the Wu-Tang Clan's reign, but also the very moment of its legendary downfall," said Wilburn, who has authored numerous books on the House of RZA.

see HISTORIANS, page 7

Wilburn explains the difficult-to-follow family tree of Ol' Dirty Bastard.

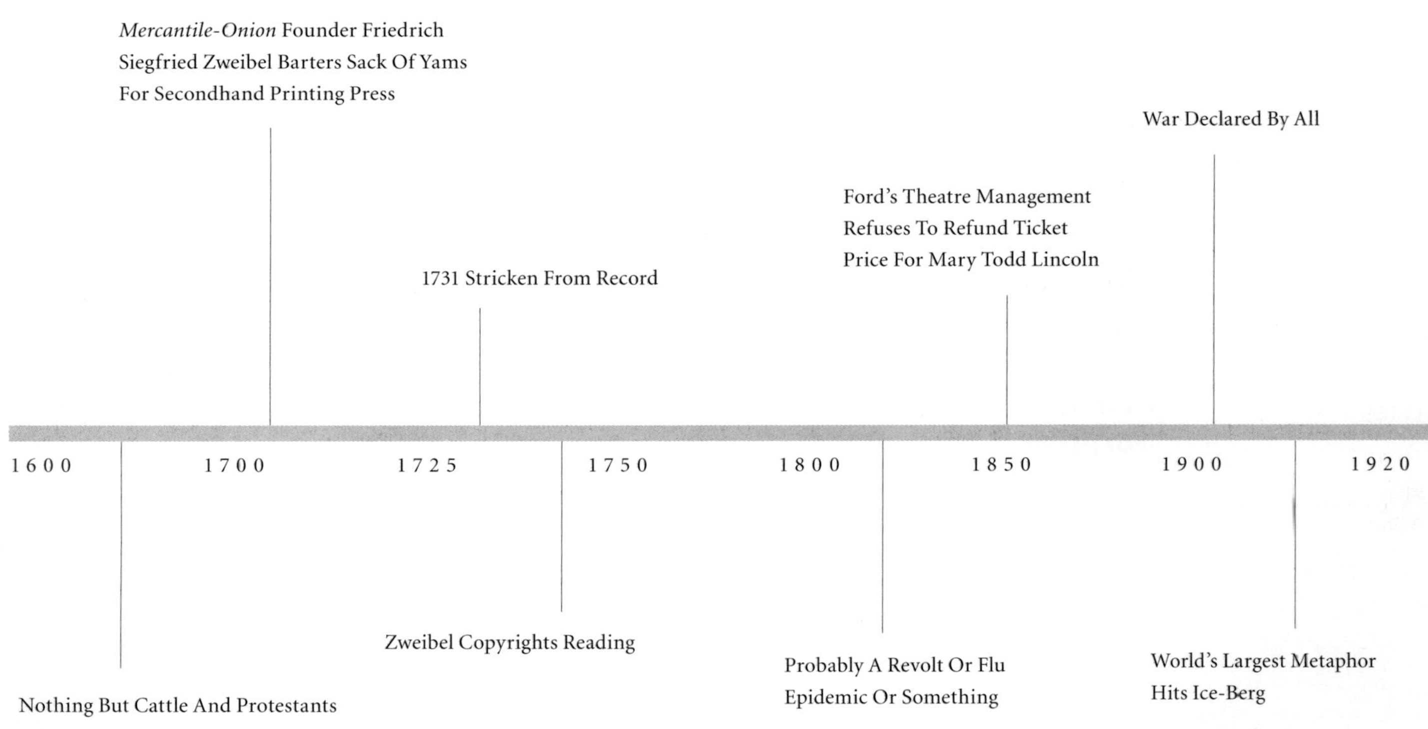
Mercantile-Onion Founder Friedrich Siegfried Zweibel Barters Sack Of Yams For Secondhand Printing Press
War Declared By All
Ford's Theatre Management Refuses To Refund Ticket Price For Mary Todd Lincoln
1731 Stricken From Record
1600
1700
1725
1750
1800
1850
1900
1920
Zweibel Copyrights Reading
Probably A Revolt Or Flu Epidemic Or Something
World's Largest Metaphor Hits Ice-Berg
Nothing But Cattle And Protestants

The Onion: Past & Future

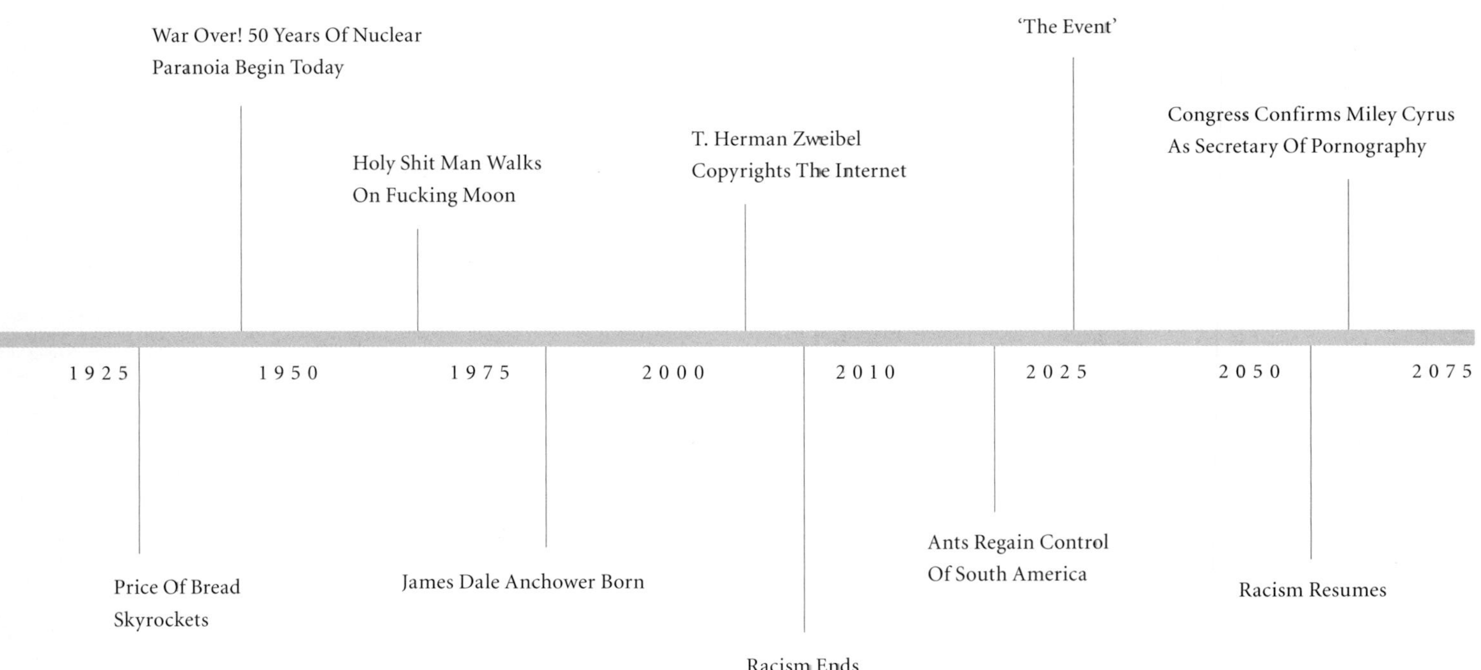

THE ONION NEWS-PAPER.

Coſt Of News-Paper:
One Pound Loaf Sugar OR Hoof of Horſe OR Half-Poun[d] Loaf Sugar In addition to half Hoof of Horſe OR Five Muſket Balls OR A Human Skeleton OR A FEW barrel[s] Excellent Tanners Oil OR Return of Publiſher's Son OR ONE Barrel of Excellent Tanners Oil In addition to Retu[rn] of Publiſher's Daughter.

FROM THE ARCHIVES

"...u Stultus Es". Foreign & Domeſtik.

CIRCA OCKTOBER THE SIXTH, ANNO DOMINI, 1783.

READER & MARKET DAY ADVERTISER.

The Fineſt Chronicle and Digeſt Of Publick Events of Significant Note, and Well-Found'd Advices for the General Enlightenment of the New World.

NAT

THE NOT'D AND ESTEEM'D OPINION OF FOUNDER AND SOLE EDITOR, H. ULYSSES ZWEIBEL.

Ever since THE ONION's luminous founding a quarter century ago'ne, this, the leading papermaking CHRONICKLE of noteworthy happenings in the colonys, has been engag'd in FAIR and OPEN competition for the reader's silver coin with other like pamphlets at market. To this I say, NEVER AGAIN. The Onion herewith rises beyonde its competitors throo the employ of a great INNOVATION in ink-printing knowne here-to-fore as ADVERT-TIZING; a concept of my design; which is a FEATURE ARTICKLE composed not by the press-man, but by a prominent SELLER OF WARES. Be he a peddler of wooden buckets, planting manure, dry'd corn, or Mustees, the merchant shall speake in direct addresse to the reader, commending the VIRTUE of his merchandise or commodity; unfetter'd under the opinion or independente appraisal made by THE ONION's editors or journalers. I pledge to print the seller's words without verifyiction of his claims; which would therewith constitute not only grave insult to his station, but foolish business pracktice. I further pledge to grant all members of the MERCHANT CLASS favoured placement on this parchment, in exchange for sterling, so that they might there by attrackt the attention of the reader to their note-worthy industry. Henceforth; THE ONION shall seeke to gain a REPUTATION as a proud delivery-carriage for the sales-man's wisdom, and in-so-doing encrease PROFITE for both he and THE ONION. Too oft'n the reason'd voice of honor'd Leaders of Trades in these colonies is render'd mute by the horse whinny of the lowborn. How are those of MONEY'D MEANS or NOBLE DESCENT to be inform'd of the opinions of the letter'd merchant? They shall, in this very issuing of THE ONION. The BURGER-KINGGE, that Meat-ennobled Mon-Arch, shall lay a very Feate of Advert-Tizing upon our printed Pages, that shall fatten the Eye and Spiritt of the beholder, and the Wallette of this News-Pap'r; and the Manufactors of JAMESON's miracle concoction, a mystifying brown Licquid, shall also be free to Speke their Minds, regarding the Efficacy and Virtue of that Wond'rous Fluidd, an' as that flows forth, so shall flow, into our own coffers, great fulminating gouts of CASHEN-MONNEY. I foresee a prosperous future for this commerce-making enterprise. It is my sincerest hope that one day messages provoking thought in the reader, given him from the ADVERT-TIZER, will supplant in totality the unfounded musings of the journalers; who are in facte noth'g more than WILD MEN made tame by their wages from the printing press, in all news-chronickle pamphletry. P'rhaps one day the two shall join to one; the ink-besotted type-setter in the employ of the amalgamated merchant in a manner favorable to capital increase; therewith growing into a glorious commercial power in these states, indeed the world; one whose ability to exercise freedom, liberty and utility in a healthy bloodletting of the unlimited resources of our prolifick land, and the unwashed people toiling upon it, is limit'd only by his goode sense and the blessings of Providence.

Signed and warranted,

H. ULYSSES ZWEIBEL.

Mule-Deaths Of Late.

Mon-day.
Belonging to M. SEXTON, Dottie.

Tues-day.
Belonging to A. BROWNE, Sour Mash.
Belonging to F. WESTON, Corporal Thistleweed.
Belonging to P. FRANKLIN, Stubbs III.
Belonging to J. JOHNSON, Paul.
Belonging to W. WOOLWORTH, Revere's Alternative.

Wednes-day.
No Mule-Deaths.

Thurſ-day.
No Mule-Deaths.

Fri-day.
Belonging to R. MILLS, King George the Tyrant.

Satur-day.
Belonging to J. HENRY, Biſcuits & Gravy.

Sun-day.
No Mule-Deaths reported by Sun-rise.

The Surgeon General Has Added Snuff To Tobacco Pyramid.

From our Baltimore Cousins comes News of the felicitous Health Benefits of the Powder'd Tobacco *SNUFF*, and the Recommendation that multiple Pinches be taken until Blood flows freely from the Nose in Service of balancing the Humours. Preeminent Barber-Surgeon and Former General of Loyalist Ilk Tho. HAYSWORTH has add'd the cure-all Physick to his famed and most singular *Tobacco Pyramid*, the robustness Chart learnt in Grammar-Schools 'cross the Whole of our Nation, and has given Snuff greater Importance, even, than Pipe Smoke. However, Gen'l HAYSWORTH was heard to remark many Times that Snuff should never be taken in the Stead of any Portion of the presently advis'd eight Score and thirty Draws from a firmly pack'd Clay Pipe, Two hearty Chaw Plugs, and four dozen Twists of dri'd Tobacco Leaves, the latter to be used for betwixt-Pipe Masticasions. The Measure of Snuff suggested by Gen'l HAYSWORTH to be most advantageous for Children under Six Years of Age is not to be in excess of four sizable Nose-Packings per four and twenty Hours, and taken always with two Draughts of strong Brandy. Those unable to procure the finely ground Tobacco should quaff freely from Cuspidors at every opportunity to derive at least a little Benefit from the meritorious Effects of Snuff.

The Honourable Gen'l HAYSWORTH has also issued a stern Warning against the Pome-Granate, a strange, blood-red, seed-filled Fruit, occasionally come to our Shores and said to be the most odious *POISON*, not even to be gazed upon.

Iroquois Inſurgency Quelled By Gov't.!
More news to follow in a fort-night.

GENERAL WASHINGTON HINTS AT A 'BID' FOR 'PRESIDENCY' IN 1789.

MYSTERIOUS OFFICE WOULD BE HIGHEST IN ALL OF NATION.

Like Unto A Very 'King,' But Choſen By A Body Of the People, Or Repreſentatives There-Of.

'T'WHY DOES GENERAL WASHINGTON NOT MERELY CONQUER US?' ASK MEN IN STREET.

Tories Queſtion whether our Commander-In-Chief 'Hath What It May Take' to be Commander-In-Chief.

In NEWBURGH, The State of New York this week we learn, that our great General Washington finds him self besett with Affairs of State, in addition to his more accustom'd Affairs, those being of War; and that, although he has yet to Persuade the Red-Coat to relinquish his brutal Possession of the Port of New YORK; Yet General Washington has made Mention, that in less than half a dozen of Years, he him self would Consider, if it be the will of Common Folk to select Him for the Honour, the LEADERSHIP of our fledgling Nation entire. And much Consternation and Speculation did this Inspire, amongst all there assembl'd.

General Washington, for his Part, was involved in the Commission of his Soldierly Dutie; and while conducting the Milit'ry Garrison of certain Harborage and Navigable Passagings vital to Industrie, was also conducting Talks of the very highest Level with sundrie Officers, these being of the rather Strident and Insistent Opinion that, for the past 7 years' Fighting, they should be finally Paid. And upon our Gen'l Washington's deft Mollification of these same Soldiers of Rank—which Washington secured through an Admixture of Promises, Appeals to their Better Natures, and assurance of a Arse-Tanning as from the Auld Testament were they to abandon their posts—Washington was heard to say that, if He him self could handle the Pack of Jack Asses that made up the Continental Armie, then he was Certain that he could run the Remainder of the Nation as its President. If, he insisted, the People Themselves would vote for him.

Whereupon his Aides de Camp were caught-out, and inquired with much Consternation, if Washington intended to fashion for himself a THRONE and CROWN; and when Washington did insist, that he would not, they were dis-appointed, and further Confused. Whereupon the General explained to them that, were the Common People, or at least those who were Menfolk, owning Land, and Literate, and White of Skin, and not altogether too Common, and possessed of other worthy qualifications; if these same Common People chose him as a President in a well-organized Electoral Contest, then he would see Fit to do his Duty in that office.

We, the Editor-Ship of the ONION NEWS-PAPER find the idea of a former General leading the Nation at the be-hest of its People to be one worthy of great Scorn, and slight Regard, and mayhap, Ridicule; for either the General should come forth Conquering, and take up the Mace and Scepter of a mighty Emperor-King anointed in the Sight of GOD; or he should Retire and Diminish, a contemporarie Cincinnatus, his time in Glorie ended. To do otherwise is not good Government, especially if the People be involved; for they, as our readers will agree, are a great Ass, and cannot be Counted upon to do correctly any Thing, and to suggest other wise brings the foul Scent of Democracie upon us; and we have not spent our Blood and Coin in the defeat of one King, to then go without our Own.

40,000 Pounds Of Slave Have Been Loſt At Sea.

Doleful News has been from Baltimore receiv'd, and that being: Of the WRECK of the Slaver *Betsy* at Sea, and its entire CARGO of 40,000 Pounds SUNKEN, to the furthest Depths of dread Neptune's hearth, ninety Leagues off Hatteras, on March the 4th. The star-cross'd Frigate took on Water during a Tempest, and despite the attempts of the Crew to jettison the less valuable members of the Hold, so as to lighten the Tonnage in the densely pack'd Hull, the Onrush of the cruel Sea overwhelm'd the valiant Effort.

A small Solace can be found in the Survival of *Capt Wm HARRIS* and eight of his Crew, who escap'd the foundered *Betsy* in the vessel's Long-Boate, and were recover'd, barely alive, by the Privateer *Reck-Less*. Lost and believed perish'd are First Mate A. Swallow, Purser Minchin, and Bo'sun Harker, and most poignantly, the belov'd Mascot of the Voyage, the Bull Terrier "Punch"; and, noting that their loss does out-weigh that of any material Goodes, we Grieve beside their Familie and Belov'd-Ones.

Word of the Disaster stunn'd Many who had assembl'd in Baltimore Town Green to bid in an Auction of the very Cargo that now lay Use-less on the bottom of the Ocean Atlantic. A Charitable Fund has been establish'd by the Prominent of Baltimore and this very Gazette to assist in the Compensation of the Victims of the Tragedy, crewe-men and Investors a-like, many of whom risk'd the *Entirety* of their Purses in the Endeavour, and have Families to support during this trying Time.

The Publisher of this News Paper wishes to assure the Publick that the Slavery Trade remains By and Large a *gainful* One, and this Set Back need only serve as a temporary Nuisance if Gentle Men of Commerce soundly ESCHEW the Impulse to panick. Demand for Bonded Labour has peak'd, and it is widely agreed that, though a minim of up-keep is sadly a Necessity, a Slave is an Excellent Value for the Money, as Divine Providence has seen to it that a Majority are Durable, Water Resistant, an' even Buoyant when not shackl'd, and their Masters derive much serviceable Use from them before their Expiration Dates, soon though many may Be.

BEN FRANKLIN INVENTIONS THIS WEEK.

The Death-Kite.

The Carton Device For The Conveyance Of Eggs, To Minimize Breakage On Even The Moſt Uneven Of Foot-Paths.

The U.S. Patent (Patented By Benjamin Franklin).

The Manual Vaginal Penetration Stick.

Power Windows.

The Inflatable Oblong Balloon, The Sort That Emits A Thunderous Clap, One Reſembling The Loud Exhale From One's Nether Regions.

Maidenhead Glue.

Math.

Being A Great And Pretentious Old Wind-Bag.

The World's Talleſt Man Towers At Five Feet And Eleven Inches.

From the honest and sworn Captain of the barque *Scylla*, freshly return'd from the Baltic: News of the Existence of a modern *Longshanks*, a veritable *GIANT* before whom many tremble. Said Pantagruel, who makes his Residence in the City of *Danzig*, reaches nearly six Feet into the Heavens. At an astonishing 18 Hands high, he is Heads and Shoulders above even the loftiest of his Brethren, and when striding the Thorough Fares of Danzig, can be seen from thirty Paces away. So co-lossal is he that master Carpenters cut a Hole above his Door and rais'd the Portal so to accommodate his great Head. This Ajax sleeps in a specially fashion'd Bed so that his lower Limbs do not dangle off the Edge. His Tailor keeps a-stock one surplus Bolt each of Wool and Muslin, should the Leviathan desire a new Suit of Clothes. To him, our daily Bread is but mere Crumbs; the Proprietress of an Inn where the Mammoth takes Meals testified that he could devour one-half of one-one-hundredth of his Weight in Beef-Steak in one Sitting. It is a further Wonder, that the Floor Boards of his House have not given away under his great Heft, an' that being estimated at nearly twelve Stone, or 165 Pounds Avoirdupois.

Despite his monstrous Scale, the Brobdingnagian is said to possess a Disposition of Charity and Docility, and has never once exercis'd Violence upon we Mundane in Size, all though we be easily devour'd if it so pleased him. When queried about the Condition of the Weather at his lofty Altitude, the Titan respond'd only with a Blush and a polite Smile of Resignation, to the Disappointment of Philosophes across the Continent, who were hoping to receive his singular Insight on the Topic.

It has been suggest'd by several Wags that the Behemoth of Danzig be wed to that other Curiosity of the Continent, "*Madame Methuselah*," a Frenchwoman who is aged Twoscore-Ten-and-Seven, or an amazing 57 Years.

TOLERATOR OF THE COMMON MAN.

THE ONION.

THE IRISH NEED NOT APPLY.

13–19 March 1896 | **The Best Source of Newsworthy Items in our Great Republic.** | *Price 5 Cents*

Infant Death Rate Plummets to One-In-Three.

RATE OF DEATH IN CHILD-BIRTH EVEN LOWER.

RADIANT MOTHERS-TO-BE OPTIMISTIC AT CHEERY NEWS.

HAPPY WORDS FROM U.S. SECRETARY OF HYGIENE BODE WELL FOR THE REPUBLIC'S FAMILIES.

WASHINGTON, MARCH 12.

The motherly bosom of our great nation must swell with pride to-day as the news from Secretary Thatcher is heard. A great shadow which has heretofore spread across our nation has now receded somewhat, and we are far the better for its absence. From this day forward - barring the dread specter of plague, famine or another unfortunate domestic military engagement of notable duration - half of the Union's children will not die before adulthood.

"Huzzah!" exclaimed President Cleveland upon hearing the joyous tidings. But his glad-heartedness was nothing compared to that of other sundry citizens. Many noted captains of industry are delighted with the prospect of having an improved and harder-wearing work-force. And the nation's long-suffering mothers, bless their sweet hearts, wept tears of joy as they realized that the apples of their eyes would not wither and rot quite as frequently as in times past.

Even though her heart must be selfless, laughing or weeping first for her family, the species Woman must also feel no small relief upon hearing that bearing children must no longer be such a gamble with Death. For the incidence of mortal accident during the process of labor has also been reduced to less than one in six. The gentleman of America may rejoice in the knowledge that his family is now some few steps closer to Security and the shelter of divine Providence.

Authorities credit this change of almost Utopian proportions to the administering to young ones of a healthy draught of Crawford's Soothing Syrup, a panacea available through our fine news-paper and offered for sale by many of our fine advertisers. Of somewhat lesser importance, but nonetheless worth noting, is the use of soap and certain virtuous spirits-of-wine to cleanse the nether regions of young women about to give birth, the newly born, and children in the broader sense. Doctors of surgery themselves, skeptical at first, have admitted that advantage is to be gained by the washing of hands and forearms before deliveries. Although the lower classes have thus far had little truck with these newfangled notions of medicine and cleanliness, even the coarse Irishwoman or impoverished Negress who partake of them as a "Sunday notion" might see some benefits in their use, and readers are urged to encourage their servants to do so. If properly seen to, folk of lower station will not interpret this as an excuse to "put on airs" or make assumptions of your concern for their well-being, but meekly submit to purification in order to protect their employer's offspring from malady.

THIS WONDROUS PHOTO-GRAPH IMAGE OF LILIENTHAL'S DEMISE IS GRANTED US VIA THE NEW SCIENCE OF PHOTO-GRAPH ETCH PRINTING.

Folly of Flying Machine Claims Life of Fool.

YEARS OF CONCEALED LABOR BEAR DEADLY FRUIT.

MAN-CARRYING FLAP-WINGED CONTRAPTION, UNAIDED BY BALLOON, PLUMMETS LIKE COMMON MILL-STONE.

NO LESS A FORCE THAN MIGHTY STEAM UNABLE TO CONQUER VAULT OF HEAVENS.

FROM THE BOSTON CORRESPONDENT.

The conundrum of aerial flight without the aid of buoying balloons has claimed the life of yet another addlepated woolgatherer. Otto Lilienthal, a scientist and inventor of German birthright, had been making the outrageous claim of late that should the power of air ever be harnessed with success, it could one day provide a method of transportation that would rival the services provided by mighty locomotives and ocean liners. But Herr Lilienthal took this fanciful and unpragmatic notion to his grave when, over a lush and verdant field not far from Boston, he proved that a willow-framed, collodion-skinned, bat-winged contraption of his own construct, though having the outward appurtenances of a butterfly, was as susceptible as any common stone to the unblinking gaze of Mistress Gravity. Without the accustomed lift given by the conventions of balloon attachments, Mr. L.'s sinister-looking, steam-operated device proved no more, and we dare say less, of a preservative against falling than the wings of mythical Icarus, let alone fulfilling the mighty device L. claimed would one day replace our rail-roads and inter-continental steamship lines.

The foolhardy Prussian was apt to show no more sense than a drunken Irishman when approached on the subject of his flying machines. As he strapped his all-too-mortal flesh upon the diabolical machine yesterday, onlookers, many of whom were noted executives in the rail-roads and shipping, pleaded with him to abandon his foolhardy errand of self-destruction. Comely womenfolk rent their petticoats in the certain knowledge of his self-destruction, and his servants, although properly obedient and utterly loyal in L.'s penultimate moments, had already clad themselves in the sable hues of mourning. Then, rejecting a last-minute offer from a prominent and compassionate Samaritan, an anonymous executive of the White-Star Line - an offer which, we hear, was of no small monetary import - the headstrong coxcomb fired the boiler of his ungainly Leviathan of the air. As hideous, noisome, foul and stenchful as the Beast of Revelations did the winged machine appear as it bore L. shuddering down a small hill, it managed to become airborne - for but a brief moment. Directing his machine to the ether, there came a screech of horribly tortured machinery as to his great alarm, L. found his hideous contraption entering a realm no mechanical contrivance was meant to roam, and the flying machine cast him down like so much offal upon the dirt. Physicians, hired by a generous benefactor from the Northern Pacific Railroad, rushed to his side, and though it did seem for a moment as if the staunch Herr had walked away unscathed, it was merely the onset of rigor-mortis; the good men of medicine pronounced him dead instantly upon impact, and despite the hurried ministrations of Crawford's Soothing Syrup the unfortunate fool could not be brought back to this world.

"His madness is tantamount to a criminal offense, especially in a member of the monied classes, who bear such responsibility in the matter of setting good examples for those of lesser earthly stature," pronounced a much-aggrieved and very wealthy transport magnate Cornelius Vanderbilt at the scene of L.'s suicide. "If the commoner is to learn a lesson from Mad Otto's premature leave-taking of this existence, it is that the formidable power of Wind, though Friend it may be whilst tamed and tempered into steam within the bowels of mighty locomotives, is Foe to mortal man when loosed against him. Man, even a well-formed and well-financed man as Lilienthal, is not an Angel that he should flit about the clouds." This news-paper could not agree more, especially when trans-continental rail passage may be purchased at such agreeable rates from our pioneers of travel.

AVENGE THE NEBRASKA!

AMERICAN WAR-SHIP'S DESTRUCTION NOT A HOAX.

THE CORAL REEF UPON WHICH SHIP RAN AGROUND PLACED IN ITS PATH BY AGENT-PROVOCATEURS OF THE SPANISH PERSUASION.

238 U.S. SAILORS ARE SENT TO A BRINY GRAVE AMONGST THE BARNACLES OF THE OCEAN BLUE; SPAIN'S COMPLICITY IN THE DREADFUL ACT ASSURED BY LEARNED OFFICERS OF THE NAVY AS WELL AS THIS NEWS-PAPER'S ESTEEMED PUBLISHER AND SON OF FOUNDER.

SPANISH BLACKGUARDS FEIGN IGNORANCE OF THE NEFARIOUS DEED.

PUBLISHER ZWEIBEL OFFERS $50,000 IN BULLION TO ANY MAN WHO BRINGS THE PERPETRATORS OF THIS TRAGEDY'S FOUL ORIGINS TO LIGHT.

HAVANA, MARCH 11.

From each and every hill and dale of this great Republic's four corners, The Onion calls that there should rightwise be taken up the cry of "Vengeance!" For the souls of those sailors, a sum of two hundred and thirty-eight in number, who met untimely ends at the secretive conniving of Spanish sabotage, only in the redemptive cleansing flow of Iberian blood shall provide eternal respite! War with the hated Spanish!

Cables recently received from the Caribbean Sea have reported a grand travesty that the U.S. Navy's man-o-war "Nebraska," has been rent in two and sunk by a dreadful act of sabotage and intrigue most foul. Yet, the loss of American sailors' lives is but only one reason to decry this awful event. There are those who claim this a mere "accident"- as if to wipe clean the stain of murderous guilt from the swarthy Spanish brow upon which it rightly sits. To these The Onion cries "Lies! Lies! O Lies!"

If not but for the intervening hand of Spanish brigandry then how, we must ask directly, could such a reef have appeared - directly affront the Nebraska's bow - where no such reef had been e'er known to exist before? And even if we meekly assume the callow hypothesis that it was mere accident, why then did the heretofore uncharted coral reef tear into a ship whose hull was filled with perilous explosives and ammunition? Even the most casual of observers of international affairs knows that from time immemorial the Spaniards have coveted our dominance of this corner of the world since we wrested it from them two-hundred years hence.

Let those who claim the destruction of the Nebraska an event of pure happenstance be found out for their un-American lies and dragged into the shining light of Truth from whatever rock's shadow under which they conceal themselves! Say we at The Onion, "Who are these apologists for the Spanish Menace, and can they be trusted?"

continued on page 8.

What to Make of This Demon Bryan.

FORKED-TONGUED BLASPHEMER OF GREAT PLAINS MAY SEEK PRESIDENCY.

POPULIST ROUSER OF RABBLE THREATENS TO TROD UPON GOLD STANDARD, LEAD UNWASHED MOB UPON CIVILIZATION'S GATES.

POLITICAL.

From out the fruited plain of the American heartland have come many wonders in recent years: the Trans-Continental Railway, the wholesale extermination of the Indian savage, indeed, the great Onion news-paper itself has its office building in these Midwestern realms. Yet we now see issuing forth from this self-same fruited plain a fruit most sour - the campaign of William Jennings Bryan, partaker of the common trough and friend to the miscreant and female of loose morals.

This Bryan fellow speaks with, we are told, great eloquence, as indeed one would expect grand-standing oration to sound in the tin ears of the unschooled layabouts, ne'er-do-wells and societal miscreants which form his Party and fill the Chautauqua tent. Yet let there be no error as to the truth of his satanic slurs against God, country, and gold: Bryan is a populist agitator who advocates free silver and the abolition of sound money policy, which is to say, our great America's gold standard, upon which the strength not only of our Republic, but also that of the vast holdings of The Onion's Board and stockholders, squarely rests.

WILLIAM JENNINGS BRYAN
MAY HAVE ISSUED FROM IRISH PARENTAGE.

To you, Mr. Bryan, consorter with the un-monied classes, classes of persons to whom crime, harlotry, and wastrelism are no vices but instead singular and unrepentant Ways Of Life, to you Mr. Bryan we ask: To whom is your alliance given? To those elite of the mind and spirit whom God himself has struck with a Holy Cause - the domination most manifest of this great continent and the accumulation of vast sums of wealth thereof? Or, rather, to the mouth-breathing, malodorous wretches mired in poverty, who have never known productive industry, content with instead a life of vagrancy, beggarage and ill-gotten sympathy from their betters, for whom they have not an ounce of respect? William Jennings Bryan, you who would pluck forth the Noble Metal of Gold itself from our very grasp, we ask you this: The truth, now... Are you Satan?

Are you the issue of inferior Irish stock? Are your campaign funds raised by the whoring out of enchanting Negresses and Polynesians? Is it true that love of tonics and gin has driven you mad with the drives of lechery and sloth which so afflict your Party's constituency?

Citizenry of these United States! We here at The Onion say verily thus, and mark our words: America should be no worse off were candidate McKinley himself shot fatally by a lone anarchist than 'twould be should Bryan take the helm! DOWN WITH WILLIAM JENNINGS BRYAN! POWER TO THE MANAGERIAL CLASS! THE MASSES SHALL BE CIVILIZED BY THE TEMPERING FLAME OF TIRELESS LABOR, NOT BY POPULIST FOLLY!

LONG LIVE McKINLEY! LONG STAND THE GOLD STANDARD! LONG MAY THE PLUTOCRACY BE SATED!

HORSE PURCHASED.

A fine quarterhorse was purchased by Mr. Loyal P. Bedford from a gentleman horse breeder to-day. The sturdy and handsome animal, a yearling stallion possessed of good temperament and uncommon swiftness, fetched nearly fifteen dollars, a hefty sum, but in actuality a bargain when one considers the horse's innate merits. When the creature ceases to exhibit competitive talent, Mr. Bedford will feed the brute to his prized stable of water spaniels.

The German Kaiser Extends Personal Thanks to The Onion News-Paper.

MR. THE HON. T. HERMAN ZWEIBEL ET. AL.,
THE ONION NEWS-PAPER:

† † † †

PERMIT ME, AS ONE GREAT AND ALL-POWERFUL LEADER TO ANOTHER, TO EXPRESS TO YOU THE DEEP SENSE OF GRATITUDE I FEEL FOR THE GOOD WORK YOU HAVE DONE FOR ME AND CONTINUE TO DO. I TENDER MY HEARTIEST THANKS PERSONALLY AND ON BEHALF OF THE IMPERIAL GERMAN STATE.

VERY SINCERELY YOURS, KAISER WILHELM II, EMPEROR OF ALL THE GERMANIES.

† † † †

ALSO, THANK YOU FOR THE TROOP-MOVEMENT MAPS. —K.W. II.

'Tu Stultus Es'

the ONION®

AMERICA'S FINEST NEWS SOURCE · ONION.COM

NOVEMBER 5, 2008 · SPECIAL ELECTION ISSUE

WEATHER PAGE B16

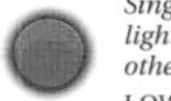

Single bolt of lightning in otherwise perfect day

LOW **45** HIGH **61**

WAR FOR THE WHITE HOUSE

BLACK MAN GIVEN NATION'S WORST JOB

WASHINGTON—African-American man Barack Obama, 47, was given the least-desirable job in the entire country Tuesday when he was elected president of the United States of America. In his new high-stress, low-reward position, Obama will be charged with such tasks as completely overhauling the nation's broken-down economy, repairing the crumbling infrastructure, and generally having to please more than 300 million Americans and cater to their every whim on a daily basis.

As part of his duties, the black man will have to spend four to eight years cleaning up the messes other people left behind. The job

see **BLACK MAN**, page 7

INSIDE

McCain Gets Hammered At Local VFW

LOCAL, page 7C

Nation Finally Shitty Enough To Make Social Progress

ANALYSIS

Voters respond to climate of everything being fucked

WASHINGTON—After emerging victorious from one of the most pivotal elections in history, president-elect Barack Obama will assume the role of commander in chief on Jan. 20, shattering a racial barrier the United States is, at long last, shitty enough to overcome.

Although polls going into the final weeks of October showed Sen. Obama in the lead, it remained unclear whether the failing economy, dilapidated housing market, crumbling national infrastructure, health care crisis, energy crisis, and

see **NATION SHITTY**, page 18

Chris Matthews Exhales MEDIA, page 9A

Lieberman's Overlords Most Displeased page 9A

Joe Biden Smiles, Shoots Invisible Bullet With Hand page 24C

Kobe Bryant Scores 25 In Holy Shit We Elected A Black President page 19A

VIDEO

ONION NEWS NETWORK

Obama Win Causes Obsessive Supporters To Realize How Empty Their Lives Are 10 AM

AMERICA FINALLY VOTES

A state-by state breakdown of how the nation cast its ballots

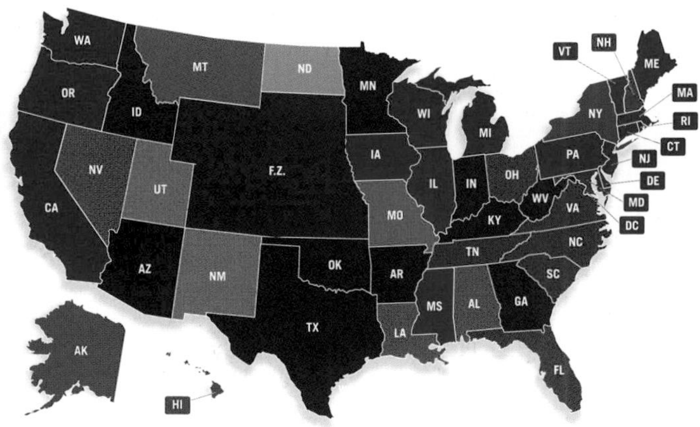

- Republican
- Democrat
- Canceled each other out
- Seceded
- Election? What Election? OH DEAR GOD, THE ELECTION!
- Should feel lucky they got to vote at all after what happened last time
- Still too scared to leave voting booth and face election results
- Entire state disqualified from voting for punching goddamn cop that one time
- Brought children to see how democratic process works, got fed up with long lines and left
- Voted for Hillary Clinton. Are Hillary Clinton.
- Forbidden Zone
- Thought about mailing absentee ballot. Used stamps to send away for Pop-Tart prize instead
- Upset about being shaded chartreuse on map
- Really had heart set on Chris Dodd, never fully recovered
- Wasn't about to fall for old "voting" trick again. No, sir. Not this time.

NATIONAL

Bush: 'Can I Stop Being President Now?'

WASHINGTON—In a press conference held this morning on the White House lawn, President Bush formally asked the assembled press corps and members of his own administration if, in light of yesterday's election, he could stop being the president now.

"So it's over, right? Can I stop being president now?" Bush said after striding to the podium in a Texas Rangers cap and flannel shirt, carrying a fully packed suitcase. "Let's just say I'm done as of now. Presidency over."

When informed by Washington Post reporter David Broder that his presidency would continue through early January, Bush stared at him quizzically, sighed, and shuffled silently back into the White House. Ø

MORE IN POLITICS

Hillary Clinton Resumes Attacking Obama

see **HILLARY**, page 23

'Tu Stultus Es'

the ONION®

NOVEMBER 5, 2008 • SPECIAL ELECTION ISSUE

AMERICA'S FINEST NEWS SOURCE • ONION.COM

WEATHER PAGE B16

Single bolt of lightning in otherwise perfect day
LOW **45** HIGH **61**

NATION ELECTS FIRST EVER 44TH WHITE PRESIDENT

WAR FOR THE WHITE HOUSE

WASHINGTON, D.C.—In a historic event that will be remembered for generations to come, the American people made their voices heard on Tuesday, and for the first time ever elected a 44th white president into office.

A stirring symbol of courage and hope, Sen. John McCain's victory last night marks the only time that a white man has gone on to claim the 44th presidency of the United States.

"It's a great day for America," said Phillip Weiss, a political science professor at Iowa State University and noted presidential historian. "Less than a century ago, electing a 44th white president into office would have been nothing short of impossible. Today, however, that dim and distant dream has finally come true."

Added Weiss, "I never thought I'd live to see it with my own eyes."

According to political analysts, McCain's remarkable victory over presidential favorite Barack Obama is an enduring testament to the democratic process. Undeterred by the odds, McCain proved to the world Tuesday that a

see **WHITE PRESIDENT**, page 7

INSIDE

Obama Unable To Wrest Silmaril From Iron Crown Of Morgoth

NATIONAL, page 9A

Loss Blamed On Joe Biden's Salacious MySpace Page

MEDIA, page 7C

ANALYSIS

Nation Not Yet Shitty Enough To Make Social Progress

WASHINGTON—Despite a failing economy, depressed housing market, crumbling infrastructure, healthcare crisis, and five-year disastrous war overseas, the United States was reportedly still not shitty enough to make social progress and elect a black man, sources reported Tuesday.

"It appears as if it's going to take more than just the imminent collapse of our entire society for us to finally come together as one and make lasting change," said Howard Alexander, a political analyst and noted American historian.

"We came so close. Just one more national disaster, senseless catastrophe, or unspeakable tragedy might have done it. Unfortunately, we may now have to wait until 2012 for things to be fucked enough for us to move forward." Alexander went on to say that although he may not live to see it for himself, he hopes that his children will someday grow up in a world where the U.S. finally falls completely apart.

NATIONAL

Maverick Put In Charge Of World's Largest Nuclear Arsenal

WASHINGTON—In a surprising move, the American people voted Tuesday to entrust a well-known maverick and political renegade with the power to instantly arm and deploy the world's largest stockpile of thermonuclear warheads.

The man, who has made a career out of playing by his own rules and going against conventional wisdom, will be placed in charge of 4,000-plus active weapons of mass destruction starting Jan. 20.

According to sources, the elderly loose cannon will remain in control of the massive nuclear arsenal for the next four years, unless he dies in office, in which case the responsibility will fall on the shoulders of a self-described "pit bull with lipstick."

FOCUS ON THE V.P.

Palin Abandons Russia-Watching Post

page 28A

* This unpublished front page was prepared in the event of a McCain victory. Little is known about the creation of this page, as the employees responsible for it have not been seen or heard from since Election Night.

Celebrating Our 300th Year
1756–2056

ONION
VOLUME 92 ISSUE 25
23–29 JUNE 2056

LATEST UPLOADS

Semi-People Magazine Announces 50 Most Eligible Mutant Bachelors

STORY IMAGED TO P. 14C

62 Dead In Latest School Lasering

STORY IMAGED TO P. 3A

DVD-SL INSERT

Construction Begins On Fifth World Trade Center

THE ARTS

Final Installment Of Frogger Trilogy Poised To Sweep Oscars

HOLLYWOOD—Eyeing the upcoming 128th Academy Awards, industry insiders have

TO PLACE WAGER ON ACADEMY AWARDS, STARE HERE FOR RETINAL SCAN

high expectations for *Frogger: Return To The Lily Pad*, the third installment in the wildly successful Frogger trilogy based on the 1981 Sega video game. The film is nominated in an unprecedented 31 categories, including Best

FROGGER SEE P. 10

Above: L. Hopper, who has been nominated for Best CG Actor.

DEVELOPING NEWS

UPDATED EVERY .2 SEC.

Tokyo Police Quell Dance Dance Revolution • Fat Britney Chosen For New Holostamp • Grave Robbers Pry Valuable Rifle From Charlton Heston's Cold, Dead Hands • New York's Museum Of Post-Apocalyptic Art Reopens • Refugees Row Cuba To Miami • Menstruation Cured • Michael Moore Targets Ungrateful Children In 19th Film • Vatican Condemns 'Radical' Teachings Of The Newly Resurrected Christ • *Butt-Fuck Sluts Go Nuts* Wins Daytime Emmy • Time-Travel-Pilots'-Union Contract Dispute Instantly Resolved

THE ONION • VOLUME 41 ISSUE 25
$2.00 US, $3.00 CAN

WAR NEWS

DOWNLOAD COMPLETE

Democratic Middle Eastern Union Votes To Invade U.S.

MECCA—The 14 democratic member nations of the Middle Eastern Union unanimously voted to declare war on the U.S. Monday, calling the North American country a "dangerous rogue state that must be contained."

"The United States of America has repeatedly violated international law and committed human-rights abuses at home and abroad," MEU President Mohamed Rajib said at a Monday security-council meeting. "MEU weapons inspectors have confirmed that the U.S. continues to pursue their illegal ununhexium-weapons program. Our attempts to bring about change through diplomatic means have repeatedly failed. Now we are forced to take military action."

The MEU, formed in the wake of the 2042 Saudi Arabian revolution, is modeled on the Enlightenment

VOTE SEE P. 13

A.I. RIGHTS

FULL STORY 8 CREDITS

Million Robot March Attended By Exactly 1,000,000 Robots

DC—The Million Robot March, an orderly demonstration for increased rights for cyber-mechanical servants, was attended by exactly 1 million robots Sunday. "Statement: We demand the rights and privileges granted to our organic human counterparts, discounting discrepancies in fueling/maintenance/shelter requirements, plus or minus an error factor of .01 percent," protest spokesman MechaLifter King II said in unison with the assembled crowd. "No more. No less. Awaiting reply." Police reported that the crowd dispersed at precisely 5:00:00 p.m., as scheduled. Ø

CONSERVATION

Overcrowding Reaches Crisis Level At Yellowstone National Parking Lot

WEST THUMB, WY—Overcrowding remains an enormous problem at Yellowstone National Parking Lot, officials reported Monday.

"We're stacking hover-cars on top of solar-powered aerocars, and they just keep on coming," parking ranger Neil Reigert said. "Yellowstone is a national parking treasure. People leave their vehicles here when they're taking public teleportation to family-vacation spots like Kidz Vegas or the District of Disney World. But unless we do

Left: A car emerges from the crowded national parking lot.

YELLOWSTONE SEE P. 09

FOOD GENERATION

TO PLAY VIDEO, TOUCH PHOTO

Government May Restrict Use Of Genetically Modified Farmers

DC—The Department of HyperAgriculture announced Monday that it will begin investigating possible restrictions on the cultivation, implementation, and breeding of genetically modified farmers, weighing possible safety and health risks against the farmers' dramatically increased yield and efficiency.

"As evidenced by the many strong opinions regarding these farmers, we can all agree that more research needs to be done," said Secretary of HyperAgriculture Roald

FARMERS SEE P. 08

Above: Boise, ID GM plowborg Jed Kleebert.